June 17–19, 2013
Montpellier, France

Association for Computing Machinery

Advancing Computing as a Science & Profession

IH&MMSec'13

Proceedings of the 2013 ACM

Information Hiding and Multimedia Security Workshop

Sponsored by:

ACM SIGMM

Supported by:

Civolution, Digimarc, Technicolor, & Université Montpellier 2

Association for Computing Machinery

Advancing Computing as a Science & Profession

ISBN: 978-1-4503-2081-8 (Digital)

ISBN: 978-1-4503-2285-0 (Print)

Additional copies may be ordered prepaid from:

ACM Order Department
PO Box 30777
New York, NY 10087-0777, USA

Phone: 1-800-342-6626 (USA and Canada)
+1-212-626-0500 (Global)
Fax: +1-212-944-1318
E-mail: acmhelp@acm.org
Hours of Operation: 8:30 am – 4:30 pm ET

Printed in the USA

ACM IHMMSEC 2013

It is our great pleasure to welcome you to the 1st ACM Workshop on Information Hiding and Multimedia Security, Montpellier, France, June 17-19, 2013.

For over a decade, two workshops have been shaping the landscape of research in multimedia security. On one hand, Information Hiding (aka. IH) was created in 1996 and focused on digital watermarking, steganography and steganalysis, anonymity and privacy, hard to intercept communications and covert/subliminal channels. On the other hand, the ACM Workshop on Multimedia and Security (aka. ACM MMSec) was initiated in 1998 and focused on data hiding, robust/perceptual hash, biometrics, video surveillance, and multimedia forensics. Key seminal works have been published in these two workshops and papers accepted for publication there attracted over 9,000 citations in total. Year after year, the two communities grew closer and the overlap between their respective scope got bigger. As a result, after 14 successful editions each, IH and ACM MMSec decided to merge in a single event in an attempt to establish synergies between the two communities while building on the reputation obtained over the years.

The 1st ACM Information Hiding and Multimedia Security Workshop (ACM IHMMSEC) is held at Montpellier, France, June 17-19, 2013. We hope that this first edition of this workshop, resulting from merging two long standing sustainable events, gives birth to an attractive research forum that will facilitate cross-fertilization of ideas among key stakeholders from academia, industry, practitioners and government agencies around the globe.

The call for papers attracted 74 submissions from Asia, South America, the United States, Africa, and Europe. The program committee accepted 27 papers (acceptance rate of 36%) that cover a variety of topics, including three invited talks and four special sessions. We hope that these proceedings will serve as a valuable reference for researchers.

Putting together ACM IHMMSEC'2013 was a team effort. We first thank the authors for providing the content of the program. We are grateful to the program committee and the steering committee, who worked very hard in reviewing papers and providing feedback for authors. Finally, we thank the hosting organization, the University of Montpellier 2, our sponsor, ACM, and our generous corporate supporters, CIVOLUTION, DIGIMARC, TECHNICOLOR and the University of Montpellier 2. We must also thank our colleagues at the University of Montpellier who "volunteered" to help with the organization, the industrial liaison chair and the international liaison chair.

We hope that you will find this program interesting and thought-provoking and that this workshop will provide you with a valuable opportunity to share ideas with other researchers and practitioners from institutions around the world.

General Chair

William Puech
LIRMM/University of Montpellier
FRANCE

Program Chairs

Marc Chaumont, University of Nîmes, France
Jana Dittmann, Otto-von-Guericke University, Germany
Patrizio Campisi, University of Roma TRE, Roma, Italy

Table of Contents

Session 5: From Biometric to Forensics

Session Chair: Chang-Tsun Li *(University of Warwick)*

Session 6: End User and Signal Processing: A Successful Synergy Towards the Assessment of Forensic Tools

Session Chair: Marco Carli *(University of Roma TRE)*,

Session 7: Media Encryption

Session Chair: Andreas Uhl *(University of Salzburg)*

Session 8: Invited Talk

Session Chair: Jana Dittman *(Otto-van-Guericke University)*

Session 9: Watermarking

Session Chair: Dinu Coltuc *(University of Targoviste)*

IH&MMSec 2013 Conference Organization

General Chair: William Puech *(LIRMM & University of Montpellier, France)*

Program Chairs: Marc Chaumont *(LIRMM & University of Nîmes, France)*
Jana Dittmann *(Otto-von-Guericke University, Germany)*
Patrizio Campisi *(University of Roma TRE, Italy)*

Industrial Liaison: Gwenaël Doërr *(Technicolor, France)*

International Liaison: Teddy Furon *(INRIA, France)*

Steering Committee: Stefan Katzenbeisser *(TU Darmstadt, Germany)*
Jana Dittmann *(Otto-von-Guericke University, Germany)*
Jessica Fridrich *(SUNY Binghamton, USA)*
George Danezis *(Microsoft Research Cambridge, UK)*
Patrizio Campisi *(University of Roma TRE, Italy)*
Balakrishnan Prabhakaran *(University of Dallas, USA)*

Program Committee: Johann Barbier *(ARX Arcéo, France)*
Morgan Barbier *(University of Caen, France)*
Mauro Barni *(Università di Siena, Italy)*
Patrick Bas *(CNRS, France)*
Rainer Böhme *(University of Münster, Germany)*
Patrizio Campisi *(University of Roma TRE, Italy)*
François Cayre *(GIPSA-lab/Grenoble INP, France)*
Ee-Chien Chang *(National University of Singapore, Singapore)*
Marc Chaumont *(LIRMM & University of Nîmes, France)*
Rémi Cogranne *(Technological University of Troyes, France)*
Christian Collberg *(University of Arizona, USA)*
George Danezis *(Microsoft Research Cambridge, UK)*
Claude Delpha *(University of South Paris, France)*
Jana Dittmann *(Otto-von-Guericke University, Germany)*
Gwenaël Doërr *(Technicolor, France)*
Tomáš Filler *(Digimarc Corporation, USA)*
Caroline Fontaine *(Télécom Bretagne, France)*
Jessica Fridrich *(SUNY Binghamton, USA)*
Teddy Furon *(INRIA, France)*
Chad Heitzenrater *(Department of Defense, USA)*
Neil F. Johnson *(Johnson & Johnson Technology Consultants, LLC, USA)*
Stefan Katzenbeisser *(TU Darmstadt, Germany)*
Andrew Ker *(University of Oxford, UK)*
Matthius Kirchner *(International Computer Science Institute, Berkeley, USA)*
Jan Kodovský *(Binghamton University, USA)*

Bayesian Inference to Evaluate Information Leakage in Complex Scenarios

Carmela Troncoso
Galician R&D Center in Advanced Telecommunications (Gradiant)
CITEXVI, Campus Universitario
Vigo, Spain
ctroncoso@gradiant.org

ABSTRACT

Common security evaluation methods require the estimation of the likelihood of a hidden state given an observation of the system. For instance: identifying the type of tampering on an image given the tampered file, identifying communication partner given an anonymous channel trace, identifying the location from where a service has been accessed given an obfuscated version of this location. In this talk we explore the suitability of Bayesian Inference techniques, specifically Markov Chain Monte Carlo methods, to evaluate information leakage in complex scenarios.

Using anonymity systems, in particular mix networks, as case study we show that casting problems in the context of Bayesian inference provides an appropriate framework to evaluate security properties (e.g., traceability of messages) in complex constraints.

We present a generative probabilistic model of mix network architectures that incorporates a number of attack techniques in the trace analysis literature. We use the model to build a Markov Chain Monte Carlo inference engine based on the Metropolis-Hastings algorithm that calculates the probabilities of who is talking to whom given an observation of network traces. Finally, we briefly overview other Bayesian techniques, such as Gibbs sampling and particle filtering, that are useful to tackle other security problems, like user profiling, or to consider dynamic behaviour.

Categories and Subject Descriptors

C.2.0 [**Computer-Communication Networks**]: General—*Security and protection*

General Terms

Security, Measurement, Theory

Keywords

Bayesian inference, Monte Carlo, Information leakage

Bio

Carmela Troncoso was born on September 17th 1982 in Vigo, Spain. She received the Master's degree in Telecommunications Engineering from the University of Vigo, Spain, in May 2006. She joined the COSIC research group at the Katholieke Universiteit Leuven, Belgium as a PhD student in October 2006 obtaining her doctoral degree in April 2011. Her thesis *Design and Analysis methods for Privacy Technologies* received the European Research Consortium for Informatics and Mathematics WG Security and Trust Management Best Ph.D. Thesis Award.

Carmela has been a research visitor at numerous worldwide known security groups amongst them Microsoft Research Cambridge, the Hatswich Research group at the University of Illinois at Urbana-Champaign, or the LCA1 lab at the École Polytechnique Féderale de Laussane. She is a co-author of more than 25 publications in peer-reviewed international conferences and journals. She has been program chair of the Hot Topics in Privacy Enhancing Technologies Workshop (HotPETs) in 2010 and 2011, and General Chair of the Privacy Enhancing Technologies Symposium in 2012. She has also served on more than 10 program committees of international conferences, and reviewed articles for numerous international journals. Since October 2012 she is a postdoctoral research at Gradiant in the framework of the LIFTGATE project.

A Simple Tracing Algorithm for Binary Fingerprinting Code under Averaging Attack

Minoru Kuribayashi
Kobe University
1-1, Rokkodai-cho, Nada-ku, Kobe
657-8501, Japan
kminoru@kobe-u.ac.jp

ABSTRACT

When a binary fingerprinting codeword is embedded into digital contents using a spread-spectrum (SS) watermarking scheme, the marking assumption is not valid anymore because it is difficult for colluders to perform the symbol-wise attack for their codewords. As discussed in the SS-type fingerprinting schemes, averaging their copies is the cost-effective attack from the signal processing point of view. In this paper, we propose an optimal detector under the averaging attack and addition of white Gaussian noise. If the detector knows the number of colluders in advance, it first estimates the variance of additive noise, and then calculates the correlation scores using a log-likelihood-based approach. However, the number of colluders is not given in a real situation. We discover in this study that the characteristic of parameters for generating codewords enables us to eliminate the number of colluders as well as the estimation of the variance of noise at the calculation of correlation score, and propose a simplified detector by analyzing the scoring function in the optimal detector. We evaluate the performance of the simplified detector through simulation using not only codewords, but also a digital image.

Categories and Subject Descriptors

D.2 [**Software Engineering**]: ManagementCopyrights

Keywords

fingerprinting, collusion attack, tracing algorithm

1. INTRODUCTION

Digital fingerprinting [22] is used to trace illegal users, where a unique ID known as a digital fingerprint is embedded into a content before distribution. When a suspicious copy is found, the owner can identify illegal users called colluders, by extracting the fingerprint. Because the fingerprinted copy slightly differs with each other, colluders will combine their differently marked copies of the same content

for the purpose of removing or changing the original fingerprint. Therefore, one of the important issues in the fingerprinting technique is the robustness against the collusion attack. Studies on collusion-resistant fingerprinting systems can be categorized into two approaches. One is based on collusion-resistant fingerprinting codes [3, 20], and the other is on the SS technique [4, 21, 11].

Boneh and Shaw [3] proposed a specific code by introducing a two-level construction in the code domain to resist up to c colluders with high probability. A drawback of the Boneh-Shaw code is its long code length, which limits its feasibility in practical applications. Recently, Tardos [20] proposed an efficient method for constructing collusion-resistant fingerprinting codes having a theoretically minimal code length with respect to the number of colluders. Among the variants of the Tardos code, Nuida et al. [19] optimized parameters to generate the codewords of the Tardos code under a limited number of colluders. At the early stage of the study, the performance of fingerprinting code has been evaluated under the well-known marking assumption [3]. An optimal detector was presented in [17] from the information theoretic analysis of collusion strategy under the marking assumption.

In a multimedia fingerprinting system, however, the marking assumption is not always valid, and the assumption should be modified to a relaxed version. For example, colluders can manipulate fingerprinted contents in the signal processing domain. In [10], a pirated copy is produced by collusion attack and it is further distorted by additive white Gaussian noise (AWGN). Because no robust watermarking scheme avoids an injection of noise into a pirated copy, it is reasonable to assume a noisy channel. Under the collusion attack and AWGN channel model, a soft decision tracing algorithm has been proposed in [12] considering a posterior probability of codeword extracted from a pirated copy.

Although the research on the fingerprinting code is mainly focusing on the symbol-wise collusion strategy, a variety of changes on the codeword could be occurred when colluders manipulate their copies in the signal processing domain. A simple, yet effective way is to average their copies. On the other hand, Yacobi [23] introduced a direct SS sequence like Cox's method [4] to modulate the codeword while embedding the fingerprints. In the SS watermarking scheme, each watermark bit is embedded into the samples of content such as DCT, DFT, and DWT coefficients. In the multi-bit embedding scenario proposed in [15], k bit watermark information is embedded into L samples randomly selected from the DCT coefficients of an image using the orthogonal frequency division multiplexing (OFDM) technique. If each symbol of a binary fingerprinting codeword is embedded based on such a SS watermarking scheme, it is difficult for colluders to classify the related samples into which each symbol is embedded. It means that colluders cannot perform a collusion strategy for symbol-by-symbol. Under such a situation, the best attack strategy could be to average their copies from the information theoretical point of view, which attenuates the embedded signal of their fingerprints. As studied in [24], various collusion attacks for the SS fingerprinting scheme can be modeled as an averaging attack and addition of white Gaussian noise. Considering the universality, we should consider the other attack model as well as the averaging strategy in order to design an optimal detector.

In this paper, we consider the fingerprinting system that encodes user's ID into a binary fingerprinting codeword and then embed each bit into samples of digital image using the SS technique. In our fingerprinting model, it is difficult for colluders to perform symbol-by-symbol attack because of the SS embedding characteristic. Hence, we focus on the averaging strategy in the code-domain and propose an optimal detector for a given number of colluders under the averaging attack. Different from the marking assumption, each symbol in a pirated codeword is not binary, there are $c + 1$ candidates when the number of colluders is c under a noiseless case. By classifying the probabilities for a given symbol of user's codeword, the Maximum A Posterior (MAP) detector is designed from the information theoretic point of view. We found that the number of colluders is not required under a noiseless case though it is inevitable under a noisy case. In order to simplify the algorithm, we study the characteristic of the parameters of Nuida code, and approximate the distribution of the symbols in a pirated codeword into a normal distribution because the original distribution is binomial. This approximation enables us to simplify the calculation of correlation score, and to eliminate the number of colluders required for the MAP detector. The validity of the simplified detector is intensively evaluated through experiments, whereas the MAP detector is assumed to know the attack strategy and the number of colluders, but not the amount of additive Gaussian noise.

Considering the management of digital content, it is reasonable to assume the following flow of attacks. At the legal purchase stage, each fingerprinted copy is compressed in order to reduce the distribution cost. Then, colluders decompress their copies and operate the averaging strategy. Finally, the averaged copy is compressed once again for the reduction of the risk to be identified as well as the redistribution cost. Under such an attack scenario, we evaluate performance of the simplified detector compared with that of the MAP detector by embedding the fingerprinting codeword into a digital image.

2. PRELIMINARIES

In this section, we briefly review the fingerprinting code and related works.

2.1 Fingerprinting Code

Let L be a length of codeword, and N be the number of users in a fingerprinting system. If at most c_{max} users collude to produce a pirated copy, at least one of them should be identified with a negligibly small false-positive probability, which is a requirement for a fingerprinting code.

Table 1: Examples of the discrete version of Nuida code's bias distribution.

c_{max}	p	q	c_{max}	p	q
1,2	0.50000	1.00000	7,8	0.06943	0.24833
3,4	0.21132	0.50000		0.33001	0.25167
	0.78868	0.50000		0.66999	0.25167
5,6	0.11270	0.33201		0.93057	0.24833
	0.50000	0.33598			
	0.88730	0.33201			

The Tardos code has a length of theoretically minimal order with respect to the number of colluders. The binary codeword of j-th user is denoted by $x_{j,i} \in \{0, 1\}$, $(1 \le i \le L)$, where $x_{j,i}$ is generated from an independently and identically distributed random number with a probability p_i such that $\Pr[x_{j,i} = 1] = p_i$ and $\Pr[x_{j,i} = 0] = 1 - p_i$. This probability p_i follows a continuous distribution over an open unit interval $(0, 1)$, which is called *bias distribution*. In order to improve the performance of the Tardos code, Nuida et al. [19] presented a discrete version of the bias distribution, which is customized for a given number c_{max} of colluders. The numerical examples are shown in Table 1, where p and q denote the output values and their emerging probabilities, respectively. It is reported in [12], the performance of Nuida code is better than that of Tardos code under a catch-many scenario. In [14], the discrete bias probability enables us to design a specified tracing algorithm considering the bias of symbols in a pirated codeword.

2.2 Collusion Attack

Suppose that c colluders attempt to produce a pirated copy from their fingerprinted copy. A coalition of colluders is denoted by $\mathcal{C} = \{j_1, j_2, \ldots, j_c\}$. The collusion attack is the process of taking sequences $x_{j_t,i}, (1 \le t \le c)$ as inputs and yielding the pirated sequence $\boldsymbol{y}$ as an output. The marking assumption states that the colluders have $y_i \in \{x_{j_t,i}\}$. It implies that they cannot change the bit in the position where all of $x_{j_t,i}$ is identical. Some typical examples of collusion strategies are "majority", "minority", "interleaving" attacks.

In [8], the collusion attack is described by the parameter vector: $\boldsymbol{\theta}_c = (\theta_0, \cdots, \theta_c)$ with $\theta_\rho = \Pr[y_i = 1 | \Phi = \rho], (0 \le \rho \le c)$, where the random variable $\Phi \in \{0, \cdots, c\}$ denotes the number of symbol "1" in the colluders' copies at a given index. The marking assumption enforces that $\theta_0 = 0$ and $\theta_c = 1$. The most damaging attack strategy is analyzed from the information theoretic point of view, which is called worst case attack(WCA), and its parameter can be represented by $\boldsymbol{\theta}_c$ (see [5] for detail). It is noted that the colluders do not need to know their symbols of codewords to perform the WCA strategy. It is sufficient for colluders to divide their codewords into each symbol, namely, symbol-by-symbol attack scenario.

In a realistic situation, each bit of a codeword is embedded into some components of a digital content using a robust watermarking scheme. From the signal processing point of view, we can further extend the collusion strategy to a generic one. Let $x_{j_t,i}, (1 \le t \le c, 1 \le i \le L)$ be an i-th element of t-th colluder's codeword. Then, a pirated codeword

y_i is produced by the following equation:

$$y_i = \sum_{t=1}^{c} \dot{w}_{t,i} x_{j_t,i}, \qquad (1)$$

where $w_{t,i}$ stands for a weighting parameter satisfying $0 \leq w_{t,i} \leq 1$ and $\sum_{t=1}^{c} w_{t,i} = 1$. It is noted that the weighting parameter can be independently selected at each element of codeword.

A simple example of the collusion strategy under the above assumption is to calculate $w_{t,i} = 1/c$, which is called "averaging strategy". In SS fingerprinting schemes, it is assumed that colluders add noise to a pirated copy which they create by combining their copies in a linear or non-linear fashion, and the effects on the pirated codeword is basically modeled as AWGN [24]. Thus, a watermark detector outputs the distorted codeword $\boldsymbol{y}^\star = \boldsymbol{y} + \boldsymbol{e}$, where $\boldsymbol{e}$ is AWGN. It is reported that the uniform linear averaging strategy is the most damaging one [9] for the SS fingerprinting scheme, which is not always true for the fingerprinting code. If a fingerprinting codeword is embedded by a spread form using a SS watermarking technique, the WCA in the code domain is difficult to perform because the symbol-by-symbol attack cannot be employed by colluders.

2.3 Tracing Algorithm

A tracing algorithm calculates a correlation score $S_i^{(j)}$ for i-th bit of j-th user, and then sums them up as the total score $S^{(j)}$. If the total score $S^{(j)}$ exceeds a threshold Z, the user is determined as guilty. Such a tracing algorithm is called "catch-many" type explained in [22].

From the original tracing algorithm proposed by Tardos [20], there are some improvements on the derivation of good score $S_i^{(j)}$ from a pirated codeword. Among them, the MAP decoder[7][17] is the optimal algorithm, which calculates the Log-Likelihood Ratio (LLR) of probabilities for a given collusion strategy.

$$S^{(j)} = \sum_{i=1}^{L} S_i^{(j)} = \sum_{i=1}^{L} \log \frac{\Pr[y_i | x_{j,i}, \boldsymbol{\theta_c}]}{\Pr[y_i | \boldsymbol{\theta_c}]}. \qquad (2)$$

The difficulty on the design of such an optimal algorithm is how to estimate the number c of colluders and the exploited collusion strategy $\boldsymbol{\theta_c}$ from a given codeword. Meerwald and Furon [18] used a Maximum Likelihood estimator, and proposed a single decoder based on a compound channel setup studied in [1]. It is reported that the single detector is provably good for tracing only one guilty user, namely detect-one scenario.

The MAP detector is customized for the number c of colluders and the given collusion strategy $\boldsymbol{\theta_c}$. In [18], they further extend the scoring function considering the addition of white Gaussian noise by accommodating the change of symbols values such as averaging strategy. The detector first estimate the attack strategy $\boldsymbol{\theta_c}$ and adopt the scoring function. Considering the universality of the tracing algorithm, the estimation of $\boldsymbol{\theta_c}$ must assume various kinds of strategy including "majority", "minority", "interleaving", "WCA", "averaging" and so on. On the other hand, if the SS watermarking technique is applied to embed a fingerprinting codeword, we exclude the attack strategies under the marking assumption because the symbol-by-symbol attack is difficult to perform. Under such a restricted assumption, we propose a MAP detector in the next section.

2.4 Design of Threshold

In a realistic situation, the number c of colluders is not always less than c_{max}. So, it is desirable to design a good detector whose false-positive probability is constant even if c exceeds c_{max}. In this paper, we forget about the limitation of the availability of fingerprinting code, and design the detector that outputs a constant false-positive probability using a properly calculated threshold.

Suppose that the maximum allowed probability of accusing a fixed innocent user is denoted by ϵ_1, and the total false-positive probability is by $\eta = 1 - (1 - \epsilon_1)^{N-c} \approx N\epsilon_1$. A simple approach to estimate the false-positive probability ϵ_1 for a threshold Z is to perform the Monte Carlo simulation. Indeed, it is not easy in general because of the heavy computational costs for estimating a tiny probability. Furon et al. [8] proposed an efficient method for estimating the probability of rare events. The method can estimate the false-positive probability ϵ_1 for a given threshold Z with a reasonable computational cost, which means that the method calculates the map $\epsilon_1 = F(Z)$. By iteratively performing the estimating method, an objective threshold for a given ϵ_1 can be obtained.

3. OPTIMAL TRACING ALGORITHM UNDER AVERAGING STRATEGY

Suppose that c colluders average their codewords to produce a pirated codeword. We begin with the noiseless case for simplicity. The pirated codeword $y_i, 0 \leq i \leq L - 1$ is represented by

$$y_i = \frac{1}{c} \sum_{t=1}^{c} x_{j_t,i}, \qquad (3)$$

where $x_{j_t,i}$ stands for the i-th symbol in t-th colluder's codeword. For convenience, we denote by $\boldsymbol{\theta^{(ave)}}$ the averaging strategy. The MAP detector calculates the correlation score $S_i^{(j)}$ for j-th user as follows:

$$S_i^{(j)} = \log \frac{\Pr\left[y_i | x_{j,i}, \boldsymbol{\theta_c^{(ave)}}\right]}{\Pr\left[y_i | \boldsymbol{\theta_c^{(ave)}}\right]}. \qquad (4)$$

For instance, when $y_i = \rho/c$, $0 \leq \rho \leq c$, the numerator in Eq.(4) is given by

$$\Pr\left[y_i = \frac{\rho}{c} \Big| \boldsymbol{\theta_c^{(ave)}}\right] = B(\rho; c, p_i) = \binom{c}{\rho} p_i^\rho (1 - p_i)^{c-\rho}. \quad (5)$$

Then, if $x_{j,i} = 0$, the denominator is

$$\Pr\left[y_i = \frac{\rho}{c} \Big| x_{j,i} = 0, \boldsymbol{\theta_c^{(ave)}}\right] = B(\rho; c - 1, p_i) \qquad (6)$$

otherwise,

$$\Pr\left[y_i = \frac{\rho}{c} \Big| x_{j,i} = 1, \boldsymbol{\theta_c^{(ave)}}\right] = B(\rho - 1; c - 1, p_i) \qquad (7)$$

Thus, the score $S_i^{(j)}$ is simplified as follows:

$$S_i^{(j)} = \begin{cases} \log \dfrac{1 - y_i}{1 - p_i} & \text{if } x_{j,i} = 0 \\[2mm] \log \dfrac{y_i}{p_i} & \text{otherwise} \end{cases} \qquad (8)$$

It is interesting to note that the number c of colluders is not involved at the calculation of the score $S_i^{(j)}$. It is because we assume $y_i = \rho/c$ with $0 \leq \rho \leq c$. Therefore, if the pirated codeword is produced only by the averaging attack, the optimal tracing algorithm is easily performed without the knowledge of c.

In a noisy case, the score $S_i^{(j)}$ is calculated from the distorted codeword $y_i^\star$. Then, the numerator in Eq.(4) is calculated by

$$\Pr\left[y_i^\star | \boldsymbol{\theta}_c^{(ave)}\right] = \sum_{\rho=0}^{c} \mathcal{N}\left(y_i^\star; \frac{\rho}{c}, \sigma_e^2\right) B(\rho; c, p_i) \quad (9)$$

where σ_e^2 stands for the variance of noise and

$$\mathcal{N}\left(y_i^\star; \frac{\rho}{c}, \sigma_e^2\right) = \frac{1}{\sqrt{2\pi\sigma_e^2}} \exp\left(-\frac{(y_i^\star - \frac{\rho}{c})^2}{2\sigma_e^2}\right). \quad (10)$$

Similarly, the denominator is

$$\Pr\left[y_i^\star | 0, \boldsymbol{\theta}_c^{(ave)}\right] = \sum_{\rho=0}^{c-1} \mathcal{N}\left(y_i^\star; \frac{\rho}{c}, \sigma_e^2\right) B(\rho; c-1, p_i) \quad (11)$$

if $x_{j,i} = 0$, otherwise;

$$\Pr\left[y_i^\star | 1, \boldsymbol{\theta}_c^{(ave)}\right] = \sum_{\rho=1}^{c} \mathcal{N}\left(y_i^\star; \frac{\rho}{c}, \sigma_e^2\right) B(\rho-1; c-1, p_i) \quad (12)$$

Note that the above probabilities are differently expressed by the vector $\boldsymbol{\theta}_c^{(ave)}$ of mode I in [18] with $y_i = \rho/c$ for $0 \leq \rho \leq c$.

In order to maximize the performance of a tracing algorithm, it is inevitable to accurately estimate the number c of colluders from the codeword $\boldsymbol{y}^\star$ and the amount of noise. Since the noise involved in $\boldsymbol{y}^\star$ is modeled as AWGN, we can simplify the issue into the estimation of parameters from the well-known Gaussian Mixture Model (GMM). The probability density function of $y_i^\star$ is given by

$$pdf(y_i^\star) = \sum_{\rho=0}^{c} a_\rho \mathcal{N}\left(y_i^\star; \frac{\rho}{c}, \sigma_e^2\right), \quad (13)$$

where $\sum_{\rho=0}^{c} a_\rho = 1$. In the above equation, we have to estimate the parameters c, $a_\rho, 0 \leq \rho \leq c$, and σ_e^2. It is known that the Expectation-Maximization(EM) algorithm [2] can estimate the parameters a_ρ if c is known. However, the estimation of c is left for an open problem.

The GMM and EM algorithm were also employed in [6] to estimate the variance of additive Gaussian noise as well as the mean value, namely y_i, under a generic collusion strategy. The above MAP detector is a kind of special case customized only for averaging strategy.

4. SIMPLIFIED MAP DETECTOR

Because of the discrete bias distribution of Nuida code, there is an interesting characteristic in the distribution of symbols in an averaged codeword.

Suppose that there are n_c candidates for the probability p_i. Let $P_\xi, 1 \leq \xi \leq n_c$ be the candidates. For example, $P_1 = 0.06943$, $P_2 = 0.33001$, $P_3 = 0.66999$, $P_4 = 0.93057$, and $n_c = 4$ when $c_{max} = 7, 8$ as shown in Table 1. Let $\mathcal{P}_\xi$ be the set of indices i satisfying $p_i = P_\xi$. By classifying the score $S_i^{(j)}$ into n_c groups, the total score $S^{(j)}$ is rewritten by

$$S^{(j)} = \sum_{\xi=1}^{n_c} \left(\sum_{i \in \mathcal{P}_\xi} S_{\xi,i}^{(j)}\right). \quad (14)$$

For ξ-th group, Eq.(5) is represented by

$$P_\xi^{(ave)}(y_i) = \Pr\left[y_i | \boldsymbol{\theta}_c^{(ave)}, \xi\right] = \sum_{\rho=0}^{c} \delta\left(y_i - \frac{\rho}{c}\right) B(\rho; c, P_\xi), \quad (15)$$

where $\delta()$ stands for the Kronecker delta function. The above equation means a binomial distribution. It is well-known that the binomial distribution can be approximated to be the normal distribution if c is large enough and P_ξ is not so close to 0 or 1. The mean and the variance is of the binomial distribution $B(\rho; c, P_\xi)$ for $0 \leq \rho \leq c$ are cP_ξ and $cP_\xi(1 - P_\xi)$, respectively; namely $\mathcal{N}(cP_\xi, cP_\xi(1 - P_\xi))$. Focusing on the variable $y_i = \rho/c$, Eq.(15) is approximated to the following equation:

$$P_\xi^{(ave)}(y_i) \approx \sum_{\rho=0}^{c} \delta\left(y_i - \frac{\rho}{c}\right) B(cy_i; c, P_\xi) \quad (16)$$

$$\approx \mathcal{N}\left(cy_i; cP_\xi, cP_\xi(1 - P_\xi)\right) \quad (17)$$

$$= \frac{1}{c}\mathcal{N}\left(y_i; P_\xi, \frac{P_\xi(1 - P_\xi)}{c}\right) = \overline{P}_\xi^{(ave)}(y_i). \quad (18)$$

When $c = 10$, the numerical examples are plotted in Fig.1. With the increase of c, the approximated probability $\overline{P}_\xi^{(ave)}(y_i)$ is asymptotically approaching to $P_\xi^{(ave)}(y_i)$. Even though c is not sufficiently large in the fingerprinting setting, it is reasonable to use the approximated distribution under the relaxed marking assumption. Because we assume that the pirated codeword is distorted by additive white Gaussian noise, the approximation error becomes relatively small.

Under the above approximation, Eq.(9) for ξ-th group is represented by the convolution of a white Gaussian noise with variance σ_e^2 and normal distribution given by $\overline{P}_\xi^{(ave)}(y_i)$. Hence, we obtain the following probability for ξ-th group.

$$\Pr\left[y_i^\star | \boldsymbol{\theta}_c^{(ave)}, \xi\right] = \frac{1}{c}\mathcal{N}(y_i^\star; P_\xi, \sigma_\xi^2), \quad (19)$$

where $\sigma_\xi^2 = \sigma_e^2 + P_\xi(1 - P_\xi)/c$. Under the condition that $x_{j,i}$ is given,

$$\Pr\left[y_i^\star | 0, \boldsymbol{\theta}_c^{(ave)}, \xi\right] = \frac{1}{c}\mathcal{N}(y_i^\star; P_\xi - \alpha_{\xi,c}^{(0)}, \tilde{\sigma}_\xi^2), \quad (20)$$

where the mean $\alpha_{\xi,c}^{(0)}$ and the variance $\tilde{\sigma}_\xi^2$ are represented by

$$\alpha_{\xi,c}^{(0)} = \frac{P_\xi}{c}, \quad (21)$$

and

$$\tilde{\sigma}_\xi^2 = \sigma_e^2 + \frac{(c-1)P_\xi(1 - P_\xi)}{c^2}, \quad (22)$$

$$= \sigma_\xi^2 - \frac{P_\xi(1 - P_\xi)}{c^2}, \quad (23)$$

respectively. If c is large or σ_e^2 is large, the term $P_\xi(1-P_\xi)/c^2$ becomes negligibly small, namely $\tilde{\sigma}_\xi^2 \approx \sigma_\xi^2$. Then if $x_{j,i} = 0$, the score $S_{\xi,i}^{(j)}$ is simplified as follows:

$$S_{\xi,i}^{(j)} = \log \frac{\mathcal{N}(y_i^\star; P_\xi - \alpha_{\xi,c}^{(0)}, \sigma_\xi^2)}{\mathcal{N}(y_i^\star; P_\xi, \sigma_\xi^2)} \quad (24)$$

$$= \log\left\{\exp\left\{\frac{-(y_i^\star - P_\xi + \alpha_{\xi,c}^{(0)})^2 + (y_i^\star - P_\xi)^2}{2\sigma_\xi^2}\right\}\right\} \quad (25)$$

$$= \frac{2\alpha_{\xi,c}^{(0)}(-y_i^\star + P_\xi) - (\alpha_{\xi,c}^{(0)})^2}{2\sigma_\xi^2}. \quad (26)$$

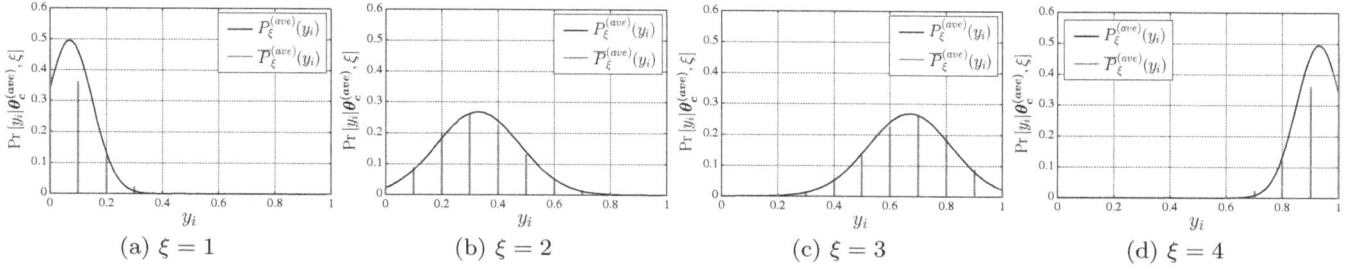

Figure 1: Approximation of binomial distribution for $c = 10$ when $c_{max} = 7, 8$ and $n_c = 4$.

(a) $\xi = 1$ (b) $\xi = 2$ (c) $\xi = 3$ (d) $\xi = 4$

Similarly, if $x_{j,i} = 1$, then

$$\Pr\left[y_i^\star | 1, \boldsymbol{\theta}_c^{(ave)}, \xi\right] = \frac{1}{c}\mathcal{N}\left(y_i^\star - \frac{1}{c}; P_\xi - \frac{P_\xi}{c}, \tilde{\sigma}_\xi^2\right), \quad (27)$$

$$= \frac{1}{c}\mathcal{N}\left(y_i^\star; P_\xi + \alpha_{\xi,c}^{(1)}, \tilde{\sigma}_\xi^2\right), \quad (28)$$

where

$$\alpha_{\xi,c}^{(1)} = \frac{1 - P_\xi}{c}. \quad (29)$$

The score is simplified as follows:

$$S_{\xi,i}^{(j)} = \frac{2\alpha_{\xi,c}^{(1)}(y_i^\star - P_\xi) - \left(\alpha_{\xi,c}^{(1)}\right)^2}{2\sigma_\xi^2}. \quad (30)$$

The above scores given by Eq.(26) and Eq.(30) can be further simplified as follows. Because of the symmetry of the bias distribution, there are following two relationships:

$$\alpha_{\xi,c}^{(0)} = \alpha_{n_c-\xi,c}^{(1)} \quad (31)$$

$$\sigma_\xi^2 = \sigma_{n_c-\xi}^2 \quad (32)$$

Therefore, for $1 \leq \xi \leq n_c$, the sum of $(\alpha_{\xi,c}^{(0)})^2/2\sigma_\xi^2$ is equal to that of $(\alpha_{\xi,c}^{(1)})^2/2\sigma_\xi^2$, and hence, these terms can be removed from Eq.(26) and Eq.(30), respectively. If c is large or σ_e^2 is large, we can roughly approximate the variance to be $\sigma_\xi^2 \approx \sigma_e^2$ because $P_\xi(1 - P_\xi)/c$ becomes relatively small. It is worthy to mention that the approximation error does not seriously degrade the performance of detector when c is small since we can identify almost all colluders in such a case. Under such an approximation, σ_ξ^2 becomes common factor in the score with respect to ξ. By removing the common mulplicative factors, we obtain the following simplified score:

$$S_{\xi,i}^{(j)} = \begin{cases} P_\xi(-y_i + P_\xi) & \text{if } x_{j,i} = 0 \\ (1 - P_\xi)(y_i - P_\xi) & \text{otherwise} \end{cases}. \quad (33)$$

It is noticed that the difference of the above scores becomes $y_i - P_\xi$ even though the multiplicative factor P_ξ or $1 - P_\xi$ is involved in the score. Therefore, the sum of the scores is not affected by the differently weighted factors. In order to achieve the simplicity, we finally formulate the following simplified score:

$$S_{\xi,i}^{(j)} = \begin{cases} -y_i + P_\xi & \text{if } x_{j,i} = 0 \\ y_i - P_\xi & \text{otherwise} \end{cases}. \quad (34)$$

It is remarkable that the above score does not involve the number c of colluders and the variance of noise. Thus, we can directly calculate the score from a pirated codeword $y_i^\star$

without complicated estimators like EM-algorithm in the MAP detector.

5. SIMULATION RESULTS

In this section, we conduct extensive simulations to illustrate the traceability of the proposed simplified detector and to compare the performance with the MAP detector knowing an attack strategy and the number of colluders, but not the variance of noise. The traceability of a detector is evaluated for the number of detectable colluders and the false-negative probability that is the probability of detecting no colluder from a pirated copy in our experiment.

5.1 Fingerprinting Code Domain

The number of users in a fingerprinting system is $N = 10^4$, and the false-positive probability is $\epsilon_1 = 10^{-8}$. Hence, the total false-positive probability is $\eta \approx 10^{-4}$ in this experiment. The results are obtained based on Monte Carlo simulations with 10^3 trials. The maximum number of colluders is set to be $c_{max} = 8$ for Nuida code in this experiment, and hence, $n_c = 4$.

A pirated codeword is produced by averaging randomly selected c codewords, and it is distorted by additive white Gaussian noise. The traceability of the simplified detector is compared with that of the MAP detector which knows c, but not σ_e^2. It is noted that the variance σ_e^2 of noise is estimated from a distorted pirated codeword $\boldsymbol{y}^\star$ using the EM algorithm under the GMM in the MAP detector. Figure 2 depicts the number of detected colluders by changing the amount of noise for $L = 1024, 2048$ and 4096. It is observed that the traceability of the simplified detector is very close to that of the MAP detector. The false-negative probability is shown in Fig.3 under the same conditions. When $L = 1024$ and $c = 6$, the performance of the simplified detector is slightly lower than that of the MAP detector. The reason mainly comes from the low accuracy of the approximation of binomial distribution to the normal distribution discussed in Sect.4.

We further compare the performance by changing the number c of colluders under a constant amount of additive noise. The number of detected colluders is depicted in Fig.4 and the false-negative probability is in Fig.5. From these experimental results, we can say that there is no remarkable disadvantage of the simplified detector.

5.2 Signal Processing Domain

We use a standard image "lena" as the host signal which have 24-bit color with a size of 512×512 pixels. In this experiments, we embed a fingerprinting codeword into the

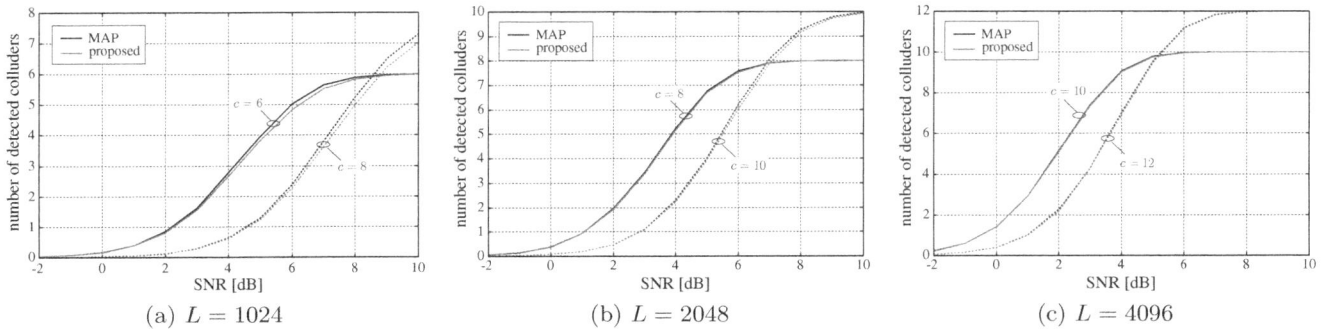

(a) $L = 1024$ (b) $L = 2048$ (c) $L = 4096$

Figure 2: Comparison of the number of detected colluders.

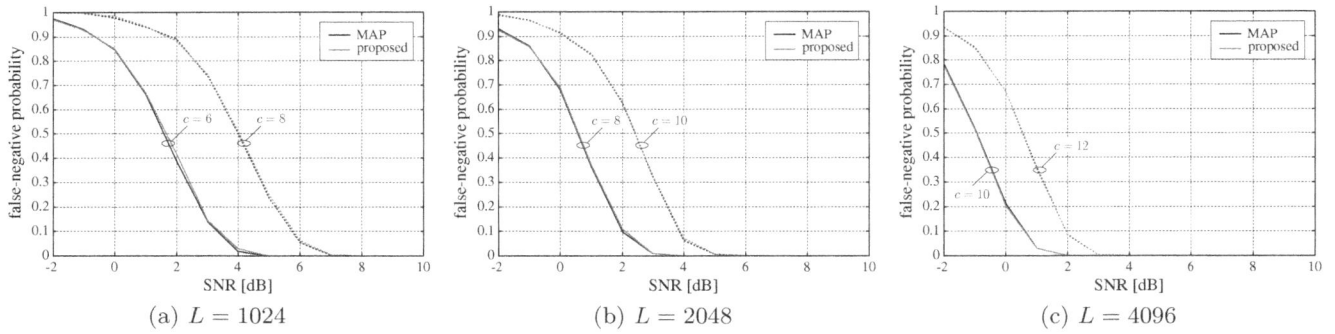

(a) $L = 1024$ (b) $L = 2048$ (c) $L = 4096$

Figure 3: Comparison of the false-negative probability.

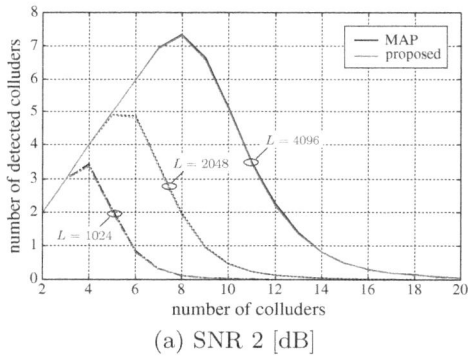

(a) SNR 2 [dB]

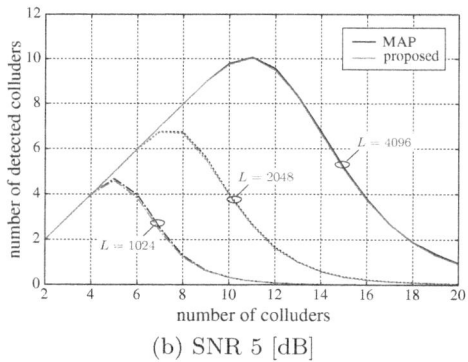

(b) SNR 5 [dB]

Figure 4: Number of detected colluders versus number of colluders.

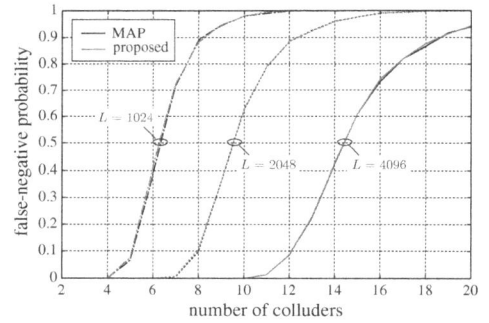

(a) SNR 2 [dB]

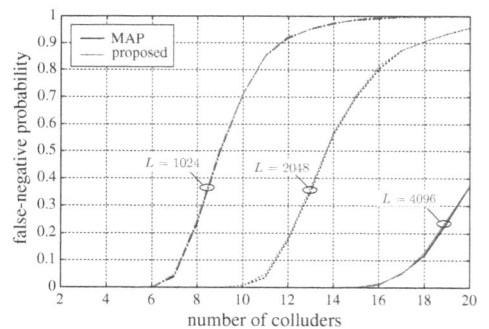

(b) SNR 5 [dB]

Figure 5: False-negative probability versus number of colluders.

luminance (Y) components of an image which is obtained by transforming RGB components of an image into YUV components. We use the basic SS-type watermarking scheme presented in IWDW2012 [15], which is a kind of SS watermarking scheme and employs the blind detection algorithm. Under the distortion constraint of fingerprinted image, each symbol in a codeword is modulated into an antipodal signal by carefully selecting its amplitude.

The procedure to embed a codeword x_j is explained below. We perform full-domain DCT to the Y components of an image, and select L DCT coefficients randomly from low and middle frequency domain using a secret key, which are regarded as a host signal denoted by v. We first modulate x_j into $\tilde{x}_j$ by BPSK modulation, and then, generate the SS sequence μ using a PN sequence pn specified by a secret key:

$$\mu = pn \otimes \text{IDCT}(\beta \tilde{x}_j), \qquad (35)$$

where $\otimes$ stands for an element-wise multiplication and β is an embedding strength. Then, we calculate the host interference h:

$$h = \text{DCT}(pn \otimes v). \qquad (36)$$

At the embedding stage, the host interference h should be removed in order to improve the robustness of a blind detector [16], which is called ISS operation. Therefore, using the above sequences, we calculate the fingerprinted host signal v' as follows:

$$v' = v + \mu - \lambda \otimes h, \qquad (37)$$

where λ stands for a control vector. By carefully tuning the parameters β and λ, we embed a fingerprinting codeword into a digital image in this experiment. At the detection, the distorted codeword $y^\star$ is calculated from the signal $v^\star$ extracted from a pirated copy.

$$y^\star = \frac{1}{\beta}\text{DCT}(pn \otimes v^\star). \qquad (38)$$

Considering the realistic situation, the number of users is $N = 10^6$, and the false-positive probability is $\epsilon_1 = 10^{-10}$, namely, $\eta \approx 10^{-4}$. We use the Nuida code with $c_{max} = 8$ in this experiment. For the evaluation of the performance, we first compress fingerprinted images using JPEG algorithm with quality factor 75%. Then, we average c images after decompression, and compress again the result with quality factor 50%. After extracting the embedded signal from the compressed and averaged copy without referring to the original copy, we attempt to detect colluders from the signal.

Under the distortion constraint with PSNR value, figures 6 and 7 show the averaged values for 10^3 trials. Because of the ISS operation at the embedding procedure, the performance is drastically dropped with the increase of PSNR value when L is large. If a non-blind detector is available, the performance is improved with the increase of L. It is observed from these figures that the traceability of the simplified detector outperforms that of the MAP detector when c is long and L is small. Because the accuracy of the estimated variance σ_e^2 in the EM algorithm is decreased with the number c of colluders, the traceability of the MAP detector which knows c, but not σ_e^2 is slightly lower than that of the simplified detector when L is small. The results indicate that the approximation error involved in the $\overline{P}_\xi^{(ave)}(y_i)$ is relatively smaller than the estimation error in the variance.

It is also confirmed from the results that the performance of the simplified detector approaches to that of the MAP detector with the increase of L. It is noted that the above performance is obtained by using an image "lena" and by tuning the embedding parameters considering the characteristic of the image. If a more robust SS watermarking scheme is applied, the performance will be improved, which is left for our future work.

5.3 Consideration

It is worth-mentioning that the performance of MAP detector is optimal under the averaging strategy if the number c of colluders and the variance σ_e^2 of noise are known. However, c and σ_e^2 are not known in a real situation. In addition, the accurate estimation of the variance of noise is inevitable. On the other hand, the simplified detector requires no additional information and estimation at the calculation of correlation score from a given pirated codeword. Because of the simplicity of the algorithm, it is advisable to use the simplified detector when a fingerprinting codeword is embedded into digital contents using a robust SS watermarking scheme. The proposed MAP and simplified detectors are specified for the averaging strategy considering the situation such that a fingerprinting codeword is embedded into a digital content using a robust SS watermarking scheme. If the other strategy is performed, the performance of these detectors is expected to be much lower than the conventional detectors [17][6].

The above experiments are conducted under the averaging attack that fixes the weights $w_{t,i} = 1/c$ because it is supposed to be the most damaging attack. The MAP detector and its simplified one are designed to be optimal under the averaging attack. However, these detectors are not optimal if the weights among c colluders are different. Suppose that one colluder takes more risk to be identified than the others, namely $w_{1,i} \gg w_{t,i}$ for $2 \leq t \leq c$. In this case, it is advisable to change the catch-many policy of the detector into the catch-one policy. When $w_{1,i} = 0.101$ and $w_{t,i} = 0.031$ for $2 \leq t \leq c = 30$ and PSNR is 38 [dB], we obtain the following results by experiments for 10^3 trials under the same conditions as Sect.5.2. Both of the detectors identify at least one colluder whose weight is $w_{1,i} = 0.101$ with a pretty small false-negative probability shown in Table 2. Different from the averaging strategy that the weight of all colluders is fixed to be $w_{t,i} = 1/c$, only one colluder's weight is much larger than the others in the above case, and hence, the colluder is much more likely to be identified from a pirated copy as confirmed by the experiment. Although this experiment only checks the extreme case of the attack strategy with different weights, we obtain a good performance using these detectors. In order to evaluate the universality of these detectors, we must study the performance for different type of weights both from the theoretical and experimental analyses, which is left for our future work.

Different from the Nuida code, the bias distribution of the Tardos code is continuous, and hence, it is difficult to apply the simplified detector directly to the probability p_i of Tardos code. In order to design the detector, the probability P_ξ is represented by a finite number (say Δ) of representative values $P_{\tilde{\xi}}$ as follows:

$$P_1 = \frac{1}{2\Delta}, \qquad (39)$$

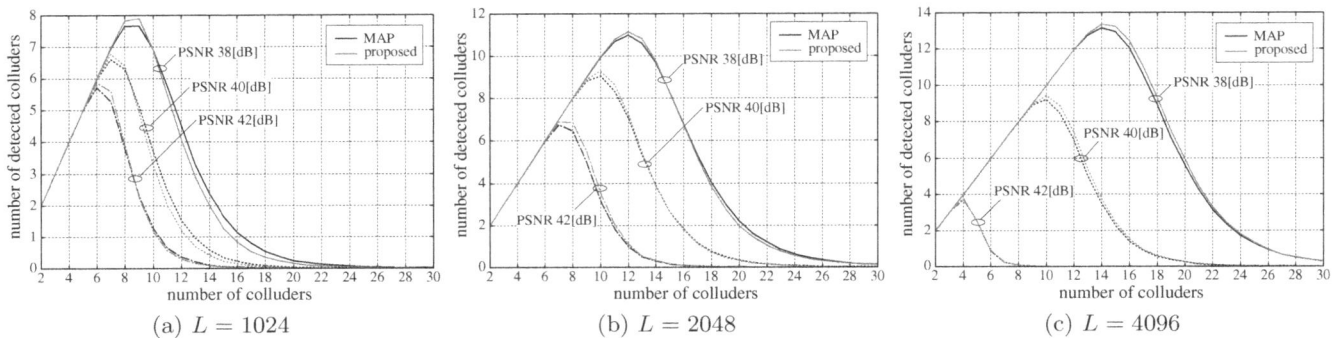

(a) $L = 1024$	(b) $L = 2048$	(c) $L = 4096$

Figure 6: Comparison of the number of detected colluders using an image "lena".

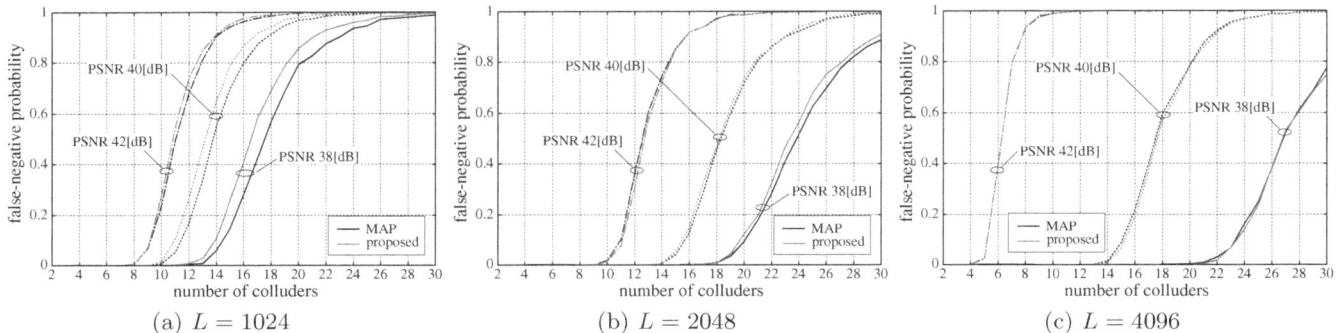

(a) $L = 1024$	(b) $L = 2048$	(c) $L = 4096$

Figure 7: Comparison of the false-negative probability using an image "lena".

Table 2: False-negative probability when $w_{1,i} = 0.101$ and $w_{t,i} = 0.031$ for $2 \leq t \leq c = 30$.

	false-negative probability	
L	MAP	proposed
1024	0.043	0.035
2048	0.003	0.002
4096	0	0

$$P_{\tilde{\xi}+1} = P_{\tilde{\xi}} + \frac{1}{\Delta}, \qquad (40)$$

for $1 \leq \tilde{\xi} \leq \Delta$, which conversion is applied in [13]. Compared with the Nuida code, however, the accuracy of the approximation of the normal distribution is decreased because of the digitized probability $P_{\tilde{\xi}}$. In addition, the traceability of Nuida code basically outperforms that of Tardos code. Therefore, it is advisable to use the Nuida code for the collusion secure fingerprinting system combined with the SS-type watermarking scheme.

6. CONCLUSION

In this paper, we proposed a MAP detector for the Nuida code under the averaging strategy. For a given number of colluders, the detector first estimates the variance of noise using the EM algorithm. The correlation score is calculated by the log-likelihood ratio of probabilities, which is information-theoretically optimal approach. Such an optimal detector must require the number of colluders in ad-

vance, and hence, its practicality is restricted in a real situation. In order to reduce the computational costs as well as to eliminate the number of colluders, we simplify the optimal detector by analyzing the characteristic of bias probabilities of Nuida code. From our intensive experiments, it is confirmed that the performance of the simplified detector is pretty close to that of the optimal detector. Furthermore, one attractive property of the simplified detector is that the number of colluders and the amount of additive noise are unnecessary at the calculation of correlation score because the performance of the MAP detector is strongly dependent on the accuracy.

7. ACKNOWLEDGMENTS

This research was partially supported by the Ministry of Education, Culture, Sports Science and Technology, Grant-in-Aid for Young Scientists (B) (24760299).

8. REFERENCES

[1] E. Abbe and L. Zheng. Linear universal decoding for compond channels. *IEEE Trans. Inform. Theory*, 56(12):5999–6013, 2010.

[2] C. M. Bishop. *Pattern Recognition and Machine Learning*. Springer, 2006.

[3] D. Boneh and J. Shaw. Collusion-secure fingerprinting for digital data. *IEEE Trans. Inform. Theory*, 44(5):1897–1905, 1998.

[4] I. J. Cox, J. Kilian, F. T. Leighton, and T. Shamson. Secure spread spectrum watermarking for multimedia. *IEEE Trans. Image Processing*, 6(12):1673–1687, 1997.

10

[5] T. Furon, A. Guyader, and F. Cérou. On the design and optimization of Tardos probabilistic fingerprinting codes. In *IH 2008*, volume 5284 of *LNCS*, pages 341–356. Springer, Heidelberg, 2008.

[6] T. Furon, A. Guyader, and F. Cérou. Decoding fingerprinting using the markov chain monte carlo method. In *WIFS - IEEE Workshop on Information Forensics and Security*. IEEE, 2012.

[7] T. Furon and L. P. Preire. EM decoding of Tardos traitor tracing codes. In *ACM Multimedia and Security*, pages 99–106, 2009.

[8] T. Furon, L. P. Preire, A. Guyader, and F. Cérou. Estimating the minimal length of Tardos code. In *IH 2009*, volume 5806 of *LNCS*, pages 176–190. Springer, Heidelberg, 2009.

[9] N. Kiyavash and P. Moulin. Regular simplex fingerprints and their optimality properties. *IEEE Trans. Inform. Forensics Security*, 4(3):318–329, 2009.

[10] M. Kuribayashi. Tardos's fingerprinting code over AWGN channel. In *IH 2010*, volume 6387 of *LNCS*, pages 103–117. Springer, Heidelberg, 2010.

[11] M. Kuribayashi. Hierarchical spread spectrum fingerprinting scheme based on the CDMA technique. *EURASIP J. Inform. Security*, (502782):16, 2011.

[12] M. Kuribayashi. A new soft decision tracing algorithm for binary fingerprinting codes,. In *IWSEC 2011*, volume 7038 of *LNCS*, pages 1–15. Springer, Heidelberg, 2011.

[13] M. Kuribayashi. Analysis of binary fingerprinting codes under relaxed marking assumption. In *Proc. 2012 Int. Symp. on Inform. Theory and its Applications, ISITA2012*, pages 643–647, 2012.

[14] M. Kuribayashi. Bias equalizer for binary probabilistic fingerprinting codes. In *IH 2012*, volume 7692 of *LNCS*, pages 269–283. Springer, Heidelberg, 2012.

[15] M. Kuribayashi. Coded spread spectrum watermarking scheme. In *IWDW 2012*, volume 7809 of *LNCS*, pages 169–183. Springer, Heidelberg, 2013.

[16] H. S. Malvar and D. A. F. Florêncio. Improved spread spectrum: a new modulation technique for robust watermarking. *IEEE Trans. Signal Processing*, 51(4):898–905, 2003.

[17] P. Meerwald and T. Furon. Group testing meets traitor tracing. In *ICASSP2011*, 2011.

[18] P. Meerwald and T. Furon. Towards practical joint decoding of binary Tardos fingerprinting codes. *IEEE Trans. Inform. Forensics and Security*, 7(4):1168–1180, 2012.

[19] K. Nuida, S. Fujitu, M. Hagiwara, T. Kitagawa, H. Watanabe, K. Ogawa, and H. Imai. An improvement of discrete Tardos fingerprinting codes. *Designs, Codes and Cryptography*, 52(3):339–362, 2009.

[20] G. Tardos. Optimal probabilistic fingerprint codes. *J. ACM*, 55(2):1–24, 2008.

[21] Z. J. Wang, M. Wu, W. Trappe, and K. J. R. Liu. Group-oriented fingerprinting for multimedia forensics. *EURASIP J. Appl. Signal Process.*, (14):2142–2162, 2004.

[22] M. Wu, W. Trappe, Z. J. Wang, and K. J. R. Liu. Collusion resistant fingerprinting for multimedia. *IEEE Signal Processing Magazine*, pages 15–27, 2004.

[23] Y. Yacobi. Improved boneh-shaw content fingerprinting. In *Proc. CT-RSA 2001*, volume 2020 of *LNCS*, pages 378–391. Springer-Verlag, 2001.

[24] H. V. Zhao, M. Wu, Z. J. Wang, and K. J. R. Liu. Forensic analysis of nonlinear collusion attacks for multimedia fingerprinting. *IEEE Trans. Image Processing*, 14(5):646–661, 2005.

Discrete Distributions in the Tardos Scheme, Revisited

Thijs Laarhoven
Eindhoven University of Technology
P.O. Box 513, 5600 MB
Eindhoven, The Netherlands
t.m.m.laarhoven@tue.nl

Benne de Weger
Eindhoven University of Technology
P.O. Box 513, 5600 MB
Eindhoven, The Netherlands
b.m.m.d.weger@tue.nl

ABSTRACT

The Tardos scheme is a well-known traitor tracing scheme to protect copyrighted content against collusion attacks. The original scheme contained some suboptimal design choices, such as the score function and the distribution function used for generating the biases. Škorić et al. previously showed that a symbol-symmetric score function leads to shorter codes, while Nuida et al. obtained the optimal distribution functions for arbitrary coalition sizes. Later, Nuida et al. showed that combining these results leads to even shorter codes when the coalition size is small. We extend their analysis to the case of large coalitions and prove that these optimal distributions converge to the arcsine distribution, thus showing that the arcsine distribution is asymptotically optimal in the symmetric Tardos scheme. We also present a new, practical alternative to the discrete distributions of Nuida et al. and give a comparison of the estimated lengths of the fingerprinting codes for each of these distributions.

Categories and Subject Descriptors

E.4 [**Data**]: Coding and Information Theory;
G.1.4 [**Mathematics of Computation**]: Numerical Analysis—*Quadrature and Numerical Differentiation*

General Terms

Design, Security, Theory

Keywords

Traitor tracing, fingerprinting, collusion-resistance, arcsine distribution, Legendre polynomials, asymptotics, quadratures

1. INTRODUCTION

To fight against copyright infringement, distributors of copyrighted content embed hidden watermarks in the data, creating a different version of the content for each user.

Then, when a user distributes his copy and the distributor finds it, the distributor extracts the watermark from this copy and traces it to the guilty user. Assuming two versions can be created for every segment of the content, it is clear that with a binary search, $\ell \approx \log_2 n$ watermarked content segments suffice to find one pirate hidden among n users.

Things become more complicated when several users *collude*, and compare their differently watermarked copies to create a new version of the content that does not exactly match any of their copies. Assuming that for each segment of the data there are two different versions, and that in each segment the colluders output one of their received versions (known in the literature as the *marking assumption*), it is impossible to trace $c \geq 2$ colluders deterministically (i.e., with no probability of error) with any fixed amount of segments. Fortunately, probabilistic schemes do exist that allow us to trace up to c colluders with at most ε probability of error, for any given $c \geq 2$ and $\varepsilon > 0$. One of the main objectives of research in this area is to construct such traitor tracing schemes, that allow us to trace colluders with as few segments ℓ as possible.

1.1 Related work

In 2003, Tardos [13] showed that the optimal length of such codes (i.e., the number of segments needed) is of the order $\ell = d_\ell c^2 \ln(n/\varepsilon_1)$ with $d_\ell = \Omega(1)$, where ε_1 is an upper bound on the probability of catching one or more innocent users.[1] In the same paper, Tardos gave a construction of a scheme with $d_\ell = 100$, which is widely known as the Tardos scheme. This shows that $d_\ell = \Theta(1)$ is optimal, and that the Tardos scheme has the optimal order code length.

Over the last ten years, improvements to the Tardos scheme have lead to a significant decrease in the code length parameter d_ℓ. We previously showed [6] that combining the symbol-symmetric score function of Škorić et al. [11] with the improved analysis of Blayer and Tassa [3] leads to an asymptotic code length constant of $d_\ell = \frac{1}{2}\pi^2 \approx 4.93$ for large c. For small coalitions, Nuida et al. [9] showed that even smaller values d_ℓ can be obtained by combining the symmetric score function with the optimized, discrete distribution functions previously obtained by Nuida et al. [10]. For large c, this lead to an asymptotic code length constant of about $d_\ell \approx 5.35$.

---

[1]Note that ε_2, commonly used for an upper bound on the probability of not catching any pirates, does not appear in the leading term of the code length for most practical values of ε_1 and ε_2.

Besides practical constructions of traitor tracing schemes, some papers have also studied absolute lower bounds on the asymptotic code lengths that any secure traitor tracing scheme must satisfy. Huang and Moulin [4] and Amiri and Tardos [2] showed that for large c, the code length constant of any scheme must satisfy $d_\ell \geq 2$, but no practical constructions of schemes achieving this lower bound are known. Huang and Moulin did show that this lower bound is tight, and that in the related min-max game between the traitors and the tracer, the optimal pirate strategy is to use the interleaving attack, and the optimal tracing strategy is to use a Tardos-like code with biases distributed according to the arcsine distribution. Note that this does not say anything about specific schemes such as the Tardos scheme, for which the related min-max games are different and may lead to a completely different optimal pirate strategy and tracing strategy.

1.2 Contributions and outline

In this paper, we show that for large coalition sizes, the discrete distributions of Nuida et al. [9, 10] converge to the arcsine distribution, thus proving that in the symmetric Tardos scheme, the arcsine distribution is asymptotically optimal. Together with results of Škorić et al. [11] and us [6], this further implies that the asymptotic code length $\ell \sim \frac{1}{2}\pi^2 c^2 \ln(n/\varepsilon_1)$ is optimal in the symmetric Tardos scheme. On the practical side, we present an alternative to the distributions of Nuida et al. with a simpler bias generation method, and conjecture that its performance is close to the performance of the distributions of Nuida et al.

The outline of this paper is as follows. In Section 2 we describe the symmetric Tardos scheme, and different choices for the distribution function F used in this scheme. In Section 3 we state our results, and we devote Section 4 to proving the main result. In Section 5 we present what we call discrete arcsine distributions, and in Section 6 we give a heuristic comparison of the lengths of the codes in the symmetric Tardos scheme when using these various distribution functions. Finally, in Section 7 we briefly discuss the results and mention a direction for future research.

2. THE SYMMETRIC TARDOS SCHEME

Before we describe the Tardos scheme, we introduce some more notation. The matrix $X = (X_{j,i})$, consisting of bits, is used to indicate which of the two versions of the ith content segment is assigned to user j, for each user $j \in \{1, \ldots, n\}$ and each segment $i \in \{1, \ldots, \ell\}$. We write $\vec{y} = (y_i)$ for the pirate output, consisting of ℓ bits.

The Tardos scheme roughly consists of two parts, which are outlined below. The scheme depends on appropriately chosen functions F and g, and constants ℓ and Z. The first part of the scheme is performed before the content is distributed, and focuses on generating the code matrix X. The second part is performed once the pirates have output a forged copy $\vec{y}$ and this copy has been detected by the distributor, and focuses on finding the guilty users.

(1) **Codeword generation**
   - For each i, generate $p_i \sim F$.
   - For each i, j, generate $X_{j,i} \sim \text{Bernoulli}(p_i)$.

(2) **Accusation algorithm**
   - For each i, j, compute $S_{j,i} = g(X_{j,i}, y_i, p_i)$.
   - For each j, accuse user j if $\sum_{i=1}^{\ell} S_{j,i} > Z$.

This description is very general, and covers (almost) any known version of the Tardos scheme. The choice of F and g, and the method to determine ℓ and Z, are what separates one scheme from another. In this paper we will focus on the class of *symmetric* Tardos schemes, which means choosing g as the symbol-symmetric score function of Škorić et al. [11]:

$$g(X_{j,i}, y_i, \dot{p}_i) = \begin{cases} +\sqrt{(1-p_i)/p_i}, & \text{if } X_{j,i} = 1, y_i = 1, \\ -\sqrt{(1-p_i)/p_i}, & \text{if } X_{j,i} = 1, y_i = 0, \\ -\sqrt{p_i/(1-p_i)}, & \text{if } X_{j,i} = 0, y_i = 1, \\ +\sqrt{p_i/(1-p_i)}, & \text{if } X_{j,i} = 0, y_i = 0. \end{cases}$$

In this paper we will not go into detail about choosing ℓ and Z, but focus on the distribution function F.

2.1 Continuous arcsine distributions

A common choice for the distribution function F is the arcsine distribution with appropriate cutoffs. More precisely, we first compute a cutoff parameter $\delta_c > 0$, and we then use the distribution function F_c defined on $[\delta_c, 1 - \delta_c]$ by:

$$F_c(p) = \frac{2 \arcsin \sqrt{p} - 2 \arcsin \sqrt{\delta_c}}{\pi - 4 \arcsin \sqrt{\delta_c}}. \qquad (\delta_c \leq p \leq 1 - \delta_c)$$

For $c = 10$, the distribution function F_{10} is shown in Figure 1. For small values of c, the parameter δ_c has to be sufficiently large for a certain proof of security to work. For large c, the cutoff δ_c tends to 0, and the distributions converge to the well-known arcsine distribution F_∞, defined on $[0, 1]$ by:

$$F_\infty(p) = \frac{2}{\pi} \arcsin \sqrt{p}. \qquad (0 \leq p \leq 1)$$

With these continuous arcsine distribution functions, we previously showed [6] that an asymptotic code length constant of $d_\ell \sim \frac{1}{2}\pi^2 \approx 4.93$ is optimal. For details, see [6].

2.2 Discrete Gauss-Legendre distributions

Nuida et al. [9, 10] showed that if the pirates aim to minimize their expected total score, the optimal distributions are in fact discrete distributions, and are related to Gauss-Legendre quadratures in numerical analysis. To define these distributions, we first need to introduce *Legendre polynomials*. For $c \geq 1$, the cth Legendre polynomial is given by

$$P_c(x) = \frac{1}{2^c c!} \left(\frac{d}{dx}\right)^c (x^2 - 1)^c.$$

This polynomial has c simple roots on $(-1, 1)$, which we will denote by $x_{1,c} < x_{2,c} < \ldots < x_{c,c}$. Now, the optimal distribution functions, for arbitrary c, are as follows. Here, optimal means that these distribution functions maximize the expected coalition score.

LEMMA 1. *[10, Theorem 3] The optimal distribution to fight against $2c - 1$ or $2c$ colluders, is*

$$F_{2c-1}(p) = F_{2c}(p) = \frac{1}{N_c} \sum_{k=1}^{c} w_{k,c} H(p - p_{k,c}), \quad (0 \leq p \leq 1)$$

where N_c is a normalizing constant, H is the Heaviside step function, and the points $p_{k,c}$ and weights $w_{k,c}$ are given by

$$p_{k,c} = \frac{x_{k,c} + 1}{2}, \qquad w_{k,c} = \frac{2}{(1 - x_{k,c}^2)^{3/2} P_c'(x_{k,c})^2}.$$

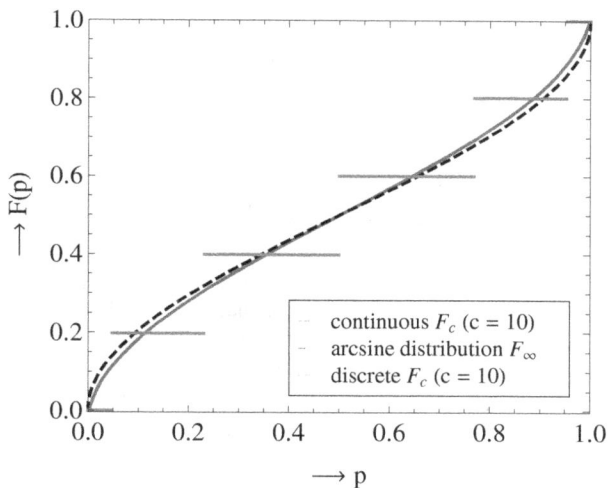

Figure 1: The continuous arcsine distribution function with cutoff $\delta_{10} \approx 0.003$ (red) and the discrete Gauss-Legendre distribution function (green), both corresponding to the case $c = 10$. The dashed curve shows the arcsine distribution function.

The Gauss-Legendre distribution designed to resist 10 colluders is shown in Figure 1. For small c, this construction gives much shorter codes than those obtained using the arcsine distributions with cutoffs. For large c, the code length parameter goes up, and Nuida et al. [9] show that their results can be extended to a construction that asymptotically achieves a code length constant of the order $d_\ell \sim K \approx 5.35$. For details on this asymptotic result and Lemma 1, we refer the reader to [9, 10].

2.3 The asymptotic optimum

As we discussed above, the asymptotic code length constant obtained by Nuida et al. [9] is slightly higher than the one obtained by us [6]. This means that the asymptotic result of Nuida et al. is not optimal. On the other hand, due to the Central Limit Theorem, the scores of innocent users (per segment) converge to the standard normal distribution with mean 0 and variance 1, while the total score of the coalition (per segment) converges to a normal distribution with some unknown mean $\tilde{\mu}$ and variance $\tilde{\sigma}^2 < \infty$, depending on the choice of F and the pirate strategy. For fixed $\varepsilon_2 > 0$ and large c, the only parameter that influences the asymptotic code length is the mean $\tilde{\mu}$, which is minimized by Nuida et al.'s choice of distribution functions. So we do expect that the asymptotic lengths of the codes in the symmetric Tardos scheme are minimized when using the distribution functions of Nuida et al. The fact that their asymptotic constant $d_\ell \approx 5.35$ is higher than the constant $d_\ell \approx 4.93$ which we showed to be sufficient for large c [6], suggests that Nuida et al.'s asymptotic analysis was not tight. Up until now, it was thus an open question what the best asymptotic distribution functions are in the symmetric Tardos scheme, as well as what their accompanying code length constants are.

3. MAIN RESULTS

We will prove that letting c tend to infinity in the class of discrete distributions of Nuida et al. leads exactly to the arc-

sine distribution. This will be done by proving the following main result.

THEOREM 1. *Let the parameters $p_{k,c}$, $w_{k,c}$, and N_c as in Lemma 1. Let $\alpha > 0$, and let k satisfy $\alpha c < k < (1-\alpha)c$. Then, as $c \to \infty$,*

$$p_{k,c} = \sin^2\left(\frac{\pi k}{2c}\right) + o(1), \tag{1}$$

$$w_{k,c} = \frac{\pi}{c} + o\left(\frac{1}{c}\right), \tag{2}$$

$$N_c = \pi - o(1). \tag{3}$$

Note that except for the points near 0 and 1, corresponding to $k = o(c)$ or $k = c - o(c)$, the leading terms of the weights are all equal. But since these points in the 'middle' carry $1 - o(1)$ weight (cf. the proof of (3)), the points near 0 and 1 have a negligible total weight. On the other hand, the points $p_{k,c}$ converge to the expected values of the corresponding order statistics of the arcsine distribution, i.e., the value y corresponding to $F_\infty(y) = \frac{k}{c}$ is exactly $y = F_\infty^{-1}(\frac{k}{c}) = \sin^2(\frac{\pi k}{2c}) = p_{k,c} + o(1)$. Since asymptotically all these points have the same weight, after k of the c points we also have $F_{2c}(p_k^{(c)}) = \frac{k}{c} + o(\frac{1}{c})$ or $F_{2c}^{-1}(\frac{k}{c}) = p_{k,c} + o(1)$. Since the set of points $\{p_{k,c}\}_{k=1}^{c}$ is dense in $(0,1)$ when c tends to infinity, these results imply that $F_{2c}(p) \to F_\infty(p)$ for each $p \in (0,1)$, proving that the arcsine distribution is asymptotically optimal in the symmetric Tardos scheme.

THEOREM 2. *In the symmetric Tardos scheme, the arcsine distribution is asymptotically optimal.*

Škorić et al. [11, Section 6] previously showed that when using the arcsine distribution, due to the Central Limit Theorem the optimal code length inevitably converges to $\ell \to \frac{1}{2}\pi^2 c^2 \ln(n/\varepsilon_1)$. So the following corollary is immediate.

COROLLARY 1. *In the symmetric Tardos scheme, the following code length is asymptotically optimal:*

$$\ell = \left(\frac{\pi^2}{2} + o(1)\right) c^2 \ln(n/\varepsilon_1).$$

In addition to these theoretical results, we present a new class of distribution functions, which can be obtained by discarding some of the order terms in Theorem 1. Compared to the Gauss-Legendre distributions, these distributions are much simpler, but still seem to achieve comparable code lengths. For details, see Sections 5 and 6.

4. PROOF OF THEOREM 1

(1): Let $\theta_{k,c} = \arccos(x_{k,c})$. From [1, Eq. (22.16.6)] we have

$$\theta_{k,c} = \left(\frac{4(c-k)+3}{4c+2}\right)\pi + o(1) = \pi - \frac{\pi k}{c} + o(1). \tag{4}$$

Using $\cos(\pi - \phi) = 2\sin^2(\frac{\phi}{2}) - 1$ for $\phi \in \mathbb{R}$, we get

$$x_{k,c} = \cos\left(\pi - \frac{\pi k}{c} + o(1)\right) = 2\sin^2\left(\frac{\pi k}{2c}\right) - 1 + o(1).$$

Since $p_{k,c} = \frac{1}{2}(x_{k,c} + 1)$, Equation (1) follows.

(2): Combining [12, Eq. (15.3.1)] and [12, Eq. (15.3.10)], and using $2\sin(\frac{\theta_{k,c}}{2})\cos(\frac{\theta_{k,c}}{2}) = \sin(\theta_{k,c})$, we get

$$\frac{2}{(1-x_{k,c}^2)P_c'(x_{k,c})^2} = \frac{\pi}{c}\sin(\theta_{k,c}) + o\left(\frac{1}{c}\right).$$

Dividing both sides by $\sqrt{1-x_{k,c}^2} = \sin\theta_{k,c}$ leads to (2).

(3): The Gauss-Legendre quadrature rule [1, Eq. (25.4.29)] states that for analytic functions f, there exist constants $A_c > 0$ and $\xi \in (-1, 1)$, with

$$\int_{-1}^1 f(x)dx = \sum_{k=1}^c \frac{2f(x_{k,c})}{(1-x_{k,c}^2)P_c'(x_{k,c})^2} + A_c f^{(2c)}(\xi).$$

Let $f(x) = (1-x^2)^{-1/2}$. Then we have $f^{(2c)}(x) > 0$ for all $x \in (-1,1)$, so in particular $f^{(2c)}(\xi) > 0$. So it follows that

$$\pi = \int_{-1}^1 \frac{dx}{\sqrt{1-x^2}} > \sum_{k=1}^c w_{k,c} = N_c. \tag{5}$$

On the other hand, from (2) and $w_{k,c} > 0$ for all k, we have

$$N_c > \sum_{k=o(c)}^{c-o(c)} w_{k,c} = (c - o(c))\left(\frac{\pi}{c} + o\left(\frac{1}{c}\right)\right) = \pi - o(1).$$

So $\pi - o(1) < N_c < \pi$, which proves (3).

5. DISCRETE ARCSINE DISTRIBUTIONS

By making a slight refinement to (1) using (4), we get that for large c and almost all values of k, the parameters of the optimal distributions satisfy

$$p_{k,c} \approx \sin^2\left(\frac{4k-1}{8c+4}\pi\right), \quad w_{k,c} \approx \frac{\pi}{c}, \quad N_c \approx \pi.$$

To get the exact values of these parameters for large c requires quite some effort, so in practice one may consider using an approximation of these distributions. An obvious approximation to the above weights and points would be

$$p_{k,c}' = \sin^2\left(\frac{4k-1}{8c+4}\pi\right), \quad w_{k,c}' = \frac{\pi}{c}, \quad N_c' = \pi.$$

Generating biases p from the associated distribution function is equivalent to drawing r uniformly at random from $\{\frac{3\pi}{8c+4}, \frac{7\pi}{8c+4}, \ldots, \frac{\pi}{2} - \frac{3\pi}{8c+4}\}$, and setting $p = \sin^2(r)$. Note that if we were to draw r uniformly at random from the complete interval $[0, \frac{\pi}{2}]$, this would correspond to the arcsine distribution, while drawing r uniformly at random from $[\arcsin(\sqrt{\delta}), \frac{\pi}{2} - \arcsin(\sqrt{\delta})]$ corresponds to the arcsine distribution with cutoff δ. So these distributions may be appropriately called *discrete arcsine distributions*, and needless to say, for large c these distributions also converge to the arcsine distribution.

Remark. Interestingly, slightly different parameters,

$$p_{k,c}'' = \sin^2\left(\frac{4k-2}{8c}\pi\right), \quad w_{k,c}'' = \frac{\pi}{c}, \quad N_c'' = \pi,$$

correspond exactly to the parameters of the so-called *Chebyshev-Gauss quadratures* [1, Eq. (25.4.38)]. These quadratures allow one to approximate integrals of the form

$$\int_{-1}^1 \frac{g(x)}{\sqrt{1-x^2}}dx \approx \sum_{k=1}^c w_{k,c}'' g(x_{k,c}''), \tag{6}$$

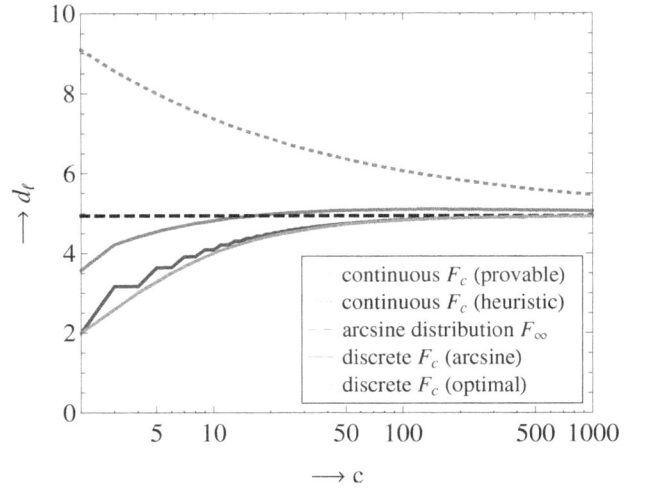

Figure 2: Estimates of the code length parameters d_ℓ for several types of distribution functions F. The dashed line shows the asymptotic optimal value $d_\ell = \frac{1}{2}\pi^2$, corresponding to the arcsine distribution F_∞.

where $x_{k,c}'' = 2p_{k,c}'' - 1$.[2] The distribution functions generated by these weights and points are very similar to the discrete arcsine distributions described above. The main difference seems to be the "cutoff", which would be about a third smaller (i.e., $\frac{2\pi}{8c}$ compared to $\frac{3\pi}{8c+4}$). Since these distributions are worse approximations of the optimal Gauss-Legendre distributions, it seems that the discrete arcsine distributions are a better alternative.

6. ESTIMATING CODELENGTHS

Let us now try to give a qualitative comparison of the several classes of discrete and continuous distribution functions, in terms of code lengths. Since the (tails of) distributions of user scores are hard to estimate, and known proof methods are not tight, we will only give a heuristic estimate of the code lengths. Getting more accurate estimates remains an open problem.

Assuming that the scores of users are Gaussian, we can get a reasonable estimate for the optimal code length parameter as $d_\ell \approx 2/\tilde{\mu}^2$, where $\tilde{\mu}$ is the expected average pirate score per content segment [11, Corollary 2]. In the case of the discrete distributions of Nuida et al., $\tilde{\mu}$ does not depend on the pirate strategy, so we can compute $\tilde{\mu}$ exactly. For the arcsine distributions with cutoffs and the discrete arcsine distributions, $\tilde{\mu}$ does depend on the pirate strategy, but by considering the attack that minimizes $\tilde{\mu}$ we can obtain lower bounds on $\tilde{\mu}$.

Figure 2 shows the resulting estimates of d_ℓ, as well as the provable upper bounds on d_ℓ of [6] (for constant ε_2). Note that the heuristic estimates for the continuous distributions are based on the arcsine distributions with cutoffs optimized for the proof technique of [6]. A different optimization of the cutoffs would lead to different (smaller) values of d_ℓ.

---

[2] Also note the resemblance between Equations (6) and (5), when $g(x) \equiv 1$ is the constant function with value 1.

7. CONCLUSION

We have shown that the optimal discrete distributions of Nuida et al. converge to the arcsine distribution, hence showing that the arcsine distribution is asymptotically optimal in the symmetric Tardos scheme. This connects the world of the discrete distributions to the world of the continuous distributions, as both converge to the same distribution.

In practice, the question remains which distribution function to choose. In the static Tardos scheme, choosing one of the discrete distributions seems logical, as this may drastically reduce the length of the fingerprinting code. On the other hand, when c is unknown, using the continuous distribution functions with cutoffs may also have its benefits, since if the coalition is slightly larger than expected, the scheme still has a good chance of catching the pirates. Recently, it was shown that the Tardos scheme can also be extended to the *dynamic* traitor tracing setting, allowing efficient tracing of pirates when the colluders broadcast their forged copy in real-time [7, 8]. The construction of the universal Tardos scheme in [7] uses the fact that the continuous distributions are very similar for different values of c, so in this setting it seems that the continuous arcsine distributions are also more practical.

An interesting open problem is what happens when the number of versions per content segment increases from 2 to q. Recent results show [5] that with unlimited computing power, the optimal asymptotic code length decreases linearly in q. This suggests that the optimal length of q-ary Tardos codes possibly decreases linearly in q as well. Škorić et al. [11] analyzed a natural generalization of the Tardos scheme to the q-ary setting, but did not obtain this linear decrease in q in their code lengths. The question remains whether their construction is suboptimal (and if so, whether this has to do with the choice of F or the choice of g), or if approaching the fingerprinting capacity for higher q with a single decoder traitor tracing scheme is simply impossible.

8. ACKNOWLEDGMENTS

We thank Jeroen Doumen, Wil Kortsmit, Jan-Jaap Oosterwijk, Georg Prokert, Berry Schoenmakers, and Boris Škorić for valuable discussions. We would also like to thank the anonymous reviewers for their useful comments.

9. REFERENCES

[1] M. Abramowitz and I.A. Stegun, editors. *Handbook of Mathematical Formulas*. Dover Publications, 1972.

[2] E. Amiri and G. Tardos. High rate fingerprinting codes and the fingerprinting capacity. In *Proc. 20th Symp. on Discrete Algorithms (SODA)*, pages 336–345, 2009.

[3] O. Blayer and T. Tassa. Improved versions of Tardos' fingerprinting scheme. *Designs, Codes and Cryptography*, 48(1):79–103, 2008.

[4] Y.-W. Huang and P. Moulin. On the saddle-point solution and the large-coalition asymptotics of fingerprinting games. *IEEE Transactions on Information Forensics and Security*, 7(1):160–175, 2012.

[5] Y.-W. Huang and P. Moulin. On fingerprinting capacity games for arbitrary alphabets and their asymptotics. In *Proc. International Symposium on Information Theory (ISIT)*, pages 2571–2575, 2012.

[6] T. Laarhoven and B. de Weger. Optimal symmetric Tardos traitor tracing schemes. *Designs, Codes and Cryptography*, 2012.

[7] T. Laarhoven, J. Doumen, P. Roelse, B. Škorić, and B. de Weger. Dynamic Tardos traitor tracing schemes. *IEEE Transactions on Information Theory*, 2013.

[8] T. Laarhoven, J.-J. Oosterwijk, and J. Doumen. Dynamic traitor tracing for arbitrary alphabets: Divide and conquer. In *Proc. 4th Workshop on Information Forensics and Security (WIFS)*, pages 240–245, 2012.

[9] K. Nuida, S. Fujitsu, M. Hagiwara, T. Kitagawa, H. Watanabe, K. Ogawa, and H. Imai. An improvement of discrete Tardos fingerprinting codes. *Designs, Codes and Cryptography*, 52(3):339–362, 2009.

[10] K. Nuida, M. Hagiwara, H. Watanabe, and H. Imai. Optimization of Tardos's fingerprinting codes in a viewpoint of memory amount. In *Proc. 9th Conf. Information Hiding (IH)*, pages 279–293, 2007.

[11] B. Škorić, S. Katzenbeisser, and M.U. Celik. Symmetric Tardos fingerprinting codes for arbitrary alphabet sizes. *Designs, Codes and Cryptography*, 46(2):137–166, 2008.

[12] G. Szegő. *Orthogonal polynomials*. American Mathematical Society, 4th Edition, 1975.

[13] G. Tardos. Optimal probabilistic fingerprint codes. In *Proc. 35th Symposium on Theory of Computing (STOC)*, pages 116–125, 2003.

Optimal Suspicion Functions
for Tardos Traitor Tracing Schemes

Jan-Jaap Oosterwijk
Eindhoven Univ. of Tech.
P.O. Box 513
5600 MB Eindhoven
The Netherlands
J.Oosterwijk@TUe.nl

Boris Škorić
Eindhoven Univ. of Tech.
P.O. Box 513
5600 MB Eindhoven
The Netherlands
B.Skoric@TUe.nl

Jeroen Doumen
Irdeto BV
P.O. Box 3047
2130 KA Hoofddorp
The Netherlands
JDoumen@Irdeto.com

ABSTRACT

We investigate alternative suspicion functions for Tardos traitor tracing schemes. In the simple decoder approach (computation of a score for every user independently) we derive suspicion functions that optimize a performance indicator related to the sufficient code length ℓ in the limit of large coalition size c. Our results hold for the Restricted-Digit Model as well as the Combined-Digit Model. The scores depend on information that is usually not available to the tracer – the attack strategy or the tallies of the symbols received by the colluders. We discuss how such results can be used in realistic contexts.

We study several combinations of coalition attack strategy versus suspicion function optimized against some attack (another attack or the same). In many of these combinations the usual scaling $\ell \propto c^2$ is replaced by a lower power of c, e.g. $c^{3/2}$. We find that the interleaving strategy is an especially powerful attack, and the suspicion function tailored against interleaving is effective against all considered attacks.

Categories and Subject Descriptors

E.4 [**Data**]: Coding and Information Theory;
G.1 [**Mathematics of Computing**]: Numerical Analysis;
G.1.6 [**Numerical Analysis**]: Optimization—*Constrained optimization, Stochastic programming*

General Terms

Design, Measurement, Security, Theory

Keywords

Traitor tracing, collusion-resistance

1. INTRODUCTION

1.1 Collusion attacks on watermarking

Forensic watermarking is a means for tracing the origin and distribution of digital content. Before distribution, the content is modified by embedding an imperceptible watermark, which plays the role of a personalized serial number. Once an unauthorized copy of the content is found, the identities of those users who participated in its creation can be determined. A tracing algorithm outputs a list of suspicious users.

The most powerful attacks against watermarking are *collusion attacks*, in which multiple attackers (the 'coalition') combine their differently watermarked versions of the same content; the observed differences point to the locations of the hidden marks.

In the past two decades several types of collusion-resistant codes have been developed. The most popular type in the recent literature is the class of *bias-based* codes. These were introduced by G. Tardos in 2003. The original paper [22] was followed by a flurry of activity, e.g. improved analyses [2, 6, 7, 10, 17, 21], code modifications [8, 14, 15], decoder modifications [1, 5, 12] and various generalizations [4, 18, 19, 23]. The advantage of bias-based versus deterministic codes is that they can achieve the asymptotically optimal relationship $\ell \propto c^2$ between the sufficient code length ℓ and the coalition size c.

Two kinds of tracing algorithm can be distinguished: (i) *simple decoders*, which assign a level of suspicion to single users and (ii) *joint decoders* [1, 5, 12], which look at sets of users. Joint decoders employ a simple decoder as a bootstrapping step.

Tardos' scheme worked with a binary code and a simple decoder. Its 'suspicion function' for computing a level of suspicion for single users was improved [18] and the scheme was generalized to q-ary alphabets. However, it turns out [20] that the suspicion function yields sub-optimal fingerprinting rates for $q > 3$, i.e. rather far below the fingerprinting capacity [3, 9] and far below the dynamic code rate [11].

Alternative suspicion functions for the binary case were introduced [5], where an Expectation Maximization (EM) algorithm was used. A candidate coalition is selected, which (if the guess is sufficiently good) makes it possible to estimate the employed attack strategy; a suspicion function is then used which is optimized against that strategy. This leads to a new ranking of users, giving a new candidate coalition, and the whole process is repeated until it converges.

1.2 Contributions

In this paper we further study suspicion functions.

- We generalize the work of Charpentier et al. [5] to q-ary alphabets. Using functional derivation methods we obtain suspicion functions that asymptotically ($c \gg 1$) maximize the expected score for the coalition, allowing the tracer to distinguish best between them and the innocent users. We present results for the Combined-Digit Model and the Restricted-Digit Model.

- We consider a set of often-considered attack strategies. We substitute these attacks into the generic formulas and obtain closed-form expressions for the optimal suspicion functions associated with these attacks.

- We tabulate the performance for each combination of attack and suspicion function. For some cases we prove theorems analytically and for all cases we have numerical results. Naturally, in case of a match the sufficient code length ℓ is small; for all considered strategies but the interleaving attack we even find $\ell \propto c^{3/2}$. For the interleaving attack and its matching suspicion function we find an asymptotic fingerprinting rate $(q-1)/(2c^2 \ln q)$, which is exactly the q-ary asymptotic fingerprinting capacity.

  In non-matching cases the results differ widely. In some cases, as expected, the mismatched defense fails completely, while in others the code length remains $\ell \propto c^2$ (often smaller than with the Tardos suspicion function), and in many cases we find $\ell \propto c^{3/2}$ even for a mismatch.

In Sections 3.1 and 7 we comment on possible ways to exploit our results for the construction of improved decoders by using several suspicion functions in parallel, and/or deploying a tally-dependent suspicion to strengthen the EM algorithm, and/or to validate candidate coalitions in general.

This paper contains a large number of lemmas and theorems. Not all the proofs are shown, due to space constraints. All proofs can be found in the ePrint version [16].

2. PRELIMINARIES

2.1 General notation

We denote random variables by capital letters and their realizations in lower case. We write vectors in boldface. We define $[\ell] = \{1, \ldots, \ell\}$. The q-ary alphabet is $\mathcal{A}$, which is sometimes set to $\mathcal{A} = \{0, \ldots, q-1\}$. We use multi-index notation, e.g. $\boldsymbol{p}^\kappa = \prod_{\alpha \in \mathcal{A}} p_\alpha^\kappa$, $\boldsymbol{p}^{\boldsymbol{m}} = \prod_{\alpha \in \mathcal{A}} p_\alpha^{m_\alpha}$, and $\binom{c}{m} = c! / \prod_{\alpha \in \mathcal{A}} m_\alpha!$. We define the norm of a vector as $|\boldsymbol{p}| = \sum_{\alpha \in \mathcal{A}} |p_\alpha|$. For probability mass/density functions we use abbreviated notation of the form $f_{y|\boldsymbol{p}} = f_{Y|\boldsymbol{P}}(y|\boldsymbol{p})$ when it does not cause ambiguity. In conditional expectation values we sometimes use the abbreviation $\mathbb{E}_{M|\boldsymbol{p}}[\cdots] = \mathbb{E}_M[\cdots | \boldsymbol{P} = \boldsymbol{p}]$. An $\mathbb{E}$ without subscripts is an expectation over *all* probabilistic degrees of freedom. We use $\delta_{x,y}$ to denote the Kronecker delta function, which is 1 when $x = y$ and 0 when $x \neq y$.

2.2 Bias-based tracing; simple decoder

The content contains ℓ abstract 'locations' into which a q-ary symbol can be embedded. For each location $i \in [\ell]$ independently, the tracer draws a bias vector $\boldsymbol{P}_i = (P_{i,\alpha})_{\alpha \in \mathcal{A}}$

from a distribution $f_{\boldsymbol{P}}$. The biases satisfy $P_{i,\alpha} \geq 0$ and $|\boldsymbol{P}_i| = 1$. In [18] a symmetric Dirichlet distribution was taken, with concentration parameter $\kappa > 0$,

$$f_{\boldsymbol{P}}(\boldsymbol{p}) = \boldsymbol{p}^{\kappa-1} \Gamma(q\kappa) / [\Gamma(\kappa)]^q. \qquad (1)$$

For $q = 2$ it is customary to set $\kappa = \frac{1}{2}$, turning (1) into the arcsine distribution for the component p_1. However, in that case the support has to be reduced to $p_1 \in [\delta, 1-\delta]$, with cutoff parameter $\delta > 0$, in order to avoid statistical problems due to extremely unlikely events. The probability density function then becomes

$$f_P(p_1) = \frac{1}{2\arcsin(1-2\delta)} \frac{1}{\sqrt{p_1(1-p_1)}}. \qquad (2)$$

As the cutoff parameter is typically chosen so small that it vanishes, we will neglect it in our analysis. The number of users is n. For each $i \in [\ell]$ and each $j \in [n]$, the tracer draws a random symbol $X_{i,j} \in \mathcal{A}$ according to the categorical distribution $\boldsymbol{P}_i$, i.e. $\Pr[X_{i,j} = \alpha | \boldsymbol{P}_i = \boldsymbol{p}_i] = p_{i,\alpha}$ independent of j. The symbol $X_{i,j}$ is embedded into the content of user j in location i.

The coalition of attackers is denoted as $\mathcal{C} \subset [n]$, with $|\mathcal{C}| = c$. In some attack models, e.g. the Combined-Digit Model (Section 2.3), they are allowed to do signal processing attacks such as introducing noise and fusing symbols. In the Restricted-Digit Model (RDM) they are only allowed to select one colluder's symbol (denoted as y_i) in location i. In the *simple decoder* approach, the tracer determines a score S_j for each user j by adding independently computed sub-scores $S_{i,j}$ for each location i; these are based on $\boldsymbol{p}_i$, $X_{i,j}$ and the colluders' output in location i. If the score exceeds a threshold, user j is suspect.

Tardos [22] introduced a (simple decoder) score system for he RDM at $q = 2$ that was later [18] symmetrized and generalized to $q > 2$. The sub-scores for each location are computed using a 'suspicion function' g as $S_{i,j} = g(x_{i,j}, y_i, \boldsymbol{p}_i)$ with

$$g(x, y, \boldsymbol{p}) = \begin{cases} \sqrt{(1-p_y)/p_y} & \text{if } x = y \\ -\sqrt{p_y/(1-p_y)} & \text{if } x \neq y. \end{cases} \qquad (3)$$

It has the special property that the $S_{i,j}$ of innocent users has expectation 0 and variance 1.

Given the symmetries present in the code generation and accusation algorithm, it is usually assumed that the attackers apply a strategy that acts at every location independently. Furthermore, we assume that the colluders take equal risks. In such an attack model, the colluders' decision in location i depends only on the tallies $M_{i,\alpha} = |\{j \in \mathcal{C} | X_{i,j} = \alpha\}|$ (with $\alpha \in \mathcal{A}$). The tallies satisfy $|\boldsymbol{M}_i| = c$, and they are multinomial-distributed, $f_{\boldsymbol{m}|\boldsymbol{p}} = \binom{c}{m} \boldsymbol{p}^{\boldsymbol{m}}$. The attack strategy may be probabilistic.

2.3 Combined-Digit Model (CDM)

The CDM [19] allows colluders to mix symbols and to introduce noise. In each location, the symbols that are mixed are assumed to have equal power. The set of symbols that the colluders choose to mix is denoted as $\boldsymbol{\Psi} \subseteq \mathcal{A}$ with $m_\alpha > 0$ for each $\alpha \in \boldsymbol{\Psi}$. The attack strategy is parametrized by a set of probabilities $f_{\boldsymbol{\psi}|\boldsymbol{m}}$. The tracer has a detector that outputs a set $\boldsymbol{\Phi} \subseteq \mathcal{A}$ of observed symbols. The joint effects of the noise and the mixing lead to probability distributions $f_{\boldsymbol{\Phi}|\boldsymbol{\Psi}}$, where it is possible that the noise introduces symbols in $\boldsymbol{\Phi}$ that are absent in $\boldsymbol{\Psi}$. Simple-decoder score systems were introduced in [19, 23].

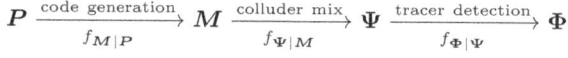

$$P \xrightarrow[f_{M|P}]{\text{code generation}} M \xrightarrow[f_{\Psi|M}]{\text{colluder mix}} \Psi \xrightarrow[f_{\Phi|\Psi}]{\text{tracer detection}} \Phi$$

Figure 1: A schematic depiction of the CDM.

The CDM reduces to the RDM when the noise strength is sent to zero and the detector unerringly observes $\boldsymbol{\Phi} = \boldsymbol{\Psi}$, forcing the colluders to output a single symbol, $\boldsymbol{\Psi} = \{Y\}$. For the RDM, a strategy is parametrized by a set of probabilities $f_{y|m}$.

2.4 Performance; moments of the scores

The performance of bias-based tracing schemes can for a large part be characterized by looking merely at the first and second moment of the innocent and guilty scores. (This holds especially at large c, where the large code length induces an almost-Gaussian shape of the score probability distributions.)

For an innocent user j, we define the mean and variance as

$$\tilde{\mu}_{\text{inn}} := \mathbb{E}[S_{i,j}] \tag{4}$$

$$\tilde{\sigma}_{\text{inn}}^2 := \text{Var}[S_{i,j}] = \mathbb{E}[(S_{i,j} - \tilde{\mu}_{\text{inn}})^2] = \mathbb{E}[S_{i,j}^2] - \tilde{\mu}_{\text{inn}}^2, \tag{5}$$

where the index $i \in [\ell]$ is arbitrary. The expectation $\mathbb{E}$ is taken over the random variables $\boldsymbol{P}_i$, $X_{i,j}$, and Y_i (in the CDM $\boldsymbol{\Psi}_i$ and $\boldsymbol{\Phi}_i$ instead of Y_i). We call a suspicion function centered if it yields $\tilde{\mu}_{\text{inn}} = 0$ and normalized if $\tilde{\sigma}_{\text{inn}}^2 = 1$. For the coalition we define $S_{i,\mathcal{C}} := \sum_{j \in \mathcal{C}} S_{i,j}$. The moments are

$$\tilde{\mu}_{\mathcal{C}} := \mathbb{E}[S_{i,\mathcal{C}}] \tag{6}$$

$$\tilde{\sigma}_{\mathcal{C}}^2 := \text{Var}[S_{i,\mathcal{C}}] = \mathbb{E}[(S_{i,\mathcal{C}} - \tilde{\mu}_{\mathcal{C}})^2] = \mathbb{E}[S_{i,\mathcal{C}}^2] - \tilde{\mu}_{\mathcal{C}}^2 \tag{7}$$

again with arbitrary index i. If the Gaussian approximation holds, then the sufficient code length is proportional to $(\tilde{\mu}_{\mathcal{C}}/\tilde{\sigma}_{\text{inn}})^{-2} c^2$ [21]. We will use the fraction $\tilde{\mu}_{\mathcal{C}}/\tilde{\sigma}_{\text{inn}}$ as a performance indicator.

3. OPTIMAL SUSPICION FUNCTIONS

We consider suspicion functions h other than the function g given in (3). We derive suspicion functions that maximize the performance indicator $\tilde{\mu}_{\mathcal{C}}/\tilde{\sigma}_{\text{inn}}$, in the CDM as well as the RDM. Without loss of generality, we will consider only suspicion functions that are centered ($\tilde{\mu}_{\text{inn}} = 0$) and normalized ($\tilde{\sigma}_{\text{inn}} = 1$). We use the standard approach of Lagrange functionals; we use constraint multipliers $\lambda_1, \lambda_2 \in \mathbb{R}$ to enforce the constraints $\tilde{\mu}_{\text{inn}} = 0$ and $\tilde{\sigma}_{\text{inn}} = 1$. We define the functional

$$L(h, \lambda_1, \lambda_2) = \tilde{\mu}_{\mathcal{C}} - \lambda_1 \tilde{\mu}_{\text{inn}} - \tfrac{1}{2}\lambda_2 (\tilde{\sigma}_{\text{inn}}^2 - 1), \tag{8}$$

where $\tilde{\mu}_{\text{inn}}$, $\tilde{\sigma}_{\text{inn}}$ and $\tilde{\mu}_{\mathcal{C}}$ depend on the function h as specified in (4-6). The optimal h is found by solving the set of equations $\delta L/\delta h = 0$, $\partial L/\partial \lambda_1 = 0$ and $\partial L/\partial \lambda_2 = 0$. The solution depends on the arguments of h: in the CDM the sub-score of user j in location i is typically a function of $X_{i,j}$, $\boldsymbol{\Phi}_i$ and $\boldsymbol{P}_i$; in the RDM a function of $X_{i,j}$, Y_i and $\boldsymbol{P}_i$.

3.1 ... in the Combined-Digit Model

We present a number of lemmas leading up to the main theorem of this section, which shows the solution obtained

by the Lagrangian approach. All proofs can be found in the ePrint version [16]. The conditional probabilities that appear in the lemmas are related as follows: $f_{\psi|\boldsymbol{p}} = \sum_{\boldsymbol{m}} f_{\psi|\boldsymbol{m}} f_{\boldsymbol{m}|\boldsymbol{p}}$ and $f_{\phi|\boldsymbol{p}} = \sum_{\psi} f_{\phi|\psi} f_{\psi|\boldsymbol{p}}$. The numbers $f_{\phi|\psi}$ are fixed parameters of the CDM independent of the strategy.

LEMMA 1. *An optimal suspicion function of the form $h(x, \boldsymbol{\phi}, \boldsymbol{\psi}, \boldsymbol{p})$ does not depend on $\boldsymbol{\phi}$. An optimal suspicion function of the form $h(x, \boldsymbol{\phi}, \boldsymbol{\psi}, \boldsymbol{m}, \boldsymbol{p})$ depends neither on $\boldsymbol{\phi}$ nor $\boldsymbol{\psi}$.*

PROOF SKETCH. The set $\boldsymbol{\psi}$ contains more information about the attackers than the set $\boldsymbol{\phi}$. Likewise, the tallies $\boldsymbol{m}$ contain more information than $\boldsymbol{\psi}$. $\square$

To determine the optimal suspicion functions of the increasingly general forms $h(x, \boldsymbol{\phi}, \boldsymbol{p})$, $h(x, \boldsymbol{\phi}, \boldsymbol{\psi}, \boldsymbol{p})$, and $h(x, \boldsymbol{\phi}, \boldsymbol{\psi}, \boldsymbol{m}, \boldsymbol{p})$, it suffices to study the forms $h_{\Phi}(x, \boldsymbol{\phi}, \boldsymbol{p})$, $h_{\Psi}(x, \boldsymbol{\psi}, \boldsymbol{p})$, and $h_M(x, \boldsymbol{m}, \boldsymbol{p})$, respectively.

LEMMA 2. *Let h be of the form $h_{\Phi}(x, \boldsymbol{\phi}, \boldsymbol{p})$ and define*

$$T_{\Phi}(x, \boldsymbol{\phi}, \boldsymbol{p}) := \frac{\mathbb{E}_{M|\boldsymbol{p}}[M_x f_{\phi|M}]}{cp_x f_{\phi|\boldsymbol{p}}} = \frac{1}{c}\frac{\partial \ln f_{\phi|\boldsymbol{p}}}{\partial p_x}\bigg|_{|\boldsymbol{p}|=1} + 1. \tag{9}$$

Then $\tilde{\mu}_{\mathcal{C}} = c \cdot \mathbb{E}[T_{\Phi} h]$ and $\mathbb{E}[T_{\Phi}] = 1$.

The notation $\frac{\partial A}{\partial p_x}\big|_{|\boldsymbol{p}|=1}$ is defined as follows. First the derivative $\partial A/\partial p_x$ is taken *without* taking the constraint $\sum_{\alpha} p_{\alpha} = 1$ into account. After differentiation the constraint is enforced.

LEMMA 3. *Let h be of the form $h_{\Psi}(x, \boldsymbol{\psi}, \boldsymbol{p})$ and define*

$$T_{\Psi}(x, \boldsymbol{\psi}, \boldsymbol{p}) := \frac{\mathbb{E}_{M|\boldsymbol{p}}[M_x f_{\psi|M}]}{cp_x f_{\psi|\boldsymbol{p}}} = \frac{1}{c}\frac{\partial \ln f_{\psi|\boldsymbol{p}}}{\partial p_x}\bigg|_{|\boldsymbol{p}|=1} + 1. \tag{10}$$

Then $\tilde{\mu}_{\mathcal{C}} = c \cdot \mathbb{E}[T_{\Psi} h]$ and $\mathbb{E}[T_{\Psi}] = 1$.

LEMMA 4. *Let h be of the form $h_M(x, \boldsymbol{m}, \boldsymbol{p})$ and define*

$$T_M(x, \boldsymbol{m}, \boldsymbol{p}) := \frac{m_x}{cp_x} = \frac{1}{c}\frac{\partial \ln f_{\boldsymbol{m}|\boldsymbol{p}}}{\partial p_x}\bigg|_{|\boldsymbol{p}|=1} + 1. \tag{11}$$

Then $\tilde{\mu}_{\mathcal{C}} = c \cdot \mathbb{E}[T_M h]$, $\mathbb{E}[T_M] = 1$, and $\text{Var}[T_M] = \frac{q-1}{c}$.

THEOREM 1. *In each of the cases above, the centered and normalized suspicion function that maximizes $\tilde{\mu}_{\mathcal{C}}$ is*

$$h = (T - \mathbb{E}[T]) / \sqrt{\text{Var}[T]} \tag{12}$$

and the expected coalition score is $\tilde{\mu}_{\mathcal{C}} = c \cdot \sqrt{\text{Var}[T]}$.

PROPOSITION 5. *For the function T in all three cases above it holds that*

$$T(x, \square, \boldsymbol{p}) \propto \frac{\Pr[j \in \mathcal{C}|x, \square, \boldsymbol{p}]}{\Pr[j \notin \mathcal{C}|x, \square, \boldsymbol{p}]}, \tag{13}$$

and thus T is a Neyman-Pearson score.

Several things are worth noting about these results.

(i) In the proof of Theorem 1 it is not necessary to specify the bias distribution. Though $\tilde{\mu}_{\mathcal{C}}$ is a functional of both h and $f_{\boldsymbol{P}}$, the optimization of h does not depend on $f_{\boldsymbol{P}}$.

(ii) In all three cases the result for h depends on information that the tracer usually does not have. (The strategy $f_{\psi|m}$ in Lemmas 2 and 3; the tallies $\boldsymbol{m}$ in Lemma 4.) When a function h_{Φ}, for some guessed strategy, is used to compute scores, there is no guarantee that the attackers are actually adhering to that guessed strategy. Such 'mismatched' situations will be discussed (for the RDM) in Section 5.

(iii) We can think of two ways in which the $\boldsymbol{m}$-dependent result of Lemma 4, $h(x, y, \boldsymbol{p}) = (\frac{m_x}{cp_x} - 1)\sqrt{\frac{c}{q-1}}$, can be used in practice. First, it could be employed in the EM algorithm [5]. The EM procedure estimates a strategy based on the symbols received by the candidate coalition, and then uses this estimate to adapt the suspicion function. Our h function could be used to directly assign scores to all users, *skipping the strategy estimation step*. This would speed up each iteration of the EM algorithm and avoid the statistical inaccuracies in the estimation. (Of course, inaccuracies due to a wrongly guessed coalition remain, and may even increase.)

Secondly, this h function can be used as a consistency check in the following way. Suppose that, by some means, a candidate coalition $\hat{\mathcal{C}}$ has been tentatively identified. Then one computes a score $(\frac{m_x}{cp_x} - 1)\sqrt{\frac{c}{q-1}}$ for all users, where the tally m_x is based on $\hat{\mathcal{C}}$ and the user's symbol x. If $\hat{\mathcal{C}}$ equals the actual coalition, one should see a huge score difference between innocent users and the colluders. Exploration of these ideas is left for future work.

(iv) The expression $\partial \ln f / \partial p_x$ in all three cases has the form of a Fisher score, being the derivative of the logarithm of a conditional probability with respect to the conditioning variable. We suspect that this form is no coincidence. However, the intuitive meaning of the associated 'game' (guessing $\boldsymbol{p}$ from y) is not immediately obvious. Asymptotically $\boldsymbol{m}$ tends to $c\boldsymbol{p}$. We hypothesize that the game 'guess $\boldsymbol{p}$ from y' is asymptotically equivalent to 'guess $\boldsymbol{m}$ from y'. The latter is a known formulation of the tracing problem.

(v) Our result in Proposition 5 is different from the Neyman-Pearson score in [12], where the whole sequence $(Y_i)_{i \in [\ell]}$ was considered.

3.2 ... in the Restricted-Digit Model

The optimal h function in the RDM case follows straightforwardly from Lemma 2 and Theorem 1 by taking the limit of zero noise and perfect detection of all mixed symbols, leading to $\Phi = \Psi = \{Y\}$, with $Y \in \mathcal{A}$.

COROLLARY 6. *Let h be of the form $h_Y(x, y, \boldsymbol{p})$ and define*

$$T_Y(x, y, \boldsymbol{p}) := \frac{\mathbb{E}_{M|\boldsymbol{p}}[M_x f_{y|M}]}{cp_x f_{y|\boldsymbol{p}}} = \frac{1}{c} \left. \frac{\partial \ln f_{y|\boldsymbol{p}}}{\partial p_x} \right|_{|\boldsymbol{p}|=1} + 1. \quad (14)$$

Then $\tilde{\mu}_{\mathcal{C}} = c \cdot \mathbb{E}[T_Y h]$ and $\mathbb{E}[T_Y] = 1$.

In the RDM, Lemma 4 and Theorem 1 hold without change. Note that the Marking Assumption is not invoked to obtain

Corollary 6. Hence Corollary 6 is valid in a more general setting, as long as the colluders produce a single symbol which is unerringly detected by the tracer.

Note also that (14) for $q = 2$ is consistent with Charpentier et al. [5].

4. MATCHES

From this point onward, we consider only the RDM. For a number of often-studied strategies we compute the optimal suspicion function. We investigate the situation where the actual attack is indeed the one for which the h-function was designed (a "match"). Mismatches are discussed in Section 5.

4.1 Arbitrary alphabets

Interleaving attack. The interleaving attack $f_{y|m} = m_y/c$ randomly selects an attacker and outputs his symbol.

PROPOSITION 7. *Against the interleaving attack, the quantity T is given by $T(x, y, \boldsymbol{p}) = 1 + (1/c)(\delta_{x,y}/p_y - 1)$, and the optimal suspicion function is*

$$h(x, y, \boldsymbol{p}) = \frac{1}{\sqrt{q-1}} \left(\frac{\delta_{x,y}}{p_y} - 1 \right). \quad (15)$$

In case of a match it holds that $\tilde{\mu}_{\mathcal{C}} = \sqrt{q-1}$ for any $f_{\boldsymbol{P}}$.

When $x = y$, the h is positive and increasing in p_y (rare events raise more suspicion). When $x \neq y$, it is negative and constant, in contrast to (3). The h is independent of c.

All-high attack. The all-high attack

$$f_{y|m} = \begin{cases} 1 & \text{if } m_y > 0 \text{ and } m_{y+1} = \cdots = m_{q-1} = 0 \\ 0 & \text{else} \end{cases} \quad (16)$$

outputs the highest symbol among those received by the coalition.

Note that this is the only attack we consider that breaks symbol symmetry and assumes an ordering of the alphabet. This is a special case of the preferred-sequence attack, in which the colluders have a predetermined ranking of the symbols. The results below generalize to the preferred-sequence attack. We will use the shorthand notation $a_k := (p_0 + \cdots + p_{k-1})$ and $a_{\mathcal{B}} = \sum_{\beta \in \mathcal{B}} p_\beta$.

PROPOSITION 8. *Against the all-high attack, the optimal suspicion function is $h = (T-1)/\sqrt{\text{Var}[T]}$, with*

$$T(x, y, \boldsymbol{p}) = \begin{cases} (a_{y+1}^{c-1} - a_y^{c-1})/(a_{y+1}^c - a_y^c) & \text{if } x < y \\ a_{y+1}^{c-1}/(a_{y+1}^c - a_y^c) & \text{if } x = y \\ 0 & \text{if } x > y. \end{cases} \quad (17)$$

In case of a match, it holds that

$$\tilde{\mu}_{\mathcal{C}} = c\sqrt{-1 + \mathbb{E}_{\boldsymbol{P}} \left[\sum_{y=0}^{q-1} \frac{A_{y+1}^{2c-1} - 2A_y^c A_{y+1}^{c-1} + A_y^{2c-1}}{A_{y+1}^c - A_y^c} \right]}. \quad (18)$$

When $x = y$, the h is positive. When $x > y$, it is negative and constant. When $x < y$, it might be negative or it might not. For instance, for $c = 2$, we find $(a_{y+1} - a_y)/(a_{y+1}^2 - a_y^2) = 1/(a_{y+1} + a_y) = 1/(p_y + 2a_y)$, in which case h is negative if and only if $p_y > 1 - 2a_y$. In particular it is negative if $a_y \geq \frac{1}{2}$. Also, h is the same for all $x < y$.

We now analyze the behaviour of $\tilde{\mu}_{\mathcal{C}}$ when the symmetric Dirichlet distribution is employed. Before we can state our result, we will need the following Lemma:

LEMMA 9. *Let $\boldsymbol{P}$ be distributed according to the symmetric Dirichlet distribution without cutoff. The joint distribution for the pair $(A_{y+1}, A_y/A_{y+1})$ is then given by*

$$J(a_{y+1}, \frac{a_y}{a_{y+1}}) = \frac{a_{y+1}^{-1+(y+1)\kappa}(1-a_{y+1})^{-1+(q-y-1)\kappa}}{B([y+1]\kappa, [q-y-1]\kappa)} \times$$
$$\frac{(a_y/a_{y+1})^{-1+y\kappa}(1-a_y/a_{y+1})^{-1+\kappa}}{B(y\kappa, \kappa)}.$$

Given this joint distribution, we can now derive our main result for the all-high attack when the symmetric Dirichlet distribution is used.

PROPOSITION 10. *Let $f_{\boldsymbol{P}}$ be the symmetric Dirichlet distribution without cutoff. If the attack is the all-high attack and the defense matches it, then, for large c,*

$$\tilde{\mu}_{\mathcal{C}} = c^{1-\kappa}\frac{\kappa\Gamma(q\kappa)\zeta(1+\kappa)}{\Gamma([q-1]\kappa)}\left[1 + \mathcal{O}(c^{-\min(1,\kappa)})\right], \quad (19)$$

where ζ is the Riemann zeta function.

Random-symbol attack. The random-symbol attack selects one of the received symbols uniformly at random. Tallies are disregarded, but a symbol can only be chosen if its tally is nonzero. The attack is parametrized by $f_{y|\boldsymbol{m}} = (1-\delta_{m_y,0})/|\{\alpha \in \mathcal{A} : m_\alpha > 0\}|$.

PROPOSITION 11. *For the random-symbol attack we find*

$$|\boldsymbol{p}|^c f_{y|\boldsymbol{p}} = \frac{a_{\mathcal{A}}^c - a_{\mathcal{A}\backslash\{y\}}^c}{q} + \sum_{\mathcal{B}\subsetneq\mathcal{A}: y\in\mathcal{B}}\frac{a_{\mathcal{B}}^c - a_{\mathcal{B}\backslash\{y\}}^c}{|\mathcal{B}|(|\mathcal{B}|+1)}. \quad (20)$$

The optimal suspicion function is $h = (T-1)/\sqrt{\mathrm{Var}[T]}$, with

$$T(x,y,\boldsymbol{p}) = \frac{1}{c}\frac{\partial \ln(|\boldsymbol{p}|^c f_{y|\boldsymbol{p}})}{\partial p_x}\bigg|_{|\boldsymbol{p}|=1} = \quad (21)$$

$$\begin{cases} \frac{1}{f_{y|\boldsymbol{p}}}\left(\frac{1}{q} + \sum_{\mathcal{B}\subsetneq\mathcal{A}:\, y\in\mathcal{B}}\frac{a_{\mathcal{B}}^{c-1}}{|\mathcal{B}|(|\mathcal{B}|+1)}\right) & if\ x=y \\ \frac{1}{f_{y|\boldsymbol{p}}}\left(\frac{1-(1-p_y)^{c-1}}{q} + \sum_{\substack{\mathcal{B}\subsetneq\mathcal{A} \\ x,y\in\mathcal{B}}}\frac{a_{\mathcal{B}}^{c-1} - a_{\mathcal{B}\backslash\{y\}}^{c-1}}{|\mathcal{B}|(|\mathcal{B}|+1)}\right) & if\ x\neq y \end{cases}$$
$$(22)$$

4.2 Binary alphabet ($q=2$)

All-1 attack. The binary all-high attack is known as the all-1 attack. It has $f_{1|\boldsymbol{m}} = 1$ whenever $m_1 > 0$ and $f_{1|\boldsymbol{m}} = 0$ when $m_1 = 0$.

COROLLARY 12. *Against the all-1 attack, the optimal suspicion function is $h = (T-1)/\sqrt{\mathrm{Var}[T]}$, with*

$$T(x,y,\boldsymbol{p}) = \begin{cases} (1-p_0^{c-1})/(1-p_0^c) & if\ (x,y)=(0,1) \\ 1/(1-p_0^c) & if\ (x,y)=(1,1) \\ 1/p_0 & if\ (x,y)=(0,0) \\ 0 & if\ (x,y)=(1,0). \end{cases} \quad (23)$$

In case of a match it holds that

$$\tilde{\mu}_{\mathcal{C}} = c\sqrt{\mathbb{E}_{\boldsymbol{P}}[P_0^{c-1}(1-P_0)/(1-P_0^c)]}. \quad (24)$$

When $x < y$, the h is positive for any c, in contrast to the q-ary case.

COROLLARY 13. *Let $f_{\boldsymbol{P}}$ be the symmetric Dirichlet distribution with $\kappa = \frac{1}{2}$ and cutoff $\delta = 0$. Against the all-1 attack, the optimal suspicion function attains $\tilde{\mu}_{\mathcal{C}} \propto c^{1/4}$ for large c.*

Coin-flip attack. The binary random-symbol attack is known as the coin-flip attack, and is parametrized as $f_{y|\boldsymbol{m}} = \frac{1}{2}(1 - \delta_{m_y,0} + \delta_{m_y,c})$.

PROPOSITION 14. *Against the coin-flip attack, the optimal suspicion function is $h = (T-1)/\sqrt{\mathrm{Var}[T]}$, with*

$$T(x,y,\boldsymbol{p}) = \begin{cases} (1+p_y^{c-1})/(1+p_y^c - p_{1-y}^c) & if\ x=y \\ (1-p_{1-y}^{c-1})/(1+p_y^c - p_{1-y}^c) & if\ x\neq y. \end{cases} \quad (25)$$

When $x=y$, the h is positive. When $x \neq y$, it is negative, since $-p_{1-y}^{c-1} < p_y^{c-1}$, so $p_{1-y}^{c-1}(p_{1-y}-1) < p_y^c$, and thus $1 - p_{1-y}^{c-1} < 1 + p_y^c - p_{1-y}^c$.

Majority-vote attack. The majority-vote attack outputs the symbol with the highest tally. In case of a tie, a uniform choice is made from the winners.

$$f_{y|\boldsymbol{m}} = \begin{cases} 1 & if\ m_y > \frac{1}{2}c \\ \frac{1}{2} & if\ m_y = \frac{1}{2}c \\ 0 & if\ m_y < \frac{1}{2}c. \end{cases} \quad (26)$$

Minority-vote attack. The minority-vote attack outputs the symbol with the lowest *nonzero* tally. In case of a tie, a uniform choice is made from the winners.

$$f_{y|\boldsymbol{m}} = \begin{cases} 1 & if\ 0 < m_y < \frac{1}{2}c\ or\ m_y = c \\ \frac{1}{2} & if\ m_y = \frac{1}{2}c \\ 0 & if\ m_y = 0\ or\ \frac{1}{2}c < m_y < c. \end{cases} \quad (27)$$

We have analytical expressions for the majority-vote and minority-vote attack, but we do not write them down here because of lack of space.

5. MISMATCHES

In this section, we analyze what happens when the coalition mounts a different attack than the tracer expected. We call the "optimal suspicion function against strategy A" the A-defense. We show that even when the score function does not match the pirate strategy, the optimal score functions derived in the previous section remain centered but not necessarily normalized. The main results of this section are analytical expressions for the performance indicator in case of a mismatch for the Tardos defense, the interleaving defense, and the interleaving attack.

Recall that $\tilde{\mu}_{\mathcal{C}} = c \cdot \mathbb{E}[T \cdot h]$. This expression remains valid in the case of a mismatch, where T is for the actual attack and h is the function that is used as defense.

We call a suspicion function $h(x,y,\boldsymbol{p})$ *strongly centered* if $\mathbb{E}_{X|\boldsymbol{p}}[h(X,y,\boldsymbol{p})] = 0$ and *strongly normalized* if $\mathbb{E}_{X|\boldsymbol{p}}[h^2(X,y,\boldsymbol{p})] = 1$.

LEMMA 15. *Each optimal suspicion function (see Theorem 1) is strongly centered. So is the symmetric Tardos function.*

5.1 Tardos Suspicion Function

We start by considering the traditional symmetric Tardos suspicion function.

LEMMA 16. *If the tracer uses the symmetric Tardos suspicion function, then*

$$\tilde{\mu}_{\mathcal{C}} = c\, \mathbb{E}_{\boldsymbol{P}} \mathbb{E}_{Y|\boldsymbol{P}} \left[P_Y \left(\sqrt{\frac{1-P_Y}{P_Y}} - \sqrt{\frac{P_Y}{1-P_Y}} \right) T(Y, Y, \boldsymbol{P}) - \sqrt{\frac{P_Y}{1-P_Y}} \right]. \tag{28}$$

Against the interleaving attack, the symmetric Tardos suspicion function does not perform well for large q:

PROPOSITION 17. *If the tracer uses the symmetric Tardos suspicion function and the coalition uses the interleaving attack, then* $\tilde{\mu}_{\mathcal{C}} = \sum_{y \in \mathcal{A}} \mathbb{E}_{\boldsymbol{P}}[\sqrt{P_y(1-P_y)}]$. *When* $\boldsymbol{P}$ *has a symmetric Dirichlet distribution with concentration parameter* $\kappa = \frac{1}{q}$ *and no cutoff is used,*

$$\tilde{\mu}_{\mathcal{C}} = \begin{cases} \frac{2}{\pi} & \text{for } q = 2 \\ \frac{1}{2}(q-2)\tan(\frac{\pi}{q}) & \text{for } q > 2 \\ \frac{\pi}{2} & \text{as } q \to \infty \end{cases} \tag{29}$$

We see that $\tilde{\mu}_{\mathcal{C}}$ is a slowly increasing function of q, which is bad for the code rate.

PROPOSITION 18. *If the tracer uses the symmetric Tardos suspicion function and the coalition uses the all-high attack, then*

$$\tilde{\mu}_{\mathcal{C}} = c \sum_{y=0}^{q-1} \mathbb{E}_{\boldsymbol{P}} \left[P_y \left(\sqrt{\frac{1-P_y}{P_y}} - \sqrt{\frac{P_y}{1-P_y}} \right) A_{y+1}^{c-1} - \sqrt{\frac{P_y}{1-P_y}} (A_{y+1}^c - A_y^c) \right]. \tag{30}$$

PROPOSITION 19. *If the tracer uses the symmetric Tardos suspicion function and the coalition uses the random-symbol attack, then*

$$\tilde{\mu}_{\mathcal{C}} = c \sum_{y=0}^{q-1} \mathbb{E}_{\boldsymbol{P}} \Bigg[P_y \left[\sqrt{\frac{1-P_y}{P_y}} - \sqrt{\frac{P_y}{1-P_y}} \right] \left[\frac{1}{q} + \sum_{\mathcal{B} \subset \mathcal{A}:\, y \in \mathcal{B}} \frac{a_{\mathcal{B}}^{c-1}}{|\mathcal{B}|(|\mathcal{B}|+1)} \right] - \sqrt{\frac{P_y}{1-P_y}} \left(\frac{1-(1-P_y)^c}{q} + \sum_{\mathcal{B} \subset \mathcal{A}:\, y \in \mathcal{B}} \frac{a_{\mathcal{B}}^c - a_{\mathcal{B} \setminus \{y\}}^c}{|\mathcal{B}|(|\mathcal{B}|+1)} \right) \Bigg]. \tag{31}$$

In the binary case the Tardos defense has a constant $\tilde{\mu}_{\mathcal{C}}$:

PROPOSITION 20. *[18] Let* $q = 2$ *and* $f_{\boldsymbol{P}}$ *be the symmetric Dirichlet distribution with parameter* $\kappa = \frac{1}{2}$ *without cutoff. If the tracer uses the symmetric Tardos defense, then* $\tilde{\mu}_{\mathcal{C}} = \frac{2}{\pi}$, *no matter what attack the coalition uses.*

5.2 Interleaving defense

We now turn our attention to the interleaving defense.

LEMMA 21. *If the tracer uses the interleaving defense, then, no matter what attack is used,*

$$\tilde{\mu}_{\mathcal{C}} = \frac{c}{\sqrt{q-1}} \left(-1 + \mathbb{E}_{\boldsymbol{P}} \mathbb{E}_{Y|\boldsymbol{P}} \left[T(Y, Y, \boldsymbol{P}) \right] \right) \tag{32}$$

and

$$\tilde{\sigma}_{inn}^2 = \frac{1}{q-1} \left(-1 + \mathbb{E}_{\boldsymbol{P}} \mathbb{E}_{Y|\boldsymbol{P}} \left[\frac{1}{P_Y} \right] \right). \tag{33}$$

where T *belongs to the attack.*

We can explicitly calculate the performance against the all-high attack:

PROPOSITION 22. *If the tracer uses the interleaving defense, but the coalition uses the all-high attack, then*

$$\tilde{\mu}_{\mathcal{C}} = \frac{c}{\sqrt{q-1}} \sum_{y=0}^{q-2} \mathbb{E}_{\boldsymbol{P}} \left[A_{y+1}^{c-1} \right], \quad \text{and} \tag{34}$$

$$\tilde{\sigma}_{\text{inn}}^2 = \frac{1}{q-1} \left(-1 + \sum_{y=0}^{q-1} \mathbb{E}_{\boldsymbol{P}} \left[\frac{A_{y+1}^c - A_y^c}{P_y} \right] \right). \tag{35}$$

If the Dirichlet distribution is used $\tilde{\mu}_{\mathcal{C}}$ will scale as $c^{1-\kappa}$ for large coalitions:

PROPOSITION 23. *Let* $f_{\boldsymbol{P}}$ *be the symmetric Dirichlet distribution with cutoff* $\delta = 0$. *If the tracer uses the interleaving defense, but the colluders use the all-high attack, then*

$$\tilde{\mu}_{\mathcal{C}} = \frac{\Gamma(q\kappa)}{\Gamma([q-1]\kappa)} \frac{c^{1-\kappa}}{\sqrt{q-1}} [1 + \mathcal{O}(1/c)]. \tag{36}$$

We now investigate the binary case $q = 2$. We can then rephrase Proposition 22 as

COROLLARY 24. *For* $q = 2$, *if the tracer uses the interleaving defense, but the coalition uses the all-1 attack, then* $\tilde{\mu}_{\mathcal{C}} = c\, \mathbb{E}_{\boldsymbol{P}} \left[P_0^{c-1} \right]$ *and* $\tilde{\sigma}_{\text{inn}}^2 = -1 + \mathbb{E}_{\boldsymbol{P}} \left[P_0^{c-1} + \frac{1-P_0^c}{P_1} \right]$.

In the binary case, we obtain explicit results for the coin-flip attack against the interleaving defense:

PROPOSITION 25. *For* $q = 2$, *if the tracer uses the interleaving defense, but the coalition uses the random coin-flip attack, then*

$$\tilde{\mu}_{\mathcal{C}} = \frac{1}{2} c\, \mathbb{E}_{\boldsymbol{P}} \left[P_0^{c-1} + P_1^{c-1} \right] \text{ and} \tag{37}$$

$$\tilde{\sigma}_{\text{inn}}^2 = -1 + \mathbb{E}_{\boldsymbol{P}} \left[\frac{1 + P_0^c - P_1^c}{2P_0} + \frac{1 + P_1^c - P_0^c}{2P_1} \right]. \tag{38}$$

Note the similarity between the coin-flip attack and the all-1 attack. For the Dirichlet distribution, this can be analytically shown:

PROPOSITION 26. *Let* $q = 2$ *and* $f_{\boldsymbol{P}}$ *be the symmetric Dirichlet distribution with parameter* $\kappa = \frac{1}{2}$ *without cutoff. If the tracer uses the interleaving defense and the coalition uses either the all-1 or the random coin-flip attack, then*

$$\tilde{\mu}_{\mathcal{C}} = c \cdot B(\kappa, \kappa + c - 1) / B(\kappa, \kappa) \quad \text{and} \tag{39}$$

$$\tilde{\sigma}_{\text{inn}}^2 = -1 + \frac{c}{1-\kappa} \frac{\Gamma(2\kappa)}{\Gamma(\kappa)} \frac{\Gamma(c+\kappa-1)}{\Gamma(c+2\kappa-1)} + \frac{1-2\kappa}{1-\kappa}. \tag{40}$$

For large c *these behave as* $\tilde{\mu}_{\mathcal{C}} \propto c^{1-\kappa}$ *and* $\tilde{\sigma}_{\text{inn}}^2 \propto c^{1-\kappa}$.

	interleaving	all-1	coin-flip	majority vote	minority vote
Tardos defense	$2/\pi$	$2/\pi$	$2/\pi$	$2/\pi$	$2/\pi$
interleaving defense	1.0	$0.61c^{0.23}$	$0.61c^{0.23}$	1.2	$0.75c^{0.25}$
all-1 defense	0.71	$0.86c^{0.25}$	$0.44c^{0.23}$	0.84	$0.54c^{0.25}$
coin-flip defense	$5.1c^{-0.71}$	$0.72c^{0.25}$	$0.72c^{0.25}$	0.0	$1.1c^{0.25}$
majority vote defense	0.91	$0.66c^{0.22}$	$0.66c^{0.22}$	$0.77c^{0.25}$	$0.90c^{0.23}$
minority vote defense	-0.08	$3.2c^{-0.51}$	$3.2c^{-0.51}$	$-1.9c^{-0.52}$	$1.4c^{0.25}$

Table 1: Numerical trends for the performance indicator $\tilde{\mu}_{\mathcal{C}}/\tilde{\sigma}_{\text{inn}}$ in the binary case $q = 2$ for large c.

5.3 Interleaving attack

Finally, we will analyze the interleaving attack.

LEMMA 27. *If the tracer uses a strongly centered score function and the coalition uses the interleaving attack, then*

$$\tilde{\mu}_{\mathcal{C}} = \sum_{y \in \mathcal{A}} \mathbb{E}_{\boldsymbol{P}}[P_y \, h(y, y, \boldsymbol{P})]. \tag{41}$$

The performance of the all-high defense against the interleaving attack can be analyzed as

PROPOSITION 28. *If the tracer uses the all-high defense but the coalition uses the interleaving attack, then*

$$\tilde{\mu}_{\mathcal{C}} = \frac{1}{\sqrt{\text{Var}[T]}} \, \mathbb{E}_{\boldsymbol{P}} \left[\sum_{y=1}^{q-1} \frac{P_y A_{y+1}^{c-1}}{A_{y+1}^c - A_y^c} \right] \tag{42}$$

where T belongs to the all-high defense.

PROOF.

$$\tilde{\mu}_{\mathcal{C}} = \frac{1}{\sqrt{\text{Var}[T]}} \left(-1 + \mathbb{E}_{\boldsymbol{P}} \left[\sum_{y \in \mathcal{A}} \frac{P_y A_{y+1}^{c-1}}{A_{y+1}^c - A_y^c} \right] \right) \tag{43}$$

$$= \frac{1}{\sqrt{\text{Var}[T]}} \, \mathbb{E}_{\boldsymbol{P}} \left[\sum_{y=1}^{q-1} \frac{P_y A_{y+1}^{c-1}}{A_{y+1}^c - A_y^c} \right]. \tag{44}$$

□

In the binary case this reduces to

PROPOSITION 29. *For $q = 2$, if the tracer uses the all-1 defense, but the coalition uses the interleaving attack, then*

$$\tilde{\mu}_{\mathcal{C}} = \frac{1}{\sqrt{\text{Var}[T]}} \mathbb{E}_{\boldsymbol{P}} \left[P_1 \sum_{k=0}^{\infty} P_0^{kc} \right]. \tag{45}$$

PROOF.

$$\tilde{\mu}_{\mathcal{C}} = \frac{1}{\sqrt{\text{Var}[T]}} \left(-1 + \mathbb{E}_{\boldsymbol{P}} \left[1 + \frac{P_1}{1 - P_0^c} \right] \right) \tag{46}$$

□

The scaling behaviour for large c is

LEMMA 30. *Let $q = 2$ and $f_{\boldsymbol{P}}$ be the symmetric Dirichlet distribution with parameter $\kappa = \frac{1}{2}$ without cutoff. If the tracer uses the all-1 defense, but the coalition uses the interleaving attack, then*

$$\tilde{\mu}_{\mathcal{C}} = \frac{\Gamma(\kappa + 1)}{B(\kappa, \kappa)\sqrt{\text{Var}[T]}} \sum_{t=0}^{\infty} \frac{\Gamma(tc + \kappa)}{\Gamma(tc + 2\kappa + 1)}. \tag{47}$$

For large c, this scales as $c^{(\kappa+1)/2}$.

The interleaving attack against coin-flip defense behaves as follows in the binary case:

LEMMA 31. *For $q = 2$, if the tracer uses the coin-flip defense, but the coalition uses the interleaving attack, then*

$$\tilde{\mu}_{\mathcal{C}} = \frac{1}{\sqrt{\text{Var}[T]}} \left[-1 + \mathbb{E}_{\boldsymbol{P}} \left[\frac{P_0(1 + P_0)^{c-1}}{1 + P_0^c - P_1^c} + \frac{P_1(1 + P_1)^{c-1}}{1 + P_1^c - P_0^c} \right] \right]. \tag{48}$$

6. NUMERICAL RESULTS

To verify our theory and its practical applicability, we ran simulations for the binary case and the arcsine distribution (without cut-off). We chose to simulate the five described attacks (interleaving, all-1, coin-flip, majority-vote, and minority-vote) and their optimal defenses. Both the cases where the defense matches the colluder strategy and the mismatches were simulated to obtain the $\tilde{\mu}_{\mathcal{C}}$ and the $\tilde{\sigma}_{\text{inn}}$ for $1 \le c \le 200$. We then analyzed this data to obtain the leading-order term in c. The results can be found in Table 1. The matching cases for each considered attack are shown in Figure 2. The interleaving defense and attack values are depicted in Figures 3 and 4. Since for mismatches the innocent score is no longer normalised ($\tilde{\sigma}_{\text{inn}} \neq 1$), we present the numeric results for $\tilde{\mu}_{\mathcal{C}}/\tilde{\sigma}_{\text{inn}}$ to make a fair comparison.

Looking at the diagonal elements of the table above, only the interleaving attack keeps a constant $\tilde{\mu}_{\mathcal{C}}$. For the other four attacks analysed, $\tilde{\mu}_{\mathcal{C}}$ seems to grow as $c^{1/4}$. We were able to prove this only for the all-1 attack. The mismatches bring even more surprises. As expected, in some cases the defense fails completely against different attacks with $\tilde{\mu}_{\mathcal{C}}/\tilde{\sigma}_{\text{inn}}$ tending to 0 (majority-vote attack against coin-flip defense) or even negative (interleaving and majority-vote attacks against the minority vote defense). Other cases tend to a constant $\tilde{\mu}_{\mathcal{C}}/\tilde{\sigma}_{\text{inn}}$ and many cases even still grow as $c^{1/4}$.

Surprisingly, we often see $\tilde{\mu}_{\mathcal{C}}/\tilde{\sigma}_{\text{inn}} > 2/\pi$, the value for the Tardos score function. There are two exceptions seen in the defenses: firstly, the minority vote defense is an exception to this, as it only seems to work well against the minority vote attack, and is of little or no use against other attacks. Secondly, the coin-flip defense also fails against the majority-vote attack, and seems to scale as approximately $c^{-3/4}$ against the interleaving attack. We do stress that these five attacks are by no means exhaustive, so we do expect more exceptions to this observation.

Another intriguing pattern from the numerical data is the similarity of the all-1 and coin-flip attacks. Except against the all-1 defense, they have the exact same numerical results. Even though for the all-1 attack against the coin-flip defense $\tilde{\sigma}_{\text{inn}} \neq 1$, the normalized $\tilde{\mu}_{\mathcal{C}}/\tilde{\sigma}_{\text{inn}}$ values are again the same. We have proven this against the interleaving defense in Proposition 26. This similarity can be explained by realizing that after the collusion attack is performed, the tracer can flip all symbols in the positions where the coalition produced a 0. This transforms the coin-flip attack into the all-1 attack, with the caveat that the coalition then never can receive the **0** vector. Naturally, this does apply to the all-1 defense, as this score function is not symmetric.

We do stress that in the case of mismatches, $\tilde{\sigma}_{\mathrm{inn}} \neq 1$. This means that to use our optimal score functions in a practical Tardos traitor tracing system, we need to add an additional step to the accusation phase. After calculating the user scores, we will need to estimate $\tilde{\sigma}_{\mathrm{inn}}$ and normalize the scores before we can check them against the Tardos threshold.

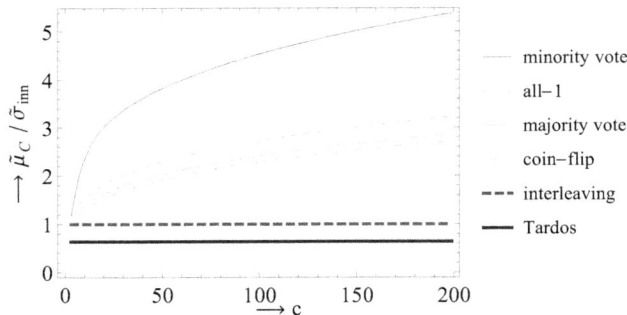

Figure 2: **Matches in the binary case.**

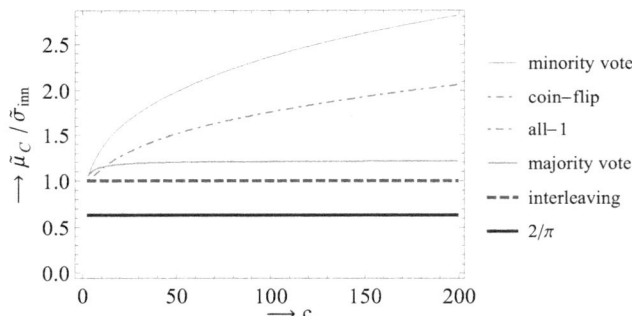

Figure 3: **Optimal interleaving defense against various attacks in the binary case.**

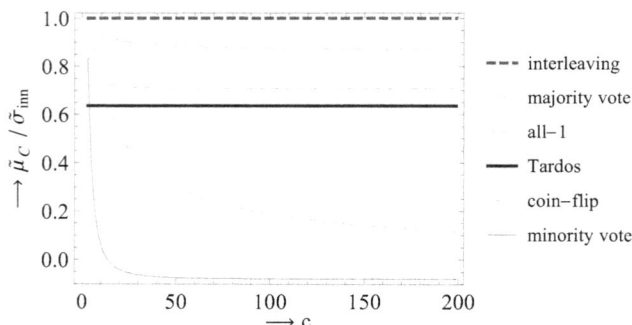

Figure 4: **Interleaving attack against various defenses in the binary case.**

7. DISCUSSION

We have investigated the optimization of the performance indicator $\tilde{\mu}_{\mathcal{C}}/\tilde{\sigma}_{\mathrm{inn}}$ for bias-based traitor tracing in the simple-decoder setting. A straightforward Lagrangian approach yields a simple expression (Theorem 1) for the optimal suspicion function in a wide variety of contexts, e.g. CDM and RDM, binary and q-ary. The result is a Neyman-Pearson score for the hypothesis $j \in \mathcal{C}$ based on single-position information. It also has the form of a Fisher score, though without a fully understood interpretation.

The h function we obtain with the Lagrangian method depends either on the collusion strategy or on the coalition's symbol tallies $\boldsymbol{m}$. These quantities are usually unknown to the tracer. Our optimization approach does not allow for deriving suspicion functions that are based purely on data known to the tracer.

In Section 3.1 we speculated on the use of the $\boldsymbol{m}$-dependent suspicion function in the EM algorithm or as a consistency check for candidate coalitions. Further exploration is left for future work.

For several binary and q-ary attacks in the RDM we have derived the optimal suspicion function. We have investigated the performance indicator $\tilde{\mu}_{\mathcal{C}}/\tilde{\sigma}_{\mathrm{inn}}$ in many combinations of suspicion function and attack strategy. In some cases analytic results are obtained. Notably, the matching case of the q-ary interleaving attack gives $\tilde{\mu}_{\mathcal{C}}/\tilde{\sigma}_{\mathrm{inn}} = \tilde{\mu}_{\mathcal{C}} = \sqrt{q-1}$, asymptotically ($c \to \infty$) yielding a code rate precisely equal to the channel capacity [3]. For $q = 2$ the results are summarized in Table 1. We observe that the interleaving defense, all-1 defense and majority voting defense outperform the Tardos suspicion function for all the considered attacks. In many cases even the power of c is changed from $\ell \propto c^2$ to $c^{3/2}$, which is a huge reduction. It is dangerous to draw general conclusions from the table, however, since not all possible attacks are listed.

The results of Sections 4–6 give us hope that the strategy-dependent suspicion functions can be used advantageously in a practical tracing scheme. We envisage a decoder that runs the Tardos function and a small battery of our h functions in parallel (one for every known 'basic' strategy, e.g. the ones discussed in this paper). Whenever the colluders use one of the basic strategies, the associated h function will quickly distinguish them from the innocent users; for other strategies, the Tardos function still does the job. The challenge is to combine the different score systems into an effective decoder. Here it has to be borne in mind that both the computational load and the total false positive probability grow with the number of incorporated h functions.

Future work will focus on (a) more precise performance indicators such as false positive and false negative error probability; (b) attacks targeted against the special suspicion functions derived in this paper (c) simulations using multiple suspicion functions in parallel (d) iterative joint decoders employing the m-dependent suspicion functions.

Acknowledgements

This research was supported by the Dutch Technology Foundation STW. We would like to thank Dion Boesten, Thijs Laarhoven, Antonino Simone and Benne de Weger for valuable discussions and comments.

8. REFERENCES

[1] E. Amiri and G. Tardos. High rate fingerprinting codes and the fingerprinting capacity. In *Proc. 20th Annual ACM-SIAM Symposium on Discrete Algorithms (SODA)*, pages 336–345, 2009.

[2] O. Blayer and T. Tassa. Improved versions of Tardos' fingerprinting scheme. *Designs, Codes and Cryptography*, 48(1):79–103, 2008.

[3] D. Boesten and B. Škorić. Asymptotic fingerprinting capacity for non-binary alphabets. In *Information Hiding 2011*, volume 6958 of *LNCS*, pages 1–13. Springer, 2011.

[4] A. Charpentier, C. Fontaine, T. Furon, and I. Cox. An asymmetric fingerprinting scheme based on Tardos codes. In *Information Hiding*, volume 6958 of *LNCS*, pages 43–58. Springer, 2011.

[5] A. Charpentier, F. Xie, C. Fontaine, and T. Furon. Expectation maximization decoding of Tardos probabilistic fingerprinting code. In *Media Forensics and Security*, volume 7254 of *SPIE Proceedings*, page 72540, 2009.

[6] T. Furon, A. Guyader, and F. Cérou. On the design and optimization of Tardos probabilistic fingerprinting codes. In *Information Hiding*, volume 5284 of *Lecture Notes in Computer Science*, pages 341–356. Springer, 2008.

[7] T. Furon, L. Pérez-Freire, A. Guyader, and F. Cérou. Estimating the minimal length of Tardos code. In *Information Hiding*, volume 5806 of *LNCS*, pages 176–190, 2009.

[8] Y.-W. Huang and P. Moulin. Capacity-achieving fingerprint decoding. In *IEEE Workshop on Information Forensics and Security*, pages 51–55, 2009.

[9] Y.-W. Huang and P. Moulin. On fingerprinting capacity games for arbitrary alphabets and their asymptotics. In *IEEE International Symposium on Information Theory (ISIT)*, pages 2571–2575, July 2012.

[10] T. Laarhoven and B. de Weger. Optimal symmetric Tardos traitor tracing schemes. *Designs, Codes and Cryptography*, pages 1–21, 2012.

[11] T. Laarhoven, J.-J. Oosterwijk, and J. Doumen. Dynamic traitor tracing for arbitrary alphabets: Divide and conquer. In *Information Forensics and Security (WIFS), 2012 IEEE International Workshop on*, pages 240–245, dec. 2012.

[12] P. Meerwald and T. Furon. Towards joint Tardos decoding: the 'Don Quixote' algorithm. In *Information Hiding*, volume 6958 of *LNCS*, pages 28–42. Springer, 2011.

[13] J. Neyman and E.S. Pearson. On the problem of the most efficient tests of statistical hypotheses. *Philosophical Transactions of the Royal Society of London. Series A, Containing Papers of a Mathematical or Physical Character*, 231(694-706):289–337, 1933.

[14] K. Nuida. Short collusion-secure fingerprint codes against three pirates. In *Information Hiding*, volume 6387 of *LNCS*, pages 86–102. Springer, 2010.

[15] K. Nuida, S. Fujitsu, M. Hagiwara, T. Kitagawa, H. Watanabe, K. Ogawa, and H. Imai. An improvement of discrete Tardos fingerprinting codes. *Des. Codes Cryptography*, 52(3):339–362, 2009.

[16] J.-J. Oosterwijk, B. Škorić, and J. Doumen. Optimal suspicion functions for Tardos traitor tracing schemes - full version. Cryptology ePrint Archive, Report 2013/154, 2013.

[17] A. Simone and B. Škorić. Accusation probabilities in Tardos codes: beyond the Gaussian approximation. *Designs, Codes and Cryptography*, 63(3):379–412, 2012.

[18] B. Škorić, S. Katzenbeisser, and M.U. Celik. Symmetric Tardos Fingerprinting Codes for Arbitrary Alphabet Sizes. *Designs, Codes and Cryptography*, 46(2):137–166, 2008.

[19] B. Škorić, S. Katzenbeisser, H.G. Schaathun, and M.U. Celik. Tardos Fingerprinting Codes in the Combined Digit Model. *IEEE Transactions on Information Forensics and Security*, 6(3):906–919, 2011.

[20] B. Škorić and J.-J. Oosterwijk. Binary and q-ary Tardos codes, revisited. Cryptology ePrint Archive, Report 2012/249, 2012.

[21] B. Škorić, T.U. Vladimirova, M.U. Celik, and J.C. Talstra. Tardos Fingerprinting is Better Than We Thought. *IEEE Transactions on Information Theory*, 54(8):3663–3676, 2008.

[22] G. Tardos. Optimal Probabilistic Fingerprint Codes. In *Proceedings of the Thirty-Fifth Annual ACM Symposium on Theory of Computing (STOC '03)*, pages 116–125, 2003.

[23] F. Xie, T. Furon, and C. Fontaine. On-off keying modulation and Tardos fingerprinting. In *Proc. 10th Workshop on Multimedia & Security (MM&Sec)*, pages 101–106. ACM, 2008.

Leakage Detection and Tracing for Databases

Waldemar Berchtold, Marcel Schäfer, Martin Steinebach
Fraunhofer Institute for Secure Information Technology SIT
Rheinstr. 25, 64295 Darmstadt, Germany
{berchtold,schaefer,steinebach}@sit.fraunhofer.de

ABSTRACT

This work presents a new approach for hash database individualization by blending pre-calculated dummy hashes for each user to their databases. This individualization is necessary to detect a leak after the distribution of for example Whitelists or Blacklists. The proposed code is based on collusion secure fingerprinting codes and provides resistance against intuitive attacks for databases as well as attacks for which users collaborate. Both, code generation and tracing requires minimal effort and the distributor is able to control the robustness desired. Advantages compared to *salting* are improved effort and leakage detection without access to the hash database. A combination of salting and the proposed approach is possible.

Categories and Subject Descriptors

H.2.4 [**Systems**]: Distributed databases; E.4 [**Coding and Information Theory**]: Nonsecret encoding schemes

General Terms

Algorithms, Security, Verification

Keywords

database individualization; leakage detection; Blacklisting/Whitelisting; Tardos Fingerprinting

1. INTRODUCTION

The leakage of databases is an important issue wherever databases are exchanged. With the possibility to detect the leakage, the illegal distribution could be constricted directly at its root before the content arrives at the hands of numerous end-users. There exists a variety of different databases. However, this work is reduced to datasets of cryptographic hash databases.

Collections of cryptographic hashes appear in several application scenarios. In IT-forensics, cryptographic hashes allow to efficiently scan through big data sets in terms of *Blacklisting* or *Whitelisting*. Blacklisting describes browsing through big data sets searching for illegal content. Whitelisting describes the process of filtering legal content out of big data sets.

One Blacklisting example is the generation of hash tables to scan quickly for child-pornographic material during Forensic examinations for a first evaluation of evidence. Large Whitelists for example provide cryptographic hashes of all components from some known software.

A useful application scenario could be a company, whose in-house Firewall automatically prohibits access to illegal image files with the help of such a list. Furthermore, anti-virus programs could benefit from these hashes by blocking or deleting illegal data material.

Besides these advantages of cryptographic hashes, there also exists a high risk that these lists are misused. A person who has access to a Blacklist could easily determine whether specific data is included in this list by computing the hash of the data and using it to scan through the list. This makes cryptographic hashes a strong tool for misuse, in fact, many Internet-crawler provide searching for content whose hashes match to the hashes of a Blacklist and therewith potentially access its content. For this reason Blacklists are rarely distributed.

This work proposes a new method that, in case the list is found, allows tracing back illegal transmission of Blacklists and Whitelists by individualizing each list. This means, for example, if several providers of anti-virus programs purchased such a list, the list would be individualized for every provider. Therewith, if one of these providers distributed his list and it appeared at an illegal location, it is possible to trace it back to him. The result could be that this provider gets informed to improve his protection methods.

2. RELATED WORK

The upcoming subsections describe the state of the art of database watermarking, alternative hash individualization by salting, and collusion secure fingerprinting codes.

2.1 Database Watermarking

A first well-known database watermarking scheme for watermarking numerical values in relational databases issued by Agrawal and Kiernan [1] is based on the assumption that the watermarked database can tolerate a small amount of errors. For watermark embedding, a least significant bit approach is used, where numerical values are changed. The work in [15] is an extension for categorical data. Here a categorical attribute is selected and changed to other values of the attribute e.g. "blue" is changed to "yellow" if this change is tolerable in certain applications. In [10] the authors introduce a distortion-free scheme for watermarking categorical data, where database depositions are arranged in a key-dependent way. Their results are high probability detection and also the possibility for localization of modification in the watermarked data.

For cryptographic hashes this approach is not possible. If a cryptographic hash is modified, it is useless for White- and Blacklists. Distortion-free approaches are easy to obviate by e.g. a random hash permutation. After the permutation the watermark detector will not find the embedded information while the database is still the same.

2.2 Salting

Salting is a well-known alternative to individualize cryptographic hashes. A random binary sequence is added to the data to be hashed or encrypted to ensure that the hash or cipher message differs from other versions made from the same data. When used with hashing, the salt is made public to enable the verification of the hash. The primary goal of salting is to increase the security of passwords by making lookup-tables impractical to use [14]. In combination with cryptographic hashes salting also can be used to individualize those hashes by simply adding the salt to the data to be hashed [5]. Thereby common files like OS libraries cannot be recognized in salted hash sets without re-calculating their hash together with the known salt. This makes the process of recognition much more complex.

Salting, on the other hand, also increases the complexity of the hash-set generation. In case of massive data collections re-hashing all data with a salt would be very expensive. Even just adding the salt to the original hash and re-hash both can be a time-consuming operation when many copies of a hash set consisting of 100,000 files or more are distributed.

2.3 Collusion Secure Fingerprinting

In a multimedia watermarking scenario an individual watermark message is embedded into each distributed multimedia file. If a user of one watermarked multimedia file redistributes a copy of his purchased and individualized version, once the copy is found, the embedded message can be detected again. Comparing the detected message to all distributed messages, the legitimate owner is able to trace back to the responsible user.

This is no longer true if several users of the same multimedia content collaborate and perform a so called *collusion attack*: They compare their purchased copies of the same content and detect positions where their copies differ from each other. Therewith, they can create a copy of high quality with a manipulated watermark message that is no longer able to trace back to one or more responsible attackers. The resulting error is named *False Negative error*. Even worse is the occurrence of the so called *False Positive error*, at which the attacked watermark message is manipulated in a way that it traces back to an innocent user.

To be resistant against collusion attacks, multimedia copyright protection methods using digital watermarking make use of *Collusion Secure Fingerprinting Codes*. In this manner, these probabilistic codes are treated like common transaction watermarking messages and are embedded as such into the multimedia files. To trace back an illegally distributed copy of a watermarked multimedia file, the owner detects the message embedded in the copied file and starts the fingerprinting tracing algorithm that, within a predefined error rate, identifies one or more responsible traitors.

Various approaches for collusion secure fingerprinting codes have been proposed. Most follow the so called *Marking Assumption* first mentioned in 1998 by *Boneh* and *Shaw* [7]. It states that only at the positions where the individual marked copies differ from each other, the colluders are able to manipulate the embedded code in a way that the resulting copy still provides comparably high quality.

Related to watermarking techniques for multimedia copyright protection, embedding messages of the required length is solely possible for very large multimedia files. Therefore a variety of approaches have been published during the last decade that focused on the reduction of the code length.

One milestone approach was published in 2003 by *Tardos*, it achieved code lengths of $O\left(c_0^2 \cdot \ln(1/\varepsilon_1)\right)$ [17] for a chosen False Positive error rate ε_1, where previous works achieved code lengths around $O\left(c_0^4\right)$. Several theoretic and stochastic approaches followed this coding technique, e.g. [16], [6].

Recently, *Meerwald* and *Furon* proposed an approach for Tardos' fingerprinting codes to be resistant against 2 to 8 colluders using a joint decoding strategy to further reduce the code length [11].

Information theoretic publications focus on the *max-min game* between attackers and code designers, e.g. [3], [2], [9], [8]. This means they search for the theoretical best attack strategy colluders can choose and the optimal fingerprint generation technique to counter the attacks. Therefore, the goal for code designers is to achieve rates that come close to the asymptotical *fingerprinting capacity*, which was first mentioned by *Moulin* and *O'Sullivan* in [13], and its definition is attributed to *Moulin* in [12].

3. HASHTABLE FINGERPRINTING

The focus of this work is on hash tables such as Blacklists or Whitelists. The challenge is to provide leakage detection even if the distributor has no access to the leaked hash database. In addition, since the contact and handling with sensible data should be reduced as much as possible, a blind scheme, a scheme for which the original hash database is not needed for the detection process, respectively, is strongly preferable. In the following is described the main idea of the proposed work.

3.1 The Scenario

In a scenario where several users or parties have access to hash tables, misuse is hardly traceable. Individualization of these hash tables is advantageous, but until now hardly secure and/or incapable efficient for practical applications. The ability to individualize hash tables using Collusion Secure Fingerprinting algorithms promises a new method satisfying the corresponding requirements regarding security, robustness and performance. To start the generation process for the fingerprints, the following parameters have to be chosen:

- The number of users, the number of individual hash tables respectively, which is denoted as n.

- The fingerprint length m, which represents the number of dummy hashes embedded into each hash table.

- The maximum number of attackers/colluders c_0 the scheme promises resistance against.

- The False Positive error rate ε_1, which bounds the probability of accusing innocents.

Note that the False Negative error rate, which bounds the probability of not accusing any responsible at all, is not needed for the generation process of the Tardos code.

3.2 Fingerprint Matrix Generation

The fingerprinting generation algorithm used here is taken from the so called *Tardos Code* [17]. The matrix of fingerprints X, in which each row represents one fingerprint, is generated in two steps: First, the distributor picks m independent numbers $\{p_i\}_{i=1}^m$ over the interval $p_i \in [t, 1-t]$, with $t = (300c_0)^{-1}$, where c_0 is the maximum number of colluders to be resistant against and m is the fingerprint length defined as

$$m := 2 \cdot (\frac{\sigma \cdot c_0}{\mu})^2 \text{Erfc}^{\text{inv}}(\varepsilon_1)^2 . \tag{1}$$

where σ^2 stands for the scaled variance

$$\sigma^2 = \sum_{j=1}^n (\mu - S_j)^2 (n\sqrt{m})^{-1},$$

of the accusation scores S_j defined in equation 3, and μ stands for its mean value. The parameter ε_1 represents the number of distributed hash tables and $Erfc^{inv}$ denotes the Inverse Complementary Error Function.

Each $p_i = \sin^2(r_i)$ is selected by picking uniformly at random the value $r_i \in [\bar{t}, \frac{\pi}{2} - \bar{t}]$ with $0 < \bar{t} < \frac{\pi}{4}$, where $\sin^2(\bar{t}) = t$.

In the second step, the matrix X is selected, by picking each entry X_{ji} independently from the binary alphabet $\{0, 1\}$ according to $\mathbf{P}[X_{ji} == 1] = p_i$.

Tardos' choice of the distribution for p_i is biased toward the values close to '0' or '1' which is motivated by the *Marking Assumption* already mentioned in section 2. This distribution is realized by a probability density function f which is symmetric around 0.5 and heavily biased towards values of p_i close to the limits of the interval $[t, 1-t]$.

$$f(p) = \frac{1}{2\arcsin(1-2t)} \frac{1}{\sqrt{p(1-p)}}, \quad p \in [t, 1-t]. \tag{2}$$

3.3 Blending Dummy Hashes into Database

Before the embedding process starts, $2 \times m$ dummy hashes are generated once. These hashes can be built arbitrarily, the only requirement is an appropriate fitting within the entries of the original hash table. Obviously, without the knowledge of these dummies it must be impossible for attackers to detect them.

Further, the fingerprinting matrix X is generated as described in subsection 3.2 with m columns and n rows, which is the expected number of users. To individualize a hash database for example for *user #1*, the dummy hashes corresponding to the first line of the matrix $X(1, 1, ..., m)$ are blended into arbitrary positions in the hash database. This is also shown in Figure 1.

Each dummy hash represents a symbol $\alpha \in \{0, 1\}$ as well as a position β_i , $i \in \{1, ..., m\}$. This means, for every column $i \in \{1, ..., m\}$ of the fingerprint matrix X there exists

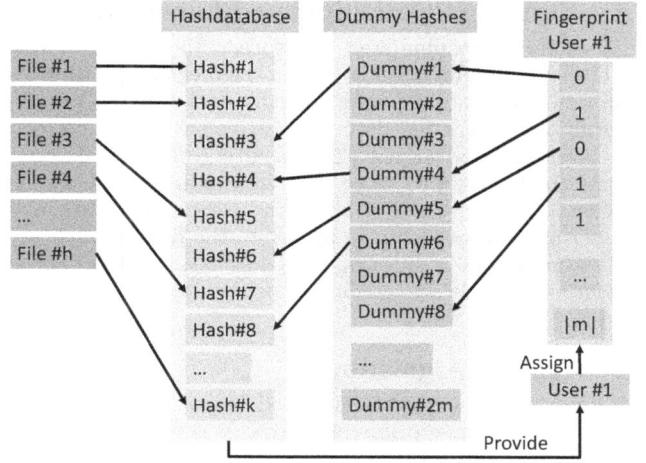

Figure 1: Hashtable Individualization Scheme

one dummy hash representing a 0, denoted by $d_{i,0}$, and one dummy hash representing a 1, $d_{i,1}$.

To embed the fingerprinting code X_j that represents user j into the hash table H_j, which is allocated to him, the dummy hashes carrying the corresponding fingerprint information are blended into H_j. For example, to embed fingerprint $X_j = (1, 0, 0, 1, 0, 1, ...)$, the dummy hash set $\{d_{1,1}, d_{2,0}, d_{3,0}, d_{4,1}, d_{5,0}, d_{6,1}, ...\}$ is blended into H_j. For obvious security reasons, the dummy hashes should be blended uniformly distributed into the hash table and via random permutation.

This way is proceeded for every fingerprint X_j. The result is an individualized hash table for each user.

For reasons of blurry evidence or in case the distributor has no access to the list, the authors recommend to use $2 \times m$ e.g. dummy images for the hash calculation. Therewith, in case of an inaccessible database, leakage detection is still possible for the distributor. That is a scenario where a salt can not help to find a leak.

Following the example of Blacklisting, this list might be consisting of hashes from child-pornography content and is leaked for crawler optimization purposes. The criminals do not emit the hash database, which means the hash comparison must be rendered on a server hosted from the criminals. To trace back whose Blacklist it is, the distributor uploads those dummy images to the Internet that were used to generate the dummy hashes. Now, the crawler searches for the uploaded dummy images starting from the uploading page. A report from the crawler shows the set of those dummy images which are blended in the leaked database and out of these the distributor is able to identify the malicious user. Figure 2 depicts this scenario.

4. DETECTION AND TRACING

The security of the scheme is based on the list of dummy hashes and their correct allocation. Only the holder of this list, in the following denoted as K according to its application as secret key, is able to reconstruct the correct message out of the hash table.

In case one of the fingerprinted hash tables is redistributed illegally, the secret allocation list allows its holder to find out the corresponding user.

4.1 Building the manipulated Fingerprint

To built the manipulated fingerprint, the holder of the list filters all dummy hash entries of the illegally distributed hash table that can be found. To achieve the embedded fingerprint, he orders the dummy hash values in the correct way prescribed by the list. The resulting binary code represents the fingerprint. Note that, in a reduced hash table, for example, if only 1/2 of all entries were distributed, the number of dummy hashes to be found, the fingerprint positions respectively, is accordingly reduced. This results in a discontinuous code, the tracing algorithm needs to consider as well.

4.2 Tracing Algorithm

If the comparison of the detected fingerprint to each of the distributed fingerprints of matrix X is without results, the tracing algorithm starts.

A well known tracing algorithm for probabilistically generated fingerprinting codes, that is also based on the *Tardos Code*, is given by *Škorić* et al. in [16]. There, each position of the manipulated fingerprint y is compared to each corresponding fingerprint position of all fingerprints in matrix X. For each user j a score is calculated out of his fingerprint X_j and y. Finally, all users whose fingerprint scores exceed a predefined threshold Z are considered to be part of the manipulation.

In [16], the accusation score S_j for user j is defined as follows:

$$S_j := \sum_{i=1}^{m} \delta_{y_i X_{ji}} g_1(p_{y_i}^{(i)}) + [1 - \delta_{y_i X_{ji}}] g_0(p_{y_i}^{(i)}). \quad (3)$$

Here, $\delta_{y_i X_{ji}}$ denotes the Kronecker Delta, y_i represents the symbol that appears in the manipulated fingerprint y at position i. The value p_i comes from the generation process of matrix X, described in section 3.2. Thus, p_{y_i} is the probability of the symbol y_i in position i. The so called accusation functions g_1 and g_0 are defined as

$$g_1(p) := \sqrt{(1-p)/p} \quad \text{and} \quad g_0(p) := -\sqrt{p/(1-p)}.$$

The accusation functions g_1 and g_0 based on [17] have specific properties: The more p increases, the smaller $g_1(p)$ becomes. This means, the higher the probability of the symbol at this position, the smaller the positive amount given to the according accusation score S_j, and vice versa.

Thus, the fingerprints that achieve the highest accusation scores are allocated to the most probable suspicious one. To decide which fingerprint is considered to be suspicious and which is considered to be innocent, a threshold Z is computed.

The proposed scheme makes use of the idea in [4] in which a threshold is computed that is adjusted to the actual derivation of the accusation scores,

$$Z := \sigma \sqrt{2} \, \text{Erfc}^{\text{inv}} \left(n^{-1} \right),$$

where σ stands for the scaled standard deviation

$$\sum_{j=1}^{n} \sqrt{(\mu - S_j)^2 (n\sqrt{m})^{-1}},$$

and μ is the mean of the accusation scores. The parameter n represents the number of distributed hash tables.

Finally, all fingerprints whose accusation score exceeds the threshold Z are accused to have partaken in the manipulation.

5. ATTACK MODELS

This section discusses potential attack models. All attack models are analyzed under the condition $c \leq c_0$ and based on the assumption that each attacker contributes approximately equal parts to the attacked database. For the case the attackers contribute unbalanced parts, the detector finds much easier at least one of the malicious users.

Comparing their databases, the attackers find some of the hash entries which do not appear in all colluders' databases. These hashes obviously belong to the number of dummy hashes utilized for the database individualization and therefore are called 'detectable dummy hashes' (DD-hash) in the following. However, a serious number of dummy hashes is not detected due to their appearance in each colluders' database. Thus, these are called 'undetected dummy hashes' (UD-hash). The union set of the original hashes and the UD-hashes is denoted as 'intersection set'. The mean number of UD-hashes for an arbitrary set of colluders is

$$|UD - hashes(c)| = \frac{2\Gamma[\frac{1}{2} + c]}{\sqrt{\pi}\Gamma[1 + c]} \cdot m,$$

where $\Gamma[z] := \int_0^\infty e^{-t} t^{z-1} dt$ represents the *Euler Gamma Function*. The mean number for DD-hashes is given by

$$|DD - hashes(c)| = m - |UD - hashes(c)|.$$

For example, in case of $c_0 = c = 10$ colluders, 35% of the dummy hashes are undetectable. With these 35%, sufficient information is provided for the detector to allow successfully tracing back to the colluders.

- Intersection Attack For an *Intersection attack* the colluders simply discard all DD-hashes and thus take the intersection set of all their hashes for the attacked database. The security of the proposed scheme then only relies on the undetected dummy hashes.

- Cropping Attack To avoid being traced back, instead of relaying the whole database, for this attack the colluders distribute only parts of it. In this work, the assumption is taken that cropping the database reduces the number of UD-hashes proportionally to the whole database. This means, in case the colluders select only 1/2 of the original database (whether of the intersection set or of the union set of all colluders' hashes) for distribution, the number of UD-hashes would be reduced by the factor 1/2 as well.

- Minority Adding In order to set the tracers on the wrong track, the colluders may also add some of their DD-hashes to the distributed version.

  The case, where both, colluder a's DD-hash d_a and colluder b's DD-hash d_b are added to the list to be distributed and in addition, d_a represents a '0' and d_b represents a '1' of the same fingerprint position, this position is denoted as *double position*.

  To avoid the possibility of double positions within the integrated fingerprint of the attacked database, only (some of) the DD-hashes are added which appear in less than $\lfloor c/2 \rfloor$ times in the colluder's databases.

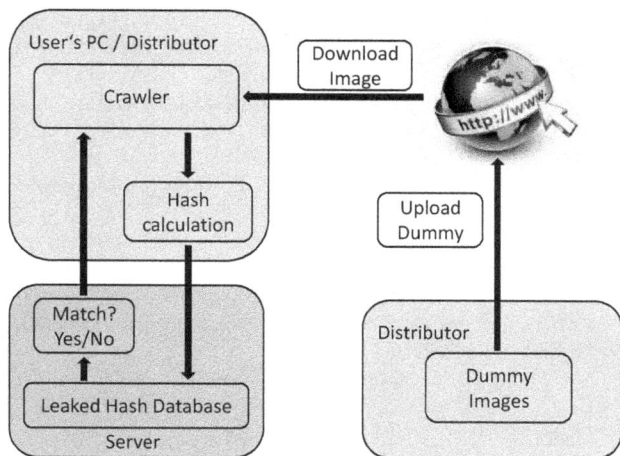

Figure 2: Leakage detection without access to the Hash database

- Majority Adding Refers to the attack that arbitrarily adds some of the DD-hashes which appear in more than $\lceil c/2 \rceil$ times in the colluders' databases. In this way the possibility of a double position is avoided as well.

- Full Minority Adding In the *full minority adding* attack, the colluders add all DD-hashes to the list to be distributed which appear less than $\lfloor c/2 \rfloor$ times in the colluders' databases.

- Full Majority Adding For the *full majority adding* attack, the colluders simply add all DD-hashes which occur more than $\lceil c/2 \rceil$ times.

6. EVALUATION AND DISCUSSION

The tests covered different numbers of users n, numbers of colluders c and number of dummy hashes m per individualized hashtable. Table 1 presents the resulting errors FP, which is the false positive error rate and the false negative error rate FN that can occur after attacks on the hash database applying different attack strategies. The FP error rate represents the probability that innocent users get accused. The FFN error rate denotes the probability of not accusing any involved colluder. Note that, the scheme is independent from the number of hashes in the database.

A reduction of the error rates can be achieved easily by increasing the number of dummy hashes. The higher the number of dummy hashes the lower the error rates. Here a trade-off between robustness against attacks and capability for adding hashes need to be found. A limit of the rate between dummy hashes and hash database should not exceed a certain bound. In equation 1 the minimal fingerprint length is given to be resistant against the attacks discussed in section 5.

Note that, other attacks such as *mixture, mix and match, subset alteration* and *hash adding* are not specified in our evaluation, because the proposed code is resistant against these attacks by construction.

Table 1: Code length comparison for small c_0

attack strategy	users	c_0	m	FP	FN
intersection	100	5	760	0	0
intersection	5000	5	854	0	0
intersection	1000	10	2672	0	0
intersection	5000	15	7679	0	0
cropping 1/2	100	5	568	0	0
cropping 1/4	100	5	760	$35 \cdot 10^{-6}$	0
cropping 1/2	5000	5	954	10^{-6}	18.8%
cropping 1/4	5000	5	1908	0	8.6%
cropping 1/2	1000	10	2672	10^{-6}	0
cropping 1/4	1000	10	5344	0	3.6%
cropping 1/2	5000	15	7679	0	0
cropping 1/4	5000	15	15358	0	3.3%
minority	100	5	760	10^{-6}	0
minority	5000	5	854	0	0
minority	1000	10	2672	$32 \cdot 10^{-6}$	0
minority	5000	15	7679	0	0
majority	100	5	760	0	0
majority	5000	5	854	0	3.3%
majority	1000	10	2672	$38 \cdot 10^{-6}$	0
majority	5000	15	7679	0	0

7. CONCLUSION AND FUTURE WORK

This paper presents a new strategy to trace back leakage in Blacklists or Whitelists after the distribution process. An individualization of the same list for different users can be done on the fly by adding appropriate dummy hashes to arbitrary positions of the existing hash database. Each of the dummy hashes represents one bit of the fingerprint code and is calculated only once in advance. The proposed code is independent from the size of the hash database.

The introduced approach is an alternative to *salting*. The individualization of hash tables by salting demands recalculation of individual random values for every user. This takes significantly more time than copying the hash database and blending the dummy hashes into the database to individualize each user's database. In case of a leak of the salted hash table, a recalculation of all distributed hash tables is necessary. On the contrary, the proposed code has to calculate accusation scores for each user's fingerprint and decides whether the corresponding user is involved in the leakage by a threshold accusation. It is possible to combine the proposed approach with salting.

Some watermarking approaches, for example embedding information by permuting the hash database, are erasable easily. Other approaches based on distortion patterns cannot be realized in this context of cryptographic hashes, because of their sensitivity. Generally transaction watermarking schemes that rely on randomly generated watermark messages are not resistant against collusion attacks. In case of a collusion attack the watermark detector is unable detect a valid message or, even worse, a user not involved in the collusion is detected as malicious.

The proposed approach could be seen as a collusion secure transaction watermarking scheme for hash databases. The tracing scheme applied is a simple example showing the possibility of the use of fingerprinting codes in a new scenario. Indeed, there is room for the use of more sophisticated approaches, adjusted to this application of databases. Future work could for example focus on the attack models to define the worst case attack for this specific scenario. Furthermore, since the dummy hashes are not somehow connected to the symbols of the fingerprints, the use of higher alphabets could be adapted easily, providing more embedded information for the same number of blended dummy hashes. However, this amount of more information also induces yet a higher variety of different attack models.

In the future we plan to expand this approach to general databases such as categorical data or numerical values.

8. ACKNOWLEDGMENTS

This work was supported by the CASED Center for Advanced Security Research Darmstadt, Germany, funded by the German state government of Hessen under the LOEWE grant programme (http://www.cased.de).

9. REFERENCES

[1] R. Agrawal and J. Kiernan. Watermarking relational databases. *VLDB*, pages 155–166, 2002.

[2] E. Amiri and G. Tardos. High rate fingerprinting codes and the fingerprinting capacity. In *Proceedings of the twentieth Annual ACM-SIAM Symposium on Discrete Algorithms*, SODA '09, pages 336–345, Philadelphia, PA, USA, 2009. Society for Industrial and Applied Mathematics.

[3] N. P. Anthapadmanabhan, A. Barg, and I. Dumer. Fingerprinting capacity under the marking assumption. In *Information Theory, 2007. ISIT 2007. IEEE International Symposium on*, pages 706 –710, june 2007.

[4] W. Berchtold and M. Schäfer. Rebound on Symmetric Tardos Codes. In *Intelligent Information Hiding and Multimedia Signal Processing, 2012. IIHMSP '12 International Conference on*, 2012.

[5] E. Biham and O. Dunkelman. A framework for iterative hash functions. *ePrint report 2007/278 HAIFA*, 2007.

[6] O. Blayer and T. Tassa. Improved versions of Tardos' fingerprinting scheme. *Designs, Codes and Cryptography*, 48:79–103, 2008. 10.1007/s10623-008-9200-z.

[7] D. Boneh and J. Shaw. Collusion-secure fingerprinting for digital data. *IEEE Transactions on Information Theory*, 44(5):1897–1905, Sept. 1998.

[8] T. Furon and L. Perez-Freire. Worst case attacks against binary probabilistic traitor tracing codes. In *Information Forensics and Security, 2009. WIFS 2009. First IEEE International Workshop on*, pages 56 –60, dec. 2009.

[9] Y.-W. Huang and P. Moulin. Saddle-point solution of the fingerprinting capacity game under the marking assumption. In *Information Theory, 2009. ISIT 2009. IEEE International Symposium on*, pages 2256 –2260, 28 2009-july 3 2009.

[10] Y. Li and R. H. Deng. Publicly verifiable ownership protection for relational databases. *ASIACCS*, pages 78–89, 2006.

[11] P. Meerwald and T. Furon. Towards joint decoding of tardos fingerprinting codes. *CoRR*, abs/1104.5616, 2011.

[12] P. Moulin. Universal fingerprinting: Capacity and random-coding exponents. *CoRR*, abs/0801.3837, 2008.

[13] P. Moulin and J. O'Sullivan. Information-theoretic analysis of information hiding. *Information Theory, IEEE Transactions on*, 49(3):563 – 593, mar 2003.

[14] B. Schneier and C. Hall. An improved e-mail security protocol. *Computer Security Applications Conference*, pages 227–230, 1997.

[15] R. Sion. Proving ownership over categorical data. *IEEE International Conference on Data Engineering*, pages 584–596, 2004.

[16] B. Skorić, S. Katzenbeisser, and M. Celik. Symmetric Tardos fingerprinting codes for arbitrary alphabet sizes. *Designs, Codes and Cryptography*, 46:137–166, 2008. 10.1007/s10623-007-9142-x.

[17] G. Tardos. Optimal probabilistic fingerprinting codes. In *Proceedings of the 35th Annual ACM Symposium on Theory of Computing (STOC), pp. 116-125*, 2003.

An Asymmetric Fingerprinting Code for Collusion-Resistant Buyer-Seller Watermarking

Serdar Pehlivanoglu
Computer Engineering
Zirve University
Gaziantep, Turkey
spehlivan38@gmail.com

ABSTRACT

A buyer seller watermarking protocol is intended to ensure copyright protection, privacy and security for both the buyer and seller simultaneously in an e-commerce application. A traitor should not be able to deny his responsibility of a copyright violation caused by him in such protocols. This feature is identified as non-repudiation in the literature. An efficient approach taken is through secure embedding of watermarks in an encrypted domain by using dither modulation and homomorphic encryption. To support non-repudiation along with collusion resistance, one needs an asymmetric collusion resistant fingerprinting code that is compatible with the watermarking technique. The design of such codes has not yet studied thoroughly with an exception of a recent work by Charpentier et. al. in [4].

In this paper, we propose an asymmetric binary fingerprinting code based on Boneh-Shaw code. When applied to the secure embedding of watermarks, we show that our code outperforms the code introduced by [4]: (i) we achieve constant communication round, (ii) we do not require any oblivious transfer protocol and (iii) we do not require any public Write Once Read Many (WORM) directory.

Categories and Subject Descriptors

K.4.4 [**Computers and Society**]: Electronic Commerce—
distributed commercial transactions; security
; E.3 [**Data**]: Data Encryption

General Terms

Theory, Security

Keywords

Asymmetric Fingerprinting; Non-repudiation; Buyer-seller Watermarking

1. INTRODUCTION

Fingerprinting Codes. A fingerprinting code is a mathematical tool to deter the unauthorized leakage of the protected content. An immediate application of a fingerprinting code is introduced by [5] and later formalized by [3] to perform key-distribution to differentiate the set of keys each receiver is assigned. Subsequent works (e.g. [22, 23, 24, 26]) on improving the code constructions have been very much related to the application of the key distribution and employed in the tracing mechanisms (including but not limited to [2, 5, 10, 11, 13, 15, 24, 25]).

An important consideration in the setting of fingerprinting systems is non-repudiation: the impossibility of a piracy collaborator(we call traitor) to deny his responsibility of a copyright violation caused by him. Indeed, it might be possible for a user that is accused to participate on a certain content leaking incident to deny her involvement and instead claim that is being framed by the tracing procedure. This scenario is plausible as in the context of such systems the accuser is the entity holding all system initialization parameters and as such is capable of fabricating a certain leakage incident that incriminates a user. This concern motivated the concept of asymmetric fingerprinting that was put forth in [18] and further elaborated on [1, 4, 19, 20].

Buyer Seller Watermarking Protocols. The enormous increase in the production of digital content is shaping our our everyday experiences, communication, entertainment, learning and commerce behaviors. The distribution of the digital content now requires a delicate handling as the content-consumers can more than ever engage in piracy and in redistribution of the digital content. Watermarking has been employed for more than a decade to personalize the content so that the pirated copy reveals the identity of the users took role in the piracy (that we call traitor). The personalization would be possible by embedding buyers information (that uniquely binds the buyer) in the distributed content. In the classical setting, this requires a trust on the content seller (or in some cases producer or distributor) such that they would perform watermarking honestly or not distribute content illegally.

Buyer-seller watermarking protocols are introduced to weaken the trust assumption as a malicious seller may frame an innocent buyer or a buyer that is involved in a piracy may repudiate his guilty by invoking the possibility of framing by the seller. An essential sub-component of these protocols is the secure embedding of the watermarks. Introduced by Memon and Wong in [16], this is achieved by having secure watermarking in the encrypted domain for which an encryption scheme with additive homomorphism is employed.

Codes	Coalition Size	Code Length(ℓ)	Buyer Enc.	Round Comp.	OT Cost	Additional Requirements
[4]	w	$O(w^2 \log n/\varepsilon)$	$O(w^2 \log n/\varepsilon)$	$O(\ell)$	$O(\ell)$ many $OT_{1:N}$	Public WORM Directory of Size $N\ell$
[4]	n	$O(n^2 \log n/\varepsilon)$	$O(n^2 \log n/\varepsilon)$	$O(\ell)$	$O(\ell)$ many $OT_{1:N}$	Public WORM Directory of Size $N\ell$
Our Code (Section 2.4)	w	$O(w^4 \log n/\varepsilon)$	$O(w^2 \log n/\varepsilon)$	$O(1)$	None	None
Our Code (Section 2.2)	n	$O(n^3 \log n/\varepsilon)$	$O(n^2 \log n/\varepsilon)$	$O(1)$	None	None

Table 1: A comparison between the asymmetric fingerprinting codes: n is the number of codewords and N is the discretization factor of the probability distribution of Tardos code and ε is the security parameter.

There are different proposals for buyer-seller protocols: Many works (including but not limited to [9, 16]) rely on a trusted party that is called Watermarking authority which embeds the watermarking and sends to the buyer. Attempts to remove such trusted party leads to the proposals with double-watermarking techniques as in pretty much all earlier works including but not limited to [21, 27]. Double watermarking is discussed to be vulnerable to many deficiencies like quality degradation or ambiguity attacks. [6]. A more recent and efficient approach is based on dither modulation techniques and homomorphic cryptosystems as proposed in [14, 17] and further studied in the protocols of [7, 8].

Collusion-Resistant Buyer-Seller Watermarking It is believed that the secure watermarking protocols of [7, 8, 14, 17] can be extended to resist against a coalition of traitors with the application of a collusion resistant fingerprinting code. However, this puts forth a trust assumption as is stated[1] clearly in the work of [17] and this would not be immediately possible as is overlooked[2] in the work of [8].

The fingerprinting code that will be integrated into the secure watermarking technique should satisfy two more features: (i) being asymmetric, i.e. supporting the non-repudiation feature and (ii) being capable of cooperating with the dither modulation techniques of the above works. An asymmetric variant of Tardos code has recently published in [4] with a goal of satisfying these two features.

Our Results Our main result is to present an asymmetric binary fingerprinting code based on the Boneh-Shaw code. We provide for the first time a rigorous formalization of the asymmetric fingerprinting codes and describe our code in this model. We also present an efficient application of the code in the context of buyer seller watermarking protocols. Our code can be embedded in secure watermarking to strengthen the buyer-seller watermarking protocols with collusion resistance.

We make a comparison of our code with the asymmetric fingerprinting code of [4] in Table 1. The code of [4] requires heavy computation of $O(\ell)$ many $OT_{1:N}$ Oblivious Transfer protocols where N is the discretization factor of the probability distribution of Tardos code and ε is the security parameter. The number of rounds in the buyer-seller

communication is also far away from being practical as it is linear in the length of the code. The code also requires a public Write Once Read Many (WORM) directory whose access is granted to all users. In comparison, the adaptation of our asymmetric fingerprinting code would not result in such efficiency losses.

2. AN ASYMMETRIC FINGERPRINTING BASED ON BONEH-SHAW CODE

In this section we present our asymmetric fingerprinting scheme that is based on the Boneh-Shaw code [3]. We first present the model in subsection 2.1, introduce our construction in 2.2, provide the security analysis in 2.3 and finally expand the length of the code with concatenation techniques in subsection 2.4.

2.1 The Model

A codeword x over an alphabet Q is an ℓ-tuple $\langle x_1, \ldots, x_\ell \rangle$ where $x_i \in Q$ for $1 \leq i \leq \ell$. We call a set of codewords $\mathcal{C} \subseteq Q^\ell$ with size n by (ℓ, n, q)-code given that the size of the alphabet is q, i.e. $|Q| = q$.

Each codeword x in an (ℓ, n, q)-code $\mathcal{C}$ can be considered as providing a unique way of accessing to some specific object or functionality. In such setting, an adversary is modeled as corrupting a number of users (called *traitors*) and retrieving their codewords. The adversary, then, runs a **Forge** algorithm that produces a non-user codeword Q^ℓ that provides an access to the same functionality. This codeword is called *pirate codeword*. A fingerprinting code is designed to identify a traitor that took role in the forgery.

Fingerprinting codes are defined by two algorithms:

CodeGen(1^n) This algorithm outputs a pair $(\mathcal{C}, tk)$ where $\mathcal{C}$ is an (ℓ, n, q)-code with alphabet Q such that $|Q| = q$, and tk is a secret key to be used for identifying purposes.

Identify($\mathcal{C}, tk, c$) On input of a pirate codeword $c \in Q^\ell$, this algorithm either fails to identify, i.e. outputs $\perp$, or outputs a codeword index $t \in [n]$ which is accused of being an index of a traitor.

We say that the fingerprinting code is (α, w)-identifier, if the **Identify** algorithm, given a pirate codeword that is produced by a coalition of at most w traitors, is successful in identifying a traitor with probability at least $1 - \alpha$. We refer an interesting reader to the Chapter 1 of [12] for a comprehensive review of the fingerprinting codes.

---

[1]from [17]: "Although this (Authors' note: the trust assumption) might not be practical in real applications, it provides a theoretical solution to the problem of collusion."
[2]from [8]: "We focus on the watermarking embedding and detection scheme, but we will not explain anti-collusion fingerprints further."

Asymmetric Fingerprinting Code. An asymmetric fingerprinting code (introduced by [18]), in addition to the identifying capability, supports two additional features. Informally speaking, these features are (i) non-repudiation: a traitor can not deny its responsibility in the generation of a pirate codeword if it is indeed involved in such a piracy and (ii) non-framing: a malicious code designer can not frame an innocent user by distributing a pirate copy which incriminates that particular user.

In the asymmetric setting, the non-framing feature would be supported only if the code designer is not fully aware of any particular user codeword, since otherwise it would be easy to incriminate an innocent user. Producing a user codeword in cooperation with an additional private input from the user is one possible way of disallowing the code designer from the knowledge of the codeword. This cooperation can be implemented in various ways depending on the application, e.g. it can be considered as a secure two party computation and can be secured by generic methods like Yao's garbled circuit. We would like to isolate the conceptual definition of asymmetric fingerprinting from its implementation. Hence, we continue with formal definition and later introduce an asymmetric fingerprinting code that fits into our definitional framework. We finally discuss an application of our new code and its secure implementation in isolation from its formal definition.

An asymmetric fingerprinting code consists of three algorithms: code generation, identification and arbitration algorithms. We next define those algorithms:

AsymCodeGen$(1^n, \{X^i\}_{i\in[n]})$ The pair of $(\mathcal{C}, tk)$ is produced where $\mathcal{C}$ is an (ℓ, n, q)-code with alphabet Q such that $|Q| = q$, and tk is a secret key to be used for identifying purposes. The input X^i, for each $i \in [n]$, is used in the generation of the i-th codeword of the code $\mathcal{C}$.

A traitor, involving in the production of a pirate codeword, will inescapably put some footprints of its private input. The Identification algorithm, in addition to finding a traitor identity, discovers those footprints and computes some kind of a proof argument that is believed to reveal, otherwise impossible, information on the private input of the identified traitor. We call this proof by arbiter-proof as it will be the evidence of the proof of the traitor involvement in the case of arbitration. In this model, we define the Identification algorithm as follows:

AsymIdentify(tk, c) On input of a pirate codeword $c \in Q^\ell$, this algorithm either fails to identify and outputs $\bot$, or outputs a codeword index $t \in [n]$ along with an arbiter proof Ω. The t-th user will be accused of being a traitor.

The last algorithm **ArbiterPredicate** checks the validity of the pair (t, Ω) computed by the identification algorithm. We say the proof is valid if the arbiter proof Ω reveals some non-trivial information on the private input X^t of the t-th user. The arbitration procedure is based on some correlation computation between the user private information and the arbiter proof.

ArbiterPredicate$(tk, \{X^i\}_{i\in[n]}, t, \Omega)$ This predicate returns 1 if the proof Ω contains some non-trivial information on X^t and returns 0 otherwise.

Since X^i is private to the i-th user, it should be hard to produce a valid proof that results in a high correlation.

This hardness implies that the tracer can not produce an arbiter proof for arbitrary user (i.e. non-framing feature) and a valid proof can not be refuted by an accused traitor (i.e. non-repudiation feature).

We are now ready to describe our asymmetric binary fingerprinting code based on Boneh-Shaw code. We provide a stand-alone description of our code, i.e. in an isolation from any possible application of the code.

2.2 The Construction

Asymmetric Code Generation: The input to the code generation algorithm is a collection of $\{X^i\}_{i\in[n]}$ which are supposed to be drawn independently and randomly from the set of all binary strings of length d where $d = 8n^2\lambda$ holds for some $\lambda = \ln(1/\varepsilon)$ that is the security parameter and n is the number of codewords. The algorithm will produce a code of length $\ell = d \cdot 2n$.

Similar to the Boneh-Shaw code, the **AsymCodeGen** algorithm first constructs a binary master-matrix $\mathbf{M}_d$ of size $n \times \ell$. In this construction, the i-th user input is embedded into the i-th row of the matrix as follows:

$$\mathbf{M}_d(i,j) = \begin{cases} 0, & \text{if } j < 2(i-1)d + 1 \\ X^i_{j-2(i-1)d} & \text{if } 2(i-1)d + 1 \leq j \leq 2id \\ 1, & \text{if } j > 2id \end{cases}$$

where $X^i = \langle X^i_1, X^i_2, \ldots, X^i_d \rangle$ is a binary string of length d. The master-matrix is depicted in Figure 1, which consists of $2n$ blocks each of size d.

The code generation algorithm, then, samples a permutation $\pi \in_R \mathsf{Perm}(2dn)$ and permutes the columns of $\mathbf{M}_d$ according to the permutation π. The resulting matrix $\mathbf{M}_{d,\pi}$ would satisfy the following: $\mathbf{M}_{d,\pi}(i,j) = \mathbf{M}_d(i, \pi^{-1}(j))$. A codeword w^i for $1 \leq i \leq n$ is defined as an $2dn$-tuple where $\mathsf{w}^i_j = \mathbf{M}_{d,\pi}(i,j)$.

The output of the **AsymCodeGen** algorithm consists of π (which will serve as the tracing key) and the $(2dn, n, 2)$-code $\mathcal{C} = \{\mathsf{w}^1, \ldots, \mathsf{w}^n\}$.

Asymmetric Identification Algorithm: This algorithm has again some similarities with the original identification algorithm of the Boneh-Shaw code. Given a pirate codeword $\mathsf{p} \in \{0,1\}^{2dn}$ and π, it first applies the inverse permutation π^{-1} on p so that the resulting vector $\mathsf{x} \in \{0,1\}^{2dn}$ satisfies $\mathsf{x}_i = \mathsf{p}_{\pi(i)}$. The **AsymIdentify** algorithm will then partition x into $2n$ blocks of length d. We denote the i-th block by B_i and the number of 1's in B_i by k_i (we define $k_0 = 0$). As a notation we call k_i as the weight of block B_i. Before we present the algorithm formally, we first give some intuition.

Regarding the $2i, 2i+1$ and $(2i+2)$-th blocks we have the following observation: (i) these blocks consist of all 1's in rows from 1 to i, and (ii) these blocks consist all 0's in rows from $i+2$ to n. Consider a column that lies in one of these three blocks, the conclusion drawn from the observations is immediate: if $i+1$ is not in the traitor coalition, the permutation π will mask on which block the column lies in. Hence, regardless on how the traitor strategy is, we expect roughy equal weights in the pirate codeword blocks B_{2i}, B_{2i+1} and B_{2i+2}.

In addition to the above observation, if $k_2 > 0$ then the first user and if $k_{2n} < d$, then the n-th user can be accused of being a traitor. In other words, a wise traitor strategy (if the first or/and the n-th user is in the coalition) would try to have $k_2 = 0$ and $k_{2n} = d$. In this case, similar to

M	$[1,d]$	$[d+1,2d]$	$[2d+1,3d]$	$\ldots$	$[2id+1,(2i+1)d]$	$\ldots$	$[(2n-2)d+1,(2n-1)d]$	$[(2n-1)d+1,(2n)d]$
1	X^1	(1)	(1)	$\ldots$	(1)	$\ldots$	(1)	(1)
2	(0)	(0)	X^2	$\ldots$	(1)	$\ldots$	(1)	(1)
$\vdots$	$\vdots$	$\vdots$	$\vdots$	$\vdots$	$\vdots$	$\vdots$	$\vdots$	$\vdots$
$i+1$	(0)	(0)	(0)	$\ldots$	X^{i+1}	$\ldots$	(1)	(1)
$\vdots$	$\vdots$	$\vdots$	$\vdots$	$\vdots$	$\vdots$	$\vdots$	$\vdots$	$\vdots$
n	(0)	(0)	(0)	$\ldots$	(0)	$\ldots$	X^n	(1)
Block	1	2	3	$\ldots$	$2i+1$	$\ldots$	$2n-1$	$2n$

Figure 1: The master matrix of the asymmetric binary fingerprinting code. (0) and (1) represents a binary string of all 0 and 1 respectively while X^i, for each $i \in [n]$, is a binary string of length d

the analysis discussed in Boneh-Shaw of [3], for the choice of $d = 8n^2\lambda$, eventually a non-negligible gap will occur between the weights of consecutive blocks B_{2i} and B_{2i+2} for some i value. This will let us to identify a traitor.

However, the challenge is still there, we need a proof that convinces the arbiter that identified user is indeed a traitor. First, recall that the $(2i+1)$-th block of the $(i+1)$-th user is the private input X^{i+1} of the user. If the weight k_{2i+1} of block B_{2i+1} is closer to k_{2i+2}, the difference between k_{2i} and k_{2i+1} will make us to believe that the 1's of the private input X^{i+1} is used extensively in the construction of the pirate block B_{2i+1}. In this case we set the arbiter proof Ω to be the pair $(B_{2i+1}, 1)$. On the contrary, if k_{2i+1} is closer to k_{2i}, the difference between k_{2i+1} and k_{2i+2} will make us to believe that the 0's of the private input X^{i+1} is used extensively in the construction of the pirate block B_{2i+1}. In this case we set the arbiter proof Ω to be the pair $(B_{2i+1}, 0)$.

Having said the intuition, we rigorously present the identification algorithm:

1. Find minimal $s \in \{0, 1, \ldots, n-1\}$ that satisfies $k_{2s+2} \geq 8n(s+1)\lambda$. Such choice will make the difference $k_{2s+2} - k_{2s} > 8n\lambda$. Hence, $s+1$ will be accused as a traitor index.

2. if $k_{2s+1} \geq (8ns + 2\sqrt{8ns} + 2)\lambda$ then set $\Omega = (B_{2s+1}, 1)$ as an arbiter proof for the accusation of the index $s+1$.

3. if $k_{2s+1} < (8ns + 2\sqrt{8ns} + 2)\lambda$ then set $\Omega = (B_{2s+1}, 0)$ as an arbiter proof for the accusation of the index $s+1$.

4. Otherwise fail.

We will formally prove, later in Section 4.1, that the above algorithm outputs a traitor index and its proof Ω is enough to convince our arbiter that we introduce next:

Arbiter Predicate In addition to the tracing key tk of the code and the collection of private inputs $\{X^i\}_{i \in [n]}$, the predicate takes an arbiter proof $\Omega = (arb, b) \in \{0, 1\}^d \times \{0, 1\}$ and the index $h \in \{1, \ldots, n\}$ of the accused user as input. The goal of the predicate is to check whether the proof Ω contains some non-trivial information on X^h or not.

We call a position is b-marked in a string if the string contains bit b in that position. For instance, the third position is a 1-marked in binary string 101000. Let us denote the number of b-marked positions in arb by p.

Assuming that X^h is chosen randomly and the string arb is chosen without any proof of tracing, we would expect to see an average $d/2$ number of matching positions of the

strings arb and X^h. Similarly, we would expect to see an average of $p/2$ number of matchings in b-marked positions of the strings arb and X^h. Any substantial deviation from these expected numbers would be enough to be a proof of accusation since it implies that the string arb is not any string but reveals some non-trivial information on the private input X^h.

More specifically, the predicate checks the following conditions:

(i) computes the number of matchings in b-marked positions of the strings arb and X^h: say $\psi = |\{x \mid arb[x] = X^h[x] = b\}|$. The predicate returns true if $|\psi - \frac{p}{2}| > \frac{\sqrt{\lambda p}}{16}$.
or

(ii) computes the number of matching positions of the strings arb and X^h: say $\omega = |\{x \mid arb[x] = X^h[x]\}|$. The predicate returns true if $\omega \geq \frac{d}{2} + \frac{\sqrt{d\lambda}}{8}$.

We will formally prove, later in Section 4.1, that it is impossible to convince the arbiter by a guessing of the private input X^h.

2.3 Analysis of Our Code

As motivated and introduced in the model (Section 2.1), we require our code to satisfy traceability, non-repudiation and non-framing. Let us rephrase these features within our definitional framework:

Traceability: The **AsymIdentify** algorithm, outputting (t, Ω), is successful in identifying a traitor, i.e. t is among the traitor codeword indices.

Non-repudiation: The **ArbiterPredicate** returns true on input (t, Ω) with high probability, i.e. the proof Ω contains non-trivial information on the private input X^t.

Non-framing: A malicious tracer or code designer should not be able to produce an arbiter proof Ω' for any index t' that makes the arbiter predicate returns true for (t', Ω') even if it has access to all private inputs but $X^{t'}$, i.e. it should be difficult to compute an arbiter proof without actual evidence of piracy.

Our construction satisfies the following security claims regarding the above features:

THEOREM 1. *The binary asymmetric fingerprinting code presented in Section 2.2, for the choice of $d = 8\lambda n^2$, $\lambda = \ln 1/\varepsilon$ and $1 > \varepsilon > 0$, would be of length $\ell = 16n^3 \ln 1/\varepsilon$ and satisfies the following:*

- *Traceability: For any probabilistic polynomial time algorithm **Forging** and for any $T \subseteq [n]$, it holds that*
$$\mathbf{Prob}[\{t\} \subseteq T] \geq 1 - 2\varepsilon$$
*where $(t, \Omega) \leftarrow \mathbf{AsymIdentify}(ik, \mathsf{p})$, and $\mathsf{p} \in \mathsf{desc}(\mathcal{C}_T)$ is the output of the **Forging** algorithm that is given $\{X^j\}_{j \in T}$ and $\mathcal{C}_T = \{\mathsf{c}^j \mid j \in T\}$.*

- *Non-repudiation: It further holds that*

$$\mathbf{Prob}[\mathbf{ArbiterPredicate}(\pi, \{(X^i)\}_{i \in [n]}, t, \Omega) = 1] \geq 1 - \varepsilon^{1/112}$$

- *Non-Framing: For any probabilistic polynomial time algorithm **Framing** and for any $t' \in [n]$, it holds that*

$$\mathbf{Prob}[\mathbf{ArbiterPredicate}(\pi, \{(X^i)\}_{i \in [n]}, t', \Omega') = 1] < 4\varepsilon^{1/384}$$

*where Ω' is an arbiter proof computed by the **Framing** algorithm on input π and $\{(X^i)\}_{i \in [n] \setminus \{t'\}}$.*

With the above parameters for any traitor coalition size, we say the code is $(2\varepsilon, \varepsilon^{1/112}, 4\varepsilon^{1/384}, n)$-identifer. If there is an upper bound w on the size of the traitor coalition $T \subseteq [n]$, then we say the code is $(\cdot, \cdot, \cdot, w)$-identifer. For the readability of our paper, we leave the full proof of theorem 1 in Section 4.1. As a corollary, we present the above construction with simplifying parameters:

Corollary 1. *The binary asymmetric fingerprinting code presented in Section 2.2, for the choice of $d = 8(384\lambda)n^2$, , $\lambda = \ln 1/\varepsilon$ and $1 > \varepsilon > 0$, is $(\varepsilon, \varepsilon, \varepsilon, n)$-identifer in the sense of Theorem 1. The length of the code is $\ell = 6144n^3 \ln 1/\varepsilon$. We say simply it is (ε, n)-identifer.*

The proof is straightforward given that $2\varepsilon^{384} < 2\varepsilon^3 < 4\varepsilon$, which is correct for any reasonable choice of ε, i.e. $\varepsilon < 1/2$. However, note that this simplifying parameters increases the constant factor in the length of the code and presented in here for simply illustrative purposes.

2.4 Code Concatenation

As in the case of original Boneh-Shaw code [3], the length of our asymmetric fingerprinting code is cubic in the number of codewords. Generating a code with shorter length and smaller alphabet size is a common challenge in the design of fingerprinting codes. Code concatenation is a technique utilized extensively in coding theory and is also proven effective in shortening code lengths in the domain of fingerprinting codes.

Code concatenation entails the composition of two codes: an 'inner' code with an 'outer' code. The composition is feasible as long as the codes adhere to a suitable structural characteristic. The end effect is that the codewords of the inner code substitute the alphabet symbols of the outer code. In general, the inner code is chosen to be resistant against any size of traitor coalition, while the the resistance of outer code is parameterized by some w value. The concatenated code supports collusion resistance against traitor coalitions of size less than or equal to w.

We concatenate our asymmetric fingerprinting code (as an inner code) with a w-identifer Chor-Fiat-Naor fingerprinting code[5] (as an outer code), we obtain a shorter asymmetric fingerprinting code. More precisely, we obtain:

Theorem 2. *There is a concatenated asymmetric binary fingerprinting code of length $O(w^4 \log \frac{w}{\varepsilon} \log \frac{n}{\varepsilon})$ which is (ε, w)-identifer (i.e. $(\varepsilon, \varepsilon, \varepsilon, w)$-identifer in the sense of Theorem 1). We use our code presented in Corollary 1 as inner code, and secret Chor-Fiat-Naor code from [5] as outer code.*

We elaborate on the details of the concatenation and present the proof of Theorem 2 in Section 4.2.

3. APPLICATION: BUYER-SELLER WATERMARKING PROTOCOL

3.1 Secure Watermarking in the Encrypted Domain

In this section, we provide the basis of the secure watermarking in the encrypted domain which is based on dither modulation techniques and homomorphic cryptosystems as proposed in [14, 17] and employed in the protocols of [7, 8].

We assume that a vector of host features x, of size m, has been extracted from the original content and we denote the i-th feature by x_i for $i \in [m]$. Out of these host features some number of them, say ℓ of them, are chosen by the content owner: denoting the chosen set of indices by $C = \{c_1, \ldots, c_\ell\} \subseteq [m]$, the corresponding watermarked features, for $i \in [\ell]$, using a scalar binary dither modulation can be expressed as

$$y_{c_i} = f(x_{c_i}, x) + w_i \cdot \Delta(x_{c_i}, x)$$

where $f(x_{c_i}, x)$ and $\Delta(x_{c_i}, x)$ denoting respectively a suitable function of the original feature and a signal dependent quantization step, change according to the chosen embedding technique. Here $w_i \in \{0, 1\}$ is the bit embedded in the content. Not to interfere with our main results, we refer reader to [14, 17] for the actual choices of f and Δ functions.

The watermarked features above are not suitable for processing through a homomorphic system since they are represented as real values. An integer valued watermarked feature is the obtained as

$$\begin{aligned} z_{c_i} &= \lceil f(x_{c_i}, x) \cdot Q \rceil + w_i \cdot \lceil \Delta(x_{c_i}, x) \cdot Q \rceil \\ &= f_Q(x_{c_i}, x) + w_i \cdot \Delta_Q(x_{c_i}, x) \end{aligned}$$

where $\lceil \cdot \rceil$ is the rounding function and Q is a scale factor that can be adjusted according to the required precision. By assuming an additively homomorphic cryptosystem, the above equation can be translated into the encrypted domain as follows where $E(\cdot)$ is an additively homomorphic public key cryptosystem:

$$E(z_{c_i}) = E(f_Q(x_{c_i}, x)) \cdot E(w_i)^{\Delta_Q(x_{c_i}, x)}$$

In a typical application of the above technique, we assume that the buyer possesses the secret key of the homomorphic encryption scheme. The buyer watermark $E(w_i)$ is produced by the buyer and transmitted to the seller. The seller, being the content owner, knows the plaintext version of x and can compute both $f_Q(x_{c_i}, x)$ and $\Delta_Q(x_{c_i}, x)$ in clear and compute the above equation relying only on the homomorphic properties of the underlying cryptosystem. Finally, the buyer can decrypt and retrieve z_{c_i} that is the watermarked host feature. The protocol of [8] improves this basic idea with a joint watermarking of the buyer and seller to support the ground for non-repudiation and non-framing features.

Remarks: As discussed above, only ℓ features out of m host features are chosen to be watermarked. The chosen features should be kept secret to ensure the robustness of the watermarking. For this purpose, all host features are transmitted in the encrypted form. To decrease the computation cost, a practical implementation with a composite signal representation is given in [7]. For simplification of the further presentation, we consider as if all host features are used in the watermarking process without loss of generality.

3.2 Collusion-Secure Watermarking

In the early works of [7, 8, 14, 17], the watermarking schemes are not collusion resistant; i.e. a number of corrupted buyers may be able to remove the watermark by comparing or composing their differently watermarked copies or they may produce a different copy not initially available to them. This is overlooked in those works by simply referring to anti-collusion fingerprinting or collusion secure codes like [3] or [26].

However, an immediate application of these conventional collusion resistant fingerprinting codes do not support non-repudiation and will not be very much useful in the buyer-seller watermarking protocol. An asymmetric variant of Tardos code has recently published in [4] with a goal of fulfilling the need on collusion resistant asymmetric fingerprinting code. Our novel binary asymmetric fingerprinting code of Section 2 can be efficiently employed in the context of buyer-seller watermarking to support collusion resistance and non-repudiation. In the next section we detail the application and compare it with the work of [4].

3.3 Secure Watermarking with Our Asymmetric Fingerprinting Code

In this section, we apply our collusion resistant asymmetric fingerprinting in the context of secure watermarking embedding. For the simplicity, we consider the basic fully-collusion resistant code. We will follow a joint watermarking of our code into the host features of the content as follows:

Setup: As an initialization, the seller picks $\ell = 2n \times d$ number of host features from the content. The same set of host features will be used for every buyer of the content. The seller also specifies a permutation π. Each buyer will randomly choose his/her private input: for the $i-th$ user we denote it by a binary string $X^i = X_1^i X_2^i \ldots X_d^i$ of length $d = 8n^2\lambda$. Each user also picks a pair of public-secret keys for an additively homomorphic public key cryptosystem $E(\cdot)$.

After the above setup, we execute a 2-round secure watermarking that takes place between a buyer, say the i-th buyer, and the seller:

Buyer Watermark: The i-th buyer will compute the encryption of each bit of its private input, i.e. computes $E(X_k^i)$ for $k = 1, \ldots, d$ with its public key. These bits are transmitted to the seller.

Seller Watermark: Adapting the master matrix (see figure 1) of our asymmetric fingerprinting code, the seller first computes the following watermarks for the i-th buyer:

$$
E(w_j) = \begin{cases} E(0), & if\ j < 2(i-1)d+1 \\ E(X_{j-2(i-1)d}^i), & if\ 2(i-1)d+1 \leq j \leq 2id \\ E(1), & if\ j > 2id \end{cases}
$$

The seller then permutes the encrypted watermarks and embeds the j-th watermark into the $\pi(j)$-th host-feature. This step matches with the permutation step our code generation algorithm. At the end of this step, the seller would have

$$
E(z_j) = E(f_Q(x_j, x)) \cdot E(w_{\pi^{-1}(j)})^{\Delta_Q(x_j, x)}
$$

for the j-th host feature.

The seller transmits the watermarked content to the buyer. The buyer, by using his secret key, will be able to decrypt $E(z_j)$, for $j = 1, \ldots \ell$, and obtains his watermarked copy. Upon observation of a pirate copy of the content, the seller extracts the watermarks from the host features of the pirate copy. These made up a pirate codeword $\mathsf{p} \in \{0, 1\}^\ell$. We call our asymmetric identification algorithm on input p and identify a traitor along with an arbiter proof.

As it is immediate in the above procedure, the watermarking protocol above satisfies both non-repudiation and non-framing by inheriting those features from our asymmetric code. The adaptation of our code requires no extra effort, simply fits into the model of secure watermark embedding of [7, 8, 14, 17]. The protocol consists of a constant round of communication, and $O(n^2)$ many encryptions on both of the sides. The concatenated code of Section 2.4 can also be adapted to the above secure watermarking protocol: this will provide a trade-of between the size of the traitor coalition and the code length (and the number of encryptions processed on the buyer side).

We make a comparison of our code with the asymmetric fingerprinting code of [4]. (see Table 1 in the Introduction) The code of [4] requires heavy computation of $O(\ell)$ many $OT_{1:N}$ Oblivious Transfer protocols where N is the discretization factor of the probability distribution of Tardos code. The number of rounds in the buyer-seller communication is also far away from being practical as it is linear in the length of the code. The code also requires a public Write Once Read Many (WORM) directory whose access is granted to all users.

In comparison, the adaptation of our asymmetric fingerprinting code would not result in such efficiency losses. The only drawback of our system, as is the case in the variants of the Boneh-Shaw codes, is that the code is longer compared to the Tardos based asymmetric fingerprinting code of [4]. Such increase in the length can be tolerable for sufficiently large host data. Despite the longer length, we do not require the buyer to prepare encryptions linear in the length of the code: fortunately, the number of encryptions at the buyer side (i.e. that is the length of the private input X) is same with the number of buyer-encryptions in the code of [4].

Remark on Bit Encryption: One crucial remark is on the reliability of the Buyer sending encryption of the bits. This kind of issue appears in all Buyer-Seller protocols: it can be addressed by the use of zero-knowledge protocols as in the example of [7, 8]. We can avoid this complexity by simply forcing the Buyer to reveal a portion of its encrypted-bits so that the Buyer is caught in the case of cheating. Asking for half of the bits to be revealed will increase the size of the private-input by a factor of two while failure of catching a cheating Buyer would be bounded by a probability of 2^{-k} for k many non-bit encryptions. The rest of the non-revealed portion of the private input can be used in joint computation of the watermark embedding procedure.

4. PROOFS

4.1 The Proof of Theorem 1

We next prove the above theorem separately for each property specified above. In the proof, we will frequently utilize the exponentially decreasing bounds on the tails of a class of related distributions commonly referred to as Chernoff Bounds. Whenever we need these tails, we will refer to them in the text and leave the detailed discussions to e.g., Chapter 1 of [12]. Before proceeding we present a general lemma that will be useful throughout the proof.

LEMMA 1. *We sample a binary string of length $2d$ from the set of strings with Hamming weight k. Let k_L and k_R be the hamming weight of left and right halves respectively. $k_R - k_L \geq 2\sqrt{\frac{k}{2}\lambda}$ holds with probability at most $2e^{-\lambda}$.*

PROOF. Suppose that we have $k_R - k_L \geq 2\sqrt{\frac{k}{2}\lambda}$, then it holds that $k_L \leq \frac{k}{2} - \sqrt{\frac{k}{2}\lambda}$. We next prove that the latter happens with probability at most $e^{-\lambda}$.

Denote the random variable X that is the weight k_L conditioning on the event that the total Hamming weight is k. The probability that $X = r$ equals:

$$\mathbf{Prob}[X = r] = \frac{\binom{d}{r}\binom{d}{k-r}}{\binom{2d}{k}}$$

Consider a random variable Y which is a binomial distribution of k successive experiments with success probability $1/2$, hence $\mathbf{Prob}[Y = r] = \frac{\binom{k}{r}}{2^k}$. It is easy to see the following(just substitute and do regular computation):

$$\mathbf{Prob}[X = r] \leq 2 \cdot \mathbf{Prob}[Y = r]$$

Note that $E[Y] = k/2$. By applying the Chernoff bound we have the following for some $0 < \alpha < k/2$.

$$\mathbf{Prob}[Y \leq k/2 - \alpha] \leq e^{-2\alpha^2/k}$$

Substituting $\alpha = \sqrt{\frac{k\lambda}{2}}$, we will see with what probability the left half has a weight $\leq k/2 - \sqrt{\frac{k\lambda}{2}}$:

$$\begin{aligned} \mathbf{Prob}[X \leq k/2 - \sqrt{\tfrac{k\lambda}{2}}] &\leq 2 \cdot \mathbf{Prob}[Y \leq k/2 - \sqrt{\tfrac{k\lambda}{2}}] \\ &\leq 2 \cdot e^{\frac{-2}{k} \cdot \frac{k\lambda}{2}} \\ &= 2 \cdot e^{-\lambda} \end{aligned}$$

This will complete the proof. ∎

Traceability: Correctness of the Identification. We, first, argue that the **AsymIdentify** algorithm outputs an index from the set $[n]$.

LEMMA 2. *The **AsymIdentify** algorithm always outputs an index from the set $[n]$.*

PROOF. The proof is straightforward given the fact that $d = 8\lambda n^2$. The index n will be output in the worst case. ∎

Let s be the minimal index computed by the **AsymIdentify** algorithm that satisfies $k_{2s+2} \geq 8n(s+1)\lambda$, it further holds that $k_{2s} < 8ns\lambda$ (to count the case $s = 0$ we say $k_{2s} \leq 8ns\lambda$ without loss of generality). We have two cases either (i) $k_{2s+1} \geq (8ns + 2\sqrt{8ns} + 2)\lambda$ or (ii) $k_{2s+1} < (8ns + 2\sqrt{8ns} + 2)\lambda$. In both cases the user $s+1$ is accused. We will study both of these cases separately and argue the failure probability in accusation.

(i) Case $k_{2s+1} \geq (8ns + 2\sqrt{8ns} + 2)\lambda$ holds and user $s+1$ is accused. Observe from the master matrix in Figure 1 that if the user-codeword $\mathbf{w}^{s+1}$ is not available to the traitor coalition, then the traitors will not be able to differentiate

the block B_{2s+1} and B_{2s}: in both of these blocks traitors with smaller indices are marked with 1 while the traitors with larger instances are marked with 0. Hence, $|k_{2s+1} - k_{2s}|$ is expected to be close to to 0. Fortunately we have $k_{2s+1} \geq (8ns + 2\sqrt{8ns} + 2)\lambda$ and $k_{2s} \leq 8ns\lambda$.

Let $k_{2s+1} + k_{2s} = k$. We next claim that the difference $k_{2s+1} - k_{2s}$ is at least $2\sqrt{\frac{k}{2}\lambda}$:

Let $k_{2s} = a^2\lambda$ holds for some $a < \sqrt{8ns}$. The claim is easily satisfied for the $s = 0$ or $a = 0$ cases: indeed we have $k_{2s} = 0$ and $k_{2s+1} = k \geq 2\lambda$ for which $k \geq 2\sqrt{\frac{k}{2}\lambda}$ holds trivially. Hence we investigate the $s > 0$ and $a > 0$ cases.

If $a > 0$ holds, then we have $k_{2s+1} = (a^2 + 2a + y)\lambda$ for some $y \geq 2$ which is obvious based on the fact that $k_{2s+1} \geq (8ns + 2\sqrt{8ns} + 2)\lambda$. We then have $\frac{k}{2} = (a^2 + a + y/2)\lambda$.

$$\begin{aligned} k_{2s+1} - k_{2s} &= (2a + y)\lambda \\ &= \sqrt{(4a^2 + 4ay + y^2)\lambda^2} \\ &\geq \sqrt{(4a^2 + 4a + 2y)\lambda^2} \\ &\geq 2\sqrt{(a^2 + a + y/2)\lambda^2} \\ &\geq 2\sqrt{\tfrac{k}{2}\lambda} \end{aligned}$$

The above can happen with probability at most $2e^{-\lambda} = 2\varepsilon$ as it is implied by Lemma 1. The conclusion is immediate: the codeword $\mathbf{w}^{s+1}$ is a traitor codeword with probability at least $1 - 2\varepsilon$. The arbiter proof Ω is set to be $(B_{2s+1}, 1)$. Note for future reference that B_{2s+1} would have k_{2s+1} many 1-marked positions.

(ii) Case $k_{2s+1} < (8ns + 2\sqrt{8ns} + 2)\lambda$ holds and user $s+1$ is accused. In this case, we consider the number of 0-marked positions in the blocks B_{2s+1} and B_{2s+2}. Denoting the numbers by m_{2s+1} and m_{2s+2}, they satisfy $m_{2s+1} = 8n^2\lambda - k_{2s+1}$ and $m_{2s+2} = 8n^2\lambda - k_{2s+2}$. Considering the assumed constraints on k_{2s+1} and k_{2s+2} we obtain $m_{2s+1} \geq (8n^2 - 8ns - 2\sqrt{8ns} - 2)\lambda$ and $m_{2s+2} \leq (8n^2 - 8n(s+1))\lambda$.

As before if the user-codeword $\mathbf{w}^{s+1}$ is not available to the traitor coalition, then the traitors will not be able to differentiate the block B_{2s+2} and B_{2s+1}: in both of these blocks traitors with smaller indices are marked with 1 while the traitors with larger instances are marked with 0. Hence, $|m_{2s+2} - m_{2s+1}|$ is expected to be close to 0 unless $\mathbf{w}^{s+1}$ is a traitor codeword.

Let $m_{2s+2} + m_{2s+1} = m$. We next claim that the difference $m_{2s+1} - m_{2s+2}$ is at least $2\sqrt{\frac{m}{2}\lambda}$:

Let $m_{2s+2} = a^2\lambda$ holds for some $a < \sqrt{8n^2 - 8n(s+1)}$. The claim again is easily satisfied for the case $a = m_{2s+2} = 0$ case: indeed we have $m_{2s+1} = m \geq (8n^2 - 8n(n-1) - 2\sqrt{8n(n-1)} - 2)\lambda = (8n - 2\sqrt{8n^2 - 8n} - 2)\lambda$. A further analysis will lead to the fact that $m \geq 2\lambda$ for which $m \geq 2\sqrt{\frac{m}{2}\lambda}$ holds trivially. Hence we investigate the $a, m_{2s+2} > 0$ cases.

If $a > 0$ holds, then we next prove that $m_{2s+1} = (a^2 + 2a + y)\lambda$ for some $y \geq 2$:

$$\begin{aligned} m_{2s+1} - m_{2s+2} &\geq (8n - 2\sqrt{8ns} - 2)\lambda \\ (2a + y)\lambda &\geq (8n - 2\sqrt{8ns} - 2)\lambda \\ 2\sqrt{8n^2 - 8n(s+1)} + y &\geq 8n - 2\sqrt{8ns} - 2 \\ y &\geq 8n - 2 - 2(\sqrt{8ns} + \sqrt{8n^2 - 8n(s+1)}) \\ y &\geq 8n - 2 - 2\sqrt{2(8ns + 8n^2 - 8n(s+1))} \\ y &\geq 8n - 2 - 2\sqrt{16n^2 - 16n} \\ y &\geq 8n - 2 - 2\sqrt{16n^2 - 16n + 4} \\ y &\geq 8n - 2 - 2(4n - 2) \\ y &\geq 2 \end{aligned}$$

Based on the above computation we obtain $\frac{m}{2} = (a^2 + a + y/2)\lambda$ for $y \geq 2$. Hence, the difference $m_{2s+1} - m_{2s+2}$ is at least $2\sqrt{\frac{m}{2}}\lambda$ based on exact same analysis made in the first case. This can happen with probability with at most $2e^{-\lambda} = 2\varepsilon$ as it is implied by Lemma 1(a variant of the lemma). The conclusion is immediate: the codeword $\mathbf{w}^{s+1}$ is a traitor codeword with probability at least $1 - 2\varepsilon$. The arbiter proof Ω is set to be $(B_{2s+1}, 0)$. Note for future reference that B_{2s+1} would have m_{2s+1} many 0-marked positions.

Non-repudiation: Convincing the Arbiter. We consider the arbiter proof $\Omega = (B_{2s+1}, \sigma)$ produced above for the traitor index $s + 1$. Based on the analysis above, the number of σ-marked positions in block B_{2s+1} is equal to $Q \overset{def}{=} (a^2 + 2a + y)\lambda$ for some $0 < a < \sqrt{8n^2}$ and $y \geq 2$ while the number of σ-marked positions in block $B_{2s+2\tau}$ is equal to $L \overset{def}{=} a^2\lambda$ where $\tau = 1 - \sigma$. For simplicity of notation, we also define $S \overset{def}{=} 8n^2\lambda$.

To convince the arbiter that $s + 1$ is a traitor index (we denote the accused traitor by T), we need to prove one of the following: either (1) the number of matches in σ-marks between B_{2s+1} and X^{s+1} is outside the interval $[\frac{Q}{2} - \frac{\sqrt{\lambda Q}}{16}, \frac{Q}{2} + \frac{\sqrt{\lambda Q}}{16}]$ or (2) the number of matches in any mark(0 or 1 marks) between B_{2s+1} and X^{s+1}, i.e. the hamming weight of $B_{2s+1} \oplus X^{s+1}$, is at least $\frac{S}{2} + \frac{\sqrt{S\lambda}}{8}$.

Before we continue let us fix some notations to make the analysis easier. We denote $p_{i,j}$ by the cardinal/size of the set $\{x \in [d] \mid B_{2s+1}[x] = i \wedge X^{s+1}[x] = j\}$ for $(i, j) \in \{0, 1\}^2$. $p_{i,j}$ is essentially the number of positions where B_{2s+1} has i-mark while X^{s+1} has j-mark.

The requirements for convincing the arbiter(non-repudiation) in terms of the new notation can be restated as follows: either (1) $p_{\sigma,\sigma}$ is outside the interval $[\frac{Q}{2} - \frac{\sqrt{\lambda Q}}{16}, \frac{Q}{2} + \frac{\sqrt{\lambda Q}}{16}]$ or (2) $p_{\sigma,\sigma} + p_{\tau,\tau}$ is at least $\frac{S}{2} + \frac{\sqrt{S\lambda}}{8}$.

We proceed with proof by contradiction. Let us assume that arbiter proof $\Omega = (B_{2s+1}, \sigma)$ is not enough to convince the arbiter. Hence, we assume that:
$$\frac{Q}{2} + \frac{\sqrt{\lambda Q}}{16} \geq p_{\sigma,\sigma} \geq \frac{Q}{2} - \frac{\sqrt{\lambda Q}}{16}$$
$$p_{\sigma,\sigma} + p_{\tau,\tau} < \frac{S}{2} + \frac{\sqrt{S\lambda}}{8}$$

Since the number of σ-marked positions in block B_{2s+1} is equal to Q, we obtain $p_{\sigma,\tau} + p_{\sigma,\sigma} = Q$. This will result in the following:
$$\frac{Q}{2} + \frac{\sqrt{\lambda Q}}{16} \geq p_{\sigma,\tau} \geq \frac{Q}{2} - \frac{\sqrt{\lambda Q}}{16}$$
$$p_{\sigma,\tau} - p_{\sigma,\sigma} < \frac{\sqrt{\lambda Q}}{8} \leq \frac{\sqrt{S\lambda}}{8}$$

From above, we obtain $Q_\tau \overset{def}{=} p_{\sigma,\tau} + p_{\tau,\tau} < \frac{S}{2} + \frac{\sqrt{S\lambda}}{4}$. We next argue that this can happen only with probability ..... .

At this phase of the proof, we introduce another notation for brevity: we denote the j-th block of an i-th receiver in the master matrix of the figure 1 by $M_{i,j}$ for $i \in [n]$ and $j \in [2n]$. The master matrix satisfies the following property:
If $j \leq 2i - 2$ then $M_{i,j}$ consist of all 0-marks.
If $j \geq 2i$ then $M_{i,j}$ consists of all 1-marks
$M_{i,2i-1}$ is equal to the private input X^i.
Due to the property above, the number of τ-marked positions in block $M_{s+1,2s+2\tau}$ is equal to S and the number of τ-marked positions in block $M_{s+1,2s+1} = X^{s+1}$ is equal to $Q_\tau = p_{\sigma,\tau} + p_{\tau,\tau}$.

Considering again the property of the master matrix presented above, let us elaborate on the view of traitors on the $(2s + 1)$-th and $(2s + 2\tau)$-th blocks of the master matrix.

Any traitor with a smaller index $k < s + 1$ are assigned full σ-marks in blocks $M_{k,2s+2\tau}$ and $M_{k,2s+1}$, while any traitor with a larger index $l > s + 1$ are assigned full τ-marks in both of the blocks $M_{l,2s+2\tau}$ and $M_{l,2s+1}$.

Since, the columns of the master matrix is permuted randomly during the code generation, the τ-marked positions in the blocks of $M_{s+1,2s+2\tau}$ and $M_{s+1,2s+1}$ are masked with that permutation. In other words, the traitor coalition will not be able to differentiate a τ-marked position in block $M_{s+1,2s+2\tau}$ from a τ-marked position in block $M_{s+1,2s+1}$.

Let us call a position/column in $(2s+1)$-th or $(2s+2\tau)$-th block to be good, if that position is σ-marked in pirate copy (i.e. $B_{2s+2\tau}$ or B_{2s+1}, say B-blocks) and τ-marked in the original blocks of the $s+1$-th user (i.e. $M_{2s+2\tau}$ or M_{2s+1}, say M-blocks). The distribution of the good positions over the pirate B-blocks is expected to be equal to the distribution of the τ-marked positions over the user M-blocks. This is true because of the indistinguishability of τ-marks in M-blocks discussed above.

Following our notation, the number of good positions in block $B_{2s+2\tau}$ is equal to L and the number of good positions in block B_{2s+1} is equal to $p_{\sigma,\tau}$. From earlier discussions, we know that $p_{\sigma,\tau} > \frac{Q}{2} - \frac{\sqrt{\lambda Q}}{16} > \frac{(a^2+a)\lambda}{2} = \frac{L + \sqrt{L\lambda}}{2}$.

Let us fix the total number of good positions to be K, i.e. $K \overset{def}{=} L + p_{\sigma,\tau} > \frac{3L + \sqrt{L\lambda}}{2}$. K good positions are chosen by the traitor coalition from a total of $S + Q_\tau$ many τ-marked positions of M-blocks. Let us denote the probability of observing a good position in block $B_{2s+2\tau}$ by q, we have $q = \frac{S}{S+Q_\tau}$. Applying what we already know, we obtain:
$$q = \frac{S}{S+Q_\tau} > \frac{4S}{6S+\sqrt{S\lambda}} > \frac{4L}{6L+\sqrt{L\lambda}}$$

Let Z be a random variable that is the number of good positions in block $B_{2s+2\tau}$: we define $Prob[Z \leq L|K, q]$ to be the probability of observing at most L good positions conditioned on the probability q and the total number of good positions K. If we consider $\frac{3L+\sqrt{L\lambda}}{2} < K$ many trials, we would have:
$$Prob[Z \leq L|K, q] \leq Prob\left[Z \leq L \Big| \frac{3L + \sqrt{L\lambda}}{2}, q\right]$$

If we further decrease the probability q to $\frac{4L}{6L+\sqrt{L\lambda}}$, we obtain:
$$Prob[Z \leq L|K, q] \leq Prob\left[Z \leq L \Big| \frac{3L + \sqrt{L\lambda}}{2}, \frac{4L}{6L+\sqrt{L\lambda}}\right]$$

We next apply the Chernoff bound that holds
$$\mathbf{Prob}[Z \leq \mu - F] < e^{-\frac{F^2}{2\mu}}$$

where μ is the expected number and F is the deviation from the expected number. Setting $L = \mu - F$ and $\mu = \frac{3L+\sqrt{L\lambda}}{2} \cdot \frac{4L}{6L+\sqrt{L\lambda}}$ we compute $F = \frac{L\sqrt{L\lambda}}{6L+\sqrt{L\lambda}}$. We next bound the probability, by bounding $\frac{F^2}{\mu}$:
$$\frac{F^2}{\mu} = \frac{L^2 L\lambda}{6L+\sqrt{L\lambda}} \cdot \frac{2(6L+\sqrt{L\lambda})}{4L(3L+\sqrt{L\lambda})}$$
$$= \frac{1}{2} \cdot \frac{L^2\lambda}{(6L+\sqrt{L\lambda})(3L+\sqrt{L\lambda})}$$
$$= \frac{1}{2} \cdot \frac{a^4\lambda^3}{(6a^2\lambda+\sqrt{a^2\lambda^2})(3a^2\lambda+\sqrt{a^2\lambda^2})}$$
$$= \frac{\lambda}{2} \cdot \frac{1}{(6+1/a)(3+1/a)}$$
$$\geq \frac{\lambda}{56}$$

Hence, we bound the error probability by $e^{-\frac{\lambda}{112}} = \epsilon^{1/112}$

Non-framing: Hardness of Framing an Innocent. The **Framing** algorithm produces an arbiter proof $(arb_{t'}, b) \in \{0,1\}^d \times \{0,1\}$ for index $t' \in \{1, \ldots, n\}$ independently from the binary string $X^{t'}$. Let the number of positions with b in arb be p. The predicate then computes the number of matches with the string $arb_{t'}$ and the input string $X^{t'}$. The predicate returns true if and only if one of the following holds:

(i) If the number of the matches over b-positions substantially deviate from the expected average of $p/2$, i.e. if either $|\{x \mid arb[x] = X^{t'}[x] = b\}| < \frac{p}{2} - \frac{\sqrt{p\lambda}}{16}$ or $|\{x \mid arb[x] = X^{t'}[x] = b\}| > \frac{p}{2} + \frac{\sqrt{p\lambda}}{16}$ holds.
or

(ii) If the total number of matches substantially exceeds $d/2$, i.e. $|\{x \mid arb[x] = X^{t'}[x]\}| \geq \frac{d}{2} + \frac{\sqrt{d\lambda}}{8}$.

We will bound the probability of the above conditions hold by using the Chernoff bounds applying on the positions we make a comparison.

We list the positions where we check for the matching between $arb_{t'}$ and $X^{t'}$: denoting the sequence of positions by $j_1, \ldots, j_s$, we define Y_{j_i} to be a random variable such that $Y_{j_i} = 1$ if $arb_{t'}[j_i] = X_{t'}[j_i]$ and $Y_i = 0$ otherwise. Observe the following (i) $\mathbf{Prob}(Y_{j_i} = 0) = \mathbf{Prob}(Y_{j_i} = 1) = \frac{1}{2}$ for $i = 1, \ldots, s$ and (ii) the sum $Y = \sum_{i=1}^{s} Y_{j_i}$ of these independent variables is the number of matches between $arb_{t'}$ and the binary string $X_{t'}$. Due to the Chernoff Bounds for any $0 < a < s/2$,

$$\mathbf{Prob}[|Y - s/2| \geq a] \leq 2e^{-2a^2/3s},$$

For the choices of $s = p$ and $a = \frac{\sqrt{p\lambda}}{16}$, the first condition holds with at most probability $2e^{\frac{-\lambda}{384}} = 2\epsilon^{1/384}$.

Similarly, for the choices of $s = d$ and $a = \frac{\sqrt{d\lambda}}{8}$, the second condition holds with at most probability $2e^{\frac{-\lambda}{96}} = 2\epsilon^{1/96}$.

Hence, a successful framing can happen with probability at most $4\epsilon^{1/384}$.

4.2 The Proof of Theorem 2

Before we proceed with the proof of the Theorem, we first recall Chor-Fiat-Naor secret fingerprinting code based on the parameters of [12]: for an alphabet size of $2w$, where w is the size of the traitor coalition, and a length of $\ell_1 = 4w \log \left(\frac{n}{\varepsilon_1} \right)$, the failure probability of identification is bounded by ε_1. The codewords are generated totally in a random fashion by assigning a random symbol from the alphabet for each codeword position. Upon observing a pirate codeword, the number of matches between each original codeword is computed, the maximum match (i.e. score) will identify a traitor. The rationale of the accusation lies on the fact that $4 \log \left(\frac{n}{\varepsilon_1} \right)$ number of matches is unlikely while on the other hand a traitor coalition of w will, regardless of the pirate strategy, lead one of them to have a score of such number.

We concatenate our asymmetric fingerprinting code (as an inner code) with a w-identifier Chor-Fiat-Naor fingerprinting code[5] (as an outer code). To achieve the parameters of the theorem we set $\varepsilon_1 = \varepsilon/2$ and $\varepsilon_2 = \frac{\varepsilon}{2\ell_1}$ in the following description the concatenation algorithms.

We next describe the resulting algorithms of the concatenation.

Code Generation: We first generate an $(\ell_1, n, 2w)$-code from secret Chor-Fiat-Naor code where the symbols of the code is chosen from the set $\{1, 2, \ldots, 2w\}$. We call this code by outer code. Each user is associated with a codeword from the outer code. This codeword is called to be the outer codeword of that user. More specifically, we assign the k-th codeword to the k-th user.

We choose ℓ_1 many permutations, randomly, over the set $\{1, 2, \ldots, 2wd\}$ where $d \stackrel{def}{=} 8(2w)^2 \ln 1/\varepsilon_2$ and $\ell_2 \stackrel{def}{=} 2wd$. Let us denote the permutations by $\pi_1, \ldots, \pi_{\ell_1}$. For each permutation π_j, we build private-input free version of the master matrices M_{d, π_j} of Figure 1 with $2w$ many rows. When we say private-input free version, we mean the blocks with private-inputs are left empty at this stage. Let us call these blocks by empty-slots.

Let $\langle c_1, \ldots, c_{\ell_1} \rangle$ be the outer codeword of a user U, and let $X^U \in \{0,1\}^d$ be the private input of user U. We generate the overall codeword of that user as follows:

For each $0 < j \leq \ell_1$, the private input X^U is placed in the empty-slot of the c_j-th row of the master matrix M_{d, π_j} as our code suggests in Section 2. Denoting this row as u_j: the resulting codeword of user U after concatenation would be $\langle u_1, \ldots, u_{\ell_1} \rangle$. Let us name these blocks at the outer level by outer-blocks, i.e. the j-th outer-block of U's codeword would be u_j.

Each receiver plugs its private input, that is of length $d = 8(2w)^2 \ln 1/\varepsilon_2$, into each symbol of its outer codeword. In other words, the same private input X is repeatedly used ℓ_1 times for each symbol of the outer codeword. The resulting code after concatenation would be a $(\ell_1 \cdot \ell_2, n, 2)$-code.

Identification: Upon obtaining a pirate codeword P we first chop the pirate codeword into ℓ_1 outer-blocks, denoted by $P = \langle p_1, \ldots, p_{\ell_1} \rangle$. Each outer-block of the pirate codeword corresponds to a pirate codeword at the inner code level. Hence, we run, in parallel, the identification algorithm of the inner code(i.e. our asymmetric code of Section 2) for each outer block: more specifically for the inputs p_i and π_i, the identification algorithm returns an index $h_i \in [2w]$ and produces $\Omega_i = (arb_i, b_i)$ as an arbiter proof.

After the above stage, we obtain a vector $\langle h_1, h_2, \ldots, h_{\ell_1} \rangle$ as a pirate codeword at the outer code level. We run the identification algorithm of the outer code which outputs a traitor index $h \in [n]$. This accused traitor, due to the correctness of the outer code, is responsible of piracy in ℓ_1/w many outer-blocks the pirate codeword P. Let us denote the indices of those outer-blocks by $\{r_1, \ldots, r_{\ell_1/w}\} \subseteq [\ell_1]$. The identification procedure of the concatenated code will accuse the receiver with index $h \in [n]$ as a traitor and output $\Omega = \{\Omega_{r_i}\}_{i \in [\ell_1/w]}$ as the arbiter proof.

ArbiterPredicate: Upon receiving $(tk, \{X^j\}_{j \in [n]}, h, \Omega)$ where tk is the tracing key (the secret information generated at the code generation phase due to both inner and outer codes), we run, in parallel, the arbitration algorithm of the inner code(i.e. our asymmetric code of Section 2) for each sub-arbiter proof Ω_{r_i}: more specifically we run the arbiter predicate with input $(\pi_{r_i}, \{X^j\}_{j \in [n]}, h, \Omega_{r_i})$. This essentially, makes a comparison between the private input X^h of the h-th user with the string (arb_{r_i}). If at least one of these protocol-runs outputs true then we also return true.

We finally provide a sketch of the analysis for the above concatenation with the selected choices:

(i) Traceability: the correctness of the traceability merely relies on the correctness of the underlying codes. Hence, the failure probability will be bounded by $2\ell_1\varepsilon_2 + \varepsilon_1$.

(ii) Non-repudiation: Based on the identification algorithms, the accused traitor with index h has found to have at least ℓ_1/w many matchings with the pirate codeword at the outer level. However, this does not necessarily mean that the traitor was actively using its private input in all of these ℓ_1/w affiliated pirate inner codewords. Indeed, a number of other traitors, with the same symbol at the outer level, might also actively use their private inputs (even to the extent that the accused traitor may not be active for that symbol). For such arbiter proof, the arbiter predicate will probably return false. What we need is at least one position where the accused traitor found to be single in having its symbol, i.e. all other traitors get a different symbol (otherwise we say a collusion of type h occurs). We now claim that finding a position without type h collusion is very likely given the parameters of the concatenation.

For one particular outer-block, the probability of the existence of a traitor having the same symbol what the h-th user (who has been accused of being traitor) has would be at most $\frac{w-1}{2w} < 1/2$. This is indeed because the outer-codewords are chosen randomly for our choice of $2w$ alphabet size where w is the size of the traitor coalition. Hence the probability that there are collisions of type h at all ℓ_1/w positions is bounded by $(1/2)^{4\log n/\varepsilon_1} = (\frac{\varepsilon_1}{n})^4$.

For such position where the traitor with index h obtains a different symbol from the rest of the traitors, the arbiter predicate will return true, i.e. the correlation of the arbiter string to the private input of h-th receiver will be suffice to accuse, with a non-repudiation error of at most $\varepsilon_2^{1/112}$. Hence, the overall non-repudiation error is bounded by $(\frac{\varepsilon_1}{n})^4 + \varepsilon_2^{1/112}$.

(iii) Non-framing: The ArbiterPredicate is provided $\ell_1/w = 4\log n/\varepsilon_1$ many guesses for the private input of the accused traitor. Hence, the probability of a framing success would be bounded by $4\log n/\varepsilon_1$ many times of the single framing success. Hence, a malicious code designer will be able to frame with at most $4\frac{\ell_1}{w}\varepsilon_2^{1/384}$ probability.

5. ACKNOWLEDGMENTS

This research is conducted in part while at Nanyang Technological University; supported by The Singapore National Research Foundation under Research Grant NRF-CRP2-2007-03. The author thanks to Prof. San Ling and Prof. Huaxiong Wang for the fruitful discussions.

6. REFERENCES

[1] I. Biehl, B. Meyer: Protocols for Collusion-Secure Asymmetric Fingerprinting STACS 1997: 399-412

[2] D. Boneh and M. Naor: Traitor tracing with constant size ciphertext. In proceedings of the 15th ACM conference on Computer and Communications Security (CCS '08), pp. 501–510, 2008.

[3] D. Boneh, J. Shaw: Collusion-Secure Fingerprinting for Digital Data (Extended Abstract). CRYPTO 1995

[4] A. Charpentier, C. Fontaine, T. Furon, I. J. Cox: An Asymmetric Fingerprinting Scheme based on Tardos Codes. Information Hiding 2011: 43-58

[5] B. Chor, A. Fiat, M. Naor: Tracing Traitors. CRYPTO 1994: 257-270

[6] S. Craver, N. Memon, B. Yeo, and M. M. Yeung. Resolving rightful ownerships with invisible watermarking techniques: Limitations, attacks, and implications. IEEE Journal on Selected Areas in Communications, 16(4):573-586, May 1998.

[7] M. Deng, T. Bianchi, A. Piva and B. Preneel: An Efficient Buyer-Seller Watermarking Protocol based on composite signal representation. 11th ACM Workshop on Multimedia and Security, Princeton, NJ, 2009, pp. 9-18

[8] M. Deng, L. Weng, B. Preneel: Anonymous Buyer-Seller Watermarking Protocol with Additive Homomorphism. SIGMAP 2008: 300-307

[9] Ju, H. S., Kim, H. J., Lee, D. H., and Lim, J. I. (2002). An anonymous buyer-seller watermarking protocol with anonymity control. Information security and cryptology ICISC 2002

[10] H. Jin, J. Lotspiech: Renewable Traitor Tracing: A Trace-Revoke-Trace System For Anonymous Attack. ESORICS 2007: 563-577

[11] A. Kiayias, S. Pehlivanoglu: Tracing and Revoking Pirate Rebroadcasts. ACNS 2009: 253-271

[12] A. Kiayias and S. Pehlivanoglu. Encryption for Digital Content, volume 52 of Advances in Information Security. Springer, 2010.

[13] A. Kiayias, S. Pehlivanoglu: Improving the Round Complexity of Traitor Tracing Schemes. ACNS 2010

[14] M. Kuribayashi, H. Tanaka: Fingerprinting protocol for images based on additive homomorphic property. IEEE Transactions on Image Processing 14(12), 2005

[15] A. Kiayias and M. Yung, On Crafty Pirates and Foxy Tracers, ACM CCS-8 Workshop DRM 2001

[16] N. D. Memon, P. W. Wong: A buyer-seller watermarking protocol. IEEE Transactions on Image Processing 10(4): 643-649 (2001)

[17] J. P. Prins, Z. Erkin, R. L. Lagendijk: Anonymous Fingerprinting with Robust QIM Watermarking Techniques. EURASIP J. Information Security 2007

[18] B. Pfitzmann, M. Schunter: Asymmetric Fingerprinting. EUROCRYPT 1996: 84-95

[19] B. Pfitzmann, M. Waidner: Asymmetric Fingerprinting for Larger Collusions. ACM Conference on Computer and Communications Security 1997

[20] B. Pfitzmann, M. Waidner: Anonymous Fingerprinting. EUROCRYPT 1997: 88-102

[21] Min-Hua Shao. A privacy-preserving buyer-seller watermarking protocol with semi- trust third party. In Trust, Privacy and Security in Digital Business, 2007

[22] J. Staddon, D. R. Stinson, R. Wei: Combinatorial properties of frameproof and traceability codes. IEEE Transactions on Information Theory 47(3) 2001

[23] D. R. Stinson, R. Wei: Combinatorial Properties and Constructions of Traceability Schemes and Frameproof Codes. SIAM J. Discrete Math. 11(1): 41-53 (1998)

[24] R. Safavi-Naini, Y. Wang: New results on frame-proof codes and traceability schemes. IEEE Transactions on Information Theory 47(7): 3029-3033 (2001)

[25] Z. Jane Wang, Min Wu, H. Vicky Zhao, Wade Trappe, K. J. Ray Liu: Anti-collusion forensics of multimedia fingerprinting using orthogonal modulation. IEEE Transactions on Image Processing 14(6), 2005

[26] Gabor Tardos: Optimal probabilistic fingerprint codes. J. ACM 55(2): (2008)

[27] J. Zhang, W. Kou, and K. Fan. Secure buyer-seller watermarking protocol. IEE Proceedings Information Security, 153(1):15-18, March 2006.

Moving Steganography and Steganalysis from the Laboratory into the Real World

Andrew D. Ker
Dept. of Computer Science
University of Oxford
Oxford OX1 3QD, UK
adk@cs.ox.ac.uk

Patrick Bas
LAGIS CNRS
Ecole Centrale de Lille
59651 Villeneuve d'Ascq, FR
patrick.bas@ec-lille.fr

Rainer Böhme
University of Münster
Leonardo-Campus 3
48149 Münster, Germany
rainer.boehme@wwu.de

Rémi Cogranne
LM2S - UMR STMR CNRS
Troyes Univ. of Technology
10004 Troyes, France
remi.cogranne@utt.fr

Scott Craver
Dept. of ECE
Binghamton University
Binghamton, NY 13902
scraver@binghamton.edu

Tomáš Filler
Digimarc Corporation
9405 SW Gemini Drive
Beaverton, OR 97008
tomas.filler@digimarc.com

Jessica Fridrich
Dept. of ECE
Binghamton University
Binghamton, NY 13902
fridrich@binghamton.edu

Tomáš Pevný
Agent Technology Group
CTU in Prague
Prague 16627, Czech Rep.
pevnak@gmail.com

ABSTRACT

There has been an explosion of academic literature on steganography and steganalysis in the past two decades. With a few exceptions, such papers address abstractions of the hiding and detection problems, which arguably have become disconnected from the real world. Most published results, including by the authors of this paper, apply "in laboratory conditions" and some are heavily hedged by assumptions and caveats; significant challenges remain unsolved in order to implement good steganography and steganalysis in practice. This position paper sets out some of the important questions which have been left unanswered, as well as highlighting some that have already been addressed successfully, for steganography and steganalysis to be used in the real world.

Categories and Subject Descriptors

D.2.11 [**Software Engineering**]: Software Architectures—*Information hiding*; H.1.1 [**Models and Principles**]: Systems and Information Theory—*Information theory*

Keywords

Steganography; Steganalysis; Security Models; Minimal Distortion; Optimal Detection; Game Theory

1. INTRODUCTION

Steganography is now a fairly standard concept in computer science. One occasionally reads, in mainstream media, of criminals hiding information in digital media ([1, 4], see [3] for other links) and, recently, of malware using it to conceal communications with command and control servers [5]. In the 1990s, the possibility of digital steganography served as an argument in debates about regulating cryptography, and it allegedly convinced some European governments to liberalize the use of cryptography [31]. We also read of the desire for certain privacy-enhancing technologies to use steganography to evade censorship [67]. If steganography becomes commonly used, so should steganalysis, though the concept is not as well recognized in nonspecialist circles.

However, where details of real-world use of steganography are known, it is apparent that they bear little resemblance to techniques described in modern literature. Indeed, they often suffer from flaws known to researchers for more than a decade. How has practice become so disconnected from research? The situation is even more stark in steganalysis, where most researchers would agree that their detectors work well only in laboratory conditions: unlike steganography, even if practitioners wanted and were technically able to implement state-of-the-art detectors, their accuracy would be uneven and unreliable.

The starting point for scientific research is to make a *model* of the problem. The real world is a messy place, and the model is an abstraction which removes ambiguities, sets certain parameters, and makes the problem amenable to mathematical analysis or empirical study. In this paper we contend that *knowledge* is the most important component in a model of the steganography and steganalysis problems. Does the steganographer have perfect knowledge about their source of covers? Does the steganalyst know the embedding method used by the steganographer? There are many questions of this type, often left implicit in early research.

By considering different levels of knowledge, we identify a number of models of the steganography and steganalysis problems. Some of them have been well-studied but, naturally enough, it is usually the simplest models which have received the most attention. Simple models may (or may not) provide robust theoretical results giving lower or upper bounds, and they increase our understanding of the fundamental problems, but they are tied to the laboratory. In this paper we identify the models which bring both steganography and steganalysis nearer to the real world. In many cases the scientific community has barely scratched their surface, and we highlight open problems which are, in the view of the authors, important to address in future research.

At the present time, steganography and steganalysis research divides into two cover types: digital media (primarily compressed and uncompressed images, but also video and audio) and network traffic (timing channels and the content of web traffic). The authors of this paper have their interest mainly in the former, and we contend that steganography and steganalysis is significantly more sophisticated in this domain than in network channels. Although network-based steganography is perhaps closer to real-world implementation, we will argue that the field needs to learn lessons from digital media steganography.

Many of the principles in this paper apply to any type of cover, but we shall be motivated by some general properties of digital media: the complexity of the cover and the lack of perfect models, the relative ease of (visual) *imperceptibility* as opposed to *undetectability*, and large capacity per object. When, in examples, we refer to *spatial domain* we mean uncompressed images, and *DCT* or *transform domain* refers to JPEG-compressed images, both grayscale unless otherwise mentioned.

The paper has a simple structure. In section 2 we discuss current solutions, and open problems, relevant to applying steganography in the real world. In section 3 we do the same for steganalysis.

The Steganography Problem

We briefly recapitulate the steganography problem, refining Simmons' original Prisoners' Problem [92] to the contemporary definition of steganography against a passive warden.

A sender, often called Alice but who will throughout the paper be known as *the steganographer*, wishes to send a covert communication or *payload* to a recipient. She possesses a source of *covers* drawn from a larger set of possible communications, and there exists a *channel* for the communications (for most purposes we may as well suppose that the communication is unidirectional). The channel is monitored by an adversary, also known as an attacker or Warden but for the purposes of this paper called *the steganalyst*, who wishes to determine whether payload is present or not.

One solution is to use a channel that the adversary is not aware of. This is how traditional steganography has reportedly been practiced since ancient times, and most likely prevails in the Internet age [46]. Examples include tools that hide information in metadata structures, at the end of files where standard parsers ignore it [103], or modifying network packet headers such as TCP time stamps [37]. (See [74] for a systematic discussion.)

However, this approach is not satisfactory because it relies on the adversary's ignorance, a form of "security through obscurity". In Simmons' formulation, inspired by conservative

assumptions typical in cryptology, the steganalyst is granted wide knowledge: the contents of the channel is perfectly observable by both parties, writable by the steganographer, and (for the "passive Warden" case which dominates this paper) read-only by the steganalyst. To enable undetectability, we must assume that cover messages run through the channel irrespective of whether hidden communication takes place or not, but this is something that we will need to make more precise later. The intended recipient of the covert payload is distinguished from the steganalyst by sharing a secret key with the steganographer (how such a key might be shared will be covered in section 2.5).

As we shall see later, this model is still imprecise: the Warden's aims, the parties' knowledge about the cover source, and even their knowledge about each others' knowledge, all create different versions of the steganography and steganalysis problems.

We fix some notation used throughout the paper. Cover objects generated by Alice's source will be denoted by $\mathbf{X}$, broken down where necessary into n elements (e.g. pixels in the spatial domain pixels, or DCT coefficients in the transform domain) $X_1, \ldots, X_n$. The objects emitted by the steganographer – which may be unchanged covers or payload-carrying stego objects – will be denoted $\mathbf{Y}$, or sometimes $\mathbf{Y}_\beta$ where β denotes the size of the payload relative to the size of the cover (the exact scaling factor will be irrelevant). Thus $\mathbf{Y}_0$ denotes a cover object emitted by the steganographer.

In parts of the paper we will assume a probability distribution for cover and stego objects (even though, as we argue in section 2.1, this distribution is unknowable precisely): the distribution of $\mathbf{Y}_\beta$ will be denoted P_β, or if the distribution depends on other parameters $\boldsymbol{\theta}$ then $P_\beta^{\boldsymbol{\theta}}$. Thus P_0 is the distribution of cover objects from the steganographer's source.

2. STEGANOGRAPHY

Steganographic embedding in a single grayscale image could be implemented in the real world, with a high degree of undetectability against contemporary steganalysis, if practitioners were to use today's state of art. In this section we begin by outlining that state of art, and highlighting the open problems for its further improvement. However, the same cannot be said of creating a steganographic channel in a stream of multiple objects — which is, after all, the essential aim for systems supporting censorship resistance — nor for robust key exchange, and our discussion is mainly of open problems barely treated by the literature.

We begin, in section 2.1, with some results which live purely in the laboratory. They apply to the security model in which the steganographer understands her cover source perfectly, or has exponential amounts of time to wait for a perfect cover. In section 2.2 we move closer to the real world, describing methods which help a steganographer to be *less* detectable when embedding a given payload. They require, however, the steganographer to know a tractably-optimizable *distortion function*, which is really a property of her enemy. Such research was far from the real world until recently, and is moving to practical applicability at the present time. But it does not tell the steganographer whether her size of payload is likely to be detectable; some purely theoretical research is discussed in section 2.3, which gives rules of thumb for how payload should scale as properties of the cover vary, but it remains an open problem to determine an appropriate payload for a given cover.

In section 2.4 we modify the original steganography model to better account for the repeated nature of communications: if the steganographer wants to create a covert channel, as opposed to a one-shot covert communication, new considerations arise. There are many open research problems in this area. Section 2.5 addresses the key exchange between the steganographer and her participant. The problem is well-understood with a passive warden opponent, but in the presence of an active warden it may even be impossible.

Section 2.6 briefly surveys other ways in which weaknesses may arise in practice, having been omitted from the model, and section 2.7 discusses whether the steganographer can encourage real-world situations favourable to her.

2.1 The laboratory: perfect steganography

One can safely say that perfectly secure steganography is now well understood. It requires that the distribution of stego objects be identical to that of cover objects.

In a model where the covers are sequences (usually of fixed length) of symbols from a fixed alphabet, the steganographer fully understands the cover source if they know the distribution of the symbols, including any conditional dependence between them. In such a case, perfect steganography is a coding problem and the capacity or rate (the number of bits per cover symbol) of perfectly secure steganography is bounded by the entropy of the cover distribution. Constructions for such coding have been proposed, including the cases of a distortion-limited sender (the sender is limited in how much the cover can be modified) and even a power-limited active Warden (the Warden can inject a distortion of limited power), for i. i. d. and Markov sources [101].

However, such a model of covers is necessarily *artificial*. The distinction between artificial and *empirical* cover sources has been proposed in [14] and is pivotal to the study of steganography in digital media. Artificial sources prescribe a probability distribution from which cover objects are drawn, whereas empirical sources take this distribution as given somewhere outside the steganographic system, which we could call *reality*. The steganographer can sample an empirical distribution, thereby obtaining projections of parts of reality; she can estimate salient features to devise, calibrate, and test models of reality; but she arguably can never fully know it. The perfect security of the preceding constructions rests on perfect knowledge of the cover source, and any violation of this assumption breaks the security proof. In practical situations, it is difficult to guarantee such an assumption. In other words, secure steganography exists for artificial sources, but we can never be sure if the artificial source exists in practice. More figuratively, artificial channels sit in the corner of the laboratory farthest away from the real world. But they can still be useful as starting points for new theories or as benchmarks.

Perfect steganography is still possible, albeit at higher cost, with empirical cover sources. If (1) secure cryptographic one-way functions exist, (2) the steganalyst is at most equally limited in her knowledge about the cover source as the steganographer, and (3) the cover source can be efficiently sampled, then perfect steganography is possible (the *rejection sampler*), but embedding requires an exponential number of samples in the message length [14, Ch. 3]. Some authors work around the inconvenient embedding complexity by tightening the third assumption and requiring that sampling is efficient conditional to any possible history of

transmitted cover objects [41, 85, 44], which is arguably as strong as solving the original steganography problem.

2.2 Optimal embedding

If the steganographer has to use *imperfect steganography*, which does not preserve exactly the distribution of objects, how should she embed to be less detectable? Designing steganography for empirical cover sources is challenging, but there has been great progress in recent years. The steganographer must find a proxy for detectability, which we call *distortion*. Then message embedding is formulated as source coding with a fidelity constraint [91] – the sender hides her message while minimizing an embedding distortion [58, 79, 39]. As well as providing a framework for good embedding, this permits one to compute the largest payload embeddable below a given embedding distortion, and thus evaluate the efficiency of a specific implementation (coding method).

There are two challenges here: to design a good distortion function, and to find a method for encoding the message to minimize the distortion. We consider the latter problem first.

Early steganographic methods were severely limited by their ability to minimize distortion tractably. The most popular idea was to embed the payload while minimizing the *number* of changes caused (*matrix embedding* [21]). Counting the embedding changes, however, implicitly assumes that each change contributes equally to detectability, which does not coincide with experimental experience.

The idea of *adaptive embedding*, where each cover element is assigned a different embedding *cost*, dates to the early days of digital steganography [31]. A breakthrough technique was to use syndrome-trellis codes (STCs) [29], which solve certain versions of the adaptive embedding problem. The designer defines an additive distortion between the cover and stego objects in the form

$$D(\mathbf{X}, \mathbf{Y}) = \sum_i \rho_i(\mathbf{X}, Y_i), \qquad (1)$$

where $\rho_i \geq 0$ is a local distortion measure that is zero if $Y_i = X_i$, and then embeds her message using STCs, which minimize distortion between cover and stego objects for a given payload.

STCs only directly solve the embedding problem for distortion functions that are *additive* in the above sense, or where an additive approximation is suitable. Recently, suboptimal coding schemes able to minimize non-additive distortion functions were proposed, thereby modelling interactions among embedding changes, using the *Gibbs construction*. This can be used to implement embedding with an arbitrary distortion that can be written as a sum of *locally supported potentials* [27]. Unfortunately, such schemes can only reach the rate-distortion bound for additive distortion measures. Moving to wider classes of distortion function, along with provably optimal and practical coding algorithms, is an area of current research.

Open Problem 1 Design efficient coding schemes for non-additive distortion functions.

How, then, to define the distortion function? For the steganographer, the distortion function is a property of her enemy, the steganalyst. If she were to know what steganalysis she is up against then it would be tempting to use the same feature representation as her opponent, defining $D(\mathbf{X}, \mathbf{Y}) = ||f(\mathbf{X}) - f(\mathbf{Y})||$, where f is the feature extraction function. Such a distortion function, however, is non-additive and non-local in just about all feature spaces used in steganalysis, which typically include histograms and high-order co-occurrences, created by a variety of local filters. One option is to make an additive approximation. Another, proposed in [27], is to create an upper bound to the distortion function, by writing its macroscopic features as a sum of locally-supported functions (for example, the elements of a co-occurrence matrix can be written as the sum of indicator functions operating on pairs of pixels). In such a case, the distortion function can be bounded, using the triangle inequality, leading to a tractable objective function for STCs.

Even if the coding problem can be solved, such embedding presupposes knowledge of the right distortion function. An alternative is to design a distortion function which reflects statistical detectability (against an optimal detector), but this is difficult to do, let alone the constraints of our current coding techniques. First attempts in these directions adjusted parameters of a heuristically-defined distortion function, to give the smallest margin between classes in a selected feature space [28]. However, unless the feature space is a complete statistical descriptor of the empirical source [61], such optimized schemes may, paradoxically, end up being more detectable [65], which brings us back to the main and rather difficult problem: modelling the source.

Open Problem 2 Design a distortion function relating to statistical detectability, e.g. via KL divergence (sect. 2.3).

Design of *heuristic* distortion functions is currently a highly active research direction. It seems that the key is to assign high costs to changes to areas of a cover which are "predictable" from other parts of the stego object or other information available to the steganalyst. For example, one may use local variance to compute pixel costs in spatial domain images [97]. The embedding algorithm HUGO [79] uses an additive approximation of a weighted norm between cover and stego features in the SPAM feature space [78], with high weights assigned to well-populated feature bins and low weights to sparsely populated bins that correspond to more complex content. An alternative distortion function called WOW (Wavelet Obtained Weights) [40] uses a bank of directional high-pass filters to assign high distortion where the content is predictable in *at least one* direction. It has been shown to resist steganalysis using rich models [35]. A further development is published in these proceedings.

One can expected that future research will turn to computer vision literature, where image models based on Markov Random Fields [102, 87, 94] are commonly trained and then utilized in various Bayesian inference problems.

In the domain of grayscale JPEG images, by far the most successful paradigm is to minimize the distortion w.r.t. the raw, uncompressed cover image, if available [58, 86, 100, 43]. In fact, this "side-informed embedding" can be applied whenever the sender possesses a higher-quality "precover" that was quantized to obtain the cover. Currently, the most secure embedding method for JPEG images that does not use any side information is the heuristically-built Uniform Embedding Distortion [39] that substantially improved the previous state of the art: the nsF5 algorithm [36].

Open Problem 3 Distortion functions which take account of side information.

We conclude by highlighting the scale of research advances seen in embedding into grayscale (compressed or uncom-

pressed) images. The earliest aims to reduce distortion attempted to correct macroscopic properties (e.g., an image histogram) by compensating embedding changes with additional correction changes, but in doing so made themselves more detectable, not less. We have progressed through a painful period where distortion minimization could not tractably be performed, to the most recent adaptive methods. However, we know of no literature addressing the parallel problems:

Open Problem 4 Distortion functions for colour images and video, which take account of correlations in these media.

Network steganography has received substantial attention from the information theory community through the analysis of *covert timing channels* [6, 98], which uses delays between network packets to embed the payload. However, the implementations are usually naive, using no distortion with respect to delays of normal data [16, 12]. The design of the embedding schemes focuses mainly on robustness with respect to the network itself, because network steganography is an active steganography problem. To the knowledge of the authors, the only work that considers a statistical distortion between normal and stego traffic is provided in [9].

2.3 Scaling laws

In this section we discuss some theory which has relevance to real-world considerations. These results rest on some information theory: the data processing theorem for Kullback-Leibler (KL) divergence [69]. We are interested in KL divergence between cover objects and stego objects, which we will denote $D_{\mathrm{KL}}(P_0 || P_\beta)$. Cachin [17] described how an upper bound on this KL divergence implies an upper bound on the performance of *any* detector; we do not repeat the argument here. What matters is that we can analyze KL divergence, for a range of artificial models of covers and embedding, and obtain interesting conclusions.

As long as the family of distributions $P_\beta^{\boldsymbol{\theta}}$ satisfies certain smoothness assumptions, for fixed cover parameters $\boldsymbol{\theta}$ the Taylor expansion to the right of $\beta = 0$ is

$$D_{\mathrm{KL}}(P_0^{\boldsymbol{\theta}} || P_\beta^{\boldsymbol{\theta}}) \sim \frac{n}{2} \beta^2 I^{\boldsymbol{\theta}}(0), \qquad (2)$$

where n is the size of the objects and $I^{\boldsymbol{\theta}}(0)$ is the so-called *Fisher information*. This can be interpreted in the following manner: in order to keep the same level of statistical detectability as the cover length n grows, the sender must adjust the embedding rate so that $n\beta^2$ remains constant. This means that the total payload, which is $n\beta$, must be proportional to $\sqrt{n}$. This is known as the *square root law* of imperfect steganography. Its effects were observed experimentally long before it was formally discovered first within the context of batch steganography [50], experimentally confirmed [57], and finally derived for sources with memory [30], where the reader should look for a precise formulation.

The law also tells us that the proper measure of secure payload is the constant of proportionality, $I^{\boldsymbol{\theta}}(0)$, the Fisher information. The larger $I^{\boldsymbol{\theta}}(0)$, the smaller the secure payload that can be embedded and vice versa. When practitioners design their steganographic schemes for empirical covers, one can say that they are trying to minimize $I^{\boldsymbol{\theta}}(0)$, and it would be of immense value if the Fisher information could be determined for practical embedding methods. But it depends heavily on the cover source, and particularly on the likelihood of *rare* covers, which by definition is difficult to estimate empirically, and there has as yet been limited progress in this area, benchmarking [26] and optimizing [53] simple embedding only in restrictive artificial cover models.

Open Problem 5 Robust empirical estimate of steganographic Fisher information.

What is remarkable about the square root law is that, although both asymptotic and proved only for artificial sources, it is robust and manifests in real life. This is despite the fact that practitioners detect steganography using empirical classifiers which are unlikely to approach the bound given by KL divergence, and the fact that empirical sources do not match artificial models. Beware, though, that it tells us how the secure payload scales when changing the number of cover elements, without changing their statistical properties — e.g. when cropping homogeneous images or creating a panorama by simple composition — but not when a cover is resized, because resizing changes the statistical properties of the cover pixels by weakening (if downscaling without antialiasing) or strengthening (if using a resampling kernel) their dependencies.

We can still say something about resized images, if we accept a Markov chain cover model. When nearest neighbour resizing is used, one can compute numerically $I^{\theta}(0)$ as a function of the resizing factor (which should be thought of as part of θ) [64]. This allows the steganographer to adjust her payload size with rescaling of the cover, and the theory aligns robustly with experimental results.

Open Problem 6 Derivation of Fisher information for other rescaling algorithms, and richer cover models.

Finally, one can ask about the impact of quantization. This is relevant as practically all digital media are obtained by processing and quantizing the output of some analogue sensor, and a JPEG image is obtained from a raw image by quantizing the real-valued output of a transform. For example, how much larger payload can one embed in 10-bit grayscale images than in 8-bit? (Provided that both bit depths are equally plausible on the channel.) How much more data can be hidden in a JPEG with quality factor 98 than quality factor 75? We can derive (in an appropriate limit) $I^{\theta}(0) \sim \triangle^{s}$, where $\triangle > 0$ is the quantization step and s is the quantization scaling exponent that can be calculated from the embedding operation and the smoothness of the unquantized distribution [32]. In general, the smoother the unquantized distribution, the larger s is and the smaller the Fisher information (larger secure payload). The exponent s is also larger for embedding operations that have a smoothing effect. Because the KL divergence is an error exponent, quantization has a profound effect on security. The experiments in [32] indicate that even simple LSB matching may be practically undetectable in 10–12 bit grayscale images. However, unlike the scaling predicted by the square root law, since the result for quantization depends strongly on the distribution of the unquantized image, it cannot quantitatively explain real life experiments.

2.4 Multiple objects

Simmons' 1983 paper used the term "subliminal channel", but the steganography we have been describing is not fully a channel: it focused on embedding a certain length payload in *one* cover object. For a *channel*, there must be infinitely many stego objects (perhaps mixed with infinitely many innocent cover objects) transmitted by the steganographer.

How do we adapt steganographic methods for embedding in one object to embedding in many? How should one allocate payload between multiple objects? There has been very little research on this important problem, which is particularly relevant to hiding in network channels, where communication is naturally repeated.

In some versions of the model, this is fundamentally no different from the simple steganography problem in one object. Take the case, for example, where the steganographer has a fixed number of covers, and decides how to allocate payload amongst them (the *batch steganography* problem posed in [48]). Treating the collection as a single large object is possible if the full message and all covers are instantly available and go through the same channel (e. g., stay on the same disk as a steganographic file system). In principle, this reduces the problem to what has been said above. It is worth pointing out that local statistical properties are more likely to change between covers than between symbols within one cover. However, almost all empirical practical cover sources are *heterogeneous* (non-stationary): samplers and distortion functions have to deal with this fact anyway. And knowing the boundaries between cover objects is just another kind of side information.

The situation is more complicated in the presence of real-time constraints, such as requirements to embed and communicate before the full message is known or before all covers are drawn. This happens, for example, when tunnelling bilateral protocols through steganographic channels. Few publications have addressed the *stream steganography* problem (in analogy to stream ciphers) [31, 52]. One interesting result is known for payload allocation in infinite streams with imperfect embedding (and applies only to an artificial setup where distortion is exactly square in the amount of payload per object): the higher the rate that payload is sent early, the lower the eventual asymptotic square root rate [52].

A further generalization is to replace the "channel" by a "network" communications model, where the steganographer serves multiple channels, each governed by specific cover source conventions, and with realtime constraints emerging from related communications. Assuming a global passive steganalyst who can relate evidence from all communications, this becomes a very hard instance of a steganography problem, and one that seems relevant for censorship-resistant multiparty communication or to tunnel covert collaboration [10].

Open Problem 7 Theoretical approaches and practical implementations for embedding in multiple objects in the presence of realtime constraints.

2.5 Key exchange

A curious problem in a steganographic environment is that of key exchange. If a reliable steganographic system exists, can parties use that channel to communicate, without first sharing a secret key? In the cryptographic world, Alice and Bob use a public-key cryptosystem to effect a secret key exchange, and then communicate with a symmetric cipher; one would assume that some similar exchange would enable communication with a symmetric stegosystem. However, a steganographic channel is fundamentally different from a traditional communications channel, due to its extra constraint of undetectability. This constraint also limits our ability to transmit datagrams for key establishment.

Key exchange has been addressed with several protocols and, paradoxically, negative results. The first protocol for key exchange under a passive warden [7] was later augmented to survive an active warden [8]. Here Alice and Bob use a public embedding key to transmit traditional key exchange datagrams: first a public encryption key, and then a session key encrypted with that public key. These datagrams are visible to the warden, but they are designed to resemble channel noise so that the warden cannot tell if the channel is in use. This requires a complete lack of observable structure in the keys.

To prevent an *active* warden from altering the datagrams, the public embedding key is made temporarily private: first a datagram is sent with a secret embedding key, and then this key is publicly broadcast after the stego object passes the warden. In [22] it was argued that a key broadcast is not allowed in a steganographic setting, but that a key could be encoded as semantic content of a cover.

This may seem to settle the problem, but recent results argue that these protocols, and perhaps any such protocols, are practically impossible because the datagrams are sensitive to even a single bit error. If an active warden can inflict a few errors, we have a problem due to a fundamental difference between steganographic and traditional communication channels: *we cannot use traditional error correction*, because its presence is observable structure that betrays the existence of a message. In [71], it was shown that this fragility cannot be fixed in general: most strings are a few surgical errors away from a failed transmission; this allows key exchange to be derailed with an asymptotically vanishing error rate. It is not clear who will have the upper hand in practice: an ever-vigilant warden can indefinitely postpone key exchange with little error, but a brief opportunity to transmit some uncorrupted datagrams results in successful key transmission, whereupon the warden loses.

A final problem in steganographic key exchange is the state of ignorance of sender and receiver, and the massive computational burden this implies. Because key datagrams must resemble channel noise, nobody can tell if or when they are being transmitted; by the constraints of the problem, neither Alice nor the warden can tell if Bob is participating in a protocol, or innocently transmitting empty covers. This is solved by brute force: Bob assumes that the channel noise of every image is a public key, and sends a reply. Alice makes similar assumptions, both repeatedly attempting to generate a shared key until they produce one that works.

Open Problem 8 Is this monstrous amount of computation necessary, or is there a protocol with more efficient guesswork to allow Alice and Bob to converge on a key?

2.6 Basic security principles

Finally, even when a steganographic method is secure, its security can be broken if there is information leakage of the secret key, or of the steganography software. We recall some basic principles that should be followed by the steganographer, in order to avoid security pitfalls.
- Her embedding key must be long enough to avoid exhaustion attacks [34], and any pseudorandom numbers generated from it must be strong.
- Whenever she wants to embed a payload in several images, she must avoid using the same embedding locations for each. Otherwise the steganalyst can use noise residuals to estimate the embedding locations, reducing the entropy of the secret

key [51]. One way to force the locations to vary is to add a robust hash of the cover to the seed.
- She must act identically to any casual user of the communication channel, which implies hiding also the use of steganographic software, and deleting temporary cover and stego objects. An actor that performs cover selection by emitting only contents that are known to be difficult to analyze (such as textured images) can seem suspicious in itself.

Open Problem 9 How to perform cover selection, if at all? How to detect cover selection?

- She has to beware of the pre- and post-processing operations that can be associated with embedding. Double compression can be easily detected [80] and forensic details, such as the ordering of different parts of a JPEG file, can expose the processing path [38].
- She should benchmark her embedding appropriately. In the case of digital images for example, it is not because the software produces *imperceptible* embedding that the payload is undetectable. Image quality metrics such as the PSNR and psychovisual metrics are of little interest in steganography.
- Her device capturing the cover should be trusted, and contents generated from this device should also stay hidden. Covers must not be re-used.

Several general principles should be kept in mind when designing a secure system. These include:
- The Kerckhoffs Principle, that a system should remain secure under the assumption that the adversary knows the system, although interpretations for steganography differ in whether this includes knowledge of the cover source or not.
- The Usability Principle (also due to Kerckhoffs), that a system should be easy for a layperson to use correctly. For example, steganographic software should enforce a square root law rather than expecting an end user to apply it.
- The Law of Leaky Abstractions [93], which requires us to be aware of, for example, statistical models of cover sources, assumptions about the adversary, or the abstraction of steganography as a generic communication channel. Even if we have provable security within the model, reality may deviate from the model in a way that causes a security weakness.
- The fact that steganographic channels are not communications channels in the traditional sense, and their limitations are different. Challenges of capacity, fidelity, and key exchange must be examined anew.

Open Problem 10 Are there abstractions that hold for steganography? Are its building blocks securely composable?

2.7 Engineering the real world for steganography

If we perfectly understood our cover sources, secure steganography would reduce to a coding problem. Engineering secure steganography for the real world is so difficult precisely because it requires us to understand the real world as well as our artificial models. If there is a consensus that the real world needs secure steganography, a completely different approach could be to engineer the real world so that parts of it match the assumptions needed for security proofs. This implies changing the conventions, via protocols and norms, towards more randomness in everyday communications, so that more artificial channels knowingly exist in the real world. For example, random nonces in certain protocols, or synthetic pseudorandom textures in video-games (if implemented with trustworthy randomness) already provide opportunities for steganographic channels. Adding more of these increases the secure capacity ([23] proposes a concrete system). But this approach creates new challenges, many outside the domain of typical engineering, such as the social coordination problem of giving up bandwidth across the board to protect others' communication relations, or the difficulty of verifying the quality of randomness.

Open Problem 11 Technical and societal aspects of inducing randomness in communications to simplify steganography.

3. STEGANALYSIS

Approaches to the steganalysis problem depend heavily on the security model, and particularly on the steganalyst's knowledge about the cover source and the behaviour of his opponent. The most studied models are quite far from real-world application, and (unlike steganography) most researchers would agree that state of the art steganalysis *could not* yet be used effectively in the real world.

Laboratory conditions apply in section 3.1, where we assume that the steganalyst has perfect knowledge of (1) the cover source, (2) the embedding algorithm used by the steganographer, and (3) which object they should examine. This is as unrealistic as the parallel conditions in section 2.1, but the laboratory work provides a conservative attack model, and still gives interesting insights into practice. Almost all current steganalysis literature adheres to the model described in section 3.2, which weakens (1) so that the steganalyst can only learn about the cover source by empirical samples; it is usually assumed that something similar to (2) still holds, and (3) must hold. This line of steganalysis research, which rests on binary classification, is highly refined, but weakening even slightly the security model leads to difficult problems about learning.

In section 3.3 we ask how a steganalyst could widen the application of binary classifiers by using them in combination, and in 3.4 by moving to a model with complete ignorance of the embedding method (and empirical knowledge of the covers). Although these problems are known in machine learning literature, there have been few steganalysis applications.

In section 3.5 we open the model still further, weakening assumption (3), above, so that the steganalyst no longer knows exactly where to look: first, against one steganographer making many communications, and then when monitoring an entire network. This parallels section 2.4, and reveals an essentially game-theoretic nature of steganography and steganalysis, which is the topic of section 3.6. Again, there are many open problems.

Finally, section 3.7 goes beyond steganalysis, to ask what further information can be gleaned from stego objects.

3.1 Optimal detection

The most favourable scenario for the steganalyst occurs when the exact embedding algorithm is known, and there is a statistical model for covers. In this case it is possible to create optimal detection using statistical decision theory, although the framework is not (yet) very robust under less favourable conditions.

The inspected medium $\mathbf{Y} = (Y_1, \ldots, Y_N)$ is considered as a set of N digital samples (not necessarily independent), and P_β^θ the distribution of stego object $\mathbf{Y}_\beta$, after embedding

at rate β. We are separating one parameter controlling the embedding, β, from other parameters of the cover source θ which in images might include size, camera settings, colour space, and so on.

When the embedding rate β and all cover parameters θ are known, the steganalysis problem is to choose between the following hypotheses: $\mathcal{H}_0 = \{\mathbf{Y} \sim P_0^\theta\}$ vs $\mathcal{H}_1 = \{\mathbf{Y} \sim P_\beta^\theta\}$. These are two simple hypotheses, for which the Neyman-Pearson Lemma [70, Th. 3.2.1] provides a simple way to design an optimal test, the Likelihood Ratio Test (LRT):

$$\delta^{\mathrm{LRT}} = \begin{cases} \mathcal{H}_0 \text{ if } \Lambda(\mathbf{Y}) = \dfrac{P_\beta^\theta[\mathbf{Y}]}{P_0^\theta[\mathbf{Y}]} < \tau \\[2ex] \mathcal{H}_1 \text{ if } \Lambda(\mathbf{Y}) = \dfrac{P_\beta^\theta[\mathbf{Y}]}{P_0^\theta[\mathbf{Y}]} \geq \tau, \end{cases} \tag{3}$$

with Λ the likelihood Ratio (LR) and τ a decision threshold.

The LRT is optimal in the following sense: among all the tests which guarantee a maximum false-alarm probability $\alpha \in (0, 1)$ the LRT maximizes the correct detection probability. This is not the only possible measure of optimality, which we return to in section 3.6.

Accepting, for a moment, the optimal detection framework, we can deduce some interesting "laboratory" results. Assume that pixels from a digital image are i.i.d.: then the statistical distribution P^θ of an image is its histogram. If cover samples follow a Gaussian distribution $X_i \sim \mathcal{N}(\mu_i, \sigma_i^2)$, it has been shown [107] that the LR for the LSB replacement scheme can be written: $\Lambda(\mathbf{Y}) \propto \sum_i (y_i - \bar{y}_i)(y_i - \mu_i)/\sigma_i^2$, where $\bar{k} = k + (-1)^k$ is the integer k with flipped LSB. This LR is similar to the well-known Weighted Stego-image statistic [33, 54] and justifies it *post hoc* as an optimal hypothesis test. Similarly, the LR for the LSB matching scheme can be written [18]: $\Lambda(\mathbf{Y}) \propto \sum_i ((y_i - \mu_i)^2 - \frac{1}{12})/\sigma_i^4$. This shows that optimal detection of LSB matching is essentially based on pixel variance. Particularly since LSB matching has the effect of masking the true cover variance, this explains it has proved a tougher nut to crack than LSB replacement.

However, the assumption that pixels can be modelled as i.i.d. random variables is unrealistic. Similarly, the model of statistically independent pixels following a Gaussian distribution (with different expectation and variance) is of limited interest in the real world.

The description of the steganalysis problem in the framework of hypothesis testing theory emphasizes the practical difficulties. First, it seems highly unlikely that the embedding rate β would be known to a steganalyst, unless they already know that steganography is being used. And when β is unknown the design of an optimal statistical test becomes much harder because the alternative hypothesis $\mathcal{H}_1$ is *composite*: it gathers different hypotheses, for each of which a different most powerful test exists.

There are two approaches to overcome this difficulty: design a test which is *locally optimal* around a target embedding rate [19, 107] (again these tests rely on a statistical model of pixels); or design a test which is universally optimal for any embedding rate [18] (unfortunately their optimality assumptions are seldom met outside "the laboratory").

Open Problem 12 Theoretically well-founded, and practically applicable, detection of payload of unknown length.

Second, it is also unrealistic to assume that the vector parameter θ, which defines the statistical distribution of the whole inspected medium, is perfectly known. In practice, these parameters are unknown and would have to be estimated using a model. Here one could employ the Generalized Likelihood Ratio Test (GLRT), which estimates unknown parameters in the LRT by the method of maximum likelihood. Unfortunately, maximum likelihood estimators again depend on a particular models of covers, and furthermore the GLRT is not usually optimal.

Although models of digital media are not entirely convincing, a few have been used for steganalysis, e.g. [20], as well as models of camera post-acquisition processing such as demosaicking and colour correction [95]. Much is unexplored.

Open Problem 13 Apply models from the digital imaging community, which do not require independence of pixels, to the optimal detection framework.

However, it is sobering to observe that a well-developed detector based on testing theory and Laplacian model of DCT coefficients [106] performs poorly in practice compared to the rather simple WS detector adapted to the JPEG domain [13]. As we have repeatedly stated, digital media steganography is a particularly difficult domain in which to understand the covers.

3.2   Binary classification

Absent a model of covers, currently the best image steganalyzers are built using feature-based steganalysis and machine learning. They rest on the assumption that the steganalyst has some samples from the steganographer's cover source, so that its statistical properties can be learned, and also that they can create or otherwise obtain stego objects from these covers (for example by knowing the exact embedding algorithm). Typically, one starts by representing the media using a feature of a much smaller dimensionality, usually designed by hand using heuristic arguments. Then, a training database is created from the cover and stego examples, and a binary classifier is trained to distinguish the two classes.

Machine-learning steganalysis is fundamentally different from statistical signal processing approaches because one does not need to estimate the distribution of cover and stego images. Instead, this problem is replaced with a much simpler one: merely to distinguish the two classes. Thus, one can build classifiers that use high-dimensional features even with a limited number of training examples. When trained on the correct cover source, feature-based steganalysis usually achieves significantly better detection accuracy than analytically derived detectors (with the exception of LSB replacement).

There are two components to this approach: the features, and the classification algorithm.

Image steganalysis features have been well-studied in the literature. In the spatial domain, one usually starts by computing *noise residuals*, by creating and then subtracting an estimate of each cover pixel using its neighbours. The pixel predictors are usually built from linear filters, such as local polynomial models or 2-dimensional neighbourhoods, and can incorporate nonlinearity using the operations of maximum and minimum. The residuals improve the SNR (stego signal to image content). Typically, residuals are truncated and quantized into $2T + 1$ bins, and the final feature vector is the joint probability mass function (co-occurrence) or conditional probability distribution (transition matrix) of D neighbouring quantized residuals [78]. The dimensionality of this feature vector is $(2T + 1)^D$, which quickly grows especially with the co-occurrence order D, though it can somewhat be reduced by exploiting symmetry.

In the JPEG domain, one can think of the DCT coefficients already as residuals and form co-occurrences directly from their quantized values. Since there exist dependencies among neighbouring DCT coefficients both within a single 8×8 block as well as across blocks, one usually builds features as two-dimensional intra-block and inter-block co-occurrences [60]. It is also possible to build the co-occurrences only for specific pairs of DCT modes [62]. A comprehensive list of source code for feature vectors for raw and compressed images, along with references, is available at [2]. The current state of art in feature sets are unions of co-occurrences of different filter residuals, so-called *rich models*. They tend to be high-dimensional (e.g., 30 000 or more) but they also tend to exhibit the highest detection accuracy [35, 63].

We note that, in parallel to the steganography situation, steganalysis literature is mostly specialized to grayscale images: there exists only a little literature on steganalysis in video, e.g. [15, 47], and for various kinds of network traffic analysis [16, 104, 12]. The latter methods only use basic statistics such as the variance of inter-packet delays or quantiles of differences between arrival times. There is scope to transfer lessons from grayscale image steganalysis to these domains.

Open Problem 14 Design features for colour images and video, which take account of correlations in these media, and rich features for network steganalysis.

Another problem specific to steganalysis of network traffic is the difficulty of acquiring large and diverse data sets.

The second component, the machine learning tool, is a very important part. When the training sets and feature spaces are small, the tool of choice is the support vector machine (SVM) [88] with Gaussian kernel, and this was predominant in the literature to 2011. But with growing feature dimensionality, one also needs larger training sets, and it becomes computationally unfeasible to search for hyperparameters. Thus, recently, simpler classifiers have become more popular. An example is the ensemble classifier [66], a collection of weak linear base learners trained on random subspaces of the feature space and on bootstrap samples of the training set. The ensemble reaches its decision by combining the decisions of individual base learners. (In contrast, decision trees are not suitable for steganalysis, because among the features there is none that is strong alone.) When trying to move the tools from the laboratory to the real world, one likely needs to further expand the training set, which may necessitate *online learning* such as the simple perceptron and its variants [72]. There has been little research in this direction. Online learning also requires fast extraction of features, which is in tension with the trend towards using many different convolution filters.

Although highly refined, the paradigm of training a binary classifier has some limitations. First, it is essentially a binary problem, which presupposes that the steganalyst knows exactly the embedding method *and payload size* used by their attacker. Dealing with unknown payload sizes has been approached in two ways: quantitative steganalysis (see section 3.7), or effectively using a uniform prior by creating the stego training set with random payload lengths [77]. An unknown embedding method is more difficult and changes to the problem to either a multi-class classification (computationally expensive [76]) or one-class anomaly detection (section 3.4).

A more serious weakness is that the classifier is only as good as its training data. Although it is possible, in the real world, that the steganalyst has access to the steganographer's cover source (e.g. he arrests her and seizes her camera), it seems an unlikely situation. Thus the steganographer must train the classifier on some other source. This leads to *cover source mismatch*, and the resulting classifier suffers from decreased accuracy. The extent of this decrease depends on the features and the classifier, in a way not yet fully understood. It is fallacious to try to train on a large heterogeneous data set as somehow "representative" of mixed sources, because it guarantees a mismatch and may still be an unrepresentative mixture.

Machine learning literature refers to the problem of *domain adaptation*, which could perhaps be applied to this challenge.

Open Problem 15 Attenuate the problems of cover source mismatch.

A final issue in moving machine-learning steganalysis to the real world is the measure of detection accuracy. Popular measures such as $\min \frac{1}{2}(P_{FP} + P_{FN})$ correspond to the minimal Bayes risk under *equally likely cover and stego images*, which is doubtful in practice. Indeed, one might expect that real-world steganography is relatively rarely observed, so real-world steganalysis should be required to have very low false positive rates, yet steganalysis with very low false positive rates has hardly been studied. Even having a *reliable* false positive rate would be a good start, and there has been some research designing detectors with constant false-alarm rate (CFAR) [68], but it relies on artificial cover models and is also vulnerable to cover source mismatch. It should be noted that establishing classification error probabilities remains unsolved in general [90].

3.3 Adaptive classification

Suppose that, for different cover parameters θ, we have trained different specialized binary classifiers. One possibility is to select the optimal classifier for each observed stego object. This approach has been used to tackle images which have double JPEG compression, and those with different JPEG quality factors (in the absence of quantization-blind features, such images have to be considered as coming from completely different sources) [76]. A similar approach specializing detectors to different covers has been pursued in [42].

This is a special case of *fusion*, where multiple classifiers have their answers combined in some weighted fashion. It presupposes that the cover parameters θ can reliably be estimated from the observed stego image, and that training data was available for all reasonable combinations of parameters. It is also very expensive in terms of training. In machine learning this architecture is known as a *mixture of experts* [105].

Open Problem 16 Apply other fusion techniques to steganalysis.

3.4 Universal steganalysis

It is not always realistic to assume that the embedder knows anything about the embedding algorithm used by the steganographer. *Universal* steganalysis focuses on such a scenario, assuming that the steganalyst can draw empirically from the cover source but is otherwise ignorant. Despite being almost neglected by the community, such a problem is important for deployment of steganalysis in the real world.

Universal steganalysis considers the following hypothesis test: $\mathcal{H}_0 = \{\mathbf{Y} \sim P_0^\theta\}$ vs $\mathcal{H}_1 = \{\mathbf{Y} \nsim P_0^\theta\}$. We can distinguish two cases: either the cover source is entirely known to the detector (θ is known and $\mathcal{H}_0$ is simple), or not (both hypotheses are composite). The first version of the problem is unrealistic in the real world, for the reasons we previously cited. The second shows that detector design is about modelling a cover source, and practical approaches resort to modelling the distribution of cover images in a space determined by steganographic features. In comparison with the binary hypothesis testing scenario of section 3.2, this problem is much more difficult, because learning a probability distribution is unavoidably more difficult than learning a classifier [96]. We must expect that universal steganalyzers have inferior performance to targeted binary classifiers. In fact it is not straightforward to benchmark universal steganalysis, because there is no well-defined alternative hypothesis class from which to test for false negatives.

Universal steganalysis can be divided into two types: supervised and unsupervised. The former uses samples from the cover-source to create the cover model, e.g. by using one-class support vector machines [88] designed to solve the above hypothesis test under a false positive constraint. This approach has been investigated in [82, 73]. Obviously, the accuracy of supervised steganalysis is limited if the training data is not perfectly representative of the steganographer's cover source and, if mismatched, the accuracy might be as bad as random guessing.

Unsupervised universal steganalysis tries to circumvent the problem of model mismatch by postponing building a cover model until the classification phase. It analyses *multiple* images at once, assuming that most of them are covers, and is therefore a form of outlier detection. To our knowledge there is no literature dealing with this scenario in steganalysis, though there are works dealing with it on the level of *actors*, treated in section 3.5.

Open Problem 17 Unsupervised universal steganalysis.

The accuracy of universal steganalysis is to a large extent determined by the steganographic features, and features suitable for binary classification are not necessarily right for universal steganalysis. The features should be sensitive to changes caused by embedding, yet insensitive to variations between covers (including perhaps unnatural but non-steganographic processing techniques). Particularly in the case of unsupervised learning, the latter condition requires them to have low dimension, because unsupervised learning cannot learn to ignore irrelevant noise. A small number of features also facilitates training of supervised detectors, as it decreases the required number of samples to learn the probability distribution. An unstudied problem is therefore:

Open Problem 18 Design of features suitable for universal steganalysis.

3.5 Pooled and multi-actor steganalysis

So far, the security models have assumed that the steganalyst has one object to classify, or if they have many then they know exactly which one to look at. This is highly unrealistic and if steganalysis is to move to the real world it will have to address the problem of *pooled steganalysis* [48]: combining evidence from multiple objects to say whether they collectively contain payload. It is in opposition to the steganographic channel of section 2.4.

Although posed in 2006, there has been little success in attacking this problem. One might say that it is no different to binary steganalysis: simply train a classifier on multiple images. But there are many practical problems to overcome: should the feature set be the sum total of features from individual images (if so, this loses information), or concatenated (in which case how does one impose symmetry under permutation)? To our knowledge, there has been no such detector proposed in the literature, except for simple examples studied when the problem was first posed [48, 49].

A related problem which, to the best of our knowledge, has never been studied is *sequential* detection. When inspecting VOIP traffic, for instance, it would be interesting to perform online detection. The theoretically optimal detection is more complex because time-to-decision also has to be taken into account. The statistical framework of sequential hypothesis tests should be applicable [99].

Open Problem 19 Any detector for multiple objects, or based on sequential hypothesis tests.

We can widen the steganalysis model still further, to a realistic scenario relevant to network monitoring, if the steganalyst does not know even which user to examine. In this situation the steganalyst intercepts many objects each from many actors (e.g. social network users); their problem is to determine which actor(s), if any, are using steganography in some or all of their images.

This is the most challenging version of steganalysis, but recent work [56, 55] has shown that the size of the problem can be turned to the steganalyst's advantage: by calibrating the behaviour of actors (as measured through steganalysis features) by the behaviour of the majority, steganographers can potentially be determined in an unsupervised and universal way. It amounts to an anomaly detection where the unit is the actor, not the individual object. This can be related to unsupervised intrusion detection systems [24].

This is a new direction in steganalysis and we say no more about it here, but highlight the danger of false accusations:

Open Problem 20 Can steganographers be distinguished from unusual (non-stego) cover sources, by a detector which remains universal?

3.6 Game theoretic approaches

The pooled steganalysis problem exposes an essentially game-theoretic situation. When a (batch) steganographer hides all their payload in one object, a certain type of detector is optimal; when they spread their payload in many objects, a different detector is optimal. These statements can be proved in artificial models and observed in practice. Indeed, the same can be said of *single* images: if the embedder always hides in noisy areas, the detector can focus their attention there, and *vice versa*. A parallel situation most likely exists in non-media covers.

Game theory offers an interesting perspective from which to study steganography. If both steganographer and steganalyst know the cover source and are computationally unconstrained, the steganographer can embed perfectly; with a shorter key if the steganalyst is computationally bounded.

If the steganographer is computationally bounded, but not the steganalyst, the best she can do is to minimize the KL divergence, subject to her constraints. Another way to frame this is that she plays a minimax strategy against the best-possible detector [45].

This may not add a lot of insight in the lab. But once we step out into the real world, where knowledge of the cover source is incomplete and computational constraints defy finding globally optimal distortion functions or detectors, then game theory becomes very useful. It offers a wealth of solution concepts for situations where no maximin or minimax strategies exist. A popular one is the notion of a Nash equilibrium. It essentially says that among two sets of strategies, one for the steganographer (choice of embedding operation, distortion function, parameters etc.) and one for the steganalyst (feature space, detector, parameters such as local weights, etc.), there exist combinations where no player can improve his or her outcome unilaterally. Although exploitation of game theory for steganography has just begun, and we are aware of only four independent approaches [25, 49, 75, 89], it seems to be a promising framework which allows us to justify certain design choices, such as payload distribution in batch steganography or distortion functions in adaptive steganography. This is a welcome step to replace heuristics with (some) rigor in the messy scenarios of limited knowledge and computational power, as we find them in the real world.

However, game theory for steganography is in its infancy, and there are substantial obstacles to be overcome, such as:

Open Problem 21 Find equilibria for practical covers, and transfer insights of game-theoretic solutions from current toy models to the real world.

3.7 Forensic steganalysis

Finally, what does the steganalyst do after detecting hidden data in an object? The next steps might be called *forensic* steganalysis, and only a few aspects have been studied in the literature.

If the aim of the steganalyst is to find targets for further surveillance, or to confirm the existence of already-suspected covert communication, circumstantial evidence such as statistical steganalysis is probably sufficient in itself. But for law enforcement it is probably necessary to demonstrate the content of a message by extracting it, in which case the first step is to determine the embedding algorithm. This problem, largely neglected, has been studied in [81] for JPEG images. The detection of different algorithms based on statistical properties will not be perfect, as methods with similar distortion functions and embedding changes are likely to be confused, but this has not been studied for recent adaptive embedding methods.

Open Problem 22 Can statistical steganalysis recognize different adaptive embedding algorithms?

Some identify a specific implementation by a signature, effectively relying on implementation mistakes [11, 103], but this is unsatisfactory in general.

Once the embedding method is known, the next step is a brute-force search for the embedding key. Very little research has been done in this area, though two complementary approaches have been identified: using headers to verify the correctness of a key [84], and comparing statistics along potential embedding paths [34] in which the correct key deviates from the rest.

Open Problem 23 Is there a statistical approach to key brute-forcing, for adaptive steganography?

Additionally, forensic steganalysis includes estimation of the length of the hidden message (*quantitative steganalysis*). This knowledge is useful to prevent "plausible deniability", where the steganographer hides two messages, one of which is not incriminating and can be disclosed if forced. Such a scheme is uncovered if the total embedded payload can be estimated. Quantitative steganalysis is a regression problem parallel to binary classification, and the state of the art applies regression techniques to existing steganalysis features [83, 59].

4. CONCLUSIONS

Over the last ten years, ad-hoc solutions to steganography and steganalysis problems have evolved into more refined techniques. There has been a disparity in the rate of progress: grayscale images have received most of the attention, which should be transferred to colour images, video, other digital media, and non-media covers such as network traffic. Such transfer would bring both steganography and steganalysis closer to real-world implementation.

For steganography, we have stressed the distortion-minimization paradigm, which only became practical with recent developments in coding. There is no good reason not to use such a technique: there are efficiencies from the coding, and if there is a fear that current distortion functions might make detection paradoxically easier, one can use this feedback to redesign the distortion function, and continue the cycle of development. We expect further advances in coding to widen the applicability of such techniques.

For steganalysis, the binary classification case is well-developed, but there is a need to develop techniques that work with unknown algorithms, multiple objects, and multiple actors. Even the theoretical framework which we have highlighted, that of KL divergence as a fundamental measure of security, has yet to be adapted to these domains.

Acknowledgments

The work of A. Ker and T. Pevný is supported by European Office of Aerospace Research and Development under the research grant numbers FA8655-11-3035 and FA8655-13-1-3020, respectively. The work of S. Craver and J. Fridrich is supported by Air Force Office of Scientific Research under the research grant numbers FA9950-12-1-0124 and FA9550-09-1-0666, respectively. The U.S. Government is authorized to reproduce and distribute reprints for Governmental purposes notwithstanding any copyright notation thereon. The views and conclusions contained herein are those of the authors and should not be interpreted as necessarily representing the official policies, either expressed or implied, of EOARD, AFOSR, or the U.S. Government.

The work of R. Cogranne is funded by Troyes University of Technology (UTT) strategic program COLUMBO. The work of T. Pevný is also supported by the Grant Agency of Czech Republic under the project P103/12/P514.

5. REFERENCES

[1] Documents reveal Al Qaeda's plans for seizing cruise ships, carnage in europe. CNN, April 2012. `http://edition.cnn.com/2012/04/30/world/al-qaeda-documents-future/index.html`, accessed February 2012.

[2] Feature extractors for steganalysis. `http://dde.binghamton.edu/download/feature_extractors/`, accessed February 2012.

[3] MIT Technology Review: Steganography. `http://www.technologyreview.com/search/site/steganography/`, accessed February 2012.

[4] Russian spies' use of steganography is just the beginning. MIT Technology Review, July 2010. `http://www.technologyreview.com/view/419833/russian-spies-use-of-steganography-is-just-the-beginning/`, accessed February 2012.

[5] D. Alperovitch. Revealed: Operation Shady RAT. McAfee White Paper, 2011. `http://www.mcafee.com/us/resources/white-papers/wp-operation-shady-rat.pdf`, accessed February 2012.

[6] V. Anantharam and S. Verdu. Bits through queues. *IEEE Trans. Inf. Theory*, 42(1):4–18, 1996.

[7] R. Anderson. Stretching the limits of steganography. In *Information Hiding, 1st International Workshop*, volume 1174 of *LNCS*, pages 39–48. Springer-Verlag, 1996.

[8] R. J. Anderson and F. A. P. Petitcolas. On the limits of steganography. *IEEE J. Sel. Areas Commun.*, 16(4):474–481, 1998.

[9] A. Aviv, G. Shah, and M. Blaze. Steganographic timing channels. Technical report, University of Pennsylvania, 2011.

[10] A. Baliga and J. Kilian. On covert collaboration. In *Proceedings of the 9th ACM Multimedia & Security Workshop*, pages 25–34, 2007.

[11] G. Bell and Y.-K. Lee. A method for automatic identification of signatures of steganography software. *IEEE Trans. Inf. Forensics Security*, 5(2):354–358, 2010.

[12] V. Berk, A. Giana, G. Cybenko, and N. Hanover. Detection of covert channel encoding in network packet delays, 2005.

[13] R. Böhme. Weighted stego-image steganalysis for JPEG covers. In *Information Hiding, 10th International Workshop*, volume 5284 of *LNCS*, pages 178–194. Springer-Verlag, 2007.

[14] R. Böhme. *Advanced Statistical Steganalysis*. Springer-Verlag, 2010.

[15] U. Budhia, D. Kundur, and T. Zourntos. Digital video steganalysis exploiting statistical visibility in the temporal domain. *IEEE Trans. Inf. Forensics Security*, 1(4):502–516, 2006.

[16] S. Cabuk, C. E. Brodley, and C. Shields. Ip covert timing channels: design and detection. In *Proceedings of the 11th ACM conference on Computer and communications security*, pages 178–187. ACM, 2004.

[17] C. Cachin. An information-theoretic model for steganography. In *Information Hiding, 2nd International Workshop*, volume 1525 of *LNCS*, pages 306–318. Springer-Verlag, 1998.

[18] R. Cogranne and F. Retraint. An asymptotically uniformly most powerful test for LSB matching

detection. *IEEE Trans. Inf. Forensics Security*, 8(3):464–476, 2013.

[19] R. Cogranne, C. Zitzmann, L. Fillatre, F. Retraint, I. Nikiforov, and P. Cornu. Statistical decision by using quantized observations. In *International Symposium on Information Theory*, pages 1135–1139. IEEE, 2011.

[20] R. Cogranne, C. Zitzmann, F. Retraint, I. Nikiforov, P. Cornu, and L. Fillatre. A locally adapted model of natural images for almost optimal hidden data detection. *IEEE Trans. Image Process.*, 2013. (to appear).

[21] R. Crandall. Some notes on steganography. *Steganography Mailing List*, 1998. available from `http://os.inf.tu-dresden.de/~westfeld/crandall.pdf`.

[22] S. Craver. On public-key steganography in the presence of an active warden. In *Information Hiding, 2nd International Workshop*, volume 1525, pages 355–368, 1998.

[23] S. Craver, E. Li, J. Yu, and I. Atalki. A supraliminal channel in a videoconferencing application. In *Information Hiding, 10th International Workshop*, volume 5284 of *LNCS*, pages 283–293. Springer-Verlag, 2008.

[24] D. E. Denning. An intrusion-detection model. *IEEE Trans. Softw. Eng.*, SE-13(2):222–232, 1987.

[25] M. Ettinger. Steganalysis and game equilibria. In *Information Hiding, 2nd International Workshop*, volume 1525 of *LNCS*, pages 319–328. Springer-Verlag, 1998.

[26] T. Filler and J. Fridrich. Fisher information determines capacity of ϵ-secure steganography. In *Information Hiding, 11th International Conference*, volume 5806 of *LNCS*, pages 31–47. Springer-Verlag, 2009.

[27] T. Filler and J. Fridrich. Gibbs construction in steganography. *IEEE Trans. Inf. Forensics Security*, 5(4):705–720, 2010.

[28] T. Filler and J. Fridrich. Design of adaptive steganographic schemes for digital images. In *Media Watermarking, Security and Forensics XIII*, volume 7880 of *Proc. SPIE*, pages OF 1–14, 2011.

[29] T. Filler, J. Judas, and J. Fridrich. Minimizing additive distortion in steganography using syndrome-trellis codes. *IEEE Trans. Inf. Forensics Security*, 6(3):920–935, 2011.

[30] T. Filler, A. D. Ker, and J. Fridrich. The Square Root Law of steganographic capacity for Markov covers. In *Security and Forensics of Multimedia XI*, volume 7254 of *Proc. SPIE*, pages 08 1–11, 2009.

[31] E. Franz, A. Jerichow, S. Möller, A. Pfitzmann, and I. Stierand. Computer based steganography: How it works and why therefore any restrictions on cryptography are nonsense, at best. In *Information Hiding, 1st International Workshop*, volume 1174 of *LNCS*, pages 7–21. Springer-Verlag, 1996.

[32] J. Fridrich. Effect of cover quantization on steganographic fisher information. *IEEE Trans. Inf. Forensics Security*, 8(2):361–372, 2013.

[33] J. Fridrich and M. Goljan. On estimation of secret message length in LSB steganography in spatial domain. In *Security, Steganography, and Watermarking of Multimedia Contents VI*, volume 5306 of *Proc. SPIE*, pages 23–34, 2004.

[34] J. Fridrich, M. Goljan, and D. Soukal. Searching for the stego key. In *Security, Steganography, and Watermarking of Multimedia Contents VI*, volume 5306, pages 70–82, 2004.

[35] J. Fridrich and J. Kodovský. Rich models for steganalysis of digital images. *IEEE Trans. Inf. Forensics Security*, 7(3):868–882, 2011.

[36] J. Fridrich, T. Pevný, and J. Kodovský. Statistically undetectable JPEG steganography: Dead ends, challenges, and opportunities. In *Proceedings of the 9th ACM Multimedia & Security Workshop*, pages 3–14, 2007.

[37] J. Giffin, R. Greenstadt, P. Litwack, and R. Tibbetts. Covert messaging through TCP timestamps. In *Privacy Enhancing Technologies*, volume 2482 of *LNCS*, pages 194–208. Springer-Verlag, 2002.

[38] T. Gloe. Forensic analysis of ordered data structures on the example of JPEG files. In *Information Forensics and Security, 4th International Workshop*, pages 139–144. IEEE, 2012.

[39] L. Guo, J. Ni, and Y.-Q. Shi. An efficient JPEG steganographic scheme using uniform embedding. In *Information Forensics and Security, 4th International Workshop*, pages 169–174. IEEE, 2012.

[40] V. Holub and J. Fridrich. Designing steganographic distortion using directional filters. In *Information Forensics and Security, 4th International Workshop*, pages 234–239. IEEE, 2012.

[41] N. J. Hopper, J. Langford, and L. von Ahn. Provably secure steganography. In *Advances in Cryptology, CRYPTO '02*, volume 2442 of *LNCS*, pages 77–92. Springer-Verlag, 2002.

[42] X. Hou, T. Zhang, G. Xiong, and B. Wan. Forensics aided steganalysis of heterogeneous bitmap images with different compression history. In *Multimedia Information Networking and Security, 4th International Conference*, pages 874–877, 2012.

[43] F. Huang, J. Huang, and Y.-Q. Shi. New channel selection rule for JPEG steganography. *IEEE Trans. Inf. Forensics Security*, 7(4):1181–1191, 2012.

[44] C. Hundt, M. Liskiewicz, and U. Wölfel. Provably secure steganography and the complexity of sampling. In *Algorithms and Computation*, volume 4317 of *LNCS*, pages 754–763. Springer-Verlag, 2006.

[45] B. Johnson, P. Schöttle, and R. Böhme. Where to hide the bits? In J. Grossklags and J. Walrand, editors, *Decision and Game Theory for Security*, volume 7638 of *LNCS*, pages 1–17. Springer-Verlag, 2012.

[46] D. Kahn. *The Codebreakers: The Comprehensive History of Secret Communication from Ancient Times to the Internet*. Scribner, revised edition, 1996.

[47] K. Kancherla and S. Mukkamala. Video steganalysis using motion estimation. In *International Joint Conference on Neural Networks*, pages 1510–1515. IEEE, 2009.

[48] A. D. Ker. Batch steganography and pooled steganalysis. In *Information Hiding, 8th*

International Workshop, volume 4437 of *LNCS*, pages 265–281. Springer-Verlag, 2006.

[49] A. D. Ker. Batch steganography and the threshold game. In *Security, Steganography, and Watermarking of of Multimedia Contents IX*, volume 6505 of *Proc. SPIE*, pages 04 1–13, 2007.

[50] A. D. Ker. A capacity result for batch steganography. *IEEE Signal Process. Lett.*, 14(8):525–528, 2007.

[51] A. D. Ker. Locating steganographic payload via ws residuals. In *Proceedings of the 10th ACM Multimedia & Security Workshop*, pages 27–32. ACM, 2008.

[52] A. D. Ker. Steganographic strategies for a square distortion function. In *Security, Forensics, Steganography, and Watermarking of Multimedia Contents X*, volume 6819 of *Proc. SPIE*, pages 04 1–13, 2008.

[53] A. D. Ker. Estimating the information theoretic optimal stego noise. In *Digital Watermarking, 8th International Workshop*, volume 5703 of *LNCS*, pages 184–198. Springer-Verlag, 2009.

[54] A. D. Ker and R. Böhme. Revisiting weighted stego-image steganalysis. In *Security, Forensics, Steganography, and Watermarking of Multimedia Contents X*, volume 6819 of *Proc. SPIE*, pages 05 1–17, 2008.

[55] A. D. Ker and T. Pevný. Batch steganography in the real world. In *Proceedings of the 14th ACM Multimedia & Security Workshop*, pages 1–10. ACM, 2012.

[56] A. D. Ker and T. Pevný. Identifying a steganographer in realistic and heterogeneous data sets. In *Media Watermarking, Security, and Forensics XIV*, volume 8303 of *Proc. SPIE*, pages 0N 1–13, 2012.

[57] A. D. Ker, T. Pevný, J. Kodovský, and J. Fridrich. The Square Root Law of steganographic capacity. In *Proceedings of the 10th ACM Multimedia & Security Workshop*, pages 107–116, 2008.

[58] Y. Kim, Z. Duric, and D. Richards. Modified matrix encoding technique for minimal distortion steganography. In *Information Hiding, 8th International Workshop*, volume 4437 of *LNCS*, pages 314–327. Springer-Verlag, 2006.

[59] Kodovský and J. Fridrich. Quantitative steganalysis using rich models. In *Media Watermarking, Security, and Forensics 2013*, Proc. SPIE, 2013. (to appear).

[60] J. Kodovský. *Steganalysis of Digital Images Using Rich Image Representations and Ensemble Classifiers*. PhD thesis, Electrical and Computer Engineering Department, 2012.

[61] J. Kodovský and J. Fridrich. On completeness of feature spaces in blind steganalysis. In *Proceedings of the 10th ACM Multimedia & Security Workshop*, pages 123–132, 2008.

[62] J. Kodovský and J. Fridrich. Steganalysis in high dimensions: Fusing classifiers built on random subspaces. In *Media Watermarking, Security and Forensics XIII*, volume 7880, pages OL 1–13, 2011.

[63] J. Kodovský and J. Fridrich. Steganalysis of JPEG images using rich models. In *Media Watermarking, Security, and Forensics 2012*, volume 8303 of *Proc. SPIE*, pages 0A 1–13, 2012.

[64] J. Kodovský and J. Fridrich. Steganalysis in resized images. In *International Conference on Acoustics, Speech, and Signal Processing*. IEEE, 2013. (to appear).

[65] J. Kodovský, J. Fridrich, and V. Holub. On dangers of overtraining steganography to incomplete cover model. In *Proceedings of the 13th ACM Multimedia & Security Workshop*, pages 69–76, 2011.

[66] J. Kodovský, J. Fridrich, and V. Holub. Ensemble classifiers for steganalysis of digital media. *IEEE Trans. Inf. Forensics Security*, 7(2):432–444, 2012.

[67] S. Köpsell and U. Hillig. How to achieve blocking resistance for existing systems enabling anonymous web surfing. In *Privacy in the Electronic Society, ACM Workshop*, pages 47–58. ACM, 2004.

[68] S. Kraut and L. L. Scharf. The CFAR adaptive subspace detector is a scale-invariant GLRT. *IEEE Trans. Sig. Proc.*, 47(9):2538–2541, 1999.

[69] S. Kullback. *Information Theory and Statistics*. Dover, 1968.

[70] E. Lehmann and J. Romano. *Testing Statistical Hypotheses*. Springer, 3rd edition, 2005.

[71] E. Li and S. Craver. A square-root law for active wardens. In *Proceedings of the 13th ACM Multimedia & Security Workshop*, pages 87–92. ACM, 2011.

[72] I. Lubenko and A. D. Ker. Going from small to large data sets in steganalysis. In *Media Watermarking, Security, and Forensics 2012*, volume 8303 of *Proc. SPIE*, pages OM 1–10, 2012.

[73] S. Lyu and H. Farid. Steganalysis using higher-order image statistics. *IEEE Trans. Inf. Forensics Security*, 1(1):111–119, 2006.

[74] S. J. Murdoch and S. Lewis. Embedding covert channels in TCP/IP. In *Information Hiding, 7th International Workshop*, volume 3727 of *LNCS*, pages 247–261. Springer-Verlag, 2005.

[75] A. Orsdemir, O. Altun, G. Sharma, and M. Bocko. Steganalysis-aware steganography: Statistical indistinguishability despite high distortion. In *Security, Forensics, Steganography, and Watermarking of Multimedia Contents X*, volume 6819 of *Proc. SPIE*, pages 15 1–19, 2008.

[76] T. Pevný. *Kernel Methods in Steganalysis*. PhD thesis, Binghamton University, SUNY, 2008.

[77] T. Pevný. Detecting messages of unknown length. In *Media Watermarking, Security and Forensics XIII*, volume 7880 of *Proc. SPIE*, pages OT 1–12, 2011.

[78] T. Pevný, P. Bas, and J. Fridrich. Steganalysis by subtractive pixel adjacency matrix. *IEEE Trans. Inf. Forensics Security*, 5(2):215–224, 2010.

[79] T. Pevný, T. Filler, and P. Bas. Using high-dimensional image models to perform highly undetectable steganography. In *Information Hiding, 12th International Conference*, volume 6387 of *LNCS*, pages 161–177. Springer-Verlag, 2010.

[80] T. Pevny and J. Fridrich. Detection of double-compression in JPEG images for applications in steganography. *IEEE Trans. Inf. Forensics Security*, 3(2):247–258, 2008.

[81] T. Pevný and J. Fridrich. Multiclass detector of current steganographic methods for JPEG format.

IEEE Trans. Inf. Forensics Security, 3(4):635–650, 2008.

[82] T. Pevný and J. Fridrich. Novelty detection in blind steganalysis. In *Proceedings of the 10th ACM Multimedia & Security Workshop*, pages 167–176, 2008.

[83] T. Pevny, J. Fridrich, and A. D. Ker. From blind to quantitative steganalysis. *IEEE Trans. Inf. Forensics Security*, 7(2):445–454, 2012.

[84] N. Provos and P. Honeyman. Detecting steganographic content on the internet. Technical Report CITI Technical Report 01-11, University of Michigan, 2001.

[85] L. Reyzin and S. Russell. Simple stateless steganography. IACR Eprint archive, 2003. http://eprint.iacr.org/2003/093.

[86] V. Sachnev, H. J. Kim, and R. Zhang. Less detectable JPEG steganography method based on heuristic optimization and BCH syndrome coding. In *Proceedings of the 11th ACM Multimedia & Security Workshop*, pages 131–140, 2009.

[87] U. Schmidt, Q. Gao, and S. Roth. A generative perspective on MRFs in low-level vision. In *Computer Vision and Pattern Recognition*, pages 1751–1758. IEEE, 2010.

[88] B. Schölkopf and A. Smola. *Learning with Kernels: Support Vector Machines, Regularization, Optimization, and Beyond*. MIT Press, 2001.

[89] P. Schöttle and R. Böhme. A game-theoretic approach to content-adaptive steganography. In *Information Hiding, 14th International Conference*, volume 7692 of *LNCS*, pages 125–141. Springer-Verlag, 2012.

[90] C. Scott and R. Nowak. A Neyman-Pearson approach to statistical learning. *IEEE Trans. Inf. Theory*, 51(8):3806–3819, 2005.

[91] C. E. Shannon. Coding theorems for a discrete source with a fidelity criterion. *IRE Nat. Conv. Rec.*, 4:142–163, 1959.

[92] G. J. Simmons. The prisoner's problem and the subliminal channel. In *Advances in Cryptology, CRYPTO '83*, pages 51–67. Plenum Press, 1983.

[93] J. Spolsky. *Joel on Software: Selected Essays*. APress, 2004.

[94] J. Sun and M. F. Tappen. Learning non-local range Markov random field for image restoration. In *Computer Vision and Pattern Recognition*, pages 2745–2752. IEEE, 2011.

[95] T. H. Thai, F. Retrait, and R. Cogranne. Statistical model of natural images. In *Proceedings IEEE, International Conference on Image Processing, ICIP 2012*, pages 2525–2528. IEEE, 2012.

[96] V. N. Vapnik. *Statistical learning theory*. Wiley, 1998.

[97] S. Voloshynovskiy, A. Herrigel, N. Baumgaertner, and T. Pun. A stochastic approach to content adaptive digital image watermarking. In *Information Hiding, 3rd International Workshop*, volume 1768 of *LNCS*, pages 211–236. Springer-Verlag, 2000.

[98] A. B. Wagner and V. Anantharam. Information theory of covert timing channels. In *Proceedings of the 2005 NATO/ASI Workshop on Network Security and Intrusion Detection*, pages 292–296. IOS Press, 2008.

[99] A. Wald. Sequential tests of statistical hypotheses. *Ann. Math. Stat.*, 16(2):117–186, 1945.

[100] C. Wang and J. Ni. An efficient JPEG steganographic scheme based on the block–entropy of DCT coefficents. In *International Conference on Acoustics, Speech, and Signal Processing*, pages 1785–1788. IEEE, 2012.

[101] Y. Wang and P. Moulin. Perfectly secure steganography: Capacity, error exponents, and code constructions. *IEEE Trans. Inf. Theory*, 55(6):2706–2722, 2008.

[102] Y. Weiss and W. T. Freeman. What makes a good model of natural images? In *Computer Vision and Pattern Recognition*, pages 1–8. IEEE, 2007.

[103] A. Westfeld. Steganalysis in the presence of weak cryptography and encoding. In *Digital Watermarking, 5th International Workshop*, volume 4283 of *LNCS*, pages 19–34. Springer-Verlag, 2006.

[104] L. Yao, X. Zi, L. Pan, and J. Li. A study of on/off timing channel based on packet delay distribution. *Computers & Security*, 28(8):785–794, 2009.

[105] S. Yuksel, J. Wilson, and P. Gader. Twenty years of mixture of experts. *IEEE Trans. Neural Netw. Learn. Syst.*, 23(8):1177–1193, 2012.

[106] C. Zitzmann, R. Cogranne, L. Fillatre, I. Nikiforov, F. Retrait, and P. Cornu. Hidden information detection based on quantized Laplacian distribution. In *International Conference on Acoustics, Speech, and Signal Processing*, pages 1793–1796. IEEE, 2012.

[107] C. Zitzmann, R. Cogranne, F. Retrait, I. Nikiforov, L. Fillatre, and P. Cornu. Statistical decision methods in hidden information detection. In *Information Hiding, 13th International Conference*, LNCS, pages 163–177. Springer-Verlag, 2011.

Digital Image Steganography Using Universal Distortion

Vojtěch Holub
Binghamton University
Department of ECE
Binghamton, NY 13902-6000
vholub1@
binghamton.edu

Jessica Fridrich
Binghamton University
Department of ECE
Binghamton, NY 13902-6000
fridrich@
binghamton.edu

ABSTRACT

Currently, the most secure practical steganographic schemes for empirical cover sources embed their payload while minimizing a distortion function designed to capture statistical detectability. Since there exists a general framework for this embedding paradigm with established payload–distortion bounds as well as near-optimal practical coding schemes, building an embedding scheme has been essentially reduced to the distortion design. This is not an easy task as relating distortion to statistical detectability is a hard and open problem. In this article, we propose an innovative idea to measure the embedding distortion in one fixed domain independently of the domain where the embedding changes (and coding) are carried out. The proposed universal distortion is additive and evaluates the cost of changing an image element (e.g., pixel or DCT coefficient) from directional residuals obtained using a Daubechies wavelet filter bank. The intuition is to limit the embedding changes only to those parts of the cover that are difficult to model in multiple directions while avoiding smooth regions and clean edges. The utility of the universal distortion is demonstrated by constructing steganographic schemes in the spatial, JPEG, and side-informed JPEG domains, and comparing their security to current state-of-the-art methods using classifiers trained with rich media models.

Categories and Subject Descriptors

I.4.9 [**Computing Methodologies**]: Image Processing and Computer Vision—*Applications*

General Terms

Security, Algorithms, Theory

Keywords

Steganography, distortion function, JPEG, side-informed embedding

1. MOTIVATION

The lack of accurate models for complex sources, such as digital media, significantly complicates the construction of secure steganographic schemes. One may even argue that, fundamentally, perfect steganographic security in such empirical sources is not possible [1]. Postulating this as an assumption gave birth to the study of imperfect steganography as a subdiscipline that better corresponds to real-world conditions and lead to fundamental new results, such as scaling laws of secure payload w.r.t. various cover source attributes, such as the length (the square root law [16, 21, 6]), quantization [8], and resolution [24]. Steganographic capacity of imperfect steganography is zero as the secure payload scales sublinearly with cover length.[1] Thus, one can say that in practice, steganographers merely try to increase the steganographic Fisher information, which defines the root rate [18, 19, 2] – the proper measure of secure payload for imperfect steganography.

The mainstream (and by far the most successful) approach is framing the embedding as source coding with a fidelity constraint [30] and build the embedding around a distortion function that is minimized to embed a desired payload [5, 3, 22, 31, 28, 13, 15]. Upon closer inspection of these references, one discovers that the distortion functions are always designed either in the embedding domain or in a selected model (feature) space. The first alternative can be rightfully challenged as, for example, changing a DCT coefficient has an effect on an entire block of pixels, and the detectability of this embedding change needs to consider this fact. Designing distortion in a model space [28, 4] is more appealing but can only succeed with a sufficiently comprehensive source model to avoid creating security holes for the Warden who chooses to work outside of the model [25].

In this paper, we propose a distortion function that allows careful analysis of the impact of making an embedding change on the local content and thus introduce less detectable artifacts. We work with a wavelet representation of the cover image (if the image is represented in some other domain, such as JPEG, it is first decompressed to the spatial domain prior to the wavelet transform), which can be viewed as a representation obtained using a bank of directional filters. Interpreting the highest frequency undecimated subbands as directional residuals, one can assess the impact of an embedding change in multiple directions, which allows us to constrain the embedding changes to textures and noisy regions of the image while avoiding smooth content as well

---

[1]This result was derived for a fully-informed Warden and it may change, depending on Warden's ignorance [20].

as clean edges. This is a model-free approach as we do not work with a feature representation of the cover image.

We implement three versions of one embedding algorithm depending on the cover representation – spatial, JPEG, and side-informed JPEG domains. To prove the merit of our construction, a comparison to the current state-of-the-art steganographic algorithms is included for each domain. Since the proposed distortion is in the form of a sum of *relative* changes between the stego and cover images represented in the wavelet domain, we named it UNIversal WAvelet Relative Distortion (UNIWARD). We would like to point out that this paper is a shortened version of our recent journal submission to IEEE TIFS, which differs from this article in several aspects. The journal version contains a thorough analysis of embedding using the Gibbs construction with the non-additive version of UNIWARD in the spatial domain. Furthermore, to stay within the page limits of this workshop, we steered this article more towards the JPEG domain and limited the scale of experiments in the spatial domain. The wording in this article has also been altered to avoid copyright conflicts and the flow restructured to give it a form that is more suitable for a workshop article and more likely to elicit audience discussions.

The purpose of Section 2 is to introduce notation and basic concepts. In Section (3), we describe the UNIWARD costs for images represented in an arbitrary domain as well as for side-informed JPEG steganography when the sender has the raw, uncompressed cover available and wishes to embed in its JPEG compressed form. The common core of all experiments is summarized in Section 4, where we provide details about the cover source, machine learning, and the measure used for empirical evaluation of security. Section 5 contains the results of all experiments in the spatial, JPEG, and side-informed JPEG domains including the comparison with previous art. The paper is concluded in Section 6.

2. NOTATION AND BASIC CONCEPTS

To improve the readability of this article, we adopt the following conventions. Capital and lower-case boldface symbols will be used solely for matrices and vectors, respectively. The symbols $\mathbf{X} = (X_{ij}), \mathbf{Y} = (Y_{ij}) \in \{0, \dots, 255\}^{n_1 \times n_2}$ will always stand for matrices representing a cover and the corresponding stego image with $n_1 \times n_2$ pixels/DCT coefficients. For simplicity we only work with 8-bit grayscale images, which means that $X_{ij}, Y_{ij} \in \{0, \dots, 255\}$. For JPEG images, $X_{ij}, Y_{ij} \in \{-1024, \dots, 1023\}$ stand for quantized JPEG DCT coefficients arranged into an $n_1 \times n_2$ matrix by replacing each 8×8 pixel block with the corresponding block of quantized DCT coefficients. For simplicity and without any loss on generality, we will assume that n_1 and n_2 are integer multiples of 8.

For matrix $\mathbf{A}$, its transpose is $\mathbf{A}^{\mathrm{T}}$, while $|\mathbf{A}| = (|a_{ij}|)$ is the matrix of absolute values. Furthermore, we reserve the indices i, j to index pixels or DCT coefficients, while u, v will always index wavelet decomposition coefficients. The abbreviation 'w.r.t.' stands for "with respect to." Finally, $[S]$ is the Iverson bracket equal to 1 when the statement S is true and 0 when S is false.

2.1 JPEG compression

The raw image before JPEG compression will be denoted as $\mathbf{P} = (P_{ij}) \in \{0, \dots, 255\}^{n_1 \times n_2}$. When applying JPEG compression to $\mathbf{P}$, first a blockwise DCT transform is ap-

plied to each 8×8 block of pixels from a fixed non-overlapping grid. Then, the DCT coefficients are divided by quantization steps and rounded to integers. Formally, let $\mathbf{P}^{(b)}$ be the bth 8×8 block when ordering the blocks, e.g., in a row-by-row fashion ($b = 1, \dots, n_1 \times n_2/64$). With an 8×8 luminance quantization matrix $\mathbf{Q} = \{Q_{kl}\}$, $1 \leq k, l \leq 8$, we denote $\mathbf{D}^{(b)} = \mathrm{DCT}(\mathbf{P}^{(b)})./\mathbf{Q}$ the raw (non-rounded) values of DCT coefficients. Here, the operation './' is elementwise division of matrices and $\mathrm{DCT}(.)$ is the DCT transform used in the JPEG compressor. Finally, we denote by $\mathbf{X}^{(b)} = \mathrm{round}(\mathbf{D}^{(b)})$ the quantized DCT coefficients rounded to integers. We use the symbols $\mathbf{D}$ and $\mathbf{X}$ to denote the arrays of all raw and quantized DCT coefficients when arranging all blocks $\mathbf{D}^{(b)}$ and $\mathbf{X}^{(b)}$ in the same manner as the 8×8 pixel blocks in the uncompressed image.

2.2 DCT transform

The JPEG format allows several different implementations of the DCT transform, $\mathrm{DCT}(.)$, which may especially impact the security of side-informed steganographic methods that assign costs based on the DCT coefficients' rounding errors. In this work, we use the $\mathrm{DCT}(.)$ implemented as 'dct2' in Matlab with the input matrix of pixel values represented as 'double'. In particular, a block of 8×8 DCT coefficients is computed from a block $\mathbf{P}^{(b)}$ as

$$\mathrm{DCT}(\mathbf{P}^{(b)})_{kl} = \sum_{i,j=0}^{7} \frac{w_k w_l}{4} \cos \frac{\pi k (2i + 1)}{16}$$
$$\times \cos \frac{\pi l (2j + 1)}{16} P_{ij}^{(b)}, \quad (1)$$

where $k, l \in \{0, \dots, 7\}$ index the DCT mode (spatial frequency) and $w_0 = 1/\sqrt{2}$, $w_k = 1$ for $k > 0$.

To make sure that both the cover and stego images were created using the same JPEG compressor and to guarantee that our steganalyzers will not be detecting compressor artifacts but only the impact of embedding, we adopt the following procedure for all steganographic algorithms that output JPEG stego images. To obtain an actual JPEG image from a two-dimensional array of quantized DCT coefficients $\mathbf{X}$ (cover) or $\mathbf{Y}$ (stego), we first create an (arbitrary) JPEG image of the same dimensions $n_1 \times n_2$ using Matlab's 'imwrite' with the same quality factor, read its JPEG data structure using 'jpeg_read' from Sallee's JPEG Toolbox (http://www.philsallee.com/jpegtbx/index.html) and then merely replace the array of quantized coefficients in this structure with $\mathbf{X}$ and $\mathbf{Y}$ to obtain the corresponding cover and stego images.

3. UNIVERSAL DISTORTION FUNCTION

In this section, we describe the universal distortion function UNIWARD that will be used to construct steganographic schemes in all embedding domains. To this end, in Section 3.1 we first introduce the wavelet directional filter bank using which UNIWARD is built and then, in Sections 3.2–3.3 we define the distortion between cover and stego images as a sum of relative changes between wavelet coefficients. We do so separately for steganography in the spatial and JPEG domains and for side-informed JPEG domain when the sender has an uncompressed image available. Since the distortion defined in this manner is non-additive, in Section 3.4 we explain a general procedure (originally introduced in [3]) that gives UNIWARD an additive form to be able to embed in practice near the payload–distortion bound using Syndrome–Trellis Codes (STCs) [5].

3.1 Wavelet directional filter bank

For a given image $\mathbf{X}$ represented in the spatial domain, we evaluate its smoothness in multiple directions using the Daubechies 8-tap Wavelet Directional Filter Bank (D-WDFB) $\mathcal{B} = \{\mathbf{K}^{(1)}, \mathbf{K}^{(2)}, \mathbf{K}^{(3)}\}$ consisting of the LH, HL, and HH directional high-pass filters (kernels $\mathbf{K}$). These three filters are built from one-dimensional low-pass ($\mathbf{h}$) and high-pass ($\mathbf{g}$) decomposition filters shown in Table 1:

$$\mathbf{K}^{(1)} = \mathbf{h} \cdot \mathbf{g}^{\mathrm{T}}, \ \ \mathbf{K}^{(2)} = \mathbf{g} \cdot \mathbf{h}^{\mathrm{T}}, \ \ \mathbf{K}^{(3)} = \mathbf{g} \cdot \mathbf{g}^{\mathrm{T}}. \quad (2)$$

Observe from Table 1 that the support of each one-dimensional filter is 16, which gives the kernels the size of 16×16. We define the kth *directional residual* as $\mathbf{R}^{(k)} = \mathbf{K}^{(k)} \star \mathbf{X}$, $k = 1, 2, 3$, where '$\star$' is a mirror-padded convolution that gives each $\mathbf{R}^{(k)}$ the dimension of $n_1 \times n_2$. The purpose of the mirror-padding is to prevent introducing embedding artifacts at the image boundary. Also notice that the directional residuals are essentially the first-level[2] *undecimated* wavelet LH, HL, and HH directional decomposition of $\mathbf{X}$. The reason for selecting this filter bank for constructing UNIWARD is found in [14], where, among the Daubechies wavelets, the authors studied several different filter banks, including the Sobel edge detector, non-directional kernels, and Haar wavelets. Since the Daubechies wavelets gave consistently the best results, we use this filter bank in this article as well.

3.2 UNIWARD for spatial and JPEG domains

Given a pair of cover and stego images, $\mathbf{X}$, and $\mathbf{Y}$, we will denote with $W_{uv}^{(k)}(\mathbf{X})$ and $W_{uv}^{(k)}(\mathbf{Y})$ the uvth wavelet coefficient in the kth decomposition obtained using kernels (2). If $\mathbf{X}$, and $\mathbf{Y}$ are JPEG images, they are first decompressed to the spatial domain and then the wavelet transform is applied. The distortion between both images is the sum of relative changes of the wavelet coefficients w.r.t. the cover image:

$$D(\mathbf{X}, \mathbf{Y}) \triangleq \sum_{k=1}^{3} \sum_{u,v} \frac{|W_{uv}^{(k)}(\mathbf{X}) - W_{uv}^{(k)}(\mathbf{Y})|}{\varepsilon + |W_{uv}^{(k)}(\mathbf{X})|}, \quad (3)$$

where the sum over uv is taken over all $n_1 \times n_2$ subband coefficients and $\varepsilon > 0$ is a stabilizing constant to avoid dividing by zero. In our implementation, we set $\varepsilon = 10 \times$ eps (in Matlab), which means that $\varepsilon \approx 10^{-15}$. From experiments, we found out that the security of embedding using UNIWARD is rather insensitive to the exact value of this parameter.

To understand the logic behind this definition, realize that the ratio in (3) is smaller when a large cover wavelet coefficient is changed, which will happen in textures/noisy regions and near edges. On the other hand, if at least one coefficient, which is small, is changed by a relatively large amount, the distortion value will also be large. Thus, (3) discourages making changes in regions where the content is smooth (and thus modelable) in at least one direction.

---

[2]Experiments with multiple decomposition levels did not improve security in any noticeable manner.

3.3 UNIWARD for side-informed JPEG embedding

In general, by side-informed embedding we understand any embedding method where the sender has a higher-quality version of the cover available (the so-called 'precover'). Historically, the first method that used precover was the Embedding by Dithering algorithm [9] that utilized a true-color image on its input to embed while converting the image to a 256-color palette GIF. The term precover is due to Ker [17].

Specifically in the JPEG domain, the precover attains the form of the unquantized DCT coefficients D_{ij} obtained from the raw precover image $\mathbf{P}$. In this case, the embedder may choose to round D_{ij} "up" or "down" to modulate its parity (e.g., the least significant bit of the rounded value). When compressing the precover $\mathbf{P}$ to the cover image $\mathbf{X}$, the rounding error for the ijth DCT coefficient is

$$e_{ij} = |D_{ij} - X_{ij}|, \quad e_{ij} \in [0, 0.5]. \quad (4)$$

By rounding "to the other side," the sender introduces the following embedding change

$$Y_{ij} = X_{ij} + \text{sign}(D_{ij} - X_{ij}), \quad (5)$$

which corresponds to a "rounding error" of $1 - e_{ij}$. Therefore, every embedding change increases the distortion *w.r.t. the precover* by the *difference* between both rounding errors:

$$|D_{ij} - Y_{ij}| - |D_{ij} - X_{ij}| = 1 - 2e_{ij}. \quad (6)$$

It is thus natural to define the distortion for side-informed embedding in JPEG domain as the difference:

$$D^{(\text{SI})}(\mathbf{X}, \mathbf{Y}) \triangleq D(\mathbf{P}, \mathbf{Y}) - D(\mathbf{P}, \mathbf{X})$$
$$= \sum_{k=1}^{3} \sum_{u,v} \frac{|W_{uv}^{(k)}(\mathbf{P}) - W_{uv}^{(k)}(\mathbf{Y})| - |W_{uv}^{(k)}(\mathbf{P}) - W_{uv}^{(k)}(\mathbf{X})|}{\varepsilon + |W_{uv}^{(k)}(\mathbf{P})|}. \quad (7)$$

We would like to point out that the linearity of DCT and the wavelet transforms guarantee that $D^{(\text{SI})}(\mathbf{X}, \mathbf{Y}) \geq 0$. This is because rounding a DCT coefficient to obtain a cover $\mathbf{X}$ corresponds to adding a certain two-dimensional 8×8 pattern in the spatial domain, which depends on the modified DCT mode, and thus a 23×23 pattern in the wavelet domain because the support of the 8-tap Daubechies wavelets is 16×16. On the other hand, rounding "to the other side" to obtain the stego image $\mathbf{Y}$ corresponds to *subtracting* the same pattern but with a *larger* amplitude, which is why $|W_{uv}^{(k)}(\mathbf{P}) - W_{uv}^{(k)}(\mathbf{Y})| - |W_{uv}^{(k)}(\mathbf{P}) - W_{uv}^{(k)}(\mathbf{X})| \geq 0$.

3.3.1 Relationship of UNIWARD to prior art

Equation (7) bears some similarity to the distortion utilized in the recently proposed Normalized Perturbed Quantization (NPQ) [15]. There, the authors also proposed to compute the embedding distortion as a *relative* change of cover DCT coefficients. What distinguishes UNIWARD from the distortion function of NPQ is the fact that we compute the distortion using a directional filter bank in the wavelet domain, which brings in a very important ingredient – directional sensitivity – and thus potentially better content adaptability. Furthermore, in our approach we treat all DCT coefficients equivalently and do not exclude those that are zeros in the cover. UNIWARD also naturally incorporates the influence of the quantization step because the

Table 1: One-dimensional filters used to construct the kernels of the D-WDFB using (2).

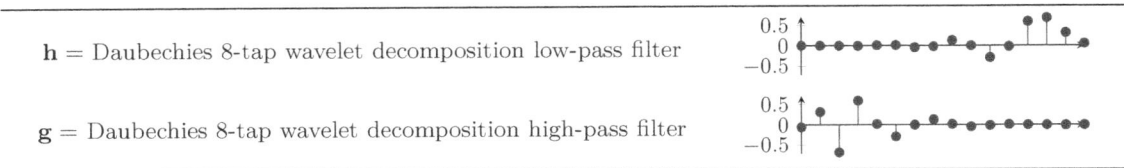

h = Daubechies 8-tap wavelet decomposition low-pass filter	
g = Daubechies 8-tap wavelet decomposition high-pass filter	

wavelet coefficients are computed from the decompressed JPEG image.

Also, distortion (3) is built similarly as the embedding distortion used in WOW [14] in that it is also capable of assessing local cover content using directional residuals computed in the wavelet domain. The pixel costs of WOW are, however, obtained in a different manner. First, for every subband and every pixel it computes the so-called embedding suitabilities, which are sums of weighted changes of wavelet coefficients. Then, the suitabilities are aggregated using a reciprocal Hölder norm to obtain costs with the property that if at least one suitability is zero (or very small), the embedding cost is infinite (very large). We refer the reader to the original publication for more details.

3.4 Additive form of UNIWARD

Note that both (3) and (7) are non-additive because changing pixel X_{ij} will affect a 16×16 neighborhood of wavelet coefficients (the support size of the Daubechies 8-tap wavelet). As already mentioned above, for images represented in the JPEG domain, changing a JPEG coefficient X_{ij} will affect a block of 8×8 pixels and thus 23×23 wavelet coefficients. Therefore, when changing neighboring pixels (or DCT coefficients), the embedding patterns overlap and the changes "interact," causing the non-additivity of D. Even though there exist methods for embedding using non-additive distortion functions (e.g., the Gibbs construction [3]), realizing the embedding using additive distortion is significantly easier. Moreover, in the case of UNIWARD, it appears that the interactions among nearby embedding changes are strong enough to make the Gibbs construction ineffective in practice. The Gibbs construction is only capable of embedding the so-called erasure entropy but with a distortion corresponding to the actual entropy of the Markov field. The stronger the interactions among embedding changes are, the larger is the difference between both entropies, and the less effective the Gibbs construction becomes. Detailed technical explanation of this issue supported with experiments on real images appears in the journal version of this paper.

As shown in [3], any distortion function $D(\mathbf{X}, \mathbf{Y})$ can be used for embedding in its so-called *additive approximation* by using D to compute the cost of changing each pixel/DCT coefficient. In particular, the cost, ρ_{ij}, of changing X_{ij} to Y_{ij} when leaving all other cover elements unchanged is:

$$\rho_{ij}(\mathbf{X}, Y_{ij}) \triangleq D(\mathbf{X}, \mathbf{X}_{\sim ij} Y_{ij}), \qquad (8)$$

where $\mathbf{X}_{\sim ij} Y_{ij}$ is the cover image $\mathbf{X}$ with only its ijth element changed: $X_{ij} \to Y_{ij}$.[3] Note that $\rho_{ij} = 0$ when $\mathbf{X} = \mathbf{Y}$. We will denote the additive approximations to (3) and (7) with a subscript "A." For example, the additive approxima-

tion to $D(\mathbf{X}, \mathbf{Y})$ is:

$$D_{\mathrm{A}}(\mathbf{X}, \mathbf{Y}) = \sum_{i=1}^{n_1} \sum_{j=1}^{n_2} \rho_{ij}(\mathbf{X}, Y_{ij})[X_{ij} \neq Y_{ij}]. \qquad (9)$$

Note that the presence of absolute values in $D(\mathbf{X}, \mathbf{Y})$ (3) implies

$$\rho_{ij}(\mathbf{X}, X_{ij} + 1) = \rho_{ij}(\mathbf{X}, X_{ij} - 1), \quad \forall i, j, \text{ and } X_{ij}, \quad (10)$$

which permits us to use a *ternary* embedding operation for the spatial and JPEG domains. Practical embedding algorithms can be constructed using the ternary multi-layered version of STCs (Section IV in [5]). One might seemingly rightfully argue that the embedding cost should depend on the polarity of the change, however the equal cost for both possible changes is given by the distortion function. Moreover, since UNIWARD restricts the embedding changes to textures, the potential disadvantage of having equal costs for both polarities is reduced and it allows us to reduce the embedding distortion for a fixed payload by utilizing stronger ternary codes. This is expected to become especially advantageous for larger payloads. Finally, note that for the side-informed JPEG steganography, $D_{\mathrm{A}}^{(\mathrm{SI})}(\mathbf{X}, \mathbf{Y})$ is inherently limited to a *binary* embedding operation because the sender has only two options – either rounding X_{ij} up or down.

The embedding methods that use the additive approximations of UNIWARD for the spatial, JPEG, and side-informed JPEG domain will be called S-UNIWARD, J-UNIWARD, and SI-UNIWARD, respectively.

4. SETUP OF ALL EXPERIMENTS

Before reporting the experimental results of embedding with UNIWARD in all three domains in the next section, we summarize the common core of all experiments.

4.1 Cover source

All experiments are conducted on the BOSSbase database ver. 1.01 [7] containing 10,000 512×512 8-bit grayscale images coming from eight different cameras. This database is very convenient for our purposes because it contains uncompressed images that serve as precovers for side-informed JPEG embedding that can be compressed to any desirable quality factor for the JPEG domain. The fact that the images are downsampled rather than raw has an effect on the statistical detectability, especially for algorithms operating in the spatial domain. According to the study carried out in [24], downsampling without antialiasing (that is with a fixed-size interpolation kernel) as is done for the BOSSbase makes detection of steganography *more difficult*

---

[3]This notation was used in [3] and is also standard in the literature on Markov random fields [32].

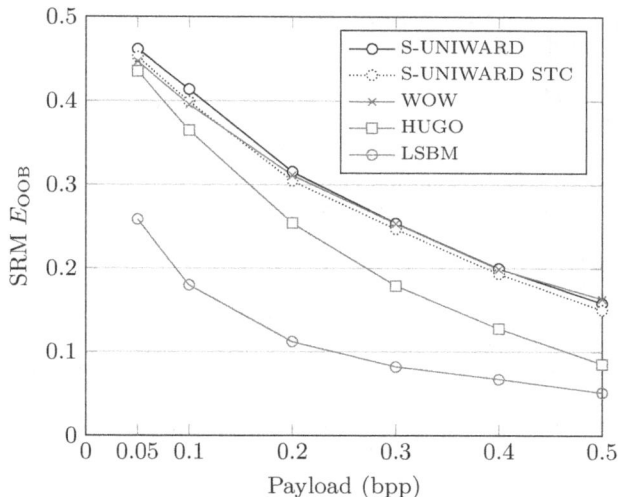

Figure 1: Detection error E_{OOB} as a function of relative payload for S-UNIWARD, HUGO, and LSBM. The dotted curve shows the performance of UNIWARD when implemented with STCs with constraint height $h = 12$.

rather than easier[4] despite the presence of resizing artifacts that might aid detection. This is because resizing in general decreases statistical dependencies between adjacent pixels, which seems to have a much stronger effect than the weak resizing artifacts. Perhaps a more careful statement would be to say that current empirical steganalyzers built using rich models are unable to utilize the resizing artifacts to the point that would outweigh the lowered dependencies among pixels.

The steganographic security is evaluated empirically using binary classifiers trained on a given cover source and its stego version embedded with a fixed payload. Even though this setup is artificial and does not correspond to real-life applications, it allows assessment of security w.r.t. the payload size, which is the goal of academic investigations of this type.

4.2 Features and machine learning

Spatial-domain steganography methods will be analyzed using the Spatial Rich Model (SRM) [11] consisting of 39 symmetrized sub-models quantized with three different quantization factors with a total dimension of $34,671$. JPEG-domain methods (including the side-informed algorithms) will be steganalyzed using the union of a downscaled version of the SRM with a single quantization step $q = 1$ (SRMQ1) with dimension $12,753$ and the JPEG Rich Model (JRM) [23] with dimension $22,510$, giving the total feature dimension of $35,263$.

All classifiers were implemented using the ensemble [26] with Fisher linear discriminant as the base learner. Security is quantified using the ensemble's "out-of-bag" (OOB) error E_{OOB}, which is an unbiased estimate of the minimal total *testing* error under equal priors [26] (equal a priori probabilities of encountering a cover or stego image):

$$P_{\mathrm{E}} = \min_{P_{\mathrm{FA}}} \frac{1}{2}(P_{\mathrm{FA}} + P_{\mathrm{MD}}). \qquad (11)$$

To show how the statistical detectability increases with payload, we produce graphs showing E_{OOB} as a function of the relative payload. With the feature dimensionality and the database size, the statistical scatter of E_{OOB} over multiple ensemble runs with different seeds was typically so small that drawing error bars around the data points in the graphs would not show two visually discernible horizontal lines, which is why we omit this information in our graphs. As will be seen later, the differences in detectability between the proposed methods and prior art are so large that there should be no doubt about the statistical significance of the improvement. The code for extractors of all rich models as well as the ensemble is available at http://dde.binghamton.edu/download.

5. EXPERIMENTS AND COMPARISON TO PRIOR ART

This section contains the results of all experiments carried out with the costs obtained from the additive approximation of UNIWARD for all three embedding domains – spatial, JPEG, and side-informed JPEG. Spatial-domain methods are tested for relative payloads $0.05, 0.1, 0.2, \ldots, 0.5$ bits per pixel (bpp), while JPEG-domain and side-informed JPEG methods will be tested on the same payloads expressed in bits per non-zero cover AC DCT coefficient (bpnzAC). Even though J-UNIWARD and SI-UNIWARD embed into DC modes and zero coefficients, we express the payload in terms of bpnzAC in order to be compatible with previous art.

Figure 2: Embedding probability for payload 0.4 bpp using HUGO (top right), WOW (bottom left), and S-UNIWARD (bottom right) for a 128×128 grayscale cover image shown in top left.

---

[4]For a fixed root rate [2], embedding in resized images is more difficult to detect than in cropped images.

5.1 Spatial domain

In the spatial domain, we compare S-UNIWARD with HUGO [28], Wavelet Obtained Weights (WOW) [14], and LSB Matching (LSBM). HUGO [28] embeds by minimizing an embedding distortion defined as a weighted norm between the features of the cover and stego image in the SPAM feature space [27]. It assigns large weights to well-populated feature bins and low weights to sparsely populated bins that correspond to more complex content. We used the HUGO embedding simulator [7] with default settings $\gamma = 1$, $\sigma = 1$, and the switch --T with $T = 255$ to remove the weakness reported in [25].

Given the similarity of distortion functions employed in WOW and S-UNIWARD (see Section 3.3.1 on comparison to prior art), one can expect a correspondingly similar performance of both algorithms, which is confirmed below. Since both algorithms are highly adaptive, they are expected to better resists steganalysis using rich models [11] than HUGO.

We report the results of all algorithms for their embedding simulators that operate at the theoretical payload–distortion bound. The non-adaptive LSBM was simulated at the ternary bound corresponding to uniform costs, $\rho_{ij} = 1$ for all i, j. The only algorithm that we implemented using STCs (with constraint height $h = 12$) to assess the coding loss is the proposed S-UNIWARD method.

Figure 1 shows the E_{OOB} error for all stego methods as a function of the relative payload expressed in bpp. As expected, the security of the S-UNIWARD and WOW is practically the same due to the similarity of their distortion functions. The improvement over HUGO is, however, quite significant especially for large payloads. As expected, the non-adaptive LSBM performs poorly across all payloads.

5.1.1 Content adaptivity

In Figure 2, we contrast the placement of embedding changes for HUGO, WOW, and S-UNIWARD. Observe that the cover image has numerous horizontal and vertical edges and also some textured areas. While HUGO embeds with high probability into the pillar edges as well as the horizontal lines above the pillars, S-UNIWARD directional costs force the changes solely into the textured areas.

While the placement of embedding changes for WOW and S-UNIWARD is quite similar, S-UNIWARD seems to be more discriminative than WOW. This higher sensitivity to content is due to the fact that it only takes one wavelet coefficient (among 3×16^2 coefficients affected by changing a single pixel $X_{ij} \rightarrow Y_{ij}$) to be close to zero to have a very large embedding cost ρ_{ij}. In contrast, in WOW, the costs are obtained by adding reciprocal values of three "embedding suitabilities," which are themselves sums over many wavelet coefficients. This makes encountering a high embedding cost less likely than in S-UNIWARD.

Upon closer inspection of the embedding probabilities for S-UNIWARD in Figure 2, one observes alternating short streaks with large differences in embedding probabilities. This is caused by the properties of the Daubechies 8-tap filter bank, which has proved to be ideal for compression of natural images due to its ability to produce many small coefficients even in textured regions. In combination with the oscillation of its high-pass component between positive and negative values, it creates the streaks as well as some small low-probability areas in textured regions. While the streaks

may increase the statistical detectability, steganalysis with rich media models showed no evidence for this.

5.2 JPEG domain

To the best knowledge of the authors, currently the most secure embedding method for JPEG images that does not use any side information is the heuristic Uniform Embedding Distortion UED method [13]. It offers a substantially better empirical security than the nsF5 algorithm [12]. The authors of UED implemented their algorithm with binary codes. However, since the UED costs do not depend on the polarity of the embedding change direction, we included for comparison the UED implemented using *ternary* codes rather than binary as this is likely to produce an even more secure method.[5]

All methods were again simulated at their corresponding payload–distortion bounds. The costs for nsF5 were uniform over all non-zero DCTs with zeros assigned infinite costs (the so-called wet elements [10]). Figure 3 shows the results for JPEG quality factors 75, 85, and 95. J-UNIWARD clearly outperforms nsF5 as well as both versions of UED by a sizeable margin across all three quality factors. Furthermore, the coding loss of J-UNIWARD implemented using STCs with constraint height $h = 12$ appears rather negligible.

5.3 Side-informed JPEG domain

In the JPEG domain, by far the most successful paradigm is to minimize the distortion w.r.t. the raw, uncompressed image, if available [22, 29, 31, 15]. In this section, we compare SI-UNIWARD with three other side-informed JPEG steganographic schemes that constitute the current state of the art. The first is the Entropy Block Steganography (EBS) [31] with the cost of DCT coefficient ij corresponding to the DCT mode kl:

$$\rho_{ij}^{(kl)} = \left(\frac{q_{kl}(0.5 - |e_{ij}|)}{H(\mathbf{X}^{(b)})} \right)^2, \tag{12}$$

where $H(\mathbf{X}^{(b)})$ is the block entropy defined as $H(\mathbf{X}^{(b)}) = -\sum_m h_m^{(b)} \log h_m^{(b)}$, where $h_m^{(b)}$ is the normalized histogram of all non-zero DCT coefficients in block $\mathbf{X}^{(b)}$. EBS embeds into all DCT coefficients, including the DC term and coefficients that would otherwise round to zero ($X_{ij} = 0$).

The second method is the already mentioned Normalized Perturbed Quantization (NPQ) [15] with embedding costs

$$\rho_{ij}^{(kl)} = \frac{q_{kl}^{\lambda_1}(1 - 2|e_{ij}|)}{(\mu + |X_{ij}|)^{\lambda_2}}, \tag{13}$$

where, per the experiments reported in [15], we set $\mu = 0$ as NPQ embeds only in non-zero AC DCT coefficients. We also set $\lambda_1 = \lambda_2 = 1/2$ as this setting seemed to produce the most secure scheme across a wide range of payloads when tested with various feature sets.

The third algorithm is the BCHopt [29] introduced in 2009. We refer the reader to this publication for more details about its cost assignment and the actual coding.

5.3.1 Problem with zero embedding costs

We want to point out that the cost ρ_{ij} for all three prior-art methods as well as for SI-UNIWARD is equal to zero

---

[5]The authors of UED were apparently unaware of this possibility to further boost the security of their algorithm using ternary codes.

when the rounding error $e_{ij} = 1/2$. This, however, inevitably leads to a technical problem that, to the best knowledge of the authors, has not been disclosed elsewhere. It is connected to the fact that when $e_{ij} = 1/2$ the cost of rounding D_{ij} "down" instead of "up" should not be zero because, after all, this does constitute an embedding change. This does not affect security much when the number of such DCT coefficients is small. With an increasing number of coefficients with $e_{ij} = 1/2$ (we will call them 1/2-coefficients), however, the distortion is no longer a good measure of statistical detectability and one starts observing a rather pathological behavior – with payload approaching zero, the detection error does not saturate at 50% (random guessing) but rather at a lower value and only reaches 50% for payloads nearly equal to zero.[6] The strength with which this phenomenon manifests depends on how many 1/2-coefficients are in the image, which in turn depends on the implementation of the DCT used to compute the costs and the JPEG quality factor.

The slow DCT (implemented using 'dct2' in Matlab) typically produces a negligible number of 1/2-coefficients to cause any pathological behavior with the exception of high quality factors (see below). However, in the fast-integer implementation of DCT (e.g., Matlab's 'imwrite'), all D_{ij} are multiples of 1/8, which increases the number of 1/2-coefficients especially for high JPEG quality factors. To avoid dealing with this issue in this paper, we computed the embedding costs using the slow DCT implemented using Matlab's 'dct2' as explained in Section 2.2.

Even with the slow DCT implementation, however, the effect of 1/2-coefficients does not disappear. As can be easily verified from the formula for the DCT (1), when $k, l \in \{0, 4\}$, the value of D_{kl} is always a rational number because the cosines are either 1 or $\sqrt{2}/2$, which, together with the multiplicative weights $\mathbf{w}$, gives again a rational number. In particular, the DC coefficient (mode 00) is always a multiple of 1/4, the coefficients of modes 04 and 40 are multiples of 1/8, and the coefficients corresponding to mode 44 are multiples of 1/16. For all other combinations of $k, l \in \{0, \ldots, 7\}$, D_{ij} is an irrational number. In practice, *any* embedding whose costs are zero for 1/2-coefficients will thus strongly prefer these four DCT modes, which will cause a highly uneven distribution of embedding changes among the DCT coefficients. Because rich JPEG models [23] utilize statistics collected for each mode separately, they are capable of detecting this statistical peculiarity even at low payloads.

To demonstrate the pathological behavior of all four embedding schemes due to concentrating their embedding changes in DCT modes 00, 04, 40, and 44, we subjected all embedding methods to steganalysis using the JRM+SRMQ1 rich media model (see Section 4.2) for the JPEG quality factor 95. The results displayed in Figure 4 clearly show the saturation of the testing error at $\sim 25-30\%$ for small–medium payloads. Note that NPQ and BCHopt do not exhibit the pathological error saturation as strongly because they do not embed into the DC term (mode 00).

To eliminate this problem, we decided to modify all four side-informed JPEG embedding schemes in the following manner. We prohibit embedding changes into all 1/2-coefficients in modes 00, 04, 40, and 44.[7]

---

[6]This is because the embedding strongly prefers 1/2-coefficients.

[7]In practice, we assign very large costs to such coefficients.

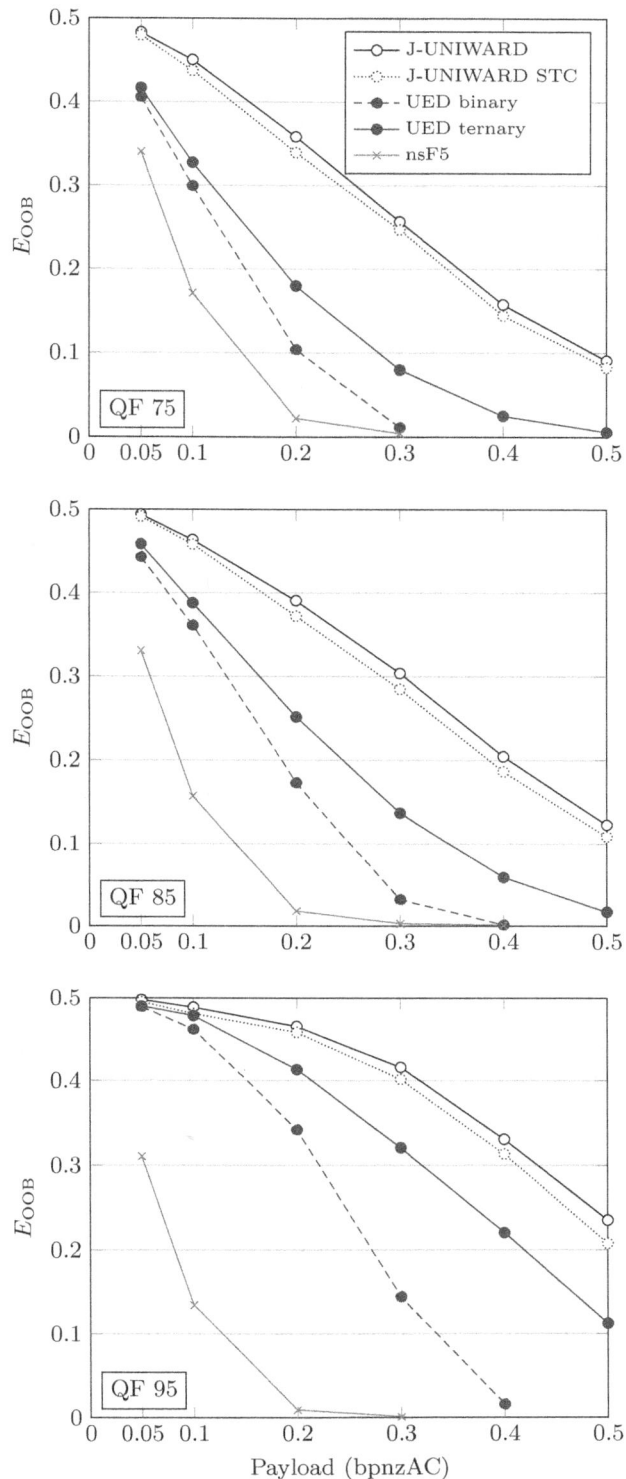

Figure 3: Testing error E_{OOB} for **J-UNIWARD, nsF5, and binary (ternary) UED on BOSSbase 1.01 with the union of SRMQ1 and JRM and ensemble classifier for quality factors 75, 85, and 95.**

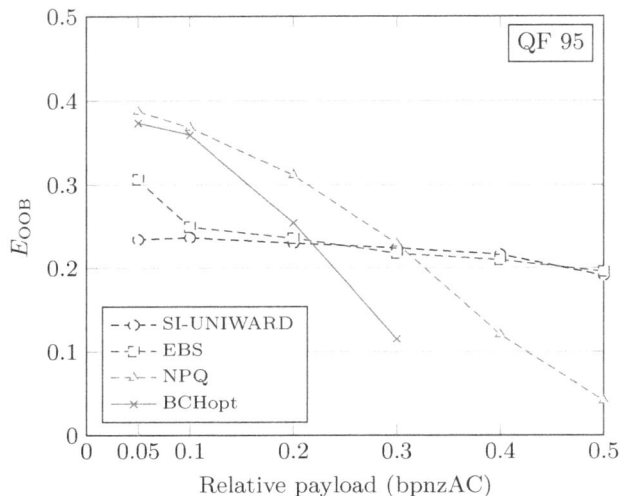

Figure 4: Pathological behavior of all four embedding schemes with zero embedding cost for 1/2-coefficients (JPEG quality factor 95). Notice that the testing error saturates for small–middle payloads due to the fact that the embedding strongly prefers DCT coefficients with zero costs, which are mostly located in DCT modes: 00, 04, 40, and 44. NPQ and BCHopt exhibit this phenomenon to a lesser degree because they avoid embedding in the DC term.

While this measure seems to have largely solved the problem (see Figure 5), we are obviously facing a much more fundamental problem, which is how exactly the side-information in the form of an uncompressed image should be utilized for the design of steganographic distortion functions. The authors postpone a detailed study of this quite intriguing problem to a separate paper.

Figure 5 shows that SI-UNIWARD achieves the best security among the tested methods for all payloads and all JPEG quality factors while its coding loss is quite small.

6. CONCLUSION

The modern paradigm for building steganographic schemes in empirical cover sources is to formulate the data hiding problem as source coding with a fidelity constraint and implement the embedding using existing codes operating near the rate–distortion bound. Technically, in imperfect steganography one minimizes the steganographic Fisher information or, equivalently, embeds as large payload at a given level of statistical detectability as possible. In practice, one first defines the fidelity measure (embedding distortion) and obtains feedback regarding the statistical detectability empirically on a given source (database of images) using a steganalyzer built using machine-learning and the best available cover models.

The main contribution of this paper is a clean, parameter-free, universal design of the distortion function called UNIWARD. What distinguishes our approach from previous art is that UNIWARD evaluates the embedding impact independently of the embedding domain. Whether one embeds

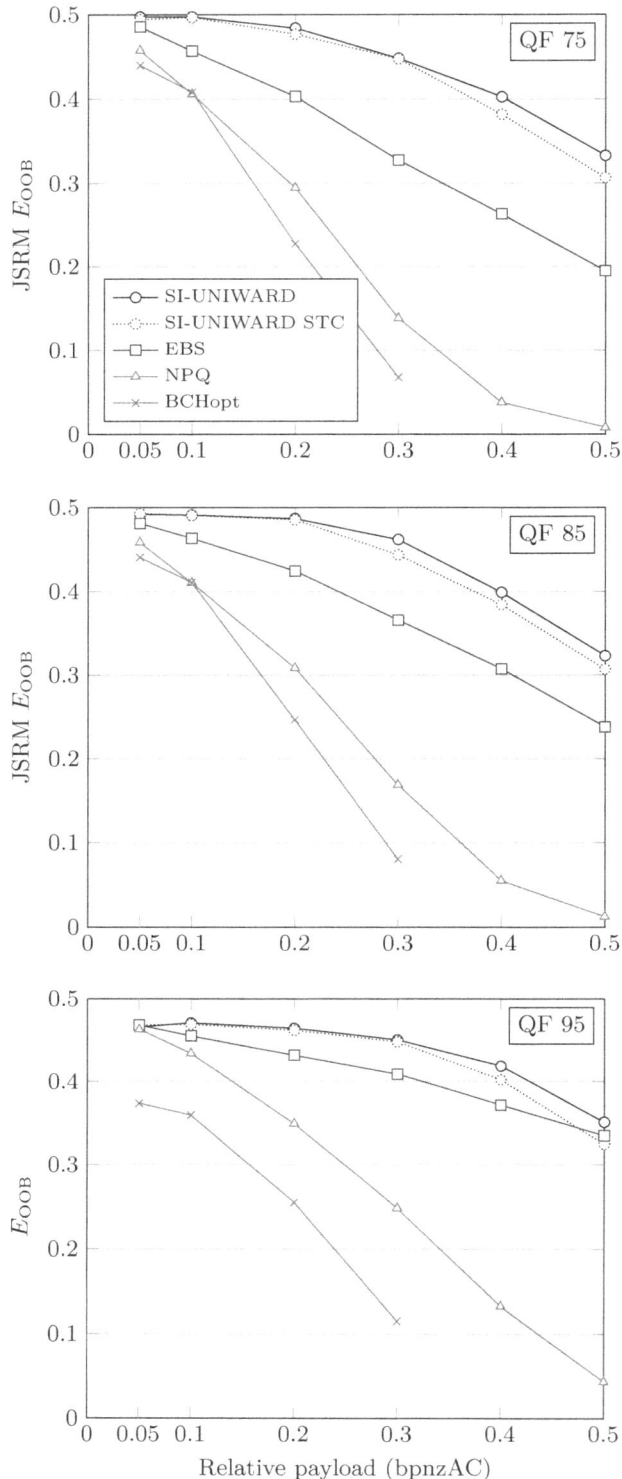

Figure 5: Testing error E_{OOB} for SI-UNIWARD and three other methods with the union of SRMQ1 and JRM and the ensemble classifier for JPEG quality factors 75, 85, and 95.

in the spatial or JPEG domain, the distortion is always computed in the wavelet domain as a sum of relative changes of wavelet coefficients in the highest frequency undecimated subbands. Since the wavelet basis functions are directional, UNIWARD can assess the neighborhood of each pixel (DCT block) for the presence of discontinuities in multiple directions and directs the embedding into the most complex textures and "noisy" regions in the cover image. In particular, UNIWARD discourages embedding in regions that can be modeled along at least one direction, such as "clean edges."

We implemented this model-free heuristic approach in the spatial, JPEG, and side-informed JPEG domains. The merit of the proposed construction is proved in this article by showing (sometimes quite significant) improvement over previous art when detecting steganography using rich media models. This applies especially to the JPEG and side-informed JPEG domains. The innovative concept to assess the costs of changing a JPEG coefficient in an alternative domain is, indeed, quite promising.

Finally, we have discovered that side-informed JPEG steganographic schemes that assign zero embedding distortion when the quantization error of DCT coefficients is 1/2 exhibit a pathological behavior that is especially striking for high quality factors and for fast integer implementation of the DCT. This is because any embedding that minimizes distortion starts introducing embedding artifacts that are quite detectable using the JPEG rich model. This finding raises an important question, which is how to best utilize the side information in the form of an uncompressed image when embedding data into the JPEG compressed form. The authors postpone detailed investigation of this open problem to their future effort.

Matlab, MEX, and C++ code for all three UNIWARD algorithms is available at http://dde.binghamton.edu/download/stego_algorithms/.

7. ACKNOWLEDGMENTS

The work on this paper was supported by Air Force Office of Scientific Research under the research grant number FA9950-12-1-0124. The U.S. Government is authorized to reproduce and distribute reprints for Governmental purposes notwithstanding any copyright notation there on. The views and conclusions contained herein are those of the authors and should not be interpreted as necessarily representing the official policies, either expressed or implied of AFOSR or the U.S. Government. The authors would like to thank Tomáš Filler and Jan Kodovský for useful discussions.

8. REFERENCES

[1] R. Böhme. *Advanced Statistical Steganalysis*. Springer-Verlag, Berlin Heidelberg, 2010.

[2] T. Filler and J. Fridrich. Fisher information determines capacity of ϵ-secure steganography. In S. Katzenbeisser and A.-R. Sadeghi, editors, *Information Hiding, 11th International Conference*, volume 5806 of *Lecture Notes in Computer Science*, pages 31–47, Darmstadt, Germany, June 7–10, 2009. Springer-Verlag, New York.

[3] T. Filler and J. Fridrich. Gibbs construction in steganography. *IEEE Transactions on Information Forensics and Security*, 5(4):705–720, 2010.

[4] T. Filler and J. Fridrich. Design of adaptive steganographic schemes for digital images. In A. Alattar, N. D. Memon, E. J. Delp, and J. Dittmann, editors, *Proceedings SPIE, Electronic Imaging, Media Watermarking, Security and Forensics of Multimedia XIII*, volume 7880, pages OF 1–14, San Francisco, CA, January 23–26, 2011.

[5] T. Filler, J. Judas, and J. Fridrich. Minimizing additive distortion in steganography using syndrome-trellis codes. *IEEE Transactions on Information Forensics and Security*, 6(3):920–935, September 2011.

[6] T. Filler, A. D. Ker, and J. Fridrich. The Square Root Law of steganographic capacity for Markov covers. In N. D. Memon, E. J. Delp, P. W. Wong, and J. Dittmann, editors, *Proceedings SPIE, Electronic Imaging, Security and Forensics of Multimedia XI*, volume 7254, pages 08 1–11, San Jose, CA, January 18–21, 2009.

[7] T. Filler, T. Pevný, and P. Bas. BOSS (Break Our Steganography System). http://www.agents.cz/boss, July 2010.

[8] J. Fridrich. Effect of cover quantization on steganographic fisher information. *IEEE Transactions on Information Forensics and Security*, 2013. To appear.

[9] J. Fridrich and R. Du. Secure steganographic methods for palette images. In A. Pfitzmann, editor, *Information Hiding, 3rd International Workshop*, volume 1768 of *Lecture Notes in Computer Science*, pages 47–60, Dresden, Germany, September 29–October 1, 1999. Springer-Verlag, New York.

[10] J. Fridrich, M. Goljan, D. Soukal, and P. Lisoněk. Writing on wet paper. In T. Kalker and P. Moulin, editors, *IEEE Transactions on Signal Processing, Special Issue on Media Security*, volume 53, pages 3923–3935, October 2005. (journal version).

[11] J. Fridrich and J. Kodovský. Rich models for steganalysis of digital images. *IEEE Transactions on Information Forensics and Security*, 7(3):868–882, June 2011.

[12] J. Fridrich, T. Pevný, and J. Kodovský. Statistically undetectable JPEG steganography: Dead ends, challenges, and opportunities. In J. Dittmann and J. Fridrich, editors, *Proceedings of the 9th ACM Multimedia & Security Workshop*, pages 3–14, Dallas, TX, September 20–21, 2007.

[13] L. Guo, J. Ni, and Y.-Q. Shi. An efficient JPEG steganographic scheme using uniform embedding. In *Fourth IEEE International Workshop on Information Forensics and Security*, Tenerife, Spain, December 2–5, 2012.

[14] V. Holub and J. Fridrich. Designing steganographic distortion using directional filters. In *Fourth IEEE International Workshop on Information Forensics and Security*, Tenerife, Spain, December 2–5, 2012.

[15] F. Huang, J. Huang, and Y.-Q. Shi. New channel selection rule for JPEG steganography. *IEEE Transactions on Information Forensics and Security*, 7(4):1181–1191, August 2012.

[16] A. D. Ker. A capacity result for batch steganography. *IEEE Signal Processing Letters*, 14(8):525–528, 2007.

[17] A. D. Ker. A fusion of maximal likelihood and structural steganalysis. In T. Furon, F. Cayre,

G. Doërr, and P. Bas, editors, *Information Hiding, 9th International Workshop*, volume 4567 of *Lecture Notes in Computer Science*, pages 204–219, Saint Malo, France, June 11–13, 2007. Springer-Verlag, Berlin.

[18] A. D. Ker. The ultimate steganalysis benchmark? In J. Dittmann and J. Fridrich, editors, *Proceedings of the 9th ACM Multimedia & Security Workshop*, pages 141–148, Dallas, TX, September 20–21, 2007.

[19] A. D. Ker. Estimating steganographic fisher information in real images. In S. Katzenbeisser and A.-R. Sadeghi, editors, *Information Hiding, 11th International Conference*, volume 5806 of *Lecture Notes in Computer Science*, pages 73–88, Darmstadt, Germany, June 7–10, 2009. Springer-Verlag, New York.

[20] A. D. Ker. The square root law in stegosystems with imperfect information. In R. Böhme and R. Safavi-Naini, editors, *Information Hiding, 12th International Conference*, volume 6387 of *Lecture Notes in Computer Science*, pages 145–160, Calgary, Canada, June 28–30, 2010. Springer-Verlag, New York.

[21] A. D. Ker, T. Pevný, J. Kodovský, and J. Fridrich. The Square Root Law of steganographic capacity. In A. D. Ker, J. Dittmann, and J. Fridrich, editors, *Proceedings of the 10th ACM Multimedia & Security Workshop*, pages 107–116, Oxford, UK, September 22–23, 2008.

[22] Y. Kim, Z. Duric, and D. Richards. Modified matrix encoding technique for minimal distortion steganography. In J. L. Camenisch, C. S. Collberg, N. F. Johnson, and P. Sallee, editors, *Information Hiding, 8th International Workshop*, volume 4437 of *Lecture Notes in Computer Science*, pages 314–327, Alexandria, VA, July 10–12, 2006. Springer-Verlag, New York.

[23] J. Kodovský and J. Fridrich. Steganalysis of JPEG images using rich models. In A. Alattar, N. D. Memon, and E. J. Delp, editors, *Proceedings SPIE, Electronic Imaging, Media Watermarking, Security, and Forensics of Multimedia XIV*, volume 8303, pages 0A 1–13, San Francisco, CA, January 23–26, 2012.

[24] J. Kodovský and J. Fridrich. Steganalysis in resized images. In *Proc. of IEEE ICASSP*, Vancouver, Canada, May 26–31, 2013. Under review.

[25] J. Kodovský, J. Fridrich, and V. Holub. On dangers of overtraining steganography to incomplete cover model. In J. Dittmann, S. Craver, and C. Heitzenrater, editors, *Proceedings of the 13th ACM Multimedia & Security Workshop*, pages 69–76, Niagara Falls, NY, September 29–30, 2011.

[26] J. Kodovský, J. Fridrich, and V. Holub. Ensemble classifiers for steganalysis of digital media. *IEEE Transactions on Information Forensics and Security*, 7(2):432–444, 2012.

[27] T. Pevný, P. Bas, and J. Fridrich. Steganalysis by subtractive pixel adjacency matrix. *IEEE Transactions on Information Forensics and Security*, 5(2):215–224, June 2010.

[28] T. Pevný, T. Filler, and P. Bas. Using high-dimensional image models to perform highly undetectable steganography. In R. Böhme and R. Safavi-Naini, editors, *Information Hiding, 12th International Conference*, volume 6387 of *Lecture Notes in Computer Science*, pages 161–177, Calgary, Canada, June 28–30, 2010. Springer-Verlag, New York.

[29] V. Sachnev, H. J. Kim, and R. Zhang. Less detectable JPEG steganography method based on heuristic optimization and BCH syndrome coding. In J. Dittmann, S. Craver, and J. Fridrich, editors, *Proceedings of the 11th ACM Multimedia & Security Workshop*, pages 131–140, Princeton, NJ, September 7–8, 2009.

[30] C. E. Shannon. Coding theorems for a discrete source with a fidelity criterion. *IRE Nat. Conv. Rec.*, 4:142–163, 1959.

[31] C. Wang and J. Ni. An efficient JPEG steganographic scheme based on the block–entropy of DCT coefficents. In *Proc. of IEEE ICASSP*, Kyoto, Japan, March 25–30, 2012.

[32] G. Winkler. *Image Analysis, Random Fields and Markov Chain Monte Carlo Methods: A Mathematical Introduction (Stochastic Modelling and Applied Probability)*. Springer-Verlag, Berlin Heidelberg, 2nd edition, 2003.

Distortion Function Designing for JPEG Steganography with Uncompressed Side-image

Fangjun Huang
School of Information Science and Technology,
Sun Yat-Sen University, GD 510006, China
huangfj@mail.sysu.edu.cn

Weiqi Luo
School of Software,
Sun Yat-Sen University, GD 510006, China
weiqi.luo@yahoo.com

Jiwu Huang
School of Information Science and Technology,
Sun Yat-Sen University, GD 510006, China
isshjw@mail.sysu.edu.cn

Yun-Qing Shi
Department of Electrical and Computer Engineering,
New Jersey Institute of Technology, NJ 07102, USA
shi@njit.edu

ABSTRACT

In this paper, we present a new framework for designing distortion functions of joint photographic experts group (JPEG) steganography with uncompressed side-image. In our framework, the discrete cosine transform (DCT) coefficients, including all direct current (DC) coefficients and alternating current (AC) coefficients, are divided into two groups: first-priority group (FPG) and second-priority group (SPG). Different strategies are established to associate the distortion values to the coefficients in FPG and SPG, respectively. In this paper, three scenarios for dividing the coefficients into FPG and SPG are exemplified, which can be utilized to form a series of new distortion functions. Experimental results demonstrate that while applying these generated distortion functions to JPEG steganography, the intrinsic statistical characteristics of the carrier image will be preserved better than the prior-art, and consequently the security performance of the corresponding JPEG steganography can be improved significantly.

Categories and Subject Descriptors

I.4 [**Image Processing and computer vision**]

Keywords

JPEG, steganography, steganalyzer, distortion function

1. INTRODUCTION

The key concept behind the security of steganographic systems is the statistical un-detectability. It may be influenced by many factors [1], such as the choice of cover object, the type of modification operation on cover elements, the number of embedding changes (related to the payload), and the distortion functions used to identify individual elements of cover that could be modified during embedding. Assume that the first three factors mentioned above are the same, designing the distortion function will be an important approach to minimizing the impact caused by embedding, and thus improve the security performance of steganography.

To minimize the impact caused by data embedding, the sender should choose to modify those elements (pixels/coefficients) in such a way that the caused detectable distortion is as small as possible. Embedding the secret message bits under the guidance of minimizing distortion function can improve the security performance of steganography and has been known for a long time. In [2], Fridrich et al. presented the perturbed quantization (PQ) steganography. As a specific case, they pointed out that the sender can constrain the embedding changes to those DCT coefficients that experience the largest quantization error, i.e., the coefficients with the quantization error of $0.5 \pm \square$ ($\square$ is a small positive number). Such kind of coefficients, when rounded to the other value, may leave the smallest embedding distortion. In [3], another two adaptive versions of PQ, i.e., texture-adaptive PQ (PQt) and energy-adaptive PQ (PQe) have been presented. Through considering the local block content such as texture complexity and energy capacity, JPEG steganography with higher security performance can be obtained. In [4-6], the authors have combined quantization step with quantization error in their distortion function to improve the security performance of JPEG steganography. Besides the quantization step, Wang and Ni [7] presented a new JPEG distortion function with consideration of the block entropy, and the experimental results demonstrate that this new distortion function may lead to less detectability of steganalyzers. Recently, Huang et al. [8] presented another distortion function for JPEG steganography, which is called new PQ (NPQ). Three factors are considered, i.e., the quantization error, the quantization step and the magnitude of quantized DCT coefficients to be modified. Via nonlinearly combining these three different factors, the new distortion function, NPQ, can improve the security performance of JPEG steganography significantly as demonstrated in [8].

All the aforementioned distortion functions are employed to find the DCT coefficients that may result in less detectable distortion after modification. Generally, they are applied together with the utilization of matrix encoding (embedding) technology [9, 10]. For example, in [2] Fridrich et al. have exemplified how to implement PQ distortion function in JPEG steganography with the help of Wet paper codes [11, 12]. In [13], Kim et al. provided a simple and practical scheme to apply PQ distortion function with matrix encoding, which is based on modified binary Hamming codes [14]. This new matrix encoding strategy allows more than one embedding change in each coefficient block. Via a brute-force search, the modifications are made on those coefficients that may introduce minimal detectable distortion, and thus improving the security performance of the corresponding JPEG steganography. According to the number of allowable changing bits in each coefficient block, these modified matrix encoding (MME) schemes are called MME2, MME3, *etc.* Similar approach can also be made based on BCH (Bose, Chaudhuri and Hocquenghem) codes [14] to improve the embedding efficiency of matrix encoding as described in [4, 6, 15, 16]. However, since the decoding of BCH codes is much more complicated than Hamming codes, some specific techniques need to be adopted by the sender to reduce the time complexity and storage complexity in the embedding process. In [5], Filler *et al.* provided the syndrome-trellis codes (STCs), which can be utilized for embedding while minimizing an arbitrary additive distortion function with a performance near the theoretical bound. This new methodology can directly improve the security performance of many existing steganographic schemes, allowing them to communicate larger payloads at the same embedding distortion or to decrease the distortion for a given payload.

In this paper, we present a new framework for designing distortion functions with uncompressed side-image, which can be applied to JPEG steganography using any of the above mentioned matrix encoding strategies. In our framework, the DCT coefficients, including the direct current (DC) coefficients and all the alternating current (AC) coefficients of JPEG image are divided into two groups: first-priority group (FPG) and second-priority group (SPG). Different strategies will be established to associate the distortion values to the coefficients in FPG and SPG, respectively. Generally, the coefficients that may result in less detectable distortion in the embedding process are grouped into FPG and the rest are into SPG. Note that in our framework, all DCT coefficients are utilized for matrix encoding, and we believe that any DCT coefficient can be modified in the embedding process. In an extreme case, we can change any single coefficient in a given JPEG image and the introduced distortion will not be perceived by today's most powerful JPEG steganalyzers. Thus in our framework, no coefficient is considered as un-changeable, and any DCT coefficient can be modified if needed in the embedding process. That is also the main difference between the distortion functions generated from our framework and those previously presented in the literature. In this paper, three different scenarios for dividing the coefficients into FPG and SPG are exemplified, which can be utilized to form a series of new distortion functions. Via applying these generated distortion functions in JPEG steganography with matrix encoding, the modifications will mainly be made on those coefficients that may result in less detectable distortion in the embedding process. Thus JPEG steganography with higher security performance can be obtained.

The rest of this paper is organized as follows. In Section II, the proposed new framework is introduced. Experimental results and analysis are illustrated in Section III, and the conclusion is drawn in Section IV.

2. PROPOSED FRAMEWORK

Suppose the raw, uncompressed side-image is available to the sender. The DCT coefficients that have been divided by quantization steps and not yet rounded are called un-rounded DCT coefficients, and those that have been divided by the quantization steps and rounded are called quantized DCT coefficients, respectively. To facilitate the explanation, the existing distortion functions such as PQ [2] and NPQ [8] are referred to as ordinary distortion functions, and those to be proposed below in this paper are referred to as advanced distortion functions. To make this paper self-contained, we will introduce the PQ and NPQ distortion functions firstly.

2.1 PQ and NPQ

Without loss of generality, the quantized coefficients and un-rounded DCT coefficients utilized for data hiding are represented by $C = (c_1, c_2, \ldots, c_N)$ and $C' = (c'_1, c'_2, \ldots, c'_N)$, respectively, where N represents the number of DCT coefficients in the quantized and un-rounded coefficient sequence. The relationship between $c_i (1 \leq i \leq N)$ and $c'_i (1 \leq i \leq N)$ is as follows.

$$c_i = round(c'_i) \tag{1}$$

where $round(x)$ is a function that rounds the element x to the nearest integer. Note that in Equation (1), c_i represents the quantized DCT coefficient that is obtained in JPEG compression without secret message embedding. Suppose that while embedding the secret message the modification needs to be made on c_i, and the coefficient after being modified is represented by s_i. The PQ distortion function is represented as follows.

$$d_{c_i}^{PQ} = \left\| |c_i - c'_i| - |s_i - c'_i| \right\| \tag{2}$$

where $|x|$ is a function that returns the absolute value of the corresponding element x. For any coefficient c_i, the PQ distortion value $d_{c_i}^{PQ}$ can be computed according to Equation (2). As pointed out in [2, 13], while embedding the secret message bits, the sender should select those coefficients with minimal PQ distortion values for modification.

NPQ can be regarded as an improved version of PQ considering the quantization step and the magnitude of the quantized DCT coefficients to be modified. Suppose the quantization step associated with the coefficient c_i is q_i. According to [8], the NPQ distortion function is represented as follows.

$$d_{c_i}^{NPQ} = d_{c_i}^{PQ} \times (q_i)^{\lambda_1} / (\mu + |c_i|)^{\lambda_2} \tag{3}$$

where λ_1 and λ_2 are two parameters that are used to control the impacts caused by q_i and $|c_i|$, respectively. As recommended in [8], the two control parameters λ_1 and λ_2 can be selected in the rage of (0, 1]. The parameter μ is utilized to avoid the zero divisors in Equation (3). When NPQ is only utilized to compute the distortion value corresponding to the non-zero DCT coefficients, μ is selected as 0. Otherwise, the parameter μ can be selected as a small number, e.g., the number of 1. For any coefficient c_i, the NPQ distortion value $d_{c_i}^{NPQ}$ can be computed according to Equation (3). As pointed out in [8], while embedding the secret message bits, the sender can select those coefficients with minimal NPQ distortion values for modification to obtain JPEG steganography with high security performance.

2.2 The Proposed Distortion function

As mentioned above, in our new framework the DCT coefficients are divided into two groups: FPG and SPG. The coefficients in FPG and SPG are associated with distortion values calculated via using different strategies. Firstly, the impact caused by the modifications of coefficients in FPG and SPG are measured using some ordinary distortion functions. Secondly, those obtained distortion values associated with the coefficients in SPG are multiplied by a penalty factor, which is a big value. Thus the distortion values associated with the coefficients in FPG may be much less than that in SPG in general in our advanced distortion function. When conducting matrix encoding with some syndrome codes as in [4-8, 13, 16], several alternative solutions may be produced and those coefficients in FPG that may result in less distortion in the embedding process will take precedence for modification. Even if all the alternative solutions are restricted to those coefficients in SPG, the coefficients in SPG associated with smaller ordinary distortion values will still take precedence for modification. That is, the advanced distortion functions generated from our framework can orientate us to make as less distortion as possible in embedding the secret message bits, and thus the security performance of JPEG steganography will be improved. The proposed advanced distortion function is defined in Equation (4).

$$d_{c_i}^{ADV} = d_{c_i}^{ORD} \times (1 + \rho) \qquad (4)$$

In Equation (4), the $d_{c_i}^{ORD}$ represents the impact caused by modification operation on coefficient c_i, which is computed according to the ordinary (abbreviated as "ORD") distortion functions such as PQ, NPQ and some others. The penalty factor ρ is selected as a big value (e.g., 10^6) if the coefficient $c_i \in SPG$, otherwise it is selected as 0. According to Equation (4), for any coefficient c_i in the input image, the advanced (abbreviated as "ADV") distortion value $d_{c_i}^{ADV}$ can be easily computed.

Via applying the advanced distortion functions generated from our framework to JPEG steganography, no special processing needs to be made on those DCT coefficients with the values of +1 and -1 as that in [7, 8, 13]. Note that in [7, 8, 13], the distortion functions have only been applied on the non-zero AC DCT coefficients. If the coefficient with value of +1 or -1 is flipped to 0, the recipient will not be able to accurately locate the corresponding non-zero coefficients utilized for matrix encoding in the transmitting end, and the embedded secret message bits may not be extracted successfully. Thus special modification operation should be made by the sender on those coefficients with the quantized values of +1 and -1. For example, in [7, 8, 13] the coefficients with the quantized values of +1 and -1 can only be flipped to +2 and -2, respectively. Since the distortion functions generated from framework are applied on all the DCT coefficients, i.e., all the DCT coefficients are utilized for matrix encoding, no such special modification operation needs to be made while

applying our advanced distortion functions to JPEG steganography. For any coefficient $c_i (1 \le i \le N)$ to be modified, the operation is conducted as follows.

$$s_i = \begin{cases} c_i + 1, & \text{if } (c_i - c'_i) \le 0 \\ c_i - 1, & \text{if } (c_i - c'_i) > 0 \end{cases} \qquad (5)$$

where s_i is the coefficient after having been modified.

Furthermore, since all the DCT coefficients (including DC coefficients and numerous zero AC coefficients besides the non-zero AC coefficients) are included in our framework while applying those advanced distortion functions to JPEG steganography, the embedding efficiency (the number of bits embedded per embedding change [17]) of matrix encoding will be improved significantly. For example, if we select MME2 embedding strategy for matrix encoding, with the usage of $[2^k - 1, k] (k \ge 1)$ modified binary Hamming codes, k secret message bits can be embedded into $2^k - 1$ quantized DCT coefficients by changing at most two of them. That is, the larger the k, more efficiently the matrix encoding will be accomplished. According to [8, 9, 13], the parameter k of Hamming codes is determined by the number of secret message bits (represented by n) and the number of DCT coefficients (represented by N) utilized for matrix encoding. In general we will select the maximum k that qualifies the inequality $\dfrac{k}{2^k - 1} > \dfrac{n}{N}$. It is obviously that with embedding the same number of secret message bits, the algorithms utilizing more DCT coefficients for data hiding will result in a more efficient matrix encoding.

Note that in order to exchange the secret message bits successfully, both the sender and recipient should utilize the same coefficients to accomplish the matrix encoding. For example, in [7, 8, 13], the recipient needs to accurately locate the non-zero AC DCT that have been used in the embedding process to conduct the matrix encoding, otherwise the secret message bits cannot be extracted accurately. A special note of interest is that while applying those advanced distortion functions generated from our framework to JPEG steganography, the sender should first divide all the DCT coefficients into FPG and SPG. However, the sender does not need to share the dividing scenario with the recipient, since they (i.e., the sender and recipient) both use all the DCT coefficients to conduct matrix encoding. The recipient does not need to locate the DCT coefficients in FPG or SFG in the receiving end, and he/she can exchange the secret message with the sender easily via selecting the same matrix encoding strategy.

2.3 Three Different Scenarios for Dividing FPG and SPG

The statistics of DCT coefficients are complicated and they may interact with each other while being modified. Moreover the statistics of DCT coefficients may also have a close relationship with the secret message bits to be embedded, and the type of embedding operation that modifies the coefficients, *etc.* It is not easy to derive an optimal strategy for dividing the coefficients into FPG and SPG. However, a series of suboptimal scenarios can be found easily.

In the following, three scenarios for dividing the coefficients into FPG and SPG are exemplified. Scenario 1 is a simple and direct way. Its separation performance may not be as good as the following two scenarios. However, our experiments in next section will demonstrate that with appropriate selection of the ordinary distortion function, high secure performance can still be obtained. The fundamental idea of the next two scenarios is that in the texture area of a carrier image more coefficients will be divided into FPG, and in the flat area fewer coefficients will be divided into FPG. In Scenario 2, the first-priority and second-priority coefficients are classified according to the statistics of coefficients in DCT domain. In Scenario 3, the coefficients are divided into FPG and SPG with resorting to the statistics of JPEG image in spatial domain.

Scenario 1: The AC DCT coefficients are considered as first-priority coefficients, and the DC DCT coefficients are classified as the second-priority coefficients.

Scenario 2: Compute the standard deviation $D_i(1 \leq i \leq N)$ of the quantized AC DCT coefficients in each 8×8 block of JPEG image, where N represents the total number of 8×8 blocks in JPEG image. The average value of all the standard deviations is $\overline{D} = \dfrac{1}{N} \sum_{i=1}^{N} D_i$, and the maximum value among all the standard deviations is $D_{max} = \max(D_1, D_2, \ldots, D_N)$. In each block, the number of AC DCT coefficients that belongs to FPG is computed as follows.

$$A_i = \begin{cases} 1, & \text{if } D_i < \dfrac{1}{32}\overline{D} \\ \left\lfloor \dfrac{1}{2} \times 64 \times (D_i / \overline{D}) \right\rfloor, & \text{if } \dfrac{1}{32}\overline{D} \leq D_i < \overline{D} \\ \left\lfloor \dfrac{1}{2} \times 64 \times (1 + D_i / D_{max}) \right\rfloor, & \text{if } \overline{D} \leq D_i < D_{max} \\ 63, & \text{if } \overline{D} = D_{max} \end{cases} \quad (6)$$

where $A_i(1 \leq i \leq N)$ represents the number of AC DCT coefficients that should be divided in FPG in each 8×8 block, and $\lfloor x \rfloor$ is a function that rounds the element x to its nearest integer less than or equal to x.

In Equation (6), the number 64 represents that there are 64 DCT coefficients in each 8×8 block. As we pointed above, any DCT coefficient can be modified, and we can change any single coefficient in a given JPEG image in the embedding process. Other methods for dividing the coefficients into FPG and SPG may still work, e.g., we can change the number 32 to 31 or 30 in Equation (6), and the obtained distortion function may still result in JPEG steganography with high security performance. Here, we only try to illustrate the applicability of our framework and do not try to make a clear boundary between FPG and SPG.

Scenario 3: Compute the standard deviation $P_i(1 \leq i \leq N)$ of pixel values in each 8×8 block of the decompressed JPEG image,

where N represents the total number of 8×8 blocks in JPEG image. The average value of all the standard deviations is $\overline{P} = \dfrac{1}{N} \sum_{i=1}^{N} P_i$, and the maximum value among all the standard deviations is $P_{max} = \max(P_1, P_2, \ldots, P_N)$. In each block, the number of AC DCT coefficients that belongs to FPG is computed as follows.

$$B_i = \begin{cases} 1, & \text{if } P_i < \dfrac{1}{32}\overline{P} \\ \left\lfloor \dfrac{1}{2} \times 64 \times (P_i / \overline{P}) \right\rfloor, & \text{if } \dfrac{1}{32}\overline{P} \leq P_i < \overline{P} \\ \left\lfloor \dfrac{1}{2} \times 64 \times (1 + P_i / P_{max}) \right\rfloor, & \text{if } \overline{P} \leq P_i < P_{max} \\ 63, & \text{if } \overline{P} = P_{max} \end{cases} \quad (7)$$

where $B_i(1 \leq i \leq N)$ represents the number of AC DCT coefficients that should be divided in FPG in each 8×8 block.

As seen, the philosophy for choosing the first-priority coefficients in Equation (7) is similar to that in Equation (6). Differently, in Scenario 3 the DCT coefficients are divided into FPG and SPG according to the statistical characteristics of JPEG image in spatial domain. Since decompressing the JPEG image is a nonlinear process (including de-quantization and rounding process [18]), the selected first-priority coefficients in Scenario 3 will be different from that in Scenario 2. In Scenario 3, the $B_i(1 \leq i \leq N)$ first-priority coefficients in each block are also selected according to the *zig-zag* scanning order, and the rest AC and DC coefficients are considered as second-priority coefficients.

In this section, we have introduced two ordinary distortion functions and exemplified three different dividing scenarios. According to Equation (4), six different advanced distortion functions can be generated via combining those different ordinary distortion functions and dividing scenarios. Note that the framework proposed in this paper is an open system. Firstly, PQ, NPQ and any other ordinary distortion function can be used on our framework. For instance, in Equation (4) the superscript "ORD" stands for the ordinary distortion function. Secondly, more advanced scenarios for splitting the DCT coefficients into FPG and SPG can also be used in our framework. For example, if the more advanced scenario is found, the FPG and SPG in Equation (4) may be updated accordingly.

3. EXPERIMENTAL RESULTS
In this section, experimental results and analysis are presented to demonstrate the efficiency of our proposed framework. The test image set consists of 10000 uncompressed images which are downloaded from the BOSSBase image dataset [19]. All the images are with the size of 512×512. In the following, the uncompressed image is called input image and the JPEG compressed image without any message embedding is called cover image. The cover and stego images are created using the same JPEG encoder [20], and the quality factor is selected as 75 in all of our testing. The secret message bits are randomly

generated, and the embedding rates are represented in terms of *bpac* (bits per non-zero quantized AC DCT coefficients) values.

The efficiency of our proposed distortion functions is tested with three state-of-the-art feature-based steganalyzers, which are called CC-PEV (Cartesian-calibrated Pevný) [21], SPAM (subtractive pixel adjacency matrix) [22] and CDF (cross domain feature) [23], respectively. The 548-dimensional CC-PEV feature vector is mainly extracted from JPEG domain, which is extended to twice its size by Cartesian calibration from the 274 feature vector designed for JPEG images [24]. The 686-dimensional SPAM feature vector is extracted from spatial domain, which is the second-order Markov model of pixel differences. Through combing the CC-PEV and SPAM feature vector, we can get the 1,234-dimensional CDF feature vector. Those feature vectors or their improved versions are popularly utilized [25-28] in detecting the classical algorithms such as F5 [5] and MB1 [29], and some modern steganographic schemes [30-33]. Since the CDF feature vector is extracted in cross domain, it may have better detection performance than CC-PEV and SPAM in general.

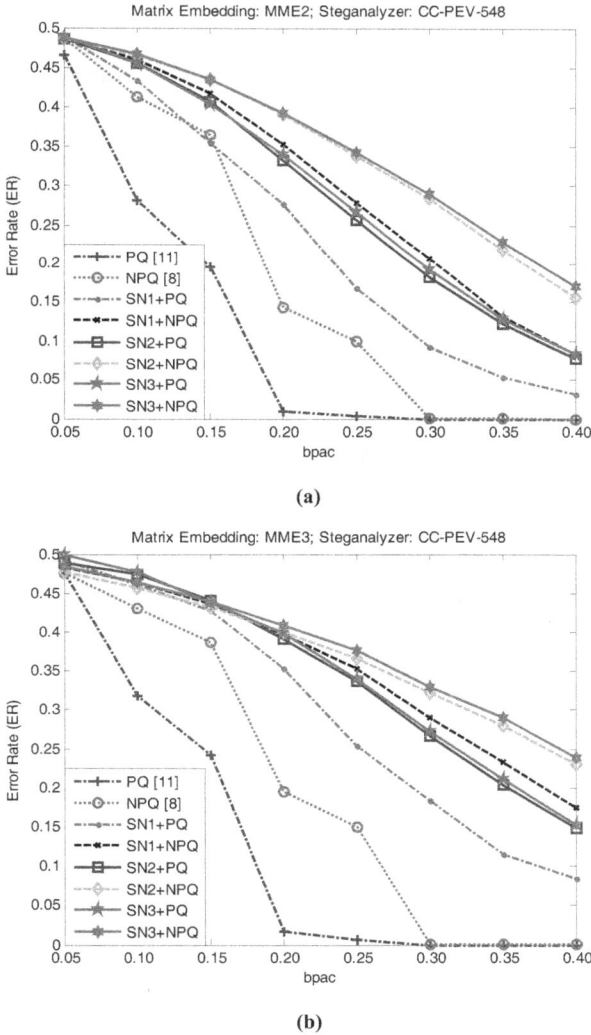

The ensemble classifier presented in [34] is employed in our testing with default parameters. It is a fully automatic framework with an efficient utilization of out-of-bag (OOB) error estimates for stopping criterion. As pointed out in [25], the proposed ensemble classifier consists of a lot of base learners independently trained on a set of cover and stego images. The decision threshold of each base learner is adjusted to minimize the total detection error under equal priors on the training set:

$$P_E = \min_{P_{FA}} \frac{1}{2}(P_{FA} + P_{MD}(P_{FA})) \qquad (8)$$

where P_{FA}, P_{MD} are the probabilities of false alarms and missed detection, respectively.

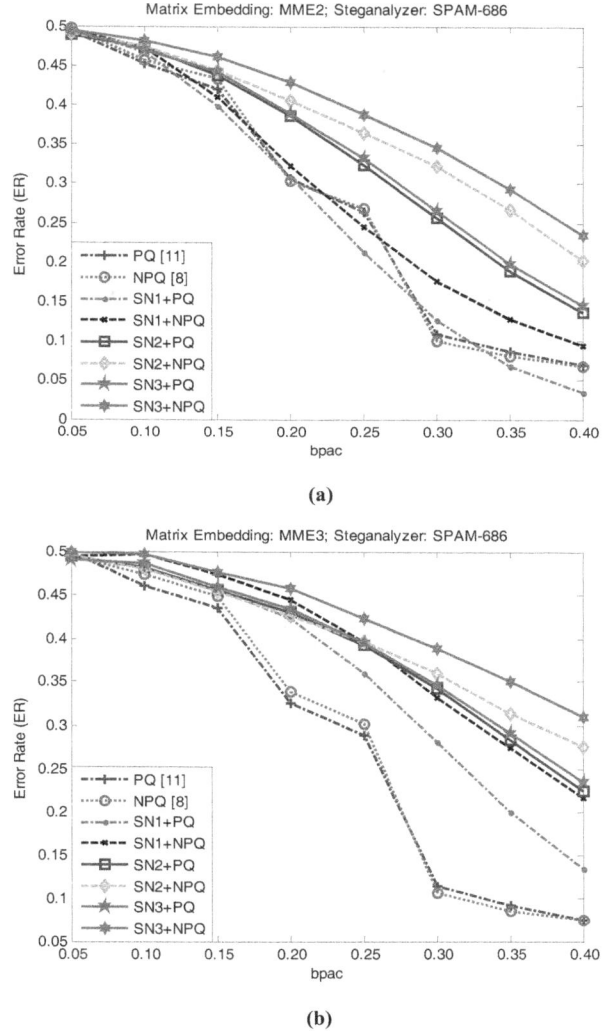

(a)

(b)

Fig. 2 The detection error rates with the steganalyzer SPAM-686. (a) MME2 embedding strategy. (b) MME3 embedding strategy.

(a)

(b)

Fig. 1 The detection error rates with the steganalyzer CC-PEV-548. (a) MME2 embedding strategy. (b) MME3 embedding strategy.

Firstly, we have applied the advanced distortion functions to JPEG steganography with MME2 and MME3 embedding strategies for a detail comparison. The PQ and NPQ are selected as the ordinary distortion functions for a demonstration. In Section 2.3, we have exemplified three scenarios for dividing the DCT coefficients into FPG and SPG. The algorithms resulted from different dividing scenarios (abbreviated as "SN") and ordinary distortion functions are represented as "SN1+PQ", "SN1+NPQ", "SN2+PQ" "SN2+NPQ", "SN3+PQ", "SN3+NPQ", respectively. The original PQ and NPQ distortion functions are applied with MME2 and MME3 embedding strategies as in [8, 13]. Totally there are sixteen different steganographic schemes. Half of them are conducted with MME2 embedding strategy, and the other half are conducted with MME3 embedding strategy. Note that in all our testing, the two control parameters of NPQ are selected as $(\lambda_1 = 0.5, \lambda_2 = 0.2)$.

The detection error rates (ERs) corresponding to the three steganalyzers CC-PEV, SPAM, and CDF are illustrated in Figs. 1, 2 and 3, respectively. In these three figures, the horizontal axes represent the *bpac* values, and the vertical axes represent the detection error rates. For the aforementioned sixteen steganographic schemes, the embedding rates are increased from 0.05 *bpac* to 0.40 *bpac* with the step size of 0.05. The embedding strategy and the steganalyzer with the dimension size of feature vector are illustrated in the title of each figure.

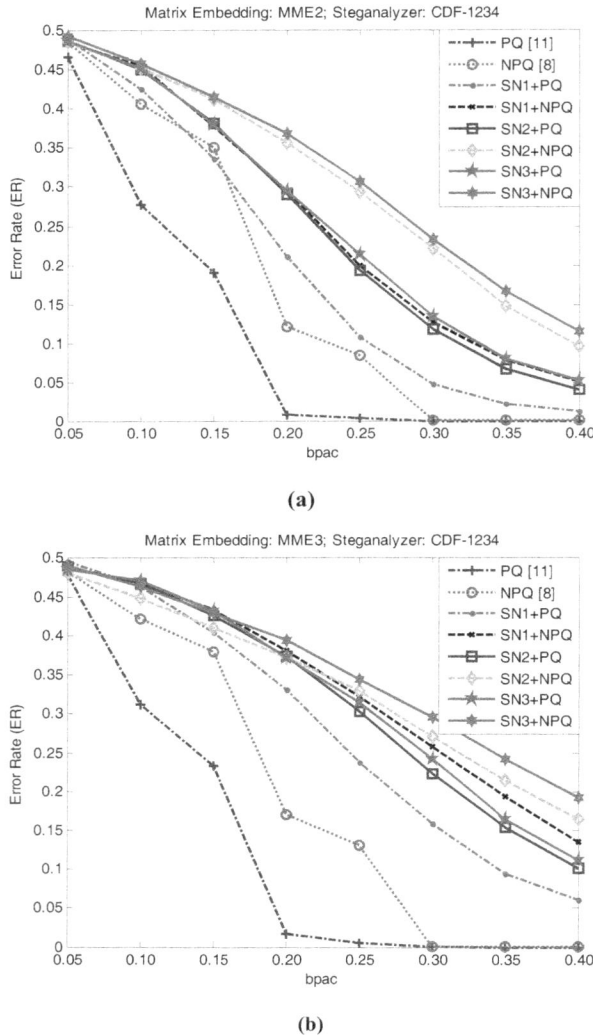

(a)

(b)

Fig. 3 The detection error rates with the steganalyzer CDF-1234. (a) MME2 embedding strategy. (b) MME3 embedding strategy.

It is observed from Figs. 1, 2 and 3 that whichever dividing scenario or ordinary distortion function is selected, the security performance of the obtained JPEG steganography may be greatly improved under the guidance of those distortion functions generated from our framework. Our experimental results also demonstrate that the selection of dividing scenarios and ordinary distortion functions may have great importance in our framework. Different dividing scenarios and ordinary distortion functions may result in JPEG steganography with different security performance. As seen, with using the same ordinary distortion function, JPEG steganography resulted from Scenario 2 and Scenario 3 may have higher security performance than that from Scenario 1. With adopting the same dividing scenario, PQ and NPQ may result in JPEG steganography with different security performance too. Fortunately, via using our proposed framework, the different dividing scenarios and ordinary distortion functions can easily be combined to form efficient advanced distortion functions, even though the dividing scenarios and ordinary distortion functions are not optimal.

Secondly, in order to demonstrate the universality of our proposed framework, we have applied those generated distortion functions to JPEG steganography with STC. The Wang and Ni's method [7] has also been conducted for a comparison, which is one of the most secure JPEG steganographic schemes with using STC. The steganalyzer CDF is selected for testing, and the experimental results are shown in Fig. 4. The horizontal axes represent the *bpac* values, the vertical axes represent the detection error rates, and the distortion functions are shown on the legend. As seen, when the embedding rate is no more than 0.25 *bpac*, all the steganographic schemes resulted from our proposed and Wang and Ni's method have the similar security performance, and the obtained detection accuracy rates are near random guessing. However, with the increasing of embedding rate, the JPEG steganographic schemes resulted from our proposed distortion function may have much better security performance than that resulted from Wang and Ni's method. Via comparing Fig. 4 and Fig. 3, we can also find out that via using more efficient embedding strategy, the security performance of JPEG steganography resulted from our advanced distortion function can be improved further.

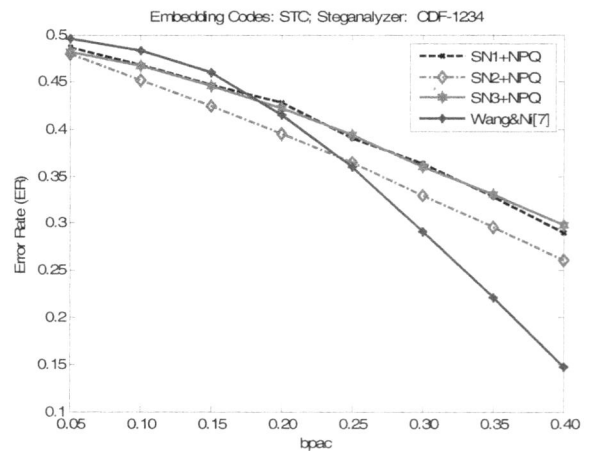

Fig. 4 The efficiency of our proposed framework with using STC.

4. CONCLUSIONS

In this paper, we have presented a new framework for designing distortion functions of JPEG steganography with uncompressed side-image, and a series of advanced distortion functions that may result in high secure JPEG steganography are exemplified. Note that our proposed framework is an open system. It will not be constrained to the aforementioned dividing scenarios and ordinary distortion functions. Other dividing scenarios and ordinary distortion functions can be adopted easily in our framework to form a series of new distortion functions.

5. ACKNOWLEDGEMENTS

This work was supported by the National Natural Science Foundation of China (61173147, U1135001), the 973 Program of China (2011CB302204), the Key Projects in the National Science & Technology Pillar Program (2012BAK16B06), the Fundamental Research Funds for Central Universities (12lgpy31), and the Project Sponsored by the Scientific Research Foundation for the Returned Overseas Chinese Scholars, State Education Ministry ([2012]1707).

6. REFERENCES

[1] J. Fridrich, P. Lisoněk and D. Soukal, "On Steganographic embedding efficiency," in *Proc. Information Hiding Workshop* 2006, *LNCS* 4437, pp. 282-296, 2007

[2] J. Fridrich, M. Goljan and D. Soukal, "Perturbed quantization steganography with wet paper codes," in *Proc. the ACM Workshop on Multimedia & Security*, Magdeburg, Germany, September 20-21, pp. 4-15, 2004.

[3] J. Fridrich, T. Pevný and J. Kodovský, "Statistically undetectable JPEG steganography: dead ends, challenges, and opportunities," in *Proc. the ACM Workshop on Multimedia and Security*, Dallas, Texas, September 20-21, pp. 3-14, 2007.

[4] V. Sachnev, H. J. Kim, and R. Zhang, "Less detectable JPEG steganography method based on heuristic optimization and BCH syndrome coding," in *Proc. the ACM Workshop on Multimedia & Security*, Princeton, New Jersey, Sep. 7-9, pp. 131–140, 2009.

[5] T. Filler, J. Judas, and J. Fridrich, "Minimizing additive distortion in steganography using Syndrome-Trellis Codes," *IEEE Transactions on Information Forensics and Security*, vol. 6, no. 3, pp. 920-935, 2010.

[6] V. Sachnev, H. J. Kim, "Modified BCH data hiding scheme for JPEG steganography," *Eurasip Journal on advances in signal processing*, vol. 2012, no. 1, pp. 89-98, 2012

[7] C. Wang, J. Ni, "An efficient JPEG steganographic scheme based on block-entropy of DCT coefficients," in *Proc. of IEEE ICASSP*, Kyoto, Japan, Mar. 25-30, pp. 1785-1788, 2012

[8] F. Huang, J. Huang, and Y. Q. Shi, "New channel selection rule for JPEG steganography," *IEEE Trans. Information Forensics and Security*, vol. 7, no. 4, pp. 1181-1191, 2012.

[9] R. Crandall, "Some notes on steganography", Posted on Steganography Mailing List, 1998. http://os.inf.tu-dresden.de/~westfeld/crandall.pdf

[10] A. Westfeld, "High capacity despite better steganalysis (F5-a steganographic algorithm)", in *Proc. Information Hiding, 4th International Workshop*, volume 2137 of *Lecture Notes in Computer Science*, pp. 289-302, 2001.

[11] J. Fridrich, M. Goljan, P. Lisoněk, and D. Soukal, "Writing on wet paper," *IEEE Trans. Signal Processing*, vol. 53, no. 10, pp. 3923-3935, 2005.

[12] J. Fridrich, M. Goljan and D. Soukal, "Wet paper codes with improved embedding efficiency," *IEEE Trans. Information Forensics and Security*, vol. 1, no. 1, pp. 102-110, 2006.

[13] Y. Kim, Z. Duric and D. Richards, "Modified matrix encoding technique for minimal distortion steganography," in *Proc. Information Hiding Workshop 2006, LNCS* 4437, pp. 314-327, 2007.

[14] T. K. Moon, *Error Correction Coding, Mathematical Methods and Algorithms*. Hoboken, NJ: Wiley, 2005.

[15] D. Schönfeld, A. Winkler, "Embedding with syndrome coding based on BCH codes," in *Proc. the ACM Workshop on Multimedia & Security*, Geneva, Switzerland, Sep. 26-27, pp. 214–223, 2006

[16] R. Zhang, V. Sachnev, and H. J. Kim, "Fast BCH syndrome coding for steganography," in *Proc. Information Hiding Workshop 2009, LNCS* 5806, pp. 48-58, 2009.

[17] J. Fridrich, and D. Soukal, "Matrix embedding for large payloads," *IEEE Trans. Information Forensics and Security*, vol. 1, no. 3, pp. 390-395, 2006.

[18] F. Huang, J. Huang, and Y. Q. Shi, "Detecting double JPEG compression with the same quantization matrix," *IEEE Trans. Information Forensics and Security*, vol. 5, no. 4, pp. 848-856, 2010.

[19] T. Filler, T. Pevny, and P. Bas. BOSS (Break Our Steganography System). http://www.agents.cz/boss, July 2010.

[20] P. Shllee, Matlab JPEG Toolbox [Online]. Available: http://www.philsallee.com/jpegtbx/index.html

[21] J. Kodovský and J. Fridrich, "Calibration revisited," in *Proc. the ACM Multimedia & Security Workshop*, Princeton, New Jersey, Sep. 7-9, pp. 63-74, 2009.

[22] T. Pevný, P. Bas, ad J. Fridrich, "Steganalysis by subtractive pixel adjacency matrix," *IEEE Trans. Information Forensics and Security*, vol. 52, no. 2, pp. 215-224, 2010

[23] J. Kodovský, T. Pevný, and J. Fridrich, "Modern steganalysis can detect YASS," in *Proc. SPIE, Electronic Imaging, Security Forensics of Multimedia XII*, San Jose, California, Jan. 17–21, 2010, vol. 7541, pp. 0201–0211.

[24] T. Pevný and J. Fridrich, "Merging Markov and DCT features for multi-class JPEG steganalysis," in *Proc. SPIE Electronic Imaging, Security, Steganography, and Watermarking of Multimedia Contents IX*, San Jose, California, Jan. 28 - Feb. 1, 2007, vol. 6505, pp. 03.1-03.13

[25] F. Huang, J. Huang, and Y. Q. Shi, "An experimental study on the security performance of YASS," *IEEE Trans. Information Forensics and Security*, vol. 5, no. 3, pp. 374-380, 2010.

[26] J. Kodovský and J. Fridrich, "Steganalysis of JPEG images using rich models," in *Proc. SPIE, Electronic Imaging,*

Media Watermarking, Security, and Forensics of Multimedia XIV, San Francisco, CA, Jan. 23–25, 2012, vol. 8303, pp. A-1-A-13.

[27] J. Fridrich and J. Kodovský, "Rich models for steganalysis of digital images," *IEEE Trans. Information Forensics and Security,* vol. 7, no. 3, pp. 868-882, 2012.

[28] Q. Liu , A. Sung, and M. Qiao, "Neighboring joint density-based JPEG Steganalysis," *ACM Transactions on Intelligent Systems and Technology*, vol. 2, no. 2, pp. 1-16, 2011.

[29] P. Sallee, "Model based methods for steganography and steganalysis," *International Journal of Image Graphics*, vol. 5, no. 1, pp. 167-190, 2005.

[30] W. Luo, F. Huang, and J. Huang, "Edge adaptive image steganography based on LSB matching revisited," *IEEE Trans. Information Forensics and Security,* vol. 5, no. 2, pp. 201-214, 2010.

[31] T. Pevný, T. Filler, and P. Bas, "Using high-dimensional image models to perform highly undetectable steganography," in *Proc. Information Hiding Workshop 2010, LNCS* 6387, pp. 161–177, 2010

[32] K. Solanki, A. Sarkar, and B. S. Manjunath, "YASS: Yet another steganographic scheme that resists blind steganalysis," in *Proc. Information Hiding Workshop 2007, LNCS 4567*, pp. 16-31, 2007.

[33] A. Sarkar, K. Solanki, and B. S. Manjunath, "Further study on YASS: Steganography based on randomized embedding to resist blind steganalysis," in *Proc. SPIE Electronic Imaging, Security, Steganography, and Watermarking of Multimedia Contents IX*, 2008, vol. 6819, pp. 17.1–17.11.

[34] J. Kodovský, J. Fridrich and V. Holub, "Ensemble calssifiers for steganalysis of digital media," *IEEE Trans. Information Forensics and Security*, vol. 2, no. 7, pp. 432-444, 2012

Embedding Change Rate Estimation based on Ensemble Learning

Zhenyu Li[*]
State Key Laboratory of
Mathematical Engineering and
Advanced Computing
Zhengzhou 450002, China
zheenyuli@gmail.com

Zongyun Hu
Zhengzhou Institute of
Information Science and
Technology
Zhengzhou 450002, China
zongyunhu@126.com

Xiangyang Luo[†]
State Key Laboratory of
Information Security,
Institute of Information
Engineering,Chinese
Academy of Sciences
Beijing 100093,China
xiangyangluo@126.com

Bin Lu
Zhengzhou Institute of
Information Science and
Technology
Zhengzhou 450002, China
stoneclever@gmail.com

ABSTRACT

In order to achieve higher estimation accuracy of the embedding change rate of a stego object, an ensemble learning-based estimation method is presented. First of all, a framework of embedding change rate estimation based on estimator ensemble is proposed. Then an algorithm of building the estimator ensemble, the core of the framework, is concretely described. Finally, a pruning method for estimator ensemble is proposed in consideration of both the diversity among the base estimators and accuracy of each of them. The experimental results for three modern steganographic algorithms (nsF5, PQ and PQt) indicate that the proposed method acquired better performance than the existed typical method. Furthermore, the pruned estimator ensemble with less base estimators maintained, even slightly improved the estimation accuracy, compared to the one without purning.

Categories and Subject Descriptors

I.4.9 [**Computing Methodologies**]: Image Processing and Computer Vision—*Applications*

---

[*]Zhenyu Li is also a graduate student at Zhengzhou Institute of Information Science and Technology.

[†]Xiangyang Luo, the corresponding author, is also an Associate Professor at Zhengzhou Institute of Information Science and Technology.

IH&MMSec'13, June 17–19, 2013, Montpellier, France.
Copyright 2013 ACM 978-1-4503-2081-8/13/06 ...$15.00.

General Terms

Algorithms, Design, Security

Keywords

Quantitative steganalysis, embedding change, ensemble learning, ensemble pruning, steganography

1. INTRUCTION

Steganography makes communication behavior invisible by embedding secret messages into texts, images, audio, video or other digital files. The research of steganalysis contains not only the detection of the presence of secret message, but also quantitative steganalysis, that is estimation of secret message length or embedding change rate. Compared to detecting the presence of secret message, more attached information will be gained by quantitative steganalysis.

The early study of quantitative steganalysis required full knowledge of the steganographic algorithms. The steganalysts need to analyze a steganographic algorithm in detail, so that they might design a quantitative steganalysis method specifically for it. Many typical quantitative steganalysis methods were developed in this way, for instance, the RS (Regular Singular) [9] and SPA (Sample Pair Analysis) [6] methods for LSB (Least Significant Bit) replacement in spatial domain, JPairs [24] for Jsteg (LSB replacement for JPEG images). However, there are still few specific quantitative steganalyzers for the modern steganographic algorithms with higher security, such as nsF5 (no-shrinkage F5) [11], PQ (Perturbed Quantization) [10] steganagraphy, PQt (texture-adaptive PQ) [11] and many others. It is interesting that the secret messages embedded by these steganographic algorithms can be reliably detected using blind detectors. Noticing this, Penvý et al. [22] made a breakthrough by applying the features, previously only utilized in blind steganalysis, to quantitative steganalysis with a statistical learning technique, regression. In their method, regression is used to learn the quantitative relationship between the feature vectors and the embedding change rates on a training set, and then a change rate estimator is explicitly constructed. Their estimators acquired good performance for several steganographic algorithms, especially the ones for JPEG images.

This paper presents an embedding change rate estimation method based on ensemble learning. In the framework of the method, the final estimation result is the combination of the results generated by multiple base estimators in the ensemble. As for the estimator ensemble construction algorithm, firstly, multiple training sets were generated with the help of random subspace and bootstrap methods. Subsequently, each base estimator is trained by the SVR (Support Vector Regression) with Gaussian kernel on one training set. Finally, the base estimators are combined with the same weight forming the estimator ensemble. In addition, aiming at reducing the computational complexity of the estimation, the ensemble is pruned in consideration of both the diversity among the base estimators and accuracy of each of them. The experimental results indicate that the embedding change rate estimation method proposed in this paper has a higher estimation accuracy than the existed typical method for three steganographic algorithms, namely nsF5, PQ and PQt. Furthermore, the pruned estimator ensemble with less base estimators maintained, even slightly improved the estimation accuracy, compared with the one without purning.

2. THE FRAMEWORK OF EMBEDDING CHANGE RATE ESTIMATION

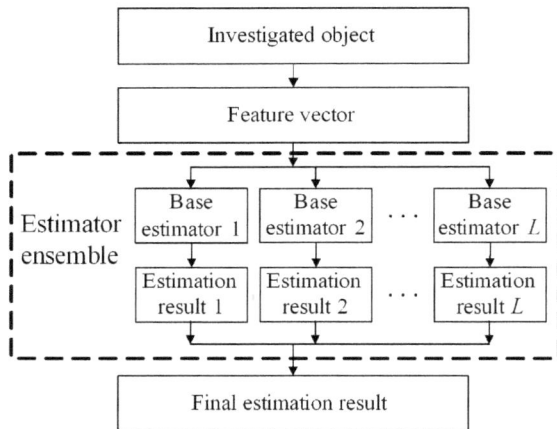

Figure 1: The framework of the estimation method

It is well known that with the help of ensemble methods, better generalization ability will be achieved. Kodovský et al.[16] developed an ensemble of FLD (Fisher Linear Discriminant) for detecting the presence of secret message. Inspired by their work, here we present an embedding change rate estimation method based on ensemble learning, whose core is an ensemble of multiple base estimators. As illustrated in Figure 1, the feature vector that extracted from the investigated object, for instance, a digital image, will be the input of the estimator ensemble. Using different subvectors

of the feature vector, multiple base estimators generate independent estimation results. The output of the estimator ensemble, the final estimation result, is the weighted combination of the results from multiple base estimators. Note that embedding change rate denotes the number of embedding modifications divided by the number of cover elements.

3. THE CONSTRUCTION OF ESTIMATOR ENSEMBLE

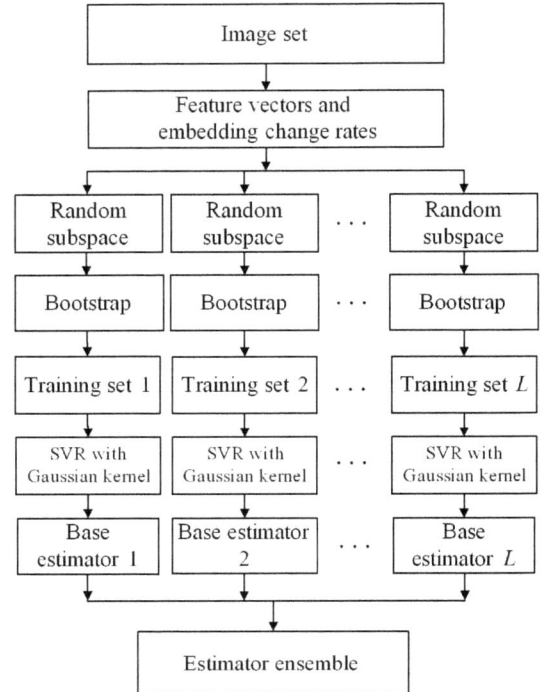

Figure 2: The construction of estimator ensemble

The construction procedure of the ensemble is illustrated in Figure 2. Although the method is explained on the example of digital images, but it can be readily applied to other digital media objects, such as audio or video files. Usually, the training image set is constructed by the steganalysts who embed certain length of messages into the images, so that the change rate will be known. The feature vectors which consist of a lot of statistics of the images along with corresponding embedding change rates are the samples. Then, it randomly selects the subspace from the feature space and resamples the instances with replacement to form the multiple training sets. Furthermore, L base estimators are trained by SVR with Gaussian kernel on the training sets independently. Finally, the L base estimators are weighted combined forming the estimator ensemble.

3.1 Generation of the training sets

The sample set is derived from the training image set. Extracting the feature vector from an image can be captured with a mapping $\mathbf{g} : \mathcal{C} \mapsto \mathrm{R}^m$ from the space of training image set, $\mathcal{C}$, to a m-dimensional Euclidean feature space. The sample set $\mathcal{D} = \{(\mathbf{x}_i, y_i) | i = 1, ..., N\}$ is developed from the training image set which consists of N images, where

$\mathbf{x}_i = \mathbf{g}(c_i) = (\mathrm{x}_{1_i}, \mathrm{x}_{2_i}, ..., \mathrm{x}_{m_i}) \in \mathrm{R}^m$ denotes the feature vector computed from the image with the embedding change rate $y_i \in [0,1]$.

Multiple training sets are fundamental to the base estimators. The generation of the training sets is based on random subspace and bootstrap methods. Positive correlation has been demonstrated between the diversity among the base estimators and accuracy of ensemble in practice [5, 12, 17]. Furthermore, it is already known that the random subspace [13] and bootstrap methods [7] widely used in ensemble learning can increase the diversity among the base learners.

As the generation processes are similar, here we take the l-th training set for example. To begin with, a m_{sub}-dimensional feature subspace $\mathbb{R}^{|\theta_l|}$, where $\theta_l \subset \{1, 2, ..., m\}$, $|\theta_l| = m_{sub} < m$, is randomly selected from the original m-dimensional feature space. Then a sample set $\mathcal{D}^{(\theta_l)} = \{(\mathbf{x}_i^{(\theta_l)}, y_i) | i = 1, ..., N\}$ is obtained, where $\mathbf{x}_i^{(\theta_l)} \in \mathbb{R}^{|\theta_l|}$ is the feature vector of the i-th image with components in the subspace and $y_i \in [0,1]$ is the corresponding embedding change rate. Afterward, a bootstrap replicate $\mathcal{D}_b^{(\theta_l)} = \{(\mathbf{x}_i^{(\theta_l)}, y_i) | i = 1, ..., N\}$ is formed by uniformly resampling with replacement from set $\mathcal{D}^{(\theta_l)}$, and it is just the training set for the l-th base estimator.

3.2 Training of multiple base estimators

The training of base estimator is solving a regression problem. Functions $f_l : \mathbb{R}^{|\theta_l|} \mapsto [0,1]$, where $l = 1, 2, ..., L$, reflects the quantitative relationship between feature vector $\mathbf{x}_i^{(\theta_l)}$ and the embedding change rate $y_i \in [0,1]$. The l-th base estimator $\hat{f}_l$ is an approximation to the function f_l, that minimizes the error on $\mathcal{D}_b^{(\theta_l)} = \{(\mathbf{x}_i^{(\theta_l)}, y_i) | i = 1, ..., N\}$, or

$$\hat{f}_l = \arg \min_{f_l \in \mathcal{F}} \frac{1}{N} \sum_{i=1}^{N} e(f_l(\mathbf{x}_i^{(\theta_l)}), y_i), \qquad (1)$$

where $e(\hat{y}, y)$ is an error function (also called a loss function) measuring the error between the true value y and the estimated value $\hat{y}$, and $\mathcal{F}$ is a properly selected class of functions.

In solving the regression problem mentioned above, the choice of error function $e(\hat{y}, y)$ and function class $\mathcal{F}$ will influence the accuracy of the base estimators. We choose the SVR with Gaussian kernel, where the loss function is ϵ-insensitive function, to train multiple base estimators, because this learning technique can learn the complicated nonlinear relationships. Besides, the experimental results in [22] showed that the estimators trained by the SVR with Gaussian kernel had better performance than the ones trained by the ordinary linear least squares regression for most steganographic algorithms. As SVR is widely used in machine learning, there is no need to introduce the basic principle of it here. For the details of SVR we refer to [23].

Three hyper-parameters need to be set before the training of the base estimators: the penalization parameter C, the width of the Gaussian kernel γ, and the insensitivity of the loss function ϵ. In consideration of the significant influence of the hyper-parameters on the generalization performance, a search for the optimal hyper-parameters is commonly needed.

After the training process, the estimator ensemble is weighted combined by multiple base estimators. The finally generated estimator ensemble is

$$\hat{f} = \sum_{l=1}^{L} w_l \hat{f}_l, \qquad (2)$$

where $0 \leq w_l \leq 1, \sum_{l=1}^{L} w_l = 1$. In implementation of the algorithm, we use the simple and low computational complexity fusion method, averaging, that is combining multiple base estimators with the same weight.

This algorithm of building an estimator ensemble is named EN-SVR and summarized in Algorithm 1.

Algorithm 1 The EN-SVR algorithm.

Input:

    Training image set, $\mathcal{C}$;

    Embedding change rates of the images in training image set, $\mathbf{y}$;

    Feature extraction function, $\mathbf{g}$;

    Number of base estimator, L;

    Dimensionality of the feature subspace, m_{sub}.

Output: Estimator ensemble, $\hat{f}$.

1: extract the feature vectors from the images in training image set, $\mathbf{x} = \mathbf{g}(\mathcal{C})$;

2: label the feature vectors with corresponding change rate, $\mathcal{D} = (\mathbf{x}, \mathbf{y})$;

3: generate $\mathcal{D}^{(\theta_l)}$ by randomly selecting m_{sub}-dimensional subspace;

4: create bootstrap sample set, $\mathcal{D}_b^{(\theta_l)}$, by uniformly resampling $\mathcal{D}^{(\theta_l)}$ with replacement;

5: obtain a base estimator $\hat{f}_l$ trained by SVR with Gaussian kernel on $\mathcal{D}_b^{(\theta_l)}$;

6: go to step 3 until L base estimators are generated;

7: $\hat{f} = \frac{1}{L} \sum_{l=1}^{L} \hat{f}_l$;

---

4. ENSEMBLE PRUNING

Apparently, with the large volume of digital data transmitted through various channels, reducing the computational complexity is of great importance to making the steganalysis practically feasible in the real world. With respect to the embedding change rate estimation using the estimator ensemble, a smaller number of base estimator will of course lead to a lower computational complexity of the estimation process. Many studies [26, 3, 1, 25, 18] in the ensemble learning have shown that the performance could be maintained, even improved by merely using part of the independently built base estimators as an ensemble. The selection process of the base estimators can be viewed as pruning the ensemble.

In this paper, a variant of diversity regularized ensemble pruning method [18] is proposed to prune the estimator ensemble. During the pruning process, two factors are considered, the accuracy of the base estimators and the diversity among them. Before the pruning, two parameters need to be set. One is the tradeoff parameter, q, for finding a counterbalance between the accuracy and the diversity. The other one is the number of base estimator L' in the pruned ensemble. To begin with, it initializes the set P, which consists of the base estimators to be selected, with the base estimator that has the highest accuracy. Entering the loop, it sorts the base estimators outside the set P in the descending order of their differences with the set P and obtains the sequence S. Then, it selects the most accurate base estimator from the first $\lceil q \cdot |S| \rceil$ base estimators of S and puts it into set P. The iteration will be stopped until the size of set P reaches L'. Finally, the pruned estimator ensemble consists of the base estimators in the set P.

We have to note that the measurements of the accuracy and the diversity are not the same as the ones in [18]. In the proposed method, the accuracy of the base estimator is reflected on the OOB (Out Of Bag) error. As the bootstrap method resamples with replacement,there will be some instances not included in the bootstrap sample, and these instances form the OOB sample set $\mathcal{D}_{oob}^{(\theta_l)}$, that is $\mathcal{D}_{oob}^{(\theta_l)} = \mathcal{D}^{(\theta_l)} - \mathcal{D}_b^{(\theta_l)}$. OOB error is the estimation error of the base estimator on the OOB sample set. Here we use the squared-error loss function, and the OOB error of the l-th base estimator is

$$E_l = \frac{1}{N_l} \sum_{i=1}^{N_l} (y_i - \hat{f}_l(\mathbf{x}_i^{(\theta_l)}))^2, \qquad (3)$$

where $(\mathbf{x}_i^{(\theta_l)}, y_i) \in \mathcal{D}_{oob}^{(\theta_l)}$, $N_l = \left| \mathcal{D}_{oob}^{(\theta_l)} \right| < N$.

To measure the diversity among base estimators, we assume that the difference between two base estimators has positive correlation with the difference between the two subspaces that selected in forming the corresponding training sets. The different subspaces convey various statistics of the images and lead to different training sets. Obviously, the base estimator varies with its training set, so the assumption above is likely to be satisfied. In the implementation, we use the difference between two subspaces to approximate the difference between the two base estimator, that is

$$\text{DIFF}(\hat{f}_i, \hat{f}_j) \approx diff(\theta_i, \theta_j) = (\mathbf{h}^{(\theta_i)} - \mathbf{h}^{(\theta_j)})^{\text{T}} (\mathbf{h}^{(\theta_i)} - \mathbf{h}^{(\theta_j)}), \qquad (4)$$

where $\mathbf{h}^{(\theta)} = (h_1, h_2, ..., h_m)^{\text{T}}$, and if $k \in \theta$ then $h_k = 1$, otherwise $h_k = 0$. The difference between individual base estimator and set P is the average of the differences between this base estimator and the ones in set P, that is

$$\text{DIFF}(\hat{f}_i, \text{P}) = \text{Ave} \sum_{\hat{f}_j \in \text{P}} \text{DIFF}(\hat{f}_i, \hat{f}_j), \qquad (5)$$

where $\hat{f}_i \notin \text{P}$.

The algorithm of constructing a pruned estimator ensemble is named PEN-SVR, and it is summarized in Algorithm 2.

5. EXPERIMENTAL RESULTS AND ANALYSIS

For the purpose of knowing the effectiveness of the proposed algorithm in practical, we evaluated the performance of the estimator ensembles constructed by the two algorithms above (denoted EN-SVR estimator ensemble and PEN-SVR estimator ensemble respectively), simultaneously compared to the typical estimator based on the SVR with Gaussian kernel method in [22] (denoted SVR estimator), for three modern steganographic algorithms: nsF5, PQ and PQt.

Algorithm 2 The PEN-SVR algorithm.

Input:
    Training image set, $\mathcal{C}$;
    Embedding change rates of the images in training image set, $\mathbf{y}$;
    Feature extraction function, $\mathbf{g}$;
    Dimensionality of the feature subspace, m_{sub}.
    Number of base estimator, L;
    Number of base estimator in the pruned ensemble, L';
    A tradeoff parameter in ensemble pruning, q;
Output: Pruned estimator ensemble $\hat{f}$.
1: extract the feature vectors from the images in training image set, $\mathbf{x} = \mathbf{g}(\mathcal{C})$;
2: label the feature vectors with corresponding change rate, $\mathcal{D} = (\mathbf{x}, \mathbf{y})$;
3: generate $\mathcal{D}^{(\theta_l)}$ by randomly selecting m_{sub}-dimensional subspace;
4: create bootstrap sample set, $\mathcal{D}_b^{(\theta_l)}$, by uniformly resampling $\mathcal{D}^{(\theta_l)}$ with replacement;
5: obtain a base estimator $\hat{f}_l$ trained by SVR with Gaussian kernel on $\mathcal{D}_b^{(\theta_l)}$;
6: test the base estimator $\hat{f}_l$ on $\mathcal{D}_{oob}^{(\theta_l)}$ to get the OOB error E_l;
7: go to step 3 until L base estimators are generated;
8: initialize the set P with the base estimator with the smallest E_l;
9: calculate the difference between each base estimator $\hat{f}_i$ and the set P, $\text{DIFF}(\hat{f}_i, \text{P})$, $\hat{f}_i \notin \text{P}$;
10: sort the base estimators outside P in the descending order of their differences with set P and get the sequence S;
11: select the base estimator with the smallest E_l from the first $\lceil q \cdot |S| \rceil$ base estimators of S and put it into the set P;
12: go to step 9 until the size of P reaches L';
13: $\hat{f} = \frac{1}{L'} \sum_{l=1}^{L'} \hat{f}_l$;

5.1 Materials and parameters

The mother database for the experiments was BOSSBase (v1.01) [2] database with 10000 images, a widely used image database in steganalysis research. In the experiment with nsF5, all the PGM images in BOSSBase were compressed to JPEG with quality factor 75 using the MATLAB's command *imwrite*. Then we used the nsF5 simulator[1] developed by Dr. Kodovský which makes embedding operations as if an optimal binary matrix coding scheme was used, with the relative payloads uniformly distributed over [0,1] bpac (bit per nonzero AC DCT coefficient). In the experiments with PQ and PQt, the cover images were double-compressed with primary quality factor 85 and secondary quality factor 70. To avoid the prior setted relative payloads exceeding the maximal embedding capacity of the cover images, the distribution of payloads was set to be uniform over [0,0.3] bpac. Counting the differences of the nonzero AC DCT coefficients between the covers and stegos, the accurate embedding change rates were obtained. For the quantitative steganalysis of each steganography, 5000 stego images were

---

[1]Obtained from http://dde.binghamton.edu/download.

randomly selected for training, and the other 5000 stego images were the testing images.

As for the feature set extracted by function **g**, we used the 548-dimensional CC-PEV feature [14], which had been demonstrated superior to the 274-PEV feature used in [21]. All the features were normalized by the same method in [22] to have zero mean and unit variance.

The estimation algorithms were implemented in MAT-LAB with the usage of LIBSVM [4]. The optimal hyper-parameters $(C, \gamma, \varepsilon)_1$ used in training SVR estimator were searched by the same method in [22]. Thereafter, we made some adjustment of $(C, \gamma, \varepsilon)_1$ and got $(C, \gamma, \varepsilon)_2$, which were applied to the training of each base estimator in the EN-SVR and PEN-SVR estimator ensembles. Searching for the optimal hyper-parameters for the base estimators over each training set repeatedly would lead to unacceptable computational complexity.

There are some other parameters need to be set prior to the construction of the EN-SVR and PEN-SVR estimator ensembles: the number of base estimator L, the dimensionality of the feature subspace m_{sub}. What's more, for PEN-SVR estimator ensemble, the number of base estimator in the pruned ensemble L' and a tradeoff parameter q in ensemble pruning are necessary. In the experiments, we set the dimensionality of the feature subspace m_{sub}=274. The dimensionality of the feature subspace m_{sub} has significant influence on the estimation accuracy, and Ho [13] recommended that relatively good results would be obtained, when the dimensionality of the feature subspace was half of that of the total feature space.

According to the experiments with the number of base estimator increasing, the estimation error would be relatively stable after the L reaching 50. So we set the number of base estimator L=50. What's more, in the experiments to be presented, $L' = 20$ and q=0.5, which is based on the heuristics. We also constructed a EN-SVR estimator ensemble with L=20 that consisted of the same number of base estimator as the PEN-SVR estimator ensemble did.

The performance was evaluated using three statistics: mean squared error (denoted MSE), interquartile range of the observed error (denoted IQR), and the bias (defined as mean observed error). In order to avoid the influence of randomness and give a more accurate evaluation of the EN-SVR and PEN-SVR estimator ensemble, the statistics were the average result over 10 independent splits, and the standard deviation of the statistics over different splits were also calculated. All the experiments were performed on a 64-bit Intel i3 2.2GHz computer with 8GB of RAM.

5.2 Results and analysis

Figure 3-5 show the MSE of the EN-SVR estimator ensemble, displayed as error bars, and that of SVR estimator for three steganographic algorithms. As the number of base estimator increases, the MSE of the estimator ensemble first quickly decreases and then slows down, approaching a relatively stable level. It is shown that the average performance of estimator ensemble would be better than the SVR estimator when the number of base estimator is larger than 10. At the same time, the standard deviation of the MSE also becomes smaller, which indicates that the stability of the estimator ensemble is enhanced.

Experimental results for three embedding algorithms are summarized in Table 1. As for the estimator ensembles,

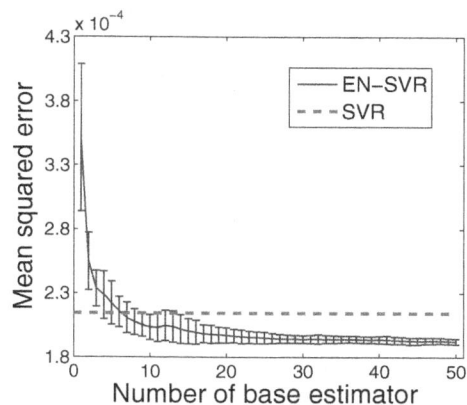

Figure 3: The MSE of EN-SVR estimator ensemble and SVR estimator for nsF5.

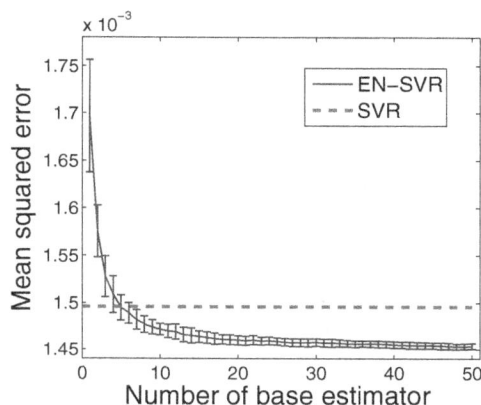

Figure 4: The MSE of EN-SVR estimator ensemble and SVR estimator for PQ.

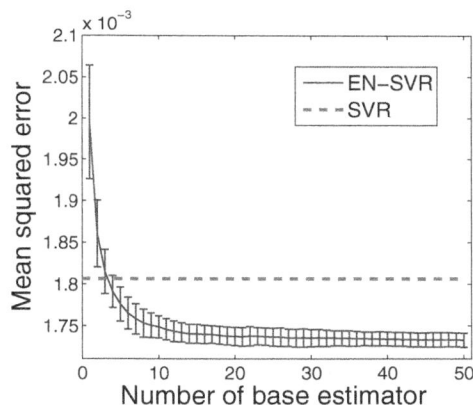

Figure 5: The MSE of EN-SVR estimator ensemble and SVR estimator for PQt.

EN-SVR(L=50), EN-SVR(L=20), PEN-SVR, not only the mean value of the statistics, but also the standard deviations of the statistics are explicitly presented. Compared to the SVR estimator, all the estimator ensembles acquired smaller MSE and IQR for all the tested algorithms. Mean-

	Estimator (ensemble)	MSE	IQR	Bias
nsF5	SVR	$2.144 \cdot 10^{-4}$	$1.591 \cdot 10^{-2}$	$-1.543 \cdot 10^{-4}$
	EN-SVR(L=50)	$(1.923 \pm .021) \cdot 10^{-4}$	$(1.467 \pm .010) \cdot 10^{-2}$	$(1.552 \pm .311) \cdot 10^{-4}$
	EN-SVR(L=20)	$(1.965 \pm .045) \cdot 10^{-4}$	$(1.475 \pm .012) \cdot 10^{-2}$	$(1.399 \pm .816) \cdot 10^{-4}$
	PEN-SVR	$(1.913 \pm .056) \cdot 10^{-4}$	$(1.472 \pm .009) \cdot 10^{-2}$	$(1.187 \pm .064) \cdot 10^{-4}$
PQ	SVR	$1.496 \cdot 10^{-3}$	$6.243 \cdot 10^{-2}$	$-1.919 \cdot 10^{-4}$
	EN-SVR(L=50)	$(1.454 \pm .003) \cdot 10^{-3}$	$(6.112 \pm .037) \cdot 10^{-2}$	$(-3.450 \pm 1.080) \cdot 10^{-4}$
	EN-SVR(L=20)	$(1.463 \pm .003) \cdot 10^{-3}$	$(6.125 \pm .057) \cdot 10^{-2}$	$(-2.538 \pm 1.221) \cdot 10^{-4}$
	PEN-SVR	$(1.459 \pm .008) \cdot 10^{-3}$	$(6.080 \pm .015) \cdot 10^{-2}$	$(-2.881 \pm 1.467) \cdot 10^{-4}$
PQt	SVR	$1.807 \cdot 10^{-3}$	$6.962 \cdot 10^{-2}$	$5.129 \cdot 10^{-4}$
	EN-SVR(L=50)	$(1.733 \pm .009) \cdot 10^{-3}$	$(6.741 \pm .087) \cdot 10^{-2}$	$(1.038 \pm 1.769) \cdot 10^{-4}$
	EN-SVR(L=20)	$(1.754 \pm .009) \cdot 10^{-3}$	$(6.639 \pm .044) \cdot 10^{-2}$	$(2.142 \pm 1.857) \cdot 10^{-4}$
	PEN-SVR	$(1.732 \pm .005) \cdot 10^{-3}$	$(6.798 \pm .035) \cdot 10^{-2}$	$(-0.879 \pm 2.277) \cdot 10^{-4}$

Table 1: The MSE, IQR and bias of the SVR estimator, EN-SVR(L=50), EN-SVR(L=20) and PEN-SVR estimator ensembles for nsF5, PQ and PQt.

while, the biases of the estimator ensembles are commonly lower or at the same level to that of the SVR estimator for nsF5 and PQt, except PQ. In addition, in comparison with EN-SVR(L=20), PEN-SVR estimator ensemble showed a closer performance to that of EN-SVR(L=50), although the PEN-SVR estimator ensemble also consisted of 20 base estimators. Additionally, the PEN-SVR estimator ensemble sometimes acquired slightly better performance than EN-SVR(L=50) in certain aspects.

We notice that the bias of the estimator ensemble fluctuates between a relatively large range, especially in the experiments for PQ and PQt. On the one hand, it was reported in [22] that the cluster of PQ stego-image feature vectors seriously deforms with increasing payload and this phenomenon makes it difficult for the estimator to learn the relationship between cover and stego features as a function of the change rate. On the other hand, since the averaging strategy is used for the combination of multiple base estimators both in EN-SVR and PEN-SVR algorithms, the bias of the estimator ensemble is identical to the average of the biases of multiple base estimators. However, the multiple base estimators were trained with the fixed hyper-parameters, despite the fact that the base estimators operated in different feature subspace. This probably makes the biases of the base estimators unstable, ultimately leading to a high fluctuation of the bias of the estimator ensemble.

	EN-SVR(L=50)	PEN-SVR	Reduction ratio
nsF5	639.61s	255.16s	60.1%
PQ	697.97s	273.65s	60.7%
PQt	434.37s	187.18s	56.9%

Table 2: Testing time for the embedding algorithms and the reduction ratio.

Table 2 shows the running time of the estimation process of the EN-SVR(L=50) and PEN-SVR estimator ensembles, along with the reduction ratios of the testing time for the embedding algorithms. As the number of base estimator of PEN-SVR estimator ensemble is 30 less than that of EN-SVR(L=50), it is easy to understand why the reduction ratios are all around 60%.

6. CONCLUSIONS

In this paper, we proposed an embedding change rate estimation method based on ensemble learning. Inspired by the ensemble classifier in blind detection, a framework for embedding change rate estimation based on estimator ensemble is presented. Then an algorithm, namely the EN-SVR algorithm, building the estimator ensemble is concretely described. Finally, a pruned estimator ensemble with less base estimators is constructed by the PEN-SVR algorithm. According to the experimental results for three modern steganographic algorithms (nsF5, PQ, and PQt), the proposed estimator ensembles achieved higher estimation accuracy, compared to the estimators based on the typical and advanced method. Moreover, the ensemble pruning played a role in decreasing the computational complexity of estimation while without damaging, even slightly improving the performance.

Note that although the proposed method can be easily parallelized and performed on the high-performance computer, there still exist many hurdles in using it for quantitative steganalysis in real world. For example, it is really in need of a better way to set the hyper-parameters for the base estimators. In the experiments, the setting of the hyper-parameters for the base estimators mostly relied on heuristics and all the base estimators were trained with the same parameters, which might lead to suboptimal results. Additionally, the optimal or near-optimal dimensionality of the random subspace will be different when other powerful high-dimensional features (e.g., 22,510-dimensional CC-JRM feature [15]) are applied in our estimation framework. In the future, we will research the problems above to make the proposed estimation method more practical and effective. Besides, the estimator ensembles for some other adaptive embedding algorithms, such as EA [19], HUGO [20] and MOD [8], will be constructed later.

7. ACKNOWLEDGEMETNS

We would like to thank Prof. Fridrich and Dr. Kodovský for generously providing the codes for implementation of the embedding algorithms and CC-PEV feature on their website, which contributed a lot to our research. This work is supported by the National Natural Science Foundation of China (Grant No. 61272489, 61170032, 61250007), the Strategic Priority Research Program of Chinese Academy of Sciences (Grant No. XDA06030601), the Innovation Scientists and Technicians Troop Construction Projects of Zhengzhou City (Grant No. 10LJRC182), and China Postdoctoral Science Foundation (Grant No. 2012T50842).

8. REFERENCES

[1] R. E. Banfield, L. O. Hall, K. W. Bowyer, and W. P. Kegelmeyer. Ensemble diversity measures and their application to thinning. *Information Fusion*, 6(1):49–62, 2005.

[2] P. Bas, T. Filler, and T. Pevný. Break our steganographic system — the ins and outs of organizing boss. In T. Filler, T. Pevný, S. Craver, and A. Ker, editors, *Information Hiding, 13th International Workshop*, volume 6958 of *Lecture Notes in Computer Science*, pages 59–70, Prague, Czech Republic, May 18–20, 2011. Springer.

[3] R. Caruana, A. Niculescu-Mizil, G. Crew, and A. Ksikes. Ensemble selection from libraries of models. In *Proceedings of the twenty-first international conference on Machine learning*, pages 18–26. ACM, 2004.

[4] C.-C. Chang and C.-J. Lin. LIBSVM: A library for support vector machines. *ACM Transactions on Intelligent Systems and Technology*, 2:27:1–27:27, 2011. Software available at http://www.csie.ntu.edu.tw/~cjlin/libsvm.

[5] T. Dietterich. An experimental comparison of three methods for constructing ensembles of decision trees: Bagging, boosting, and randomization. *Machine learning*, 40(2):139–157, 2000.

[6] S. Dumitrescu, X. Wu, and Z. Wang. Detection of lsb steganography via sample pair analysis. In F. Petitcolas, editor, *Information Hiding, 5th International Workshop*, volume 2578 of *Lecture Notes in Computer Science*, pages 355–372, Noordwijkerhout, The Netherlands, October 7–9, 2003. Springer.

[7] B. Efron and R. Tibshirani. *An introduction to the bootstrap*, volume 57. Chapman & Hall/CRC, 1994.

[8] T. Filler and J. Fridrich. Design of adaptive steganographic schemes for digital images. *Proceedings of Media Watermarking, Security and Forensics III, SPIE*, 7880:78800F–1, 2011.

[9] J. Fridrich, M. Goljan, and R. Du. Detecting lsb steganography in color, and gray-scale images. *Multimedia, IEEE*, 8(4):22–28, 2001.

[10] J. Fridrich, M. Goljan, and D. Soukal. Perturbed quantization steganography. *Multimedia Systems*, 11(2):98–107, 2005.

[11] J. Fridrich, T. Pevný, and J. Kodovský. Statistically undetectable jpeg steganography: dead ends challenges, and opportunities. In *Proceedings of the 9th workshop on Multimedia & security*, pages 3–14. ACM, 2007.

[12] G. Fumera and F. Roli. A theoretical and experimental analysis of linear combiners for multiple classifier systems. *Pattern Analysis and Machine Intelligence, IEEE Transactions on*, 27(6):942–956, 2005.

[13] T. Ho. The random subspace method for constructing decision forests. *Pattern Analysis and Machine Intelligence, IEEE Transactions on*, 20(8):832–844, 1998.

[14] J. Kodovský and J. Fridrich. Calibration revisited. In *Proceedings of the 11th ACM Multimedia & Security Workshop*, pages 63–74. Princeton, NJ, 2009.

[15] J. Kodovský and J. Fridrich. Steganalysis of jpeg images using rich models. In *IS&T/SPIE Electronic Imaging*, pages 83030A–83030A. International Society for Optics and Photonics, 2012.

[16] J. Kodovský, J. Fridrich, and V. Holub. Ensemble classifiers for steganalysis of digital media. *Information Forensics and Security, IEEE Transactions on*, 7(2):432–444, 2012.

[17] L. Kuncheva, C. Whitaker, C. Shipp, and R. Duin. Limits on the majority vote accuracy in classifier fusion. *Pattern Analysis & Applications*, 6(1):22–31, 2003.

[18] N. Li, Y. Yu, and Z. Zhou. Diversity regularized ensemble pruning. In *Machine Learning and Knowledge Discovery in Databases*, volume 7523 of *Lecture Notes in Computer Science*, pages 330–345, Bristol, UK, September 2012. Springer.

[19] W. Luo, F. Huang, and J. Huang. Edge adaptive image steganography based on lsb matching revisited. *Information Forensics and Security, IEEE Transactions on*, 5(2):201–214, 2010.

[20] T. Pevný, T. Filler, and P. Bas. Using high-dimensional image models to perform highly undetectable steganography. In R. Böhme, P. W. Fong, and R. Safavi-Naini, editors, *Information Hiding, 12th International Conference*, volume 6387 of *Lecture Notes in Computer Science*, pages 161–177, Calgary, AB, Canada, June 28–30, 2010. Springer.

[21] T. Pevný and J. Fridrich. Merging markov and dct features for multi-class jpeg steganalysis. *Proceedings SPIE, Electronic Imaging, Security, Steganography, and Watermarking of Multimedia Contents IX*, 6505:3, 2007.

[22] T. Pevný, J. Fridrich, and A. Ker. From blind to quantitative steganalysis. *Information Forensics and Security, IEEE Transactions on*, 7(2):445–454, 2012.

[23] A. Smola and B. Schölkopf. A tutorial on support vector regression. *Statistics and computing*, 14(3):199–222, 2004.

[24] A. Westfeld. Generic adoption of spatial steganalysis to transformed domain. In K. Solanki, K. Sullivan, and U. Madhow, editors, *Information Hiding, 10th International Workshop*, volume 5284 of *Lecture Notes in Computer Science*, pages 161–177, Santa Barbara, CA, USA, May 19–21, 2008. Springer.

[25] Z. Zhou. *Ensemble Methods: Foundations and Algorithms*. Chapman & Hall, 2012.

[26] Z. Zhou, J. Wu, and W. Tang. Ensembling neural networks: many could be better than all. *Artificial intelligence*, 137(1):239–263, 2002.

Privacy and Security Challenges in the Smart Grid User Domain

Dominik Engel
Josef Ressel Center for
User-Centric Smart Grid Privacy, Security and Control
Salzburg University of Applied Sciences
Urstein Süd 1, A–5412 Urstein/Salzburg, Austria
dominik.engel@en-trust.at

ABSTRACT

The term "smart grids" is used to describe the next-generation intelligent energy systems. Smart grids employ state-of-the-art information and communication technology to control generation, distribution and consumption of energy. With smart grids, the power network organization moves from a hierarchical to a decentralized structure and communication flow moves from largely uni-directional to bi-directional. The degree of information needed on network status is vastly more accurate compared to traditional power networks, and needs to be available in fine granularity in near real-time. The availability of such fine-grained data raises severe privacy concerns in the end-user domain. For example, the application of non-intrusive load monitoring techniques to high-resolution load profiles allows inferring details on user behavior such as presence, sleep-and-wake cycles and the brands of used appliances. Another challenge in the widespread adoption of smart grid technologies lies in the domain of security. Recent reports of smart meters that can easily be hacked and used to remotely control energy availability in the connected household have not helped to increase user trust.

In this talk, the main challenges in the area of smart grid privacy and security from an end-user perspective will be reviewed. At the example of smart metering, selected solutions will be discussed in detail, with a focal point on leveraging insights and methods from multimedia security to provide security and privacy in the smart grid user domain. These include signal processing in the encrypted domain / secure signal processing, homomorphic encryption, conditional access based on multi-resolution analysis, as well as watermarking techniques.

Categories and Subject Descriptors

K.4 [**Computers and Society**]: Privacy; E.3 [**Data**]: Data Encryption

Keywords

Smart Grids, Security, Privacy

Short Bio

Dominik Engel is a professor at the Salzburg University of Applied Sciences in Austria, where he heads the Josef Ressel Center for User-Centric Smart Grid Privacy, Security and Control. He holds a PhD degree in Computer Science from the University of Salzburg. Prior to joining Salzburg University of Applied Sciences, Dominik Engel was a researcher at the Universities of Bremen and Salzburg and product manager at Sony DADC, where he was responsible for video content security. His research interests include smart grid security, multimedia security and technological methods for enhancing end-user trust.

References

[1] D. Engel. Conditional access smart meter privacy based on multi-resolution wavelet analysis. In *Proceedings of the 4th International Symposium on Applied Sciences in Biomedical and Communication Technologies*, pages 45:1–45:5, Barcelona, Spain, 2011. ACM.

[2] D. Engel. Wavelet-based load profile representation for smart meter privacy. In *Proc. IEEE PES Innovative Smart Grid Technologies (ISGT'13)*, pages 1–6, Washington, D.C., USA, Feb. 2013. IEEE.

Document Authentication Using Graphical Codes: Impacts of the Channel Model

Anh Thu Phan Ho
LAGIS UMR 8219 CNRS
Inst. Telecom, Telecom Lille1
59000 Villeneuve d'Ascq, FR
phanho@telecom-
lille1.eu

Bao An Mai Hoang
LAGIS UMR 8219 CNRS
Telecom Lille1
59000 Villeneuve d'Ascq, FR
maihoang@telecom-
lille1.eu

Wadih Sawaya
LAGIS UMR 8219 CNRS
Inst. Telecom, Telecom-Lille1
59000 Villeneuve d'Ascq, FR
wadih.sawaya@telecom-
lille1.eu

Patrick Bas
LAGIS UMR 8219 CNRS
Ecole Centrale de Lille
59651 Villeneuve d'Ascq, FR
patrick.bas@ec-lille.fr

ABSTRACT

This paper proposes to investigate the impact of the channel model for authentication systems based on codes that are corrupted by a physically unclonable noise such as the one emitted by a printing process. The core of such a system is the comparison for the receiver between an original binary code, an original corrupted code and a copy of the original code. We analyze two strategies, depending on whether or not the receiver use a binary version of its observation to perform its authentication test. By deriving the optimal test within a Neyman-Pearson setup, a theoretical analysis shows that a thresholding of the code induces a loss of performance. This study also highlights the fact that the probability of the type I and type II errors can be better approximated, by several orders of magnitude, computing Chernoff bounds instead of the Gaussian approximation. Finally we evaluate the impact of an uncertainty for the receiver on the opponent channel and show that the authentication is still possible whenever the receiver can observe forged codes and uses them to estimate the parameters of the model.

Categories and Subject Descriptors

K.6.5.0 [**Management of Computing and Information Systems**]: Computer Security and Protection—*Authentication* ; H.1.1 [**Models and Principles**]: Systems and Information Theory—*Information theory*

Keywords

Authentication, Statistical Analysis, Hypothesis testing, Binary thresholding

1. INTRODUCTION

Authentication of physical products such as documents, goods, drugs, jewels, is a major concern in a world of global exchanges. According to the Organization for Economic Co-operation and Development (OECD), international trade in counterfeit and pirated goods reached more than US \$250 billion in 2009 [10], additionally the World Health Organization in 2005 claimed that nearly 25% of medicines in developing countries are forgeries [9].

One way to perform authentication of physical products is to rely on the stochastic structure of the material that composes the product. Authentication can be performed for example by recording the random patterns of the fiber of a paper [6], but such a system is practically heavy to deploy since each product needs to be linked to its high definition capture stored in a database. Another solution is to rely on the degradation induced by the interaction between the product and a physical process such as printing, marking, embossing, carving ... Because of both the defaults of the physical process and the stochastic nature of the mater, this interaction can be considered as a Physically Unclonable Function (PUF) [12] that cannot be reproduced by the forger and can consequently be used to perform authentication. In [5], the authors measure the degradation of the inks within printed color-tiles, and use discrepancy between the statistics of the authentic and print-and-scan tiles to perform authentication. Other marking techniques can also be used, in [11] the authors propose to characterize the random profiles of laser marks on materials such as metals (the technique is called LPUF for Laser-written PUF) and to use them as authentication features.

We study in this paper an authentication system which uses the fact that a printing process at very high resolution can be seen as a stochastic process due to the nature of different elements such as the paper fibers, the ink heterogeneity, or the dot addressability of the printer. Such an authentication system has been proposed by Picard et al. [8, 7] and uses 2D pseudo random binary codes that are printed at the native resolution of the printer (2400 dpi on a standard offset printer or 812 dpi on digital HP Indigo printer). The whole system is depicted on Fig. 1: once printed on a package to be authenticated, the degraded code can be scanned and thresholded by an opponent (the forger). Note that at this stage the thresholding is necessary because the industrial printers can only print dots, e.g. binary versions of the scanned code. The opponent will produce a printed copy of the original code to manufacture his forgery and the receiver will compare the scanned (and potentially post-processed) version of the original code with the scanned (and potentially post-processed) version of the copied code in order to perform authentication. One advantage of this system over previously cited ones is that it is easy to deploy since the authentication process needs only a scan of the graphical code under scrutiny and the seed used to generate the original one, no fingerprint database is required.

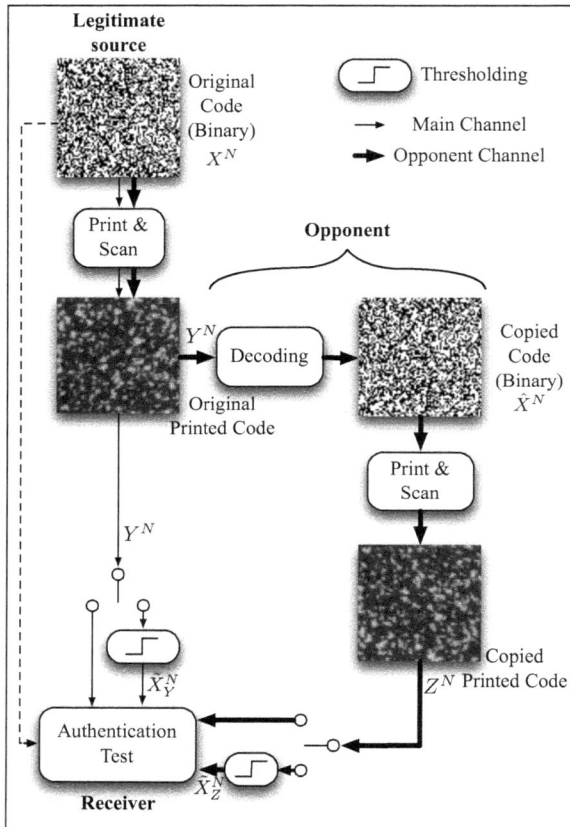

Figure 1: Principle of authentication using graphical codes.

The security of this system solely relies on the use of a PUF, i.e. the impossibility for the opponent to accurately estimate the original binary code. Different security analysis have already been performed w.r.t. this authentication system, or to very similar ones. In [1], the authors have studied the impact of multiple printed observations of same graphical codes and the authors have shown that the power of the noise due to the printing process can be reduced in this particular setup. In [3], the authors use machine learning tools in order to try to infer the original code from an observation of the printed code, their study shows that the estimation accuracy can be increased without recovering perfectly the original code. In [2], the authors consider the security analysis in the rather similar setup of passive fingerprinting using binary fingerprints under informed attacks (the channel between the original code and the copied code is assumed to be a Binary Symmetric Channel), they show that the security increase with the code length and they propose a practical threshold when type I error (original detected as a forgery) and type II error (forgery detected as an original) are equal.

The goal of this paper is to analyze what are the different strategies for the receiver with respect to the post-processing step. We assume that the strategy of the opponent is fixed and that the copied binary code suffers a binary input binary output channel. We show that it is in the receiver's interest to process directly the scanned grayscale code instead of a binary version and we evaluate the impact of the Gaussian approximation of the test with respect to its asymptotic expression. We also investigate the impact of the estimation of the opponent printing channel over the authentication performances.

2. AUTHENTICATION CHANNEL

2.1 Notations

We designate sets by calligraphic font e.g. $\mathcal{X}$ and random variables (RV) ranging over these sets by the same italic capitals e.g. X. The cardinality of the set $\mathcal{X}$ is denoted by $|\mathcal{X}|$. The sequence of N variables $(X_1, X_2, ..., X_N)$ is denoted X^N.

2.2 The setup

The authentication sequence is a binary sequence X^N chosen at random from the message set $\mathcal{X}^N$, and is shared secretly with the legitimate receiver. In our authentication model, X^N is published as a noisy version Y^N, taking values in the set of points $\mathcal{V}^N$ (see Fig. 1). An opponent may observe Y^N and, naturally, tries to retrieve the original authentication sequence. He obtains an estimated sequence $\hat{X}^N$ and prints it to forge a fake sequence Z^N hoping that it will be accepted by the receiver as coming from the legitimate source. The receiver observes then a sequence $\mathcal{O}^N$ which may be one of the two possible sequences Y^N or Z^N, and has to decide whether it comes from the legitimate source or not.

The authentication model may then be viewed as a secret communication problem involving two channels $\mathcal{X} \to (\mathcal{Y}, \mathcal{Z})$, where unreliable communication is desired for one of them (the opponent channel), and perfect communication for the second one (the main channel). We define the main channel as the channel between the legitimate source and the receiver, and the opponent channel as the channel between the legitimate source and the receiver but passing through the counterfeiter channel (see Fig. 1).

2.3 Channel modeling

Let $P_{V/X}$ be the generic transition matrix modeling the whole physical processes used here, precisely printing and scanning devices. The entries of this matrix are conditional probabilities $P_{V/X}(v/x)$ relating the input alphabet $\mathcal{X}$ and the output alphabet $\mathcal{V}$ of the whole processes. In practical and realistic situations, $\mathcal{X}$ is a binary alphabet standing with black (0) and white (1) elements of a digital code and the channel output set $\mathcal{V}$ stands for the set of gray level values with cardinality K (for printed and scanned images, $K = 256$). Transition matrix $P_{V/X}$ may be any discrete distribution over the set $\mathcal{V}$. In our global authentication model, the two channels $\mathcal{X} \rightarrow (\mathcal{Y}, \mathcal{Z})$ are considered being discrete and memoryless with conditional probability distribution $P_{YZ/X}(y, z/x)$. The marginal channels $P_{Y/X}$ and $P_{Z/X}$ constitute the transition probability matrices of the main channel and the opponent channel respectively. While $P_{Y/X} = P_{V/X}$, $P_{Z/X}$ depends on the opponent processing. We aim here at expressing this marginal distribution considering that the opponent tries to restore the original sequence before publishing his fraudulent sequence Z^N.

When performing a detection to obtain an estimated sequence $\hat{X}^N$ of the original code, the opponent undergoes errors. These errors are evaluated with probabilities $P_{e,W}$ when confusing an original white dot with a black and $P_{e,B}$ when confusing an original black dot with a white. This distinction is due to the fact that the channel distribution $P_{V/X}$ of the physical devices is arbitrary and not necessarily symmetric. Let $\mathcal{D}_{\mathcal{W}}$ and $\mathcal{D}_{\mathcal{W}}^c$ be respectively the optimal decision regions for decoding white or black, obtained after using classical maximum likelihood decoding. As the opponent observes Y^N (we assume that all the physical processes involved are identical for the main channel and the opponent channel), the decision regions will be defined as:

$$\mathcal{D}_{\mathcal{W}} = \{ v \in \mathcal{V} : P_{V/X}(v/X = 1) > P_{V/X}(v/X = 0) \}. \quad (1)$$

Recalling that $P_{Y/X} = P_{V/X}$, error probabilities $P_{e,W}$ and $P_{e,B}$ are equal to:

$$P_{e,W} = \sum_{v \in \mathcal{D}_{\mathcal{W}}^c} P_{Y/X}(v/X = 1), \quad (2)$$

$$P_{e,B} = \sum_{v \in \mathcal{D}_{\mathcal{W}}} P_{Y/X}(v/X = 0). \quad (3)$$

The channel $X \rightarrow \hat{X}$ can be modeled as a Binary Input Binary Output channel (BIBO) with transition probability matrix $P_{\hat{X}/X}$:

$$\begin{bmatrix} 1 - P_{e,B} & P_{e,B} \\ P_{e,W} & 1 - P_{e,W} \end{bmatrix} \quad (4)$$

As we can see in Fig. 1, the opponent channel $\mathcal{X} \rightarrow Z$ is a physically degraded version of the main channel. Thus, $X \rightarrow \hat{X} \rightarrow Z$ forms a Markov chain with the relation $P_{\hat{X}Z/X}(\hat{x}, z/x) = P_{\hat{X}/X}(\hat{x}/x) P_{Z/\hat{X}}(z/\hat{x})$. Components of the marginal channel matrix $P_{Z/X}$ are:

$$P_{Z/X}(Z = v/x) = \sum_{\hat{x}=0,1} P_{\hat{X}Z/X}(\hat{x}, Z = v/x)$$
$$= \sum_{\hat{x}=0,1} P_{\hat{X}/X}(\hat{x}/x) P_{Z/\hat{X}}(Z = v/\hat{x}). \quad (5)$$

If we assume that the physical processes are identical for the main channel and the opponent channel ($P_{Z/\hat{X}} = P_{Y/X} = P_{V/X}$) the components of the marginal channel matrix $P_{Z/X}$ will be expressed as:

$$P_{Z/X}(Z = v/X = 0) = (1 - P_{e,B}) P_{V/X}(v/X = 0) \\ + P_{e,B} P_{V/X}(v/X = 1), \quad (6)$$

$$P_{Z/X}(Z = v/X = 1) = (1 - P_{e,W}) P_{V/X}(v/X = 1) \\ + P_{e,W} P_{V/X}(v/X = 0). \quad (7)$$

2.4 Receiver's strategies

Two strategies are possible for the receiver.

2.4.1 Binary thresholding:

As a first strategy the receiver decodes the observed sequence $\mathcal{O}^N$ using maximum likelihood criterion and restores a binary version $\tilde{X}^N$ of the original message X^N. Error probabilities in the main channel, i.e. when $\mathcal{O}^N = Y^N$, are the same as (2) and (3). In the opponent channel, i.e. when $\mathcal{O}^N = Z^N$, these probabilities are:

$$\tilde{P}_{e,W} = \sum_{v \in \mathcal{D}_{\mathcal{W}}^c} P_{Z/X}(v/X = 1), \quad (8)$$

$$\tilde{P}_{e,W} = \sum_{v \in \mathcal{D}_{\mathcal{W}}^c} (1 - P_{e,W}) P_{V/X}(v/X = 1) \\ + P_{e,W} P_{V/X}(v/X = 0).$$

Finally we have:

$$\tilde{P}_{e,W} = (1 - P_{e,W}) P_{e,W} + P_{e,W}(1 - P_{e,B}). \quad (9)$$

The same development yields:

$$\tilde{P}_{e,B} = (1 - P_{e,B}) P_{e,B} + P_{e,B}(1 - P_{e,W}). \quad (10)$$

For this first strategy, the opponent channel may be viewed as the cascade of two binary input/binary output channels:

$$\begin{bmatrix} 1 - \tilde{P}_{e,B} & \tilde{P}_{e,B} \\ \tilde{P}_{e,W} & 1 - \tilde{P}_{e,W} \end{bmatrix} =$$

$$\begin{bmatrix} 1 - P_{e,B} & P_{e,B} \\ P_{e,W} & 1 - P_{e,W} \end{bmatrix} \times \begin{bmatrix} 1 - P_{e,B} & P_{e,B} \\ P_{e,W} & 1 - P_{e,W} \end{bmatrix}. \quad (11)$$

When the channel distribution $P_{V/X}$ is symmetric, we have $P_{e,W} = P_{e,B} = p$, and expressions (9) and (10) are unified giving $\tilde{p} = 2p(1 - p)$. We recognize here the cross over probability of two cascaded binary symmetric channels with cross probability p. As we will see in the next section, the test that the receiver will perform to decide whether the observed decoded sequence $\tilde{X}^N$ comes from the legitimate source or not is tantamount to counting the number of errors in this case.

2.4.2 Grey level observations:

In the second strategy, the receiver performs his test directly on the received sequence $\mathcal{O}^N$ without any given decoding. We will see in the next section that this strategy is better than the previous one for authentication.

3. HYPOTHESIS TESTING

As the observed sequence may come from the legitimate receiver or from a counterfeiter, the receiver considers two hypothesis H_0 and H_1 corresponding respectively to each of the former cases. This problem is formulated by the fact that the observed sequence may be described by two probabilities, say Q_0 and Q_1. A decision rule will assign one of the two hypothesis for each possible observed sequence and the observed sequence space will then be partitioned into two regions $\mathcal{H}_0$ and $\mathcal{H}_1$. Accepting hypothesis H_0 while it is actually a fake (H_1 is true) leads to an error of type II having probability β. Rejecting hypothesis H_0 while actually the observed sequence comes from the legitimate source (H_0 is true) leads to an error of type I with probability α. An optimal decision rule will be given by the Neyman Pearson criterion. The eponymous theorem states that under the constraint $\alpha \leq \alpha^*$, β is minimized when the choice of H_0 is done if only if the following log-likelihood test is verified:

$$\log \frac{Q_0(v^N)}{Q_1(v^N)} \geq \gamma, \tag{12}$$

where γ is a threshold verifying the constraint $\alpha \leq \alpha^*$.

3.1 Binary thresholding:

In the first strategy, the final observed data is $\tilde{X}^N$ and the original sequence X^N is a side information containing two types of data ("0" and "1"). The distribution of each component $(\tilde{X}_i, X_i)$ of the sequence $(\tilde{X}^N, X^N)$ is the same for each of these types. We derive now the probabilities that describe $\tilde{X}^N$ for each of the two possible hypothesis. Under hypothesis H_j, $j \in \{0, 1\}$, these probabilities are expressed conditionally to the known original code:

$$P(\tilde{X}^N = \tilde{x}^N / X^N = x^N, H_j) = \prod_{i/X_i=0}^{N_B} P(\tilde{x}_i / X_i = 0, H_j)$$
$$\times \prod_{i/X_i=1}^{N_W} P(\tilde{x}_i / X_i = 1, H_j),$$

where N_B and N_W are respectively the number of black and white components in the original code.

- Under hypothesis H_0 the channel $X \to \hat{X}$ has distributions given by (2) and (3) and we have:

$$P\left(\tilde{x}^N / x^N, H_0\right) = (P_{e,B})^{n_{e,B}} (1 - P_{e,B})^{N_B - n_{e,B}}$$
$$\times (P_{e,W})^{n_{e,W}} (1 - P_{e,W})^{N_W - n_{e,W}},$$

where $n_{e,B}$ and $n_{e,W}$ are the number of errors ($\tilde{x}_i \neq x_i$) when black is decoded into white and when white is decoded into black respectively.

- Under hypothesis H_1, the channel $X \to \hat{X}$ has distributions given by (9) and (10) and we have:

$$P\left(\tilde{x}^N / x^N\ H_1\right) = (\tilde{P}_{e,B})^{n_{e,B}} (1 - \tilde{P}_{e,B})^{N_B - n_{e,B}}$$
$$\times (\tilde{P}_{e,W})^{n_{e,W}} (1 - \tilde{P}_{e,W})^{N_W - n_{e,W}}.$$

Applying now the Neyman Pearson criterion (12) the test is expressed as:

$$L_1 = \log \frac{P\left(\tilde{X}^N = \tilde{x}^N / X^N = x^N, H_1\right)}{P\left(\tilde{X}^N = \tilde{x}^N / X^N = x^N, H_0\right)} \underset{H0}{\overset{H1}{\gtrless}} \gamma, \tag{13}$$

$$L_1 = n_{e,B} \log \left(\frac{\tilde{P}_{e,B}(1 - P_{e,B})}{P_{e,B}(1 - \tilde{P}_{e,B})}\right)$$
$$+ n_{e,W} \log \left(\frac{\tilde{P}_{e,W}(1 - P_{e,W})}{P_{e,W}(1 - \tilde{P}_{e,W})}\right) \underset{H0}{\overset{H1}{\gtrless}} \lambda_1, \tag{14}$$

where $\lambda_1 = \gamma - N_B \log\left(\frac{1-\tilde{P}_B}{1-P_B}\right) - N_W \log\left(\frac{1-\tilde{P}_W}{1-P_W}\right)$. For symmetric channels, this expression is simplified by

$$n_{e,B} + n_{e,W} \underset{H0}{\overset{H1}{\gtrless}} \lambda_1'. \tag{15}$$

This expression of the test has the practical advantage to only count the number of errors in order to perform the authentication task without even knowing the opponent channel, but at a cost of a loss of optimality.

3.2 Grey level observations:

In the second strategy, the observed data is $\mathcal{O}^N$. Here again, the distribution of each component $(\mathcal{O}_i, X_i)$ of the sequence $(\mathcal{O}^N, X^N)$ is the same for each type of data of X. The Neyman Pearson test is expressed as:

$$L_2 = \log \frac{P(\mathcal{O}^N = v^N / X^N = x^N, H_1)}{P(\mathcal{O}^N = v^N / X^N = x^N, H_0)} \underset{H0}{\overset{H1}{\gtrless}} \lambda_2, \tag{16}$$

which can be developed as

$$L_2 = \sum_{i/X_i=1}^{N_W} \log \frac{P_{Z/X}(\mathcal{O}_i = v / X_i = 1)}{P_{Y/X}(\mathcal{O}_i = v / X_i = 1)} \tag{17}$$
$$+ \sum_{i/X_i=0}^{N_B} \log \frac{P_{Z/X}(\mathcal{O}_i = v / X_i = 0)}{P_{Y/X}(\mathcal{O}_i = v / X_i = 0)} \underset{H0}{\overset{H1}{\gtrless}} \lambda_2,$$

$$L_2 = \sum_{i/X_i=1}^{N_W} \log \left(1 - P_{e,W} + P_{e,W} \frac{P_{V/X}(\mathcal{O}_i/0)}{P_{V/X}(\mathcal{O}_i/1)}\right) +$$
$$\sum_{i/X_i=0}^{N_B} \log \left(1 - P_{e,B} + P_{e,B} \frac{P_{V/X}(\mathcal{O}_i/1)}{P_{V/X}(\mathcal{O}_i/0)}\right) \underset{H0}{\overset{H1}{\gtrless}} \lambda_2. \tag{18}$$

Note that here the expressions of the channel models $P_{V/X}(\mathcal{O}_i/X_i)$ are required in order to perform the optimal test.

3.3 Performance of hypothesis testing

3.3.1 The Gaussian approximation

In the previous section we have expressed the Neyman-Pearson test for the two proposed strategies resumed by (14) and (18). These tests may then be practically performed on the observed sequence in order to make a decision about its authenticity. We aim now at expressing the error probabilities of type I and II, and comparing the two possible strategies described previously. Let $m = 1, 2$ be the index denoting the strategy, a straightforward calculation gives

$$\alpha_m = \sum_{l > \lambda_m} P_{L_m}(l/H_0), \tag{19}$$

$$\beta_m = \sum_{l < \lambda_m} P_{L_m}(l/H_1). \tag{20}$$

As the length N of the sequence is generally large, we use the central limit theorem to study the distributions P_{L_m}, $m = 1, 2$.

For the binary thresholding strategy, the observed sequence is $\hat{X}^N$. In (14) $n_{e,W}$ and $n_{e,B}$ are binomial random variables, with parameters depending on the source of the observed sequence, i.e. if it comes from the legitimate source or from the counterfeiter. Let N_x and $P_{e,x}$ stand respectively for the number data of type x in the original code and the cross over probabilities of the BIBO channels (4) and (11). When N is large enough, the binomial random variables are approximated with a Gaussian distribution. We have:

$$n_{e,x} \sim \mathcal{N}(N_x P_{e,x}, \ N_x P_{e,x}(1 - P_{e,x})). \quad (21)$$

One can obviously now deduce the parameters of the normal approximation describing the log-likelihood L_1.

For the second strategy, i.e. when the receiver tests directly the observed gray level sequence, the log-likelihood L_2 Eq. (18) may be expressed as two sums of i.i.d. and becomes:

$$L_2 = \sum_{i/X_i=1}^{N_W} \ell(\mathcal{O}_i;\ 1) + \sum_{i/X_i=0}^{N_B} \ell(\mathcal{O}_i;\ 0) \underset{H0}{\overset{H1}{\gtrless}} \lambda_2, \quad (22)$$

where $\ell(v;\ x)$ is a function $\ell : \mathcal{V} \to \mathbb{R}$ with parameter $x = 0, 1$ and having some distribution with mean and variance equal to:

$$\mu_x = E[\ell(V;\ x) \mid H_j] = \sum_{v \in \mathcal{V}} \ell(v,\ x) P_{V/X}(v/x), \quad (23)$$

and

$$\mathrm{var}[\ell(V;\ x) \mid H_j] = \sum_{v \in \mathcal{V}} (\ell(v,\ x) - \mu_x)^2 P_{V/X}(v/x), \quad (24)$$

with $P_{V/X} = P_{Y/X}$ (resp. $P_{V/X} = P_{Z/X}$) for $j = 0$ (resp. 1) . The central limit theorem is then used again for the distribution of L_2 to compute the type I and type II error probabilities.

3.3.2 Asymptotic expression

One important problem is the fact that the Gaussian approximation proposed previously provides inaccurate error probabilities when the threshold λ_m in (19) and (20) is far from the mean of the random variable L_m. Chernoff bound and asymptotic expression are preferred in this context as very small error probabilities of type I and II may be desired [4]. Given a real number s the Chernoff bound on type I and II errors may be expressed for $m = 1, 2$ as:

$$\alpha_m = \Pr(L_m \geq \lambda_m) \leq e^{-s\lambda_m} g_{L_m}(s) \ \text{for any } s > 0, \quad (25)$$

$$\beta_m = \Pr(L_m \leq \lambda_m) \leq e^{-s\lambda_m} g_{L_m}(s) \ \text{for any } s < 0, \quad (26)$$

where the function $g_{L_m}(s)$ is the moment generating function of L_m defined as:

$$g_{L_m}(s) = E_{L_m}\left[e^{sL_m} \right]. \quad (27)$$

These bounds are significant for λ_m far from $E[L_m]$, namely when bounding the tails of a distribution. The tightest bound is obtained by finding the value of s that provides the minimum of the RHS of (25) and (26), i.e. the minimum of $e^{-s\lambda_m} g_{L_m}(s)$. Taking the derivative, the value s that provides the tightest bound is such that[1]:

$$\lambda_m = \frac{\frac{dg_{L_m}(s)}{ds}}{g_{L_m}(s)} = \frac{d}{ds} \ln g_{L_m}(s). \quad (28)$$

---
[1](one can show that $e^{-s\lambda_m} g_{L_m}(s)$ is convex)

Reminding that L_m is a sum of N independant random variables, asymptotic analysis in probability theory (when N is large enough) shows that bounds similar to (25) and (26) are much more appropriate for estimating α_m and β_m than the Gaussian approximation. To make this more clear, we will introduce the semi-invariant moment generating function after an acute observation of the identity (28). The semi-invariant moment generating function of L_m is $\mu_{L_m}(s) = \ln g_{L_m}(s)$. This function has many interesting properties that ease the extraction of an asymptotic expression for (25) and (26) [4]. For instance, this function is additive for the sum of independant random variables, which yields for example for $m = 2$:

$$\mu_{L_2}(s) = \sum_{i/X_i=1}^{N_W} \mu_{\ell_{i/1}}(s) + \sum_{i/X_i=0}^{N_B} \mu_{\ell_{i/0}}(s), \quad (29)$$

where $\mu_{\ell_i/x}(s)$ is the semi-invariant moment generating function of the random variable $\ell_{i/x} = \ell(\mathcal{O}_i;\ x)$. In addition, the s optimizing the bound and obtained from (28) may be driven from the sum of the derivatives:

$$\lambda_m = \sum_{i/X_i=1}^{N_W} \mu'_{\ell_i/1}(s) + \sum_{i/X_i=0}^{N_B} \mu'_{\ell_i/0}(s). \quad (30)$$

Chernoff bounds on type I and II errors (25) and (26) may then be expresses as:

$$\alpha_m = \Pr(L_m \geq \lambda_m)$$
$$\leq \exp\left[\sum_{i/X_i=1}^{N_W} \left(\mu_{\ell_i/1}(s) - s\mu'_{\ell_i/1}(s) \right) \right. \quad (31)$$
$$\left. + \sum_{i/X_i=0}^{N_B} \left(\mu_{\ell_i/0}(s) - s\mu'_{\ell_i/1}(s) \right) \right] \ \text{for any } s > 0,$$

and

$$\beta_m = \Pr(L_m \leq \lambda_m)$$
$$\leq \exp\left[\sum_{i/X_i=1}^{N_W} \left(\mu_{\ell_i/1}(s) - s\mu'_{\ell_i/1}(s) \right) \right. \quad (32)$$
$$\left. + \sum_{i/X_i=0}^{N_B} \left(\mu_{\ell_i/0}(s) - s\mu'_{\ell_i/1}(s) \right) \right] \ \text{for any } s < 0.$$

The distribution of each component $(\mathcal{O}_i, X_i)$ of the sequence $(\mathcal{O}^N, X^N)$ is the same for each type of data of X, and $\mu_{\ell_i/x}(s) = \mu_{\ell/x}(s)$ is independent from i for a given type of data $x = 0, 1$. The RHS in (31) and (32) can be simplified as:

$$\exp\left[N_W \left(\mu_{\ell/1}(s) - s\mu'_{\ell/1}(s) \right) + N_B \left(\mu_{\ell/0}(s) - s\mu'_{\ell/0}(s) \right) \right]. \quad (33)$$

The asymptotic expression is evaluated (see [4], Appendix 5A) for the sum of i.i.d and for large N we have (for $N_B \approx N_W \approx N/2$), for $s > 0$:

$$\alpha_m = \Pr(L_m \geq \lambda_m)$$
$$\underset{N \to \infty}{\to} \frac{1}{|s|\sqrt{N\pi\mu''_\ell(s)}} \exp\left\{ \frac{N}{2} [\mu_\ell(s) - s\mu'_\ell(s)] \right\}. \quad (34)$$

and for $s < 0$:

$$\beta_m = \Pr(L_m \le \lambda_m)$$
$$\underset{N\to\infty}{\rightarrow} \frac{1}{|s|\sqrt{N\pi\mu_\ell''(s)}} \exp\left\{\frac{N}{2}\left[\mu_\ell(s) - s\mu_\ell'(s)\right]\right\}. \tag{35}$$

where $\mu_\ell(s) = \mu_{\ell/0}(s) + \mu_{\ell/1}(s)$, $\mu'_\ell(s) = \mu'_{\ell/0}(s) + \mu'_{\ell/1}(s)$, and $\mu_\ell''(s) = \mu_{\ell/0}''(s) + \mu_{\ell/1}''(s)$ is the second derivative of the semi invariant moment generating function of random variable $\ell(v; x)$ defined by:

$$\ell(v; 0) = \log\left(1 - P_{e,W} + P_{e,W}\frac{P_{V/X}(v/0)}{P_{V/X}(v/1)}\right),$$
$$\ell(v; 1) = \log\left(1 - P_{e,B} + P_{e,B}\frac{P_{V/X}(v/1)}{P_{V/X}(v/0)}\right).$$

Fig. 2 illustrates the gap between the estimation of α and β using the Gaussian approximation and the asymptotic expression. The Monte-Carlo simulations confirm the fact that the derived Chernoff bounds are tight.

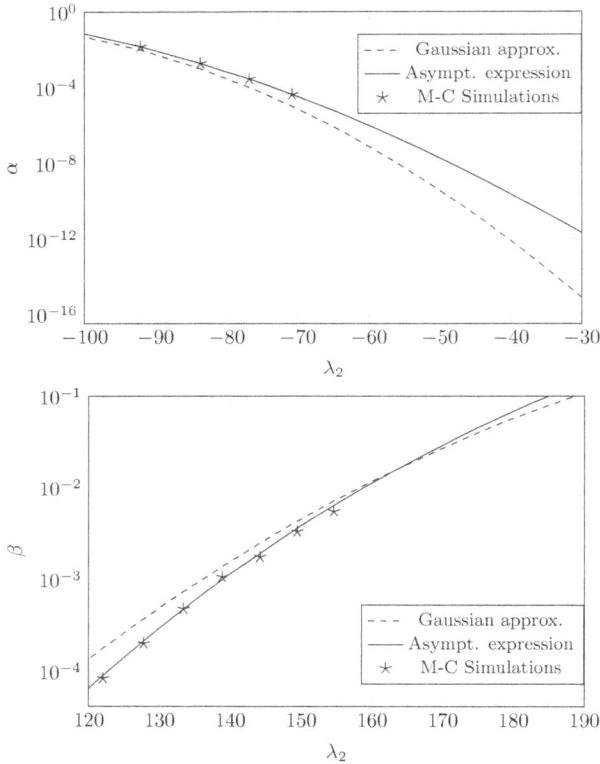

Figure 2: Comparison between the Gaussian approximation, the asymptotic expression and Monte-Carlo simulations (10^6 trials) for the second strategy, $N = 2000$, $\sigma = 50$.

3.4 Comparison between the two strategies

In this setup and without loss of generality, we assume that the print and scan channel is modeled by a discreet non-symmetric and memoryless channel with binary input alphabet $\mathcal{X}$ and grey level outputs $\mathcal{V}$, generated from a normalized discrete Gaussian distribution $P_{V/x}(v/x)$. For $x = 0, 1$:

$$P_{V/x}(v/x) = \frac{\exp(-(v-\mu_x)^2/2\sigma^2)}{\sum\limits_{v\in\mathcal{V}}\exp(-(v-\mu_x)^2/2\sigma^2)}. \tag{36}$$

Fig. 3 compares the Receiver Operating Characteristic (ROC) curves associated with the two different strategies, and the impact of the Gaussian approximation. We can notice that the gap between the two strategies is important, this is not a surprise since the binary thresholding removes information about the forged code Y, yet this has a practical impact because one practitioner can be tempted to use the weighted bit error rate given in (15) as an authentication score for its easy implementation.

Moreover, as we will see in the next section, the plain scan of the graphical code can be used whenever the receiver needs to estimate the opponent's channel.

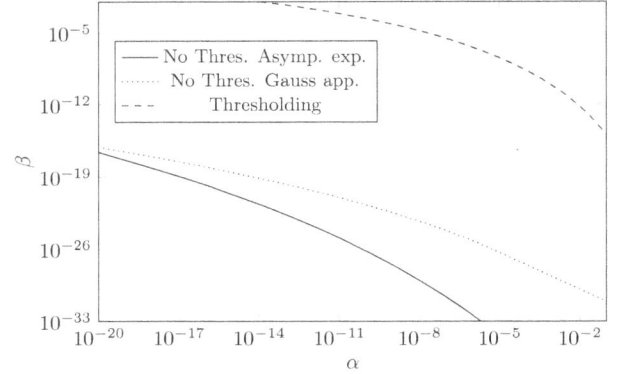

Figure 3: ROC curves for the two different strategies ($N = 2000$, $\sigma = 52$).

4. IMPACT OF THE ESTIMATION OF THE PRINT AND SCAN CHANNEL

The previous scenarios assume that the receiver has a full knowledge of the print and scan channel. Here we assume that the receiver has also to estimate the opponent channel before performing authentication. From the estimated parameters, the receiver will compute a threshold and a test according to a Neyman-Pearson strategy. Depending of the number of observations N_o, the estimated model and test will decrease the performance of the authentication system.

We consider now that the opponent uses different printing device. According to (6) and (7), the parameters to be estimated are $P_{e,W}$, $P_{e,B}$, μ_0, μ_1 and σ. We use the classical Expectation Maximization (E.M.) algorithm combined with the Newton's method to solve the maximization step.

Fig. 4 shows the authentication performances using model estimation for $N_o = 2000$ observed symbols. We can notice that the performance (and the estimated parameters) are very close to an exact knowledge of the model. This analysis shows also that if the receiver has some assumptions of the opponent channel and enough observations, he should perform model estimation instead of using the thresholding strategy. Fig. 5 shows the importance of model estimation when comparing it to a blind authentication test when the receiver assumes that both the opponent channel and his channel are identical.

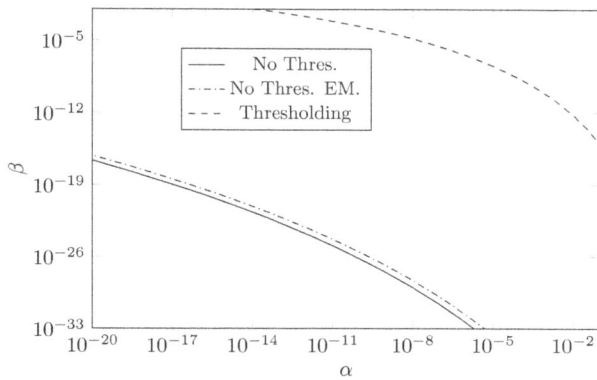

Figure 4: Authentication performance using model estimation with the EM algorithm ($N = 2000$, $N_o = 2000$, $\sigma = 52$, $\mu_0 = 50$, $\mu_1 = 150$). The asymptotic expression is used to derive the error probabilities.

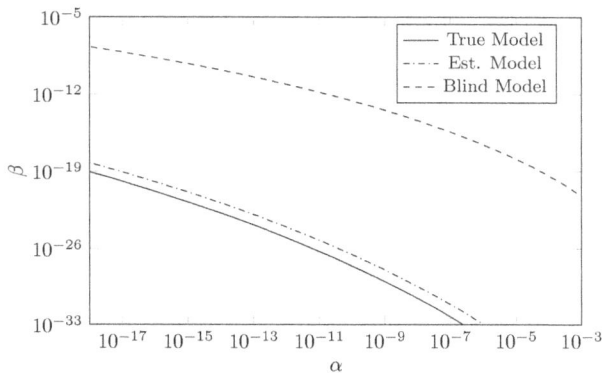

Figure 5: ROC curves comparing different knowledges about the channel while the opponent uses a different printing process ($\sigma = 40$, $\mu_0 = 40$, $\mu_1 = 160$). "True model": the receiver knows exactly this model, "Blind model": the receiver uses his printing process model as the opponent model, "Est. model": the receiver estimates the opponent channel using $N_o = 2000$ observations.

5. CONCLUSIONS AND PERSPECTIVES

This papers brings numerous conclusions on the authentication using binary codes corrupted by a manufacturing stochastic noise:

- The nature of the receiver's input is of upmost importance and thresholding is a bad strategy with respect to getting an accurate version of the genuine or forged code, except if the system requires it.

- The Gaussian approximations used to compute the ROC of the authentication system are not valuable anymore for very low type I or type II errors. Chernoff bounds have to be used instead.

- If the opponent's print and scan channel remains unknown for the receiver, he can use estimation techniques such as the E.M algorithm in order to estimate the channel.

- The proposed methodology is not impacted by the nature of the noise, and can be applied for different memoryless channels that are more realistic for modeling the printing process.

Our futures works plan to address the potential benefits for authentication of structured codes such as error-correcting codes.

6. ACKNOWLEDGEMENTS

This work was partly supported by the National French project ANR-10-CORD-019 "Estampille".

7. REFERENCES

[1] C. Baras, F. Cayre, et al. 2D bar-codes for authentication: A security approach. *Proceedings of EUSIPCO 2012*, 2012.

[2] F. Beekhof, S. Voloshynovskiy, and F. Farhadzadeh. Content authentication and identification under informed attacks. In *Information Forensics and Security (WIFS), 2012 IEEE International Workshop on*, pages 133–138. IEEE, 2012.

[3] M. Diong, P. Bas, C. Pelle, and W. Sawaya. Document authentication using 2D codes: Maximizing the decoding performance using statistical inference. In *Communications and Multimedia Security*, pages 39–54. Springer, 2012.

[4] R.G. Gallager. *Information theory and reliable communication*, volume 15. Wiley, 1968.

[5] M.D. Gaubatz, S.J. Simske, and S. Gibson. Distortion metrics for predicting authentication functionality of printed security deterrents. In *Image Processing (ICIP), 2009 16th IEEE International Conference on*, pages 1489–1492. IEEE, 2009.

[6] T. Haist and H.J. Tiziani. Optical detection of random features for high security applications. *Optics communications*, 147(1-3):173–179, 1998.

[7] J. Picard, C. Vielhauer, and N. Thorwirth. Towards fraud-proof id documents using multiple data hiding technologies and biometrics. *SPIE Proceedings–Electronic Imaging, Security and Watermarking of Multimedia Contents VI*, pages 123–234, 2004.

[8] J. Picard and J. Zhao. Improved techniques for detecting, analyzing, and using visible authentication patterns, July 28 2005. WO Patent WO/2005/067,586.

[9] WCO Press. Global congress addresses international counterfeits threat immediate action required to combat threat to finance/health, 2005. "http://www.wcoomd.org/en/media/newsroom/2005/november".

[10] WCO Press. Counterfeiting and piracy endangers global economic recovery, say global congress leaders, 2009. "http://www.wipo.int/pressroom/en/articles/2009/article_0054.html".

[11] S.S. Shariati, F.X. Standaert, L. Jacques, B. Macq, M.A. Salhi, and P. Antoine. Random profiles of laser marks. In *Proceedings of the 31st WIC Symposium on Information Theory in the Benelux*, 2010.

[12] G.E. Suh and S. Devadas. Physical unclonable functions for device authentication and secret key generation. In *Proceedings of the 44th annual Design Automation Conference*, pages 9–14. ACM, 2007.

First Investigation of Latent Fingerprints Long-term Aging using Chromatic White Light Sensors

[1]Ronny Merkel, [1]Karen Otte, [1]Robert Clausing, [1]Jana Dittmann, [1,2]Claus Vielhauer,
[3]Anja Bräutigam

[1]Research Group Multimedia & Security, Otto-von-Guericke-University of Magdeburg, Germany
[2]Department of Informatics and Media, Brandenburg University of Applied Sciences, Germany
[3]State Police Headquarters of Saxony-Anhalt, Germany

[1]{merkel,dittmann}@iti.cs.uni-magdeburg.de, [1]{karen.otte,robert.clausing}@st.ovgu.de
[2]claus.vielhauer@fh-brandenburg.de, [3]anja.braeutigam@polizei.sachsen-anhalt.de

ABSTRACT

Non-invasive high-resolution Chromatic White Light (CWL) measurement devices offer great potential for solving the challenge of latent fingerprints age determination. In this paper, we place 40 prints from different subjects on hard disk platters and capture them from three different indoor locations every week over 1.5 years, acquiring high-resolution time series (10 µm and 20 µm). In contrast to prior findings from Popa et al. (using glass substrates) we show that the ridge thickness of our very precise images does not significantly decrease over time (test goal 1). We furthermore show that pores exhibit a significant loss in contrast and contour, which might lead to the impression of becoming bigger and fewer (test goal 2). Computing the contrast based Binary Pixel aging feature (test goal 3), we observe very characteristic results, leading to the conclusion that the dominant aging property seems to be an overall loss of image contrast rather than a specific change of ridge thickness or pore size. Comparing our findings between three different indoor locations (test goal 4) and discussing them from a police point of view, we conclude that sweat composition, environmental influences and scan parameters have a significant impact on fingerprints long-term aging.

Categories and Subject Descriptors

I.5.2 [**Pattern Recognition**]: Design Methodology – *Feature evaluation and selection.*

General Terms

Algorithms, Measurement, Performance, Design, Experimentation

Keywords

Latent Prints, Crime Scene Forensics, Age Determination, Long-term Aging, Ridge Thickness, Pores, Binary Pixel, CWL Sensor.

1. INTRODUCTION

When lifting latent fingerprints from crime scenes, the age of a print is in many cases of great interest to forensic experts. In contrast to Biometrics, where 'age' usually refers to the length of time during which a human has existed or a biometric template has been enrolled [1], a traces age in the forensic context de-

scribes the time which has passed from leaving the trace (fingerprint application) until its capture by the police (lifting of the print). Determining the age of a fingerprint in such forensic context, which is subject to investigation within this paper, is an unresolved challenge since many decades. Researchers from different areas have tried to find chemical or morphological properties of latent prints, which exhibit characteristic changes during aging. However, so far no reliable results could be achieved. Reasons for this seem to originate in the huge variability between the aging behavior of different prints (mainly caused by chemical composition and environmental influences) and the obscurity of the initial state of certain features. Other reasons are the requirement of physical print development (preventing the creation of time series) and a lack of using digital processing methods.

The approaches investigated in this paper are based on digital acquisition and processing techniques and can therefore be considered as part of computational forensics [2]. However, as we are looking into the special case of non-invasive, digital trace acquisition and processing exclusively in the digital domain, we refer to the term digitized forensics, where traces are digitized contactless and non-invasively at the crime scene itself and can be left in their original context for further investigations.

Three similar, non-invasive CWL sensors [3] are used to capture high-resolution (10 µm and 20 µm) latent print time series from 40 different test subjects at three different locations over a time period of about 1.5 years. We evaluate different morphological as well as statistical aging features using digital processing techniques. The evaluation includes ridge thickness, pore brightness, amount and average size of pores as well as the statistical Binary Pixel aging feature, which has been shown in prior work [4] [5] [6] to be very characteristic for to the short-term aging of a few hours up to a few days. Our contribution is in particular:

- For the first time we evaluate the long-term aging of latent fingerprints over 1.5 years using high-resolution, non-invasive optical CWL sensors and the concept of time series.
- Using digital preprocessing and feature extraction techniques, we evaluate characteristic changes in fingerprint properties in a formal and automated way.
- Discussing the significant influence of dust on the preprocessing and feature extraction over such long period, we adapt the used digital methods to reduce the dust influence.
- Using visual comparison and automated segmentation, we show that the ridge thickness of prints does not significantly decrease during aging on hard disk platter surfaces, in contrast to earlier work of Popa et al. [7] using glass substrates.
- Evaluating changes of pore brightness, amount of pores and average pore size we show in a visual as well as automated

formal way that some changes do occur, which seem to be the result of loss in contrast and contour of the pore regions.

- Evaluating the aging behavior of the statistical Binary Pixel feature, we show that a loss of contrast and contour does occur throughout the complete fingerprint image, making this aging feature the most promising at this point in time.
- Comparing the aging behavior of the investigated features between three different capturing locations, we show that different influences from the environment, sweat composition and capturing parameters seem to have a significant impact on the aging behavior and lifting process of latent prints.
- We evaluate our findings from a police point of view and discuss potential implications to a practical application in forensic crime scene investigations.

For our evaluation, we define the following four test goals:

- Test goal 1 (TG1): Investigation of characteristic changes in the average ridge thickness over 1.5 years and a comparison with the related work of Popa et al. [7].
- Test goal 2 (TG2): Evaluation of changes in brightness of pore regions as well as the amount and average size of pores during 1.5 years of aging.
- Test goal 3 (TG3): Transfer of the Binary Pixel aging feature from the short-term aging [4] to the long-term aging over 1.5 years and a practical evaluation of its performance.
- Test goal 4 (TG4): Comparison of the results of *TG1 - TG3* between the three used capturing locations.

The remainder of this paper is structured as follows: Section 2 gives a brief introduction into state of the art approaches concerning fingerprint age estimation and the used preprocessing methods. Our test setup is then introduced in section 3, followed by a detailed description of our processing pipeline in section 4. Section 5 presents and discusses the experimental results. In section 6, the findings of this paper are discussed from a police perspective. Section 7 concludes the paper and lists potential future work.

2. STATE OF THE ART

Many fingerprint age estimation approaches have focused on chemical features, i.e. targeting changes in the chemical composition over time, as summarized in [8]. However, no reliable age estimation schemes could be developed so far. Only a few approaches have targeted physical properties, i.e. changes in the physical appearance of fingerprints during aging. Such approaches include a manual comparison of the fingerprint appearance with a reference database of prints at different aging stages [9], which could not deliver objective and reliable results. Popa et al. have investigated changes in ridge thickness and pores on glass surfaces over 0.5 years using cameras and microscopes [7], showing that ridges seem to become thinner over time, closed pores open up and single pores merge with other ones. Their results are considered comparable to our experimental studies, since glass as well as hard disk platter substrates are non-absorbing surfaces with similar structure and reflection behavior, as preliminary studies confirm. Unfortunately, they do not report the mean ridge thickness of their experiments, only the range is given. Furthermore, it is not clear how the ridge thickness was obtained, e.g. if the similar ridge location was used for all temporal images or how many distances were collected from each image. To provide at least some means of comparison, we average the ridge thickness range reported by Popa et al. directly after print application and after 0.5 years. This simplification of their results leads to a ridge thickness decrease of 60 µm (20%) and will be used for comparison with our experimental results (*TG1*).

For investigating changes in ridge thickness (*TG1*), we use the ridge segmentation algorithm proposed by Hong et al. [10] and its implementation in Matlab by Kovesi et al. [11], optimized for 500 dpi images. The algorithm uses orientation and frequency fields to apply a block based Gabor filtering for the enhancement of fingerprint ridges. We implement such algorithm in C++/OpenCV and adapt it (e.g. by linear scaling of the filter kernels) to segment ridges in our high-resolution, digitized latent fingerprint images (see also section 4.4.1). For the extraction of pores (*TG2*, see also section 4.4.2), we use a Mexican Hat filter as proposed by Jain et al. [12], showing a strong filter response to pores as well as ridge edges.

In prior work [4] [5] [6], we have investigated a novel aging feature called Binary Pixel, which observes changes in the relative amount of background pixels in non-invasively captured and binarized fingerprint time series. The feature shows a very promising logarithmic aging tendency (i.e. fingerprint pixels disappear over time in a logarithmic manner). However, such feature was only investigated for the short-term aging (a few hours up to a few days) and is here applied for the first time to investigate the long-term aging behavior of fingerprints (*TG3*, see also section 4.4.3).

3. OUR TEST SETUP

Our experimental test setup consists of 40 latent prints from the left or right index finger of different subjects. Fingers were not pre-treated in any way (such as washing or touching the forehead) and the application process (e.g. contact time or pressure) was not controlled, to achieve a realistic distribution of samples. Samples are applied to well-reflecting hard disk platters (metal coated disk from hard disks, ideal surface for the used capturing device). The samples were let to dry for at least 24 hours, to exclude the comparatively strong aging response during the drying process of the prints and to distinguish the investigated long-term aging of the Binary Pixel feature from the strong logarithmic aging tendency of its short-term aging observed in prior work [4].

Three FRT MicroProf 200 CWL 600 measurement devices [3] are used in parallel, capturing the prints at three different locations *A* (University of Magdeburg), *B* (University of Applied Sciences Brandenburg) and *C* (State Police Head Quarters Saxony-Anhalt). Each sample is captured in regular time intervals of approximately one week (depending on sensor maintenance and holidays) for about 18 month (*1 month = 30 days*, $t_{max} \approx 1.5$ *years*). This leads to a total of 66 - 77 temporal samples per time series (the total time period t_{max} varies between 16 and 20 month for the three different capturing locations). Samples are aligned by gluing the used hard disk platters onto metal plates, which are attached to the measurement table by screws. If necessary, samples are manually aligned with an accuracy of about ±10 µm. Only the intensity images produced by the sensor are used, since they are of higher quality than the topographic images for our specific case. The complete test setup is given in table 1.

Table 1. Our experimental test setup.

	Location A	Location B	Location C
Period	31.03.11 – 08.12.12	09.06.11 – 08.12.12	24.08.11 – 19.12.12
Temp.	µ = 24.4°C σ = 1.9°C	µ = 23.8°C σ = 1.5°C	µ = 25.1°C σ = 2.7°C
Hum.	µ = 41.3%; σ = 6.2%	µ = 46.9% σ = 6.8%	µ = 32.2% σ = 7.2%
Subjects	9 males / 1 female	8 males / 2 females	9 males / 11 females
Age	26 – 38	24 - 42	28 – 57
TG1	10 time series 8 x 8 mm, 10 µm	10 time series 8 x 8 mm, 10 µm	20 time series 4 x 4 mm, 20 µm
TG2	Pores visible: 5 series	Pores visible: 3 series	No pores visible
TG3	10 time series 4 x 4 mm, 10 µm	10 time series 4 x 4 mm, 10 µm	20 time series 4 x 4 mm, 20 µm

In total, 40 time series are available from all three locations for the investigation of test goals *TG1*, *TG3* and *TG4*. For the evaluation of pores in *TG2*, only 8 time series are used, since pores are not present on the other images. As described in section 4.4.1, images are cropped during preprocessing from 800 x 800 pixels to 560 x 560 pixels or 200 x 200 pixels to 80 x 80 pixels respectively. For the investigation of the Binary Pixel feature (*TG3*), a size of 4 x 4 mm was used for all three locations, since it was shown in prior work [13] that this measured area size is sufficient.

4. OUR APPROACH FOR THE EXTRACTION OF LONG-TERM AGING FEATURES

For the evaluation of long-term fingerprint aging features, we first define a processing pipeline, which describes different steps from the capture of fingerprint time series until the evaluation of characteristic aging features. It furthermore models a print's aging as well as influences on the aging and capturing process (see fig. 1).

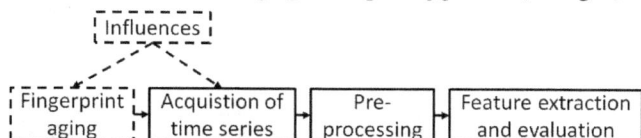

Figure 1. Our processing pipeline (solid boxes) and its input (dashed boxes) for the evaluation of print long-term aging.

In future work, the pipeline might be extended by an *age classification* step, in which rule based or machine learning based methods are applied to assign a fingerprint to well defined time classes. However, such *age classification* step remains subject to future work, since it requires the identification of characteristic aging features prior to successful age estimation.

4.1 The Fingerprint Aging Process

Fingerprint aging is a natural process, which leads to changes in the morphology as well as the chemical composition of fingerprints. In the scope of our experiments, the focus lies on the investigation of morphological changes during aging, which are captured non-invasively. Exemplary images of two captured time series are depicted in fig. 2. It can be seen that a loss of image contrast seems to occur over time. However, the strength of this loss seems to vary strongly between the time series of different fingerprint samples, probably caused by a different chemical composition of the prints. It is to note that the first image ($t = 1d$) is captured after one day, where the fingerprint has dried up already and therefore the strong logarithmic increase in background pixel values observed by the Binary Pixel feature for the short-term aging (see prior work [4]) has mostly passed.

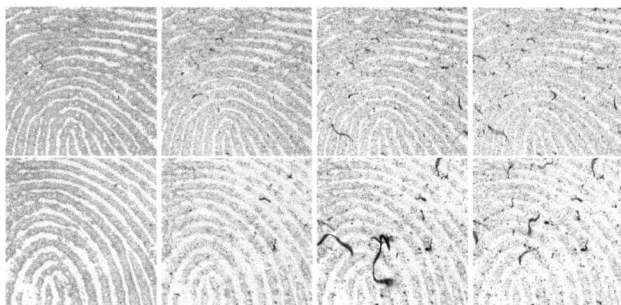

Figure 2. Exemplary images (5.6 x 5.6 mm, 10 μm) of two captured time series *S1* and *S2* (from left to right: $t = 1d$, $t = 0.5y$, $t = 1y$, $t = 1.5y$).

Furthermore, dust can clearly be seen in fig. 2 to settle on the prints over time (and also disappear again), which is discussed in

the following sections. Changes of ridges and pores cannot clearly be observed without additional magnification (for that purpose see fig. 9 and 11) and it cannot easily be distinguished whether the reduced amount of visible pores over time is caused by pores disappearing or by the loss of contrast. However, the presence and visibility of pores seem to vary between different samples. In our exemplary time series of fig. 2, pores are visible in both series (slightly better for series *S1*, upper row). In other images, pores cannot be observed at all. This is an important difference to exemplary fingerprints, where pores are usually very well visible.

4.2 Acquisition of Fingerprint Time Series

In the acquisition step of our processing pipeline, we capture latent fingerprint samples in regular time intervals of approximately one week ($\Delta t \approx 1w$) over a total time period of about 1.5 years ($t_{max} \approx 1.5y$). Three FRT MicroProf 200 CWL 600 [3] surface measurement devices are used, which are based on the chromatic aberration of lenses and can capture high-resolution intensity as well as topography images with a lateral resolution of up to 2 μm and a longitudinal resolution of 20 nm. To study the aging behavior in such way is only possible because the capturing process is non-invasive and the fingerprints are not subject to any pre-treatment. If development would be applied prior to the capturing process or if the lifting itself would be invasive, prints would be altered and therefore could not be captured again at a later point in time for the extraction of changes caused by aging. This is a very important improvement in comparison to common lifting methods, since only consecutive scans from non-modified fingerprint samples can provide accurate results for aging studies.

4.3 Influences on Aging & Capturing Process

A complex network of different factors influences the aging behavior as well as the capturing process of latent fingerprints. Apart from the chemical composition of fingerprints, environmental influences (e.g. temperature, humidity, vibrations), surface characteristics (e.g. reflection properties, structure, texture), scan settings (e.g. resolution, size of the measured area) and characteristic differences in the way a print is applied (e.g. contact time, contact pressure, smearing) impact the aging as well as the capturing process. It is not realistic to investigate such complex network of influences in the limited scope of this paper. Therefore, we refer to first qualitative studies of the issue conducted in [4].

Sweat/sebum composition and fingerprint application characteristics are strongly dependent on the individual leaving the print and cannot be determined or estimated at a practical crime scene. We therefore need to accept such influences as natural sources of variability in the aging behavior of latent prints. We do not control them during our experiments, to investigate aging under such natural fluctuations.

Environmental influences might be estimated from a crime scene under certain circumstances. However, such estimation is very limited. In the scope of this paper, we conduct our experiments at three different, non-climatized laboratories (simulating indoor crime scenes), where certain fluctuations in temperature and humidity do occur (see section 3). We compare the aging behavior between these three 'crime scenes' in test goal *TG4*, to see if significant differences in the aging behavior can be observed under such moderate climate variations.

One of the most significant environmental influences on the calculation of aging features is dust. Dust may settle on the latent print at random times and locations during the aging period and might also be removed by air circulation at random times (see also fig. 2). It might also impact different features with different strength. We therefore need to design specific preprocessing methods to erase or at least limit the influence of dust, which is discussed in section 4.4.

The surface influence is set constant during our experiments by the use of a fixed set of similar, well reflecting hard disk platters. Other surfaces are of importance and need to be investigated in future work. The scan settings are set constant by fixing the dot distance and size of measured area as described in section 3.

4.4 Preprocessing of Fingerprint Images

The preprocessing is the most complex and computationally expensive step of our processing pipeline. The used methods are applied to all images of a time series in the same manner, except for the first image, which is often processed in a different way and used for creating a mask. To remove artifacts from samples not laying totally planar on the measurement table, each input image is planarized by a best-fit plane subtraction. The planarized images are then preprocessed in different ways, depending on the investigated features for *TG1* - *TG3*. Our test goal *TG4* compares the results between the three different locations and therefore does not need any specific preprocessing.

4.4.1 Preprocessing for Ridge Extraction (TG1)

In the scope of test goal *TG1*, we investigate changes in ridge thickness during aging, which has been stated by Popa et al. [7] to decrease over time for glass substrates. In particular, we use the print enhancement algorithm proposed by Hong et al. [10], based on the calculation of orientation and frequency fields and a block-based Gabor filtering. The method is not openly available, but has been re-implemented in Matlab by Kovesi et al. [11]. However, the algorithm is optimized for resolutions of 500 dpi and performs suboptimal on our high-resolution CWL images of 2540 dpi (10 μm) and 1270 dpi (20 μm). We therefore implement the algorithm in C++/OpenCV and adapt it to high-resolution images.

In our implementation, the most important aspect can be seen in the linear scalability of the used filter kernels for different resolutions, which are adapted in respect to their original values from [10] and [11]. This is important to avoid the loss of image quality caused by downscaling to 500 dpi. However, the significantly higher image resolution leads to ridges being split, especially around pores, even when using scaled filter kernels. Therefore, we apply a Gaussian Blur (*kernelsize = dpi/100*) to the normalized fingerprint images, which is effectively resolving the problem.

After normalization and blurring of a fingerprint image, the orientation field is calculated according to [10] and [11] by using Gauss gradients and convolution. Furthermore, the frequency field is computed by an orthogonal projection of blocks in respect to the ridge orientation and the wavelengths within these blocks are calculated. Apart from a linear scaling of the projected blocks, the given confidence interval for wavelengths was removed, since larger kernel sizes seem to produce a wider variation of wavelengths. As suggested in [11] we use the median frequency of all blocks instead of their individual frequencies to provide better results for the final Gabor filtering. As described in [10] and [11], images are Gabor filtered in a block based manner and the filter response is binarized by a threshold of *th = 0.85*. To remove artifacts of different filtering steps at the image edges, 120 pixels (for 10 μm images) or 60 pixels (for 20 μm images) are cropped from each edge, resulting in a final size of 560 x 560 pixels for 10 μm images and 80 x 80 pixels for 20 μm images (see fig. 3).

It can be seen from fig. 3 (enhanced ridges) and fig. 2 (corresponding original images) that the algorithm enhances the ridges quite well for *t = 1d* (left images) with a certain margin of error.

Such error may occur at areas of distortions, e.g. where neighboring ridges are located very close to each other. Here, minutiae might be added or removed, leading to adjacent ridges being joined or vice versa. Comparing the ridge enhancement performance for different points in time *t* (see fig. 2 and 3 from left to right), it can be seen that the increased settlement of dust poses a major challenge to a successful ridge extraction, since it changes the orientation of image regions and therefore leads to false minutiae and ridges. To avoid this problem, we reduce the influence of dust by computing the orientation map only from the first image of a time series and use this map for all following images, keeping the orientations constant while not interfering with the ridge thickness. This adaption is feasible since at this point our interest is only in the general presence of a characteristic ridge thickness decrease during aging. In case no significant decrease exists (as is shown in section 5.1), the feature might be excluded from future study. Only in case a characteristic ridge thickness decrease would be observed, a practical determination of ridge thickness at crime scenes would be necessary, requiring additional methods for the exclusion of dust.

Figure 3. Exemplary images (5.6 x 5.6 mm, 10 μm) of two captured time series *S1* and *S2*, enhanced using our adaption of the algorithm from [10] and [11] (from left to right: *t = 1d*, *t = 0.5y*, *t = 1y*, *t = 1.5y*).

Figure 4. Exemplary images (5.6 x 5.6 mm, 10 μm) of two captured time series *S1* and *S2*, enhanced using our adaption of the algorithm from [10] and [11] by applying the orientation field of the first image to all consecutive images of a time series (from left to right: *t = 1d*, *t = 0.5y*, *t = 1y*, *t = 1.5y*).

Fig. 4 illustrates that this adaption does remove most distortions introduced by dust and the loss of contrast when aging, leaving a few minor distortions. Apart from reusing the orientation map, the algorithm is applied to each temporal image of a time series independently. The segmented fingerprint ridges can then be used in the feature extraction step of our processing pipeline for computing the average ridge thickness for *TG1*.

4.4.2 Preprocessing for Pores Extraction (TG2)

For segmenting pores from our captured time series, we use a Mexican Hat filter as proposed by Jain et al. [12]. Essentially, the parameterization of such Mexican Hat filter is based on a scale factor sigma, which is suggested to be 1.32 for live scans (1000 dpi) in [12]. For our high-resolution latent fingerprints (2540 dpi), we observed good results using a sigma of 5.2. Exemplary results of such filter application are depicted in fig. 5 (rows 1 and 4).

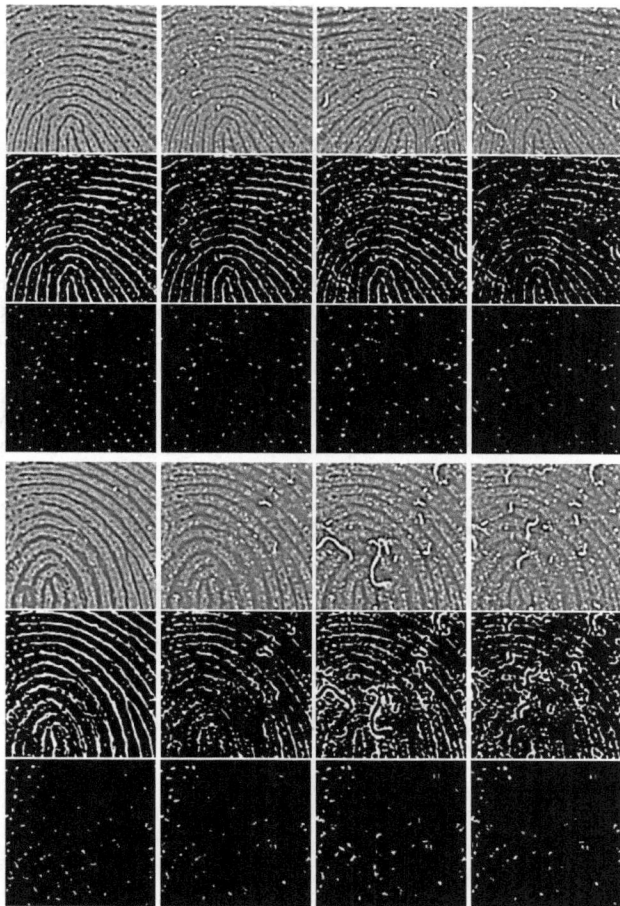

Figure 5. Exemplary images (5.6 x 5.6 mm, 10 µm) of two captured time series *S1* and *S2*, processed using our adaption of the Mexican Hat filter proposed in [12] (rows 1 and 4), followed by normalization and binarization (rows 2 and 5) and the removal of ridge edges and pores of invalid size (rows 3 and 6). From left to right: *t = 1d, t = 0.5y, t = 1y, t = 1.5y.*

To extract pores from the Mexican Hat filter response, a fixed range of the image histogram is used to normalize the image to the interval [0;1]. Such interval is calculated for the first image of a time series and then fixed for all other images of the series, excluding 1% outermost histogram values to erase outliers. After normalization, a fixed threshold of $th = 0.32$ is applied for binarization. Exemplary resulting images are depicted in fig. 5, rows 2 and 5. It can be seen that ridgeline edges often show a similar strong response to the Mexican Hat filter than pores. Therefore, such edges should explicitly be excluded from the image. This is done by using the segmented ridges from section 4.4.1. The valleys of the first ridge image of a time series are dilated two times (with kernelsize 3) and then applied as a mask to the binarized pores image, effectively removing ridgeline edge artifacts from it. Pores with a size *20 pixels < s < 100 pixels* (first image) and *s < 20 pixels* (all consecutive images) are removed and the images are cropped analog to the ridge enhancement of section 4.4.1 to exclude filtering artifacts at the edges. The cropped images depict the pores segmented from each input image. For our two exem-

plary time series, the detected pores (white) are overlaid with the binarized original images (gray) in fig. 6 for a manual verification of the pore segmentation approach.

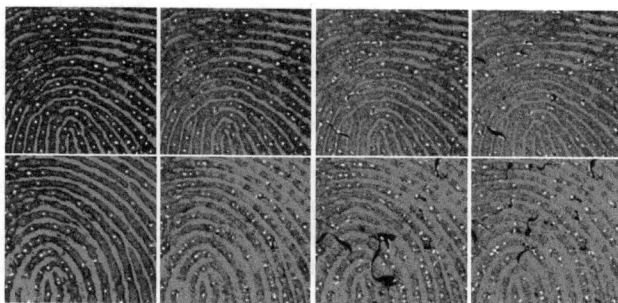

Figure 6. Exemplary binarized images (5.6 x 5.6 mm, 10 µm) of two captured time series *S1* and *S2* with enhanced pores (fingerprint: dark gray, background: light gray, pores: white). From left to right: *t = 1d, t = 0.5y, t = 1y, t = 1.5y.*

As can be seen from fig. 6, our segmentation approach can successfully identify pores from the time series. However, as a manual inspection of different time series shows, by far not all latent fingerprints exhibit pores. In such case, neither the pore detection algorithm nor a human observer can clearly identify them. This is an important difference to approaches extracting pores from exemplary fingerprint images, which are of much better quality. We therefore have to carefully select time series, which do contain pores and investigate only those series. Moreover, our interest is only on false positives (not false negatives), since for investigating the aging behavior of pores, a subset of all pores of an image is sufficient. However, it is important that the segmented pores are indeed pores. At this point in time, only a human observer can produce a reliable ground truth in that respect. Using a manual comparison of the first image of each time series with its corresponding original image and a determination of its false positives rate, we only consider series with a true positives rate *TPR > 0.7*, assuring that more than two thirds of segmented objects are indeed pores. From our complete test set, we receive 8 time series in total, which are feasible for pore evaluation. Only images with a dot distance of 10 µm seem to be of sufficient quality for that purpose, excluding all 20 µm time series (see also section 3).

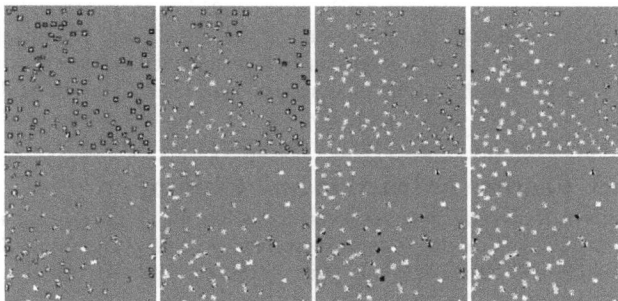

Figure 7. Exemplary images (5.6 x 5.6 mm, 10 µm) of two time series *S1* and *S2* binarized and overlaid with our computed pore mask (from left to right: *t = 1d, t = 0.5y, t = 1y, t = 1.5y*).

When studying the images of fig. 6, it can be seen that for increasing times *t*, pores might disappear and additional pore-like objects appear. This behavior seems to be caused by changes in the image contrast when aging, as well as dust particles. Therefore, a certain amount of pores should be identified in the first image and then exclusively be investigated over time, ignoring all later appearing pores and other particles. We achieve this by segmenting pores in the first image of a time series and creating a pore mask to be applied to all consecutive images. To investigate also the close proximity of a pore, we dilate each found pore six times (with kernelsize 3), creating the final pore mask. To illustrate such procedure using our two exemplary time series, we overlay the binarized original images with the created pore mask in fig. 7. It can be seen that the pores identified by our mask seem to become brighter and/or bigger over time (pixels in the mask turn white) and in some cases disappear (pixels in the mask turn black), which will be discussed in section 5. Having successfully segmented pores and their adjacent regions, aging features can be calculated.

4.4.3 Preprocessing for Binary Pixel Feature (TG3)

As a statistical feature, the Binary Pixel aging feature has the potential to capture all changes in a fingerprint image at the same time, may they occur at ridges, pores or other regions of the image. The feature allows for two different normalization methods, referred to as dynamic and static normalization [4]. In both cases, 1% of the outermost gray values from the image histogram are excluded to erase outliers and the pixel values are normalized to the interval [0;1]. A normalized image is then binarized using a fixed threshold of $th = 0.8$, resulting in a segmentation of fingerprint pixels from background pixels. It is to note that this segmentation is different from the one computed in section 4.4.1 for the ridge thickness calculation, since the latter one requires a continuous progression of the ridge, whereas the Binary Pixel feature only needs to differentiate fingerprint pixels from background pixels, which occur as irregular particles, droplets or puddles.

The main difference between the dynamic and static normalization method lies in the selection of the gray value range used for normalization. While the dynamic normalization adaptively adjusts this range to include 99% of inner histogram gray values for each temporal image of a time series, the static normalization computes such range only for the first image and applies the determined range to all consecutive images. Dynamic normalization can successfully exclude shifts of the complete histogram, whereas static normalization provides robustness against partial changes. When investigating the changes of the lower and upper histogram bounds of a dynamically normalized time series during aging, it can be observed that the lower bound shows a very characteristic decrease in gray values over time for most time series. It appears that such decrease is caused by dust settling on the image, which is represented by very dark image pixels and is therefore added to the lower end of the histogram. Therefore, dynamic normalization is subject to a systematic decrease of the lower bound of the histogram range and hence should not be used. However, using static normalization can successfully exclude such influence of dust, since the range of the histogram is fixed.

4.5 Feature Extraction and Evaluation

After a successful preprocessing, including image planarization, normalization, ridges or pores segmentation, binarization or mask creation and - especially important - dust reduction, we can compute the aging features used in our investigations. From the temporal fingerprint images of a time series, the calculated features are combined to experimental aging curves, depicting the change of feature values in respect to time. The curves are then evaluated for all test series to investigate if characteristic changes during aging exist, where characteristic aging behavior of a feature is mainly defined by the monotony of its curves. If a curve is monotonic increasing or decreasing over the complete investigated time period and if other time series show similar trends, the feature might be feasible for age determination. Similar to section 4.4, only the features for test goals *T1 - T3* are calculated, which are then compared between the three different locations in *TG4*.

4.5.1 Ridge Thickness Extraction (TG1)

For our test goal *TG1*, we compute the average ridge thickness *thick(I)* of a fingerprint image *I*. Our algorithm is based on the general definition of skeletons described in [14]. In our implementation of such algorithm, the skeleton of a fingerprint ridge consists of all center points c of valid circles *valid(c)* along the ridges. Only points between the edges of a ridge (based on the segmentation of section 4.4.1) are considered. A valid circle *valid(c)* has exactly two intersection points s_c with the ridge edges and its diameter $d(c)$ is equal to the distance between the two intersections $s1_c$ and $s2_c$ of the circle with the ridge edges:

$$valid(c) = \begin{cases} true, & if \ |s_c| = 2 \ and \ |\overrightarrow{s1_c s2_c}| = d(c) \\ false, & else \end{cases} \quad (1)$$

Formula (1) ensures that the diameter $d(c)$ of a circle centered in the middle of the ridge is equal to the diameter of the ridge, since circles with more than two intersections s_c have a larger diameter than the ridge and circles with less than two intersections have a smaller one. Ensuring that the distance between the two intersecting points $s1_c$ and $s2_c$ is equal to the diameter $d(c)$ effectively excludes circles with center points c not lying in the middle of a ridge as well as circles lying inside bifurcations. The skeletonized ridges of two exemplary, partial fingerprints are depicted in fig. 8.

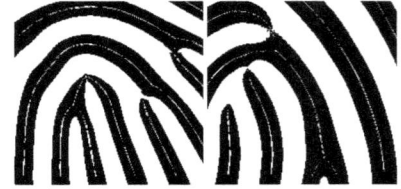

Figure 8. Exemplary visualization (2 x 2 mm, 10 μm) of skeletonized images ($t = 1d$) of time series S1 (left) and S2 (right).

From the n extracted valid circles *valid(c)* of a skeletonized fingerprint image, the average ridge thickness *thick(I)* is computed:

$$thick(I) = \frac{1}{n} \cdot \sum_{x=1}^{n} d(c_x) \quad (2)$$

4.5.2 Brightness, Amount and Size of Pores (TG2)

For evaluating test goal *TG2*, we first determine the relative amount of white pixels *pbright(I)* from the binarized original images I_B of size $n \ x \ m$ for all pore areas (pores and their vicinity as described in the dilated pore mask I_M from the preprocessing output of section 4.4.2). The goal of this brightness calculation is to formally verify our observation from fig. 7 that the pores and their surrounding area become brighter over time:

$$pbright(I) = \frac{1}{n \cdot m} \cdot \sum_{x=1, y=1}^{n,m} I_M(x,y) \cdot I_B(x,y) \quad (3)$$

We then compute the amount of pores *pcnt* from the segmented pores I_P (see section 4.4.2 and fig. 5, rows 3 and 6):

$$pcnt(I) = CountObjects(I_P) \quad (4)$$

Furthermore, the average size *psize* of a pore is calculated from the amount of white (pore) pixels in the binarized pores image I_P:

$$psize(I) = \frac{\sum_{x=1, y=1}^{n,m} I_P(x,y)}{pcnt} \quad (5)$$

4.5.3 Binary Pixel Feature Calculation (TG3)

Test goal *TG3* is investigated by calculating the Binary Pixel feature value *bp(I)* for each image *I* (size $n \ x \ m$) of a time series. It is defined as the relative amount of (white) background pixels of the binarized fingerprint image I_B, computed in section 4.4.3:

$$bp(I) = \frac{1}{n \cdot m} \cdot \sum_{x=1, y=1}^{n,m} I_B(x,y) \quad (6)$$

5. EXPERIMENTAL RESULTS

In this section we present the experimental result for our test goals of determining characteristic changes in ridge thickness (*TG1*), pores (*TG2*) and the Binary Pixel feature (*TG3*) and compare them between different indoor application scenarios (*TG4*).

5.1 Changes in Ridge Thickness (TG1)

When manually comparing the ridge thickness of different samples between different points in time using temporally mixed images (see fig. 9), we cannot observe a significant difference.

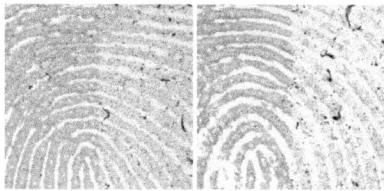

Figure 9. Temporally mixed grayscale images (5.6 x 5.6 mm, 10 µm, left side of each image: *t = 1d*, right side of each image: *t = 1.5y*) of the exemplary time series *S1* and *S2* for manual comparison of ridge thickness changes during aging.

In the scope of our experiments, the pixel size is 10 µm (locations *A* and *B*) or 20 µm (location *C*). Therefore, a loss in ridge thickness of 60 µm (20%) as reported by Popa et al. in [7] for glass substrates equals 6 or 3 pixels of ridge diameter decrease in our experiments. Popa et al. observed this maximum decrease over a period of 0.5 years. Therefore, the ridge thickness decrease in our 1.5 years long experiments should be significantly higher. Fig. 10 shows the ridge thickness over time for all 10 test series of location *A* and *B* and 10 exemplary series of location *C*. From the figure it can be seen that for the samples captured with 10 µm (upper two images), we observe in most cases a decrease in ridge thickness of less than one pixel (10 µm). We can therefore not confirm the observation of Popa et al. of a significant decrease in ridge thickness for our investigated hard disk platter surfaces. However, it remains a subject of future research to investigate if the different surfaces used (glass vs. hard disk platter) have an influence on such different observations).

Instead of a decrease in ridge thickness, it rather seems to be the case that the contrast of the ridges decreases significantly over time, where pixels become brighter and finally disappear all over the complete fingerprint image in a similar manner. Such loss of contrast (which is targeted by the later investigated Binary Pixel feature) is corrugating the edges of the ridges and might lead to the false conclusion of a decrease in ridge width. It can furthermore be seen from fig. 10, that in one case of the samples from location *B* (dotted line), a sharp decrease of ridge thickness can be observed after about 10 months, which is caused by different dust fluffs settling on the image and disappearing again, changing the enhanced ridges several times and therefore leading to a distortion of the results.

For the 20 µm samples of location *C* (lower image of fig. 10), it can be seen that the curves seem to be very smooth in some cases (and do not show any decrease of ridge thickness), but very noisy in others. This is caused by the comparatively small fingerprint area left for investigation (the block-based Gabor filter and other preprocessing steps lead to a decrease of the filtered image size from 200 x 200 pixels to 80 x 80 pixels), which contains only a few blocks of ridge enhancement in comparison to the images of location *A* and *B* (where the image size is 560 x 560 pixels after preprocessing, see also section 4.4.1). Images from location *C* therefore depict the comparatively constant nature of the ridge

thickness very well (if not distorted) or very poor (in case a dust fluff settles on the evaluated area).

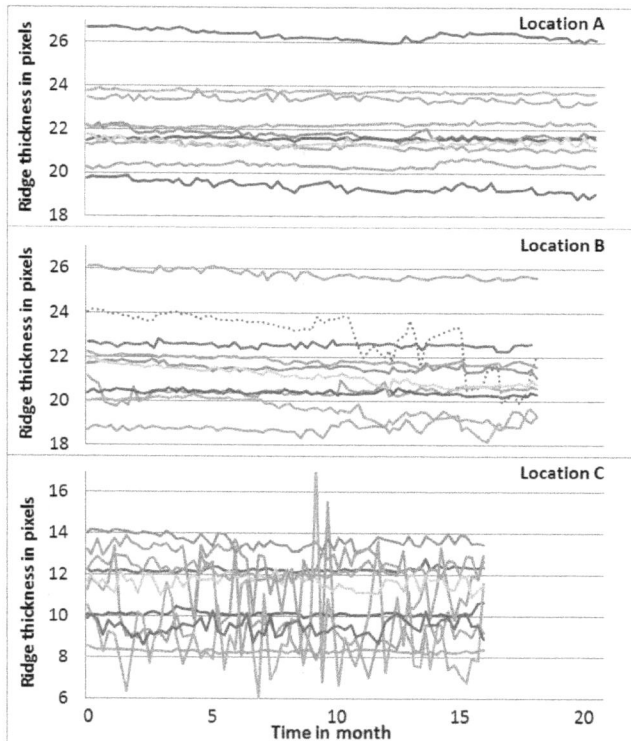

Figure 10. Mean fingerprint ridge thickness in pixels in respect to time, 10 exemplary curves for locations *A*, *B* (1 pixel ≜ 10 µm) and *C* (1 pixel ≜ 20 µm).

5.2 Changes of Pores (TG2)

As introduced in section 4.4.2, we manually inspect the first image of each time series and select only those series where detected pores seem to a human observer to be indeed real pores (true positives) for at least 70% of cases. The resulting 8 series (exclusively 10 µm samples) are used for the following evaluation.

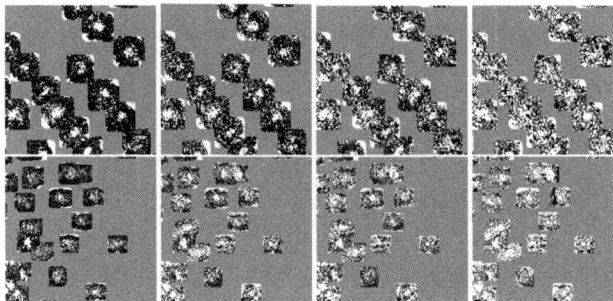

Figure 11. Enlarged image blocks (upper row: 1.6 x 1.6 mm, 10 µm, lower row: 2.4 x 2.4 mm, 10 µm) of masked pores (12 dilate operations for better visualization, overlay with binarized original image) from the two captured time series *S1* and *S2* (from left to right: *t = 1d*, *t = 0.5y*, *t = 1y*, *t = 1.5y*).

When manually inspecting the changes of pores and their close proximity (see fig. 11), a significant loss of contrast around the pores can be observed, where pixels become brighter or disappear at random, corrugating the edges of the pores and leading to a decrease in their visibility. However, such increased brightness does not seem to occur in a systematic manner (e.g. by a systematic increase of pore size), but rather at random throughout the complete ridge area, leading to a loss of form and sharpness of the pores edges, finally rendering them invisible. This loss of contrast is formally shown in fig. 12, which depicts the relative frequency of white pixels from the masked and binarized areas around the pores in respect to time.

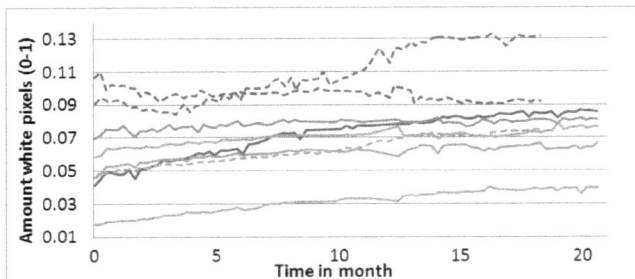

Figure 12. Relative amount of white pixels from masked and binarized pore regions in respect to the time (location A: five solid curves, location B: three dashed curves).

It can be seen from fig. 12 that for all but one sample (where several pores are covered with dust fluffs during aging), the amount of white pixels of the masked and binarized pore regions increases over time, supporting our earlier finding of a significant increase in brightness of the ridge area around the pores.

For investigating the amount and average size of pores during aging, a visual inspection can be performed using fig. 5, 7 and 11. For our 8 time series containing pores, the amount of pores within an image as well as the average size of such pores is depicted in fig. 13 in relation to time. It can be seen for location A (upper image) that the total amount of pores seems to decrease over time. This is most likely caused by the loss of image contrast and contour of the pores from the corrugation of their edges, which leads to a decreased detectability by the segmentation algorithm. After a certain time, it is even for the human eye very hard to identify the pores (see also fig. 11). This trend is complemented by an increase in the pores average size (fig. 13, second image from top). Such increase seems to be caused by corrugated edges of the pores, leading to bigger areas being identified as pores by the segmentation algorithm, rather than a real and continuous increase in the pore size.

For location B (fig. 13, lower two images), this characteristic trend seems to be distorted at some points. Small changes in brightness and contour seem to cause significant changes in the Mexican Hat filter response, where the pores size and detectability changes. The algorithm therefore seems to be quite vulnerable to changes of image contrast and pore contour, which renders it infeasible for a practical age determination, requiring a certain level of robustness. However, the much clearer aging characteristic of location A shows that also other influences contribute to such distortion. One of this influences might be dust falling on the print, e.g. due to an increased amount of polluted air at location B.

To summarize our evaluation of changes in pores, we conclude that a decrease of image contrast over time as well as the increased corrugation of pore edges leads to less pores being correctly identified by a human observer as well as our preprocessing algorithm. The pores which can still be segmented after some time seem to become bigger, however, this seems to be rather a result of corrugated edges than of a real increase of the pores size, as can be seen in fig. 11. The most dominant aging characteristic of pores therefore does not seem to be a change of size, but rather the loss of contrast and edge contour. However, the macroscopic appearance of pores is strongly dependent on the sensitivity of the

applied lifting technique. A loss in pore contour might be interpreted as enlargement or merging of pores [7].

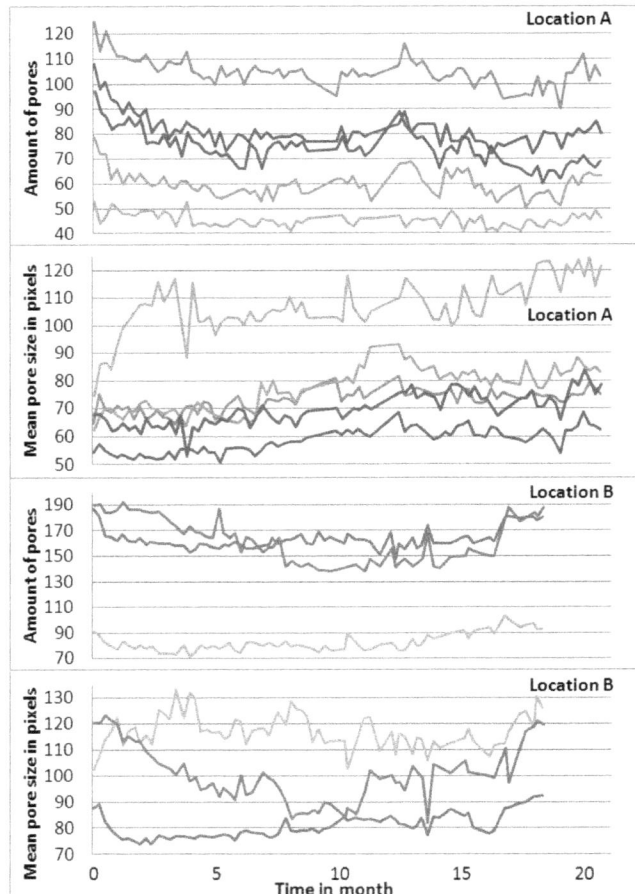

Figure 13. Amount of pores and mean pore size in pixels in respect to time (location A: 5 series, location B: 3 series).

5.3 Changes of Binary Pixel Feature (TG3)

From the evaluation of ridge thickness and changes of pores, we conclude that the most dominant source of changes during aging seems to be the loss of image contrast, which occurs over the complete image. This loss of contrast is targeted by the Binary Pixel aging feature, whose experimental results are depicted in fig. 14 for all time series of the locations A and B and 10 exemplary series of location C. The results show a clear increasing tendency for most aging curves of all three locations (including both resolutions), which is often similar to a logarithmic progression. It is to note here that the first image was captured after at least 24 hours, meaning the steep logarithmic increase of the aging curve within the first few hours (short-term aging, see also [4]) is already excluded. It can also be seen that not all curves have a similarly high slope, meaning the aging speed of different fingerprint samples is very different, most likely depending on the chemical composition of the print.

A few curves of fig. 14 also show distortions or even a decreasing trend. Distortions are mainly caused by dust particles or dust fluffs settling on the sample or disappearing at random. While the influence of dust on the normalization interval is successfully excluded by using static normalization, an influence on the aging feature calculation still exists due to dust covering (white) background pixels with (black) dust pixels. Small particles seem to be very minor in their influence, however, bigger particles such as dust fluffs or hairs can change a significant amount of pixels from white to black or vice versa, which can be recognized by abrupt changes in the curves progression. For location *C*, a sudden drop of the Binary Pixel value after 13 months can be observed for several curves. Such distortion might either be caused by hairs settling on the measurement table, covering different samples simultaneously or by other influences, e.g. from the environment or the capturing device.

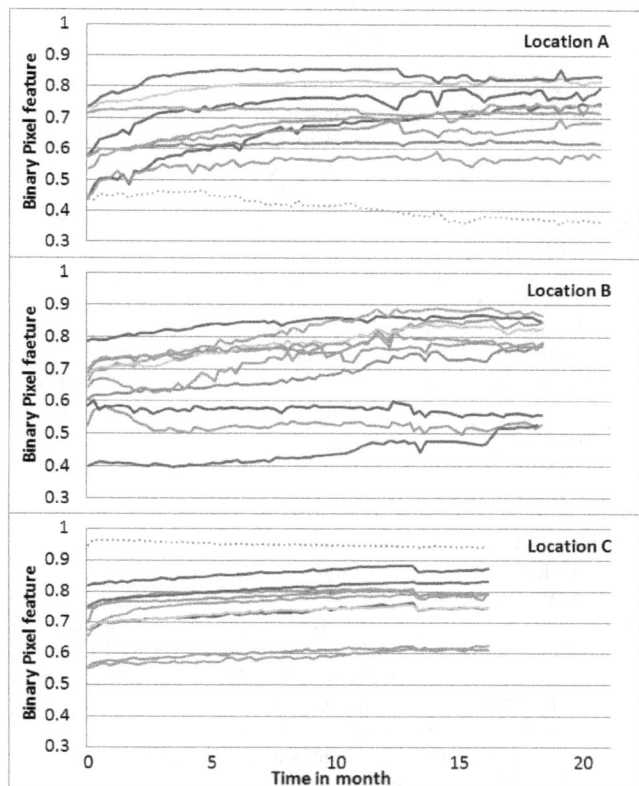

Figure 14. The Binary Pixel feature in respect to time, 10 exemplary curves for locations *A*, *B* and *C*.

In few cases, curves might show a decreasing aging behavior. This can be caused by very poor sample quality, as is the case for the dotted curve of location *C* (fig. 14, lower image). In this case, the captured image consists of so few fingerprint pixels that the experimental curve is mainly measuring the amount of dust which settles on the platter over time, which would be similar to investigating the aging of an empty surface. In one case of location *A* (fig. 14, dotted curve in upper image), a decreasing trend is produced by the darkening of a certain region within the print. This might be caused by certain distortions of the capturing process or a certain (maybe external) chemical substance within the residue.

Overall, the Binary Pixel feature seems to exhibit a very characteristic, logarithmic aging behavior for the long-term aging, confirming prior results of short-term aging studies. However, additional distortions occur, such as dust.

5.4 Different Locations Aging Behavior (TG4)
Comparing the aging behavior of ridge thickness, pores and the Binary Pixel feature between the three different locations *A*, *B*, and *C*, it can be concluded that especially the decreased image resolution of location *C* leads to much more distorted results for this location, especially for the ridge thickness evaluation (fig. 10) and the pore evaluation, where pores with a dot distance of 20 μm

could not be extracted at all. For the Binary Pixel feature evaluation (fig. 14), 20 μm seem to be sufficient for good quality results.

Comparing the locations *A* and *B*, which have used the same capturing resolution, much more distorted results are obtained from location *B* for the ridge thickness (fig. 10) and the pores aging behavior (fig. 13). Results for the Binary Pixel feature are comparatively similar between location *A* and *B* (fig. 14) although one might argue that also here the results of location *B* are slightly more distorted. When investigating possible reasons for the lower quality of the aging curves of location *B* in some cases, dust might be an influence factor.

The Binary Pixel feature seems to perform equally well for 20 μm and 10 μm resolutions. It can therefore be used to compare environmental influences and sweat composition between all three locations. The average value and variation of the temperature seems to be comparatively similar between the three locations (see section 3), whereas humidity is significantly lower at location *C*. This might lead to an increase in aging speed (higher slope of aging curves) according to first findings of [4], which, however, cannot be observed from fig. 14. Therefore, additional influences seem to exist, e.g. the sweat composition, which have a significant impact on the aging speed.

Summarizing our findings, the main difference in captured aging properties at specific geographical locations seems to be caused by the different environmental conditions (e.g. dust, temperature, humidity), different sweat compositions as well as different capturing parameters used. Such influences need to be investigated in more detail in future work.

6. DISCUSSION OF RESULTS FROM A POLICE AUTHORITY PERSPECTIVE
A first practical application scenario for long-term age determination are cases of long intervals between crime and its discovery. For example, for people with poor social contact there might be long post mortem intervals until finding of their corpses (e.g. up to one year [15]). Furthermore burglaries of seldom used estates are discovered with delay of months sometimes.

A second practical application is the exclusion or inclusion of detected prints, if the date of offense is known. Exclusion of non-relevant prints might improve data privacy protection of non-involved persons and reduce the amount of traces, which have to be examined for identification [16]. If a suspect states that he was present at the crime scene before or after the act, this could be verified or falsified for each trace.

In respect to *TG1* and *TG2*, ridge thickness and pores (size and amount) which seemed to be suitable tools for age determination of latent prints [7], figured out as not very promising after a formal and automated examination in this work. But even the exclusion of these features is an important step towards reliable long-term age determination.

Only the contrast based Binary Pixel model (*TG3*), which was introduced for short-term aging [4], shows a certain tendency over time. The loss of contrast of CWL images over time is probably caused by evaporation of substances, which are volatile at storage conditions. For short time spans reasonable substances might be water or low molecular organic compounds, which are originally part of skin exudates (sweat, sebum). During longer time spans some initial fingerprint compounds degrade. Decomposition products might have different reflection properties and/or evaporate, leading to changes in contrast. Fig. 14 shows that there are some outliers, which might be explained by appearance and disappearance of dust. In practice, this source of error could be minimized by manual excision of dusty regions from evaluation or in an automated way using edge detection. For whole prints enough material, free of visible dust, should be left for analysis.

A challenge for the Binary Pixel model (*TG4*) is the different slope for each test subject, even at similar environmental conditions. The reason for this seems to be the variance of qualitative and quantitative substance composition between test subjects. To normalize this, an additional chemical analysis of the reasonable compounds might be necessary.

7. CONCLUSIONS & FUTURE WORK
In the scope of this paper, we have investigated different morphological features in respect to the long-term aging of latent fingerprints over approximately 1.5 years. Using non-invasively captured high-resolution fingerprint time series (10 µm and 20 µm) and automated digital preprocessing and feature extraction methods, we have shown that the morphological feature of ridge thickness does not exhibit a significant change during aging on hard disk platter surfaces. This is in contrast to what was reported before in [7] for a manual investigation of fingerprints on glass substrates over 0.5 years. Furthermore, we have shown that the amount and average size of pores seems to slightly change over time. However, we have also demonstrated that this is a result of the loss of contrast and contour of the pores rather than a change in their actual morphology. Having extracted a very characteristic response for the global contrast based Binary Pixel feature as well as for the brightness around pores, we conclude that the dominant aging property for latent fingerprints seems to be a global loss in contrast, equally distributed over the complete fingerprint area, where pixel values become brighter and finally disappear in a random like fashion. All observed changes in pores over time seem to clearly be a result of such loss in global contrast, leading to the extraction algorithm not being able to detect pores any more or to spill over the pores edges during segmentation. Taking furthermore into account that pores are detectable only in less than half of the 10 µm time series and in none of the 20 µm series (with automated segmentation algorithms as well as manual inspection), we conclude that pores are at this point not feasible for a practical age estimation. The so far evaluated ridges and pores features seem to be a mere result of global, statistical changes, as measured by the Binary Pixel feature.

We have furthermore demonstrated that different influences, such as sweat composition, environmental conditions and sensor settings seem to greatly impact the aging behavior and capturing process, especially for the long-term aging. It therefore seems to be a major challenge of future work to investigate such influences in detail, especially the impact of dust, temperature, humidity, capturing resolution and internal as well as external chemical substances within the prints. Further studies have to be complemented by the investigation of different surfaces, which might be found at crime scenes. Once different influences on the aging process of the Binary Pixel feature are well understood and can be taken into account, rule based or machine learning based classification approaches should be investigated to evaluate the practical long-term age estimation performance of such method. A combination with additional, most likely also statistical features might be used to further increase the age estimation performance.

8. ACKNOWLEDGMENTS
The work in this paper has been funded in part by the German Federal Ministry of Education and Science (BMBF) through the Research Programme under Contract No. FKZ: 13N10816, FKZ: 13N10818 and FKZ: 13N10822. We also thank Stefan Gruhn for his support in conducting the scans.

9. REFERENCES
[1] Fairhurst, M. and Erbilek, M. 2011. Analysis of physical ageing effects in iris biometrics. Computer Vision, IET, vol.5, no.6, pp.358-366.

[2] Srihari, S.N. 2010. Computing the scene of a crime. IEEE Spectrum, vol.47, no.12, pp.38-43.

[3] Fries Research & Technology: www.frt-gmbh.com/en/, www.frtofamerica.com/us, last accessed on 21.01.2013.

[4] Merkel, R., Gruhn, S., Dittmann, J., Vielhauer, C. and Bräutigam, A. 2012. On non-invasive 2D and 3D Chromatic White Light image sensors for age determination of latent fingerprints. Forensic Sci Int 222 (1-3), pp. 52-70, Elsevier.

[5] Merkel, R. and Vielhauer, C. 2012. On using flat bed scanners for the age determination of latent fingerprints: first results for the binary pixel feature. Proceedings of the 14th ACM Workshop on Multimedia and security, pp. 39-46.

[6] Merkel, R., Dittmann, J. and Vielhauer, C. 2012. Novel fingerprint aging features using binary pixel sub-tendencies: A comparison of contactless CLSM and CWL sensors. Proceedings of the 2012 IEEE International Workshop on Information Forensics and Security (WIFS), pp. 7-12.

[7] Popa, G., Potorac, R. and Preda, N. 2010. Method for fingerprints age determination. Romanian Journal of Legal Medicine, Vol. 18, Issue 2, June 2010, pp 149-154.

[8] Girod, A., Ramotowski, R. and Weyermann, C. 2012. Composition of fingermark residue: A qualitative and quantitative review, Forensic Sci Int 223 (1–3), pp. 10-24.

[9] Baniuk, K. 1990. Determination of Age of Fingerprints. Forensic Science International, (46) 1990, pp.133-137.

[10] Hong, L., Wan, Y. and Jain, A. K. 1998. Fingerprint image enhancement: Algorithm and performance evaluation. IEEE Trans. Pattern Anal. Mach. Intell., 29(8):777, 790.

[11] Kovesi, P. and Thai, R. Fingerprint enhancement (matlab-code). http://www.csse.uwa.edu.au/~pk/research/matlabfns/index.html#fingerprints, last accessed on 30.01.2013.

[12] Jain, A. K., Chen, Y. and Demirkus M. 2007. Pores and ridges: High-resolution fingerprint matching using level 3 features. IEEE Transactions on Pattern Analysis and Machine Intelligence, 29(1):15 – 28.

[13] Merkel, R., Krapyvskyy, A., Leich, M., Dittmann, J. and Vielhauer, C. 2011. A first framework for the development of age determination schemes for latent biometric fingerprint traces using a chromatic white light (CWL) sensor. Proceedings of SPIE Security+Defence, 0001;():81890T-81890T-15.

[14] Toennies, K. D. 2005. Grundlagen der Bildverarbeitung. Pearson, pp. 287-288.

[15] Ito, T., Tamiya, N., Takahashi, H., Yamazaki, K., Yamamoto, H., Sakano, S., Kashiwagi, M. and Miyaishi, S. 2012. Factors that prolong the 'postmortem interval until finding' (PMI-f) among community-dwelling elderly individuals in Japan: analysis of registration data. BMJ Open, Sep 27 2012, 2(5).

[16] Merkel, R., Pocs, M., Dittmann, J. and Vielhauer, C. 2013. Proposal of Non-invasive Fingerprint Age Determination to Improve Data Privacy Management in Police Work from a Legal Perspective Using the Example of Germany. In: Pietro, R., Herranz, J., Damiani, E. and State, R. (Ed.): Lecture Notes in Computer Science 7731: Data Privacy Management and Autonomous Spontaneous Security, pp. 61-74, Springer.

Non-Invertible and Revocable Iris Templates using Key-dependent Wavelet Transforms

Jutta Hämmerle-Uhl, Elias Pschernig, Andreas Uhl
University of Salzburg
Department of Computer Sciences
Jakob-Haringer-Straße 2
Salzburg, Austria
uhl@cosy.sbg.ac.at

ABSTRACT

A technique to generate non-invertible and revocable iris templates is proposed employing key-dependent wavelet transforms. In particular, parametrised wavelet filters and wavelet packets are used in feature extraction in replacement of a pyramidal D4 wavelet transform. Since the template generation process is non-invertible by design, the overall scheme is non-invertible as well. Recognition accuracy is found to be high as long as personal tokens remain secret, templates can be revoked by simply exchanging the wavelet transform applied in the feature extraction process.

Categories and Subject Descriptors

I.4.9 [**Image Processing and Computer Vision**]: Applications; K.6.5 [**Management of Computing and Information Systems**]: Security and Protection

General Terms

Algorithms, Security, Experimentation

Keywords

iris recognition, wavelet transform, wavelet packets, filter parameterisation, cancelable biometrics, biometric salting

1. INTRODUCTION

Security threats against biometric systems and possible countermeasures have been identified systematically [19, 16]. Among the most critical attacks is sensor spoofing, where faked biometric traits of a genuine user are used to fool a sensor. Another attack point are biometric template databases in which genuine user template data are stored. A problem of a compromised template database is not only that the stolen templates may be directly injected fraudulently into a biometric system at some place, but there is the potential danger that "raw" biometric sample data may be recon-

structed from stored template data, thus enabling a spoofing attack.

To cope with this potential danger, template protection mechanisms [12] have been developed to facilitate a matching in some encrypted domain – e.g. biometric cryptosystems in various flavours [18] or applying homomorphic encryption [5, 22] – such that templates do not have to be stored or accessed in plaintext.

Indeed, it has been shown that a (re)construction of biometric sample data from template data is possible: For fingerprint data, this has been demonstrated based on minutiae and phase type template data [1, 20, 6]. First attacks against iris templates have been based on a systematic construction of approximate iris codes exploiting system responses to authentication attempts [9, 17]. Only quite recently, also iris texture reconstruction / synthetisation using iris codes have been demonstrated [23, 7].

In this paper we propose a technique to generate non-invertible and revocable iris templates. Contrasting to classical cancelable biometrics approaches, non-invertibility is not a result of applying non-invertible transforms, but is a result of a non-invertible template generation process. Revocability and sufficiently high accuracy are achieved by user specific key-dependent wavelet transforms. Thus, contrasting to typical biometric salting techniques (see [11] for a recent example using parameterised wavelet filters and [18] for a general overview), a compromise of the key material does not result in invertibility of the templates, but in a decrease of recognition accuracy only.

Section 2 describes the non-invertible feature extraction and template generation process. In Section 3, we review two types of potential key-dependent wavelet transforms which are employed to facilitate revocability of the templates and do provide an improved recognition accuracy to the overall system as long as user specific keys are not compromised. Section 4 presents experimental results with respect to recognition accuracy and key sensitivity, while Section 5 concludes the paper.

2. IRIS RECOGNITION AS TEXTURE CLASSIFICATION

Zhu et al. [25] describe an algorithm where they use mean values and standard deviations of multiple 2D-wavelet subbands as features. A pyramidal wavelet subdivision (see Fig. 3.a) using the standard Daubechies D4 wavelet in 5 decomposition levels is performed on iris textures, which are obtained from a polar mapping of the region between the pupil circle and outer iris circle. Following the suggestion of Ma et al. [14], we assume the texture to be the area between the two almost concentric circles of the pupil and the outer iris. These two circles are found by contrast adjustment, followed by Canny edge detection and Hough transformation. After the circles are detected, unwrapping along polar coordinates is done to obtain a rectangular texture of the iris. In our case, we always resample the texture to a size of 512x64 pixels. The features of the subbands of the 4 lowest decomposition levels (i.e. 13 subbands) are extracted by computing coefficients' mean value and standard deviation for each subband. In this way, from each iris picture a feature vector is obtained which contains 26 floating point values, one mean value and one standard deviation for each subband (see Fig. 1.d). To get a similarity score of such a feature vector against an iris contained in the database, a weighted Euclidean distance (WED) is used involving a number of enrolment training samples to find per-class weights for comparing the features:

$$WED(k) = \sum_{i=1}^{N} \frac{(f_i - f_i^{(k)})^2}{(\delta_i^{(k)})^2} \ ,$$

where N is the number of elements in the feature vector, k is the iris class in the biometric database to compare against, and f is the feature vector of the unknown sample. $f^{(k)}$ and $\delta^{(k)}$ are a feature vector and per-feature standard deviation obtained during training the enrolled samples for iris class k. There is no attempt made to compensate for rotation, but the parts of the iris texture corresponding to the upper and lower quarter of the iris circle are cut off as these usually contain most of the noise resulting from overlap by lids or eyelashes.

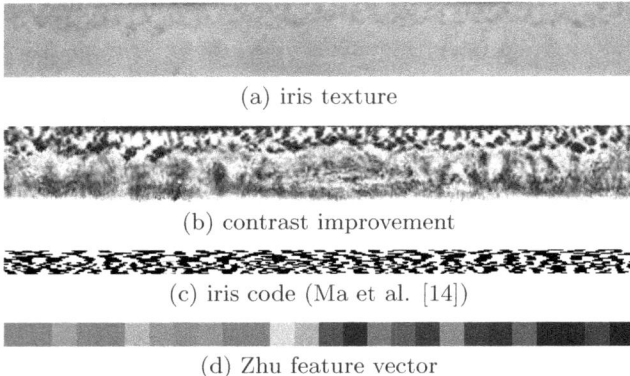

(a) iris texture

(b) contrast improvement

(c) iris code (Ma et al. [14])

(d) Zhu feature vector

Figure 1: Generation of the iris templates.

Fig. 1 illustrates the process of generating the template data. In particular, we illustrate the difference between the rather simply structured template data as proposed by the algorithm of Zhu et al. (Fig. 1.d) and the binary iris code generated following the suggestion of Ma et al. [14] (to show the much more complicated structure and much higher information content of a typical state-of-the-art iris code scheme, see Fig. 1.c) – it is clearly visible that the amount of information being present in the Zhu template can be expected to be much lower as compared to the iris code, also due to the entire absence of any information related to spatial position. Therefore, recognition accuracy is is expected to be

much lower using this approach. It is interesting to note that feature vectors of the "Zhu type" are classically used in texture classification and are derived from various (wavelet) transform domains (see e.g. [10]). In this application context, features of this type are expressive enough to determine membership with respect to few classes very reliably, however, the aim in texture classification is not to identify individual textures.

On the other hand, the information contained in the Zhu template is not at all sufficient to (re)construct human iris texture in a way that human operators or other feature extraction / template generation schemes could be fooled by the synthetic data. Thus, this type of template generation can be safely rated to be non-invertible. In the next section, we introduce key-dependent wavelet transforms which are meant to replace the pyramidal subdivision using the D4 wavelet to result in (a) revocable templates and (b) higher recognition accuracy as compared to the original approach. Revocable templates are implemented by simply changing transformations once a template gets compromised. Recognition accuracy is expected to improve since inter-class distances will increase due to the additional individual key-material used by the employed "personalised" transforms. As a consequence, the FMR is expected to decrease thereby improving overall ROC behaviour.

3. KEY-DEPENDENT WAVELET TRANSFORMS

Contrasting to the Fourier- or Walsh-Hadamard transforms, the wavelet transform is not exactly defined but denotes a wide class of different transforms. The corresponding multiple degrees of freedom in defining wavelet transforms have been exploited for designing wavelet transforms for specific applications, e.g. in biometrics custom wavelet transforms for compressing fingerprint sample data have been suggested – optimised filters in the classical pyramidal decomposition [8] and adaptive wavelet packet subband structures [15]. A further application domain exploiting the wide variety of available wavelet transforms is media security, e.g. providing key-dependency for watermarking schemes [3] or design of lightweight media encryption schemes where the security resides in a secret transform domain [4]. Probably the existing application related most to cancelable biometrics is to provide key-dependency for robust media hashing authentication schemes [13], since biometric templates share many properties with robust media hashes.

3.1 Parameterised Wavelet Filters

One parameterisation of wavelets with a simple recursive implementation is described by Schneid and Pittner [21], based on work by Zou and Tewfik [26] and an idea by Pollen. To construct compactly supported orthonormal wavelets, they find coefficients c_k for the dilation equation of the scaling function:

$$\phi(t) = \sum_{k=0}^{N} c_k \phi(2t - k) \qquad (N \in \mathbb{N}, c_k \in \mathbb{R})$$

Two additional conditions are necessary for the coefficients:

$$\sum_{k \in \mathbb{Z}} c_k = 2,$$

$$\sum_{k \in \mathbb{Z}} c_k c_{k+2l} = 2\delta_{0l} \qquad (l \in \mathbb{Z})$$

The solution by Schneid and Pittner finds c_k given n parameters $\alpha_0, ..., \alpha_{n-1}$ with $\alpha_i \in [-\pi, \pi]$ and $2*n+1 = N$ with the following recursion:

$$
\begin{aligned}
c_k^{N+2} &= 0.5 * (c_{k-2}^N + c_k^N) \\
&+ 0.5 * (c_{k-2}^N - c_k^N) \cos \alpha_{(N+1)/2} \\
&+ 0.5 (c_{N-k+2}^N - c_{N-k}^N (-1)^k) \sin \alpha_{(N+1)/2} \\
c_k^1 &= \begin{cases} 1/2 \text{ if } k \in [0, N], \\ 0 \text{ otherwise.} \end{cases}
\end{aligned}
$$

The filter coefficients h and g for the lowpass and highpass filters of the DWT can be directly derived from the coefficients c_k. Fig. 2 shows examples for $n = 1, 2, 3$ which make it immediately obvious that not all these wavelet filters generated by the parametrisation scheme will be equally well suited for applications and might therefore affect recognition accuracy when applied for feature extraction.

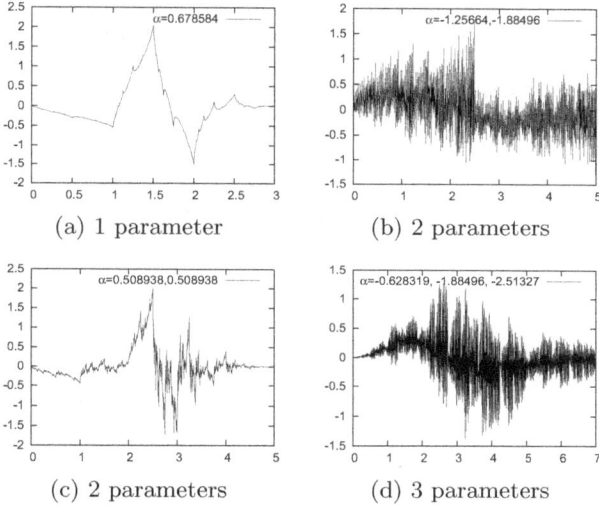

Figure 2: Examples of parameterised Schneid and Pittner wavelet functions.

Obviously, using a parametrisation approach a wide class of wavelet transforms can be considered, and of course, the selection which transform should be applied can be made dependent on some key material.

3.2 Wavelet Packets

Another way to get different wavelets depending on a used parameter are wavelet packets (WP) [24]. Looking only from a high-level view, the wavelet packet transformation changes the sub-division scheme used in a pyramidal wavelet transformation (see Fig. 3.a) to not only use the result of the lowpass filter in the subsequent step, but also the result of the highpass filter (Fig. 3.b shows an example of a 5 decomposition level subband structure of the size of a normalised iris texture used in this study as shown in Figs. 1.a&b). Instead of fixed results for all subbands, there are now many

possibilities of how to cascade through the wavelet filter tree, and each choice of tree is a different overall transformation.

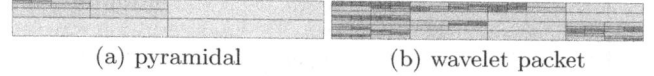

(a) pyramidal   (b) wavelet packet

Figure 3: Subband structures of the wavelet transform.

Thus, a wide class of different and potentially key-dependent wavelet transforms is available following the WP approach.

4. EXPERIMENTS

4.1 Experimental Settings

For testing, we used the *Interval* dataset out of the *CASIA Iris V3 database*, which consists of 2653 images in 396 classes (i.e. irises). We first analyse the behaviour of our implementation of the original approach of Zhu et al. [25]. As the algorithm needs a number of training samples for each class, we used the first 5 pictures of each class for training and the remaining pictures for testing. Using only the classes with at least 10 samples available (79 classes with 829 samples), we first enrolled the 79 classes with 5 pictures each (395 pictures), then matched the remaining 434 pictures to all classes. The shown distance is the WED described above, normalised to the range 0..1 as $\frac{WED}{1+WED}$. Fig. 4.b displays the matching score distribution which exhibits a significant overlap of inter- and intra-class matching scores, leading to the relatively high EER=6.34% when assessing verification mode.

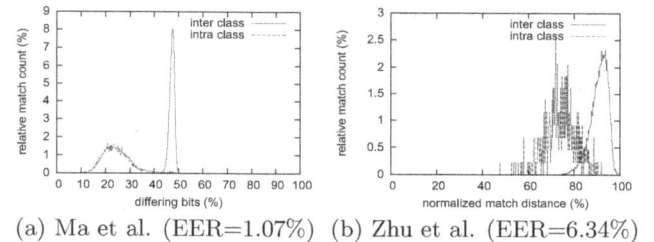

(a) Ma et al. (EER=1.07%) (b) Zhu et al. (EER=6.34%)

Figure 4: Matching score distributions.

For comparison to a more state-of-the-art scheme, we also display the matching score distribution of the Ma et al. approach over the entire CASIA V3 Interval dataset in Fig. 4.a. It can be clearly observed that the distributions' overlap is very small, leading to the much better value of EER=1.07%. So the recognition accuracy behaves as expected, i.e. it is much better for the binary iris code as compared to the Zhu template. This is also confirmed in identification mode: Rank-one recognition rate is 97.8% for Ma et al. vs. 80.4% for the Zhu approach.

4.2 Experimental Results

The aim of the subsequent experiments is twofold: First, to verify if key-dependent wavelet transforms can actually lead to better recognition results (i.e. ROC behaviour), and second, to investigate the security of the scheme which is done by conducting key-sensitivity analysis. Wavelet filter parameterisations of the Schneid type are assessed first with respect to both aims.

4.2.1 Parameterised Wavelet Filters

To assess ROC behaviour, we create 1000 different keys by sampling the parameter α_0 at 1000 equidistant-distant points in the range of $-\pi : \pi$ ($n = 1$). Each resulting wavelet is then used instead of the original D4 wavelet and the iris recognition system is run in verification mode, finally, EER is determined.

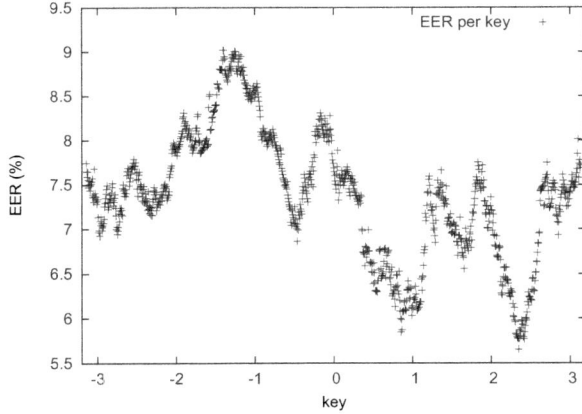

Figure 5: EERs with Schneid parametrisation and $n = 1$.

Fig. 5 shows that the resulting EERs are between 5.5% and 9%, compared to ERR=6.34% for the D4 wavelet in the original scheme. We notice that EER fluctuates for different parameter values and has some particularly high values around $\alpha_0 = -1.0$, $\alpha_0 = 0.0$, and $\alpha_0 = 2.0$. On the other hand, overall, the approximative EER magnitude is preserved for a large number of parameters.

The parameterisation also works for larger filters, Fig. 6 uses filters resulting from two parameters ($n = 2$) in the range $-\pi : \pi$ (filter length 6). EERs are found to vary between 5% and 14%. A peak in the EER surface is found in case both parameters are around a value of -1.0 – Fig. 2.b shows an example filter from this area, the shape of which does not make it a surprise to find EER clearly increased. The plot also clearly shows that the range of parameters leading to poor EER can be identified and easily excluded from a key generation process (of course, for an actual application the notion of "range" has to be identified exactly).

To see the effect of using parametrisation as user specific keys, we assign a random key to each iris class. The resulting EER are 6.4% for $n = 1$ and 6.0% for $n = 2$, respectively, the ROC behaviour is shown in Fig. 7. The different performance is due to the different properties of the filters as generated by the parameterisation scheme for different values of n. It has also to be noted that extremely poor performing keys have been excluded based on the results as displayed in Figs. 5 and 6. When comparing this result with EER=6.34% for the original fixed D4 filter, we may conclude that Schneid parametrisation does not lead to a significantly better separation of inter- and intra-class matches, even though a distinct filter is used for each class. So, the first aim (improvement of recognition accuracy) cannot be met with this parametrisation technique.

In order to study the effect of eventual similar keys in case of too fine parameter space discretisation (and get information about the actual key-space available), we conduct

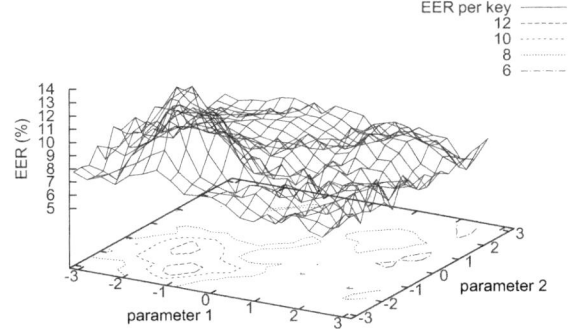

Figure 6: EERs with Schneid parametrisation and $n = 2$.

a specific experiment to reveal potential performance degradations. We use the dataset with 79 classes as before, but each class is copied 100 times. The copied classes are treated as different iris classes, and again, a distinct key is assigned to each class. Contrasting to the experiment before, now most classes are only different in terms of the used filter but share identical underlying iris textures. Fig. 7 shows that the ROC behaviour is better as compared to the setup without copied classes (which is due to the larger dataset this experiment is conducted on).

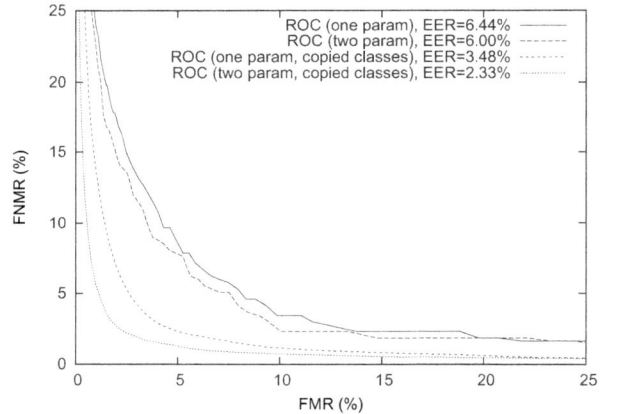

Figure 7: ROC of Zhu et al. using Schneid parametrisation and copied classes.

However, when considering the matching score distributions as visualised in Fig. 8 for $n = 1, 2$, we find the distributions' overlap to be smaller as compared to the original Zhu et al. scheme with fixed D4 wavelet (see Fig. 4). This means that while not improving recognition accuracy in terms of EER, we get a reasonably sized keyspace which can be used to generate revocable templates.

Next, we look at using random wavelet packets instead of pyramidal wavelet subdivision.

4.2.2 Wavelet Packets

Instead of the fixed 13 subbands from which mean value and standard deviation are used as features in the original

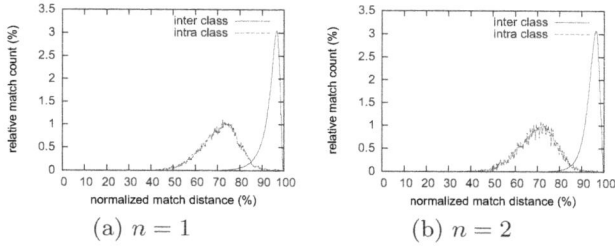

(a) $n = 1$ (b) $n = 2$

Figure 8: Matching score distributions of Zhu et al. with Schneid parametrisation and copied classes.

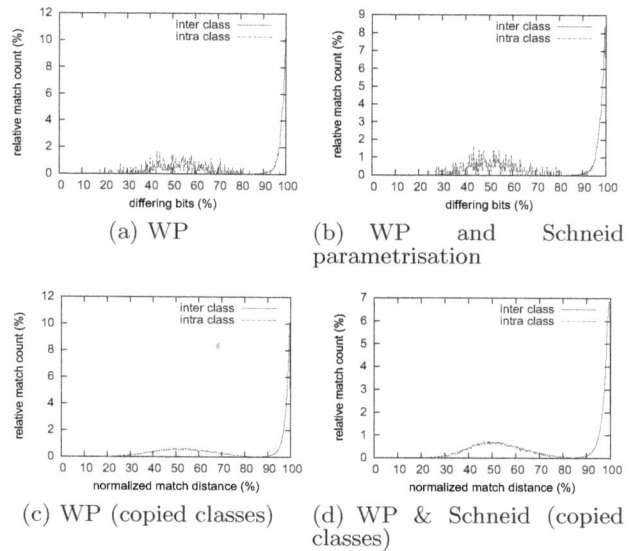

(a) WP   (b) WP and Schneid parametrisation

(c) WP (copied classes)   (d) WP & Schneid (copied classes)

Figure 9: Matching score distributions of Zhu et al. using WP and Schneid parametrisation.

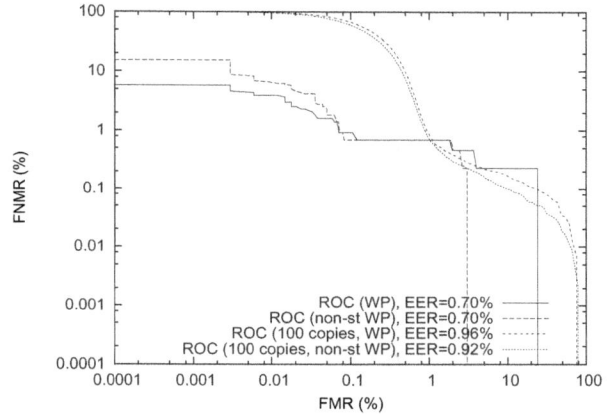

Figure 10: ROC of Zhu et al. using WP and Schneid parametrisation.

algorithm (and in the version using parameterised filters), there are $4^1 + 4^2 + 4^3 + 4^4 + 4^5 = 1364$ possible subbands, when stopping decomposition after the 5th decomposition level (which is suggested due to the limited resolution of the normalised texture in radial direction, see Figs. 1.a&b). Out of these 1364 subbands, we randomly select 13 for feature extraction. For the generation of the random wavelet packet tree, we follow an algorithm outlined in [4]. The resulting feature vector has the same size as the one in the original algorithm. The original (pyramidal) algorithm corresponds to one single possible key. Because we select 13 subbands out of 1364 possible ones, there are around 2^{135} possible keys. If those of them representing almost the same wavelet packet structure also result in highly similar feature vectors remains to be seen in the subsequent experiments.

In order to assess ROC behaviour, in Fig. 9.a we display the matching score distribution in case random WP structures are used for each class instead of the pyramidal decomposition. Contrasting to the distributions of the original scheme and the approach using Schneid parametrisation (see Figs. 4.b and 8) we notice separated intra- and inter-class distributions caused by a shift of both distributions. It is also possible to combine both techniques by using differently parametrised Schneid filters for each single decomposition stage in the WP tree, denoted as non-stationary (NS) subdivision scheme [2]. This strategy of course results in a significant increase in keyspace size. Fig. 9.b shows the matching score distributions when applying this strategy, which is rather similar to the one without additional parametrisation, except that the intra-class distribution is slightly narrower for the NS case.

Key sensitivity is investigated by applying the same strategy as before in the case of parametrised filters using 100 copies of 79 iris classes and treating the copies as distinct classes, which are each assigned a dedicated random subband selection for generating the template. In Figs. 9.c and 9.d it can be clearly seen that inter- and intra-class distribution separation is still very well which means that key sensitivity can be rated as quite high. This visual impression is also confirmed by inspecting the ROC behaviour as shown in Fig. 10. Applying WP and WP with Schneid parametrisation to each iris class of the 79 class dataset perform very similar, leading to EER=0.7% as compared to EER=6.34% for the original scheme, which is a significant improvement in terms of recognition accuracy. The benefit of applying the additional parametrisation can be seen for $FNMR < 0.1\%$, where we find a clearly lower FMR for the parametrisations case.

The ROC behaviour for the case of copied classes is also clearly better as compared to the Schneid parametrisations case, e.g. EER=2.33% for Schneid parametrisation for $n = 2$ (see Fig. 7) vs. EER=0.96% for WP and EER=0.92% for NS WP, respectively. Overall, the combined WP and parametrisation scheme offers a vast keyspace, significantly improved recognition performance with respect to the original Zhu et al. scheme (as long as the personal key information is kept secret), and the possibility of revoking the templates in case of compromise. Based on the properties of the underlying template generation process, the scheme is non-invertible.

5. CONCLUSION

We have found that Schneid parametrisation alone cannot provide the desired functionalities, as its application does not lead to clearly improved recognition accuracy as compared to the original scheme, only revocability can be provided. Wavelet packets on the other hand do significantly improve recognition accuracy, key-sensitivity is found to be high and also the keyspace is very large, especially in case wavelet packets are combined with the Schneid parametrisation technique. Therefore, we recommend to use key-dependent non-stationary wavelet packets in the feature extraction stage of the original Zhu et al. technique to provide non-invertible and revocable templates with sufficiently high recognition accuracy.

6. REFERENCES

[1] R. Cappelli, A. Lumini, D. Maio, and D. Maltoni. Fingerprint image reconstruction from standard templates. *IEEE Transactions on Pattern Analysis and Machine Intelligence*, 29(9):1489–1503, 2007.

[2] A. Cohen and N. Dyn. Nonstationary subdivisions schemes and multiresolution analysis. *SIAM Journal of Mathematical Analysis*, 27(6):1745–1769, Nov. 1996.

[3] W. Dietl, P. Meerwald, and A. Uhl. Protection of wavelet-based watermarking systems using filter parametrization. *Signal Processing (Special Issue on Security of Data Hiding Technologies)*, 83(10):2095–2116, Oct. 2003.

[4] D. Engel, T. Stütz, and A. Uhl. Assessing JPEG2000 encryption with key-dependent wavelet packets. *EURASIP Journal on Information Security*, 2012(2), 2012.

[5] Z. Erkin, M. Franz, J. Guajardo, S. Katzenbeisser, I. Lagendijk, and T. Toft. Privacy-preserving face recognition. In I. Goldberg and M. Atallah, editors, *Proceedings of Privacy Enhancing Technologies (PETS'09)*, volume 5672 of *LNCS*, pages 235–253. Springer Verlag, 2009.

[6] J. Feng and A. Jain. Fingerprint reconstruction: From minutiae to phase. *IEEE Transactions on Pattern Analysis and Machine Intelligence*, 33(2):209,223, 2011.

[7] J. Galbally, A. Ross, M. Gomez-Barrero, J. Fierrez, and J. Ortega-Garcia. From the iriscode to the iris: A new vulnerability of iris recognition systems, 2012. Briefings-Talk at *blackhat* USA 2012, `http://media.blackhat.com/bh-us-12/Briefings/Galbally/BH_US_12_Galbally_Iris_Reconstruction_WP.pdf`.

[8] O. Gerek and A. Cetin. Polyphase adaptive filter banks for fingerprint image compression. *Electronics Letters*, 34:1931–1932, Oct. 1998.

[9] M. Gomez-Barrero, J. Galbally, P. Tome, and J. Fierrez. On the vulnerability of iris-based systems to a software attack based on a genetic algorithm. In *Progress in Pattern Recognition, Image Analysis, Computer Vision, and Applications*, volume 7441 of *Lecture Notes on Computer Science*, pages 114–121, Berlin, Heidelberg, 2012. Springer-Verlag.

[10] M. Häfner, R. Kwitt, A. Uhl, A. Gangl, F. Wrba, and A. Vécsei. Computer-assisted pit-pattern classification in different wavelet domains for supporting dignity assessment of colonic polyps. *Pattern Recognition*, 42(6):1180–1191, Sept. 2008.

[11] J. Hämmerle-Uhl, E. Pschernig, and A. Uhl. Cancelable iris-templates using key-dependent wavelet transforms. In *Proceedings of the 6th IAPR/IEEE International Conference on Biometrics (ICB'13)*, Madrid, Spain, June 2013. To appear.

[12] A. K. Jain, K. Nandakumar, and A. Nagar. Biometric template security. *EURASIP Journal Adv. Signal Process*, 2008:1–17, 2008.

[13] G. Laimer and A. Uhl. Key dependent JPEG2000-based robust hashing for secure image authentication. *EURASIP Journal on Information Security*, Article ID 895174:doi:10.1155/2008/895174, 19 pages, 2008.

[14] L. Ma, T. Tan, Y. Wang, and D. Zhang. Efficient iris recognition by characterizing key local variations. *IEEE Transactions on Image Processing*, 13(6):739–750, June 2004.

[15] B. Mühlbacher, T. Stütz, and A. Uhl. JPEG2000 Part 2 wavelet packet subband structures in fingerprint recognition. In P. Frossard, H. Li, F. Wu, B. Girod, S. Li, and G. Wei, editors, *Visual Communications and Image Processing 2010 (VCIP'10)*, number 7744 in Proceedings of SPIE, pages 77442C–1 – 77442C–10, Huang Shan, China, July 2010. SPIE.

[16] N. Ratha, J. Connell, and R. Bolle. Enhancing security and privacy in biometrics-based authentication systems. *IBM Systems Journal*, 40(3):614–634, Apr. 2001.

[17] C. Rathgeb and A. Uhl. Attacking iris recognition: An effcient hill-climbing technique. In *Proceedings of the 20th International Conference on Pattern Recognition (ICPR'10)*, pages 1217–1220, Istanbul, Turkey, 2010.

[18] C. Rathgeb and A. Uhl. A survey on biometric cryptosystems and cancelable biometrics. *EURASIP Journal on Information Security*, 2011(3), 2011.

[19] C. Roberts. Biometric attack vectors and defenses. *Computers & Security*, 26:14–25, 2007.

[20] A. Ross, J. Shah, and A. K. Jain. From template to image: Reconstructing fingerprints from minutiae points. *IEEE Transactions on Pattern Analysis and Machine Intelligence*, 29(4):544–560, 2007.

[21] J. Schneid and S. Pittner. On the parametrization of the coefficients of dilation equations for compactly supported wavelets. *Computing*, 51:165–173, May 1993.

[22] B. Sy. Secure computation for privacy preserving biometric data retrieval and authentication. In D. Ortiz-Arroyo et al., editors, *Intelligence and Security Informatics*, volume 5376 of *LNCS*, pages 143–154. Springer Verlag, 2008.

[23] S. Venugopalan and M. Savvides. How to generate spoofed irises from an iris code template. *IEEE Transactions of Information Forensics and Security*, 6:385–394, 2011.

[24] M. Wickerhauser. *Adapted wavelet analysis from theory to software.* A.K. Peters, Wellesley, Mass., 1994.

[25] Y. Zhu, T. Tan, and Y. Wang. Biometric personal identification based on iris patterns. In *Proceedings of the 15th International Conference on Pattern Recognition (ICPR'00)*, volume 2, pages 2801–2804. IEEE Computer Society, 2000.

[26] H. Zou and A. H. Tewfik. Parametrization of compactly supported orthonormal wavelets. *IEEE Transactions on Signal Processing*, 41(3):1423–1431, Mar. 1993.

Towards Standardised Fingerprint Matching Robustness Assessment: The StirMark Toolkit – Cross-Database Comparisons with Minutiae-based Matching

Jutta Hämmerle-Uhl, Michael Pober, Andreas Uhl
University of Salzburg
Department of Computer Sciences
Jakob-Haringer-Straße 2
Salzburg, Austria
uhl@cosy.sbg.ac.at

ABSTRACT

We propose to establish a standardised tool in fingerprint recognition robustness assessment, which is able to simulate a wide class of acquisition conditions, applicable to any given dataset and also of potential interest in forensic analysis. As an example, StirMark image manipulations (as being developed in the context of watermarking robustness assessment) are applied to fingerprint data to generate test data for robustness evaluations, thereby interpreting certain image manipulations as being highly related to realistic fingerprint acquisition conditions. Experimental results involving three different minutiae-based fingerprint matching schemes applied to FVC2004 data underline the need for standardised testing and a corresponding simulation toolset.

Categories and Subject Descriptors

I.4.9 [**Image Processing and Computer Vision**]: Applications; K.6.5 [**Management of Computing and Information Systems**]: Security and Protection

General Terms

Algorithms, Fingerprint recognition robustness, Experimentation

Keywords

fingerprint recognition, robustness in biometrics, watermarking robustness, StirMark

1. INTRODUCTION

One of the big issues in fingerprint recognition is robustness of recognition accuracy against sample image quality degradation [1, 7]. A wide variety of factors influence the quality of a fingerprint image: Skin conditions (e.g., dryness, moisture, dirt, cuts and bruises), sensor conditions (e.g., dirt, noise, size), and other acquisition conditions like user cooperation or crime scene preservation in forensic settings, etc. Some of these factors are inevitable

and some of them change over time. Therefore, it is essential to provide reliable methodology to comparatively assess fingerprint recognition robustness under varying conditions.

This issue is classically tackled by the establishment of benchmarking frameworks, which facilitate a common evaluation basis with standardised protocols for various fingerprint recognition algorithms, see e.g. the fingerprint verification contests (FVC [7]) and the BioSecure evaluation framework [1]. Usually such frameworks rely on the establishment of test data which are used to compare the different algorithms on a common basis. A very good example, specifically focusing onto the robustness issue, are the FVC (2002 and 2004) data sets. While the availability of these and similar datasets is a significant achievement, the data collection and database establishment is tedious work. Moreover, if additional acquisition conditions should be considered which have not been included into the original dataset, re-enrolment is required, involving complicated procedures for getting the original people back to enrolment. Also, it is hard to compare the different quality degradations from dataset to dataset (e.g. FVC, MCYT, BIOMET, MSU), since usually, there is no standardised manner to generate the acquisition conditions applied. Therefore, the experimental results of recognition algorithms in case applied to different datasets are hardly comparable and the results shown in many papers are difficult to interpret.

A strategy to cope with some of these issue is to generate synthetic fingerprints, the SFinGe [2] being the most well known tool for doing this. The generated fingerprints have proven to be highly realistic and serve as a sensible tool to generate large datasets for benchmarking. While SFinGe also allows to apply some manipulations to the images, e.g. noise insertion, translations, rotations and uses a skin deformation model, a simulation of specific sensor types is not foreseen.

In the area of robust watermarking, a similar situation with respect to the lack of standardised testing procedures could be observed. Each watermarking scheme presented was evaluated on a specific dataset, where especially the types of introduced image manipulations and their respective extent to prove robustness did vary from paper to paper, thus making a comparison of techniques impossible. To cope with the situation, standardised benchmark toolsets consisting of a collection of parameterisable image manipulations have been created, including StirMark [5] and CheckMark [8]. This enabled developers and authors to apply these manipulations to publicly available datasets thus making their results comparable.

In this paper, we propose to establish a standardised tool in fingerprint recognition robustness assessment, which is able to simulate a wide class of acquisition conditions, applicable to any given dataset. As an example, StirMark image manipulations are applied to fingerprint data to generate test data for robustness evaluations, also considering forensic scenarios. Since these manipulations can be applied to any dataset, the effect of manipulations on data originating from different sensors and acquisition conditions can be studied with respect to recognition accuracies of the algorithms used.

In Section 2, we explain the StirMark image manipulations and discuss the interpretation of those procedures in the context of fingerprint acquisition and quality, respectively. Experiments are covered in Section 3 where we first shortly describe the employed minutiae-based fingerprint recognition schemes, the used FVC2004 dataset, and experimental conditions with respect to evaluation protocols. Finally, we present fingerprint verification results generated on the FVC2004 dataset processed with a set of StirMark image manipulations with increasing strength. Section 4 concludes the paper.

2. THE STIRMARK TOOLKIT

The StirMark Benchmark is a generic benchmark test for evaluating the robustness of digital image watermarking methods, developed by Fabien A. P. Petitcolas et al. [4, 5]. The basic idea behind the robustness tests in the StirMark benchmark is, that a digital watermark within an image can be attacked and possibly rendered useless, by introducing small, ideally imperceptible perturbations into the marked image. To be suitable for application in a common generic benchmark, the specific types of perturbations are pre-defined and the respective intensity is adjustable via a given set of parameters. The corresponding software is currently available "StirMark Benchmark 4.0" at http://www.petitcolas.net/fabien/watermarking/stirmark/.

In the following, we describe the set of image manipulations that has been selected for this study. We explain the way each manipulation is defined, how it is parameterised to achieve varying strength of the manipulation, and we discuss which realistic fingerprint acquisition condition could be modelled by applying the manipulation to fingerprint sample images. Thus, only a subset of the complete range of StirMark tests is used, which simulate "natural" perturbations potentially appearing in real-life fingerprint application scenarios. Example images shown have been generated by applying StirMark tests with increasing intensity to a sample image taken from the FVC2004 database DB1 (see Section 3.1).

Additive Noise is introduced to the input image. The amount of noise is adjustable and can range from "none" to "completely random image", controlled by a single parameter, ranging from 0 to 100. Fig. 1 shows examples for increasing noise content.

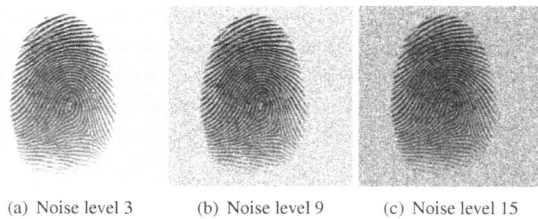

(a) Noise level 3   (b) Noise level 9   (c) Noise level 15

Figure 1: Examples for the *Additive Noise* test, applied to an image from DB1 (ID 91_2).

This test is intended to simulate noise, that might "naturally" appear in fingerprint sample images. Possible causes for this kind of noise could be actual dust on the contact area during acquisition

of the imprint, graining caused by the acquisition equipment itself (sensor noise) or any other kind of systematic error introduced during processing, transmission and/or storage of the collected images (e.g. a grainy surface the latent fingerprint has been taken off can cause noise in forensics).

Mean Filtering is applied as a special case for any kind of convolution filtering. The specific filter mask has to be defined by the user. Mean filtering is used to simulate blur in fingerprint images – the most common and renowned cause for blur is probably slight movement of the finger (or the sensor in forensics [3]) during image acquisition, but can also be the result of de-focus. We use mean filters of sizes {3, 5, 7} as larger filters lead to a blurring of the original ridge-and-furrow structure which gets too strong to still be considered "natural". See Fig. 2 for examples when applying a mean filter of increasing size.

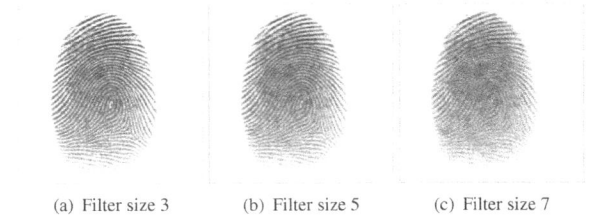

(a) Filter size 3   (b) Filter size 5   (c) Filter size 7

Figure 2: Examples for the *Mean Filtering* test, applied to an image from DB1 (ID 91_2).

Rotation rotates the image by a given angle, the set of angular values that will be inspected in the experiments is $\{-20°, -15°, -10°, -5.5°, -5°, 7°, 7.5°, 13°, 18°, 20°\}$. Examples for rotations of $-15°$, $-5.5°$, and $20°$ can be seen in Fig. 3.

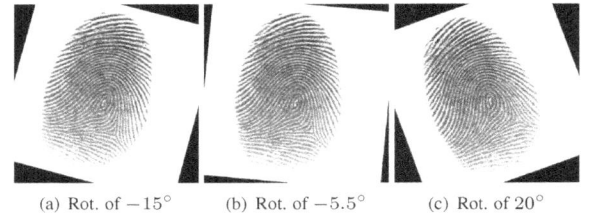

(a) Rot. of $-15°$ (b) Rot. of $-5.5°$ (c) Rot. of $20°$

Figure 3: Examples for the *Rotations* test, applied to an image from DB1 (ID 91_2).

Rotation is a very typical, not to say – omnipresent – challenge for fingerprint matching, as in very few cases a finger will be presented twice in exactly the same orientation to the contact area during image acquisition. Thus, this test provides the means for comparison of the rotational alignment capabilities of the various fingerprint matchers.

Affine Transformation is a generic manipulation for arbitrary affine image transformations. The user specifies the parameters $a, \dots, f$ of the inverse transformation matrix of the form:

$$\begin{pmatrix} x' \\ y' \end{pmatrix} = \begin{pmatrix} a & b \\ c & d \end{pmatrix} \begin{pmatrix} x \\ y \end{pmatrix} + \begin{pmatrix} e \\ f \end{pmatrix}$$

The application of affine transformations to fingerprint images is intended to simulate distortions of the entire finger imprint, that can appear in real-life situations during fingerprint acquisition, depending on the way, the finger is pressed on the contact area. As special cases, we consider *shearing* and *stretching*.

Stretching in Y-Direction is parameterised by setting $b = c = e = f = 0$ and $a = 1$, while configurations 1 - 8 set d to the values

{1.035, 1.070, 1.105, 1.140, 1.175, 1.210, 1.280, 1.350}. Configurations 1, 5, and 8 are shown in Fig. 4. While for stretching in X-Direction the fingerprint appears to be broader, Y-Direction stretching leads to a longer imprint.

(a) $d = 1.035$ (b) $d = 1.175$ (c) $d = 1.350$

Figure 4: Examples for the *Affine Transformations – Stretching in Y-Direction* test, applied to an image from DB1 (ID 91_2).

A certain *stretching* might appear in the finger imprint, when the amount of force applied while pressing the finger on the contact area is large or larger than usual. Considering the forensic scenario, stretching of a fingerprint appears if the finger was imprinted on a soft or flexible surface.

Shearing in X- and Y-direction is parameterised by setting $e = f = 0$ and $a = d = 1$, while configurations 1 - 6 set $b = c$ to the values {0.05, 0.10, 0.15, 0.20, 0.25, 0.30}. Configurations 1, 4, and 6 are shown in Fig. 5.

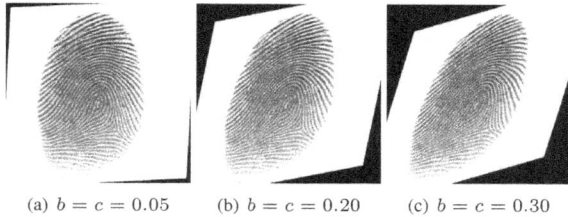

(a) $b = c = 0.05$ (b) $b = c = 0.20$ (c) $b = c = 0.30$

Figure 5: Examples for the *Affine Transformations – Shearing in X- and Y-Direction* test, applied to an image from DB1 (ID 91_2).

A *shearing* effect can occur, when the force that is exercised while pressing the finger on the contact area is not exerted perpendicular to this area. For example, when the finger is presented, with the user pushing rather in direction to the upper-right corner of the sensor, than straight downwards.

Latest Small Random Distortions *The* StirMark test. Introduced in version 4.0 of the StirMark Benchmark, this test represents a modification of the *Small Random Distortions* test. Being a combination of several basic manipulations (i.e. random minor geometric distortion followed by resampling and interpolation, a transfer function to emulate analog/digital converter imperfections, global "bending", high frequency displacement, and JPEG compression), this latter test originally aims to simulate a resampling process, i.e. the errors introduced when printing an image and then scanning it again. The involved image warping is performed both on a global, as well as on a very local level, adding even more to the "natural" and "coincidental" character of the output fingerprint images.

The "new version" of the test replaces two original, sine-function-based processing steps (gobal bending and higher frequency replacement), responsible for generating global and local image distortion, with a single procedure, employing randomised "Distortion Maps" instead. The test is conducted with parameters {0.6, 1.0, 1.4, 1.8, 2.2, 2.6, 3.0, 3.4, 3.8, 4.2} where an example for the values 0.6, 2.6, and 0.42 are visualised in Fig. 6.

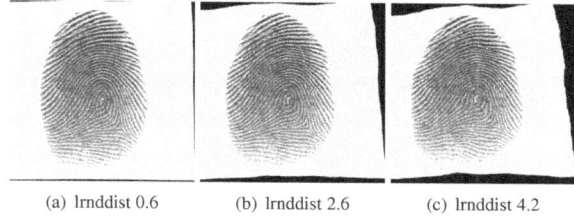

(a) lrnddist 0.6   (b) lrnddist 2.6   (c) lrnddist 4.2

Figure 6: Examples for the *Latest Small Random Distortions* test, applied to an image from DB1 (ID 91_2).

In its character of being a combination of several different image distortions, by applying this StirMark test on fingerprint images, we aim to simulate an interaction of various naturally occurring image perturbations: Foremost a random warping of the ridge lines, that in real life would be caused by e.g. unevenly distributed pressure exercised on the contact area during acquisition, or if this contact area were to be uneven by itself, i.e. a latent fingerprint scanned from an uneven surface. Also inaccuracies or errors introduced by the fingerprint scanner can be a source for this type of deformation.

3. EXPERIMENTS

We first provide details about the used minutiae-based fingerprint matching schemes and the employed FVC2004 data set. Subsequently, experimental results are presented and discussed, covering questions of robustness of recognition accuracy against various StirMark manipulations and in particular a comparison of the behaviour of the different fingerprint recognition schemes when applied to different datasets.

3.1 Experimental Settings

An interesting question is to ask if a certain type of fingerprint feature extraction method has particular strong points or weaknesses when dealing with a specific type of acquisition condition. In order to get a sensible answer we will consider different types of minutiae-based fingerprint feature extraction and matching schemes [7].

As the first minutiae-based matcher type we use *mindtct* and *bozorth3* from the "NIST Biometric Image Software" (NBIS) package (available at http://fingerprint.nist.gov/NBIS/) for minutiae detection and matching, respectively. *mindtct* generates several image quality maps and binarises the fingerprint images as a first step. Subsequently, minutiae are detected in admissible areas by detecting specified pixel patterns, followed by false minutiae removal and minutiae quality assessment. *bozorth3* is designed to be rotation and translation invariant and provides a matching score based on traversing certain inter-fingerprint compatibility tables.

As the second minutiae-based matcher type we use the *Fingerprint SDK 2009* as developed by *Griaule Biometrics* (in particular the Java version of the SDK, denoted as GF in the following, retrieved from http://www.griaulebiometrics.com/page/fingerprint_sdk). The Griaule fingerprint recognition algorithms won in the "Open Category", section "Average results over all databases", of the FVC2006, having the best Average EER. Specific to the algorithm is the determination of polygons connecting three minutiae making the considered features rotation and translation invariant. In the experiments, GF is used with a rotation alignment range of 180° (GF180) and a range of 20° (GF20) with can be selected in the SDK (the aim is to expose a possible accuracy vs. computational performance tradeoff).

As the third minutiae-based matcher type we use *VeriFinger* which is developed by *Neurotechnology*. For integration in PC- and web-based application this matcher is available in form of the *VeriFinger SDK 6.2*, denoted VF subsequently, retrieved from `http://www.neurotechnology.com/verifinger.html`. In the FVC2006, in the "Open Category", section "Average results over all databases", VF ranked 7th and was additionally having the best Average Zero FMR results among the contestants. Robustness is claimed to be very high against translation, rotations, and deformation. Identification is said to be possible even if the gallery template and the query fingerprint only have 5 – 7 similar minutiae.

We employ three out of four databases provided for the FVC2004 [6] as shown in Table 1 (the synthetic dataset is omitted), each with 500dpi resolution (DB3 with 512 dpi).

Table 1: Details on the fingerprint images in the three employed FVC2004 databases.

	Sensor Type	Model	Image Size
DB1	Optical	CrossMatch *V300*	640×480
DB2	Optical	Digital Persona *U.are.U 400*	328×364
DB3	Thermal Sweep	Atmel *FingerChip*	300×480

The procedure for performance evaluation is basically the same in all FVCs, from 2000 to 2006. We follow this specification by conducting all genuine tests and the required impostor tests for DB1, DB2, and DB3, thereby obtaining FNMR and FMR as required. Finally, equal error rate (EER) is determined and used as measure for recognition accuracy to compare different settings. Table 2 shows the result when applying the three considered minutiae matchers to the FVC2004 test data *without* having applied any StirMark manipulations.

Table 2: EERs for the considered fingerprint recognition schemes when applied to the original, "undistorted" sample image databases within the StirMark framework.

	NBIS (%)	VF (%)	GF180 (%)	GF20 (%)
DB1	14.81	5.87	11.41	13.61
DB2	11.12	5.01	11.72	12.89
DB3	6.68	3.60	6.90	5.82

It can be clearly seen that the ranking of the algorithms is heavily dependent on the used dataset, except for VF which is ranked first for each dataset. For example, NBIS is worst for DB1, second-best for DB2, and ranked third for DB3. While there is significant result variance for DB1 and DB3, the EERs are very close for DB2 (except for VF). It is also interesting to see that GF180 is outperformed by GF20 on DB3. While being contra-intuitive at first sight, this effect is observed in several settings and can be explained by the fact that GF180 inspects much more data configurations as compared to GF20 and obviously, in some cases this may end up in false positive matches.

3.2 Experimental Results

Table 3 shows the influence of additive noise on recognition performance considering DB2. Especially for a higher degree of noise content we see that all recognition systems are affected. It is especially interesting to note that VF is significantly ahead of the pack up to the one but last noise level, however, for the highest distortion level considered all four schemes perform almost equivalently, despite the much better "starting-value" of VF. NBIS slightly outperforms the two GF variants, maintaining its start advantage.

Table 3: EERs for *Additive Noise* test conducted on sample image database DB2.

Noise Level	NBIS (%)	VF (%)	GF180 (%)	GF20 (%)
unperturbed	11.12	5.01	11.72	12.89
03	10.86	5.05	13.90	14.90
07	15.03	7.07	17.27	17.91
11	20.54	14.20	22.89	21.56
15	30.78	29.24	31.17	29.40

In Table 4 we see that the situation completely changes when considering a different dataset, DB3 in this example. VF recognition results are not at all affected, also NBIS exhibits only minor impact on recognition results, even in case of a significant amount of noise, entirely contrasting to the results obtained on DB2. Only GF shows some result degradations, still not in the same order of magnitude as seen on DB2. Again we observe superior results of GF20 as compared to GF180, with the same reason as discussed before. Here, also the ranking among the different schemes changes – NBIS gets superior to GF20 although "starting" inferior.

Table 4: EERs for *Additive Noise* test conducted on sample image database DB3.

Noise Level	NBIS (%)	VF (%)	GF180 (%)	GF20 (%)
unperturbed	6.68	3.60	6.90	5.82
03	7.05	3.25	7.43	6.09
07	7.19	3.03	8.06	6.59
11	7.08	3.29	9.28	7.86
15	7.91	3.25	9.78	8.14

Fig. 7 illustrates the behaviour of VF in more detail by displaying ROC curves when applied to DB2 and DB3 data, respectively, successively increasing the introduced noise level. Expectations as induced by the EER values are entirely confirmed across the entire FMR / FNMR range.

This first example overall shows that general robustness properties and even ranking results with respect to robustness achieved on a specific database cannot be generalised but need to verified for each single dataset. This nicely illustrates the general need for systematic testing and evaluation tools.

Table 5 shows robustness results with respect to mean filtering on DB2. While VF clearly takes the lead up to a kernel size of 5×5, the next larger size can be handled better by NBIS. However, we are close to guessing with EERs of this magnitude, so the 7×7 kernel results are not relevant in practice. Overall, high sensitivity against mean filtering is observed which is critical in terms of applications since many types of blur are approximated by mean filtering.

Table 5: EERs for *Mean Filtering* test conducted on sample image database DB2.

Filter Size	NBIS (%)	VF (%)	GF180 (%)	GF20 (%)
unperturbed	11.12	5.01	11.72	12.89
03	11.99	6.50	13.44	14.16
05	20.06	13.39	19.78	19.57
07	42.10	44.22	48.23	46.62

Table 6 shows corresponding results for DB3. We observe that overall results are much better, and again VF gets highly sensitive

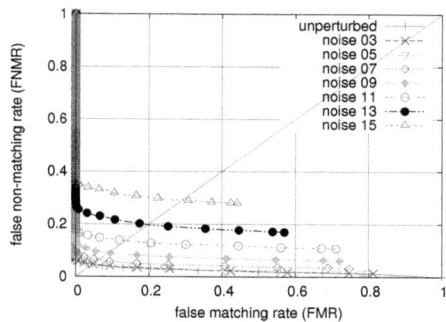

(a) DB2

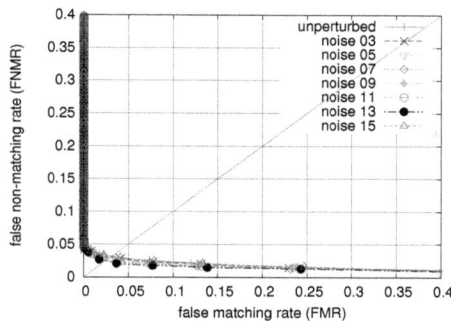

(b) DB3

Figure 7: ROC behaviour for the VeriFinger (VF) fingerprint recognition system under noise insertion.

resulting in the worst results for a larger kernel size, but here overall accuracy stays at a more realistic level. Superiority of GF20 over GF180 is confirmed again.

Table 6: EERs for *Mean Filtering* test conducted on sample image database DB3.

Filter Size	NBIS (%)	VF (%)	GF180 (%)	GF20 (%)
unperturbed	6.68	3.60	6.90	5.82
03	6.72	3.52	6.73	5.45
05	6.76	6.11	7.83	6.44
07	17.17	20.59	17.13	14.33

One of the most important robustness issues is fingerprint rotation, since this effect is omnipresent in sample acquisition. Tables 7 and 8 compare the results for DB1 and DB3.

Table 7: EERs for *Rotation* test conducted on sample image database DB1.

Rotation	NBIS (%)	VF (%)	GF180 (%)	GF20 (%)
unperturbed	14.81	5.87	11.41	13.61
-15	13.00	5.28	12.59	17.66
-5.5	12.94	5.78	11.80	14.14
13	13.05	5.89	11.62	17.02
20	13.41	5.12	12.56	22.38

The first thing to note is the excellent robustness of VF against rotation for both datasets. Also NBIS exhibits no result depreciations when applied to DB2, DB3 results show some minor im-

pact on NBIS. Also GF180 exhibits similar behaviour, being only slightly affected for DB2 but more considerable for DB3. GF20 is as consistent as VF in its results when comparing DB2 and DB3 – for both datasets, GF20 cannot handle the imposed rotations well. Again, the need for dedicated testing for each sensor type is confirmed since the extent of result impact cannot be predicted for unseen data based on the results of test data.

Table 8: EERs for *Rotation* test conducted on sample image database DB3.

Rotation	NBIS (%)	VF (%)	GF180 (%)	GF20 (%)
unperturbed	6.68	3.60	6.90	5.82
-15	6.83	3.04	7.53	9.28
-5.5	6.81	3.21	6.99	6.03
13	6.72	3.47	6.75	6.67
20	7.41	3.21	8.48	14.01

Affine transformations also model a class of very important acquisition conditions. Table 9 shows the strong effect of stretching in a single dimension only. No feature extraction type can handle this type of distortion in a sufficient degree. EERs results do continuously increase for an increasing amount of stretching, also the ranking among the different techniques is rather preserved under stretching, except for the largest distortion setting where GF20 outperforms GF180. Obviously, there is need to introduce better stretching robustness into feature sets.

Table 9: EERs for *Affine Transformations – Stretching in Y-Direction* test conducted on sample image database DB1.

Configuration	NBIS (%)	VF (%)	GF180 (%)	GF20 (%)
unperturbed	14.81	5.87	11.41	13.61
2	13.38	6.13	12.49	14.29
4	15.75	7.40	14.56	15.08
6	19.88	10.21	17.69	17.75
8	27.33	16.01	23.98	22.76

Table 10 shows corresponding results for DB2, where the overall impression is confirmed. However, the impact is much lower when compared to DB1, except for the strongest stretching settings. Contrasting to DB1 we notice that NBIS is most affected from medium to high extent of stretching, although exhibiting second best EER on the unperturbed data.

Table 10: EERs for *Affine Transformations – Stretching in Y-Direction* test conducted on sample image database DB2.

Configuration	NBIS (%)	VF (%)	GF180 (%)	GF20 (%)
unperturbed	11.12	5.01	11.72	12.89
2	11.51	5.24	12.64	13.67
4	14.19	6.76	13.62	13.99
6	18.35	8.07	16.66	15.60
8	25.24	13.66	21.48	20.58

Shearing robustness as illustrated in Table 11 is shown to be as problematic as stretching for DB1. We observe a steady increase of EERs for increasing shearing strength. The ranking among the algorithms seen on unperturbed data is preserved under the type of shearing we consider here.

Table 11: EERs for *Affine Transformations – Shearing in X- Y-Direction* test conducted on sample image database DB1.

Configuration	NBIS (%)	VF (%)	GF180 (%)	GF20 (%)
unperturbed	14.81	5.87	11.41	13.61
1	14.56	6.15	12.13	13.71
2	17.44	6.57	14.24	15.17
3	22.38	8.94	17.15	16.76
4	30.14	11.57	21.82	19.42
5	37.21	19.44	28.46	24.30
6	40.71	29.06	34.11	28.15

Table 12 displays a similar behaviour, except that NBIS develops into being clearly the worst performing algorithm for all shearing settings, being slightly superior to GF180 on unperturbed data.

Table 12: EERs for *Affine Transformations – Shearing in X- Y-Direction* test conducted on sample image database DB3.

Configuration	NBIS (%)	VF (%)	GF180 (%)	GF20 (%)
unperturbed	6.68	3.60	6.90	5.82
1	7.56	3.48	6.49	5.56
2	9.41	4.01	7.57	6.03
3	14.87	5.10	10.25	8.25
4	22.39	8.24	14.88	11.86
5	29.65	14.74	19.95	17.50
6	34.71	28.06	27.61	23.41

Finally, robustness results against a combination of manipulations are shown in Table 13. This rather localised distortions can be handled quite well by VF and GF20 where EER is increased only by $\approx 2\%$ for the strongest setting. NBIS and GF180 are affected twice as strong, the overall ranking of the algorithms on unperturbed data is almost maintained (except for GF20 and GF180).

Table 13: EERs for *Latest Small Random Distortions* test conducted on sample image database DB1.

Factor	NBIS (%)	VF (%)	GF180 (%)	GF20 (%)
unperturbed	14.81	5.87	11.41	13.61
0.6	13.60	5.88	11.24	13.49
1.0	14.00	5.24	12.31	13.71
1.8	14.04	5.71	12.12	13.72
2.6	14.76	6.37	13.49	14.00
3.4	15.99	7.15	14.29	15.05
4.2	18.13	7.88	15.82	15.53

On DB3 the situation is somewhat different. VF turns out to be very stable, GF20 shows a similar behaviour as seen on DB1. GF180 and NBIS are much stronger affected, with NBIS being clearly the worst performing scheme.

4. CONCLUSION

We have employed the StirMark benchmark testsuite to generate large scale test data to assess robustness of fingerprint recognition schemes in various acquisition conditions. Experimental results confirm a significant variability of robustness properties across different types of minutiae extraction and matching schemes **and** across

Table 14: EERs for *Latest Small Random Distortions* test conducted on sample image database DB3.

Factor	NBIS (%)	VF (%)	GF180 (%)	GF20 (%)
unperturbed	6.68	3.60	6.90	5.82
0.6	6.87	3.26	6.20	5.46
1.0	6.86	3.13	6.68	5.59
1.8	7.96	3.19	7.12	5.60
2.6	8.20	3.63	7.30	6.14
3.4	10.06	4.48	8.78	6.53
4.2	12.21	4.63	9.82	7.84

different datasets considered. As an example we refer to the VF results – while clearly being the best performing algorithm on unperturbed data for all three datasets, this is no longer true for shearing and mean filtering, where VF actually turns into the worst performing scheme for the latter type of distortions on DB3. These results underline the need for a standardised tool in fingerprint recognition robustness assessment, which is able to simulate a wide class of acquisition conditions, applicable to any given dataset.

While we have motivated the interpretation of several image manipulations contained in the StirMark benchmark as being closely related to a wide class of fingerprint acquisition conditions (including some forensic settings), these experiments only represent a first step. In fact, the aim is to establish a benchmark explicitly designed for systematic fingerprint recognition robustness evaluations, where these current StirMark based results can serve as first guidelines to model actual fingerprint acquisition conditions more accurately. For example, forensic conditions can be accurately modelled to (at least partially) resolve the urgent demand for realistic forensic testdata.

5. REFERENCES

[1] F. Alonso-Fernandes, J. Bigun, J. Fierrez, H. Fronthaler, K. Kollreider, and J. Ortega-Garcia. Fingerprint recognition. In D. Petrovska-Delacretaz, G. Chollet, and B. Dorizzi, editors, *Guide to Biometric Reference Systems and Performance Evaluation*, pages 51–88. Springer-Verlag, 2009.

[2] R. Cappelli. Synthetic fingerprint generation. In D. Maltoni, D. Maio, A. Jain, and S. Prabhakar, editors, *Handbook of Fingerprint Recognition (2nd Edition)*, pages 271–302. Springer-Verlag, 2009.

[3] S. Kiltz, J. Dittmann, and C. Vielhauer. Challenges in contact-less latent fingerprint processing in crime scenes - review of sensors and image processing investigations. In *Proceedings of the 20th European Signal Processing Conference (EUSIPCO 2012)*, pages 1504–1508, 2012.

[4] M. Kutter and F. A. P. Petitcolas. A fair benchmark for image watermarking systems. In P. W. Wong and E. J. Delp, editors, *Proceedings of the 11th SPIE Annual Symposium, Electronic Imaging '99, Security and Watermarking of Multimedia Contents*, volume 3657, pages 226–239, San Jose, CA, USA, Jan. 1999.

[5] M. Kutter and F. A. P. Petitcolas. Fair evaluation methods for image watermarking systems. *Journal of Electronic Imaging*, 9(4):445–455, Oct. 2000.

[6] D. Maio, D. Maltoni, R. Cappelli, J. L. Wayman, and A. K. Jain. FVC2004: Third Fingerprint Verification Competition. In *ICBA*, volume 3072 of *LNCS*, pages 1–7. Springer Verlag, 2004.

[7] D. Maltoni, D. Maio, A. Jain, and S. Prabhakar. *Handbook of Fingerprint Recognition (2nd Edition)*. Springer-Verlag, 2009.

[8] P. Meerwald and S. Pereira. Attacks, applications and evaluation of known watermarking algorithms with Checkmark. In P. W. Wong and E. J. Delp, editors, *Proceedings of SPIE, Electronic Imaging, Security and Watermarking of Multimedia Contents IV*, volume 4675, pages 293–304, San Jose, CA, USA, Jan. 2002. SPIE.

JPEG Anti-forensics Using Non-parametric DCT Quantization Noise Estimation and Natural Image Statistics

Wei Fan [*], Kai Wang, François Cayre
GIPSA-Lab, CNRS UMR5216,
St-Martin d'Hères, France
{wei.fan, kai.wang, francois.cayre}
@gipsa-lab.grenoble-inp.fr

Zhang Xiong
School of Computer Science and Engineering,
Beihang University, Beijing, P. R. China
xiongz@buaa.edu.cn

ABSTRACT

This paper proposes an anti-forensic method that disguises the footprints left by JPEG compression, whose objective is to fool existing JPEG forensic detectors while keeping a high visual quality of the processed image. First we examine the reliability of existing detectors and point out the potential vulnerability of the quantization table estimation based detector. Then we construct a new, non-parametric method to DCT histogram smoothing without any histogram statistical model. Finally JPEG forensic detectors are fooled by optimizing an objective function considering both the anti-forensic terms and a natural image statistical model. We show that compared to the state-of-the-art methods the proposed JPEG anti-forensic method is able to achieve a higher image visual quality while being undetectable under existing detectors.

Categories and Subject Descriptors

H.4 [**Information Systems Applications**]: Miscellaneous

General Terms

Algorithms, Reliability, Security

Keywords

Digital image forensics; anti-forensics; JPEG compression; natural image statistics; calibration

1. INTRODUCTION

The authenticity of digital images has been frequently questioned, due to the increasing popularity of easy-to-use and powerful photo-editing tools. Visually plausible fake images are appearing with a growing frequency, and in consequence image forensics has emerged over the last a few years to re-establish some credibility to digital images.

---

[*]Wei Fan is also with Beihang University.

JPEG, one of the most commonly used image compression formats today, enjoys its popularity in default camera setting, photo editing, and image processing. The artifacts left by JPEG compression are known and well studied [5], targeting at which Stamm et al. [11, 12] pioneered the work of JPEG anti-forensics. Thereafter it is possible to hide evidence of tampering or falsify the image origin by re-compressing the JPEG anti-forensically processed image [12]. Not long after Stamm et al.'s work, the research focus has been thrown upon countering JPEG anti-forensics: the analysis of weaknesses was carried out and two powerful JPEG forensic detectors were proposed [16, 15, 7].

Anti-forensics challenges the reliability of forensics, and can help researchers study the weaknesses in existing forensic techniques for further development of trustworthy digital forensics. In this paper, we continue the work of JPEG anti-forensics by trying to disguise the footprints of JPEG compression with less cost of image quality degradation, that is, we try to perform better JPEG anti-forensics. First, by running the test on a large uncompressed image dataset BOSS-Base [1], we investigate the limitations of the quantization table estimation based detector [5, 11]. We further analyze the disadvantages of using a model for DCT histogram smoothing [11], then a novel method is proposed based on estimating the quantization noise in the DCT domain using the approximate maximum *a posteriori* (MAP) based image restoration [17] and calibration [6]. For JPEG anti-forensics, we formulate the problem as the optimization of an objective function considering both the anti-forensic terms and a natural image prior model [17]. Experimental results show that our improved JPEG anti-forensics outperforms the state-of-the-art methods with a higher image quality while successfully fooling existing forensic detectors.

The remainder of this paper is organized as follows. Sec. 2 briefly reviews the related work on forensics, anti-forensics and countering anti-forensics for JPEG compression. The reliability analysis of JPEG forensic detectors is investigated in Sec. 3. The proposed improved DCT histogram smoothing method is described in Sec. 4. Sec. 5 presents the optimization problem of removing the introduced unnatural spatial-domain noise during DCT histogram smoothing, as well as fooling existing JPEG forensic detectors. We provide some discussions and conclude the paper in Sec. 6.

2. RELATED WORK

During JPEG compression (here we avoid retelling the standard JPEG compression process), two known kinds of artifacts appear, indicating the JPEG compression history of an image. The first one is *quantization artifacts* in the *DCT domain*. The DCT coefficients are clustered around integer multiples of the quantization step length, leaving a comb-like distribution of DCT coefficients in each subband. The second one is *blocking artifacts* in the *spatial domain*. There are consistent discontinuities across block borders.

Fan and de Queiroz [5] proposed an algorithm for Maximum Likelihood Estimation (MLE) of the JPEG quantization table, from a bitmap representation of the image. The method can serve as a detector (denoted as $\mathcal{D}_{F_q}$) to classify an image as never compressed, if each entry of the estimated quantization table is either 1 or "undetermined" [5, 11]. They also proposed a JPEG blocking detector $\mathcal{D}_{F_b}$ to examine JPEG blocking artifacts [5].

In order to disguise JPEG quantization artifacts, Stamm et al. [11] proposed to add a dithering signal to the DCT coefficient in each subband, so that the dithered signal approximates the distribution of unquantized coefficients (the created forgery is denoted as $\mathcal{F}_{S_q}$). For AC components, the DCT coefficients are modeled to follow the Laplacian distribution; meanwhile the quantization noise of the DC component is assumed to follow a uniform distribution. The dithering operation succeeded in fooling $\mathcal{D}_{F_q}$ [5]. After the dithering operation, Stamm et al. [12] later proposed an anti-forensic deblocking operation against $\mathcal{D}_{F_b}$ [5]. The deblocking was carried out by a combination of the median filtering and the white Gaussian noise addition. We denote the forgery created following this process as $\mathcal{F}_{S_q S_b}$.

Valenzise et al. [16, 15] claimed that the image quality of $\mathcal{F}_{S_q}$ is degraded by the dithering operation [11]. A detector $\mathcal{D}_V$ is therefore designed by measuring the noisiness of the re-compressed anti-forensic image, employing the total variation (TV) of the image as the noisiness measure.

Lai and Böhme [7] proposed another detector $\mathcal{D}_L$ to detect $\mathcal{F}_{S_q}$ [11]. They borrowed the idea of calibration from steganalysis [6] and compared the variances of high-frequency subbands (as defined in [7]) between the given image and its calibrated version by cropping the image by 4 pixels both horizontally and vertically.

3. RELIABILITY OF DETECTORS

Fan and de Queiroz [5] suggested that if each entry detected by $\mathcal{D}_{F_q}$ is either 1 or "undetermined", it is a good indication that the image has not been JPEG compressed. Therefore, the JPEG anti-forensic image $\mathcal{F}_{S_q}$ [11] is designed aiming at fooling this detector. However, as pointed out by Böhme and Kirchner [2], we lack a good prior for the false positive rate of $\mathcal{D}_{F_q}$.

In order to investigate the reliability of $\mathcal{D}_{F_q}$, we performed the experiment estimating the quantization tables of 10,000 genuine, uncompressed 512×512 PGM images generated from raw files of BOSSBase (v1.01) [1]. Table 1 lists the false positive rate P_{FP} of all the ten BOSSBase archives each of which contains 1000 images. Surprisingly, P_{FP} can reach as high as 61.50% for archive 06. The average rate 25.22% also indicates $\mathcal{D}_{F_q}$ is not very reliable to determine whether an image has been previously JPEG compressed.

Furthermore, we found that among all the "non-1" and "non-undetermined" estimated entries, 3 takes a large portion, as shown in the P_3 column in Table 1. Figure 1-(a) is a sample DCT histogram from a never compressed image, which has no comb-like quantization artifacts but is detected

Table 1: P_{FP} and P_3 for detector $\mathcal{D}_{F_q}$ on BOSSBase.

Archive	$P_{FP}(\%)$	P_3
01	18.70	$1653/1959 = 84.38\%$
02	12.40	$957/1118 = 85.60\%$
03	4.50	$175/187 = 93.58\%$
04	5.70	$111/125 = 88.80\%$
05	10.50	$986/1141 = 86.42\%$
06	61.50	$9243/11033 = 83.78\%$
07	17.50	$1084/1155 = 93.85\%$
08	43.90	$5655/6670 = 84.78\%$
09	33.20	$5062/5895 = 85.87\%$
10	44.30	$6780/7720 = 87.82\%$
Average	25.22	87.49%

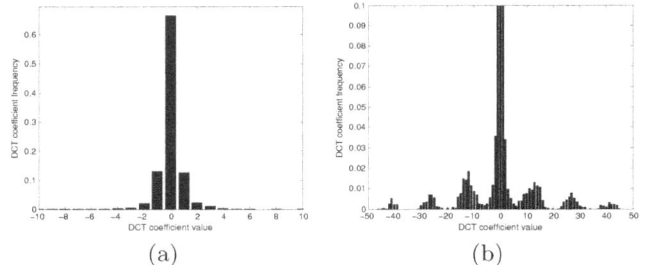

(a)   (b)

Figure 1: (a) is a sample unquantized DCT histogram which is detected as quantized by 3 according to $\mathcal{D}_{F_q}$, while the quantization step length is detected as 1 (namely never compressed) for (b).

as quantized by 3 according to $\mathcal{D}_{F_q}$. Here we go back to review the MLE of the quantization table. For the sake of simplicity, we only analyze why $\mathcal{D}_{F_q}$ picks 3 instead of 1 in this case. Based on Eq. (14) in [4] and Eq. (15) in [5], for $q = 1$, the log-likelihood is:

$$L(1) = N \times w(0,1) + N \times \log 1, \qquad (1)$$

while the log-likelihood for $q = 3$ is:

$$L(3) = p_0 \times N \times w(0,3) + (1-p_0) \times N \times w(1,3) + N \times \log 3, \quad (2)$$

where N is the total number of blocks used in estimation, and $w(i, q)$ is an even function of i defined in [4] (more details can be found in [4, 5]). We denote p_0 as the percentage of coefficients which are integer multiples of 3. $\mathcal{D}_{F_q}$ chooses 3 instead of 1 when $L(3) > L(1)$. This happens when $p_0 > 67.28\%$. For Figure 1-(a), among all the 4083 coefficients in estimation, there are 2797 coefficients which are integer multiples of 3, namely $p_0 = 68.50\%$. Hence $\mathcal{D}_{F_q}$ detects that it is quantized by 3. This frequently happens in the high-frequency subbands of relatively smooth images.

Another interesting point is that $\mathcal{D}_{F_q}$ outputs 1 for some DCT histograms which are obviously not from genuine, uncompressed images. Figure 1-(b) is from a post-processed JPEG image using our method of Sec. 4. It is obvious that the comb-like quantization artifacts still remain, but $\mathcal{D}_{F_q}$ fails to estimate the correct quantization step length.

Our large-scale test of JPEG forensics was carried out on 1338 genuine, uncompressed images of size 512×384 from the UCID corpus (v2) [10]. Here we divide UCID into two sets: the first 1000 images are put into UCIDTest for forensic testing; the last 338 images are put into UCIDTrain for training the quantization noise model and the image prior model, which will be described in Sec. 4 and used in our proposed

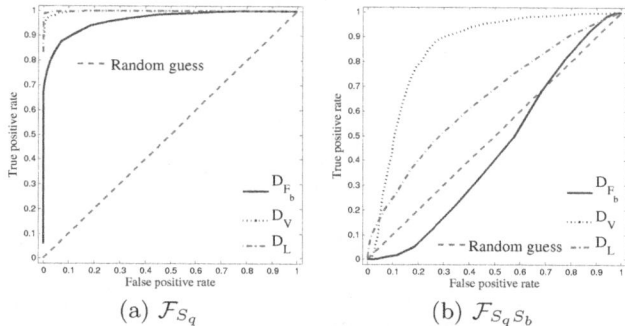

(a) $\mathcal{F}_{S_q}$ (b) $\mathcal{F}_{S_q S_b}$

Figure 2: ROC curves of Stamm et al.'s two versions of forgeries [11, 12] against the detectors.

method. Each UCIDTest image $\mathcal{I}$ is compressed[1] at a random quality factor $Q \in [30, 35, 40, 45, 50, 55, 60, 65, 70, 75, 80, 85, 90]$. Then JPEG image $\mathcal{J}$ was generated, from which all types of JPEG anti-forensic forgeries will be created.

Based on the previous reliability analysis of detector $\mathcal{D}_{F_q}$, although it is not a very reliable JPEG forensic detector, we still tested it on UCIDTest. The false positive rate is $P_{FP} = 16/1000 = 1.6\%$, and $P_3 = 15/16 = 94.74\%$. This low false positive rate may be due to two facts: 1) UCID does not contain too many images, which is also why we investigated the reliability of $\mathcal{D}_{F_q}$ on the larger dataset BOSSBase which has a richer image diversity; 2) most UCID images contain a large portion of highly textured regions, which reduce the occurrences of 3 in the quantization step length estimation. Experiments on other natural image datasets are needed to faithfully assess the performance of $\mathcal{D}_{F_q}$. In our anti-forensic work, we still consider the outputs of $\mathcal{D}_{F_q}$ trying to reduce the occurrences of 3 in the anti-forensic image on UCIDTest, which means in other words to avoid the image to be over-smoothed. The results will be later discussed in Sec. 5.

In this paper we mainly consider three JPEG forensic detectors: $\mathcal{D}_{F_b}$, $\mathcal{D}_V$ and $\mathcal{D}_L$. Figure 2 shows the ROC curves of $\mathcal{F}_{S_q}$ and $\mathcal{F}_{S_q S_b}$ [11, 12] under the three detectors. The detection reliability [14] $\rho = 2a - 1$, where a is the area under the ROC curve, is reported in Table 4. All the detectors are able to detect $\mathcal{F}_{S_q}$ but no longer perform that well on $\mathcal{F}_{S_q S_b}$. However the cost for $\mathcal{F}_{S_q S_b}$ is to lose 5.13 dB of PSNR value compared to $\mathcal{J}$ on average.

4. A NEW, NON-PARAMETRIC APPROACH TO DCT HISTOGRAM SMOOTHING

The basic assumption of Stamm et al.'s dithering-based JPEG anti-forensics [11] is that the DCT coefficients follow the Laplacian distribution for AC components. The Laplacian distribution is the dominant choice balancing simplicity of the model and fidelity to the real data. However, because of the diversity of natural images, the suitability of the Laplacian distribution model differs for different images. Figure 3-(a) shows the DCT histogram for subband $(2, 2)$ of an UCID image, and -(b) is from its corresponding forgery $\mathcal{F}_{S_q}$. The red curves are the Laplacian distribution fitting results, with the parameter $\hat{\lambda}$ obtained by the MLE [8]. Obviously, here the Laplacian model is not a very good choice for a precise description of the DCT histogram.

---

[1] All the JPEG compression and decompression operations in this paper were performed using *libjpeg* version 6b provided by Independent JPEG Group. More information can be found at http://www.ijg.org.

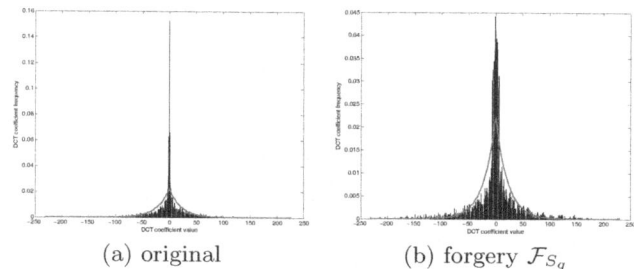

(a) original   (b) forgery $\mathcal{F}_{S_q}$

Figure 3: Two histograms of DCT coefficients of subband $(2, 2)$. The red curves are the fitting results of the Laplacian distribution model.

During the creation of $\mathcal{F}_{S_q}$ [11], the dithering signal is generated depending on $\hat{\lambda}$, and is then added to the quantized DCT coefficient *randomly* without any consideration of the local information of the image in the spatial domain. This constitutes another disadvantage of the method that would lead to a poor visual quality of $\mathcal{F}_{S_q}$ [16].

After analyzing the disadvantages of the Laplacian model-based DCT histogram smoothing strategy, we aim to find a new, non-parametric approach to DCT histogram smoothing. We wish to be able to estimate the actual DCT-domain quantization noise. The first step is to recover as much information of $\mathcal{I}$ as possible from $\mathcal{J}$.

Given a JPEG compressed image $\mathbf{x}_q$ (pixel values in vectorized form), the objective is to obtain a restored image $\hat{\mathbf{x}}$, which is the most likely to be the original uncompressed image. A MAP criterion is used to seek the solution:

$$\hat{\mathbf{x}} = \arg \max_{\mathbf{x}} p(\mathbf{x}|\mathbf{x}_q) = \arg \max_{\mathbf{x}} p(\mathbf{x}_q|\mathbf{x})p(\mathbf{x}), \quad (3)$$

where $p(\mathbf{x}_q|\mathbf{x})$ is the likelihood term describing the distortion caused by JPEG compression, and $p(\mathbf{x})$ is a prior term representing natural image statistics. A common practice for maximizing Eq. (3) is to minimize its negative log function.

JPEG compression can be modeled as a process to add spatial-domain *quantization noise* $\mathbf{n}_q$ to the original uncompressed image, then $\mathbf{x}_q = \mathbf{x} + \mathbf{n}_q$. A common assumption is to treat $\mathbf{n}_q$ as a random quantity; meanwhile $\mathbf{n}_q$ and $\mathbf{x}$ are considered to be independent [9, 13]. Then we have:

$$p(\mathbf{x}_q|\mathbf{x}) = p(\mathbf{x} + \mathbf{n}_q|\mathbf{x}) = p(\mathbf{n}_q|\mathbf{x}) = p(\mathbf{n}_q). \quad (4)$$

For the quantization noise model $p(\mathbf{n}_q)$, a 0-mean Gaussian model, whose covariance matrix can be computed from the quantization table, is used in [9, 13]. For the image prior model $p(\mathbf{x})$, Robertson and Stevenson [9] used the Huber-Markov Random Field (HMRF), while Sun and Cham [13] used a higher order Markov random field based on the Fields of Experts (FoE) framework to further improve the visual quality of the post-processed image.

In this paper, for the image prior, we follow Zoran and Weiss' [17] framework of maximizing the EPLL (Expected Patch Log Likelihood), whose idea is to find $\hat{\mathbf{x}}$ in which *every* patch is *likely* under the patch prior. We use the patch size of 8×8, the same as that of JPEG blocks. The motivation of choosing this patch-wise prior is to facilitate and speed up the learning and restoration processes, when compared with [9, 13]. We still use the 0-mean Gaussian [9] to model the quantization noise. The difference is that for a better quality of the recovered image we need to take into account all the *overlapping* patches instead of the *non-overlapping* JPEG blocks. We therefore consider 64 kinds of patches according

Table 2: PSNR results for four classical test images and three different quantization tables provided in [13].[3]

Quantization table	Lena			Peppers			Barbara			Baboon		
	Q1	Q2	Q3	Q1	Q2	Q3	Q1	Q2	Q3	Q1	Q2	Q3
JPEG image	30.71	30.08	27.45	30.72	30.17	27.66	25.95	25.60	24.05	24.32	24.14	22.14
FoE-based [13]	31.95	31.44	28.83	32.04	**31.61**	29.35	26.65	26.31	24.86	24.77	24.62	**22.61**
The proposed method	**32.06**	**31.48**	**28.94**	**32.09**	31.59	**29.40**	**26.94**	**26.56**	**25.00**	**24.84**	**24.68**	**22.61**

to their relative position with respect to JPEG blocks. The minimization problem is then formulated as:

$$\hat{\mathbf{x}} = \arg\min_{\mathbf{x}} \{\frac{\lambda}{2}\sum_{k=1}^{64}\sum_{\mathbf{P}_i \in \mathcal{S}_k}(\mathbf{P}_i(\mathbf{x}_q - \mathbf{x}))^t \mathbf{C}_k^{-1}\mathbf{P}_i(\mathbf{x}_q - \mathbf{x})$$
$$-\sum_i \log p(\mathbf{P}_i\mathbf{x})\}, \quad (5)$$

where λ is a regularization parameter, $\mathbf{P}_i$ is a matrix extracting the i-th patch from the image, $\mathcal{S}_k$ is the k-th set of matrices which extract patches having the same relative positions with respect to JPEG blocks, and $\mathbf{C}_k$ is the covariance matrix for modeling the quantization noise of the k-th group of patches. Eq. (5) has the familiar form of the negative log function of Eq. (3) (with the extra balancing parameter λ), which contains a likelihood term and a prior term. The patch prior model in use is the Gaussian Mixture Model (GMM) [17]. The optimization of Eq. (5) can be solved using an approximate MAP procedure (for more details, please refer to [17]), then a Quantization Constraint Set (QCS) projection is used to assure that the DCT coefficient of the processed image is within the same quantization bin as that of the JPEG image.

We learn a GMM prior with 200 mixture components from 338×6000 randomly sampled patches. Given a JPEG compression quality factor Q, we compress all the images in the training set, the real quantization noise is therefore obtained for learning the 64 covariance matrices $\mathbf{C}_k$. Learning was performed on UCIDTrain using Expectation Maximization (EM) with unoptimized MATLAB code[2].

Table 2 lists the PSNR results for four classical images and three quantization tables Q1, Q2 and Q3, provided by [13], for very low bit-rate compression. We can see that the proposed method is very competitive in terms of PSNR gain. In our JPEG anti-forensic work, the quality factor in use is randomly selected among 30, 35, 40, 45, 50, 55, 60, 65, 70, 75, 80, 85, and 90. We found that the PSNR gain of our JPEG decompression method is slightly lower than that of Sun and Cham's [13] method using these quality factors. However our method only requires one step of approximate MAP estimation, which is practically around ten times faster than [13] using conjugate gradient descent. As an intermediate result of our anti-forensic image creation (to be described later), the PSNR gain is already satisfying.

After the JPEG image restoration process, we hereby propose a non-parametric approach to DCT histogram smoothing based on *relaxed* calibration [6] as follows:

1. Given a JPEG compressed image $\mathcal{J}$ of quality factor Q, $\hat{\mathcal{I}}$ is recovered following the approximate MAP procedure and the QCS projection, as described above.

---

[2]http://www.mathworks.com/matlabcentral/fileexchange/26184-em-algorithm-for-gaussian-mixture-model

[3]Note that the results are slightly different from the values listed in [13]. It is because we rounded the pixel values to integers within $[0, 255]$ before calculating the PSNR value.

Table 3: The difference of the average KL divergence between $\mathcal{F}_{S_q}$ and $\mathcal{I}$, and that between $\mathcal{F}_{F_q}$ and $\mathcal{I}$ for all 64 DCT subbands. The average divergence difference over all subbands is 0.1262.

	1	2	3	4	5	6	7	8
1	−0.022	0.019	0.045	0.070	0.094	0.123	0.142	0.115
2	0.014	0.051	0.065	0.067	0.073	0.126	0.112	0.070
3	0.057	0.060	0.067	0.073	0.088	0.116	0.134	0.065
4	0.059	0.064	0.068	0.065	0.092	0.168	0.166	0.086
5	0.076	0.068	0.081	0.100	0.111	0.234	0.243	0.140
6	0.085	0.080	0.100	0.102	0.141	0.228	0.286	0.218
7	0.141	0.119	0.139	0.172	0.231	0.293	0.295	0.248
8	0.137	0.157	0.164	0.192	0.209	0.217	0.241	0.243

2. Slightly crop $\hat{\mathcal{I}}$ by 1 pixel[4] both horizontally and vertically to obtain $\hat{\mathcal{I}}_c$.

3. $\hat{\mathcal{J}}_c$ is obtained by compressing $\hat{\mathcal{I}}_c$ at quality factor Q.

4. Compute the DCT coefficients of $\hat{\mathcal{I}}_c$ and $\hat{\mathcal{J}}_c$, and the estimated DCT quantization noise $\hat{\mathcal{N}}_q$ can be obtained by subtracting their DCT coefficients.

5. $\hat{\mathcal{N}}_q$ is added to $\hat{\mathcal{I}}$ in the DCT domain, the forgery $\mathcal{F}_{F_q}$ with smoothed DCT histograms is therefore created.

In Sec. 4, we analyzed that the quality degradation of $\mathcal{F}_{S_q}$ is due to the randomness of adding dithering signal without any consideration of the image spatial-domain information. In our strategy, $\hat{\mathcal{I}}$ has already partly recovered the lost information during JPEG compression, however the DCT-domain information has not been very well recovered. A sample DCT histogram of $\hat{\mathcal{I}}$, which still has the comb-like quantization artifacts, is shown in Figure 1-(b). Based on the translation invariance of natural image statistics and the effectiveness of calibration [6], the very slight cropping helps $\hat{\mathcal{I}}_c$ get a good estimation of the original DCT histogram of $\mathcal{I}$, while taking into account certain spatial-domain information in the estimation of the DCT quantization noise. The DCT histograms of $\mathcal{F}_{F_q}$ are smoothed by adding $\hat{\mathcal{N}}_q$ without sacrificing too much image quality.

One main objective of JPEG anti-forensics is to reproduce original uncompressed DCT histograms. After our DCT histogram smoothing, the gaps left by JPEG compression are filled in $\mathcal{F}_{F_q}$. In order to give a quantitative evaluation, here we use the symmetric Kullback-Leibler (KL) divergence as the distance measure between the forged DCT histogram and the original one. Here the two DCT histograms in comparison are constructed using the same range of integers as the bin centers. We compute the average KL divergence between $\mathcal{F}_{S_q}$ and $\mathcal{I}$, and that between $\mathcal{F}_{F_q}$ and $\mathcal{I}$ for all DCT subbands. The difference of these two average KL divergence values is reported in Table 3. $\mathcal{F}_{F_q}$ performs consistently better than $\mathcal{F}_{S_q}$, with the exception of a slightly

---

[4]Note that here we only crop the image by 1 pixel instead of 4 pixels as in classical image calibration, it is empirically determined in order to attain higher image quality for $\mathcal{F}_{F_q}$.

higher divergence value for the DC component. We also examined the image quality: $\mathcal{F}_{F_q}$ achieves 2.09 dB PSNR gain and 0.0214 SSIM gain compared to $\mathcal{F}_{S_q}$ on average.

5. IMPROVED JPEG ANTI-FORENSICS

Although we are trying to estimate the actual quantization noise in the DCT domain, we are aware that the estimation cannot be very accurate in the spatial domain. The injection of $\hat{\mathcal{N}}_q$ must have introduced some extra unnatural spatial-domain noise to $\hat{\mathcal{I}}$. In this section, we will focus on the denoising on $\mathcal{F}_{F_q}$ as well as JPEG anti-forensics against the detectors. For convenience, the spatial-domain noise presented in $\mathcal{F}_{F_q}$ is assumed to be additive white Gaussian noise, with standard deviation σ_n. The forensic detectors in consideration are $\mathcal{D}_{F_b}$, $\mathcal{D}_V$ and $\mathcal{D}_L$.

We still follow Zoran and Weiss' [17] image restoration framework, yet adding some terms for JPEG anti-forensic purposes. The cost function we propose to minimize is:

$$
\begin{aligned}
\mathbf{f} \;=\; & \frac{\lambda}{2}\|\mathbf{x}-\mathbf{x}_q\|^2 + \alpha \times \iota(\mathbf{x}) \\
& + \beta \sum_{k=1}^{28} \sum_{c=0}^{7} |\nu_k(\mathbf{x}_c) - \hat{\sigma}_k^2| \\
& + \sum_i \frac{\gamma}{2}\|\mathbf{P}_i\mathbf{x}-\mathbf{z}^i\|^2 - \log p(\mathbf{z}^i), \qquad (6)
\end{aligned}
$$

where α, β and γ are regularization parameters, $\mathbf{x}_c$ is the calibrated image obtained by cropping $\mathbf{x}$ by c pixels in both horizontal and vertical directions [6, 7], and $\{\mathbf{z}^i\}$ is a set of auxiliary variables facilitating the optimization [17].

Now we explain the different terms in Eq. (6) in order. The first term is for the image fidelity control, which expects the obtained image is still close to the JPEG image. The second term is designed for $\mathcal{D}_V$ [15], and $\iota(\cdot)$ computes the TV of the image (the ℓ_1 norm of the spatial first-order derivatives). We wish the image would have low TV, in other words not very noisy. The third term is for $\mathcal{D}_L$, and $\nu_k(\cdot)$ returns the variance of the k-th high-frequency subband (defined in [7]) of the image, while $\hat{\sigma}_k^2$ is the estimated variance of the k-th high-frequency DCT subband from $\mathcal{F}_{F_q}$. As the JPEG block size is 8×8, basically we have 7 ways to crop the image along the diagonal direction by c ($c = 1, \cdots, 7$) pixel(s) in both horizontal and vertical directions. Following the main idea of $\mathcal{D}_L$, 6 other detectors can be built using the similar way by comparing the variances of high-frequency subbands between the image and its calibrated version. If the image and all its 7 calibrated versions have close variances to the estimated one in all the high-frequency subbands, $\mathcal{D}_L$ and the other 6 potential detectors described above can be fooled. The last term is the image prior term which expects every patch is likely under the prior, thanks to which the outputs of $\mathcal{D}_{F_b}$ [5] can be largely decreased.

The optimization problem can be solved using the "Half Quadratic Splitting" [17] and it consists of two sub-problems:

- $\mathbf{z}$ sub-problem, solving $\mathbf{z}$ given $\mathbf{x}$ — This is solved using the approximate MAP estimation, given the parameter γ related to the noise standard deviation σ_n [17]. The main objective of this sub-problem is to remove the introduced extra unnatural noise in $\mathcal{F}_{F_q}$, thanks to the regularization by the natural image statistical model.

- $\mathbf{x}$ sub-problem, solving $\mathbf{x}$ given $\mathbf{z}$ — This can be solved using the subgradient descent method. JPEG anti-

Table 4: From the 2nd to the 4th columns, detection reliabilities of three detectors on different types of images are listed; the 5th and 6th columns show the image quality comparison.

	$\mathcal{D}_{F_b}$	$\mathcal{D}_V$	$\mathcal{D}_L$	PSNR	SSIM
$\mathcal{J}$	0.9999	0.9865	0.9889	35.1918	0.9862
$\mathcal{F}_{S_q}$	0.9166	0.9949	0.9972	31.5105	0.9584
$\mathcal{F}_{S_q S_b}$	−0.2052	0.6824	0.1889	30.0621	0.9427
$\mathcal{F}$	−0.0365	0.1814	0.0517	34.2652	0.9745

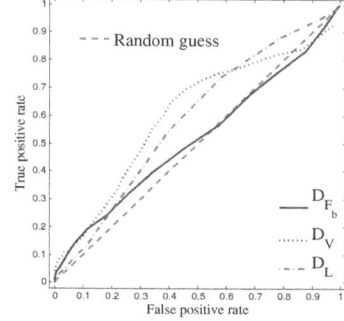

Figure 4: ROC curves of $\mathcal{F}$ against the detectors.

forensics is mainly carried out in this sub-problem, while keeping the image still close to $\mathbf{x}_q$.

Figure 4 shows the ROC curves of our forgeries (denoted as $\mathcal{F}$) against the three JPEG forensic detectors. Table 4 reports the figures of detection reliabilities and average PSNR and SSIM values compared to JPEG images, and to Stamm et al.'s two versions of forgeries [11, 12]. We also calculated the detection reliabilities of $\mathcal{F}$ against the above 6 potential detectors which are built in a similar way as $\mathcal{D}_L$, the average reliability value is −0.1285 with the standard deviation 0.1983. We can see that our forgeries achieve a better trade-off between undetectability against existing JPEG forensic detectors and the visual quality of processed images: the average PSNR value has been improved by 4.20 dB compared to $\mathcal{F}_{S_q S_b}$, and being 0.93 dB lower than $\mathcal{J}$.

Figure 5 shows the processed anti-forensic images from an example JPEG compressed image at quality factor 50. As expected, Figure 5-(e) is able to keep more details such as textures and edges than -(d) (please refer to the electronic version for a better visibility). Meanwhile we need to examine the DCT histograms of the forgery. Even though $\mathcal{D}_{F_q}$ was proven not very reliable, we still tested it on $\mathcal{F}$. The false positive rate is $P_{FP} = 5/1000 = 0.5\%$, and $P_3 = 4/5 = 80\%$. These values are close to the test results on uncompressed UCIDTest images (c.f. Sec. 3). We also examined the shape of the DCT histogram, and some example results are shown in Figure 5 (f)-(i), no noticeable artifacts appear. We furthermore compared the KL divergence, on average $\mathcal{F}$ has a divergence value 0.1104 lower than $\mathcal{F}_{S_q}$, and 0.0024 slightly higher than $\mathcal{F}_{S_q S_b}$. However, we have no explanation why $\mathcal{F}_{S_q S_b}$ processed by the median filtering combined with the white Gaussian noise addition would make the DCT histogram closer to the original one of $\mathcal{I}$ than $\mathcal{F}_{S_q}$.

6. DISCUSSION AND CONCLUSION

For solving Eq. (6), we do three iterations and the parameter setting is: $\lambda = \frac{N}{10\sigma_n^2}$, $\alpha = \frac{N}{10\sigma_n^2}$, $\beta = \frac{8N}{10\sigma_n^2}$, where N is the number of pixels in each patch, $\gamma = \frac{1}{\sigma_n^2}[1, 8, 32]$,

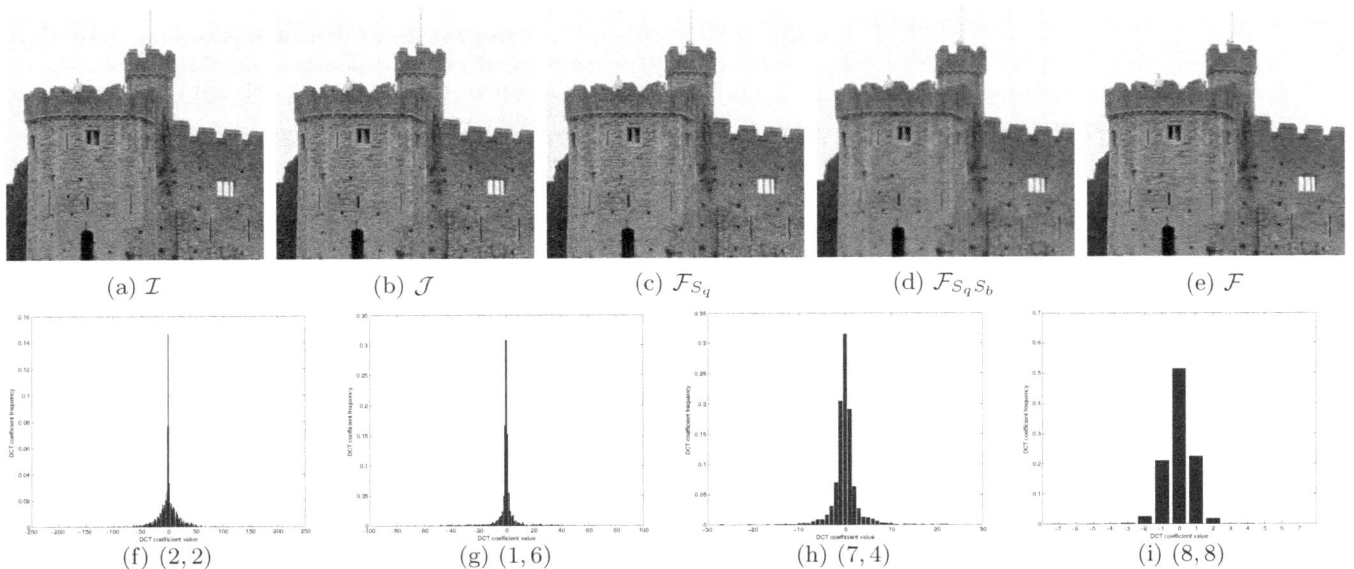

| (a) $\mathcal{I}$ | (b) $\mathcal{J}$ | (c) $\mathcal{F}_{S_q}$ | (d) $\mathcal{F}_{S_q S_b}$ | (e) $\mathcal{F}$ |

| (f) $(2,2)$ | (g) $(1,6)$ | (h) $(7,4)$ | (i) $(8,8)$ |

Figure 5: (a)-(e) are example results (close-up images) of $\mathcal{F}$ compared with $\mathcal{I}$, $\mathcal{J}$, $\mathcal{F}_{S_q}$, and $\mathcal{F}_{S_q S_b}$, where $\mathcal{J}$ is compressed at quality factor 50. (f)-(i) are example DCT histograms from -(e).

and σ_n is empirically set as $-0.1Q + 13$ according to the quality factor of $\mathcal{J}$. For each iteration of constant γ value, $\mathbf{z}$ and $\mathbf{x}$ sub-problems are solved alternatively once for either problem. In practice, we found that the output of $\mathcal{D}_L$ is not easy to be further decreased into the normal range. Moreover, images tend to be over-smoothed as $\mathcal{D}_{F_q}$ detects many 3 entries. We tackle this problem by adding a slight amount of white Gaussian noise in the middle of solving the $\mathbf{x}$ sub-problem during the last iteration. We set $\lambda = 0$, $\alpha = 0.01$ and $\beta = 1$ to emphasize on decreasing the $\mathcal{D}_L$ output. The added noise is mostly suppressed during the later subgradient iterations but can successfully reduce the occurrences of 3 in the quantization table estimation.

By using the MAP-based image restoration, calibration and a prior of natural image statistics, we created JPEG forgeries with a higher image quality than Stamm et al.'s forgeries [11, 12] as well as a good undetectability against existing detectors [5, 15, 7]. Moreover, the DCT histogram is explicitly smoothed by the proposed DCT-domain quantization noise estimation to better approximate the original one, which is also one of the main improvements compared to our previous TV-based anti-forensic method [3]. Future research could be devoted to the investigation on whether the improvement of the image quality of $\hat{\mathcal{I}}$ will lead to a better anti-forensic image $\mathcal{F}$ on the JPEG anti-forensic side, and to further study of natural image statistics to build more powerful detectors on the JPEG forensic side. We also plan to conduct larger-scale tests and comparisons on BOSSBase.

7. ACKNOWLEDGMENTS

The first author performed this work while at GIPSA-Lab on the grant from China Scholarship Council (No. 2011602067). This work was also funded, in part, by French ANR Estampille (No. ANR-10-CORD-019), International S&T Cooperation Program of China (2010DFB13350), and National High Technology Research Development Program ("863" Program) of China (2011AA010502).

8. REFERENCES

[1] P. Bas, T. Filler, and T. Pevný. Break our steganographic system — the ins and outs of organizing BOSS. In *Proc Int. Conf. on Information Hiding*, pages 59–70, 2011.

[2] R. Böhme and M. Kirchner. Counter-forensics: Attacking image forensics. In H. T. Sencar and N. Memon, editors, *Digital Image Forensics*, pages 327–366. Springer, New York, NY, USA, 2013.

[3] W. Fan, K. Wang, F. Cayre, and Z. Xiong. A variational approach to JPEG anti-forensics. In *Proc. IEEE Int. Conf. Acoust., Speech, and Signal Process.*, 2013.

[4] Z. Fan and R. L. de Queiroz. Maximum likelihood estimation of JPEG quantization table in the identification of bitmap compression history. In *Proc. IEEE Int. Conf. Image Process.*, pages 948–951, 2000.

[5] Z. Fan and R. L. de Queiroz. Identification of bitmap compression history: JPEG detection and quantizer estimation. *IEEE Trans. Image Process.*, 12(2):230–235, 2003.

[6] J. Fridrich, M. Goljan, and D. Hogea. Steganalysis of JPEG images: Breaking the F5 algorithm. In *Proc. Int. Workshop on Information Hiding*, pages 310–323, 2003.

[7] S. Lai and R. Böhme. Countering counter-forensics: the case of JPEG compression. In *Proc Int. Conf. on Information Hiding*, pages 285–298, 2011.

[8] J. R. Price and M. Rabbani. Biased reconstruction for JPEG decoding. *IEEE Signal Process. Lett.*, 6(12):297–299, 1999.

[9] M. A. Robertson and R. L. Stevenson. DCT quantization noise in compressed images. *IEEE Trans. Circuits Syst. Video Technol.*, 15(1):27–38, 2005.

[10] G. Schaefer and M. Stich. UCID - An uncompressed colour image database. In *Proc. SPIE: Storage and Retrieval Methods and Applications for Multimedia*, pages 472–480, 2004.

[11] M. Stamm, S. Tjoa, W. S. Lin, and K. J. R. Liu. Anti-forensics of JPEG compression. In *Proc. IEEE Int. Conf. Acoust., Speech, and Signal Process.*, pages 1694–1697, 2010.

[12] M. Stamm, S. Tjoa, W. S. Lin, and K. J. R. Liu. Undetectable image tampering through JPEG compression anti-forensics. In *Proc. IEEE Int. Conf. Image Process.*, pages 2109–2112, 2010.

[13] D. Sun and W.-K. Cham. Postprocessing of low bit-rate block DCT coded images based on a fields of experts prior. *IEEE Trans. Image Process.*, 16(11):2743–2751, 2007.

[14] C. Ullerich and A. Westfeld. Weaknesses of MB2. In *Proc. of Int. Workshop on Digital Watermarking*, pages 127–142, 2008.

[15] G. Valenzise, V. Nobile, M. Tagliasacchi, and S. Tubaro. Countering JPEG anti-forensics. In *Proc. IEEE Int. Conf. Image Process.*, pages 1949–1952, 2011.

[16] G. Valenzise, M. Tagliasacchi, and S. Tubaro. The cost of JPEG compression anti-forensics. In *Proc. IEEE Int. Conf. Acoust., Speech, and Signal Process.*, pages 1884–1887, 2011.

[17] D. Zoran and Y. Weiss. From learning models of natural image patches to whole image restoration. In *Proc. IEEE Int. Conf. Computer Vision*, pages 479–486, 2011.

SIFT Keypoint Removal and Injection
for Countering Matching-Based Image Forensics

Irene Amerini
Media Integration and
Communication Center
University of Florence
Firenze, Italy
irene.amerini@unifi.it

Mauro Barni
Department of Information
Engineering
University of Siena
Siena, Italy
barni@dii.unisi.it

Roberto Caldelli *
Media Integration and
Communication Center
University of Florence
Firenze, Italy
roberto.caldelli@unifi.it

Andrea Costanzo
Department of Information
Engineering
University of Siena
Siena, Italy
andreacos82@gmail.com

ABSTRACT

Scale Invariant Feature Transform (SIFT) has been widely employed in several image application domains, including Image Forensics (e.g. detection of copy-move forgery or near duplicates). Until now, the research community has focused on studying the robustness of SIFT against legitimate image processing, but rarely concerned itself with the problem of SIFT security against malicious procedures. Recently, a number of methods allowing to remove SIFT keypoints from an original image have been devised. Although quite effective, such methods produce an attacked image with very few (or no) keypoints, thus leaving cues that can be easily exploited by a forensic analyst to reveal the occurred manipulation. In this paper, we explore the topic of reintroducing fake SIFT keypoints into a previously cleaned image in order to address the main weakness of the existing removal attacks. In particular, we evaluate the fitness of locally adaptive contrast enhancement methods to the task of injecting new keypoints. The results we obtained are encouraging: (i) it is possible to effectively introduce new keypoints whose descriptors do not match with those of the original image, thus concealing the removal forgery; (ii) the perceptual quality of the image following the removal and injection attacks is comparable to the one of the original image.

Categories and Subject Descriptors

I.4 [**Image processing and computer vision**]: Applications

---

*Corresponding author

Keywords

Image forensics; SIFT keypoints; counter-forensics; keypoint injection.

1. INTRODUCTION

Counterfeiting digital images by means of photo editing tools to alter the original meaning is becoming an immediate and easy practice. Copy-move forgery is the one of the most common ways of manipulating the semantic content of a picture, whereby a portion of the image is copied and pasted once or more times elsewhere into the same image. Image forensics literature offers several examples of detectors for such manipulation [3] and, among them, the most recent and effective ones [1, 11] are those based on Scale Invariant Feature Transform (SIFT) [10]. The capability of SIFT to discover correspondences between similar visual content, in fact, allows the forensic analysis to detect even very accurate and realistic copy-move forgeries. Expectedly, a methodology so powerful has drawn the interest of *counter-forensic* research, where with the term *counter-forensics* the study of methods to counter-attack forensic techniques by concealing manipulations traces is to be intended [4]. The actual reliability of such algorithms can only be estimated by considering what an attacker can try to do to invalidate such techniques. Furthermore, since SIFT is a powerful instrument to recognize and retrieve object, an analysis on SIFT security becomes very important also in the case of Content Based Image Retrieval (CBIR) [16] systems in order to assess if an attacker is able or not to succeed in deluding the image recognition process. The first work in this sense is the one by Hsu et al. [9], in which first the impact of simple attacks is analyzed and then a method to strengthen SIFT features (or keypoints) is proposed. Following this work, Do et al. [6–8] focused on a SIFT-based Content Based Image Retrieval scenario and devised a number of interesting attacks. The aim of the previous works is to modify the SIFT feature descriptor of a keypoint but they are not interested in the complete removal of the keypoints. A pioneer work on this has been presented in [5] where an attack based on local warping techniques derived from image watermarking was proposed. All these studies have demonstrated that devising methods to attack SIFT feature is not a trivial task. SIFT features are not only robust against several non-malicious processing but also against tampering attempts.

Most attacks, in fact, though succeeding in erasing keypoints, pay a high cost in terms of visual quality degradation. Given that, anyway, there is another basic issue to be taken into account when performing keypoint deletion that an image that does not contain SIFT keypoints (or very few of them) is suspicious by itself: such absence, especially in textured areas, could be taken as a clue of tampering, thus leading to a detector whose implementation is very straightforward. Therefore, a smarter attack could greatly benefit from an additional module introducing plausible fake keypoints which could trigger false positives during the SIFT match detection. Reinserted keypoints should ideally appear in a neighborhood of the original spatial locations, but, at the same time, their SIFT descriptors should be as far as possible from the original one in the SIFT space. In addition to that, injection should achieve a number of inserted keypoints as high as possible and, also, a spatial distribution compliant with the underlying image content (a huge number of thickened keypoints could be questionable as well).This topic is crucial in a copy-move forgery detection scenario where portions of an image are to be considered. Such a main aspect is investigated in this paper by analyzing different algorithms to reinsert keypoints in a keypoint-cleaned image while still avoiding matching in the SIFT domain. The fundamental idea of the paper is to highlight the security issue of the need of keypoint injection after a previous removal, to provide some instruments to perform this action and, finally, to present an analysis on some initial results.

The paper is organized as follows: Section 2 introduces the procedure devoted to keypoint removal. Section 3 gives a glance of our idea about keypoints injection in a cleaned image. Section 4 presents experimental results to prove the effectiveness of the proposed method. Section 5 concludes the paper.

2. KEYPOINT REMOVAL

This Section briefly describes the method in [2], we used to remove SIFT keypoints in a target image. It combines, in an iterative procedure, different attacks presented in [7] and [9], on the basis of a keypoint classification; it does not deal with the issue of keypoint injection at all. The idea to adopt a classification of the keypoint typology permits to use an ad-hoc attack for each kind of them, thus maximizing performances. Classification is basically done by resorting to a histogram description of a squared neighborhood around every keypoint; on the basis of the histogram shape three classes are defined: unimodal, bimodal and multimodal. Furthermore, it has been demonstrated [8] that sometimes an attack may introduce new keypoints in its attempt to delete those already present. In such cases, a single iteration of the attack is not enough, since there is the need to deal also with the newly introduced keypoints. For this reason, we arranged our attacks into an iterative procedure. For the first part (usually one half) of the iterations we attack all the keypoints with the *Smoothing* attack and for the second part, we alter the keypoints by means of *Collage* and the *RMD* (Removal with Minimum Distortion) [7] attacks according to the previous keypoint classification. The classification-based attack terminates after a certain number of iterations or when the desired percentage of deleted keypoints is reached (ideally 100%). The *Smoothing* attack reduces the population of keypoints without a significant loss of quality. The keypoints that survive to this first round of the attack are somehow "harder" to remove and require more powerful countermeasures (i.e. *Collage* and *RMD*). In the following, we briefly review each attack taken in account.

The first attack is the *Smoothing Attack*. A light Gaussian smoothing flattens the pixel values of an image in such a way that its potential keypoints at the level of DoG are reduced. The strength of the attack can be controlled with the parameters (h, σ), i.e. the size

and the standard deviation of the Gaussian kernel. In our experiments we have found out that $h = 3$ and $\sigma = 0.7$ represent a good compromise between the removal rate and the overall visual quality after the attack. This attack has also been used in [7].

The second attack is the *Collage Attack*, which is a variant of the attack used in [9]. It consists of the substitution of the original patch with another patch of the same size. The new patch should not contain a keypoint and needs to be as similar as possible to the original one according to some criteria of similarity. To implement the collage attack we created a database of about 120000 "keypoint-free" patches extracted from a data set of 80 images characterized by very heterogeneous visual contents. We chose to measure the similarity by means of the histogram intersection distance, which has been widely used in the past in image retrieval applications [20]. Let now $patch_{orig}$ and $patch_{min}$ be respectively the original patch and the most similar counterpart stored in the database (i.e. the patch whose histogram is at minimum d_{int}); to avoid visible artifacts along the borders, we do not reinsert $patch_{min}$ directly into the original image. Instead, we reinsert the following linear combination:

$$patch_{new} = W \cdot patch_{orig} + (1 - W) \cdot patch_{min} \qquad (1)$$

where W is an empirical 8×8 weighting matrix whose elements $w_{i,j} \in [0, 1]$ are set to 1 along the patch borders and progressively decrease to 0 near the center.

The third attack is the *RMD* attack proposed by Do et al. in [7]. The idea behind this technique is to calculate a small patch ϵ that added to the neighborhood of a keypoint allows its removal. The coefficients of ϵ are chosen in such a way to reduce the contrast around the keypoint computed at the DoG level, thus invalidating the check performed by the SIFT algorithm on all potential keypoints. Moreover, it is requested that the coefficients locally introduce the minimum visual distortion and, differently from the original version of the algorithm, we used the same weighting window of Eq. (1) to replace the original neighborhoods with the new patch.

3. KEYPOINT INJECTION

In this Section, the injection of fake keypoints into the cleaned image, obtained through the procedure described in Section 2, is investigated. However, before discussing this issue in depth, a schematization of the whole attack procedure (keypoint removal and injection) is shown in Figure 1 for sake of clarity.
At the beginning an original gray-scale image I (or a region within it) is fed to the system, which starts by detecting the SIFT keypoints. Then, for each keypoint, the corresponding 8×8 patch is manipulated by means of the attack procedure described in Section 2. Finally, the manipulated patches are inserted back into the image in their original positions to achieve keypoint removal and the cleaned image I_c is obtained.
The second step of the procedure is devoted to the injection of fake keypoints into the cleaned image. We have tested several different injection algorithms (e.g. contrast enhancement, sharpening and so on) to introduce new keypoints into the cleaned image. The most specific and promising ones, taken into account in the experimental tests presented in Section 4, will be described in subsection 3.1. At this stage, the image is processed full-frame, unlike in the previous stage, so this fact has a negative impact on the visual quality of the entire image (e.g. flat areas which did not contained keypoints originally). For this reason, in a 8×8 neighborhood of each keypoint we mix this image, let us call it pre-injected image, with the original one I, in a way that is similar to what happened in Eq. (1). The obtained patches (originally keypoint-free) are then substituted onto the pre-injected image producing the final injected one

I_{inj} which now shows a better visual quality.

In the third step, it is necessary for the attacker to check how

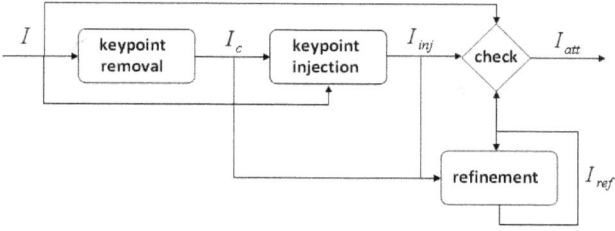

Figure 1: Schematization of the proposed framework.

many injected keypoints in the image are really valid. An injected keypoint is deemed as valid when, first of all, is located in a textured area and is spatially distributed with respect to the others and, above all, has a SIFT descriptor which is sufficiently different from its original homologue not to evidence a match. It is worth to point out that it is not so crucial to check that the new injected keypoint is or is not in the same spatial position (x,y coordinates) with respect to the original one. So, on this basis, we perform a matching detection between the original image I and the injected one I_{inj}. Ideally, it would be desirable not to obtain matches between the two images, though having in the injected image I_{inj} a plausible amount of well distributed keypoints: the final image I_{att} is obtained. It has also been foreseen, a possible refinement phase (at the moment only one loop is considered) where a selection of keypoints is made by taking the valid ones and discarding those presenting a correct match with their homologue (sometimes wrong welcomed matches are obtained, see Section 4 for details). For each discarded keypoint, a corresponding patch (16×16 pixels which is the computational window of the SIFT descriptor) of the cleaned image I_c is selected and inserted back into the image I_{inj} refining the injection procedure. The background idea is to primarily avoid a SIFT match at the expense of the loss of an injected keypoint.

3.1 Injection Algorithms

In this subsection, we briefly describe the techniques that we have employed to inject fake keypoints into an image. Their choice is justified by the following idea: we observed that smoothing techniques are quite effective in removing SIFT keypoints by lowering the image details. Therefore, we hypothesized that enhancement techniques, which exalt image details, may conversely introduce new keypoints. However, full-frame enhancement techniques, such as sharpening or global contrast enhancement, proved to be visually unsatisfactory, since they do not take into account local properties of the image. As a consequence, we needed to resort to more complex methods; hereafter four methods that have demonstrated superior performances and that have been selected for being presented within experimental result section of the paper are debated.

3.1.1 Contrast limited adaptive histogram equalization

Global contrast enhancement (GCE) techniques assume that the distribution of gray-scale pixel values is uniform over all the areas of an image. When this assumption does not hold, GCE performance are poor and the resulting image visually unpleasant. The *CLAHE* (Contrast Limited Adaptive Histogram Equalization) [21] tackles this problem in two ways: first, it adapts to the local properties of the regions of an image and, secondly, it limits the con-

trast differences across them. In a nutshell, the algorithm proceeds as follows (see [21] for details). First the image I is divided into a specified number of non-overlapping regions (tiles) and the histogram of each region is computed. Then, a clipping limit β for the contrast enhancement is obtained by means of the following Eq. (2):

$$\beta = \frac{MN}{L}\left(1 + \frac{\alpha}{100}(s_{max} - 1)\right) \tag{2}$$

where: $[M, N]$ are the size of the gray-scale image, $L = [0, 255]$ the histogram bins, $\alpha \geq 0$ is the *clipping factor* and s_{max} is the slope of the transfer function mapping the contrast from its input value to its output value; if $s_{max} = 1$ then no enhancement is performed, while larger values (usually up to 4) will result into more visible enhancements. Next, each region's histogram is clipped in such a way that its height is limited by β. At this point, it is necessary to remap the clipped values to the entire intensity range (i.e. to re-normalize the histogram of the processed image to its original area). This task can be done in several ways, the most common of which consists on redistributing the clipped pixels uniformly in all the bins of the histogram of the whole image.

3.1.2 Brightness preserving dynamic fuzzy histogram equalization

The *BPDFHE* (Brightness Preserving Dynamic Fuzzy Histogram Equalization) [14] is a method to enhance the contrast of an image while preserving its mean brightness, and thus the perceived subjective quality of the image. Similarly to other contrast enhancement techniques, the BPDFHE proposes to divide the image histogram into segments, which are then independently equalized. The partitioning, however, is not performed on the normal histogram, but rather on its fuzzy counterpart, whereby a pixel may belong to some degree to more than one of the bins, in accordance with a fuzzy membership function. Such histogram, in facts, is smoother, with no missing levels or abrupt fluctuations, thus allowing a more accurate segmentation. The membership function can be designed in different fashions, in our experiments *triangular* and *gaussian* have been considered.

The algorithm proceeds as follows (see [14] for details): (i) the fuzzy histogram $\tilde{H}(k)$, $k = [0, 255]$ is computed by assigning to each bin k the number of pixels whose value is "around k" (according with the chosen membership function); (ii) the local maxima $\{m_1, m_2, \ldots, m_n\}$ are computed and used to define histogram's segments $S = \{[\tilde{H}_{min}, m_1 - 1], [m_1, m_2 - 1], \ldots, [m_n, \tilde{H}_{max}]\}$, where $[\tilde{H}_{min}, \tilde{H}_{max}]$ is the range of $\tilde{H}$; (iii) each segment is equalized by means of a technique depending on the number of pixels belonging to the partition; (iv) in order to cope with the alterations that BPDFHE may have introduced, the resulting image's brightness is finally normalized to match the original brightness.

3.1.3 Anisotropic diffusion

The *2D-Anisotropic Diffusion* (2D-AD) is a method to enhance images by preserving the perceptual quality of semantically relevant parts (i.e. straight lines, edges, geometric shapes) [12]. In principle, it is a generalization of the scale-space transform, where an image I is iteratively convolved with a nonlinear smoothing filter which adapts to the local content to generate progressively more blurred versions of I. In this paper, we resort to the works of Weickert [18, 19], to which we refer for theoretical details.

The filter model used for anisotropic diffusion is derived by well-known operators used to extract image details. Let $I_\sigma = I * G_\sigma$ be the convolution of an image I with a Gaussian kernel ($\sigma > 0$); then, the gradient ∇I_σ can be employed to highlight structures such as the edges of I, unless they are parallel. In this case, a more accurate method is required. Let $J(\nabla I_\sigma) = \nabla I_\sigma \nabla I_\sigma^T$ be the Hessian of ∇I_σ; then, $J_\rho(\nabla I_\sigma) = J(\nabla I_\sigma) * G_\rho$, that is the convolution with a Gaussian kernel ($\rho > \sigma$), is called *tensor operator*, and it can be used to effectively highlight parallel, flow-like or T-shaped structures [18]. The eigenvectors $\{w_1, w_2\}$ of J_ρ give indications on local orientations, and the corresponding eigenvalues (μ_1, μ_2) on the local contrast along these directions. The *diffusion tensor* D, that permits to perform the anisotropic diffusion, is defined by means of the eigenvectors of J_ρ and the eigenvalues of Eq. (3-4).

$$\lambda_1 = c_1 \tag{3}$$

$$\lambda_2 = \begin{cases} c_1 & \text{if } \mu_1 = \mu_2 \\ c_1 + (1 - c_1)\exp\left(\frac{-c_2}{(\mu_1 - \mu_2)^2}\right) & \text{otherwise} \end{cases} \tag{4}$$

where $c_1 \in (0, 1)$ and $c_2 > 0$. By resorting to D, it is possible to efficiently compute blurred versions of $I(x, t)$ as numerical solutions of Eq. (5), where $t \geq 0$ is called *diffusion time*.

$$\frac{\partial I}{\partial t} = \nabla \cdot (D\nabla I) \tag{5}$$

In practice, the algorithm proceeds as follows: given $I = I(x, 0)$, first $J_\rho(\nabla I_\sigma)$ is computed and D is derived (Eq. (3-4)); then, $I(x, 1)$ is obtained (Eq. (5)). Starting from $I(x, 1)$, the process is repeated until a specified number of iterations have been reached (i.e. $t \leq t_{max}$).

Consequently, the final processed image corresponds to $I(x, t_{max})$. The tensor D ensures that each iteration will, at the same time, preserve linear structures and smooth the image along them. The model can be further refined in such a way that orientations are invariant to rotation [19].

4. EXPERIMENTAL RESULTS

In this Section, experimental tests carried out to check the performances of the proposed procedure for keypoint removal and injection are presented. A dataset of 86 digital images has been created by randomly drawing from UCID database [13] with size 512×384 pixels and with different visual content: landscapes, animals and faces. We will evaluate the performance of the proposed method both from the point of view of number of injected keypoints and of number of matches obtained after injection; an analysis on perceptual quality is provided too. In the following tests the keypoints have been computed by means of VLFeat, the Vedaldi and Fulkerson's implementation of SIFT [15] (DoG peak and edge thresholds set to 4 and 10). The threshold for keypoint matching is fixed to 0.6, as suggested by Lowe in [10]. We set a target keypoint removal percentage of 100% (perfect removal) and a maximum number of allowed iterations (i.e. $max\_iter = 40$). A higher number of iterations would have an unacceptably negative impact on quality. We continued with the iterations until we reached the desired removal percentage or the 40-th iteration. Then, after the keypoint removal, we applied the injection module. Results refer to four injection tools (*CLAHE, BPDFHE-Tri/Gauss* and *2D-AD*) presented in subsection 3.1; such methods have been used by adopting a parameter setting according to the values indicated in their reference papers. Section 4 is organized into three subsections: subsection 4.1 presents a quantitative analysis regarding the results achieved by the injection operation, while subsection 4.2 discusses some specific cases in detail, paying attention to the issue of *correct* generated matches. With this meaning *correct*, all the SIFT matches that link two keypoints, respectively belonging to two images, located in the same spatial position or, at most, within a 8×8 neighbor-

hood are intended. The last subsection 4.3 is dedicated to results regarding perceptual quality of processed images.

4.1 Effectiveness of keypoint removal-injection

In this subsection an analysis on the effectiveness of the procedure for keypoint removal-injection is presented. In Figure 2 (left column), the number of keypoints detected for each image, belonging to the selected dataset, is plotted. In particular, we have two reference trends that are common to both graphs (top-left and bottom-left): the number of keypoints existing in the original image (*Original*) which represents the upper bound and the ones remained in the cleaned image after removal (*Clean*) which, on the contrary, can be considered as the lower bound. Between these two, the trends of keypoints after injection performed with the four described tools are plotted: *BPDFHE triangular* and *gaussian* in the top-left graph, *CLAHE* and *2D-AD* in the bottom-left one (this separation has been done for sake of graph readability). It can easily be noticed how keypoint removal drastically reduces the number of keypoints which is globally close to the zero level though, in some cases, a quite consistent amount of keypoints survives, like for images 1, 5 and 8. After that, injection substantially succeeds in raising the number of keypoints per image towards the original quantities: all the four tools show similar behaviors (it is out of the scope to determine the best performing tool), with some borderline situations: sometimes no keypoints are injected (e.g. images 69 and 70 top-left), sometimes more than the original (e.g. image 30 and 49 bottom-left).

On the other side, in Figure 2 (right column, again tools *BPDFHE triangular* and *gaussian* in the top-right, *CLAHE* and *2D-AD* in the bottom-right), histograms of the deviations ($Diff$) between the number of SIFT matches obtained between the original image and the injected one, and the original image and the cleaned one are plotted. It can be observed that histograms are globally located around zero that means that, though keypoint injection has been carried out, a low amount of additional matches is actually appeared with respect to the case of the cleaned image. Negative cases indicate that an inferior number of matches is present after the injection step.

4.2 An in-depth analysis

In this subsection, we have extracted two images ($I24$ and $I83$) from the previous dataset of 86 images, trying to provide a different analysis point of view of the proposed approach; the tool *BPDFHE-Triangular* is taken into account for both. In Figure 3, the case of image $I24$, named *Dwarf*, is pictured; in top row keypoints are visualized respectively, from left to right, for original, cleaned and injected images. It can be seen that the cleaned image (top-center) contains only three keypoints while the injected one presents a higher amount of spatially distributed green circles. In particular, now keypoints appear on the nose of the dwarf, as primarily was, and, interestingly, on the top of the hood where there were not in origin. In the bottom row of Figure 3, SIFT matches are highlighted: between the original image and the cleaned one (bottom-left), between the original and the injected (bottom-right). In this favorable circumstance, after keypoint removal we obtained that three correct matches and two wrong (not horizontal lines) are left, but, after injection, we got again three correct matches, though one is different (keypoint on the dwarf nose), and one wrong. This means that injection operation does not determine an unwanted improvement in image matching detection.

In Figure 4, in the same presentation structure as before, the case of image $I83$, named *Bell Tower*, is pictured. Similar results are obtained as previously, but two aspects are interesting in this case.

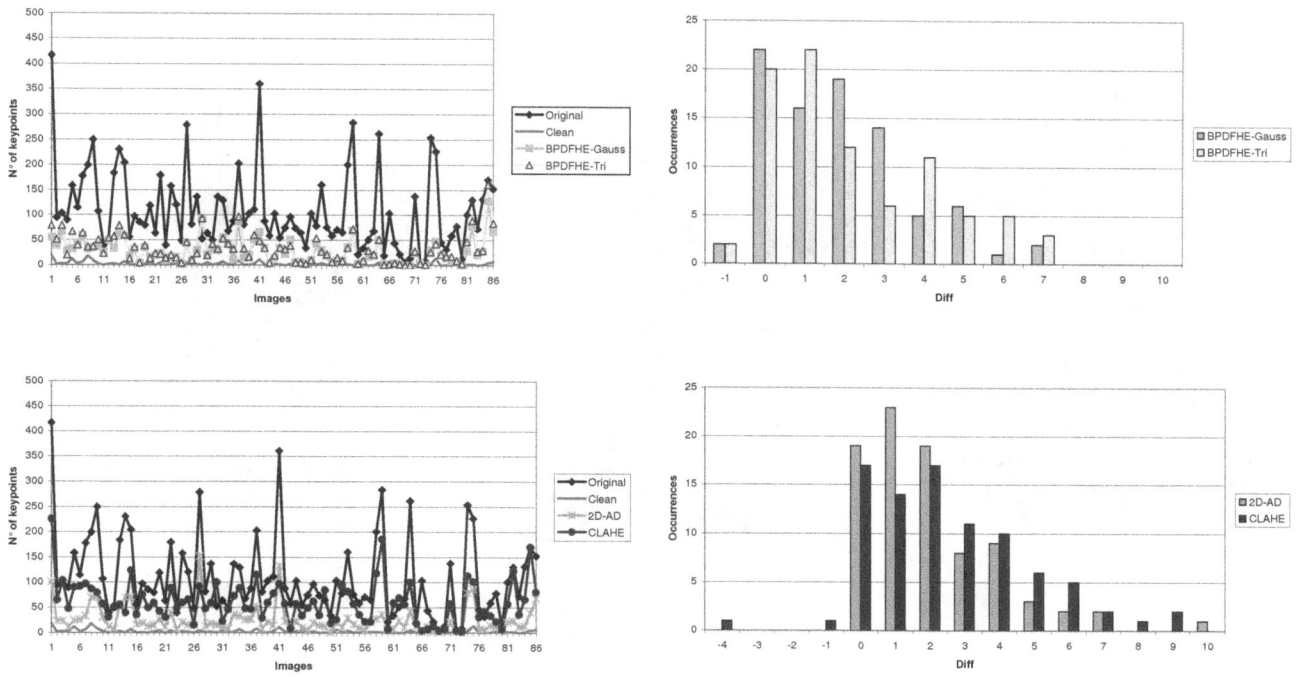

Figure 2: Graphs for keypoint removal-injection procedure. *Left column*, keypoints per image and *Right column*, variation of SIFT matches per image. With the term $Diff$, differences between the number of SIFT matches obtained between the original image and the injected one, and the original image and the cleaned are to be intended.

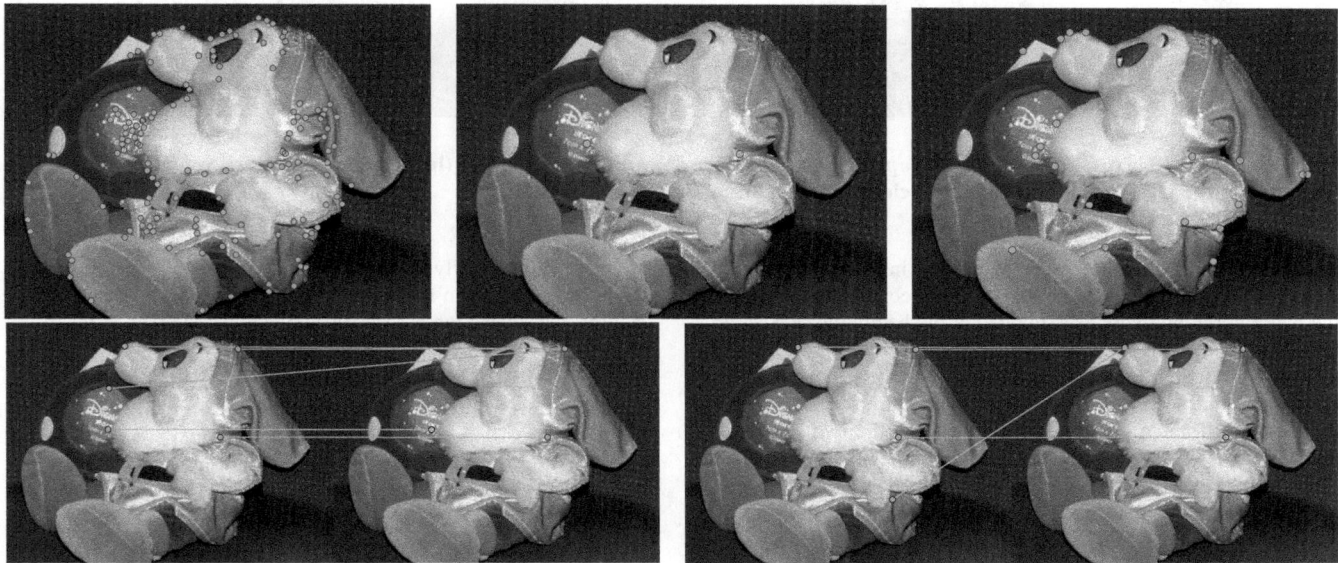

Figure 3: Image $I24$ (*Dwarf*). On the top row, keypoints are shown: original image (left); cleaned (center); injected (right). On the bottom row, SIFT matches: original vs cleaned (left); original vs injected (right).

Concerning the issue of keypoint extraction: cleaned image (Figure 4 top-center) does not contain any keypoint, that is quite suspicious per se being the image content very textured, as clearly evidenced by the original distribution of keypoints (Figure 4 top-left); instead injected image is more likely: the absence of keypoints over the clouds, which is an almost flat area, is not so strange. Concerning the issue of SIFT matches: obviously, the cleaned image, not containing any keypoint, does not produce any match with the original at all (Figure 4 bottom-left), but the injected one, which in turn has 4 matches (Figure 4 bottom-right), does not present any correct. In

Figure 4: Image *I*83 (***Bell Tower***). **On the top row, keypoints are shown: original image (left); cleaned (center); injected (right). On the bottom row, SIFT matches: original vs cleaned (left); original vs injected (right).**

fact, looking carefully at the green match line in the highest part of Figure 4 (bottom-right), it can visually be appreciated that also such line is not horizontal and, as explained at the beginning of Section 4, this means that the fake keypoint falls out of a 8×8 neighborhood with respect to the location of its possible homologue. Such an aspect could become crucial when an operation of estimate of the geometric transformation existing between the two images is carried out based on these matches; this might be necessary, for instance, for image registration or for region duplication localization in forgery detection in a forensic scenario. In such a circumstance, this would yield to a wrong computation and consequently to a misleading result.

Hereafter, detailed values, both for keypoints and for SIFT matches, referring to the two previous sample images, are provided in Table 1, to allow a numerical analysis of what visually proposed so far. In the left column of Table 1 with term *Correct SIFT matches* all the right matches, as explained previously, between the original image and the cleaned (injected) one are intended again. As already stated throughout the paper, here it can be observed that image quality (see PSNR and SSIM values at the bottom of Table 1) is not worsened after injection phase in comparison with what achieved after keypoint removal only; visual quality with respect to the original

image is satisfactorily preserved too. Indicatively, such a behavior has globally been registered for all the images of the selected dataset, see subsection 4.3 for further detail on such an issue.

4.3 An analysis on perceptual quality

In this subsection an analysis on perceptual quality of the processed images is presented; in particular, a comparison between the visual quality of each image after keypoint removal only and after removal-injection, with respect to the original image, is proposed in Figure 5. Two metrics have been computed for all the images belonging to the experimental dataset, Peak-Signal-to-Noise-Ratio (PSNR) and Structural SIMilarity (SSIM [17]); results pictured in Figure 5 refers to one of the four proposed injection methods which is *BPDFHE triangular* accordingly to what has been presented in Figures 3 and 4. In fact, all the methods seem to globally perform in a similar manner, both from the point of view of keypoint injection and from the point of view of image distortion. It can be noticed that the two lines are almost always overlapped, both for PSNR and SSIM, that indicates that the final visual quality after injection process is very close to that achieved at the end of keypoint cleaning phase. Averagely PSNR is around $40dB$ and SSIM is around 0.995. Anyway, there are some worst cases such as im-

Table 1: Performance of keypoint removal-injection attack on two sample images: $I24(Dwarf)$ and $I83(Bell\ Tower)$.

Description	I24 (*Dwarf*)	I83 (*Bell Tower*)
Original image keypoints	158	73
Cleaned image keypoints	3	0
Injected image keypoints	20	27
SIFT matches Original-vs-Cleaned	5	0
Correct SIFT matches Original-vs-Cleaned	3	0
SIFT matches Original-vs-Injected	4	5
Correct SIFT matches Original-vs-Injected	3	0
PSNR Original-Cleaned	39.12 dB	42.55 dB
PSNR Original-Injected	39.12 dB	42.02 dB
SSIM Original-Cleaned	0,9961	0,9984
SSIM Original-Injected	0,9960	0,9970

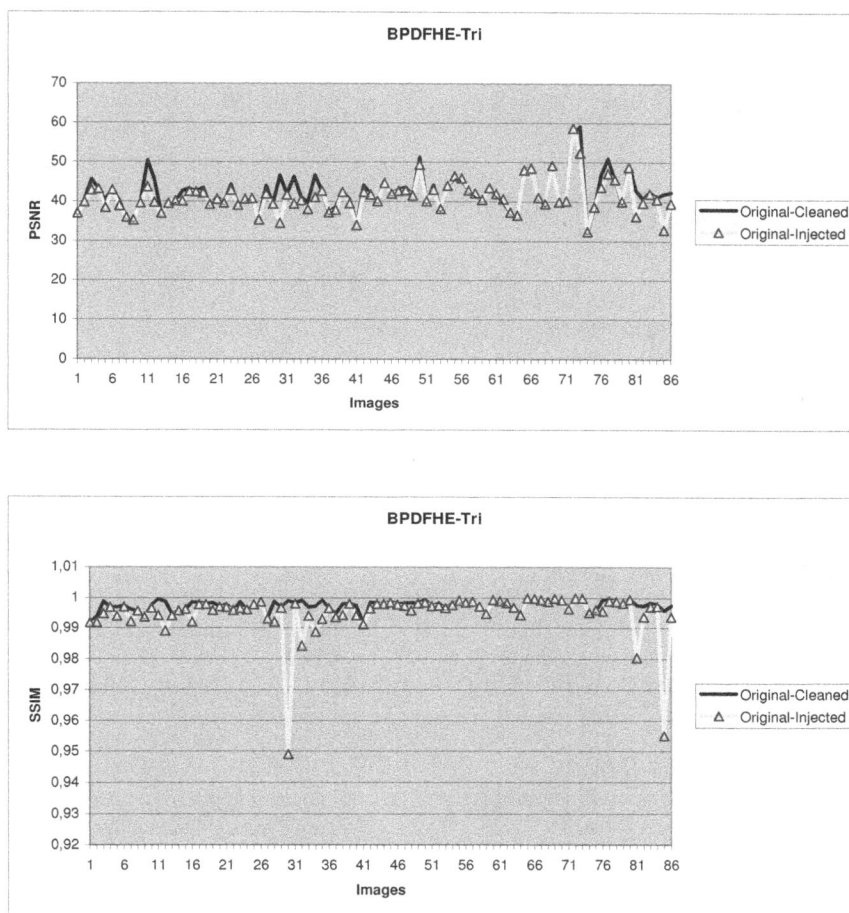

Figure 5: PSNR (top) and SSIM (bottom) computed between the original image and the cleaned one, and between the original image and the injected one. Injection has been performed by means of the method *BPDFHE triangular*.

age $I30$ and $I85$ where a stronger quality reduction is registered between original-cleaned and original-injected cases.

5. CONCLUSIONS AND FUTURE WORK

In this paper, the basic issue to inject fake SIFT keypoints in a previously cleaned image has been underlined and investigated.

This has been moved from the consideration that a complete keypoint-free image could be per se a clue of counterfeit. Furthermore, a procedure to firstly remove and then reinsert keypoints has been presented and a set of possible injection tools has been analyzed. Experimental results are encouraging and already show that injection is feasible without causing a successive detection at SIFT-matches level. Visual quality is still preserved both with respect to the original image and, particularly, in comparison with the image quality achieved after keypoint removal only. Future works will be dedicated to the research of more effective and ad-hoc injection tools and to evaluate the whole procedure in a copy-move attack forensic scenario.

Acknowledgments

This work was partially supported by the REWIND Project, funded by the Future and Emerging Technologies (FET) programme within the 7FP of the EC under grant 268478 and by the SECURE! Project, funded by the POR CreO FESR 2007-2013 programme of the Tuscany Region (Italy).

6. REFERENCES

[1] I. Amerini, L. Ballan, R. Caldelli, A. Del Bimbo, and G. Serra. A sift-based forensic method for copy move attack detection and transformation recovery. *Information Forensics and Security, IEEE Transactions on*, 6(3):1099 –1110, sept. 2011.

[2] I. Amerini, M. Barni, R. Caldelli, and A. Costanzo. Counter-forensics of SIFT-based copy-move detection by means of keypoint classification. *EURASIP Journal of Image and Video Processing - JIVP*, 2013.

[3] S. Bayram, H. Sencar, and N. Memon. A survey of copy-move forgery detection techniques. In *IEEE Western New York Image Processing Workshop*, pages 538–542, 2008.

[4] R. Böhme and M. Kirchner. Counter-forensics: Attacking image forensics. In H. T. Sencar and N. Memon, editors, *Digital Image Forensics*, pages 327–366. Springer New York, 2013.

[5] R. Caldelli, I. Amerini, L. Ballan, G. Serra, M. Barni, and A. Costanzo. On the effectiveness of local warping against SIFT-based copy-move detection. In *Proc. of Int'l Symposium on Communications, Control and Signal Processing (ISCCSP)*, Roma, Italy, May 2012.

[6] T.-T. Do, E. Kijak, L. Amsaleg, and T. Furon. Enlarging hacker's toolbox: deluding image recognition by attacking keypoint orientations. In *37th International Conference on Acoustics, Speech, and Signal Processing, ICASSP'12*, Kyoto, Japan, March 2012.

[7] T.-T. Do, E. Kijak, T. Furon, and L. Amsaleg. Deluding image recognition in sift-based cbir systems. In *Proceedings of the 2nd ACM workshop on Multimedia in forensics, security and intelligence*, MiFor '10, pages 7–12, 2010.

[8] T.-T. Do, E. Kijak, T. Furon, and L. Amsaleg. Understanding the security and robustness of sift. In *Proceedings of the international conference on Multimedia*, MM '10, pages 1195–1198, 2010.

[9] C.-Y. Hsu, C.-S. Lu, and S.-C. Pei. Secure and robust sift. In *Proceedings of the 17th ACM international conference on Multimedia*, MM '09, pages 637–640, 2009.

[10] D. G. Lowe. Distinctive image features from scale-invariant keypoints. *Int.'l Journal of Computer Vision*, 60(2):91–110, 2004.

[11] X. Pan and S. Lyu. Region duplication detection using image feature matching. *IEEE Transactions on Information Forensics and Security*, 5(4):857–867, 2010.

[12] P. Perona and J. Malik. Scale-space and edge detection using anisotropic diffusion. *Pattern Analysis and Machine Intelligence, IEEE Transactions on*, 12(7):629–639, 1990.

[13] G. Schaefer and M. Stich. UCID - An uncompressed colour image database. *Storage and Retrieval Methods and Applications for Multimedia, Proceedings of SPIE*, 5307:472–480, 2004.

[14] D. Sheet, H. Garud, A. Suveer, M. Mahadevappa, and J. Chatterjee. Brightness preserving dynamic fuzzy histogram equalization. *Consumer Electronics, IEEE Transactions on*, 56(4):2475–2480, november 2010.

[15] A. Vedaldi and B. Fulkerson. VLFeat: An open and portable library of computer vision algorithms. http://www.vlfeat.org/, 2008.

[16] R. C. Veltkamp and M. Tanase. Content-based image retrieval systems: A survey. Technical report, 2000.

[17] Z. Wang, A. Bovik, H. Sheikh, and E. Simoncelli. Image quality assessment: From error visibility to structural similarity. *Image Processing, IEEE Transactions on*, 13(4):600–612, 2004.

[18] J. Weickert. Coherence-enhancing diffusion filtering. *International Journal of Computer Vision*, 31(2):111–127, 1999.

[19] J. Weickert and H. Scharr. A scheme for coherence-enhancing diffusion filtering with optimized rotation invariance. *Journal of Visual Communication and Image Representation*, 13(1):103–118, 2002.

[20] D. Zhang and G. Lu. Evaluation of similarity measurement for image retrieval. In *Neural Networks and Signal Processing, 2003. Proceedings of the International Conference on*, volume 2, pages 928–931. IEEE, 2003.

[21] K. Zuiderveld. Graphics gems iv. chapter Contrast limited adaptive histogram equalization, pages 474–485. Academic Press Professional, Inc., San Diego, CA, USA, 1994.

Forensic Identification of GSM Mobile Phones

Jakob Hasse

dence GmbH
c/o Technische Universität Dresden
jakob.hasse@dence.de

Thomas Gloe

dence GmbH
c/o Technische Universität Dresden
thomas.gloe@dence.de

Martin Beck

Institute of Systems Architecture
Technische Universität Dresden
martin.beck1@tu-dresden.de

ABSTRACT

With the rapid growth of GSM telecommunication, special requirements arise in digital forensics to identify mobile phones operating in a GSM network. This paper introduces a novel method to identify GSM devices based on physical characteristics of the radio frequency hardware. An implementation of a specialised receiver software allows passive monitoring of GSM traffic along with physical layer burst extraction even for handover and frequency hopping techniques. We introduce time-based patterns of modulation errors as a unique device-dependent feature and carefully remove random effects of the wireless communication channel. Using our characteristics, we could distinguish 13 mobile phones at an overall success rate of 97.62 % under real-world conditions. This work proves practical feasibility of physical layer identification scenarios capable of tracking or authenticating GSM-based devices.

Categories and Subject Descriptors

K.4.2 [**Social Issues**]: Abuse and Crime Involving Computers; C.2.0 [**General**]: Security and Protection

Keywords

mobile phone identification; digital forensics; GSM; radio fingerprinting

1. INTRODUCTION

The currently most used mobile telecommunication system GSM lacks reliable mechanisms to identify end user mobile devices. Identification using the device identification number IMEI is considered insecure. Available hardware flashers allow to change and manipulate a mobile phone's software including the IMEI number. In consequence, law enforcement agencies focus on monitoring the SIM identifier IMSI, which can be changed easily by switching SIM cards.

Another method to identify GSM devices could evaluate characteristics of the transmitted wireless signal. GSM

networks use radio transmissions as communication channels, which naturally represent a shared medium. The radio transmissions can therefore be captured passively by third party receivers located within the communication range of the sending device and and do not rely on the cooperation of the sender. Inaccuracies in the manufacturing process and allowed tolerances of the radio hardware are likely to introduce identifying traces in the signal. Recent studies document possibilities to identify IEEE 802.11 devices using characteristics of the transmitted signals. Brik et al. [2] measures errors in the modulation domain to generate a fingerprint of a IEEE 802.11 based device. B. Rasmussen et al. [1] use 5 transient features of the signal amplitude to identify short range devices. Focusing on the same class of devices, D. Zanetti et al. [9] propose features of the link frequency, which is allowed to deviate between 4% and 22% according to the specification of the UHF Class 1 communication protocol. These works demonstrate the feasibility of RF device identification on the physical layer but are less important for selecting physical features for GSM. First investigations targeting GSM device identification are reported by Reising et al. [8]. Evaluating the instantaneous frequency and phase responses of the raw RF signal in transient and midamble regions, notable identification performance was achieved for a small set of 3 devices using a fixed location during training and test.

Threshold based burst extraction as performed by Reising et al. is only applicable under laboratory conditions, but not in realistic scenarios. Our work aims to evaluate identification performance in a practical environment. Because of the complex GSM radio access scheme, burst extraction is a complicated task. To extract the communication stream of an individual phone, we interpret the captured radio signal according to the GSM standard. Instead of using coarse statistical moments of the raw captured signal, we analyse the signal in the well defined domain of the Gaussian Minimum Shift Keying (GMSK) modulation, similarly to Brik et al. Based on the interpreted radio signal, we are able to derive signal features independent from the transmitted data, allowing to evaluate entire bursts instead of using only midamble and transient regions. Because GSM is a high precision communication system allowing only marginal inaccuracies of the RF hardware, modulation accuracy features used for IEEE 802.11 are not directly applicable. We propose to evaluate the modulation errors in respect to the time of one burst transmission, targeting both time dependent and constant inaccuracies of the radio hardware. Using signal processing, we carefully diminish random effects introduced by different locations or variable radio parameters. Reising et al. employed a fixed location to capture training and test data, while we prove our features are location independent. In summary our key contributions are:

- the first practical identification system of GSM devices based on radio frequency fingerprints,

- a software receiver for full extraction of bursts allocated to individual mobile devices,

- proposal of time based device characteristics based on modulation accuracy, and

- a comprehensive evaluation of our proposed methods and comparison to state-of-the art mobile device identification measures.

Our identification system allows law enforcement agencies to identify mobile phones under surveillance without the cooperation of the network. Further, these methods might be integrated in GSM base stations to improve authentication procedures and to find phones reported to be stolen. Equally, a mobile phone can identify a base station to authenticate the communication partner on the network part. When integrated in this way, implementation difficulties relating to encryption and burst extraction will become easier or obsolete.

The remainder of the paper is structured as follows. In Section 2, we introduce the most important technical details of a GSM network detailing the physical layer air interface. In the following Section 3, we describe the procedure of recording physical radio signals and common problems relating to GSM features. The signal processing applied on each burst is described in Section 4 along with an introduction of the proposed signal features. Section 5 describes the test setup for our experiments performed in Section 6. We conclude in Section 7.

2. GSM FUNDAMENTALS

A GSM network provides land based mobile communication. In contrary to satellite based systems, the communication counterpart is a base station on the ground at a fixed position. The network is run by an operator and can be connected to other networks like public switched networks or other mobile networks using gateways. Figure 1 shows an overview of the entities in a GSM network. The mobile phone communicates with the base station using the air interface. The base station provides the RF link in a fixed geographical location, known as the cell. One or more base stations are managed by a base station controller, taking care of radio channels and some features like handovers. The mobile switching center acts as a switch between all components of a fixed network, connecting to multiple base station controllers, other switching centers, databases or different phone networks.

For a seamless operation, databases like the visitor or home location register store data of subscribers currently using the network. This includes authentication data and identifiers like the IMSI or IMEI. While the IMSI identifies a SIM module with the corresponding contract between a subscriber and the network operator, the IMEI identifies the mobile phone or a similar device which is able to gain access to a GSM network. The handling of the IMEI depends on the network. Many networks query the IMEI on

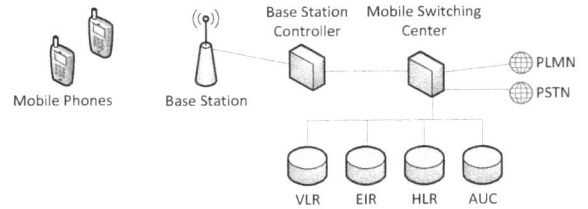

Figure 1: GSM Network Architecture

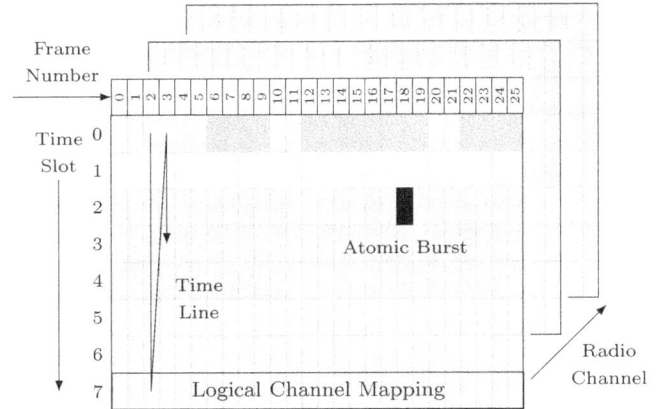

Figure 2: GSM Multiplexed Access Scheme

every connection of a mobile phone to perform a lookup in the equipment identity register, which holds the IMEIs of stolen, malfunctioning phones or IMEIs which are known to be used by criminals. The storage and transmission of the IMEI is handled by the software of the mobile phone and can be altered with a simple software patch.

When making a call, a mobile phone connects to the most powerful base station in range to establish a communication channel to the network. After authentication at the authentication center, the current location will be updated and stored in the home or visitor location register. A temporary replacement for the IMSI may be assigned to prohibit the plain transmission of the IMSI on every connection attempt. Finally, the requested call service is performed by establishing a transmission channel through multiple switching centres to the target communication partner.

To identify a mobile phone, we focus on the air interface between the mobile phone and the base station. The protocol is divided in three layers: physical, link and networking/signalling layer. For our identification method, the understanding of the physical layer including the wireless transmission channel is most important. Because of the complex access scheme for radio resources, it is a challenge to capture RF signals of an individual GSM mobile phone. On the most basic level, RF resources of a base station are multiplexed using frequency and time (see Figure 2). The frequency bands allowed to be used by the government are split into radio channels with a bandwidth of 200 kHz each.

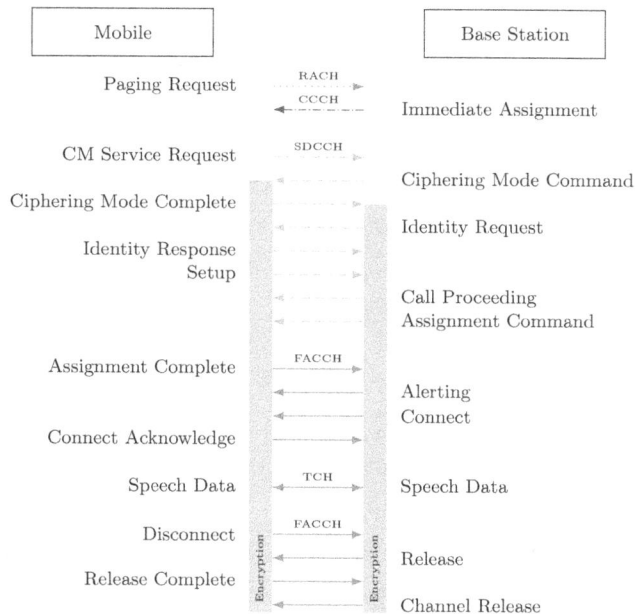

Figure 4: Protocol Flow of Making a Call

The base station decides how many radio channels to use and whether to switch between radio channels over time (frequency hopping) or not. When employing frequency hopping, a communication stream can be spread over all radio channels the base station supports. The state of the time multiplex is defined by the frame number and time slot. Each frame consists of 8 time slots, each time slot lasts for approximately $577\,\mu s$. The frame number is incremented continuously until reset after 3.5 h. The combination of radio channel, frame number and time slot defines a dedicated physical radio resource during which a mobile phone sends one radio burst. Based on the physical multiplex, logical channels are defined by fixed mappings to create communication subchannels for specific uses.

As a consequence of the access system, the mobile phone almost never transmits two bursts consecutively. Each burst is transmitted independently, so the procedure of sending a 'normal burst' (see Figure 3) is always the same for the RF hardware. At the start of a burst, the sending power ramps up to the desired signal strength. The tail bits at the beginning and end of a burst are set to zero. The data payload is split into two data segments of 57 Bit each, with a training sequence in between. The training sequence is one of the available bit sequences defined in the GSM specification [3]. The base station decides which training sequence to use for the radio transmission. The two additional stealing flags have a special meaning in some logical channels and are ignored in others. After the last tail bits, the RF hardware powers down. The burst transmission of the next time slot starts at the end of the guard period, which lasts for 8.25 Bits at GSM symbol rate. The described normal burst is modulated with the GMSK algorithm. There are specialised burst versions for specific applications which will not be analysed in detail in this work. The observed normal burst transmission performed by the mobile phone is the data source for the identification procedure described in Section 4.

When a mobile phone communicates over the air, it often changes logical channels. To extract the burst transmissions performed by an individual phone, a receiver must be able to interpret the higher protocol layers in order to follow the communication stream. Figure 4 shows the protocol flow when making a call, different logical channels are represented by different arrows. A mobile requests radio resources on the random access channel (RACH). The network assigns dedicated resources using the common control channel (CCCH) and switches the subsequent communication to a standalone dedicated control channel (SDCCH). After requesting call related services, encryption is activated. The base station may require to send the IMEI before the call is initiated. For the upcoming speech transmission, a traffic channel (TCH) is established. Now all signalling packets are sent over the fast associated control channel (FACCH). The mobile ends the call with the disconnect message and the communication channel will be released.

3. RECORDING GSM SIGNALS

The first step towards identification of mobile phones over the air is to capture the radio bursts emitted by one or more targeted mobile phones operating in a GSM network. There are two general possibilities to access these signals. The first one is to perform the identification algorithm at one communication endpoint, i.e. the base station analyses the signals emitted by the mobile phone or vice versa. The identification algorithm can be implemented as an extension to the existing GSM transceiver. The receiver's burst extraction algorithm can be reused minimising additional implementation of the GSM protocol. However, to perform experiments on public mobile networks, access to public base stations is required, but was not available in this study. The second possibility is to capture the radio signals as a third party, using a receiver which does not take part in the communication.

Reising et al. [8] capture the radio signals of mobile phones located next to the receiver using a threshold to extract transmitted bursts from these phones. Although quite simple and straight forward, this burst selection process can not be used in a practical environment with a bigger distance between the mobile phones and the receiver. Other phones might interfere and the extracted bursts of an individual phone may become mixed up with other communication streams. Instead, we used a two way receiving software defined radio (SDR) to capture GSM signals from the mobile phone and from the base station at the same time. The SDR needs to be placed in receiving range of both communication entities. That way the complete communication stream can be observed in both directions without interfering or disrupting the ongoing GSM communication.

We developed a specialised receiver software able to act as a mobile phone for the frames received from the base station and as a base station for the remaining frames. The signals of both directions are interpreted according to the GSM specification to extract the correct communication stream and the corresponding bursts of each mobile phone under test. As a side effect, our software extracts the whole protocol flow of the communication and we are able to identify the mobile phone on protocol basis to assure the correctness of the identification algorithm. Because of the special scenario, we could only reuse a small part of existing open

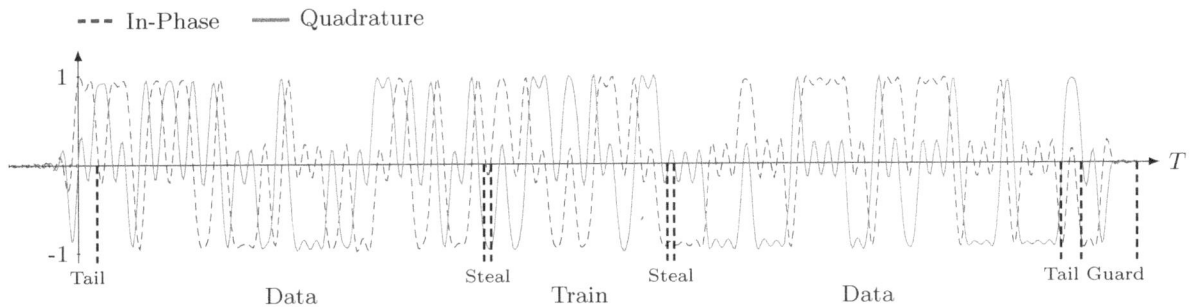

Figure 3: Structure of a Captured Normal Burst

3.1 Synchronisation

The receiver must be able to synchronise to a base station. Every base station sends a special burst containing only zeros on a regular basis on the main radio channel. After modulation, the signal contains a sine wave at a frequency of approximately 67.7 kHz. Deviations from this frequency are used to calculate clock offsets in our receiver and in mobile phones connecting to the base station. The clock of the base station acts as a common reference.

Perfect synchronisation is not possible, which introduces random frequency offsets for the mobile and our receiver on each connection. To reduce the random influence, our receiver works with a constant frequency offset which is determined once for the acquisition device. The offset stays constant even when monitoring different base stations. This is possible, because the base stations are required to have a very precise clock with frequency deviations of 0.05 ppm (parts per million) or less. Still remaining frequency offsets are compensated in the signal preprocessing stage. Time synchronisation is established using a special synchronisation burst sent by the base station, containing the current state of the time multiplex system.

3.2 Encryption

As described in Section 2, some part of the communication stream is usually protected by encryption. For every attempt to make a call, an observer can obtain at least 32 bursts from the same mobile phone before the communication switches to an unknown logical channel. For practical reasons, we want to capture a lot of packets within a short period of time. The transmitted speech data of a voice call produces up to 217 bursts per second. When encryption is activated, the logical channel and the underlying mapping to physical resources of the traffic channel is unknown. To be able to observe the bursts, the mobile phone must be able to reveal the temporary encryption key or the encryption needs to be broken.

In our experiments, all public base stations activated encryption with the A5/1 cipher algorithm. We used a known-plaintext attack proposed by Karsten Nohl [7] to calculate the temporary key with an exhaustive search for all mobile

phones under test, which were not able to reveal the key due to software limitations. To use this attack on encrypted GSM bursts, the keystream has to be determined. A plaintext predictor for special GSM messages was implemented as described by Sylvain Maut[3]. This cipher attack was successfully applied on the captured traffic of all mobile phones under test, carefully leaving out other transmissions not relating to our experiments. Although this attack is capable of calculating one key in 4 seconds on specialised hardware, our software receiver is not able to find the key in real time of the communication.

Recall that the proposed identification algorithm does not require decryption of the communication stream in principle. In case 32 bursts are not enough for identification, the correct logical channel and physical mapping of the speech data transmission could potentially be guessed for base stations which are rather idle. The decryption method was chosen for practical reasons.

3.3 Frequency Hopping

Base stations may decide to employ frequency hopping, which results in changing the radio channel for each timeframe during communication. While experimenting, some of the analysed base stations never used frequency hopping, whereas some hopped every time and others seemed to decide randomly whether to use hopping or not. Depending on the configuration of the cell, the communication stream can be spread over a wide bandwidth. To follow the hopping sequence, it would be possible to retune the receiving device in real time, like a mobile phone does, which however highly depends on the capabilities of the acquiring device. We chose to capture the whole bandwidth the communication might be spread over to be independent of real time tuning operations. However recording two bands simultaneously with a bandwidth of several MHz each requires a careful setup of the recording device to cope with the high data throughput and to avoid dropping frames.

3.4 Receiver Signal Processing

The raw captured signal needs to be preprocessed in order to demodulate the GSM signal. After recording at a wide bandwidth, the recorded signal is split into individual GSM radio channels using a polyphase filter bank channeliser. This filter is implemented in software running on a computer, which decreases performance dramatically. In later versions this task could be performed in real time by

---

[1] https://svn.berlin.ccc.de/projects/airprobe/
[2] http://wush.net/trac/rangepublic

[3] http://web.archive.org/web/20100808001500/http://lists.lists.reflextor.com/pipermail/a51/2010-July/000804.html

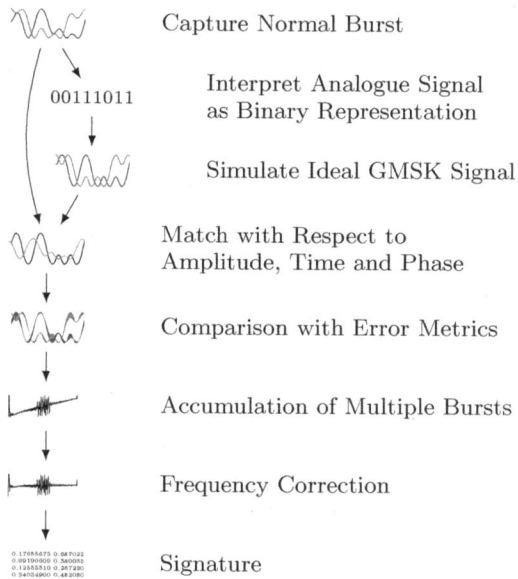

Figure 5: Overall Procedure of Feature Extraction

specialised hardware like an FPGA system. For synchronisation with the target base station, frequency offsets are corrected using a finite impulse response filter. Due to technical limitations of the acquisition device, we had to include a fractional resampler, aligning the sample rate to a multiple of the GSM symbol rate. The performed signal processing is the same for every run of the receiver and for every individual channel to minimise the introduction of new characteristics to the signal.

4. PHYSICAL CHARACTERISTICS

Every mobile phone has a RF frontend which contains hardware components working on the analogue signal. When a mobile phone sends a burst, the digital signal passes through a digital-analogue converter, a band pass filter, mixers and an amplifier. Inaccuracies in the manufacturing process result in minor physical differences of these components. Even components coming from the same stack of a manufacturing procedure do have different properties caused by random effects, slight differences in material or sub-components.

Because ideal operation of these components is not possible, they are manufactured and sold in classes of error tolerance. The tolerances in the processing chain add up to a reasonable amount of unintentionally introduced errors in the resulting RF signal. When designing a RF communication system, the allowed error tolerance of the RF signal is well specified to ensure proper operation. These errors can be measured and used to generate a unique fingerprint of a mobile phone's RF components. This fingerprint is not easy to forge, because it would involve replacing hardware components fixed on the circuit board of the mobile phone. The 'normal bursts' collected from a communication stream by the GSM receiver software are the basis for the calculation and detection of the fingerprint.

Rather than analysing the raw RF signal as done by Reising et al. [8], our analysis interprets the signal according to the Gaussian Minimum Shift Keying (GMSK) modulation.

For every extracted burst, the receiver demodulates the signal to produce a binary representation which is employed to create a mathematical ideal simulation of the modulated burst. The differences between every observed and ideal sample are used to estimate error metrics which can be employed for identification. Brik et al. [2] shows this procedure for the Quadrature Phase Shift Keying (QPSK) modulation of IEEE 802.11 and confirms applicability for robust physical device identification. The following describes the overall procedure (c.f. Fig. 5) to extract suitable characteristics from GSM normal bursts based on modulation errors.

4.1 Simulation

The simulation of GMSK is quite complex. Testing several software based implementations of GMSK modulators, we observed common systematic differences when comparing an ideal signal to the realisation of a mobile phone. The OpenBTS implementation showed the best similarity, but still required slight changes to the Gaussian pulse in order to match the general shape of the collected signals for our oversampling rate. The modulation was optimised exemplarily using the tested mobile phones as a reference and remained constant throughout all experiments. Even with this optimisation, a small portion of systematic differences remains, which results in content dependent fluctuations of the error metrics. These variations are expected to result from different practical hardware implementations of a GMSK modulator, compared to the mathematical model.

4.2 Matching

For device identification, it is essential to extract characteristics which remain stable over different dimensions and especially over time. We try to identify and remove all aspects which introduce random behaviour or which can be attributed to side effects, which the identification should be invariant of. The first varying aspect is the sending power. The base station can order the mobile phone to use different levels of sending power, depending on the current reception strength. Additionally, the reception strength varies depending on environmental conditions.

For an invariant comparison, the captured in-phase and quadrature signal is normalised. A filter detects the maximum and minimum peaks by comparing 3 neighbours for each side of a sample. The detected peaks are ordered by absolute value and a threshold decides which samples to include in averaging. The average of the selected peaks is normalised to 1, thus the maximum and minimum peaks match 1 and -1, respectively. This is based on the assumption, that the changes in amplitude due to movement of the target phone is negligible for the duration of a single burst, i.e. $577\,\mu s$. According to the GSM specification [5], a mobile phone is allowed to send a burst with an arbitrary phase offset. In our experiments, we confirmed for every mobile phone under test, that the overall phase offset of a burst behaves randomly. We remove this effect by aligning the captured signal to a simulation with a zero phase offset for all experiments. Because of the interdependency to time, we approximate the correct time t_o and phase offset ϕ_o simultaneously with an increasing precision using overall correlation as the optimisation metric. Employing prior knowledge about time alignment from the receiver software, we first match the signal on sample level and try different phase offsets of $\phi_o = \pi$ and $\phi_o = \pi/2$. After matching the

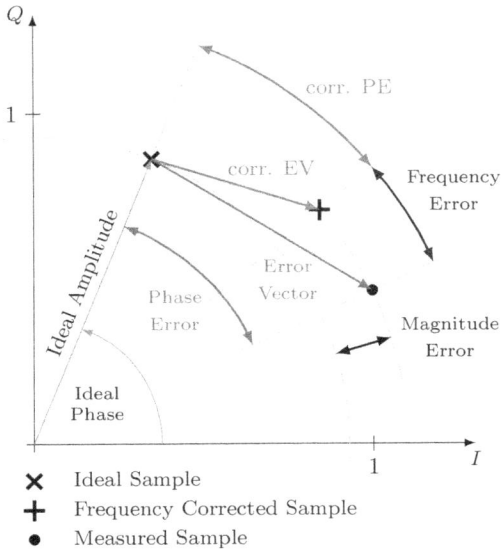

Figure 6: Error Metrics with Frequency Correction in the Inphase/Quadrature Diagram

signals on coarse precision, a more precise ϕ_o is calculated by the average difference between the ideal phase ϕ_i and observed phase ϕ, with N being the count of samples in the burst:

$$\phi_o = \frac{1}{N} \sum_{n=0}^{N} (\phi(n) - \phi_i(n)). \qquad (1)$$

The methods described here to achieve phase and time alignment can be exchanged with more sophisticated algorithms available in latest RF technology to improve computational performance. As the last preprocessing step, we align the observed and simulated signal in time on a fractional sample precision. With a fractional timing offset in the range $(-1, 1)$, a linear optimiser selects the best fractional t_o, maximising correlation. Note that the timing offset can not be used as a device identification feature, because it is dependent on the location of the mobile phone. The identification procedure should be invariant of the current location, as long as the mobile phone resides in the reception range of our receiver.

4.3 Error Metrics and Frequency Correction

When the observed signal is aligned with the simulation, different error metrics can be employed to quantise the differences between the signals. Depicting an observed sample in a constellation diagram, the length of the position vector represents the current amplitude and the angle to the I axis represents the current phase at a certain point in time (c.f. Fig. 6). When compared to an ideal sample, the difference in amplitude is called Magnitude Error (ME) and the phase difference is called Phase Error (PE). The vector between the observed and ideal sample is the Error Vector (EV) and its length the Error Vector Magnitude (EVM). These are common error metrics describing the precision of a modulated signal. In GSM, phase errors may occur up to 5° RMS[4]

---

[4]Root Mean Square, $\mathrm{RMS}(\boldsymbol{v}) = \sqrt{\frac{1}{N} \sum_i^N \boldsymbol{v}_i^2}$. ($N$ denotes the number of elements in $\boldsymbol{v}$.)

and up to 20° peak. The EVM may deviate 9-10% RMS and up to 30% peak [6, 4]. The ME is limited implicitly by the EVM and is not specified separately as a modulation error metric.

Following the approach of Brik et al., we initially tried to quantify the accuracy of a mobile phone's RF hardware using the average of the aforementioned metrics over a single collected burst to measure the accuracy of a mobile phones RF hardware as an identification characteristic. This characteristic was not stable enough for identification, because the random part of PE and ME did not allow to detect the deterministic errors of the observed signals. Taking the high precision of GSM into account, we propose to use characteristic error patterns over the time of a normal burst as a device-dependent feature.

As the process of sending a normal burst is always the same, the RF hardware introduces deterministic deviations at specific times of a burst, e.g. fluctuations of the power amplifier. With consideration of the error metrics in respect to the time of a burst, it is possible to evaluate both time-dependent and modulation-dependent characteristics. Systematic differences introduced by the modulation algorithm of different mobile phones consolidate in the training sequence and tail bits during accumulation, because the modulated bits do not change, assuming a constant training sequence. Time dependent fluctuations of the radio hardware are captured in all regions of the burst.

To improve identification performance, we accumulate the error metrics for each sample position over all available bursts of one signature. This is possible, because all bursts were aligned in time to match the individual simulation, which makes them independent of the individual time offset. When t is the sample position of a burst and M the total count of bursts contributing to one signature, the accumulated ME trajectory $\mathbf{a}_{\mathrm{ME}}$ is determined with the average at each sample position:

$$\mathbf{a}_{\mathrm{ME}}(t) = \frac{1}{M} \sum_{i=0}^{M} \mathrm{ME}_i(t). \qquad (2)$$

The $\mathbf{a}_{\mathrm{PE}}$ and $\mathbf{a}_{\mathrm{EVM}}$ are accumulated likewise. After accumulation, the $\mathbf{a}_{\mathrm{PE}}$ trajectory reveals a dependency to a linear model. The slope of this model is a remaining frequency error, which is attributed to imperfect synchronisation mechanisms in mobile phones and our receiver.

In initial experiments, we tested the frequency error as a possible characteristic for identification, but found the characteristic was unstable due to randomness of the synchronisation procedure and noise effects, compared to the required precision of the mobile phones RF hardware after synchronisation. We determine the linear frequency model with a least squares approximation and deduct the frequency related part from PE in respect to time, resulting in the frequency corrected phase error, $\mathbf{a}_{\mathrm{PEfc}}$.

As can be seen in Figure 6, the frequency error also influences the EV. Thus, we need to correct the observed samples to compensate the errors introduced by the detected frequency offset resulting in the $\mathbf{a}_{\mathrm{EVMfc}}$. Note that the frequency error has only negligible effect on the ME[5]. The $\mathbf{a}_{\mathrm{PEfc}}$, $\mathbf{a}_{\mathrm{EVMfc}}$ and $\mathbf{a}_{\mathrm{ME}}$ are the error patterns we can use as input for a classification algorithm. Each of these time de-

---

[5]The frequency error only influences the ME in combination with strong I/Q imbalance, which we did not observe.

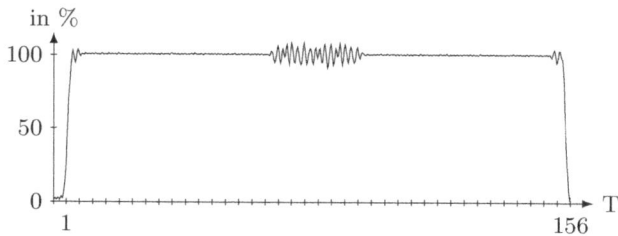

Figure 8: $\mathbf{a}_{\text{PWR}}$ Trajectory of a Motorola C118 Mobile Phone

pendent patterns contain the typical errors at specific sample positions of a normal burst. Because we used an oversampling rate of 4 at the GSM symbol rate for one burst, we end up with $148\,\text{Bit} \cdot 4 = 592$ error metrics for each trajectory.

To justify the selection of these patterns, we show two different examples relevant for device identification. In the first comparison, we calculate the $\mathbf{a}_{\text{PEfc}}$ trajectory of the same mobile phone at two different locations, accumulating over 1000 bursts each for demonstration purpose. As shown in Figure 7, the $\mathbf{a}_{\text{PEfc}}$ is very similar for the same device, regardless of the current location. In the area of the training sequence, the two trajectories are almost identical. The second comparison shows the same trajectory for two mobile phones of the same brand and model. The differences of the two trajectories represent different characteristics of the RF hardware of the individual phone. For the two phones, the differences are visible especially in the data sequences. Apart from two big and two minor spikes, the training sequences are similar. Note that systematic errors depending on the modulated bits add up in the training sequence and the tail bits, but average out in the data sequences, because the modulated bits change randomly for each burst[6]. The following experiments will evaluate the performance of these characteristics in an identification scenario.

4.4 Power Trajectory

Unlike other digital modulation schemes, GMSK has a constant envelope, i.e. the signal power does not drop to zero and remains level in the transition between different states of the constellation diagram. The GSM specification requires the mobile to keep the power level constant during the transmission of a normal burst [4]. We can use this property to obtain the amplitude related errors more easily. With the aforementioned normalisation defining the average peaks of the in-phase and quadrature signals to be 100 %, the observed signal only needs to be aligned in time in order to obtain a power trajectory PWR. In this work we used the whole burst in combination with the simulation for time synchronisation. However, time synchronisation can be achieved using the training sequence only, as done in almost all GSM receivers. This makes the PWR trajectory independent of the simulation and renders the computational intensive matching procedure obsolete for this feature. This can be crucial for identification scenarios requiring real time operation. When accumulating over M bursts, the accu-

mulated power trajectory $\mathbf{a}_{\text{PWR}}$ can be calculated for each sample position t of a normal burst using the normalised in-phase signal I and quadrature signal Q as follows:

$$\mathbf{a}_{\text{PWR}}(t) = \frac{1}{M} \sum_{i=0}^{M} \sqrt{\text{I}_i(t)^2 + \text{Q}_i(t)^2}. \qquad (3)$$

The resulting trajectory looks like depicted in Figure 8. Before and after the burst, additional time is granted to power the amplifier up and down and to adjust to the target power level just before the burst transmission starts. This trajectory is similar to the $\mathbf{a}_{\text{ME}}$, but represents the general sending power of an RF signal instead of magnitude errors in the modulation domain. By not interpreting the signal according to the modulation, the processing time is greatly reduced for amplitude based errors. Similarly to the $\mathbf{a}_{\text{ME}}$, the intentional power fluctuations of GSM add up in the training sequence whereas they average out in the data sequences. The following experiments will evaluate the performance of the presented features in an identification scenario.

5. TEST SETUP

In the following, we describe the practical details of our experiments. All parameters are summarised in Table 2. For signal acquisition, we used two USRP N210 devices operating synchronised. Each of them is equipped with a daughterboard covering an analogue bandwidth of 40 MHz. The device recording the uplink frequency band was equipped with a +3 dB 900/1800 MHz GSM antenna, the device capturing the downlink band used a general purpose antenna covering a wide frequency range. The acquisition site was inside of an office building, without any arrangements like shielding. The site was exposed to other common radio signals present in office buildings such as wireless networking at the time of acquisition.

For the selected acquisition radios, commodity hardware can record radio signals with a sample rate up to 10 MHz for two simultaneous channels. Recording with higher bandwidths is only possible with optimised hardware. When selecting a base station to monitor, we had to take the limitations of the recording capabilities into account. We selected a base station operated by T-Mobile, because of the strong signal and a recordable combination of radio channels used for frequency hopping. For the selected base station, the main radio channel and the channels used for the hopping sequence were separated by 10-15 MHz. To cover the main and the hopping channels in one recording with an available recording bandwidth of 10 MHz, we had to split each band in two different recording blocks, one capturing the main radio channel (30) and the other capturing the hopping radio channels (82-102). So recording was performed on four channels in total with a sample rate of 5 MHz each, based on two analogue radio sources. With the same technique of splitting an analogue source into two different recording blocks, it is also possible to record communication of a GSM base station with a single USRP and daughterboard only, assuming frequency hopping is deactivated and the base station sends strong enough signals in the E-GSM band.

For our experiments, we used a total of 13 mobile phones of 4 different manufacturers and 9 models (c.f. Tab. 1). Note that the Sony Ericsson J100i and all Motorola phones are designed and manufactured by Compal Inc. and sold under a branded name. They share the same system de-

---

[6]For the collected bursts, the encryption algorithm was active which produced a pseudo-random bit stream for the data sequences on physical layer.

(a) $\mathbf{a}_{PEfc}$ for the Same Mobile Phone at Different Locations

(b) $\mathbf{a}_{PEfc}$ for two Different Mobile Phones of the Same Brand and Model

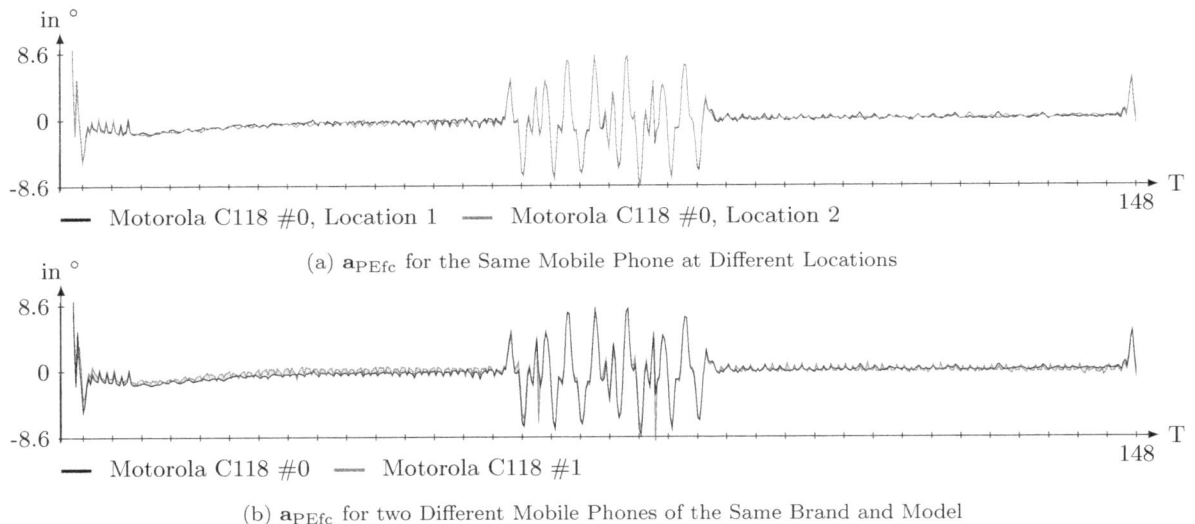

Figure 7: Two Examples of $\mathbf{a}_{PEfc}$ Trajectories

Table 1: Mobile Phones Used in Tests

Manufacturer	Model	Chipset	#
Motorola	C115	Calypso G2 (D751749ZHH)	1
Motorola	C118	Calypso G2 (D751749ZHH)	4
Motorola	C123	Calypso G2 (D751749ZHH)	1
Motorola	C139	Calypso G2 (D751749ZHH)	1
Motorola	C140	Calypso G2 (D751749ZHH)	1
Sony Ericsson	J100i	Calypso G2 (D751749ZHH)	1
Nokia	6100	UPP8M/MJOELNER S2006	1
Nokia	E51	BB5 SL2 RAPIDO	1
HTC	TyTNII	Qualcomm MSM7200	1
Palm	Pre	Qualcomm MSM6801A	1

sign and use very similar or the same RF hardware chipsets. The four Motorola C118 phones can only be distinguished by the IMEI. This selection of mobile phones was chosen to provide the most difficult identification problem due to the high amount of identical hardware chipsets. For the training stage, the phones were placed next to the receiver. While the acquisition was running, each mobile phone was voice called twice, the calls were answered and the phones transmitted for 45 seconds each call. For the test stage, the mobile phones were placed at a different location, 4 metres away from the receiver. Because the new location used in the test set is completely unknown in the training stage, the performance of the identification algorithm is evaluated location independent. Because of different ranges, the captured signals have different signal to noise ratios with 13.3 dB and 5.4 dB for train and test set, respectively. Note that our identification system ignores bursts containing massive amounts of bit errors. In order to produce a valid signature, the simulation needs to be correct. Bursts with an EVM error of more than 60 % RMS were skipped. Approximately 25 % of all frames were dropped because of this requirement due to a very basic demodulation algorithm. This can be improved by using a more sophisticated demodulator able to determine the binary representation more precisely. An

alternative would be to implement bit correction for the simulation.

For classification, each signature was accumulated using 30 passed bursts, with training and test counts of 150 and 100. The influence of these parameters is analysed in Section 6. The signatures were put into a linear Support Vector Machine (SVM) for classification. To calculate the SVM model, the training signatures were split in two equally sized parts. The first group was used to estimate the parameter of the linear kernel using a grid search with cross validation. The model was then determined using the second group of signatures. Thus, the identification model was not optimised to the new location of the test set and optimisation of the kernel was done without manual correction.

6. EXPERIMENTS

We start our practical investigations with individual evaluations of each proposed feature. The True Acceptance Rate (TAR) is used as a performance indicator. The TAR is the probability of detecting a given device correctly. The average TAR over every device under test symbolises the overall success rate of an experiment. The results in Table 3 indicate that the $\mathbf{a}_{PEfc}$ is the most successful characteristic, identifying a device correctly with an overall probability of 96.67 %. Amplitude-based features do not work as good as phase-based error metrics. The $\mathbf{a}_{ME}$ performs better than the $\mathbf{a}_{PWR}$ feature, because the $\mathbf{a}_{ME}$ can remove content dependent effects in the data sequences more efficiently by comparing to the ideal simulation instead of simple averaging of the signal power. If the computational resources are available to produce and match an ideal simulation, the $\mathbf{a}_{ME}$ should be preferred to the $\mathbf{a}_{PWR}$. The mixed characteristic $\mathbf{a}_{EVMfc}$ which is based on both amplitude and phase characteristics, performs almost as good as the $\mathbf{a}_{PEfc}$.

To further analyse synergy effects between these features, we test every possible combination and evaluate the performance using the average TAR (c.f. Tab. 3). The obvious best performing combination is $\mathbf{a}_{PEfc}$ with $\mathbf{a}_{EVMfc}$ virtually matching the performance of the individual $\mathbf{a}_{PEfc}$. Except

Table 2: Parameters of Test Setup

Acquisition	Device	USRP N210, SBX
		USRP N210, WBX
	Sample Rate	5 MHz·4
	GSM Oversampling	4
Cell	Provider	T-Mobile
	Uses Hopping	Yes
	Main Channel	30
	Hopping Channels	82-102
Phones		13
Locations	Training	At Receiver (13.3 dB)
	Test	4 m away (5.4 dB)
Classification		Linear SVM
	Bursts per Signature	30
	Training Signatures	150
	Test Signatures	100

Table 3: Overall Performance of Individual and Combined Features

a_{PWR}	a_{ME}	a_{PEfc}	a_{EVMfc}	
Individual				
60.75 %	68 %	**96.67 %**	93.33 %	TAR
Combinations				
		•	•	**96.50 %**
•		•	•	92.25 %
	•	•	•	89.50 %
•	•	•	•	89.00 %
•	•		•	87.83 %
•	•		•	87.83 %
•		•		86.33 %
	•	•		86.17 %
	•		•	85.75 %
•	•	•		85.33 %
•	•			69.83 %

for the combination of a_{PWR} and a_{ME}, the identification rates of the best individual feature was better compared to a combination with other features. Nevertheless, we used the combination of the best individual performing feature a_{PEfc} and a_{EVMfc} for the following experiments to include as many relevant device dependent characteristics as possible.

Within our second experiment we analyse the interdependency between the two classification parameters accumulation count and total amount of bursts per phone in training. The accumulation count varies from 10 to 50, while the total amount of bursts for one phone varies between 500 and 4500. The amount of training signatures is calculated by dividing the total bursts count per phone by accumulation count, e.g. for an accumulation count of 50 and a total training burst count of 4500, the number of training signatures equals 50. The count of test signatures remains constant at 100 signatures per phone for all training parameter combinations.

The results are illustrated in Figure 9 and document an overall increase of performance when using more bursts in training for each phone. When 3500 bursts or more are available for the training procedure, the chosen accumulation count has only marginal influence on the overall success rate. For lesser amounts of training bursts, it is generally

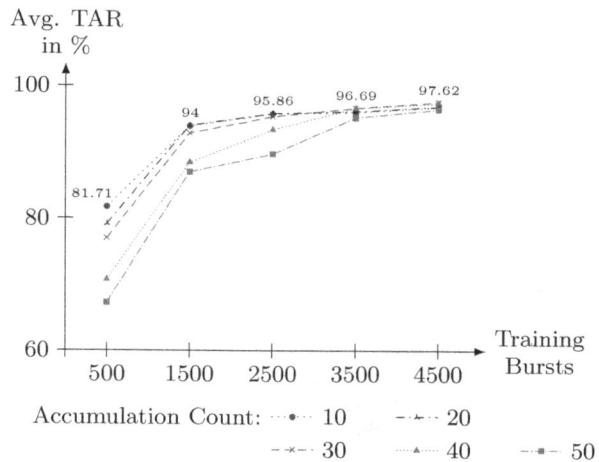

Figure 9: TAR as a Function of Accumulation Count and Total Amount of Bursts per Phone in Training

better to use a lower amount for the accumulation count in order to produce a higher number of training signatures. For 1500 and 2500 available training bursts per phone, an accumulation count of 20 is optimal while an accumulation count of 30 produces best results for 3500 and 4500 training bursts. Collecting a training set of 4500 bursts would require monitoring a voice call for 21 seconds. Note that with a low accumulation count of 30 or less, it is possible to identify a known mobile phone without the need to break the encryption of the GSM traffic. For a mobile phone to establish a communication channel, at least 30 bursts have to be transferred on a publicly known physical channel. This is enough to produce one or more test signatures, possibly using sliding windows. This way, any phone with a previously recorded model can be identified very easily.

In the last experiments, we determined the optimal configuration for a classification system. Using the best performing parameters of 30 for accumulation and 4500 for training burst count, we show the detailed results of the identification procedure in Table 4 omitting all zeroes for visual clarity. For 13 mobile phones and a total of 1300 test signatures, only 31 signatures were not classified correctly. The Motorola C123 was detected with the worst TAR of only 87 %, mistakenly detecting the Nokia 6100 in 7 % of cases. Also, the Motorola C123 and Motorola C118 #3 seem to share similarities in the selected hardware characteristics, because they are confused with each other in 4 % of cases. Six devices were identified perfectly, i.e. every available test signature was matched to the correct class. With the overall average TAR of 97.62 %, the classification performance is slightly better compared to the work of Reising et al. [8] at our noise level and clearly outperforms in the amount of classes showing the practical relevance of our approach.

7. CONCLUSION

This work is a first step in mobile forensics to identify mobile devices in a GSM network without relying on traditional identifiers like IMEI or IMSI. By targeting the air interface of GSM on physical layer, it is possible to identify mobile phones without the interaction with or recognition by the sender. We proposed to detect physical properties

Table 4: Confusion Matrix for Twelve Mobile Phones (in Percent)

		C115	C118 #0	C118 #1	C118 #2	C118 #3	C123	C139	C140	J100i	6100	E51	TyTN II	Pre
						Identified As								
Original Phone	Motorola C115	100												
	Motorola C118 #0	1	99											
	Motorola C118 #1			100										
	Motorola C118 #2			1	99									
	Motorola C118 #3					96	4							
	Motorola C123	2				4	87				7			
	Motorola C139				2			98						
	Motorola C140								100					
	Sony Ericsson J100i									100				
	Nokia 6100										100			
	Nokia E51											100		
	HTC TyTN II	1	2								3		94	
	Palm Pre										4			96

of a mobile phones RF hardware to create a unique fingerprint for every individual device. The environment of the performed experiments was chosen to be a most realistic one, passively monitoring the communication on a public GSM network. The radio signals were captured according to the GSM specification at varying locations. Based on previous work by Brik et al. [2], features of modulation accuracy originally targeting IEEE 802.11 were adopted for GSM to be used as a device identifier. These features have been improved, resulting in time based features describing a characteristic pattern of modulation deviations over the time of a normal burst. Using the improved features, a total of thirteen mobile phones have been correctly identified with an overall success rate of 97.62 %. This included four identical and nine almost identical phones, which proves the selected features to be unique for an individual device.

Compared to previous work by Reising et al. [8], we were able to improve the overall detection performance using a practically relevant implementation of the burst selection process. At the same time we increased the amount of mobile phones under test considerably. Training and test signatures were obtained at different locations assuring location independence. Our proposed model uses the well defined domain of GMSK modulation, backed by the modulation requirements of the GSM specification. We showed that identification based on RF hardware inaccuracies is possible even for a high precision communication system like GSM.

Future work should analyse the influence of environmental conditions such as temperature or movement of a target device, as well as the robustness against noise and a bigger distance between the mobile phone under test and the listening receiver. The features can potentially be improved by using additional statistical parameters other than the average during accumulation. The burst extraction process may be improved to work in real time employing digital signal processing hardware. Further analysis should target the robustness against potential attacks trying to forge a device signature.

8. ACKNOWLEDGEMENTS

Accommodation and travel was partly funded by the Federal Ministry of Economics and Technology of Germany, the European Union and the European Social Fund.

9. REFERENCES

[1] K. Bonne Rasmussen and S. Capkun. Implications of radio fingerprinting on the security of sensor networks. In *Third International Conference on Security and Privacy in Communications Networks and the Workshops (SecureComm' 2007)*, pages 331 –340, 2007.

[2] V. Brik, S. Banerjee, M. Gruteser, and S. Oh. Wireless device identification with radiometric signatures. In *Proceedings of the 14th ACM International Conference on Mobile Computing and Networking (MobiCom '08)*, pages 116–127, 2008.

[3] ETSI TS 100 908 V8.11.0 (2003-06). *Digital cellular telecommunications system (Phase 2+) — Multiplexing and Multiple Access on the Radio Path — 3GPP TS 05.02 version 8.11.0 Release 1999*, 2003.

[4] ETSI TS 100 910 V8.20.0 (2005-11). *Digital cellular telecommunications system (Phase 2+) — Radio Transmission and Reception — 3GPP TS 05.05 version 8.20.0 Release 1999*, 2005.

[5] ETSI TS 100 959 V8.4.0 (2001-11). *Digital cellular telecommunications system (Phase 2+) — Modulation — 3GPP TS 05.04 version 8.4.0 Release 1999*, 2001.

[6] P. Kimuli. Introduction to GSM and GSM mobile RF transceiver derivation. *RF DESIGN*, 26(6):12–21, 2003.

[7] K. Nohl. Attacking phone privacy. https://srlabs.de/blog/wp-content/uploads/2010/07/Attacking.Phone_.Privacy_Karsten.Nohl_1.pdf, 2010.

[8] D. R. Reising, M. A. Temple, and M. J. Mendenhall. Improved wireless security for GMSK based devices using RF fingerprinting. *International Journal of Electronic Security and Digital Forensics*, 3(1):41–59, 2010.

[9] D. Zanetti, P. Sachs, and S. Capkun. On the practicality of UHF RFID fingerprinting: How real is the RFID tracking problem? In *Privacy Enhancing Technologies*, volume 6794 of *LNCS*, pages 97–116, 2011.

Optimizing Acoustic Features for Source Cell-Phone Recognition Using Speech Signals

Cemal Hanilçi
Department of Electronic Engineering
Uludağ University
16059, Bursa, Turkey
chanilci@uludag.edu.tr

Figen Ertaş
Department of Electronic Engineering
Uludağ University
16059, Bursa, Turkey
fertas@uludag.edu.tr

ABSTRACT

This paper presents comparison and optimization of acoustic features for source cell-phone recognition using recorded speech signals. Different acoustic feature extraction methods such as Mel-frequency, linear frequency and Bark frequency cepstral coefficients (MFCC, LFCC and BFCC) and linear prediction cepstral coefficients (LPCC) are considered. In addition to different feature sets, the effect of dynamic features, delta and double-delta coefficients (Δ and Δ^2), and feature normalizations, cepstral mean normalization (CMN), cepstral variance normalization (CVN) and cepstral mean and variance normalization (CMVN) are also examined on the performance of source cell-phone recognition. The same support vector machine (SVM) classifier with fixed parameters and the same cell-phone dataset are used in the experiments in order to make a fair comparison of different features and feature normalization techniques.

Categories and Subject Descriptors

I.5.4 [**Pattern Recognition**]: Signal Processing

General Terms

Theory, Measurement, Experimentation, Verification

Keywords

Audio forensics, source cell-phone recognition, acoustic features, feature normalization

1. INTRODUCTION

Technological development in electronic devices have led to widespread use by individuals in daily life. Devices such as computers, digital cameras, cell-phones, printers and scanners have various kinds of sensors that generate digital data which are used for storing or transmitting to another device. However, these developments bring many challenging problems together. Nowadays, in many court cases, digital materials which are generated by such sophisticated hardware and software tools are presented as evidence. Thus, tracking the source of these materials would be essential for the court of law or another official venue.

Forensic research has largely focused on *image forensics* over the last decades. Source device (camera, printer or scanner) identification [13, 21, 24] - the problem of identifying the source device using images-, detection of image manipulation [3], image steganalysis which aims to detect the presence of hidden messages in images [2] are the most popular applications of image forensics. Source camera, printer and scanner identification are the most challenging applications of image forensics. For example, in [21], it was shown that sensor pattern noise can be used for identifying source cameras with high recognition accuracy and it became *state-of-the-art method* for source camera recognition in image forensic. Similar to that study, in [9], it was proposed that dust, dirt and scratches on the scanner platen can be used as signatures which characterize the source device for scanner identification.

Audio forensics [23] is another challenging area of forensic research which has been much less studied. In [23], audio forensics was categorized into three groups: i) authentication of audio evidences, ii) enhancement of audio recordings and iii) interpretation of evidences that audio recordings contain. Audio authentication is the ability of determining whether an audio recording is original and whether it has been tampered. Generally, spectral analysis, spectrogram analysis and phase continuity analysis are used for audio authentication [15, 16, 28]. Audio steganalysis, the task of detecting the presence of hidden messages in audio signals, is another interesting application of audio forensics [1, 18, 19]. Speech enhancement [20] which aims to remove unwanted additive noise from audio signals, is generally used as a pre-processing step in many speech applications such as speech and speaker recognition. Speech recognition, recognizing the context of an audio signal, speaker recognition [29], the task of recognizing the speaker from speech signal and language recognition [6] which aims to identify the language being spoken are the most popular applications of audio forensics. In another recent study, it was shown that the coding and decoding (*codec*) technique can also be identified using speech signals [31].

Forensic techniques can be used to identify the origin of a digital material. This is also known as *forensic characterization* which means identifying the type of device, model and other characteristics [14]. A source device can be identified by using the data which are produced by that particular

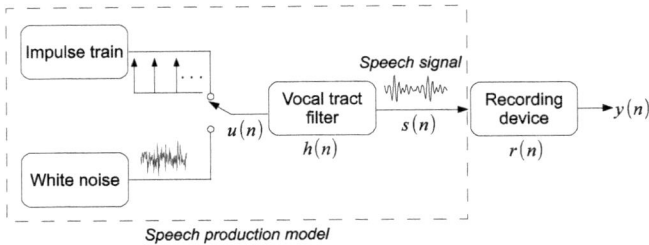

Figure 1: Speech production model and recording procedure.

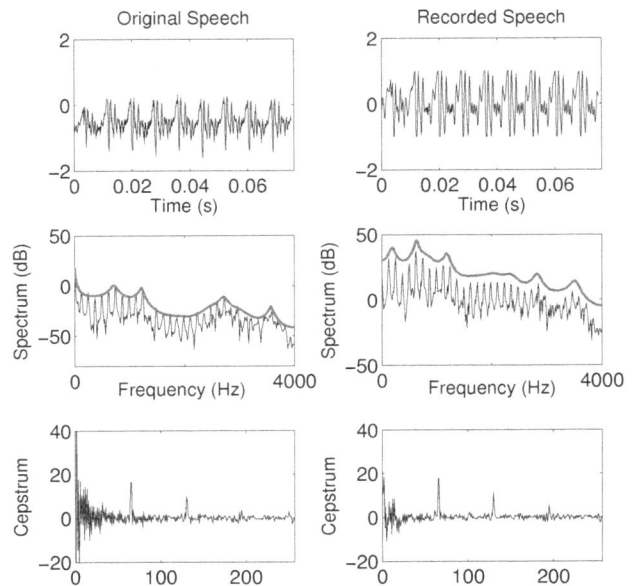

Figure 2: An example of spectrum and cepstrum representations of an original and recorded speech.

device. In our recent study, we have addressed a new problem of audio forensics, *source cell-phone identification using audio recordings* and shown that speech signal conveys information about the source recording device [12]. To the best of our knowledge, that was the first attempt for source device recognition using speech signals. In another recent study [25], it has been shown that speech signals can be used to identify landline telephone handsets (carbon-button or electret). The reason of our motivation with considering cell-phones is the fact that they have become an integral part of human life with the development in mobile technology. From forensic point of view, widespread usage of cell-phones in daily life will provide lots of evidences in speech signals recorded by cell-phones and there is an increasing trend on presenting such recordings as evidence in the court of laws. Since cell-phones have their built-in microphones which can be used as ordinary speech recorders, transfer function of different cell-phone microphones will be different from each other. Difference in transfer functions will be larger when electronic components are produced by different manufacturers. Because of the tolerances of components, there will be difference even these components are produced by the same manufacturer. Thus, each cell-phone leaves its telltale footprints on recorded speech signals and this can be used for source device recognition using recorded audio signals.

In this paper, we compare and optimize the acoustic features for source cell-phone recognition. In [12], we have shown that mel-frequency cepstral coefficients (MFCC) which is a popular acoustic feature extraction method can be used for source device recognition using speech signals. Since it was the first study in this emerging field, comparison of different features and optimizing feature parameters would be a significantly valuable step on source recognition using audio recordings. We compare MFCC features with linear-frequency cepstral coefficients (LFCC), bark-frequency cepstral coefficients (BFCC) and linear prediction cepstral coefficients (LPCC). Besides comparison of different features, we examine the effect of feature normalizations, cepstral mean, variance and mean-variance normalizations (CMN, CVN and CMVN), and dynamic features (1st and 2nd order derivatives of features, Δ and Δ^2). A database which consists of 14 cell-phones is used in the experiments with support vector machines (SVM) classifier.

2. SOURCE INFORMATION IN SPEECH

Figure 1 shows a simple speech recording procedure. Basic human speech production model is shown within dashed box in the figure. Typically, a speech signal, $s(n)$, is produced by convolution of excitation signal, $u(n)$, and time-varying vocal tract filter, $h(n)$, $s(n) = u(n) * h(n)$ [10]. Excitation signal, $u(n)$, can be a periodic impulse train or random white noise depending on the speech type being produced (voiced or unvoiced) [10]. Speech signal, $s(n)$, is then convolved with the transfer function of the recording device, $r(n)$. Thus, recorded signal is the convolution of the speech signal and recording device, $y(n) = s(n) * r(n)$. Apparently, source device information $(r(n))$ is embedded into speech signal in convolutive form in time-domain. Therefore, signal processing methods can be used to extract device specific features from recorded speech.

In frequency domain, recorded speech is represented by,

$$Y(f) = S(f)R(f), \qquad (1)$$

where, $Y(f)$, $S(f)$ and $R(f)$ correspond to Fourier transforms of $y(n)$, $s(n)$ and $r(n)$, respectively. It is seen from (1) that source information modifies the speech signal spectrum in multiplicative form. By taking the logarithm of (1)

$$\log Y(f) = \log S(f)R(f) = \log S(f) + \log R(f). \qquad (2)$$

In speech processing applications, *cepstrum* is a well-known method to decompose convolution of two signals which is computed as the inverse Fourier transform (IFT) of the logarithm of the signal spectrum [10]. Converting (1) into cepstrum domain, we obtain

$$c_y(n) = c_s(n) + c_r(n), \qquad (3)$$

where $c_y(n)$, $c_s(n)$ and $c_r(n)$ are the cepstrum representations of $y(n)$, $s(n)$ and $r(n)$, respectively. From (3) it can be seen that the source device information is embedded into speech signal in additive form in cepstral-domain. Figure 2 shows an example of an original short speech frame and its recorded counterpart. In figure it can be seen that, spectrum and cepstrum of recorded speech differ from original version and these differences helps us to recognize the source device. Feature extraction methods used for source cell-phone recognition are described briefly in the following subsections.

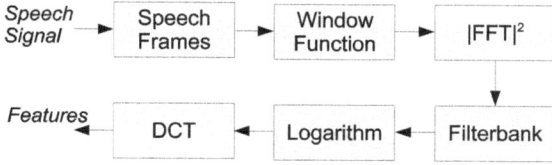

Figure 3: Speech feature extraction based on filterbank approach.

2.1 Filterbank Based Cepstral Features

Filterbank based cepstral feature extraction is used in many recognition applications based on speech signal such as speech, speaker and language recognition [4]. Figure 3 shows the filterbank based feature extraction procedure. Since speech is a dynamic signal, i.e. its amplitude and frequency content change over time, it is first divided into overlapping frames (generally 20-30 ms) and each frame is windowed using an appropriate window function (usually Hamming window). The power spectrum of each windowed frame is computed using fast Fourier transform (FFT). The spectrum is then multiplied with a filterbank which is a series of bandpass filters because the spectrum presents lots of fluctuations and mostly all these details are not of interest. The filterbank is defined by the shape of filters and localization of their frequencies (left, center and right frequencies). Usually triangular filters are used in filterbank-based feature extraction. Triangular filters can be located on different frequency scales. The most popular frequency scale to locate filters is the Mel-frequency scale. In the mel-scale, the center frequencies of the filters are computed by [4]

$$f_{\text{MEL}} = 1000 \frac{\log_{10}(1 + f_{\text{Hz}}/1000)}{\log_{10} 2}. \quad (4)$$

Triangular filters are placed according to these center frequencies. Another popular frequency scale used for filter localization is the Bark scale which models the human auditory system and center frequencies of the filters in Bark scale are computed by [30]

$$f_{\text{BARK}} = 6 \log_e \left(\frac{f_{\text{Hz}}}{600} + \sqrt{\frac{f_{\text{Hz}}}{600} + 1} \right). \quad (5)$$

Different from Mel and Bark scales, one other option to locate filters is the spacing center frequencies uniformly in Hz scale. Figure 4 shows an example of filterbank which consists of 6 triangular filters located in Mel-scale, Bark-scale and linear scale. It can be seen from the figure that filters located in low frequencies have narrow bandwidth whereas filter bandwidths are larger in high frequencies for Mel and Bark scales. However in linear scale, bandwidth of each filter is the same. Usually triangular filters are located between $f_{min} = 0$ and $f_{max} = 4$ kHz frequency band (for the signals sampled at 8kHz). However, when telephone recordings are used, locating the filters in a limited frequency band (e.g. between 300 - 3400 Hz), improves the speaker recognition performance [27]. Recently, it has been shown that placing the filters in the high frequency regions improves the recognition accuracy in audio steganalysis [18, 19].

After spectrum of each frame is multiplied with filterbank, the logarithm of filterbank outputs are taken and logarithmic outputs are converted into cepstral feature vectors by

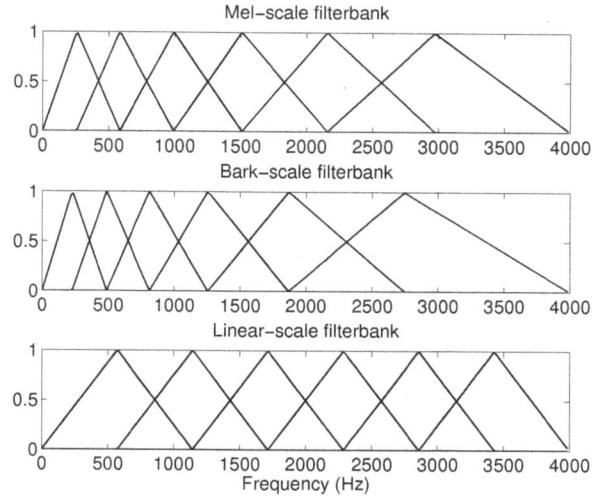

Figure 4: Triangular filters spaced in Mel, Bark and linear scales.

taking the discrete cosine transform (DCT):

$$x_i = \sum_{k=1}^{K} F_k \cos \left[n \left(k - \frac{1}{2} \right) \frac{\pi}{K} \right], \quad i = 1, \ldots, D, \quad (6)$$

where K is the number of triangular filters in the filterbank, F_k is the logarithmic output of the kth filter and D is the number of features calculated. Typically, from each speech frame, D feature coefficients are extracted which results a set of feature vectors such as $\mathbf{X} = [\mathbf{x}_1, \ldots, \mathbf{x}_T]$. Here, $\mathbf{x}_i$ is a D-dimensional feature vector extracted from the ith frame and T is the total number of frames. When filters are located in Mel-scale, the resulting features are called mel-frequency cepstral coefficients (MFCC), BFCC in Bark-scale and LFCC in linear scale.

2.2 Linear Prediction Cepstral Coefficients

Linear prediction (LP) is a popular method in speech processing which relies on the assumption that a speech sample can be estimated as a weighted sum of its p previous samples, $\hat{s}(n) = \sum_{k=1}^{p} \alpha_k s(n - k)$, where $s(n)$ is the original speech sample, $\hat{s}(n)$ is the predicted sample and p is the predictor order. LP analysis is based on the linear speech production model shown in Figure 1 and the vocal tract filter, $h(n)$, can be estimated from predictor coefficients α_k, $k = 1, \ldots, p$ [22]. Standard autocorrelation method is generally used to compute the predictor coefficients, α_k [22]. From the source device recognition point of view, LP analysis can be used to estimate the equivalent filter whose transfer function is the convolution of the vocal tract and recording device, $h(n) * r(n)$. Thus, feature vectors obtained via LP technique contains information about the source device.

Linear prediction cepstral coefficients (LPCC) features are derived from LP coefficients. First, LP coefficients, α_k, $k = 1, \ldots, p$, are calculated from each windowed speech frame. Predictor coefficients can be used to estimate spectrum envelope or to calculate cepstral feature coefficients. Spectrum envelope estimated using the α_k coefficients models the vocal tract transfer function, $h(n)$ ($h(n) * r(n)$ in our case since the signal used is a recorded speech) [22, 10]. An example

143

of estimated spectrum envelope using predictor coefficients, a_k, is shown with bolded line in the second row of Figure 2. In this study, we consider cepstral feature vectors obtained from LP coefficients which is given by [4]:

$$x_i = \begin{cases} \alpha_i + \sum_{k=1}^{i-1} \frac{k}{i} x_k \alpha_{i-k}, & 1 \le i \le p \\ \sum_{k=1}^{i-1} \frac{k}{i} x_k \alpha_{i-k}, & i > p \end{cases} \quad (7)$$

2.3 Feature Normalization

After features are extracted, they can be centered by subtracting the mean vector from each feature vector which is called cepstral mean normalization (CMN) [17, 26]. CMN is generally used in speaker recognition to remove slowly varying convolutional noises from the feature vectors. Given a set of feature vectors extracted from a speech signal, $\mathbf{X} = \{\mathbf{x}_1, \ldots, \mathbf{x}_T\}$, feature vectors after CMN is computed by

$$\mathbf{x}_i^{\text{cmn}} = \mathbf{x}_i - \frac{1}{T} \sum_{t=1}^{T} \mathbf{x}_t, \ i = 1, \ldots, T, \quad (8)$$

where, $\mathbf{x}_i$ is a D-dimensional feature vector extracted from the ith frame and T is the total number of frames.

Another frequently used method to reduce the unwanted additive noise effect from feature vectors is the cepstral variance normalization (CVN) [33]. CVN normalizes the variance of each feature vector extracted from each speech frame to one, namely

$$\mu = \frac{1}{T} \sum_{t=1}^{T} \mathbf{x}_t, \quad (9)$$

$$\sigma^2 = \frac{1}{T} \sum_{t=1}^{T} (\mathbf{x}_t - \mu)^2, \quad (10)$$

$$\mathbf{x}_i^{\text{cvn}} = \frac{\mathbf{x}_i}{\sigma}, \quad (11)$$

where μ is the mean vector and σ^2 is the variance vector of the feature set. After CVN given in (11) the variance of the feature vectors are normalized to one. CVN has more impact on reducing the effect of additive environmental noise from feature vectors than CMN operation. However, in many speech and speaker recognition studies, CMN and CVN are combined which yields to have feature vectors with zero mean and unit variance which is known as cepstral mean and variance normalization (CMVN) [4, 33]:

$$\mathbf{x}_i^{\text{cmvn}} = \frac{\mathbf{x}_i - \mu}{\sigma}. \quad (12)$$

CMVN reduces the effect of additive environmental noises from the feature vectors and it was previously shown that it improves the recognition rate in speaker recognition [33].

2.4 Dynamic Features

After feature vectors are extracted and possibly mean and variance normalized, dynamic features can also be appended to original feature vectors. Dynamic features convey information about the way of feature vectors vary in time [4]. The 1st and 2nd order time derivatives of the feature vectors (Δ and Δ^2) are mostly used as dynamic information. Δ and Δ^2 vectors of a feature vector extracted from the ith frame, $\mathbf{x}_i$, are computed as the time differences between the

Table 1: The brands and models of cell-phones used in the experiments and their class names

Class	Model	Class	Model
H1	HP IPAQ514	N5	Nokia 6670
L1	LG KE970	SA1	Samsung E250
M1	Motorola Q	SA2	Samsung E250
N1	Nokia 2730	SA3	Samsung D900
N2	Nokia 3600	SO1	Sony K750I
N3	Nokia 3600	SO2	Sony W880
N4	Nokia 6500	SO3	Sony W880

adjacant frames:

$$\Delta \mathbf{x}_i = \mathbf{x}_{i+k} - \mathbf{x}_{i-k}, \quad (13)$$

$$\Delta^2 \mathbf{x}_i = \Delta \mathbf{x}_{i+k} - \Delta \mathbf{x}_{i-k}, \quad (14)$$

where $k = 1$ or $k = 2$ are generally used. In this study we used $k = 1$ to compute dynamic features. Appending dynamic features to the baseline features are generally improves the speech and speaker recognition performances. Especially when speech recordings are collected in different sessions, dynamic features capture the information about the characteristics of the changes in the spectrum of the current frame.

3. EXPERIMENTAL SETUP

In the experiments we used a cell-phone database which consists of 14 device. The collection of brands include Nokia, Samsung, Sony Ericsson, LG, Motorola and HP. Five of Nokia, three of Samsung, one of LG, three of Sony Ericsson, one of Motorola, and one of HP models have been used in the experiments. The brand and model of the cell-phones and their class names are summarized in Table 1. We have used the pairs of cell-phones with exactly the same brand and model to explore the discrimination capability of the features and recognition system on the same units of devices. Two Nokia 3600, two Samsung E250 and two Sony W880 are the cell-phone pairs with the same brand and model. Popular speech and speaker recognition database, TIMIT [27], has been used to record voice samples using cell-phones in our database. TIMIT database consists of 630 speakers from different dialects of American English (192 females and 432 males) and each speaker reads ten sentences each of which is approximately 3 seconds long. We have selected 24 speakers from the test portion of database, and 240 sentences of these 24 speakers are played and recorded by each cell-phone in an office environment. With this, we have 240 sentences for each cell-phone and hence totalling 3360 voice samples each sampled at 8kHz. For each cell-phone, we have used randomly selected 120 sentences for training and the remaining 120 sentences for testing (a total of 1680 individual tests).

We have used popular support vector machine (SVM) classifier in our recognition experiments. SVM is a powerful classifier which have been used in many applications of pattern recognition. The most challenging application area of SVM classifier is the speech applications. Since speech signal is processed by dividing the signal into short overlapping frames, features extracted from a speech signal is a set of vectors rather than a single vector. Thus, sequence kernel approach which maps the set of feature vectors into a single high dimensional characteristic vector is

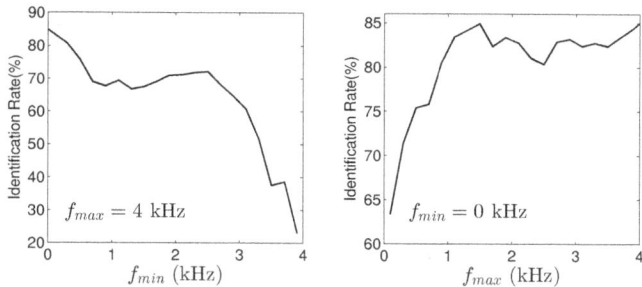

Figure 5: Identification rates for different f_{min} and f_{max} frequency values in MFCC extraction.

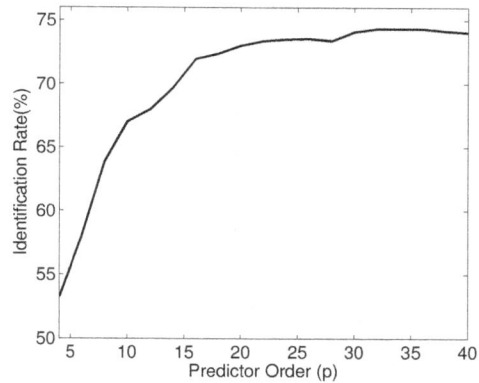

Figure 6: Effect of prediction order, p, on identification rate for LPCC features.

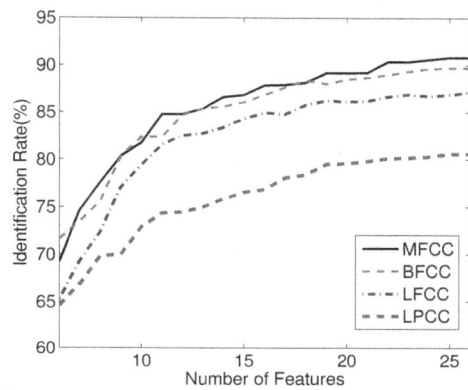

Figure 7: Comparison of MFCC, BFCC, LFCC and LPCC features.

used in speech applications of SVM [5, 8]. In this study we have used a simple but powerful generalized linear discriminant sequence (GLDS) kernel approach as the classifier. In SVM-GLDS technique, feature vectors are mapped into higher dimensional space by polynomial expansion. As an example, the 2nd order polynomial expansion of a two dimensional feature vector, $\mathbf{x} = [x_1, x_2]^T$ is given by $\mathbf{b}(\mathbf{x}) = [1, x_1, x_2, x_1^2, x_1 x_2, x_2^2]^T$. During training and test of SVM system, the set of feature vectors extracted from a speech signal, $\mathbf{X} = \{\mathbf{x}_1, \ldots, \mathbf{x}_T\}$, is represented by average expanded feature vectors, $\mathbf{b} = \frac{1}{T} \sum_{t=1}^{T} \mathbf{b}(\mathbf{x}_t)$. In the experiments we have used the 3rd order polynomial expansions of the feature vectors. The details about the SVM-GLDS can be found in [6, 11, 12]. Since we consider cell-phone identification which is a multi-class classification we have used LibSVM package [7], in which a multi-class SVM classification is available. The LibSVM uses the one-against-one approach for multi-class classification by constructing $N(N-1)/2$ classifiers where N is the number of classes. An advantage of this package is that it predicts class probability information besides the class labels. The details of implementation of multi-class SVM can be found in [32].

We have used the identification rate, which is the ratio of number of correctly recognized trial to the total number of trials, as the performance criterion. The confusion tables of the selected feature extraction methods are also presented to analyze the performance in detail.

4. RESULTS AND DISCUSSIONS

We first optimize the control parameters of feature extraction methods which are described in the previous sections. The number of features to be computed (D), the minimum and maximum frequencies (f_{min} and f_{max}) in which the triangular filters to be placed and prediction order (p) used to compute LPCC features are the control parameters that requires to be optimized. Number of features is set to $D = 12$ and we first optimize the f_{min} and f_{max} values for the MFCC features. Figure 5 shows the identification rates obtained with different values of f_{min} and f_{max}. As can be seen from the figure, the best identification rates are obtained when $f_{min} = 0$ and $f_{max} = 4$ kHz. This is expected because the speech samples in TIMIT database were collected under controlled laboratory environment using carbon button microphone and the cell-phones have been used as ordinary voice recorders. Thus there is no transmission line effects on the recordings. Interestingly, when $f_{max} = 1.5$ kHz, identification rate is slightly worse than the accuracy

obtained when $f_{max} = 4$ kHz. $f_{min} = 0$ and $f_{max} = 4$ kHz frequency values are fixed for MFCC, BFCC and LFCC features in the rest of the paper.

We next optimize the prediction order, p, to extract LPCC features. As in the previous experiments, the number of features is fixed as $D = 12$ and identification rates for different values of p varies on the range of $4 \leq p \leq 40$ is shown in Figure 6. Identification rate shows an increasing trend as p increases up to $p = 30$. Although there are slight differences on the identification performance for the values of $p \geq 30$, we further set the prediction order as $p = 32$ which yields the highest performance.

Then we study the effect of the number of features, D, on cell-phone identification performance. We compare the MFCC, BFCC, LFCC and LPCC features for different values of number of features, D, in Figure 7. Identification rates obtained with all feature sets are increasing functions of number of features and they saturate around $D = 24$. MFCC features yield the highest identification rate among the others independent from number of features. BFCC gives the same identification rate with MFCC features when $D = 13$ and $D = 17$ and it slightly outperforms MFCC when $D = 10$. Another interesting observation is that, LPCC features give the smallest accuracy in comparison to filtberbank features. In general, MFCC features are the absolute winner

Table 2: Effect of feature normalization on identification rate ($D = 24$).

Features	Identification Rate (%)
MFCC	90.59
MFCC + CMN	90.24
MFCC + CVN	**96.85**
MFCC + CMVN	96.43
BFCC	89.64
BFCC + CMN	88.69
BFCC + CVN	**96.49**
BFCC + CMVN	95.53
LFCC	86.73
LFCC + CMN	84.76
LFCC + CVN	**97.68**
LFCC + CMVN	96.49
LPCC	80.18
LPCC + CMN	78.57
LPCC + CVN	**97.68**
LPCC + CMVN	97.08

Table 3: Effect of dynamic features on identification rate ($D = 24$).

Features	Identification Rate (%)
MFCC + CVN	96.85
MFCC + CVN + Δ	**98.04**
MFCC + CVN + Δ + Δ^2	97.86
BFCC + CVN	96.49
BFCC + CVN + Δ	**97.94**
BFCC + CVN + Δ + Δ^2	97.14
LFCC + CVN	97.68
LFCC + CVN + Δ	**97.98**
LFCC + CVN + Δ + Δ^2	97.68
LPCC + CVN	97.68
LPCC + CVN + Δ	**98.15**
LPCC + CVN + Δ + Δ^2	98.04

and we fix the number of features as $D = 24$ in the rest of the experiments.

The effect of feature normalization methods, CMN, CVN and CMVN, on cell-phone identification performance are compared in Table 2. The highest recognition rates are bolded for each feature set. For all feature extraction methods, CMN slightly reduces the identification accuracy. This is probably because, since the transfer functions of recording devices are time-invariant filters, the contribution of the source device on the feature vectors varies slowly over time. Hence, normalizing the mean reduces the device information from the feature vectors. However, CVN and CMVN significantly improves the performance. The significant improvement obtained by CVN is because of the fact that, the variations in the feature vectors over all frames are mostly speaker and context information which are irrelevant for source device recognition (the source device information can be considered time-invariant) thus normalizing the variance reduces these irrelevant information. Interestingly, for LPCC features when CVN or CMVN is applied, the largest relative improvement over the baseline features is obtained (identification rate increases from 78.57% to 97.68%). While baseline LPCC features give the smallest identification rate in comparison to filterbank features (Figure 7), it shows better performance than MFCC, BFCC and LFCC features when feature normalization is applied.

Finally, we compare the effect of dynamic information on source device identification performance. Identification rates of the baseline features with and without dynamic features are summarized in Table 3. For all feature sets, appending the first order derivative of features, Δ, improves the identification rate. Second order derivatives, Δ^2, in turn, does not yield any improvement over the delta features. However, identification rates obtained by appending Δ and Δ^2 features to the baseline features yield improvement on the identification rates in comparison to the baseline features (e.g. identification rates improves from 96.85% to 97.86% when Δ and Δ^2 features are appended to baseline MFCC features). The confusion matrices for baseline LFCC features and LFCC features with Δ features and CVN are given in Tables 4, and 5, respectively. With baseline LFCC features (Table 4), recognition system makes mistakes in identifying the cell-phone pairs with exactly the same brand and models (N2-N3, SA1-SA2 and SO2-SO3 pairs). However, in case of appending delta features to baseline LFCC and applying CVN (Table 5), the system shows great performance on recognizing the cell-phone of same units and yield improvement in number of correctly identified trials for each cell-phone in comparison to baseline LFCC features (Table 4).

5. CONCLUSIONS

In this paper, we compared different acoustic features for source cell-phone recognition using recorded speech signals. It was briefly showed that speech signal conveys information about the source device in convolutive, multiplicative and additive forms in time, frequency and cepstral domains, respectively. Thus, any type of features extracted from speech signal contains information about the source in some form. Filterbank features, MFCC, BFCCs and LFCCs and LP cepstral coefficients, LPCCs, were compared. In our comparisons, it was found that baseline MFCC features outperforms the other type of acoustic features. We observed slight differences on the identification rates of the baseline MFCC and BFCC features. However, the difference on the performance of the baseline MFCCs and LPCCs is larger. It was found that, baseline filterbank features (MFCC, BFCC and LPCC) yield better performance than LPCC features (Figure 7). Applying CVN or CMVN feature normalization to the feature coefficients, showed considerable improvement on the recognition rates and in that case, the highest identification rate was obtained with LPCC features. Finally, appending the 1st order derivatives of the feature vectors, Δ features, slightly improves the identification accuracies whereas this observation does not hold for Δ^2 features. Source device recognition using speech signal with larger device dataset and under mismatched additive noise conditions would be interesting for the future work plan.

6. REFERENCES

[1] İ. Avcıbaş. Audio steganalysis with content-independent distortion measures. *IEEE Signal Processing Letters*, 13(2):92–95, Feb. 2006.

Table 4: Confusion matrix of cell-phone recognition system with baseline LFCC features

	H1	L1	M1	N1	N2	N3	N4	N5	SA1	SA2	SA3	SO1	SO2	SO3
H1	120	0	0	0	0	0	0	0	0	0	0	0	0	0
L1	0	104	0	0	0	0	0	1	8	3	1	3	0	0
M1	0	0	120	0	0	0	0	0	0	0	0	0	0	0
N1	0	0	0	116	2	0	0	0	0	0	2	0	0	0
N2	0	0	0	1	101	7	6	1	1	0	3	0	0	0
N3	0	0	0	3	4	106	3	3	0	1	0	0	0	0
N4	0	0	0	14	2	0	83	1	5	7	7	0	1	0
N5	0	4	0	0	0	1	1	103	4	2	5	0	0	0
SA1	0	1	0	0	0	0	1	0	96	3	11	1	6	1
SA2	0	0	0	0	0	3	0	0	1	108	4	0	3	1
SA3	0	0	0	0	1	0	0	0	14	1	101	0	3	0
SO1	0	1	0	0	0	0	0	2	4	0	1	109	1	2
SO2	0	1	0	0	0	0	1	1	0	4	0	1	98	14
SO3	0	0	0	0	0	0	0	11	0	0	2	11	4	92

Table 5: Confusion matrix of cell-phone recognition system with LFCC + CVN + Δ features

	H1	L1	M1	N1	N2	N3	N4	N5	SA1	SA2	SA3	SO1	SO2	SO3
H1	120	0	0	0	0	0	0	0	0	0	0	0	0	0
L1	0	120	0	0	0	0	0	0	0	0	0	0	0	0
M1	0	0	120	0	0	0	0	0	0	0	0	0	0	0
N1	0	0	0	120	0	0	0	0	0	0	0	0	0	0
N2	0	0	0	0	114	5	0	0	0	1	0	0	0	0
N3	0	0	0	0	6	114	0	0	0	0	0	0	0	0
N4	0	0	0	2	1	0	114	0	2	0	1	0	0	0
N5	0	0	0	0	0	0	0	118	1	0	0	0	1	0
SA1	0	0	0	0	0	0	0	0	117	1	2	0	0	0
SA2	0	0	0	0	0	1	0	0	0	119	0	0	0	0
SA3	0	0	0	0	0	0	0	0	0	0	120	0	0	0
SO1	0	1	0	0	0	0	0	0	0	0	0	119	1	0
SO2	0	1	0	0	0	0	0	0	0	0	0	0	113	7
SO3	0	0	0	0	0	0	0	1	0	0	0	1	0	118

[2] İ. Avcıbaş, N. D. Memon, and B. Sankur. Steganalysis using image quality metrics. *IEEE Transactions on Image Processing*, 12(2):221–229, 2003.

[3] S. Bayram, İ. Avcıbaş, B. Sankur, and N. Memon. Image manipulation detection. *Journal of Electronic Imaging*, 15(4):1–17, Dec. 2006.

[4] F. Bimbot, J.-F. Bonastre, C. Fredouille, G. Gravier, I. Magrin-Chagnolleau, S. Meignier, T. Merlin, J. Ortega-Garcia, D. Petrovska-Delacrétaz, and D. A. Reynolds. A tutorial on text-independent speaker verification. *EURASIP Journal on Applied Signal Processing.*, 2004(4):430–451, 2004.

[5] W. M. Campbell. Generalized linear discriminant sequence kernels for speaker recognition. In *Proceedings of the IEEE Int. Conf. Audio, Speech and Sig. Processing (ICASSP'02)*, pages 161–164, 2002.

[6] W. M. Campbell, J. P. Campbell, D. A. Reynolds, E. Singer, and P. A. Torres-Carrasquillo. Support vector machines for speaker and language recognition. *Computer Speech & Language*, 20(2-3):210–229, 2006.

[7] C.-C. Chang and C.-J. Lin. LIBSVM: A library for support vector machines. *ACM Transactions on Intelligent Systems and Technology*, 2(3):1–27, 2011. Software available at http://www.csie.ntu.edu.tw/~cjlin/libsvm.

[8] K. Daoudi and J. Louradour. A comparison between sequence kernels for SVM speaker verification. In *Proceedings of the IEEE Int. Conf. Audio, Speech and Sig. Processing (ICASSP'09)*, pages 4241 – 4244, 2009.

[9] A. E. Dirik, H. T. Sencar, and N. D. Memon. Flatbed scanner identification based on dust and scratches over scanner platen. In *Proceedings of the IEEE Int. Conf. Audio, Speech and Sig. Processing (ICASSP'09)*, pages 1385–1388, 2009.

[10] S. Furui. *Digital Speech Processing, Synthesis, and Recognition*. New York and Basel: Marcel Dekker, Inc., 1989.

[11] C. Hanilçi and F. Ertaş. Investigation of the effect of data duration and speaker gender on text-independent speaker recognition. *Computers &Electrical Engineering*, 39(2):441–452, 2013.

[12] C. Hanilçi, F. Ertaş, T. Ertaş, and Ö. Eskidere. Recognition of brand and model of cell-phones from recorded speech signals. *IEEE Transactions on*

Information Forensics and Security, 7(2):625–634, 2012.

[13] N. Khanna. Scanner identification using feature-based processing and analysis. *IEEE Transactions on Information Forensics and Security*, 4(1):123–139, 2009.

[14] N. Khanna, A. K. Mikkilineni, A. F. Martone, G. N. Ali, G. T. C. Chiu, J. P. Allebach, and E. J. Delp. A survey of forensic characterization methods for physical devices. *Digital Investigation*, 3:17–28, Sept. 2006.

[15] B. E. Koenig. Authentication of forensic audio recordings. *Journal of Audio Engineering Society*, 38(1-2):3–33, Jan.-Feb. 1990.

[16] B. E. Koenig and D. S. Lacey. Forensic authentication of digital audio recordings. *Journal of Audio Engineering Society*, 57(9):662–695, Sept. 2009.

[17] F.-H. Liu, R. M. Stern, X. Huang, and A. Acero. Efficient cepstral normalization for robust speech recognition. In *Proceedings of the Workshop on Human Language Technology*, pages 69–74, 1993.

[18] Q. Liu, A. H. Sung, and M. Qiao. Temporal derivative-based spectrum and mel-cepstrum audio steganalysis. *IEEE Transactions on Information Forensics and Security*, 4(3):359–368, 2009.

[19] Q. Liu, A. H. Sung, and M. Qiao. Derivative-based audio steganalysis. *ACM Transactions on Multimedia Computing, Communications and Applications*, 7(3):18:1–18:19, 2011.

[20] P. C. Loizou. *Speech Enhancement: Theory and Practice* . CRC Press, 1st edition, June 2007.

[21] J. Lukáŝ, J. Fridrich, and M. Goljan. Digital camera identification from sensor pattern noise. *IEEE Transactions on Information Forensics and Security*, 1(2):205–214, June 2006.

[22] J. Makhoul. Linear prediction: A tutorial review. *Proceedings of the IEEE*, 63(4):561–580, Apr. 1975.

[23] R. C. Mayer. Audio forensic examination. *IEEE Signal Processing Magazine*, 26(2):84–94, March 2009.

[24] A. K. Mikkilineni, N. Khanna, and E. J. Delp. Texture based attacks on intrinsic signature based printer identification. In *Proceedings of the Media Forensics and Security*, volume 7541, 2010.

[25] Y. Panagakis and C. Kotropoulos. Automatic telephone handset identification by sparse representation of random spectral features. In *Proceedings of the Multimedia and Security*, pages 91–96. ACM, 2012.

[26] D. A. Reynolds. Experimental evaluation of features for robust speaker identification. *IEEE Transactions on Speech and Audio Processing*, 2(4), Oct. 1994.

[27] D. A. Reynolds. Large Population Speaker Identification Using Clean and Telephone Speech. *IEEE Signal Processing Letters*, 2:46–48, Mar. 1995.

[28] D. P. N. Rodríguez, J. A. Apolinário, and L. W. P. Biscainho. Audio authenticity: detecting ENF discontinuity with high precision phase analysis. *IEEE Transactions on Information Forensics and Security*, 5(3):534–543, Sept. 2010.

[29] P. Rose. *Forensic Speaker Identification*. CRC Press, July 2002.

[30] B. J. Shannon and K. K. Paliwal. A comparative study of filter bank spacing for speech recognition. In *Proceedings of the Microelectronic Engineering Research Conference*, 2003.

[31] D. Sharma, P. A. Naylor, N. D. Gaubitch, and M. Brookes. Non intrusive codec identification algorithm. In *Proceedings of the IEEE Int. Conf. Audio, Speech and Sig. Processing (ICASSP-2012)*, pages 4477–4480, 2012.

[32] T.-F. Wu, C.-J. Lin, and R. C. Weng. Probability estimates for multi-class classification by pairwise coupling. *The Journal of Machine Learning Research*, 5:975–1005, 2004.

[33] R. Zheng, S. Zhang, and B. Xu. A comparative study of feature and score normalization for speaker verification. In *Proceedings of the 2006 International Conference on Advances in Biometrics*, ICB'06, pages 531–538, Berlin, Heidelberg, 2006. Springer-Verlag.

Exposing Digital Audio Forgeries in Time Domain by Using Singularity Analysis with Wavelets[*]

Jiaorong Chen
jiaorong.chen@163.com

Shijun Xiang[†]
xiangshijun@gmail.com

Weiping Liu
wpl@jnu.edu.cn

Hongbin Huang
thhb@jnu.edu.cn

School of Information Science and Technology, Jinan University, Guangzhou, 510632, China

ABSTRACT

Exposing digital audio forgeries in time domain is a significant research issue in the audio forensics community. In this paper, we develop an audio forensics method to detect and locate audio forgeries in time domain (including deletion, insertion, substitution and splicing) by analyzing singularity points of audio signals after performing discrete wavelet packet decomposition. Firstly, we observe and point out that a forgery operation in time domain will often generate a singularity point because the correlation property of those samples close to the tampering position has been degraded. Furthermore, we investigate and find that the singularity point resulted from a tampering operation often stays alone while those inherent singularity points in the original signal usually staying in the form of group. Finally, we propose an approach to expose audio forgeries in time domain by introducing Mallat *et al.*'s wavelet singularity analysis method and making a difference between a forged point and the inherent singularity points. Extensive experimental results have shown that the proposed scheme can better identify whether a given speech file has been tampered (e.g., part of the content deleted or replaced) previously and further locate the forged positions in time domain.

Categories and Subject Descriptors

K.4.4 [**Electronic Commerce**]: Security and Intellectual Property; K.6.m [**Miscellaneous**]: Security

---

[*]This work was supported in part by NSFC (No.61272414), The Science and Technology Project of Guangzhou of China (No. 2012J410010), and in part by The University-Industry-Science Partnership Project of Guangdong Province and National Education Ministry (2012B091000155).

[†]Contact author

General Terms

Algorithms, Security, Verification.

Keywords

Digital audio forensics, Audio forgeries, Singularity analysis, Wavelet, Time domain

1. INTRODUCTION

With the rapid developments of low-cost personal music players and smart phones, digital audio has become more and more popular in our daily life. In this technological age, many digital audio files are produced every day. In the meanwhile, it is becoming very common to use digital audio, especially digital speech audio, as evidence in some applications of security. However, hearing cannot be always true since the digital speech audio files can be very easily tampered according to the semantic meaning without leaving any obvious auditive clues with the help of some professional editing softwares or tools. Thus it is urgent to develop authentication technologies so that people can protect their legal rights. Digital watermarking and digital signature are two representative techniques for digital audio authentication. Nevertheless, these techniques will become powerless in many actual situations because of their need for additional information (watermarking or signature) in the process of authenticating a suspicious audio. Therefore, digital audio forensics becomes an important technique since it doesn't need any additional side information and can detect a doubtful audio only by analyzing the inherent features within the digital audio. Up to now, many digital image forensics techniques have been developed while digital audio forensics is just emerging at the last several years.

In the audio forensics research field, the existing literatures mainly focus on the following aspects. The work [1] given an overview on audio authentication ways by recalling some preliminary audio analysis methods and advanced audio authentication techniques proposed in 2012 or before. Based on extracting 63 stegoanalysis features from the audio, Kraetzer *et al* [2] used the machine learning method to determine the used microphones and the environments of recorded digital audio samples. The works [3, 4] tried to detect the recording device through analyzing the recording noise. Malik *et al* [5, 6, 7] paid their attention on acoustic reverberation in order to identify the audio recorded environments, while Ikram *et al* [8] considered the same problem from the point of view of background noise. Many other researchers [9, 10, 11, 12, 13] concentrated on revealing the double compression including up-transcoding and down-transcoding in MP3 or WMA format audio via analyzing the statistical characteristics of the MDCT coefficients. Yang *et al* [14] developed a method to defeat the fake-quality MP3 format audio by using the numbers of small MDCT coefficients. Several approaches have been put forward to resist the re-sampling attack in [15, 16, 17]. Those works above are playing a role in some application fields.

As we know, deletion and insertion in time domain for digital audio are two of the simplest and easiest operations since they can be manipulated by most even untrained users. Until now, there are no detailed technical reports on how to detect these operations in time domain. This indicates that detection of the audio tampering in time domain is an important issue. Yang *et al* [18, 19] presented a specific scheme to detect the forgeries in time domain for MP3 files by considering the effect of the forgeries on the frame offsets. However, this method cannot be used to detect the some forgeries on uncompressed audio signals in time domain (e.g., the uncompressed WAV files) since there is no frame offsets. By extracting and analyzing the electric network frequency (ENF) from audio signal, some research works [20, 21, 22] could detect the time domain forgeries and locate the forged positions. However, these methods will become powerless for the stand-alone power supply subsystems which do not connect to the electric network. Pan *et al* [23] came up with an approach to detect the splicing digital audio files by using local noise level estimation. And this method is not suitable for the deletion operations and the insertion operations from the same audio file. In accordance with the assumption that a "natural" signal has weak higher-order statistical correlations in the frequency domain and that it would introduce "unnatural" correlations in speech during the forged operations which can be regarded as non-linearity, Farid [24] used the bispectrum analysis to detect digital forgeries of speech signals. It was shown that the zero phase of bispectrum decreased a lot for a forged speech file.

In this paper, we describe a more general detection strategy to resist the forged operations in time domain including deletion, insertion, substitution and splicing. We pay our attention to determine whether a given time domain speech audio in the WAV format has been tampered and where the tampering position is. In a way, our scheme is also suitable for the other contents of audio files, such as music. Firstly, we point out that there is a strong correlation between adjacent samples for original speech signal. This correlation will be degraded due to the forged operations, and will result in new singular points. Mallat *et al.*'s singularity detection and processing strategy with wavelets [25, 26, 27] is a powerful tool for detecting and locating the forged singular points. Since there are some inherent singularity points in the original speech signal, we then investigate the difference between a forged singular point and those inherent singularity points. Finally, we develop a scheme by combining five parameters for detecting and locating a forged position in time domain. The extensive experimental results have been performed to demonstrate the effectiveness of the proposed method.

The rest of the paper is organized as follows. In Section 2, we first analyze the forged operations and the principle of the singularity analysis of the wavelet packet decomposition in detecting the audio forgery points, and then we describe our detailed technique on how to detect audio forgeries in time domain. Section 3 shows the experimental results and analysis. The conclusions and future works will be discussed in Section 4. This work is useful since it is the first work to report how to detect the forgeries on the uncompressed speech files in time domain.

2. PROPOSED METHOD

The speech audio forgeries discussing in this paper include deletion, insertion, substitution and splicing of samples in time domain. This section will introduce the effects of the forged operations and some corresponding strategies on how to detect and locate these forged operations.

2.1 Analysis of Digital Speech Forgeries

For a natural speech audio file, a sample point has a strong correlation with its neighbors. In other words, there is a substantial correlation between two adjacent samples in the original speech audio. Usually, the forged operation in time domain will break this original correlation because it artificially make two "faraway" points stay as "neighbor".

In figures 1, 2 and 3, the subfigures (a) show the wave form of the original signal and the region between two blue lines is cropped to demonstrate a tampering operation in time domain. The subfigures (b) in the three figures indicate three different kinds of artifacts due to the forged operation in different positions. The subfigures (c) in the three figures show the detection results by using singularity detection and processing with wavelet packet decomposition [25, 26, 27]. From the figures 1, 2 or 3, we have the following observations on the forged signals:

1) The forged point in magnitude is a local peak after the tampering operation and a cusp point of discontinuity at the position of the forged point is generated, as shown in Fig. 1 (b).

2) Though the forged point in magnitude is not a local peak after the tampering operation, there is a catastrophe jumping at the forged position because two faraway samples are artificially put together, as shown in Fig. 2 (b).

3) The forged region in Fig. 3 (b) is smooth visually. Even in this case, the singularity analysis method with wavelets still works well for detecting the tampering operation, as shown in Fig. 3 (c).

In figures 1, 2 or 3, the positions of the forged operations can be called as singular points in the wavelet theory [26]. That is, the points are at these positions where the signal functions are not differentiable at n-order (n could be 0, 1, 2...). Since the resulting singular points are easier to be perceived in the high frequency component because the tampering operation in time domain usually degrades the high-frequency component more than the low frequency component, we wish that in the high frequency subbands of the signal the forged operations can be effectively detected and located by using the singularity detection and processing with wavelet.

2.2 Singularity Analysis with Wavelets

Wavelet transform technique has many excellent properties. In this work, we introduce singularity detection and

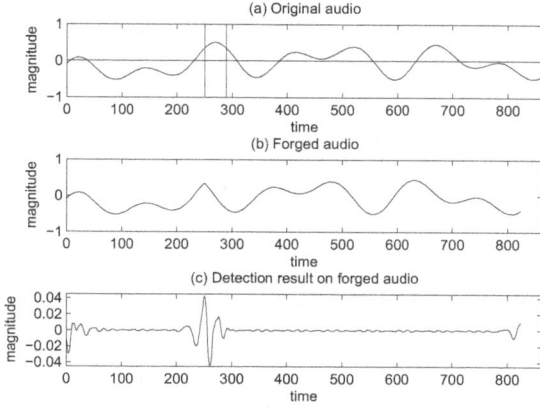

Figure 1: Illustration for generating a discontinuity cusp point at the forged position due to the forged operation. The region between two blue lines in the subfigure (a) is cropped.

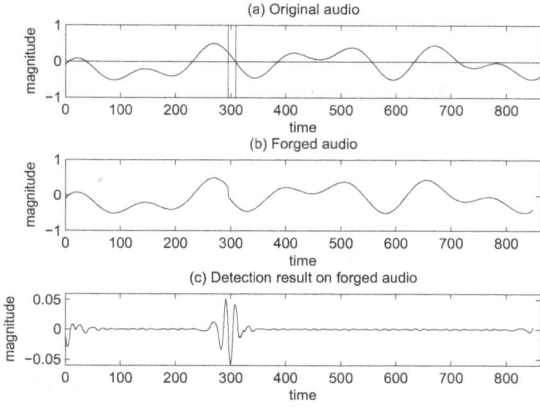

Figure 2: Illustration for generating a catastrophe jumping point at the forged position.

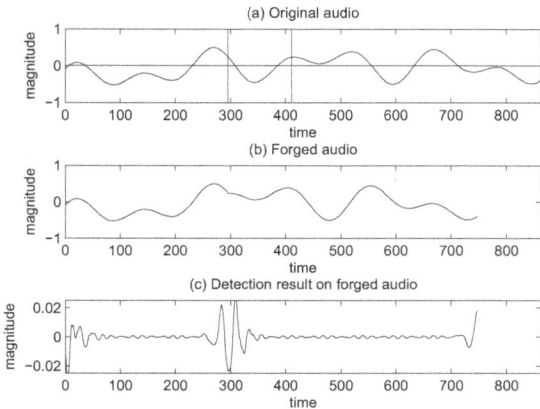

Figure 3: Illustration for generating a visually smooth transition at the forged position.

processing method with wavelets [26] for detecting and locating forgeries of digital audio in time domain.

In order to explain the principle why the wavelet transform can be used for detecting and locating the singular points in the time domain signal, we first assume that there is a real function $\theta(t)$, which can be denoted as a smoothing function if it satisfies the following equation [25]:

$$\int_{-\infty}^{\infty} \theta(t)dt = 1, \lim_{t \to \infty} \theta(t) = 0 \tag{1}$$

Due to the energy of the smoothing function $\theta(t)$ concentrates on the low frequency band, it can be viewed as the impulse response of a low-pass filter [26, 27]. One of the important examples for $\theta(t)$ is Gaussian function. We also suppose that $\theta(t)$ is twice differentiable and define $\Psi^{(1)}(t)$ and $\Psi^{(2)}(t)$ as the first- and second-order derivative of $\theta(t)$ respectively. That is:

$$\Psi^{(1)}(t) = \frac{d\theta(t)}{dt}, \Psi^{(2)}(t) = \frac{d^2\theta(t)}{dt^2} \tag{2}$$

By definition, the functions $\Psi^{(1)}(t)$ and $\Psi^{(2)}(t)$ satisfy the admissible condition:

$$\int_{-\infty}^{\infty} \Psi^{(1)}(t)dt = 0, \int_{-\infty}^{\infty} \Psi^{(2)}(t)dt = 0 \tag{3}$$

Therefore, the functions $\Psi^{(1)}(t)$ and $\Psi^{(2)}(t)$ can be served as mother wavelet according to the theory of wavelet.

In this paper, we denote the scaling function which is the dilation by a scaling factor a on a function $g(t)$.

$$g_a(t) = \frac{1}{a}g(\frac{1}{a}) \tag{4}$$

As a result, we define the convolution wavelet transforms of $x(t) \in L^2(R)$ at the scale a and position t with respect to the wavelet function $\Psi^{(1)}(t)$ is

$$W_a^{(1)}x(t) = x * \Psi^{(1)}(t) = \frac{1}{a}\int_{-\infty}^{\infty} x(\tau)\Psi^{(1)}(\frac{t-\tau}{a})d\tau \tag{5}$$

The convolution wavelet transforms of $x(t)$ with respect to $\Psi^{(2)}(t)$ is

$$W_a^{(2)}x(t) = x * \Psi^{(2)}(t) = \frac{1}{a}\int_{-\infty}^{\infty} x(\tau)\Psi^{(2)}(\frac{t-\tau}{a})d\tau \tag{6}$$

We derive that

$$W_a^{(1)}x(t) = x * (a\frac{d\theta_a}{dt})(t) = a\frac{d}{dt}(x * \theta_a)(t) \tag{7}$$

$$W_a^{(2)}x(t) = x * (a^2\frac{d^2\theta_a}{dt^2})(t) = a^2\frac{d^2}{dt^2}(x * \theta_a)(t) \tag{8}$$

The $x*\theta_a(t)$ can be considered as the result of the function $x(t)$ having been smoothed by $\theta_a(t)$. That is, as shown in equation (7) and (8), the wavelet transforms $W_a^{(1)}x(t)$ and $W_a^{(2)}x(t)$ are the first- and second-order derivative of the smoothed signal $x * \theta_a(t)$. The relations of among $x(t)$, $x * \theta_a(t)$, $W_a^{(1)}x(t)$ and $W_a^{(2)}x(t)$ can be illustrated by Fig. 4. For a fixed scale a, the sharp variation point of $x(t)$ (at t_0 and t_2) corresponds to the local peak value of $W_a^{(1)}x(t)$ and to the zero-crossing of $W_a^{(2)}x(t)$. Therefore, we can detect the

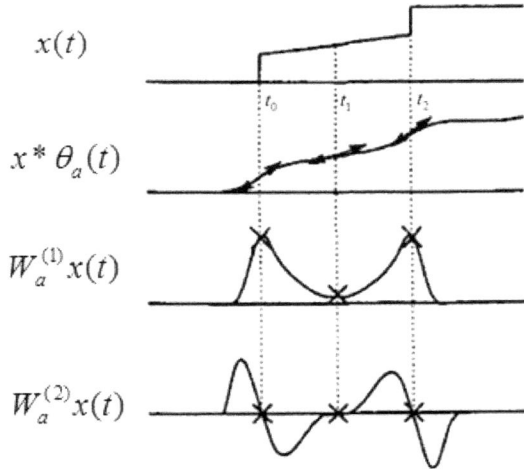

Figure 4: The relations among $x(t)$, $x * \theta_a(t)$, $W_a^{(1)}x(t)$ **and** $W_a^{(2)}x(t)$ **[26].**

local peak value of $W_a^{(1)}x(t)$ or the zero-crossing of $W_a^{(2)}x(t)$ to reveal the singular point which variation is sharp.

The procedure for detecting local peak value is similar to the detection of zero-crossing point. However, as shown Fig. 4, the zero-crossing of $W_a^{(2)}x(t)$ not only corresponds to the sharp variations point of $x(t)$ but also to the slow variation point where is t_1. Since our work is to aim at locating the forgery position in the audio signal, the local peak value of $W_a^{(1)}x(t)$ is more attractive for us compared to the zero-crossing of $W_a^{(2)}x(t)$.

For a digital speech audio signal, a forged position is highly possible to generate a singular point as the result of breaking the substantial correlation between adjacent sample points in the original speech audio. And the wavelet singularity analysis method as a powerful tool can give us a chance to detect and locate the forged singularity point (which is resulted from the forged operation) in the speech audio signal. In order to detect and locate the forged singularity point effectively, we perform wavelet packet decomposition to divide a forged speech signal into different frequency subbands. In such a way, the tampering operation can be detected in a high-frequency subband without the interference from the other frequency subbands. The lower energy of the wavelet packet subband is, the easier detection and location can be done. For a given speech audio signal, the energy of the wavelet packet subband rests with the levels of the wavelet packet decomposition by referring to the normal bandwidth of speech audio signal.

Since the length of the wavelet packet subband is different from that of the speech audio signal, we reconstruct each wavelet packet subband to make the length of the wavelet packet subband equal to the speech audio signal so that a local peak value in the subband signal can visually indicate the corresponding singularity point in position in time domain. Here, we call the reconstructed wavelet packet subband as the wavelet reconstruction subband. With the subband reconstruction step and the wavelet singularity analysis [26], we expect that a forged singularity point (a local peak value at the reconstructed high frequency subband) can be detected and located.

2.3 Detection of Digital Speech Forgeries

The speech forgeries will often result in the generation of singular points at the forged positions. And the wavelet singularity analysis can give us a hand to locate the forged positions via detecting the local peak value in a reconstructed high-frequency subband by using wavelet packet decomposition. However, for a given speech audio signal, there are many inherent singularity points because the digital speech audio files are non-stationary signal and may have severe variation in somewhere. Obviously, the inherent singularity points in the signal will cause a serious interference when we attempt to locate a forged singularity point in the speech audio. Fortunately, we observed from the extensive experiments that the inherent singularity points in the audio signal often stay together in the form of group while the forged singularity point usually stays alone, as shown in Fig. 5. In other words, in the wavelet reconstruction subband, the local peak values corresponding to the inherent singularity points are usually stay together as a group while no other local peaks staying close to the forged singularity point. Therefore, we can discriminate a forged singularity point and those inherent singularity points by judging whether a singular point stays in the form of group.

In order to discriminate a forged singularity point and the inherent singularity points in the speech audio, we design 5 parameters denoted by $N, k, n1, n2$ and P, in the wavelet reconstruction subband to form a forensics method for the tampering operation in time domain. About how to detect and process a forged singularity point with these 5 parameters is described as follows (also see Figures 5~9).

Based on experimental observation, we also find that the local peak value in the wavelet reconstruction subband, which correspond to a singular point in time domain, is larger than the absolute mean of the wavelet reconstruction subband. And most of local peak values have the same order of magnitude in the same subband, as shown in Fig. 5. What's more, the order of magnitude of a local peak value is different in different wavelet reconstruction subband since different subband has different energy according to wavelet theory.

We define LEMR as the ratio of the local peak value to the absolute mean of the wavelet reconstruction subband. For a given point in time domain, if its LEMR in the wavelet reconstruction subband is greater than a threshold N (the first designing parameter), then the point is a singular point. For the parameter N, we compute the distribution of LEMR values from 6000 tampered speech audio clips in length of 10 seconds and the result shows in Fig. 7. From Fig. 7, we can see what all the LEMR values are greater than 5 and the range of the values is from 5 to 23000. We set the initial value of N as 5. For further reducing the computational cost, we change N to half of the maximum of the LEMR values of a subband if the maximal LEMR value is larger than $k * N$, where k is a positive value, $k \in (2, 5)$.

All the singular points can be detected by using the parameter N. Furthermore, each singular point will be distinguished as an inherent singularity point or a forged singularity point. In order to distinguish a forged singularity point and those inherent singularity points in the speech audio, we use the other 3 parameters $n1, n2$ and P in the wavelet reconstruction subband. The basic method is that a given singular point is claimed as an inherent singularity point if there exists other local peak values (which have the same

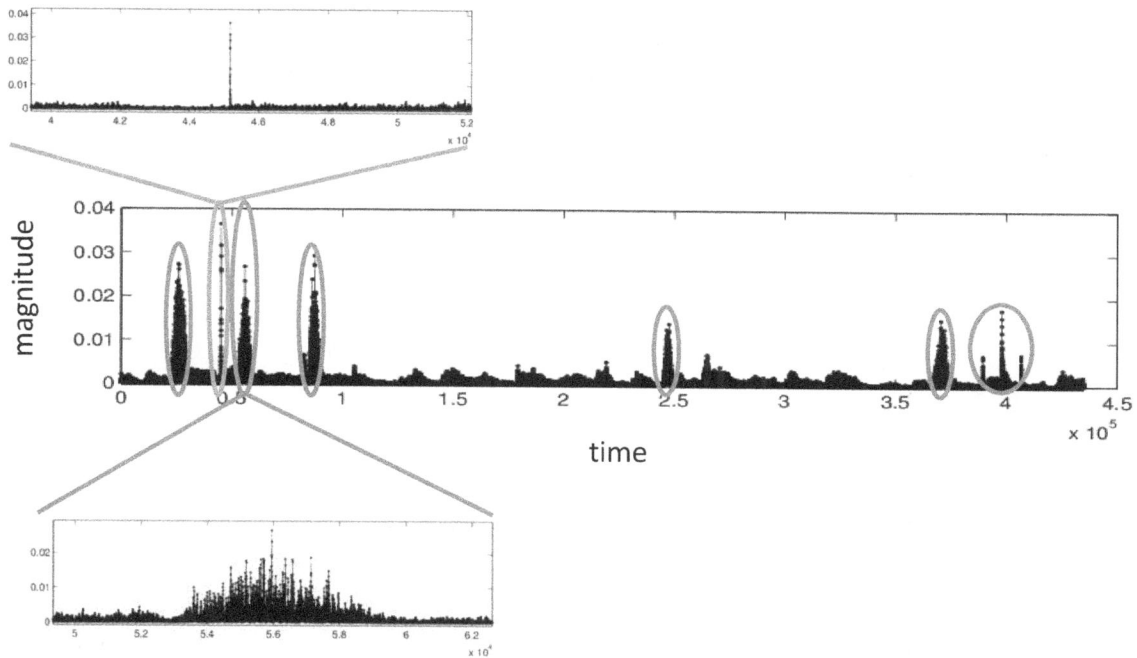

Figure 5: The difference between a forged singularity point and the inherent singularity points in the wavelet reconstruction subband. Local peak value in the second yellow circle corresponds to a forged singularity point in time domain, and the peak values in the other circles correspond to those inherent singularity points in the original audio signal. All the peak values in the circle have the same order of magnitude.

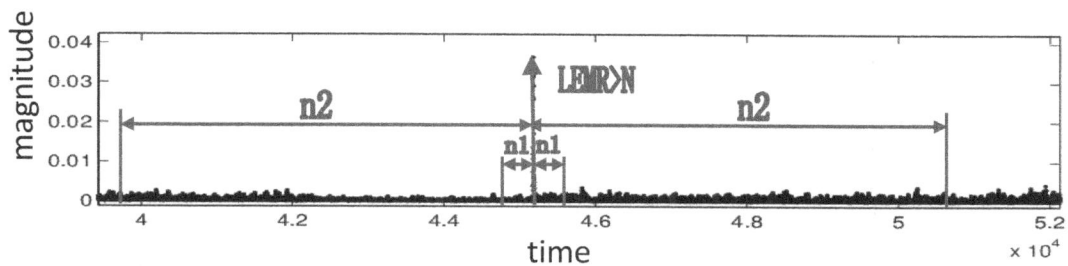

(a) The local peak value of a forged singularity point. It often stays alone.

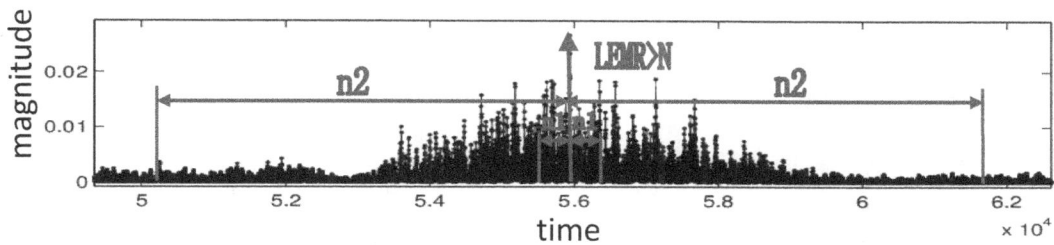

(b) The local peak values of a group of inherent singularity points

Figure 6: Illustration for the parameters $n1$ and $n2$ for a forged singularity point and for a group of inherent singularity points.

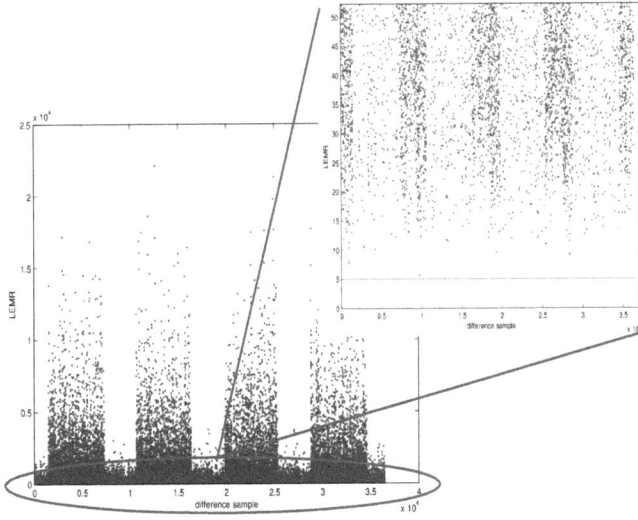

Figure 7: The statistical distribution of the LEMR values for the forged singularity points from 6000 tampered speech audio clips in length of 10s.

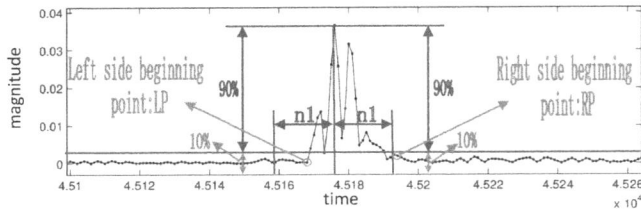

Figure 8: The illustration for computing the parameter $n1$. The $n1$ value is the bigger one in the two distances from LP and RP to the local peak.

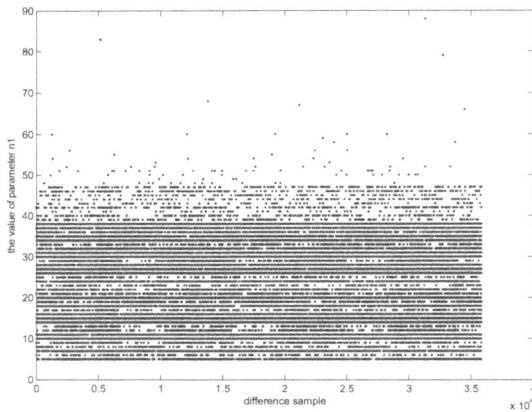

Figure 9: The value distribution of $n1$ in different subband for the forged singularity points from 6000 tampered speech audio clips of 10s.

order of magnitude as the local peak value of the given singular point) in a small region. Otherwise, the given singular point is claimed as a forged singularity point since it stays alone. The details on how to distinguish an inherent singular point and a forged singular point will be described below.

The way on how to compute the parameters $n1$ and $n2$ have been illustrated in Fig. 6. The parameter $n1$ is a distance to indicate a region including the local peak value where the points in this region in magnitude are stable and larger than 10% of the local peak value. As shown in Fig. 8, the points in left side and the right side are denoted by **LP** and **RP**, respectively. The points on the left side of the **LP** point are stable below 10% of the local peak value while the points on the right side of the **RP** point are also stable below 10% of the local peak value. The distance from the local peak value to the **LP** point may be different from that to the **RP** point. In this case, the parameter $n1$ is set to the larger one between the two distances. The reason why we design the parameter $n1$ is that there is a certain fluctuation region around the local peak value, and we compute the region in $[-n1, n1]$ (Suppose that the local peak point is origin of coordinates.) to stand for the fluctuation region.

The value distribution of parameter $n1$ is shown in Fig. 9. We can observe that most of the $n1$ values (99.2383%) are between 5 and 46. Considering a possible situation that some group of singular points may stay in a small region, the parameter $n1$ cannot be too large. Too large a $n1$ value will increase the error probability to claim an inherent singularity point as a forged singularity point. Meantime, the $n1$ cannot be too small. Too small a $n1$ value will increase the error probability to identify a forged singularity point as an inherent singularity point. In this paper, the parameter $n1$ is set to be a value between 40 and 50 for a better trade-off.

As is illustrated in Fig. 6, the parameter $n2$ is designed to indicate the other region for a given singular point. We define MLER as the ratio of the maximal value in the region ($[n1, n2]$ and $[-n2, -n1]$) around a given singular point) to the corresponding local peak value. The parameter P is defined as a threshold. We consider that there may exist other singular points if the MLER is greater than P. In other words, for a given point, if its MLER is greater than P, then the given point is claimed as an inherent singularity point since it stays together with other singular points. Otherwise, the given point is a forged singularity point because it is unique in the region.

With consideration of the parameter $n1$, the parameter P is set to be larger than 15% of the local peak value in order to save at least 5% space for improving the detection accuracy rate. Nevertheless, a larger P value increases the probability to discard some small local peak values (which may be forged points). On the basis of the experimental observation, the empirical value of P can be between 15% and 30% while $n2$ is between 800 and 1200.

Based on the analysis above, we develop a method to detect and locate a forged operation on speech audio as follows (also illustrated in Fig. 10).

1) For a given speech audio, we first decompose it into $(2^{n+1} - 2)$ subbands by performing n levels of wavelet packet decomposition.

2) Each wavelet packet subband is reconstructed to make sure that each reconstruction wavelet packet subband

has the same length as the speech audio signal so that the local peak value in a reconstruction wavelet packet subband can visually indicate the forged positions in time domain.

3) Calculate the absolute value of a wavelet reconstruction subband, and denote as $Abs\_subband$.

4) In order to better compute the forged positions, a array corresponding to the ith wavelet reconstruction subband is denoted by $SubArr_i$. The array in length is equal to the number of the samples in the speech signal. Set zeros to the array initially.

5) Compute the mean of the $Abs\_subband$ and set the parameter N as 5 first.

6) Compute the maximum value of the $Abs\_subband$ and denote as $M1$, and then get the maximum LEMR value.

7) Turn to *step* 11 if the LEMR value is less than N; Otherwise, the parameter N will be changed to half of the maximum LEMR value if the maximum LEMR value is larger than $k * N$.

8) Find the maximum value $M2$ in the ranges $[n1, n2]$ and $[-n2, -n1]$ of the $Abs\_subband$ (Suppose that the local peak point is origin of coordinates).

9) If the ratio of $M2$ to $M1$, denoted by MLER, is less than the parameter P, the element in the array $SubArr_i$ corresponding to the position of $M1$ is set to "1". In other words, if the MLER is less than P, the singular point corresponding to the $M1$ value is claimed as a forged singularity point.

10) Mark the points in the fluctuation region ($[-n1, n1]$, as shown in Fig.6) as zeros for avoiding to detect the region repeatedly. Return to the *step* 6.

11) Turn to *step* 12 if all wavelet reconstruction subbands are processed completely; Otherwise, turn to *step* 3 to process the next wavelet reconstruction subband.

12) The "1" values in the ith array indicate the forged positions detected from the ith wavelet reconstruction subband. The OR operation is performed on all arrays (a subband corresponding to a array) to output the detection results where the value "1" indicates the position of a forged operation.

3. EXPERIMENTAL RESULTS

3.1 Illustration on Time Domain Forgeries

We first illustrate an example (a sentence only consisting of numerals) with multiple deletion points to show how the proposed scheme works. This kind of deletion operations usually arises in the witness statements. In the experiments, four numbers in the sentence are cropped by using GoldWave software, as shown in Fig. 11. The detection results of the proposed method based on the singularity analysis of the wavelet packet decomposition in the doctored speech audio are shown in Fig. 11(c) and (d). We can observe that the "1" values in Fig. 11(d) can correctly indicate to the positions of the forged operations. This shows that the proposed method can resist the deletion operation in time domain.

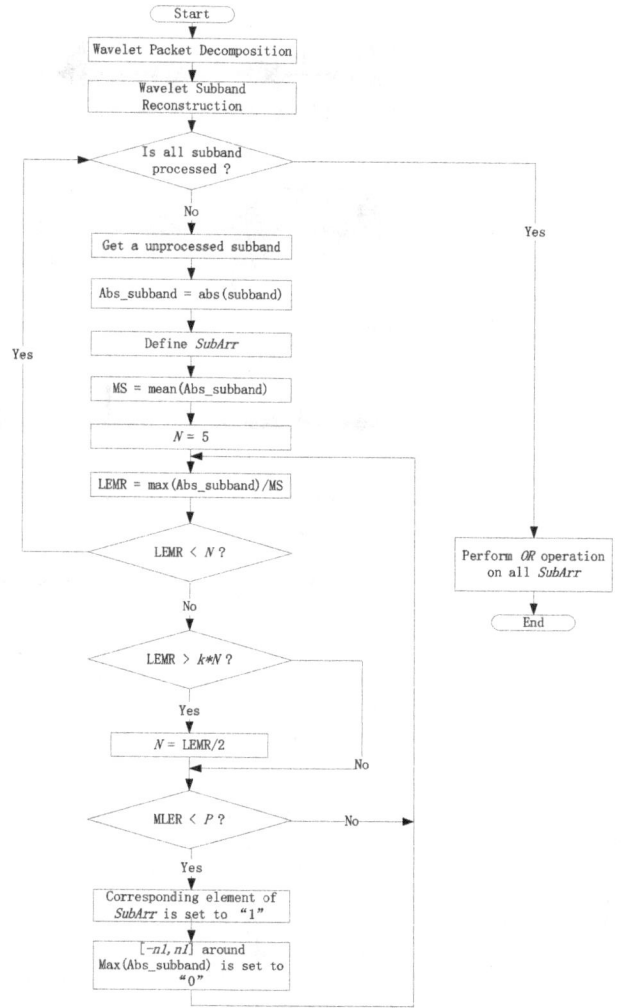

Figure 10: The processing flow chart of the proposed method.

3.2 Extensive Experiments

To test the effectiveness of the proposed method, the extensive experiment are taken to evaluate. Details for data set used, experimental setup, and experimental results are described as follows.

3.2.1 Data Set and Experimental Setup

In the experiments, we collect 3500 speech audio clips in 7 different sample rates including 44.1 kHz (for CD), 32 kHz and 24 kHz (for some soundcards), 22.05 kHz (for FM broadcasting), 16 kHz (for the ITU-T G.722 standard and DVR), 11.025 kHz and 8 kHz (for digital telephone system). All speech audio clips are 5 seconds in length, mono and randomly cut from WAV files which are downloaded from the Internet [28, 29, 30] (75% of them are MP3 format since the speech files in WAV format on the Internet are scarce, and we transform them to WAV format by using LAME software for testing). We randomly choose some of the clips to make a forged operation (that 6000 samples are deleted or inserted in a random position) by using Matlab software. Then the proposed scheme is used to detect whether the audio has

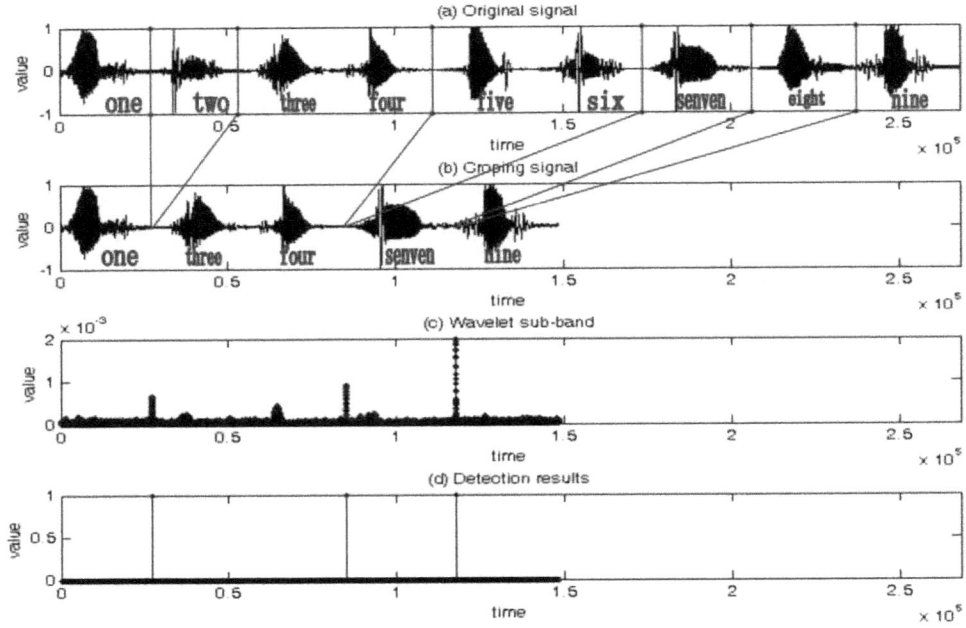

Figure 11: Example for detecting multiple deletions: Four numbers are cropped away from a series of numbers, as shown in (a) and (b). The plot (c) is the detection results in a wavelet reconstruction subband, and the plot (d) is the final detection result by considering multiple wavelet reconstruction subbands.

been cropped and where the forged position is. We set the parameters $N = 5$, $n1 = 45$, $n2 = 1000$, $P = 18\%$, $k = 3$ and perform 4 level of the wavelet packet transformation for each speech audio signal.

We denote N_{fa} as the number of audio clips tampered while N_{oa} is the number of the original (not tampered) audio clips. The detection accuracy rate for the N_{oa} original and the N_{fa} forged speech audio files are denoted as AR_o and AR_f, respectively. And we use the false positive error to measure original audio files incorrectly identified as forged audio files, while the false negative error represents the forged ones that are original. The false positive error rate and false negative rate are denoted as f_p and f_n, respectively. The accuracy detection rate AR is calculated as follows.

$$AR = (1 - \frac{f_p \times N_{oa} + f_n \times N_{fa}}{N_{oa} + N_{fa}}) \times 100\% \qquad (9)$$

or

$$AR = \frac{AR_o \times N_{oa} + AR_f \times N_{fa}}{N_{oa} + N_{fa}} \times 100\% \qquad (10)$$

3.2.2 Experimental Results and Analysis

In the experiment, for each sample rate, we have tested 500 speech audio files in turn to determine whether a given speech file is a forged one or not. And for a forged speech signal, we will locate the forged positions. The experimental results for different sample rates are shown in Table 1 and Table 2.

From Table 1 and Table 2, we can see that the best detection results are 81.55% (AR_o for insertion forgery operation at 24kHz), 94.09% (AR_f for insertion forgery operation at 44.1kHz) and 84.20%(AR for deletion forgery operation at

Table 1: Detection results for deletion forgery

Sample rate	AR_o	f_p	AR_f	f_n	AR
44.1 kHz	**76.32%**	23.68%	**90.81%**	9.19%	**84.20%**
32 kHz	**78.06%**	21.94%	**80.61%**	19.39%	**79.40%**
24 kHz	**77.91%**	22.09%	**78.09%**	21.91%	**78.00%**
22.05 kHz	**76.83%**	23.17%	**74.27%**	25.73%	**75.60%**
16 kHz	**76.51%**	23.41%	67.74%	32.26%	**72.20%**
11.025 kHz	75.76%	24.24%	42.82%	57.18%	59.40%
8kHz	81.19%	18.81%	28.32%	71.68%	54.90%

Table 2: Detection results for insertion forgery

Sample rate	AR_o	f_p	AR_f	f_n	AR
44.1 kHz	**74.90%**	25.10%	**94.09%**	5.91%	**84.00%**
32 kHz	**77.57%**	22.43%	**86.08%**	13.92%	**81.60%**
24 kHz	**81.55%**	18.45%	**83.15%**	16.85%	**82.40%**
22.05 kHz	**79.45%**	20.55%	**83.81%**	16.19%	**81.60%**
16 kHz	**77.78%**	22.22%	**75.10%**	24.90%	**76.40%**
11.025 kHz	75.50%	24.50%	49.67%	50.33%	62.50%
8kHz	79.23%	20.77%	35.81%	64.19%	57.00%

44.1kHz), respectively. For the sample rates above 16 kHz, most of the detection accuracy rates exceed 70% (which have be marked as boldface in the table). This indicates that our method can better detect the two tampering operations on the speech audio files with the sample rates of above 16 kHz.

In the Table 1 and Table 2, we also find that the detection accuracy rate for original speech audio files AR_o is relatively stable between 74% and 82% for different sample rates while the detection accuracy rate for forged speech audio files AR_f decreases as the decrease of the sample rate, which results in the accuracy rate AR decreased directly. It is obviously observed from Fig. 12 and Fig. 13. This can be explained from the fact that the speech file is a band-limited signal whose the main energy concentrates on the frequency bands between 0.2 and 3.4 kHz. So there is more energy and more inherent singular points at the same high frequency wavelet reconstruction subband for the speech audio file with the lower sample rate. Since the forged singularity points is also often present in high frequency component, for the lower sample rate speech file, the interference produced by the inherent singularity points is more serious in the process to locate a forged singularity point. The lower sample rate is, the more serious interference will be introduced for the detection. As shown in the Table 1 and 2, the AR_f decreases to below 50% as the sample rate decreases to 11.025 kHz.

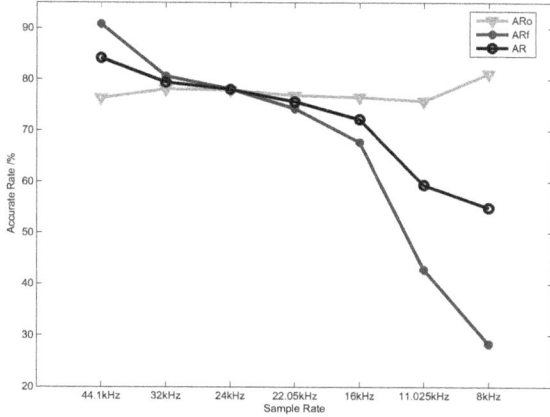

Figure 12: The accuracy detection rate for the deletion operations.

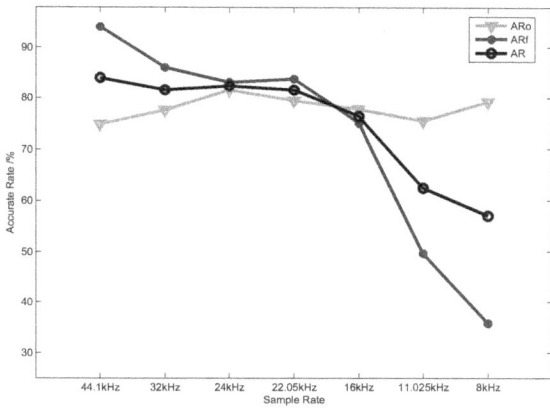

Figure 13: The accuracy detection rate for the insertion operations.

Our method is also effective for detecting the other kinds of audio files, such as music. Usually, the bandwidth of a music file is wider than a speech clip. Our method can take effect for a music file at the sample rate of 44.1 kHz (which is widely employed on CD), and the recall rate is round 83.4% (the data set for the testing inlcudes 500 music files). In the experiments, it is noting that a very small number of the forged operations will not result in the generation of singular points, and some inherent singular points in the audio signal may not stay together. The two situations will cause serious interference for the detection. For this issue, a possible way is to do more meticulous analysis on the difference between the inherent and forged singularity points so as to improve the proposed detection strategy. This is a consideration of our future works.

4. CONCLUSION

Detection of digital speech audio forgeries in time domain is an important issue in the information forensics community. By using the singularity analysis of the wavelet packet decomposition, in this paper, we propose a more general audio forensics scheme to detect speech audio forged operations in time domain.

With the help of the singularity analysis in the high frequency reconstructed subband of the wavelet packet decomposition, we can find some clues to detect and locate the forged operations in a speech audio file. By analyzing the difference between the inherent singularity points in the audio signal (which usually stay together) and the forged ones (which often stay alone) due to the forged operations, we constructed 5 parameters (denoted as $N, n1, n2, P, k$ in the paper) to form a method to effectively distinguish the two different kinds of singular points. Furthermore, we developed a method to expose digital audio forgeries by using the singularity analysis method of the wavelet packet decomposition. The experimental results have illustrated that our proposed scheme can identify whether a given speech file has been tampered previously and locate the position in time domain. The proposed method can better detect the speech audio files of above 16 kHz sample rates in a higher accuracy rate (above 72%) without any other specific side information. For the speech and music audio files at the sample rate 44.1 kHz, the accuracy rate of 84.20% and 83.4% can be achieved respectively.

In the future works, there is a room by exploring the relationship between the parameters used in this paper and the sample rate of audio signal. The other possible consideration of our future work is further to investigate the difference between the inherent singularity points and the ones due to the different forged operations.

5. REFERENCES

[1] S. Gupta, S. Cho, C.-C. Jay Kuo, Current developments and future trends in audio authentication,*IEEE MultiMedia*, 19(2):50-59, 2012.

[2] C. Kraetzer, A. Oermann, J. Dittmann, and A. Lang, Digital audio forensics: A first practical evaluation on microphone and environment classification, in Proc. of *the 9th workshop on Multimedia and Security*, pages 63-74, Dallas, USA, 2007.

[3] R. Buchhholz, C. Kraetzer, J. Dittmann, Microphone Classification Using Fourier Coefficients, in Proc. of *the 11th International Workshop on Information Hiding*, pages 235-246, Darmstadt, Germany, June 2009.

[4] S. Songnian, H. Zheng, X. Chen, S. Shaopei, Y. Xu, Research on Correlation of Digital Audio and Recording Device, *Computer Engineering*, 35(19):224-227, October, 2009.

[5] H. Malik, H. Farid, Audio forensics from acoustic reverberation, in Proc. of *ICASSP*, pages 1710-1713, Dallas, USA, March 2010.

[6] H. Malik, H. Zhao, Recording environment identification using acoustic reverberation, in Proc. of *ICASSP*, pages 1833-1836, Kyoto, Japan, March 2012.

[7] H. Zhao, H. Malik, Audio forensics using acoustic environment traces, in Proc. of *IEEE Statistical Processing Workshop*, pages 373-376, Ann Arbor, August 2012.

[8] S. Ikram, H. Malik, Digital audio forensics using background noise, in Proc. of *ICME*, pages 106-110, Suntec City, Singapore, July 2010.

[9] R. Yang, Y. Q. Shi, H. Jiwu, Detecting double compression of audio signal, in Proc. of *SPIE 7541*, Media Forensics and Security II, January, 2010.

[10] M. Qiao, A. H. Sung, Q. Liu, Revealing Real Quality of Double Compressed MP3 Audio, in Proc. of *the international conference on Multimedia*, pages 1011-1014 , New York, USA , 2010.

[11] Q. Liu. A. H. Sung. M. Qiao, Detection of Double MP3 Compression, *Cognitive Computation*, 4(2):291-296, December, 2010.

[12] G. Chen, X. Kong, W. Zhong, B. Wang, Detection of Double MP3 Compression Based on fluctuation intensity of Quantized MDCT Coefficients, in Proc. of *CIHW*, pages 164-167, Beijing, China, 2012.

[13] D. Luo, W. Luo, R. Yang, J. Huang, Compression history identification for digital audio signal, in Proc. of *ICASSP*, pages 1733-1736, Kyoto, Japan, March 2012.

[14] R. Yang, Y. Q. Shi, J. Huang, Defeating Fake-Quality MP3, in Proc. of *11th ACM Multimedia and Security Workshop, ACM Press*, pages 117-124, New York, USA, 2009.

[15] Y. Quiming, C. Peiqi, X. Guorong, Y. Zhiqiang, S. Yunqing, Audio re-sampling detection in audio forensics based on EM algorithm, *Computer Application*, 26(11):2598-2601, 2006.

[16] D. Qi, P. Xijian, Audio Tampering Detection Based on Band-Partitioning Spectral Smoothness, *Applied Sciences, Electronics and Information Engineering*, 28(2):142-146, 2010.

[17] Q. Shi, X. Ma, Detection of Audio Interpolation Based on Singular Value Decomposition, *Awareness Science and Technology (iCAST)*, pages 287-290, Dalian, 2011.

[18] R. Yang, Z. Qu, J. Huang, Detecting Digital Audio Forgeries by Checking Frame Offsets, in Proc. of *10th ACM Multimedia and Security Workshop, ACM Press*, pages 21-26, New York, USA, 2008.

[19] R. Yang, Z. Qu, J. Huang, Exposing MP3 Audio Forgeries Using Frame Offsets, *ACM Transactions on Multimedia Computing, Communications, and Applications*, 8(2):35:1-20, September 2010.

[20] C. Gigoras, Digital audio recording analysis: The electric network frequency (ENF) criterion, *The International ournal of Speech anguage and the aw*, pages 63-76, 2005.

[21] D. P. Nicolalde, J. A. Apolinario, Evaluating digital audio authenticity with spectral distances and ENF phase change, in Proc. of *ICASSP*, pages 1417-1420, Taipei, 2009.

[22] D. P. Nicolalde, J. A. Apolinario, Audio authenticity: detecting ENF discontinuity with high precision phase analysis, *IEEE Transactions on Information Forensics and Security*, 5(3):534-543, 2010.

[23] X. Pan, X. Zhang, S. Lyu, Detecting splicing in digital audios using local noise level estimation, in Proc. of *ICASSP*, pages 1841-1844, Kyoto, Japan, March 2012.

[24] H. Farid, Detecting digital forgeries using bispectral analysis, *MIT AI Memo AIM-1657, MIT*, 1999.

[25] S. Mallat, S. Zhong, Characterization of signal from multiscale edges, *IEEE Trans on PAMI*, 14(7):710-732, 1992.

[26] S. Mallat, W. L. Hwang, Singularity Detection and Processing with Wavelets, *IEEE Trans on IT*, 38(2):617-643, 1992.

[27] S. Mallat, Zero-Crossings of a Wavelet Transform, *IEEE Trans on IT*, vol. 37(4):1019-1033, 1991.

[28] http://www.51voa.com/

[29] http://www.putclub.com/

[30] http://soundlab.cs.princeton.edu/

Detection and Classification of Double Compressed MP3 Audio Tracks

Tiziano Bianchi
Dept. of Electronics and
Telecommunications
Politecnico di Torino (Italy)
tiziano.bianchi@polito.it

Alessia De Rosa
National Inter-University
Consortium for
Telecommunications
University of Florence (Italy)
alessia.derosa@unifi.it

Marco Fontani
Dept. of Information
Engineering and
Mathematical Sciences
University of Siena (Italy)
marco.fontani@unisi.it

Giovanni Rocciolo
Dept of Information
Engineering
University of Florence (Italy)
g.rocciolo@gmail.com

Alessandro Piva
Dept of Information
Engineering
University of Florence (Italy)
alessandro.piva@unifi.it

ABSTRACT

In this paper, a method to detect the presence of double compression in a MP3 audio file is proposed. By exploiting the effect of double compression in the statistical properties of quantized MDCT coefficients, a single measure is derived to decide if a MP3 file is single compressed or it has been double compressed and also to devise the bit-rate of the first compression. Experimental results confirm the performance of the detector, mainly when the bit-rate of the second compression is higher than the bit-rate of the first one.

Categories and Subject Descriptors

D.4.6 [**Software**]: Security and Protection—*Authentication*

Keywords

Audio forensics, double compression, audio tampering

1. INTRODUCTION

The presence of artifacts due to a double compression in the statistics of transformed coefficients has received a lot of attention in the image forensics field: Popescu et al. in [9] observed that consecutive quantizations introduce periodic artifacts into the histogram of DCT coefficients; these periodic artifacts are visible in the Fourier domain as strong peaks in medium and high frequencies. Their seminal work has been the basis of several works dealing with double JPEG compression, as an example we cite [4, 2, 1].

On the contrary, there are few works in the current literature dealing with MP3 audio files and with double audio compression. In [14] to defeat Fake-Quality MP3 files

(i.e. MP3 files recompressed at a higher bit-rate) authors observed that there are many more quantized MDCT coefficients with small values in a single compressed MP3 file than that in the fake-quality MP3, no matter which bit rate the fake quality MP3 is transcoded from. In particular, the detector just measures the number of MDCT coefficients assuming ± 1 values and comparing this value with a given threshold: if it is lower than the threshold, it is decided that the file is a fake-quality one, otherwise that it is a single compressed one. The same authors in [15] proposed to detect double MP3 compression through the use of support vector machine classifiers with feature vectors formed by the distributions of the first digits of the quantized MDCT coefficients; in particular, a global method is proposed, where the statistics on the first digits of all quantized MDCT coefficients is taken, and the computed probability distributions of nine digits are used as features (9 dimensions) for training of a SVM. A so called band distribution method is also proposed, where a procedure of band division is added before computing the statistics on the first digits; this modification allows to increase the performance. In [5, 10] to detect double MP3 compression, some statistical features on the MDCT are extracted and a support vector machine is applied to the extracted features for classification. In particular, a set of statistical features of zero MDCT coefficients and non-zero MDCT coefficients from the whole frequency as well as individual scale bands are adopted. In [12, 13] a forgery detection method for MP3 audio files is proposed. Based on the observation that forgeries break the original frame segmentation, frame offsets are used to locate forgeries automatically, allowing to detect most common forgeries, such as deletion, insertion, substitution, and splicing. However, experimental results are carried out in audio files that after the manipulation have not been reencoded in MP3 format. Finally, in [8] the inverse decoder problem is considered. In this scenario, only the uncompressed samples are known to the analyst and the goal is to recover the parameters of a possible previous compression.

In this work, we propose an approach exploiting the effect of double compression in the statistical properties of quantized MDCT coefficients in a MP3 compressed audio file. The method relies on a single measure derived from the statistics of MDCT coefficients, allowing us to apply a simple threshold detector to decide if a given MP3 file is single compressed or it has been double compressed. Moreover, the proposed method is able to derive the bit-rate of the first compression by means of a Nearest Neighbour classifier, as it will be described in the following.

2. THE PROPOSED METHOD

The core idea of the algorithm is to measure the similarity between the histogram of quantized MDCT coefficients of the MP3 file under analysis, that has possibly undergone a double compression, and the histogram of the coefficients computed on a single compressed version of the same file, that is of the single compressed MDCT coefficients. Intuitively, if the distance between the two distributions is low, this will indicate that the file under analysis has not been MP3 encoded twice, viceversa the file will be considered as double compressed.

Obtaining a reliable estimate of the distribution of the single quantized MDCT coefficients from the corresponding quantized or double quantized coefficients appears to be a difficult task. However, it has already been observed in the image forensic literature [6] that the DCT coefficients obtained by applying a slight shift to the grid used for computing the block DCT usually do not exhibit quantization artifacts. Hence, in a similar way the distribution of the single compressed MDCT coefficients can be approximated by considering the simulated single compressed file, achieved by removing a given number of PCM samples of the decompressed audio file and recompressing the remaining samples to the same compression quality of the file under analysis.

To demonstrate that the idea is effective, an uncompressed audio track, 4 sec long, has been MP3 compressed at several bit-rates in $[64, 96, 128, 192]$ kbit/s, and then recompressed to 160 kbit/s, in such a way to obtain 4 double compressed versions, 3 with increasing bit-rate, and one with decreasing bit-rate. Then, the uncompressed file is also single compressed to 160 kbit/s. To each of these compressed files, the previous procedure has been applied to obtain a simulated single compressed file, by removing the first 10 PCM samples to the decompressed file and recompressing the remaining samples to 160 kbit/s. Then, the histograms of MDCT coefficients for the input original files and the corresponding simulated single compressed files have been compared. In Figure 1, the histograms related to the MP3 file double compressed at 64 kbit/s and then 160 kbit/s, and to the simulated MP3 file single compressed at 160 kbit/s are shown. It is evident that the first histogram exhibits the characteristic pattern of a distribution of coefficients that have undergone a double compression, whereas in the second these artifacts have been removed. Similar results are obtained when the first compression was done with higher bit-rates, but still lower than 160 kbit/s, even if the effect of the double quantization becomes smaller. If the same procedure is applied to a single compressed MP3 file, it will happen the histograms of the input file and the corresponding simulated one are very similar, as it is shown in Figure 2. A similar situation shows up when a double compression has been applied, but with the first bit-rate (i.e. 192 kbit/s) higher than the second one (i.e. 160 kbit/s), see Figure 3.

The processing blocks composing the proposed algorithm are illustrated in Figure 4: the MP3 file is decompressed obtaining a sequence of PCM samples. The *Pattern breaker*

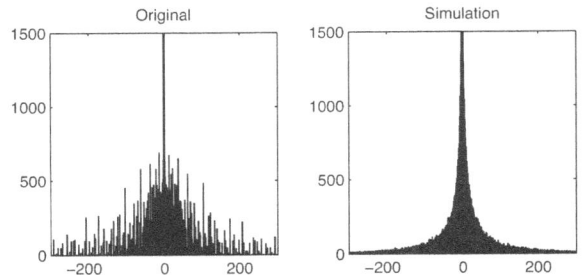

Figure 1: Histograms of MDCT coeffs of a MP3 file double compressed at 64 kbit/s and then 160 kbit/s (left), and of the corresponding simulated single compressed file at 160 kbit/s (right).

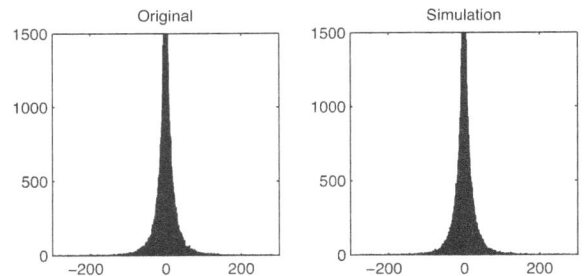

Figure 2: Histograms of MDCT coeffs of a MP3 file single compressed at 160 kb/s (left), and of the simulated single compressed file at 160 kbit/s (right).

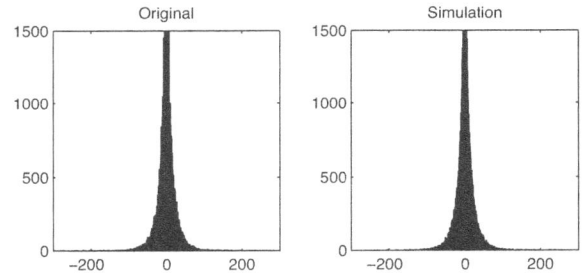

Figure 3: Histograms of MDCT coeffs of a MP3 file double compressed at 192 kb/s and then 160 kb/s (left), and of the simulated single compressed file at 160 kbit/s (right).

just removes a given number of PCM samples starting from the beginning of the PCM sequence. This operation allows to maintain the original characteristics of the signal, while removing quantization artifacts. The *Filterbank + MDCT* block takes the PCM samples and applies filtering and the MDCT transform, achieving a set of unquantized MDCT coefficients. The *Parameter extraction* allows to extract from the original MP3 bitstream the quantization parameters, i.e. the quantization pattern and the original quantization values. The quantization pattern is needed by the *Re-quantizer* to simulate a distribution of MDCT coefficients that have undergone only a single compression. In addition, the *Re-quantizer* smooths the sequence of simulated coefficients through a *Laplace Smoothing* [7], a technique used to smooth categorical data (in particular, the smoothing parameter α equal to 1 was adopted). This operation aims at filling possible empty bins present in the data histogram, and thus avoiding numerical errors in the following computations. The original quantized values and the simulated single quantized values are then compared through the *Histograms distances* block.

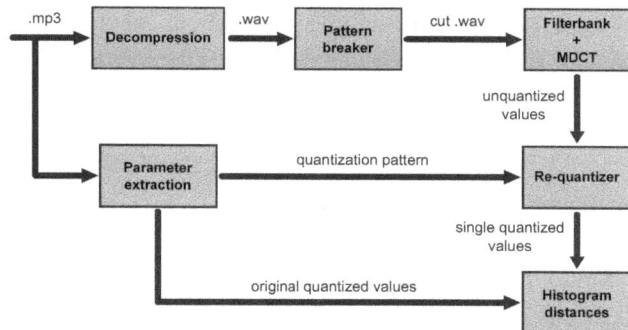

Figure 4: Scheme of the proposed method.

Indicating with X and Y respectively the observed and the simulated distributions of MDCT coefficients, their histograms are built, and a similarity measure is computed. Among the possible measures that can be used to compute the distance between two histograms, we adopted the the Chi-square distance $D_\chi(X, Y)$ [11], defined as:

$$D_\chi(X, Y) = \sum_{i=1}^{N} \frac{(X_i - Y_i)^2}{2(X_i + Y_i)} \qquad (1)$$

where N is the number of bins of the histograms.

The computed distance measure represents the feature the proposed method uses to detect if a MP3 file has been single or double compressed (i.e. when the first bit-rate is lower than the second one).

Furthermore, such a proposed feature (as it will be shown in the next Section) is able to provide additional information about the compression suffered by the analyzed MP3 file, in particular concerning the difference between the second and the first bit-rate ($\Delta = BR2 - BR1$): when such a value is positive the proposed algorithm is able to classify double compressed MP3 audio tracks with respect to the first bit-rate. In fact, the values assumed by the feature range quite differently according to the second bit-rate and the Δ factor, thus allowing to cluster double compressed MP3 audio tracks by applying a Nearest Neighbour classifier.

3. EXPERIMENTAL RESULTS

To validate the ideas proposed in the previous section, an audio dataset has been built, trying to represent as much as possible heterogeneous sources. To this aim, the database includes uncompressed audio files belonging to four different categories: *Music*: royalty free music audio tracks, with 5 different musical styles [3], *Speech*: music audio files containing dialogues, *Outdoor*: audio files relative to recording outdoors, and *Commercial*: file containing dialogues combined with music, as often happens in advertising. Each category collects about 17 minutes of audio divided into 250 segments 4 s long, for a total of 1.000 uncompressed audio files. Each file has been compressed, in dual mono, with bit-rate $BR1$

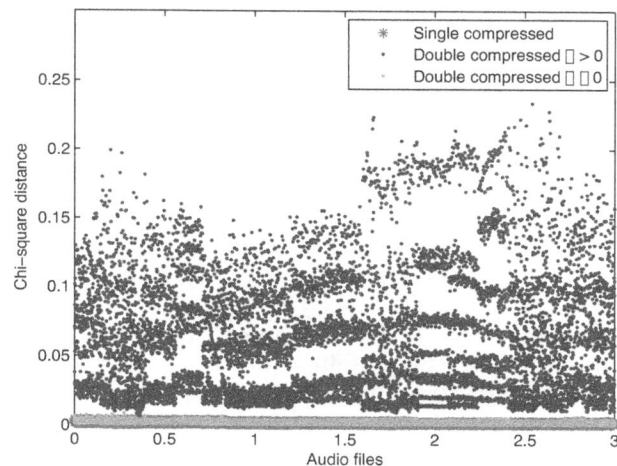

Figure 5: Chi-square distances computed for the 30.000 audio segments composing the dataset.

chosen in $[64, 96, 128, 160, 192]$ kbit/s, obtaining 5.000 single compressed MP3 files. Finally, these files have been compressed again using as $BR2$ one of the bit-rate values (also the same value as the first one was considered) achieving 25.000 MP3 double compressed files. Among these, 10.000 files have a difference $\Delta = BR2 - BR1$ between the second and the first bit-rate which is positive, taking value in $[32, 64, 96, 128]$ kbit/s; 10.000 files have a negative difference Δ taking value in $[-128, -96, -64, -32]$ kbit/s and 5.000 files have $\Delta = 0$. The overall dataset is composed by 30.000 MP3 files, including 5.000 single compressed files.

3.1 Double Compression Detection

As a first experiment, we computed the values assumed by the proposed feature for all the 30.000 files belonging to the test dataset. In Figure 5 the Chi-square distances are visualized: single compressed files and double compressed files with negative or null Δ show a distance D near to zero, whereas the other files have D rather higher than zero. By comparing D with a threshold τ is possible to discriminate these two kinds of files: double compressed files with $\Delta > 0$ and the other ones.

By adopting a variable threshold τ, we then computed a Receiver Operating Characteristic (ROC) curve, representing the capacity of the detector to separate single compressed from double compressed MP3 files (including $\Delta >$ or ≤ 0). The trend of the obtained ROC curve is shown in Figure 6 (left): it reflects the bimodal distribution of distances of double compressed files (blue and green colored in Figure 5) and highlights that the detector is able to distinguish only one of the two components (the one with $\Delta > 0$). If we separate the previous ROC in one relating to files double compressed with positive Δ, and one to files double compressed with negative or zero Δ, as is shown in Figure 6 (right), when double compressed file with positive Δ are considered, we obtain a perfect classifier, while when the cases with negative or zero Δ are analyzed, we are next to the random classifier.

As anticipated in Section 2, the distance representing the proposed feature assumes a large range of values, as it can

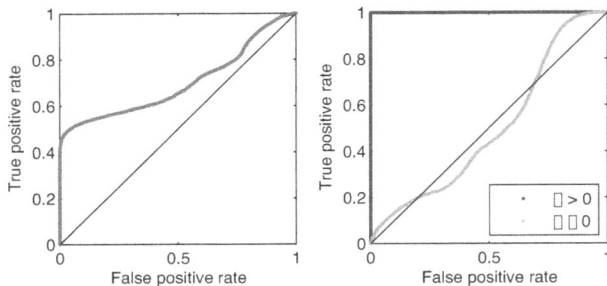

Figure 6: ROC curve obtained by varying the threshold τ of the classifier (left). Separation of cases with positive Δ and negative or zero Δ (right)

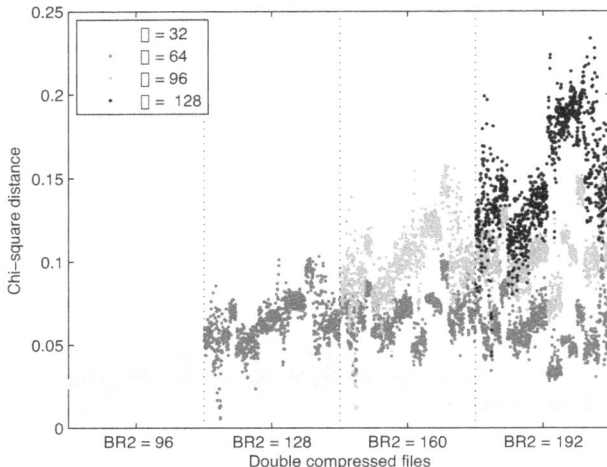

Figure 7: Chi-square distances computed for double compressed files with positive Δ, grouped according to both the values assumed by Δ and BR2.

BR1 vs BR2	64	96	128	160	192
64	-	99.9	99.9	99.9	99.9
96	49.9	-	99.9	99.9	99.9
128	49.9	49.9	-	99.9	99.9
160	69.5	47.9	49.1	-	96.7
192	56.1	66.4	57.8	67.4	-

Table 1: Detection accuracy of the proposed method for different bit-rates.

BR1 vs BR2	64	96	128	160	192
64	-	70.9	96.7	98.6	99.4
96	53.4	-	93.2	99.3	99.4
128	64.9	63.7	-	93.0	95.5
160	64.1	67.6	65.6	-	82.5
192	59.0	64.9	70.0	75.0	-

Table 2: Detection accuracy of LSQ method for different bit-rates.

BR1 vs BR2	64	96	128	160	192
64	-	99.9	99.9	99.9	99.3
96	96.2	-	99.7	99.7	98.8
128	80.2	99.0	-	99.2	98.1
160	84.5	94.1	96.3	-	98.0
192	67.6	88.5	89.9	90.3	-

Table 3: Detection accuracy of YSH method for different bit-rates.

be clearly observed in Figure 5. In order to highlight the relationship between the values taken by the feature and the compression parameters (i.e. BR2 and Δ), we examined in more detail the 10.000 double compressed files with positive Δ, plotting their Chi-square distances in Figure 7. Such values were plotted according to the different Δ: in particular there are 4.000 files with $\Delta = 32$ (yellow), 3.000 files with $\Delta = 64$ (violet), 2.000 files with $\Delta = 96$ (sky-blue), and finally 1.000 files with $\Delta = 128$ (black), and grouped for different BR2: $[96, 128, 160, 192]$. Double compressed audio tracks with same Δ factor obtain similar values of Chi-square distance (see plotting with same color) and to increasing Δ values correspond increasing Chi-square distances between the observed and simulated distribution. On the other hand, given a value of Δ, for different bit-rate of the second compression, different values of distance are obtained, since at a lower bit-rate (e.g. values for BR2=96 vs. values for BR2=192) corresponds a greater number of traces left in the content and thus a larger distance from the simulated single compression.

The dependency of the results on the bit-rate of the second compression (that is a parameter observable from the bitstream), suggests the possibility of improving the perfor-

mance of the double compression detection by taking into account a specific threshold τ for each specific BR2. With this observation in mind, we performed a set of experiments in order to compare the detection accuracy of the proposed detector with respect to the detection accuracy of the method proposed in [5, 10] by Liu, Sung, Qiao (LSQ method) and in [15] by Yang, Shi, Huang (YSH method). Corresponding results are shown in Tables 1, 2 and 3 respectively. The proposed method achieves nearly optimal performances for all combinations such that $\Delta > 0$. Also the other methods generally achieve good performances for $\Delta > 0$, however there are some bit-rate combinations for which they are slightly inferior. Conversely, for $\Delta < 0$ the proposed method is not able to reliably detect double MP3 compression, whereas the other methods have better performances, especially the YSH method that has good performances also in this scenario.

All the results shown in Tables 1, 2 and 3, have been achieved considering audio tracks 4 s long. We evaluated the degradation of the performances of the three detectors when the duration of the audio segments is reduced from 4 s to $[2, 1, 1/2, 1/4, 1/8, 1/16]$ s. The reason behind this experiment is that analyzing very small portions of audio potentially opens the door to fine-resolution splicing localization (i.e., detect if part of an audio file has been tampered). Practically, instead of taking all the MDCT coefficients of the 4 seconds long segment, only the coefficients belonging to a subpart of the segment are retained, where the subpart is just one half, one fourth and so on. For BR2=192 kbit/s and BR2=128 kbit/s the detection accuracies (averaged with respect to BR1) have been plotted with varying audio file duration in Figure 8 for our method, the LSQ method and the YSH method. The proposed method achieves a nearly

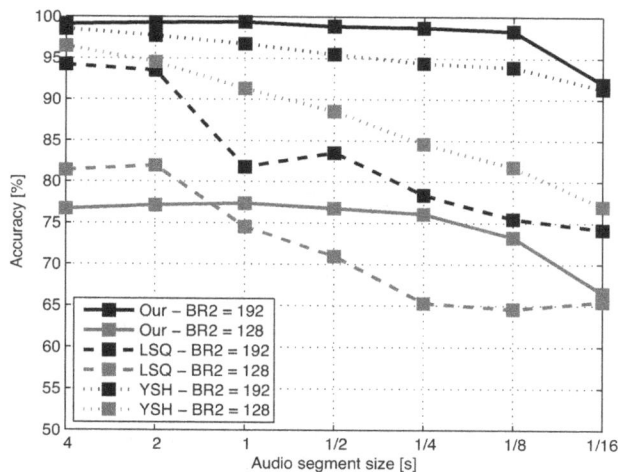

Figure 8: Detection accuracy with varying audio file duration for BR2=192 kbit/s and BR2=128 kbit/s.

constant detection performance up to 1/8 s audio segments, whereas the performance of the other methods drastically drop for audio segments under 2 s. Our method achieves very good performance in the case of high quality MP3 files. For BR2 equal to 192 kbit/s, our method achieves the best performance irrespective of the audio segment duration. For BR2 equal to 128 kbit/s, the proposed method is able to outperform the LSQ method for short audio segments, but remains inferior with respect to the YSH method.

3.2 First Compression Bit-Rate Classification

By taking into account the feature distribution highlighted in Figure 7, we considered the capability of the proposed feature to classify the double compressed file according to the first compression bit-rate, as BR1=BR2-Δ. A Nearest Neighbor classifier is adopted for each different BR2 and the corresponding classification accuracy results are shown in Table 4 for BR2=192 kbit/s and 6 for BR2=128 kbit/s. The rows of the tables represent the actual bit-rate of the first compression, and the columns the values assigned by the classifier. A comment about this experiment is in order: as shown in the previous section, the proposed method will hardly detect double compression for negative or null Δ. Similarly, the output of the classifier on double encoded files with negative or null Δ is not reliable. In particular, since a single compressed file can be considered like having undergone a (virtual) first compression at infinite quality, the classifier cannot distinguish between single encoded files and double encoded files with negative Δ.

For comparison, only the LSQ method is considered, since the YSH method was not proposed for compression classification. The corresponding results obtained on 4 s audio segments for BR2= 192, 128 kbit/s are shown in Tables 5 and 7 respectively.

In this scenario, both methods achieves similar classification performance. It is worth noting that the proposed method achieves better classification rates for higher bit-rates, whereas the LSQ method appears slightly more accurate in the case of low bit-rates.

As in the case of detection, we experimented how the classification performances vary with respect to audio file dura-

Actual vs Pred.	192	160	128	96	64
192	99.9	0.1	0.0	0.0	0.0
160	0.0	98.9	1.1	0.0	0.0
128	0.0	0.4	92.8	6.6	0.2
96	0.0	0.0	13.0	69.5	17.5
64	0.0	0.0	1.2	15.1	83.7

Table 4: Classification accuracy of the proposed method for BR2 = 192.

Actual vs Pred.	192	160	128	96	64
192	93.5	6.3	0.2	0.0	0.0
160	6.3	90.9	2.7	0.0	0.0
128	0.4	10.6	83.4	4.5	1.1
96	0.0	0.0	1.0	98.2	0.7
64	0.0	0.2	0.2	0.4	99.3

Table 5: Classification accuracy of LSQ method for BR2 = 192.

Actual vs Pred.	192	160	128	96	64
192	51.4	18.8	29.7	0.0	0.0
160	1.8	87.0	11.2	0.0	0.0
128	42.0	23.3	34.5	0.2	0.0
96	0.0	0.0	0.0	97.7	2.3
64	0.0	0.0	0.0	5.2	94.8

Table 6: Classification accuracy of the proposed method for BR2 = 128.

Actual vs Pred.	192	160	128	96	64
192	69.9	23.9	6.2	0.0	0.1
160	47.4	48.4	4.2	0.0	0.0
128	24.7	15.5	59.6	0.0	0.1
96	0.7	0.2	0.1	93.0	6.0
64	0.1	0.0	0.1	0.4	99.4

Table 7: Classification accuracy of LSQ method for BR2 = 128.

tion. The average classification accuracy for different BR2 (i.e. [192, 160, 128, 96, 64] kbit/s) and decreased audio file duration (i.e. [4, 2, 1, 1/2, 1/4, 1/8, 1/16] s) are shown in Figure 9 for both our method (a) and LSQ method (b). In the case of higher bit-rates, it is evident that the proposed method achieves better classification performance than the LSQ method. Noticeably, the performances of the proposed method suffer only a slight degradation up to 1/8 s audio segments, whereas the performances of the LSQ method usually drop for audio segments shorter than 1-2 seconds.

4. CONCLUSIONS

A method to detect the presence of double compression in a MP3 audio file has been presented. A statistical measure has been derived to measure the effect of double compression, that allows to decide if a MP3 file is single compressed or it has been double compressed and also to derive the bit-rate of the first compression. The algorithm is effective when the bit-rate of the second compression is higher than the bit-rate of the first one, and exhibits a good performance even when analyzing short temporal windows, opening the possi-

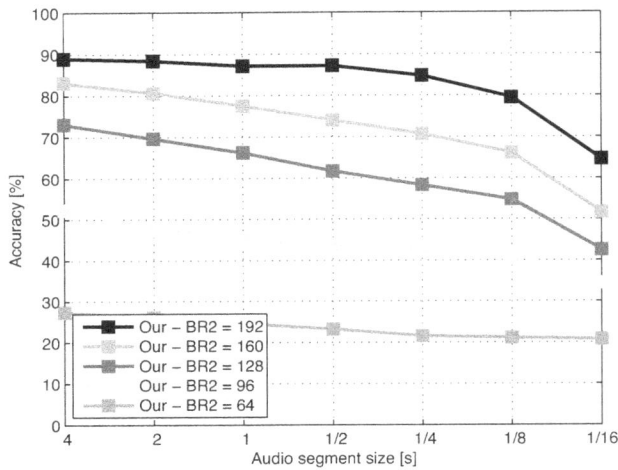

(a)

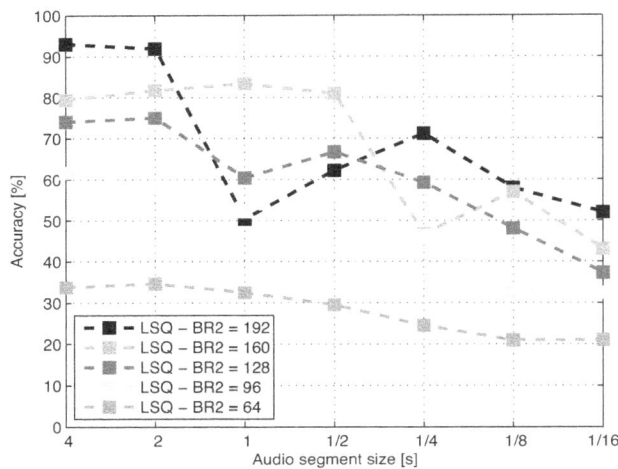

(b)

Figure 9: Accuracy of the classifiers with varying audio file duration: (a) proposed feature; (b) LSQ.

bility of using this feature for the localization of tampering in a MP3 file, whose study is left as future work.

5. ACKNOWLEDGMENTS

This work was partially supported by the REWIND Project funded by the Future and Emerging Technologies (FET) programme within the 7FP of the European Commission, under FET-Open grant number 268478.

6. REFERENCES

[1] T. Bianchi and A. Piva. Image forgery localization via block-grained analysis of JPEG artifacts. *Information Forensics and Security, IEEE Transactions on*, 7(3):1003 –1017, june 2012.

[2] T. Bianchi, A. D. Rosa, and A. Piva. Improved DCT coefficient analysis for forgery localization in JPEG images. In *Proc. of ICASSP 2011*, pages 2444–2447, May 2011.

[3] K. M. (incompetech.com). Artifact, danse macabre, just nasty, airport lounge, chee zee beach.

[4] Z. C. Lin, J. F. He, X. Tang, and C. K. Tang. Fast, automatic and fine-grained tampered JPEG image detection via DCT coefficient analysis. *Pattern Recognition*, 42(11):2492–2501, Nov. 2009.

[5] Q. Liu, A. Sung, and M. Qiao. Detection of double MP3 compression. *Cognitive Computation*, 2:291–296, 2010.

[6] J. Lukáš and J. Fridrich. Estimation of primary quantization matrix in double compressed JPEG images. In *Digital Forensic Research Workshop*, 2003.

[7] C. Manning, P. Raghavan, and H. Schütze. *Introduction to Information Retrieval*. Cambridge University Press, 2008.

[8] S. Moehrs, J. Herre, and R. Geiger. Analysing decompressed audio with the inverse decoder - towards an operative algorithm. In *Audio Engineering Society Convention 112*, 4 2002.

[9] A. C. Popescu and H. Farid. Statistical tools for digital forensics. In *In 6th International Workshop on Information Hiding*, pages 128–147. Springer-Verlag, Berlin-Heidelberg, 2004.

[10] M. Qiao, A. H. Sung, and Q. Liu. Revealing real quality of double compressed MP3 audio. In *Proceedings of the international conference on Multimedia*, MM '10, pages 1011–1014, New York, NY, USA, 2010. ACM.

[11] G. Snecdecor and W. Cochran. *Statistical Methods*. Number v. 276 in Statistical Methods. John Wiley & Sons, 1991.

[12] R. Yang, Z. Qu, and J. Huang. Detecting digital audio forgeries by checking frame offsets. In *ACM Multimedia and Security Workshop*, pages 21–26, 2008.

[13] R. Yang, Z. Qu, and J. Huang. Exposing MP3 audio forgeries using frame offsets. *ACM Trans. Multimedia Comput. Commun. Appl.*, 8(2S):35:1–35:20, Sept. 2012.

[14] R. Yang, Y. Q. Shi, and J. Huang. Defeating fake-quality MP3. In *ACM Multimedia and Security Workshop*, pages 117–124, 2009.

[15] R. Yang, Y. Q. Shi, and J. Huang. Detecting double compression of audio signal. In *SPIE Conference on Media Forensics and Security*, 2010.

Region of Interest Signalling for Encrypted JPEG Images

Dominik Engel
Salzburg University of Applied
Sciences
Urstein Süd 1
Puch/Salzburg, Austria
dengel@en-trust.at

Andreas Uhl
University of Salzburg
Dept. of Computer Sciences
Jakob-Haringer-Str. 2
Salzburg, Austria
uhl@cosy.sbg.ac.at

Andreas Unterweger
University of Salzburg
Dept. of Computer Sciences
Jakob-Haringer-Str. 2
Salzburg, Austria
aunterweg@cosy.sbg.ac.at

ABSTRACT

We propose and evaluate different methods to signal position and size of encrypted RoIs (Regions of Interest) in JPEG images. After discussing various design choices regarding the encoding of RoI coordinates with a minimal amount of bits, we discuss both, existing and newly proposed approaches to signal the encoded coordinates inside JPEG images. By evaluating the different signalling methods on various data sets, we show that several of our proposed encoding methods outperform JBIG in this special use case. Furthermore, we show that one of our proposed signalling methods allows length-preserving lossless signalling, i.e., storing RoI coordinates in a format-compliant way inside the JPEG images without quality loss or change of file size.

Categories and Subject Descriptors

E.2 [**Data**]: Data Storage Representations—*Object representation*; E.4 [**Data**]: Coding and Information Theory—*Data compaction and compression*; I.4.2 [**Image Processing and Computer Vision**]: Compression (Coding)—*JPEG*

General Terms

Algorithms, Theory, Measurement

Keywords

JPEG, Region of Interest, Coordinates, Encoding, Signalling

1. INTRODUCTION

In the last decade, a large number of region of interest encryption approaches have been proposed, especially for image and video formats using DCT-domain-based compression, like JPEG [12]. Although the human eye is capable of detecting encrypted picture regions easily, state-of-the-art software is not. There have been attempts to detect encrypted picture regions automatically [3], i.e., without the need to signal them explicitly. However, despite their reported near-100% accuracy, it is clear that perfect detection is not possible, albeit necessary for correct decryption in most cases.

Therefore, there is an immanent need to store the encrypted RoIs' coordinates inside the JPEG file in order to have them available during decryption. As the JPEG file format has no means of signalling encrypted regions, unlike JPEG2000 [1], different methods of encoding these coordinates have to be evaluated and a detailed analysis of possible signalling methods is required.

All RoI encryption approaches for JPEG proposed so far handle RoI signalling in one of three ways. The first method involves using JPEG comment segments with an unspecified coordinate encoding [2], which is straight-forward, but does not take into account that some applications do not tolerate size changes of the JPEG file. Thus, we explore different options and present solutions for a variety of typical practical contraints.

The second and most common signalling method relies on an external signalling channel [4]. As signalling RoIs in the JPEG image itself has significant advantages as compared to using a separate channel, this paper proposes and evaluates possibilities to store coordinates of encrypted RoIs inside the JPEG images themselves.

Finally, the third signalling method is to omit signalling details altogether [13], which can make decryption impossible or dependent on human RoI identification. As this is not acceptable in most cases, an analysis of encoding and signalling methods for encrypted RoIs in JPEG images is required.

This paper is structured as follows: In Section 2, we discuss design choices for RoI coordinate encodings and select a subset thereof for further evaluation. In Section 3, we propose different methods to signal the encoded coordinates inside a JPEG file. Subsequently, in Section 4, we evaluate all encoding and signalling methods in order to find appropriate combinations for different use cases before we conclude the paper in Section 5.

2. ROI COORDINATE ENCODING

Before the RoI coordinates can be signalled, they have to be encoded appropriately. As the number of signalled bits may be limited or even influence the picture quality, depending on the signalling method used, a compact encoding is desired. In this Section, we discuss several design choices for encodings, aiming at listing a set of practically useable encodings to be evaluated in Section 4.

As most state-of-the-art encryption approaches for JPEG

Name	Explicit	Value encoding	Differential	Bits per RoI	Overhead bits per file
Bitmap	–	Fixed length	N/A	0	n_{iMCU}
List	✓	Fixed length	–	$2 \cdot \lceil log_2(n_{iMCU} + 1) \rceil$	$2 \cdot \lceil log_2(n_{iMCU} + 1) \rceil$
VList	✓	Exp. Golomb	–	Variable	2
DList	✓	Signed Exp. Golomb	✓	Variable	2
ACBitmap	–	Fixed + ABAC	N/A	0	Variable
ACList	✓	Fixed + ABAC	–	Variable	Variable
ACVList	✓	Exp. G. + ABAC	–	Variable	Variable
ACDList	✓	S. Exp. G. + ABAC	✓	Variable	Variable
JBitmap	–	JBIG	–	Variable	12 (header only)

Table 1: List of coordinate encodings to be evaluated and their respective storage requirements

operate on a block [15] or iMCU (interleaved Minimum Coding Unit, multiple luminance and the corresponding chrominance blocks) level [22], coordinates are limited to iMCU granularity. Note that this limitation is also imposed – often self-imposed [3] – on format-independent encryption approaches which operate in the image domain.

Furthermore, chrominance subsampling is assumed to be 4:2:0 [14] as it is the default setting in the JPEG reference software and widely used [20]. This enforces a fixed iMCU size of six blocks, four of which are luminance blocks [12], limiting the coordinate granularity to rectangular image blocks of $16 \cdot 16$ pixels size.

Subsequently, the following variables are used: w and h denote a picture's width and height in pixels, respectively. Furthermore, the width and height in iMCUs are defined as $w_{iMCU} = \lceil \frac{w}{16} \rceil$ and $h_{iMCU} = \lceil \frac{h}{16} \rceil$, respectively. In addition, $n_{iMCU} = w_{iMCU} \cdot h_{iMCU}$ denotes the total number of iMCUs in a picture. Finally, n_{RoI} specifies the number of RoIs to be encoded. All coordinate encodings described in the subsequent subsections are summarized in Table 1 using the aforementioned variables.

2.1 Implicit vs. explicit encoding

Coordinates can be encoded either implicitly or explicitly. While implicit encoding entails deriving the actual coordinates locally, e.g., from the position of bit patterns in a bitmap, explicit encoding stores the actual coordinates globally so that they can be read directly. Hence, the simplest form of implicit encoding, i.e., a bitmap for all iMCUs where a zero bit means "not encrypted" and a one bit means "encrypted", requires n_{iMCU} bits to be stored (see Table 1: "Bitmap").

In contrast, explicit coordinate encoding requires storing a list of coordinates, specifying the location and size of each RoI. Both, location and size, are described by a horizontal and vertical component, referred to as X and Y coordinate, respectively, yielding four coordinates in total.

In addition, it is necessary to specify a special coordinate signalling the end of the coordinate list. For the sake of simplicity and practicality, we subsequently use a RoI with a size of zero to signal the end of the list. This is reflected in the per-file overhead of all explicit encodings listed in Table 1 accounting for the additional end-of-list entry as storing n_{RoI} RoIs requires $n_{RoI} + 1$ list entries in total. Each list entry consists of 4 coordinates, 2 of which are X and Y coordinates, respectively.

2.2 Component vs. index encoding

Although separate X and Y coordinates allow locating

the encrypted RoIs easily, two components (X and Y) need to be stored to specify one location. When using a fixed bit length per component, the X and Y coordinate require $\lceil log_2(w_{iMCU} + 1) \rceil$ and $\lceil log_2(h_{iMCU} + 1) \rceil$ bits of space, respectively.

Alternatively, an index can be assigned to each iMCU, starting with zero for the top-left-most iMCU and increasing in the left-to-right and top-to-bottom direction. This way, a location identified by two components (X and Y) can be specified by a single index which requires $\lceil log_2(n_{iMCU} + 1) \rceil$ bits when using a fixed bit length per index. Note that this is always shorter than or in the worst case as long as signalling two separate components since $\lceil log_2(n_{iMCU} + 1) \rceil = \lceil log_2(w_{iMCU} \cdot h_{iMCU} + 1) \rceil \leq \lceil log_2(w_{iMCU}) + log_2(h_{iMCU}) + 1 \rceil \leq \lceil log_2(w_{iMCU} + 1) \rceil + \lceil log_2(h_{iMCU} + 1) \rceil$, which is the number of bits required for two separately stored X and Y coordinates. Thus, index encoding is to be preferred over component encoding and all explicit encodings listed in Table 1 encode iMCU indices instead of X and Y coordinates.

2.3 Fixed-length vs. variable-length encoding

As the picture width and height are known, the maximum number of bits required to encode one iMCU index can be determined easily. If this fixed bit length is used for all indices, encoding one RoI requires $2 \cdot \lceil log_2(n_{iMCU}) \rceil$ bits in total (see Section 2.2), the factor of two being required to account for both, the location and size of the RoI (see Section 2.1). This way, each encoded RoI requires the same number of bits, regardless of its own size and location (see Table 1: "List").

As RoIs usually do not span the whole picture, using a constant number of bits which allows specifying the whole picture size can be disadvantageous. Similarly, RoI locations on the top-left require a high number of bits, although their corresponding iMCU start indices are small. Hence, the use of variable-length encoding for both iMCU indices, specifying the encrypted RoI's location and size, is to be evaluated. One method for variable-length coding are Exponential-Golomb codes as used e.g., for encoding a subset of H.264 syntax element values [19]. As a RoI's position and size (represented as iMCU indices) are always positive, a zeroth order (i.e., $k = 0$) unsigned Exponential-Golomb code ("ue(v)" following the notation of the H.264 standard [11]) can be used to encode them. Table 2 shows examples of values and their respective encoded bit representation.

As can be seen, a value of zero can be signalled using one bit. Hence, an end-of-list entry (with position and size being zero) can be signalled using two bits (see Table 1). Gener-

Value	ue(v) code word	se(v) code word
...	–	...
-4	–	0001001
-3	–	00111
-2	–	00101
-1	–	011
0	1	1
1	010	010
2	011	00100
3	00100	00110
4	00101	0001000
...	...	...

Table 2: List of exemplary values and their respective zeroth order Exponential-Golomb code words. Hyphens denote invalid value ranges

ally, any positive integer value x requires $2 \cdot \lceil log_2(x+2) \rceil - 1$ bits. Thus, one iMCU index requires a maximum of $2 \cdot \lceil log_2(n_{iMCU} + 2) \rceil - 1$ bits. As the actual number of bits can be smaller, depending on the actual iMCU indices to be encoded, the storage requirements per RoI are variable when using Exponential-Golomb encoded list entries (see Table 1: "VList" for variable-length coded list), possibly reducing the number of stored bits compared to fixed-length encoding.

2.4 Differential encoding

Although variable-length coding reduces the storage requirements when encoding small indices, the converse is true for large indices, i.e., indices identifying iMCUs at the bottom-right of a picture. In order to overcome this drawback, each index can be stored relative to its predecessor, replacing the actual value to be encoded by a differential value which is very likely to be smaller. For example, a location/size pair (l_2, s_2) can be encoded as $(l_2 - l_1, s_2 - s_1)$ relative to its preceding location/size pair (l_1, s_1). As all RoIs are known, their order in the RoI list can be chosen so that the differential values to be encoded are minimal in terms of size.

However, it is not guaranteed that there is an order of entries in the RoI list so that all differences are positive, thus requiring the ability to encode negative differences as well. Signed Exponential-Golomb codes which support both, positive and negative values, are described in the H.264 standard [11]. Following the latter's notation, such zeroth order codes are referred to as "se(v)". Table 2 shows examples of values and their respective encoded bit representation.

In general, any integer value x requires $2 \cdot \lceil log_2(2 \cdot |x| + 2) \rceil - 1$ bits as signed Exponential-Golomb code word, which is more than the amount required for the respective unsigned Exponential-Golomb code word. Nonetheless, we include this encoding approach as its storage requirements depend on the RoI's coordinates' differences (see Table 1: "DList" for differentially encoded list) which depend on the values and ordering of the RoIs, unlike all other encodings.

2.5 Entropy coding

Each of the encodings described above makes use of different representations and/or properties of the list of RoI coordinates. However, none of them aims at effectively eliminating redundancy. Thus, a modified version of each encoding is included in Table 1 which essentially adds an entropy

coding step after the original encoding process, indicated by a "C" (for compressed) prefix in the encoding's name.

Arithmetic coding [24] (prefixed with an additional "A") is chosen for the entropy coding step as it theoretically allows for quasi optimal, i.e., close-to-entropy, performance. As the number of different values to be encoded is equal to n_{RoI} for n_{ROI} RoI location/size pairs and smaller than or equal to $2 \cdot n_{RoI}$ for separately encoded location and size values, binary arithmetic coding (abbreviated BAC in Table 1) calculated in fixed-precision integer arithmetic as described in the JPEG standard [12] is evaluated.

As signalling the symbols' probabilities (or the corresponding subintervals) would require additional bits, adaptive coding, i.e., the dynamic adjustment of the symbol probabilities, is used to optimize coding efficiency [19]. Starting with equal probabilities for both symbols, zero and one, the subinterval ranges are adjusted according to the changing symbol frequencies during encoding. Note that end-of-stream markers can be omitted as the decoding process can stop the arithmetic decoding process as soon as the end-of-list marker (a RoI with location and size zero) is found.

2.6 Bi-level image compression

As the implicitly encoded bitmap described in Section 2.1 is in fact a bi-level image, the use of a compressor which is optimized for this type of images has to be evaluated for comparison. Due to its widespread use, we choose the JBIG compression standard [9] in combination with one of its application profiles [10] for this task (see Table 1: "JBitmap" for JBIG-compressed bitmap).

In order to compensate for its relatively large file header with a total size of 20 bytes, we shorten the former by the eight bytes which signal the image's width and height as they can also be derived otherwise, e.g., from the JPEG picture. This reduces the total per-file overhead to twelve bytes, thus allowing for a fairer comparison.

2.7 Summary

A number of choices have to be made when designing an encoding for a list of RoIs, few of which are clear without prior evaluation. As outlined in Section 2, encoding iMCU indices always requires less than or as many bits as encoding separate X and Y coordinates, Thus, all encodings to be evaluated encode iMCU indices. As most other design criteria of possible encodings depend on either the number and/or size of the RoIs and/or the picture, a selected subset of possible encodings (see Table 1) covering all of the aforementioned criteria has to be evaluated in Section 4.

3. ROI SIGNALLING

The encoded RoIs' coordinates need to be signalled in some form in order to identify the RoIs at a later point in time, e.g., during the decryption process. Thus, in this Section, we propose a number of different ways to store the encoded RoI coordinates directly inside the JPEG file. In order to account for the different needs of conceivable use cases, the proposed signalling methods are chosen to cover a number of different combinations of the following aspects:

1. **Format compliance:** The strict fulfillment of all syntactical and semantical requirements imposed by the JPEG standard [12]

2. **Losslessness**: The exact preservation of all (visible) picture data

3. **Availability**: The guarantee that the proposed method will work on every JPEG picture

4. **Length-preservation**: The guarantee that the picture's file size does not change (suitable for length-preserving encryption methods like [22])

Furthermore, the capacity, i.e., the amount of storable bits, of each signalling method is given. Note the capacity of some of the proposed methods depends on the picture and/or its metadata. As the number of RoIs is usually not known in advance for all pictures, all methods need to be evaluated in terms of usability for storing encoded RoI coordinates as proposed in Section 2, which is done in Section 4.

All proposed methods are described with regards to the aforementioned aspects and summarized in Table 3 for convenience. For reasons of practicality, we assume that all JPEG pictures are Baseline JPEG pictures [12] with three color components – Y, Cb and Cr, i.e., one luminance and two chrominance components. Note that most methods will, however, work with differently coded JPEG pictures (e.g., arithmetically coded ones) as well.

3.1 Use of COM and APP segments

The first method, the insertion of a COM (Comment) segment into the JPEG file according to Annex B of the JPEG standard [12], has already been proposed by others (e.g., [2]). One COM segment may contain up to 65533 payload bytes, plus its marker (2 bytes) and length field (2 bytes), totalling to 65537 stored bytes. As the number of COM segments is theoretically unlimited, so is the total capacity of this signalling method. Signalling n bits requires $n_{COM} = \left\lceil \frac{\left\lceil \frac{n}{8} \right\rceil}{65533} \right\rceil$ COM segments with a total of $(n_{COM} - 1 + \epsilon) \cdot 65537 + 4 + \left\lceil \left\lceil \frac{n}{8} \right\rceil \ mod \ 65533 \right\rceil$ bytes, where mod denotes the integer modulus operator and ϵ is a correction factor of 1, if there is no remainder (of the modulus operation), and 0 otherwise. The rounding to full bytes is due to the fact that a COM segment's length field is expressed in bytes, not bits.

As an alternative to the COM segment, an Application Data (APP) segment can be used, which is equivalent in terms of structure. As there are 16 different APP markers, it is theoretically possible to encode four more bits into an APP segment than into a comment segment of equal total size. As the capacity is otherwise the same, signalling n bits in APP markers requires $n_{APP} = \left\lceil \frac{\left\lceil \frac{n}{4} \right\rceil}{2 \cdot 65533.5} \right\rceil$ APP segments with a total of $(n_{APP} - 1 + \epsilon) \cdot 65537 + 4 + \left\lceil \frac{\left\lceil \left\lceil \frac{n}{4} \right\rceil \ mod \ (2 \cdot 65533.5) \right\rceil}{2} \right\rceil$ bytes. Due to the additional 4 bits per segment, APP segment signalling is to be preferred over COM segment signalling in terms of capacity. However, there may already be APP segments in the JPEG file, in which case the gain in capacity may be reduced. Moreover, there may be a border case in which all different APP segment types are already present in the file, making it impossible to store any data in this way.

One commonly used APP segment type is APP$_1$, typically storing data in the Exchangeable Image File Format (EXIF)

[6]. If such data is present, but not crucial for further processing, it can be replaced by encoded RoI coordinates. However, this method of stripping EXIF data depends on the presence of the latter and is usally very limited in terms of capacity. A more detailed description of this method and its capacity is provided in [5], which is why it is not evaluated separately herein.

3.2 Use of dummy tables

Although JPEG Baseline pictures with three components use the maximum number of Huffman tables per file, it is possible to add an arbitrary amount of dummy Tables at the end of the file by inserting Huffman table (DHT) segments containing encoded bits. One such Table can be identified easily during the decoding process. As the "defined" code words are not actually used, they do not necessarily need to be valid. Hence, it is possible to define up to 16 sets of 255 theroretically contradictory maximum length Huffman code words defining one 8-bit value each. In total, this allows storing $16 \cdot 255 \cdot 8 = 32640$ bits at the expense of $4099 \cdot 8 = 32792$ stored bits (see [12, p. 45]). Note that an additional four bytes are required for the marker (two bytes) and the length field (two bytes) per segment. As an arbitrary amount of dummy Tables with the same destination identifier can be inserted, the capacity of this approach is theoretically unlimited.

Similar to dummy Huffman tables, dummy quantization tables can be defined by inserting Quantization Table (DQT) segments. One such segment can store 8 bits for each of the 64 quantization table positions. This allows for storing $64 \cdot 8 = 512$ bits at the expense of $65 \cdot 8 = 520$ stored bits (see [12, p. 44]). Again, the four bytes of overhead for the marker (two bytes) and additional length field (two bytes) have to be accounted for once per segment. The capacity is, again, unlimited due to the theoretically unlimited amount of dummy Tables when using the same destination identifier.

3.3 Information hiding

As an alternative to bit-stream-based changes to signal the RoIs, classic information hiding approaches, especially steganographic ones, can be used. An overview of state-of-the art methods, of which we consider the widely used coefficient-based approaches, i.e., those which alter bits in the DCT domain, is given in [5]. As encrypted RoIs can typically be identified by the human eye, the main aim of using information hiding for signalling is not hiding the bits, but storing them within the image itself. Thus, hiding schemes like F5 [23] which are known to be vulnerable to attacks [7] are considered as well.

The approaches' capacities is not evaluated herein as it has been evaluated in the literature, e.g., [8] for coefficient-based information hiding. For JPEG images with one channel, i.e., grey-scale images, a capacity of 0.02 bits per non-zero AC coefficient has been reported. As we assume having three channels per image, it is safe to use the aforementioned capacity as a lower bound, requiring only to determine the average number of non-zero AC coefficients of the test data. Note that information hiding is not necessarily lossy as reversible approaches have been proposed (e.g., [16, 18]).

3.4 Length-preserving signalling

A method without overhead is the use of bits occupied by unused code words in the Huffman tables, i.e., code words

Method	Compliant	Lossless	Available	Length-preserving	Capacity (bits)
COM segment	✓	✓	✓	–	∞
APP segment	✓	✓	–	–	∞
EXIF data stripping	✓	✓*	–	✓	Variable
Dummy DHT	✓	✓	✓	–	∞
Dummy DQT	✓	✓	✓	–	∞
Steganographic (coefficients)	✓	–**	✓	Depends	Variable
Reuse of unused DHT entries	✓	✓	–	✓	Variable
DQT bit stealing	✓	Depends	–	✓	Variable
Data before first marker	–	✓	✓	–	∞
Data after last byte	–	✓	✓	–	∞

* Original EXIF data will be lost, ** Reversible techniques proposed (e.g., [16, 18])

Table 3: List of proposed methods for RoI signalling in JPEG pictures broken down by the aspects listed in Section 3

which are not used throughout the file. Although it is simple to find unused code words, even when e.g., decrypting, the number of unused code words may be very low or even zero, if the Huffman table only contains used code words or if there is no Huffman table to begin with. Even if there are unused code words, each of them only allows for storing 8 bits. Furthermore, as the number of unused code words varies from file to file, this method's capacity highly depends on the encoder which created the file and therefore has to be evaluated.

Another method of storing encoded RoI coordinates is by stealing bits from the quantization table(s), i.e., by modifying the bits of some quantization table entries, if there is a quantization table in the first place. There are two possibilities of doing so: One way is to change one bit at a time, starting at the high frequency entries of the chrominance quantization tables. After each modification, the JPEG file is decoded and compared to the version with unchanged quantization tables. Although this is computationally very expensive, it can also be done during the decoding process to find out which bits of the quantization tables were used. However, the capacity is highly dependent on the picture and possibly zero. Alternatively, if distortions are acceptable up to a certain degree, a fixed number of bits can be used, omitting the trial-and-error process described before. Although this allows for a higher capacity, it does so at the expense of picture quality, which has to be assessed.

3.5 Non-format-compliant signalling

A way to losslessly signal encoded RoI coordinates is to insert them at either the very beginning of the file, i.e., before the first marker, or at its end, i.e., after the last data byte. Adding data in this way is, however, not format compliant as the standard only allows for 0xFF fill bytes preceding each marker. In addition, in both cases, special care has to be taken in order to escape 0xFF payload bytes which would otherwise be interpreted as markers. Depending on how escaping is done, this may lead to additional overhead. As this method of signalling encoded RoI coordinates is not format compliant, most image viewers and editors will not be able to open files edited by it anymore.

4. EVALUATION

In order to evaluate the RoI signalling methods presented

in Section 3 in combination with the coordinate encoding methods proposed in Section 2, we first evaluate each aspect separately and subsequently combine them. As a practical JPEG RoI encryption application we choose the encryption of people in pictures of surveillance cameras.

In total, eleven test sets are used – three indoors and eight outdoors sets. The three indoors data sets[1] with a total of 3271 pictures with a spatial resolution of $360 \cdot 288$ pixels each are courtesy of the EPSRC funded MOTINAS project (EP/D033772/1). The eight outdoors data sets[2] with a total of 67616 pictures with a spatial resolution of $640 \cdot 480$ pixels each are courtesy of EPSRC project GR/S98146. All data sets include ground truth for people's coordinates within each picture, which is subsequently used as set of RoIs to be encoded and signalled. RoIs which exceed one or more of the pictures' borders are omitted.

4.1 Encoded RoI bit length assessment

In order to perform coordinate encoding of the data sets' RoIs, we implemented the different encoding methods presented in Section 2 in Python, except for arithmetic encoding and JBIG compression, for which we used the Python implementation of David MacKay[3] and JBIG-KIT[4], respectively. As we restrict the coordinates' accuracy to iMCUs of $16 \cdot 16$ pixels size (see Section Section 2), we rounded the data sets' RoI coordinates so that all blocks containing an RoI were considered to be encrypted as a whole. Before actually encoding the rounded coordinates, they were translated into iMCU indices as explained in Section 2.2.

Tables 4 and 5 show the average number of bits per picture required to encode the RoIs of the indoors and the outdoors data sets, respectively. As the RoI count of the pictures has a significant impact on the number of bits required, the results are grouped by RoI count, considering only pictures from the data set with the stated number of RoIs. Note that pictures without, i.e., zero, RoIs are omitted as they are discussed separately in the second part of this Section. It is clearly visible from the results of both data sets that entropy coding (in the right half of each Table) always im-

---

[1] ftp://motinas.elec.qmul.ac.uk/pub/av_people/
[2] http://groups.inf.ed.ac.uk/vision/BEHAVEDATA/INTERACTIONS/
[3] http://shedskin.googlecode.com/svn/trunk/examples/ac_encode.py
[4] http://www.cl.cam.ac.uk/~mgk25/jbigkit/

RoIs	Pictures	Bitmap	List	VList	DList	ACBitmap	ACList	ACVList	ACDList	JBitmap
1	1907	414.00	36.00	*30.94*	34.94	196.00	31.27	31.04	33.70	206.96
2	959	414.00	54.00	61.53	56.53	196.00	*52.07*	59.01	54.20	229.30
Non-0	2866	414.00	42.01	41.15	42.15	150.99	38.22	*40.38*	40.55	214.42

Table 4: Average number of bits required to encode the RoIs of each picture of the indoors data set with a given number of RoIs. The best, i.e., minimal, number of bits for each distinct picture subset is italicized

RoIs	Pictures	Bitmap	List	VList	DList	ACBitmap	ACList	ACVList	ACDList	JBitmap
1	1444	1200.00	44.00	*33.58*	37.58	138.32	35.64	34.04	36.05	212.34
2	3449	1200.00	66.00	64.72	55.80	241.83	58.78	60.92	*52.26*	231.46
3	2820	1200.00	88.00	92.81	81.97	255.98	80.66	85.31	*74.41*	238.52
4	1877	1200.00	110.00	135.89	106.16	333.66	105.88	121.25	*96.51*	245.66
5	10822	1200.00	132.00	166.46	135.98	393.94	128.51	150.00	*122.08*	260.68
6	814	1200.00	154.00	204.50	163.71	433.94	149.21	180.02	*144.71*	267.50
7	3	1200.00	176.00	232.67	168.67	430.67	177.00	208.00	*153.00*	266.67
8	2	1200.00	198.00	270.00	176.00	430.00	197.50	247.50	*158.50*	256.00
Non-0	21234	1200.00	108.38	129.92	107.54	329.75	103.34	117.70	*97.18*	248.64

Table 5: Average number of bits required to encode the RoIs of each picture of the outdoors data set with a given number of RoIs. The best, i.e., minimal, number of bits for each distinct picture subset is italicized

proves encoding efficiency, i.e., it reduces the number of bits, except in the case of only one RoI when using a list of variable-length coded indices ("VList"). Thus, implementing an entropy coding step following the actual coordinate encoding step should always be considered when encoding more than one RoI. In the case of a single RoI, variable-length coded indices ("VList") give the best results on average over all eleven test sets.

For a higher number of RoIs, the outdoors data sets (Table 5) allow for a more thorough analysis due to the data sets' widespread range of RoI counts. They clearly show that a differentially coded list of values which is entropy coded ("ACDList") always gives the best results. The higher the number of RoIs is, the higher the bit savings of this method are compared to all of the others besides "JBitmap". Note that there are only very few pictures with seven and eight RoIs, respectively, making the results only reliable for up to six RoIs. Nonetheless, averaging the number of bits spent over all pictures with RoIs (last line of Table 5) reveals that the "ACDList" encoding is optimal for data sets which contain a high number of pictures with more than one RoI. The maximum number of bits required for one list of RoIs over all data sets (not listed in the Table) is 219 bits.

Additionally considering the 959 pictures of the indoors data set (Table 4) containing two RoIs shows that an entropy coded list of indices ("ACList") yields a good performance as well, albeit only smaller by about two bits in this special case as compared to the "ACDList" encoding. Interestingly, the "ACVList" encoding shows the best overall performance over the complete indoors data sets, being 0.17 bits shorter than the "ACDList" encoding on average. This is due to the fact that the number of pictures in the indoors data set with one RoI is higher than the number of pictures with two RoIs and that the "ACVList" encoding requires the smallest number of bits for encoding one RoI as compared to all other entropy-coding-based encodings in the indoors data sets.

Surprisingly, JBIG compression performs significantly worse than most of our proposed approaches, which is mainly due to the large overhead caused by the JBIG file header. However, it is clearly visible from the outdoors data set in Table 5 that the JBIG based encoding requires fewer bits per additional RoI compared to all other approaches. While our "ACDList" approach requires on average 108.66 bits more for encoding six RoIs than it does for one RoI, "JBitmap" only requires 55.16 bits more. Thus, it is expected that JBIG compression outperforms our approaches for large numbers of RoIs.

As encoding zero RoIs, i.e., the fact that no RoIs are present, is independent of the data set used, both, Table 4 and 5, do not include pictures without RoIs. In order to assess the encoding methods' RoI encoding performance of pictures of this type in general, we used artificial images with different spatial dimensions, all of which had an aspect ratio, i.e., a width-to-height ratio, of 4:3 as is common in surveillance applications. Moreover, all image sizes were rounded to the next integer multiple of 16.

Figure 1 shows the number of bits required to encode zero RoIs for all proposed encodings with picture sizes ranging from $16 \cdot 16$ to $1920 \cdot 1440$ pixels in steps of 16 pixels in width. Although the aspect ratio is fixed (despite the small errors due to rounding), the X axis shows the square root of the image area, making the results applicable to arbitrary aspect ratios. The Y axis shows the required number of bits using a logarithmic scale.

The bit requirements for "VList" and "DList" as well as for their entropy coded variants, "ACVList" and "ACDList", are always constant, regardless of the picture's spatial dimensions, thus forming a combined line at two bits. This property makes the four encodings ideal for quasi all picture sizes, except for a size of $16 \cdot 16$, which we consider of having no practical use. Thus, each of the four encodings is recommended for encoding zero RoIs at all spatial picture dimensions used in practice.

Conversely, the "Bitmap" encoding's requirements in terms of bits increase quadratically with picture width (linearly with increasing picture area), making it inconvenient for

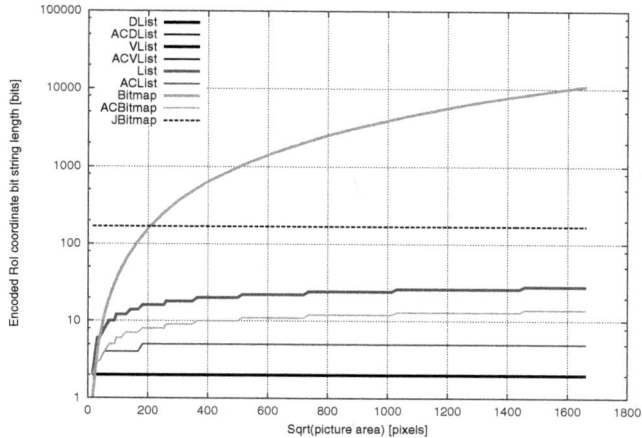

Figure 1: Number of bits required to encode zero RoIs for different spatial picture dimensions

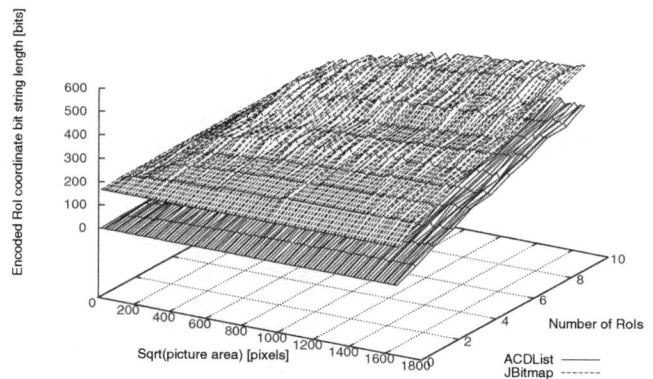

Figure 2: Number of bits required to encode a number of randomly generated, artificial RoIs for different spatial picture dimensions

practical use for pictures without RoIs. Note that entropy coding ("ACBitmap") reduces the required number of bits significantly, albeit still dependent on the picture's dimensions. The same is true for the "List" and "ACList" encodings, which are similarly inconvenient for encoding zero RoIs in practice.

Although the "JBitmap" encoding has a constant overhead, it is significantly larger (168 bits) than the overhead required by our Exponential-Golomb-based approaches described above (2 bits). Thus, it is not recommended to be used to encode zero RoIs.

As both, the indoors and the outdoors data sets, only cover a limited range of picture dimensions and RoI counts, we additionally assessed the bit length requirements of the proposed encodings using artificial test data sets. In order to artificially create RoIs that resemble real-world characteristics we use the following approach to create n_{RoI} RoIs:

- A random quadtree decomposition up to a maximum level l is created for a test image of dimensions $w \cdot h$, following the approach for creating uniformly distributed quadtree decompositions described in [17].

- n_{RoI} leaves are selected randomly from the set of all leaves (in case the number of leaves is less than n_{RoI}, a new quadtree is generated).

- For each selected leaf in the quadtree, a RoI is created with dimensions $q_w \cdot q_h$ where $q_w = \lceil f_w \cdot w \rceil$ with f_w chosen randomly such that $m \leq f_w < 1$. m denotes the minimum relative width and can be specified in $0 < m \leq 1$. q_h is chosen in an analogous manner.

- The position of the RoI is chosen randomly, ensuring that the RoI fits into the area covered by the leaf: Let (l_x, l_y) be the coordinates of the upper left-hand corner of the selected leaf with dimensions $l_w \cdot l_h$. The horizontal position of the RoI is determined as $\lfloor l_x + f_x \cdot (l_w - q_w) \rfloor$, with f_x chosen randomly and $0 \leq f_x < 1$. The vertical position of the RoI is determined in an analogous manner.

The parameters l and m can be used to tune the average size of the generated RoIs. In our test setup, we use $l = 3$ and $m = 0.2$ to simulate real-world RoIs.

Figure 2 depicts the number of bits required to encode $0 \leq n_{RoI} \leq 10$ randomly generated RoIs for various picture sizes (see above for details). Note that only "ACDList" and "JBitmap" are depicted for comparison for the sake of better graphical representation. All other encodings (not depicted) perform worse except for very small picture sizes which we do not consider being practical, as discussed above, with one exception described below. It is clearly visible that "JBitmap" does not outperform "ACDList" at any picture size or RoI count depicted. This is due to the former's large overhead, confirming that JBIG may only be suitable for a very large number of RoIs. As "ACVList" performed better than "ACDList" for a small number of RoIs, the two encodings are compared for $0 \leq n_{RoI} \leq 10$ randomly generated RoIs for various picture sizes. Figure 3 depicts the number of bits which are required by the "ACVList" encoding in addition to "ACDList"'s for any given configuration. Note that the X axis starts at 16 as a picture size of 0 is not practically useful. As in the real-world data sets, "ACDList" outperforms "ACVList" for a large number of RoIs. However, in some configurations with one or two RoIs, "ACDList" outperforms "ACVList" by a few bits. Nonetheless, the "ACDList" encoding is clearly the encoding of choice, when the number of RoIs is not known in advance and potentially large.

4.2 JPEG picture capacity assessment

As some of the signalling approaches described in Section 3 have an unknown embedding capacity, we evaluate the latter for our test data sets. The approaches considered herein are the reuse of unused DHT entries, steganographic approaches and DQT bit stealing as described in Section 3. To evaluate the embedding capacity when reusing unused DHT entries, we count the latter in the outdoors data sets' JPEG files, whose JPEG quality varies between approximately 95 and 100%. Those pictures which have a quality of approximately 100% do not have unused DHT entries at all. Conversely, the pictures which have a quality of approximately 95% allow using 214 entries on average with one byte of capacity each, i.e., 1712 bits in total. The minimum and maximum number of unused entries is 191 (corresponding to 1518 bits) and 343 (2744 bits), respectively, which, in our opinion, is surprisingly high.

As the outdoors data sets' approximate JPEG quality is

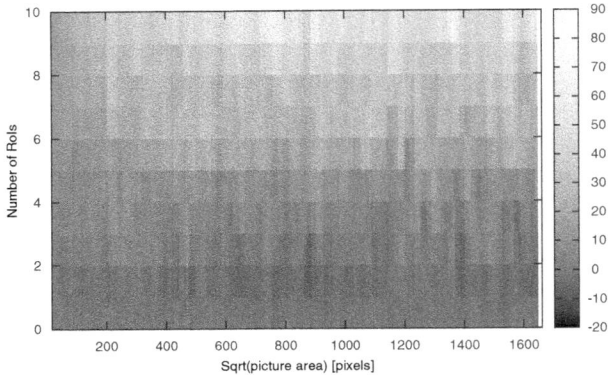

Figure 3: Additional number of bits required for the "ACVList" encoding to encode a number of randomly generated, artificial RoIs for different spatial picture dimensions compared to the "ACDList" encoding

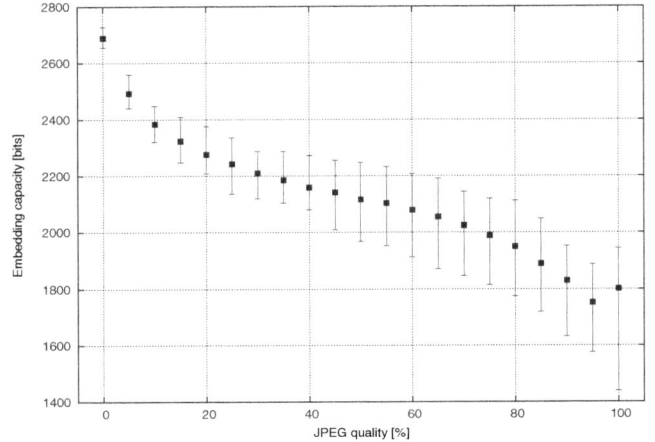

Figure 4: Average embedding capacity of the unused DHT entry reuse approach for different JPEG quality values for the pictures of the LIVE data base [21]. The bars indicate the minimum and maximum capacity for each quality value, respectively

within a very limited range, an evaluation spanning a wider range of JPEG quality values is necessary. As the indoors data sets are already compressed using a different compressor, applying JPEG compression would also recompress the existing artifacts, yielding results which are not representative. Thus, we use images from the LIVE data base [21] and compress them with the standard JPEG encoder with quality values ranging from 0 to 100% in 5% steps.

The results are depicted in Figure 4 and show that low JPEG quality values allow for a higher embedding capacity than high quality values. This is due to the standard JPEG encoder using a fixed DHT, making unused entries more likely for lower quality due to the stronger quantization and therefore longer runs with lower absolute coefficient values. Note that the embedding capacity for a quality value of 95% is approximately 1800 bits on average with a minimum value of about 1600 bits, which matches the outdoors data sets' capacity within a small bound.

To evaluate the embedding capacity of steganographic approaches, we use the approximation described in Section 3 estimating the embedding capacity as 0.02 bits per non-zero AC coefficient. Similar to the embedding method explained above, we count the non-zero AC coefficients in all JPEG images of the outdoors data sets. After omitting one image which is all black, we find an average number of about 195117 non-zero AC coefficients per file with a minimum and maximum of 49440 and 246679, respectively. This corresponds to an embedding capacity of about 3902 bits on average with a minimum of 988 bits.

Again, we also count the number of non-zero AC coefficients of the images from the LIVE data base with different JPEG quality values to cover a wider range of the latter. As can be seen in Figure 5, the number of non-zero AC coefficients and therefore the embedding capacity increases quasi linearly for increasing low JPEG quality values and exponentially with increasing high JPEG quality value (note the logarithmic Y scale). For a JPEG quality value of 95%, the embedding capacity is approximately 3000 bits on average with a minimum of about 2000 bits, which differs from the outdoors data sets' capacity, but is within the same order of magnitude.

Finally, we evaluate the DQT bit stealing approach. In or-

der to simulate a worst case bit-stealing scenario, we flip n bits of each 8-bit DQT entry from indices i_1 to i_2 in zig-zag order, i.e., in bit stream order of both, luminance and chrominance DQT.

To find suitable values for n, i_1 and i_2, we take a picture data set, decode each picture and then compare it with a decoded version with flipped QT Table entries for all possible values of n, i_1 and i_2. In order to assess the difference between the original and the modified picture, we measure the PSNR value between the two.

As the number of possible combinations of n, i_1 and i_2 is large, we evaluated them exhaustively on a smaller test set – the LIVE data base [21]. Using the JPEG reference encoder, we created Baseline JPEG images with default settings and 50, 75, 95 and 100% quality from the original, i.e., uncompressed, images.

Figure 6 shows the embedding capacity (in terms of total stolen bits, Y axis) over all images of a given JPEG quality so that the distortion of no image exceeds the depicted PSNR value (X axis). Note that the JPEG quality influences the embedding capacity significantly, as does the desired maximum distortion.

Surprisingly, the total capacity is very high, considering that changes of the DQT potentially influence all blocks of a picture. Depending on the desired target distortion, it is possible to embed several hundred bits.

Note that 100% quality does not allow embedding one bit so that no picture exceeds a distortion of 50dB. The same is true for all JPEG quality values when no distortion (∞ dB) is desired. Thus, this approach cannot be used for lossless embedding.

Attempting to verify these results for the outdoors data sets, we split the data sets into pictures with approximately 95% and 100% JPEG quality, respectively, using the obtained settings for a target quality of 35dB. Surprisingly, every picture in both sets exceeds a quality of 50dB compared to its unmodified version, indicating that the embedding capacity for a given target quality is highly dependent on the pictures themselves. Due to the lack of freely available and

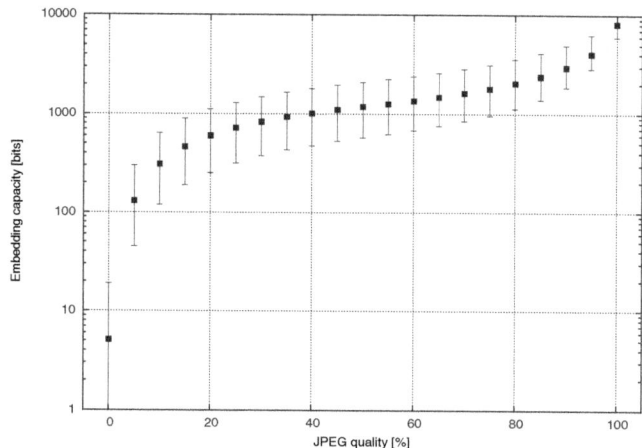

Figure 5: Average embedding capacity of steganographic approaches for different JPEG quality values for the pictures of the LIVE data base [21]. The bars indicate the minimum and maximum capacity for each quality value, respectively

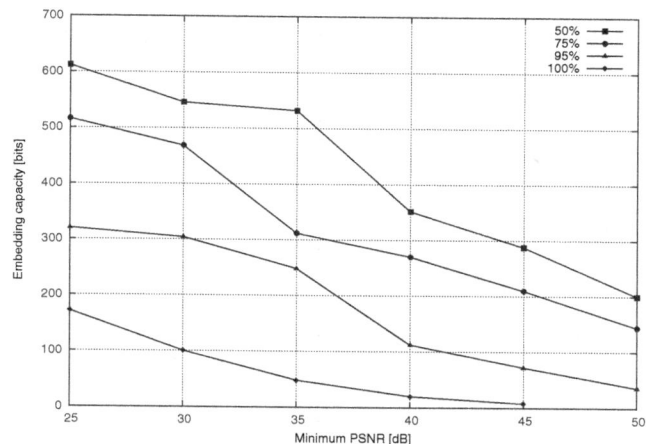

Figure 6: Embedding capacity of the DQT bit stealing approach for different JPEG quality values and maximum target distortions for the pictures of the LIVE data base [21]

practically relevant data sets, a thorough examination of this method with more pictures of different characteristics remains future work.

4.3 Combined encoding and signalling

Combining the results of the previous Sections, we subsequently evaluate the feasibility of the combined use of the proposed encoding and signalling methods in order to simulate the actual storage of RoI coordinates in the corresponding JPEG files. Due to the lack of freely available JPEG-encoded data sets with RoI ground truth, only the outdoors data sets can be assessed in this Section. Although this allows no general conclusions regarding the usefulness of the proposed approaches, it is possible to determine possible combinations of signalling and encoding methods suitable for the outdoors data sets, which cover a significant portion of practically relevant pictures and RoI counts for surveillance and encryption applications.

As the average number of bits for encoding RoI coordinates in the outdoors data sets is smallest when using our proposed "ACDList" approach (see Section 4.1), we consider the latter to be appropriate for encoding all RoIs. This choice is further supported by the fact that our "ACDList" approach is one of the few approaches which allows signalling the absence of RoIs by just two bits. Note that for data sets where zero or one RoI(s) are dominant, our "ACVList" approach allows using fewer bits.

Subsequently, we determine which of the signalling approaches described in Section 3 are able to provide enough embedding capacity to store the "ACDList"-encoded RoI coordinates for the outdoors data sets. Trivially, all approaches which offer infinite capacity can be used to signal the RoIs which require a maximum number of 219 bits with our proposed "ACDList" encoding. As format-compliant approaches are in general preferred over non-format-compliant ones, we suggest using COM segments as their overhead is smallest as compared to all other methods which offer infinite capacity (see Section 3).

The reuse of unused DHT entries allows for a largely suf-

ficient minimum capacity of 1518 bits in all pictures with approximately 95% JPEG quality, allowing for lossless and length-preserving RoI signalling. To our knowledge, this is the first time that such an approach has been proposed. However, the pictures with approximately 100% JPEG quality do not allow storing a single bit using this method, making it unusable in this scenario. Consequently, we suggest using this method instead of others whenever possible as its capacity is sufficient to store large numbers of RoIs without quality loss and change of file size.

If quality loss is acceptable, classical steganographic methods allow for a high capacity when using a generalized estimation of the embedding capacity. It is notable that the minimum estimated capacity of these approaches is lower (988 bits) than the minimum capacity provided by the reuse of unused DHT entries, if the latter is available (1518 bits). However, steganographic approaches can be used on practically any picture, making it the method of choice when quality loss is acceptable. Note that the actual capacity highly depends on the method used as well as on the desired distortion, which is outside of the scope of this paper. We refer to the available literature [5] for further details.

Finally, our proposed approach which steals bits from the DQT also allows signalling RoIs, although its capacity is limited and highly dependent on the desired quality in terms of PSNR as well as on the pictures' characteristics. As described in Section 4.2, further evaluations are required in order to determine the usefulness of this method. In general, it can be noted that its capacity is surprisingly high in all tested cases, but limited for large numbers of RoIs as well as for pictures with large spatial dimensions. As changing the DQTs typically influences all blocks of a picture, as opposed to most steganographic approaches, which operate on single blocks, steganographic approaches are recommended at this point, with our approach being an option to be considered as soon as it has been evaluated more thoroughly.

5. CONCLUSION

We proposed and evaluated several methods to encode and signal RoIs in JPEG images. Using a number of data sets, we determined that our proposed arithmetically coded differential lists of iMCU indices are superior to all other evaluated RoI coordinate encoding methods for a large range of RoI counts, outperforming JBIG in this special use case. Furthermore, we showed that using JPEG comment segments to store the encoded RoI coordinates causes the lowest overhead, if the file size is allowed to change. For scenarios which require length-preservation, we proposed a new method which reuses unused Huffman table entries. Although it is not always available, it allows for lossless and length-preserving signalling, if it is available. Finally, we showed that using quantization table bits allows for RoI signalling as well, although further tests are required in order to determine the general restrictions of this method.

6. ACKNOWLEDGMENTS

The authors would like to thank Matthew Sorell for his valuable ideas on which several of the RoI signalling methods are based. This work is supported by FFG Bridge project 832082.

7. REFERENCES

[1] M. Adams. The JPEG-2000 still image compression standard. ISO/IEC JTC 1/SC 29/WG 1 N 2412, Sept. 2001.

[2] T. E. Boult. PICO: Privacy through invertible cryptographic obscuration. In *IEEE/NFS Workshop on Computer Vision for Interactive and Intelligent Environments*, pages 27–38, Lexington, KY, USA, Nov. 2005.

[3] P. Carrillo, H. Kalva, and S. Magliveras. Compression Independent Reversible Encryption for Privacy in Video Surveillance. *EURASIP Journal on Information Security*, 2009:1–13, Jan. 2009.

[4] T. Chattopadhyay and A. Pal. Watermarking H.264 video, Nov. 2007. Available online: http://www.dspdesignline.com/202805492.

[5] A. Cheddad, J. Condell, K. Curran, and P. M. Kevitt. Digital image steganography: Survey and analysis of current methods. *Signal Processing*, 90(3):727–752, 2010.

[6] CIPA. DC-008-2010. Exchangeable image file format for digital still cameras: Exif Version 2.3, Apr. 2010. Also published as JIETA: CP-3451B.

[7] J. Fridrich, M. Goljan, and D. Hogea. Steganalysis of JPEG Images: Breaking the F5 Algorithm. In F. A. Petitcolas, editor, *Information Hiding*, volume 2578 of *Lecture Notes in Computer Science*, pages 310–323. Springer Berlin Heidelberg, 2003.

[8] J. Fridrich, T. Pevný, and J. Kodovský. Statistically Undetectable JPEG Steganography: Dead Ends, Challenges, and Opportunities. In *Proceedings of the 9th Workshop on Multimedia & Security*, MM&Sec '07, pages 3–14, New York, NY, USA, 2007. ACM.

[9] ITU. T.82: Information technology – Coded representation of picture and audio information – Progressive bi-level image compression, Mar. 1993.

[10] ITU. T.85: Application profile for Recommendation T.82 – Progressive bi-level image compression (JBIG coding scheme) for facsimile apparatus, Aug. 1995.

[11] ITU-T H.264. Advanced video coding for generic audiovisual services, Nov. 2007.

[12] ITU-T T.81. Digital compression and coding of continuous-tone still images — requirements and guidelines, Sept. 1992. Also published as ISO/IEC IS 10918-1.

[13] C. Kailasanathan. Compression performance of JPEG encryption scheme. In *Proceedings of the 14th International IEEE Conference on Digital Signal Processing, DSP '02*, July 2002.

[14] D. A. Kerr. Chrominance Subsampling in Digital Images. http://dougkerr.net/pumpkin/articles/Subsampling.pdf, Jan. 2012.

[15] M. I. Khan, V. Jeoti, and A. S. Malik. On perceptual encryption: Variants of DCT block scrambling scheme for JPEG compressed images. In T.-H. Kim, S. K. Pal, W. I. Grosky, N. Pissinou, T. K. Shih, and D. Slezak, editors, *FGIT-SIP/MulGraB*, volume 123 of *Communications in Computer and Information Science*, pages 212–223. Springer, 2010.

[16] W.-C. Kuo, S.-H. Kuo, and L.-C. Wuu. High Embedding Reversible Data Hiding Scheme for JPEG. In *Sixth International Conference on Intelligent Information Hiding and Multimedia Signal Processing (IIH-MSP)*, pages 74–77, oct. 2010.

[17] R. Kutil and D. Engel. Methods for the anisotropic wavelet packet transform. *Applied and Computational Harmonic Analysis*, 25(3):295–314, 2008.

[18] C.-C. Lin and P.-F. Shiu. DCT-based reversible data hiding scheme. In *Proceedings of the 3rd International Conference on Ubiquitous Information Management and Communication*, ICUIMC '09, pages 327–335, New York, NY, USA, 2009. ACM.

[19] D. Marpe, H. Schwarz, and T. Wiegand. Context-based adaptive binary arithmetic coding in the H.264/AVC video compression standard. *IEEE Transactions on Circuits and Systems for Video Technology*, 13(7):620–636, July 2003.

[20] W. Pennebaker and J. Mitchell. *JPEG – Still image compression standard*. Van Nostrand Reinhold, New York, 1993.

[21] H. R. Sheikh, M. F. Sabir, and A. C. Bovik. A statistical evaluation of recent full reference image quality assessment algorithms. *IEEE Transactions on Image Processing*, 15(11):3440–3451, Nov. 2006.

[22] A. Unterweger and A. Uhl. Length-preserving Bit-stream-based JPEG Encryption. In *MM&Sec'12: Proceedings of the 14th ACM Multimedia and Security Workshop*, pages 85–89. ACM, Sept. 2012.

[23] A. Westfeld. High capacity despite better steganalysis, F5 - a steganographic algorithm. In *Proceedings of the 4th Information Hiding Workshop '01*, Portland, OR, USA, Apr. 2001.

[24] I. Witten, R. Neal, and J. Cleary. Arithmetic coding for data compression. *Communications of the ACM*, 30(6):520–540, 1987.

Secure and Efficient Approximate Nearest Neighbors Search

Benjamin Mathon
INRIA Rennes, France
benjamin.mathon@inria.fr

Laurent Amsaleg
IRISA - CNRS,
Rennes, France
laurent.amsaleg@irisa.fr

Teddy Furon
INRIA Rennes, France
teddy.furon@inria.fr

Julien Bringer
MORPHO - SAFRAN
Issy-les-Moulineaux, France
julien.bringer@morpho.com

ABSTRACT

This paper presents a moderately secure but very efficient approximate nearest neighbors search. After detailing the threats pertaining to the 'honest but curious' model, our approach starts from a state-of-the-art algorithm in the domain of approximate nearest neighbors search. We gradually develop mechanisms partially blocking the attacks threatening the original algorithm. The loss of performances compared to the original algorithm is mainly an overhead of a constant computation time and communication payload which are independent of the size of the database.

Categories and Subject Descriptors

H.2.0 [**Database Management**]: General—*Security, integrity, and protection*; H.3 [**Information Storage and Retrieval**]: Information Search and Retrieval—*Retrieval models*

Keywords

Approximate Nearest Neighbors search; Privacy; Security.

1. INTRODUCTION

This paper deals with nearest neighbors search, an algorithm that finds the closest elements from a query vector within a database, according to a given distance metric. The main challenge in this field had been for a long time scalability: to retrieve the k nearest neighbors (in short k-NN) among a large database of n elements, n being extremely large ($10^6 - 10^9$), with a short time response. This challenge has been addressed in many research works proposing *approximate* nearest neighbors (k-ANN) search. The best solutions return some vectors which are likely to be the true nearest neighbors, striking a trade-off between efficiency and quality of search. There are mainly two ways. First, an approximate distance, which is faster to compute, is used instead of the given metric. Second, the database is indexed offline, i.e. it is partitioned into groups. The k-ANN is processed within the group the query vector belongs to. This speeds up the search because the cardinality of this group is smaller than n. Both solutions can be used independently or in conjunction. This article focuses on the first idea as it is based on the state-of-the-art k-ANN algorithm Product-Quantization codes (PQ-codes) [6].

Recently, other challenges have raised in this field: security and privacy. The query vector belongs to the User, the database to the Owner, and none of them is willing to share their property. This case happens for instance in biometrics identification. The main axiomatic in biometric claims that no database can be stored securely. Therefore, a Server cannot have the database of biometric templates in the clear since a pirate would steal these highly valuable data. In the same way, the User is reluctant in sending his biometric template in the clear.

The nearest neighbor search is also the pivot of some classification algorithms. A class is associated to each vector of the database, and the goal is to predict the class of the query vector from the class of its nearest neighbors. The Owner does not want to share its collection of pairs of vector and class, as this is the fruit of his know-how in collecting and assessing the quality of these data. The User is interested in the prediction value but does not want to disclose his query vector for some privacy issues. This happens in applications such as medical diagnostic (vectors are medical records like ECG) or user recommendation system (vectors are the user profiles).

Another application is Content Based Retrieval where the User looks for multimedia contents (images, videos, audio clips) perceptually similar in some sense. This technology is now deeply used in Digital Right Management systems where copyright holders are reluctant in disclosing neither their contents nor the features extracted from their contents.

There are already solutions providing secure nearest neighbors search based on cryptographic primitives such as homomorphic encryption, oblivious transfer, argument based encryption, secure multiparty computation protocol. We provide a critical overview in Sect. 3.1. In brief, we believe that these solutions put security and privacy on top of the requirements list, sacrificing a lot the scalability and the speed of the search. Scalability and speed are of utmost importance in some applications and these past solutions are just not adequate here because they are too slow. Another point is that the security levels of these cryptographic primitives are very high, whereas, in some applications, they do not prevent some basic attacks on the global system. There is no use in rising big walls if the door is weakly secured. One motto in security is 'A system is as secure as its weakest link'. This implies that using too strongly secure bricks is useless or even harmful if they degrade other features of the system, like scalability and speed in k-NN search.

This article presents a moderately secure but highly scalable and fast approximate nearest neighbors search. Our philosophy is to start from a state-of-the-art technique in this field, i.e. PQ-codes [6] presented in Sect. 3.2, to analyze the threats, and to patch it avoiding as much as possible bricks too much penalizing the scalability and the speed. On the other hand, we do not completely prevent the players to infer some knowledge, but these limitations are well explained and experimentally assessed. The experimental body uses database of size much bigger than what the past secure solutions can handle.

2. THE STARTING POINT

2.1 The framework

The framework considers an Owner having a collection of n pairs of a vector $\mathbf{x}_i \in \mathbb{R}^d$ and metadata t_i (defined in some space). Define $\mathcal{X} = \{\mathbf{x}_i\}_{i=1}^n$. The Owner subcontracts the k-NN (or k-ANN) search to an entity called the Server. For this purpose, the Owner gives a representation of each vector $h(\mathbf{x}_i)$ together with the metadata t_i (or an encrypted version of the metadata). The User has a query vector $\mathbf{q} \in \mathbb{R}^d$ and he is interested in some information about the subset $\mathcal{N}(\mathbf{q})$ of the k-NN of $\mathbf{q}$. Depending on the application, this can be their indices ($\mathcal{N}(\mathbf{q})$), the values of these vectors ($\{\mathbf{x}_i\}_{i \in \mathcal{N}(\mathbf{q})}$), or their metadata ($\{t_i\}_{i \in \mathcal{N}(\mathbf{q})}$).

For instance, in a classification application, the metadata t_i is the class associated to the vector and the prediction of the class of $\mathbf{q}$ is a function of the classes of the k-ANN vectors. In a Content Based retrieval scenario, t_i is the ID of the content from which the feature vector $\mathbf{x}_i$ has been extracted. By a voting mechanism, the most similar contents' ID are detected. In a biometric identification problem, the metadata is the user ID. An exhaustive k'-NN search over the returned k-ANN ($k' < k$) can also refine the result. The paper does not deal with this extension.

2.2 The threats

Our work adopts the 'honest but curious' model where the Server and the User follow the protocol but they might be willing to infer more information from what they know. More precisely, we explicitly list the potential threats under this model. The curious Server might want to:

S_1 Reconstruct $\mathbf{x}_i$ from $h(\mathbf{x}_i)$,

S_2 Cluster the database vectors from $\{h(\mathbf{x}_i)\}$ (i.e. by running k-ANN among vectors of the database),

S_3 Reconstruct $\mathbf{q}$ from what it receives from the User,

S_4 Detect similar queries (from one or different Users).

The curious User might want to:

U_1 Know in advance whether two similar queries $\mathbf{q}$ and $\mathbf{q}'$ yield the same k-ANN subset,

U_2 Explore efficiently a wider neighborhood of $\mathbf{q}$ by submitting few almost similar queries.

Note that this list of attacks is not exhaustive. It is worth repeating that the spirit of our work is not to prevent these threats absolutely. We enforce scalability first thanks to a moderately secure approach which yields a trade-off between the performance of the search and the feasibility of the attacks. In other words, instead of claiming that a threat is strictly impossible, we measure to which extend that threat is possible.

3. STATE OF THE ART

3.1 Secure NN search past approaches

We present some past approaches working for Euclidean distance based search. However, we omit solutions dealing with indexing (i.e. partitioning the vector space, see Sect. 1).

3.1.1 Homomorphic encryption

The Euclidean distance between the vectors of two parties can be computed without revealing them thanks to the homomorphic encryption primitive [1, 9, 7]. In a nutshell, the User sends an encrypted version of the query to the Server which, thanks to the homomorphism, sends back the encryption of the distance that the User deciphers.

This has two drawbacks. First, the Server knows $\mathcal{X}$ (threat S_1). If dishonest or if this database is stolen, exploitation of the data (threat S_2) is performed without the Owner's permission. On the other hand, threats S_3 and S_4 are impossible if the encryption is not broken. Threats U_1 and U_2 are not possible.

In practice, the computation of the Euclidean distance in the encrypted domain is slow and demands exchanging ciphers bigger in size than the vector. The search per se is exhaustive, running n times the protocol. There is no factorization between queries coming from two users since vectors must be processed by the public key of the User. This 'secure' k-NN takes in the order of 10 seconds to run the identification over a database of 320 entries [7, Tab. 3].

More general Secure Multiparty Computation (SMC) solutions have also been designed [7]. They rely on garbled circuits to securely evaluate a distance between two parties. Paper [4] introduces an efficient solution for Hamming distance based on Locality-Sensitive Hashing (LSH), which avoids the exhaustive search. However existing solutions for Euclidean distance-based search are still exhaustive and the database is stored in clear.

3.1.2 Hamming embedding

Another approach securely computes approximated distances. In the protocol of [3, Sect. IV-C], $\mathbf{x}_i$ is mapped to a binary representation $h(\mathbf{x}_i) \in \mathbb{B}^M$ ($\mathbb{B} = \{0, 1\}$) such that the Hamming distance between representations reflects the Euclidean distance between sufficiently close real vectors. This so-called Hamming embedding is parametrized by a matrix $\mathbf{A}$, a dither vector $\mathbf{w}$ and a quantization step Δ.

Since the Server needs these parameters to run the protocol, threat S_1 is possible according to [2] up to the quantization distortion. Threat S_2 is performed with the approximated distance. Nevertheless, threat S_3 is stopped because the Server never sees $h(\mathbf{q})$ in the clear ([3, Step 1]). S_4 is not feasible since $h(\mathbf{q})$ is semantically securely encrypted.

Threats U_1 and U_2 are not prevented in ([3, Step 3]) since the User controls the binary embedding of the query. Besides, the User sorts the distances ([3, Step 6]) and requires the metadata of the vectors it is interested in. The Server has no control on this selection.

The search is approximated (because based on Hamming distances) but exhaustive, requiring n homomorphic encryptions of the database representations *with the User public key* at the Server side ([3, Step 5]). This prevents the scalability of the search.

3.1.3 Attribute based encryption

Paper [8] builds a solution using attribute based encryption to avoid the last two drawbacks of 3.1.2. The User is able to decrypt the metadata t_i if and only if it knows a vector $\mathbf{q}$ such that $\|\mathbf{q} - \mathbf{x}_i\|^2 \leq \tau$ (vectors are here elements of $\mathbb{Z}^d$ and $\tau \in \mathbb{N}$). The enormous advantages follow:

- The database is composed of the metadata encrypted once for all with the Server public key,

- The Server does not store $\mathbf{x}_i$ or $h(\mathbf{x}_i)$.

Threats S_1, S_3, and S_4 are precluded. Threats U_1 and U_2 rarely occur for some specific setup. Yet, the Server which has the private key can unlock the ciphers (threat S_2).

However, the complexity is diabolic: the User must download the n encrypted metadata and perform τ decryptions (in interaction with the Server) per entry of the database to get the metadata t_i associated to the vectors $\mathbf{x}_i$ which are at most $\sqrt{\tau}$ away from $\mathbf{q}$ (if any).

3.2 An overview of PQ-codes

PQ-codes efficiently run k-ANN search at large scale [6].

3.2.1 Offline

The Owner has a database of vectors in $\mathbb{R}^d$: $\mathcal{X} = \{\mathbf{x}_i\}_{i=1}^n$. The vectors are split in into M subvectors of length ℓ. We assume $d = M\ell$ and denote $\mathbf{x}_i^{(m)} = (\mathbf{x}_i((m-1)\ell+1), \ldots, \mathbf{x}_i(m\ell))$ the m-th subvector of $\mathbf{x}_i$. Denote $[a] = \{1, \cdots, a\}$ for any $a \in \mathbb{N}^*$. Then, $\forall m \in [M]$, the Owner runs a K-means over the subvectors in $\mathcal{X}^{(m)} = \{\mathbf{x}_i^{(m)}\}_{i \in [n]}$. It consists in randomly drawing K vectors in $\mathbb{R}^\ell$ and applying the Lloyd-Max algorithm until convergence. This ends up with a codebook of K centroids $\mathcal{C}^{(m)} = \{\mathbf{c}_i^{(m)}\}_{i \in [K]}$. This defines the m-th quantizer $Q^{(m)}(\cdots) : \mathbb{R}^\ell \to [K]$ as:

$$Q^{(m)}(\mathbf{x}^{(m)}) = \arg\min_{i \in [K]} \|\mathbf{x}^{(m)} - \mathbf{c}_i^{(m)}\|, \quad \forall \mathbf{x}^{(m)} \in \mathbb{R}^\ell, \quad (1)$$

where $\|\cdot\|$ denotes the Euclidean distance. The K-means converges to a local minimum of the total reconstruction error distortion $\sum_{\mathbf{x} \in \mathcal{X}^{(m)}} \|\mathbf{x} - Q^{(m)}(\mathbf{x})\|^2$. To shorten this preparation time, the Owner applies it on a training set which is a random subset of $\mathcal{X}^{(m)}$. The results of the K-means depends on this subset, the initial random sampling, and the number of iterations. We define the global quantizer $Q(\cdot) : \mathbb{R}^d \to [K]^M$ as the product quantizer $Q^{(1)} \times \ldots \times Q^{(m)}$:

$$Q(\mathbf{x}) = (Q^{(1)}(\mathbf{x}^{(1)}), \ldots, Q^{(M)}(\mathbf{x}^{(M)})), \quad \forall \mathbf{x} \in \mathbb{R}^d. \quad (2)$$

We denote by $Q^{-1}(\cdot) : [K]^M \to \mathbb{R}^d$ the operator mapping a sequence of indices to the concatenation of centroids:

$$Q^{-1}((k_1, \ldots, k_M)) = \left(\mathbf{c}_{k_1}^{(1)^\top} \ldots \mathbf{c}_{k_M}^{(M)^\top}\right)^\top. \quad (3)$$

The Owner sends the Server the database $\mathcal{Q} = \{Q(\mathbf{x}_i)\}_{i \in [n]}$ (i.e. $h(\cdot) = Q(\cdot)$) and the set of M codebooks $\mathcal{C} = \{\mathcal{C}^{(m)}\}_{m \in [M]}$. The role of the Owner stops here.

3.2.2 Online: the symmetric search

The Server pre-computes the distances between centroids of the same codebook:

$$d_s(i, j, m) = \|\mathbf{c}_i^{(m)} - \mathbf{c}_j^{(m)}\|^2, \ \forall (i, j, m) \in [K] \times [K] \times [M]. \quad (4)$$

The matrix d_s will be used as a lookup table.

Online, when receiving a query $\mathbf{q}$ from the User, the Server first computes $Q(\mathbf{q})$. It proceeds the k-ANN search based on the approximated square distance

$$\hat{D}(\mathbf{q}, \mathbf{x}_i) = \|Q^{-1}(Q(\mathbf{q})) - Q^{-1}(Q(\mathbf{x}_i))\|^2, \quad (5)$$

instead of the true square distance $\|\mathbf{q} - \mathbf{x}_i\|^2$. This is efficiently done thanks to the lookup table:

$$\hat{D}(\mathbf{q}, \mathbf{x}_i) = \sum_{m=1}^M d_s(Q^{(m)}(\mathbf{q}^m), Q^{(m)}(\mathbf{x}_i^m), m). \quad (6)$$

The min-heap algorithm returns the indices $(i_1, \ldots, i_k)$ yielding the k smallest approximate distances. The Server sends the metadata $(t_{i_1}, \ldots, t_{i_k})$ associated to these k vectors.

There exists a variant of PQ-codes, so-called asymmetric search, which is not used in the paper.

4. SLOWLY RISING THE WALLS

The goal of this section is to underline the relationships between the threats listed in Sect. 2.2 and the key elements of PQ-codes, which are the centroids codebook $\mathcal{C}$ and the distance table d_s. We start our analysis with the original PQ-codes as presented in Sect. 3.2.

4.1 Scenario 1: original PQ-codes

First, the Server cannot reconstruct $\mathbf{x}_i$, but only an estimation $\hat{\mathbf{x}}_i = Q^{(-1)}(Q(\mathbf{x}_i))$ because it has the indices $\mathcal{Q}$ and the centroids of $\mathcal{C}$ (threat S_1). Second, the Server can run k-ANN searches without the Owner's permission, e.g. with the purpose of clustering the vectors of $\mathcal{X}$ (threat S_2). Obviously, PQ-codes are not compliant with privacy because the User sends his query $\mathbf{q}$ in the clear to the Server (threats S_3 and S_4). On the other hand, this renders the User harmless (threats U_1 and U_2 are void).

4.2 Scenario 2: confiscating the codebook

Suppose that we succeed to make the query quantization at the User side. Then, the Server no longer needs $\mathcal{C}$.

Having d_s, the Server knows the $K(K - 1)/2$ distances between the K centroids of $\mathcal{C}^{(m)}$, $\forall m \in [M]$. Since K is usually much bigger than the subspace dimension ℓ, the Server can construct a constellation of K points sharing the same inter-distances. This does not fully disclose the codebook $\mathcal{C}$, but up to an ambiguity which is an isometry of $\mathbb{R}^\ell$, i.e. a transformation of the space that preserves distances (say a rotation followed by a translation).

This ambiguity plus the quantization loss is sufficient for preventing an accurate reconstruction of the database vectors from $\mathcal{Q}$ (threat S_1) and the query vector from $Q(\mathbf{q})$ (threat S_3). The Server cannot query alone, but it can cluster the database vectors according to their approximated distances $\hat{D}(\mathbf{x}_i, \mathbf{x}_j)$ thanks to the lookup table d_s (threat

S_2). The Server can detect almost similar queries $\mathbf{q}$ and $\mathbf{q}'$ by computing $\hat{D}(\mathbf{q}, \mathbf{q}')$ (threat S_4).

To perform the quantization of the query, The User is being given the centroids. Now, he knows in advance that two queries $\mathbf{q}$ and $\mathbf{q}'$ yield the same k-ANN if $Q(\mathbf{q}) = Q(\mathbf{q}')$ (threat U_1). He can also adapt his query: forging a query $\mathbf{q}'$ which equals $\mathbf{q}$ except for one subvector pertaining to a different Voronoi cell will yield another set of k-ANN vectors. In other words, he can explore a wider neighborhood of $\mathbf{q}$ more efficiently (i.e. with less queries - threat U_2).

4.3 Scenario 3: confiscating the lookup table

Suppose now that the Server knows neither $\mathcal{C}$ nor d_s. It does not have the centroids, which prevents vector reconstruction, be it from the database (threat S_1) or the query (threat S_3). It is missing d_s to compute approximated distances between entries of $\mathcal{Q}$. Yet, it can still infer database vector neighborhood by forging the lookup table:

$$d_p(i,j,m) = 1 - \delta_{i,j}, \forall (i,j,m) \in [K] \times [K] \times [M], \quad (7)$$

where $\delta_{i,j}$ is the Kronecker function ($= 1$ if $i = j$, 0 otherwise). This method provides a very crude approximation of nearest neighbors (see Fig. 3 blue dotted line). In other words, threat S_2 seems to be barely feasible. However, the following section provides a working implementation of this scenario but this particular threat is not totally precluded.

5. OUR PROPOSAL

The previous section demonstrated that the Server can hijack information and threaten the entire system. We propose in this section several mechanisms making the job of the curious Server more difficult for threatening the security and privacy of k-ANN searches with PQ-codes. The main idea to enforce the above-mentioned Scenario 3 is the introduction of two quantizers.

5.1 The algorithm

The Owner creates offline $\mathcal{C}_S$, a set of M codebooks of K_S centroids each. This defines the product quantizer $Q_S(\cdot)$ used to create the database $\mathcal{Q} = \{Q_S(\mathbf{x}_i)\}_{i=1}^n$ given to the Server. Only the Owner knows $\mathcal{C}_S$.

The Owner also creates $\mathcal{C}_U$, a set of M codebooks of K_U centroids each, defining $Q_U(\cdot)$. $\mathcal{C}_U$ will be sent to the User to quantize $\mathbf{q}$. The Owner also computes the square distances:

$$d_{us}(i,j,m) = \|\mathbf{c}_{U,i}^{(m)} - \mathbf{c}_{S,j}^{(m)}\|^2, \forall (i,j,m) \in [K_U] \times [K_S] \times [M], \quad (8)$$

and sends this lookup table to the Server.

Online, the User gets $\mathcal{C}_U$, sends $Q_U(\mathbf{q})$ to the Server which performs the ANN search with d_{us}. Note that the quantizers may not have the same number of centroids per subspace. It is important to have a reasonable K_S because the memory footprint of $\mathcal{Q}$ at the Server side is $nM \log_2 K_S$ bits. A bigger K_U improves the quality of the approximative search, while payload of the transmission between the User and the Server, i.e. $M \log_2 K_U$, slightly increases.

5.2 Threat analysis

5.2.1 Vector reconstruction

As claimed in Sect. 4.2, the Server cannot reconstruct database vectors (threat S_1) because it misses the knowledge of $\mathcal{C}_S$. The same is true for query vectors (threat S_3)

because it does not have $\mathcal{C}_U$. Note that this holds as long as there is no collusion between a User and the Server, or as long as the Server cannot usurp the role of the User. These two cases are usually excluded in the 'honest but curious' model.

5.2.2 Similar queries detection

The Server obviously spots similar queries $\mathbf{q}$ and $\mathbf{q}'$ where $Q_U(\mathbf{q}) \approx Q_U(\mathbf{q}')$ (threat S_4). However, it has difficulty in gauging how much different are these two queries because it is missing the distance table between centroids of $\mathcal{C}_U$.

5.2.3 Clustering the database

For a given entry, the Server knows $Q_S(\mathbf{x}_i)$ whereas it would need $Q_U(\mathbf{x}_i)$ to compute the approximated distances against the other entries of $\mathcal{Q}$ thanks to d_{us}. This is the reason why we measure the averaged mutual information between results of a quantization onto $\mathcal{C}_U^{(m)}$ and $\mathcal{C}_S^{(m)}$:

$$I(Q_S; Q_U) = M^{-1} \sum_{m=1}^{M} I(Q_S^{(m)}(\mathbf{X}_i^{(m)}); Q_U^{(m)}(\mathbf{X}_i^{(m)})). \quad (9)$$

The computation of this quantity is easy since we deal with discrete random variables.

Another angle of attack is to estimate d_s defined in (4). Eq. (7) was a first attempt, but the Server can do much better thanks to d_{us} defined in (8). The idea is simple: if $d_{us}(i,j,m)$ is close to zero, it means that $\mathbf{c}_{U,i}^{(m)}$ is close to $\mathbf{c}_{S,j}^{(m)}$, therefore the distance $d_{us}(i,k,m)$ should be a good estimation of $d_s(j,k,m)$. The estimation goes as follows:

$$\hat{d}_s(j,k,m) = (d_{us}(I(j),k,m) + d_{us}(I(k),j,m))/2,$$
$$\text{with } I(j) \triangleq \arg\min_{i \in [K_U]} d_{us}(i,j,m). \quad (10)$$

The performances of the k-ANN search with this estimated distance table are slightly lower than with d_{us} (Fig. 3). This means that threat S_2 cannot be prevented. Note that our approach is close to one-way private search [5] where only the User's data are sensitive.

5.2.4 Threats from the User

Knowing $\mathcal{C}_U$ and thus the Voronoi cells associated to each subquantizer, the User knows which queries in the space will yield the same k-ANN (threat U_1): it holds for any $(\mathbf{q}, \mathbf{q}')$ such that $Q_U(\mathbf{q}) = Q_U(\mathbf{q}')$. In the same way, he can efficiently explore portion of the space by submitting queries almost identically quantized (threat U_2).

If these latter threats are annoying for the targeted application, then a secure distance computation protocol (as in Sect. 3.1.1) is a solution. The Server generates (sk_S, pk_S) for an additive homomorphic crypto-system $e(\cdot)$. The owner encrypts the $e(\mathbf{c}_{U,i}^{(m)}, pk_S)$ and $e(\|\mathbf{c}_{U,i}^{(m)}\|^2, pk_S)$ offline. These ciphers are privately sent to the User who computes and sends $e(\|\mathbf{q}^{(m)} - \mathbf{c}_{U,i}^{(m)}\|^2, pk_S)$ back to the Server. The Server decrypts and computes $Q_U(\mathbf{q})$ knowing neither $\mathbf{q}$ nor $\mathcal{C}_U$. The User no longer sees $Q_U(\mathbf{q})$. The User together with the Server have to compute in the encrypted domain $M.K_U$ distances, which is much fewer than n as proposed in 3.1.1. These secure computations last longer than the ANN search, so that the runtime is dominated by this constant duration: this does not spoil the scalability of PQ-codes.

We can even ensure that the Server learns only the value of $Q_U(\mathbf{q})$ and nothing else. To this aim, the server computes for each $m \in [M]$, $Q_U^{(m)}(\mathbf{q}^{(m)})$, i.e. the argmin of the encrypted distances $e(D_1, pk_S), \ldots, e(D_{K_U}, pk_S)$ with $D_i = \|\mathbf{q}^{(m)} - \mathbf{c}_{U,i}^{(m)}\|^2$, interactively without decrypting the distances. This prevents the Server from learning the intermediate results. First, the User encrypts the distances through El Gamal encryption $E[\cdot]$ with its public key pk_U associated to its secret key sk_U and sends the Server the results $E[e(D_1, pk_S), pk_U], \ldots, E[e(D_{K_U}, pk_S), pk_U]$. The server permutes these ciphers to randomize their order and computes, thanks to the multiplicative homomorphism of El Gamal,

$$E[e(D_{i_1}, pk_S)^\alpha, pk_U], \ldots, E[e(D_{i_{K_U}}, pk_S)^\alpha, pk_U], \quad (11)$$

with a random $\alpha > 0$. This in turn, thanks to the additive homomorphism of $e(\cdot)$, leads to:

$$E[e(\alpha.D_{i1}, pk_S), pk_U], \ldots, E[e(\alpha.D_{iK_U}, pk_S), pk_U]. \quad (12)$$

The role of α is to blind the ciphers such that the User cannot guess the permutation. The Server sends back the data to the User who decrypts those but without being able to retrieve the original order of the data.

Then, the User and the Server execute an interactive sorting algorithm by comparing the distances in the encrypted domain following the principle of Yao's millionaire problem. The secure comparison of two encrypted data $e(x, pk_S)$ and $e(y, pk_S)$ is made as follows: let R a big random element and R' significantly smaller than R, the User computes $e(R(x-y) - R', pk_S)$ thanks to the homomorphic property. The Server decrypts this message and if it gives a positive value, it decides that $x > y$. This enables the Server to determine the index of the minimum distance between the K_U distances by executing $K_U - 1$ successive secure comparisons with the User. As the order is only known by the Server, the Server obtains $Q_U^{(m)}(\mathbf{q}^{(m)})$ at the end whereas the User will not learn the result. Doing so for all m leads to $Q_U(\mathbf{q})$. This secure computation of $Q_U(\mathbf{q})$ has the advantage that the Server and the User learns the minimum level of details.

6. EXPERIMENTAL BODY

Our experiments are performed on the *ANN_SIFT1M* local SIFT descriptors database introduced in [6]. Note that the ANN_SIFT1M database consists of (i) $1,000,000$ base vectors of dimension $d = 128$, (ii) $100,000$ training vectors for running the K-means, and (iii) $10,000$ query vectors and a ground truth file which contains, for each query, the identifiers of its nearest neighbors ordered by increasing distance.

6.1 Quality of the search

PQ-codes performs a k-ANN search, meaning that the returned NN are not necessary the true ones. To gauge the quality of the output, the recall at rank $R \leq k$, denoted by 'r-recall@R' is measured. This is the proportion of query vectors for which the r-NN are ranked in the first R returned vectors. As usually done in ANN search papers, we focus on the 1-recall@R. Fig. 1 shows the 1-recall@R in percentage. On the server side, PQ-codes are performed with $M = 16$, $l = 8$, $K_S = 256$ and $N_i = 50$, the number of iterations of K-means process. The dashed line shows the performances of the original PQ-codes. In brief, the search returns almost surely the NN for R = 100. We increase the number of centroids for the quantizer Q_U (from $K_U = 64$ to 4096). This gives a better quality of search when $K_U > K_S$.

Usually, the number of centroids is a power of two, so that the memory footprint of the database is $nM \log_2 K_S$

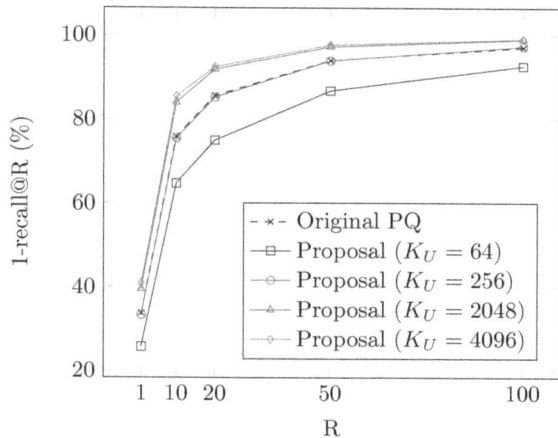

Figure 1: 1-recall@R scores for the original and proposed version of PQ-codes: $M = 16$, $l = 8$, $K_S = 256$, $N_i = 50$.

bits. This is a very compact representation of $\mathcal{X}$. The time response is linear with nM. In our setup with $n = 10^6$, $M = 16$, $K_S = 256$, the database $\mathcal{Q}$ occupies 16MB. Once $Q_U(\mathbf{q})$ is computed, one approximated search is completed within 30 ms (Core i7 platform, single threaded). Parameter K_U has almost no impact on the time response, provided d_{us} can fit in memory.

6.2 Threat S_2

The curious Server has two possibilities for running k-ANN searches within the database. A first attempt is to use d_{us}, but the database vectors are improper because they are not quantizations onto $\mathcal{C}_U$. We measure the average amount of information per quantizer $I(Q_S; Q_U)$ (see (9)) that the curious Server is missing for using d_{us}. Fig. 2 shows this amount w.r.t the number of iterations of the K-means algorithm, computed on the ANN_SIFT1M training database. The dashed line shows the entropy of $Q_S^{(m)}(\mathbf{X}^{(m)})$ when the quantization of a vector is equiprobably distributed, i.e. $\log_2(K_S)$. The black line (cross markers) shows the estimation of this entropy, which is smaller. This is due to the fact that the goal of the K-means is to minimize the mean square error, not to assure the equiprobability distribution. $I(Q_S; Q_U)$ increases with K_U, but do not reach the value of the entropy. Therefore, the curious Server is missing an amount of information which is in the order of $M.(H(Q_S) - I(Q_S; Q_U))$ bits per entry of the database to use the table d_{us}. The bigger is K_U, the bigger is the information leakage while increasing the quality of search (see Fig. 1). We can see here the price to pay for more security.

Note that for a few iterations of the K-means process, the distribution of the centroids is more random, the gap is bigger, and so the system more secure against this attack. The reconstruction error distortion is not optimal, but we have noticed that this number of iterations has no impact on the quality of search provided it is ≥ 3.

In a second attack, the curious Server either uses d_p of (7), or estimates the missing distance table d_s via (10). Fig. 3 shows the 1-recall@R scores when the Server utilizes (i) the lookup table d_{us}, (ii) the Kronecker lookup table d_p (7) and (iii) the estimated $\hat{d}_s$ (10) for different K_U (number of iterations of K-means process is 3).

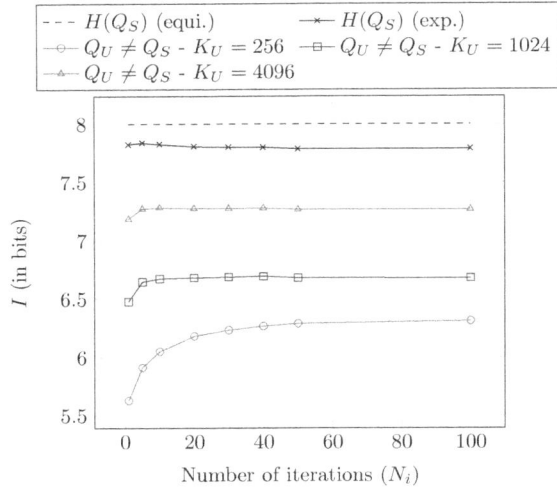

Figure 2: Empirical mutual informations between the two quantizers Q_S and Q_U w.r.t the number of iterations of the K-means with $M = 16$, $K_S = 256$.

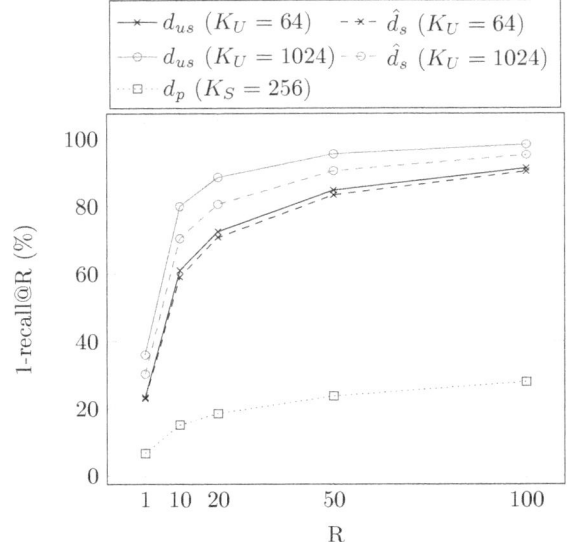

Figure 3: 1-recall@R scores computed with different lookup tables $\{d_{us}, d_p, \hat{d}_s\}$ with $M = 16$ and $K_S = 256$.

The Kronecker version yields a recall@R below 30% for any rank $R \leq 100$. The quality of search is too weak for a possible clustering of the database. The attack based on the estimation $\hat{d}_s$ works much better. A large K_U improves the accuracy of the estimation, and the performances are almost equal to the original PQ-codes with $K = K_S$. However, increasing K_U to some extend also improves the quality of search for the User (because the query is more finely quantized by Q_U). At some point, both curves do not evolve, and rising K_U even more just increases computation time and bandwidth for nothing.

6.3 Threats U_1 and U_2

Sect. 5.2.4 prevents these threats but at a huge cost in terms of computation and bandwidth. Let us roughly evaluate the bandwidth first (figures are for $K_S = 256$). The User needs the encrypted centroids and their norm, i.e. around $M(\ell+1)K_U \times 2048$ bits (10MB). This can be factorized over several queries. The User sends distances encrypted with El Gamal, i.e. $MK_U \times 4096$ bits (2MB). The Server sends back these ciphers, i.e. same amount. For the Yao protocol, the User sends $MK_U \times 2048$ bits (1MB) to the Server. As for the computation times, the User makes $O(MK_U(\ell+3))$ exponentiations ($\sim$50 sec. on a regular PC) and the Server $O(2MK_U)$ (8 sec. on a regular PC).

7. CONCLUSION

The advantages of this proposal are that (i) the database at the Server side is fixed, (ii) there is no loss w.r.t. the quality of the search, (iii) the complexity and bandwidth bottleneck depends on K_U but not on n. The preliminary protocol is a protection against threats from Users. The drawback of our proposal is that a Server can search within the database (for clustering e.g.) with a slight loss of accuracy compared to quality of search provided to the User. Note that none of past approaches protect against this threat.

8. REFERENCES

[1] M. Barni, T. Bianchi, D. Catalano, M. Di Raimondo, R. Donida Labati, P. Failla, D. Fiore, R. Lazzeretti, V. Piuri, F. Scotti, and A. Piva. Privacy-preserving fingercode authentication. In *Proceedings of the 12th ACM workshop on Multimedia and security*, MM&Sec '10, pages 231–240, New York, NY, USA, 2010. ACM.

[2] P. Boufounos. Universal rate-efficient scalar quantization. *Information Theory, IEEE Transactions on*, 58(3):1861–1872, 2012.

[3] P. Boufounos and S. Rane. Secure binary embeddings for privacy preserving nearest neighbors. In *Information Forensics and Security (WIFS), IEEE International Workshop on*, pages 1–6, 2011.

[4] J. Bringer, M. Favre, H. Chabanne, and A. Patey. Faster secure computation for biometric identification using filtering. In *Biometrics (ICB), 5th IAPR International Conference on*, pages 257–264, 2012.

[5] G. Fanti, M. Finiasz, and K. Ramchandran. One-Way Private Media Search on Public Databases: The Role of Signal Processing. *IEEE Signal Processing Magazine*, 30(2):53–61, 2013.

[6] H. Jégou, M. Douze, and C. Schmid. Product quantization for nearest neighbor search. *Pattern Analysis and Machine Intelligence, IEEE Transactions on*, 33(1):117–128, 2011.

[7] R. Lagendijk, Z. Erkin, and M. Barni. Encrypted signal processing for privacy protection: Conveying the utility of homomorphic encryption and multiparty computation. *IEEE Signal Processing Magazine*, 30(1):82–105, 2013.

[8] S. Rane and W. Sun. An attribute-based framework for privacy preserving image querying. In *Image Processing (ICIP), 19th IEEE International Conference on*, pages 2649–2652, 2012.

[9] A.-R. Sadeghi, T. Schneider, and I. Wehrenberg. Efficient privacy-preserving face recognition. In *Information, Security and Cryptology - ICISC 2009*, volume 5984 of *Lecture Notes in Computer Science*, pages 229–244. Springer Berlin Heidelberg, 2010.

XOR-Based Meaningful Visual Secret Sharing by Generalized Random Grids

Xiaotian Wu
School of Information Science
and Technology
Sun Yat-sen University
Guangzhou, China
wxt.sysu@gmai.com

Duanhao Ou
School of Information Science
and Technology
Sun Yat-sen University
Guangzhou, China
ouduanh@mail2.sysu.edu.cn

Lu Dai
School of Information Science
and Technology
Sun Yat-sen University
Guangzhou, China
dailu@mail.sysu.edu.cn

Wei Sun
School of Software
Sun Yat-sen University
Guangzhou, China
sunwei@mail.sysu.edu.cn

ABSTRACT

In recent years, random grid (RG) received much attention for constructing visual secret sharing (VSS) scheme without pixel expansion. But recovered secret image with low visual quality reveals due to the stacking operation. To improve the recovered image quality, XOR-based VSS is adopted. However, shares constructed from XOR-based VSS are random-looking. The noise-like appearance further increases the chance of suspicion on secret image communication and imposes difficulty for managing the shares. In this work, a novel $(2,2)$ generalized RG-based VSS is introduced. By adopting the $(2,2)$ VSS, we propose a XOR-based meaningful VSS where shares with meaningful contents are constructed. Moreover, superior visual quality is provided by this method as well.

Categories and Subject Descriptors

D.2.11 [**Software Engineering**]: Software Architectures—
Information hiding

General Terms

Security

Keywords

Visual secret sharing, visual cryptography, meaningful share, XOR, visual quality

1. INTRODUCTION

Visual secret sharing (VSS), which is also called visual cryptography (VC), is a technique of cryptography which prevents a secret from being modified or destructed by using the notions of perfect cipher and human visual system. For a general scheme of (k,n) threshold, a secret image is encrypted into n random-looking images, also called shares or shadows. These n shares are then distributed to n associated participants. To visually reveal the secret, any k or more shares are required to stack together. But any k or less shadows give no clue about secret. Compared with some conventional encryptions such as DES and AES, VSS offers unbreakable encryption if a meaningless share contains truly random pixels such that it can be seen as a one-time pad system. Without using a computational device and cryptographic knowledge in decryption, VSS technique is effective and suitable for certain practical applications.

An initial model of VSS was proposed by Naor and Shamir [14], where the (k,n) scheme is investigated. Inspired by Naor and Shamir's work, various studies on VSS were conducted. Constructing VSS scheme for general access structure was investigated in [1], where general access structure is used to implement complicated sharing strategy. Encoding secret images with different formats, such as grayscale and color images, was studied in [11] [10]. To manage the shadows efficiently and to reduce the chance of suspicion on secret image communication simultaneously, extended VSS [2] [13] and halftone VSS [24] [19] were proposed, where shadows with meaningful contents are constructed. For the aim of improving the reconstructed secret image quality, method for obtaining optimal contrast [3] was introduced. However, some deficiencies still remain in the above-mentioned VSS, as described as follows.

- Pixel expansion. The generated shadow is $m \geq 2$ times as big as the original secret image, where m is referred to pixel expansion. Pixel expansion further burdens the data transmission and storage.

- Tailor-made codebook required. A codebook is needed to encrypt the secret. But designing codebooks for different thresholds is not trivial.

To generate size invariant shadows, probabilistic VSS and random grid-based (RG-based) VSS are adopted. For probabilistic VSS, Ito et al. [8] presented an approach to encode a black/white pixel by using a column selected from the corresponding black/white basis matrix with equal probabilities. Yang [23] proposed constructions of probabilistic VSS for different thresholds. A secret pixel is correctly reconstructed with certain probability. Cimato et al. [7] further extended the probabilistic VSS to form a mixed model of both the classical deterministic VSS and the probabilistic VSS.

The concept of RG was initially introduced by Kafri and Keren [9] to encrypt a secret image into two noise-like images, where each image is referred as a RG. The size of a RG is the same as that of the secret image. Moreover, three distinct encryption algorithms were also presented. Inspired by Kafri and Keren, enhanced algorithms for encrypting grayscale and color images were proposed by Shyu [15], as well as the (n,n) scheme [16]. Follow-up investigations on RG-based VSS were discussed for constituting the $(2,n)$ [4], (k,n) [5] and access structure [20] schemes. Further, other studies such as improving the visual quality [21], constructing RG-based VSS with abilities of both OR and XOR decryptions [22] and user-friendly RG-based VSS [6] were presented as well.

In conventional VSS, reconstructed secret image with low image quality reveals due to the stacking operation. XOR-based VSS [18] is a new branch of VSS system that can offer better visual quality by adopting XOR operation to decrypt the secret. In the decryption phase, only some small, cheap and light-weight computational devices are needed. However, meaningless appearance of the share further increases the chance of suspicion on secret communication and imposes difficulty for managing the shares.

In this paper, a generalized RG-based VSS for $(2,2)$ case is first presented, where the average light transmission of a share becomes adjustable. Further, a (n,n) XOR-based meaningful VSS are derived, where meaningful shares are generated. Theoretical analysis and simulation results are provided as well, demonstrating the effectiveness and advantages of the XOR-based meaningful VSS.

The remaining part of this paper is organized as follows. Section 2 formulates related RG-based VSS, as well as some definitions on RG. The proposed algorithms are introduced in Section 3. Experimental results and discussions are provided in Section 4. Section 5 gives some concluding remarks.

2. RG-BASED VSS

Kafri and Keren defined a RG as a transparency comprising a two-dimensional array of pixels [9]. Each pixel can be fully transparent (white) or totally opaque (black), and the choice between the alternatives is made by a coin-flip procedure. There is no correlation between the values of different pixels in the array. Further, three sharing algorithms were proposed by Kafri and Keren, as described as follows.

Algorithm 1-3. Sharing a binary image into two RGs.
Input: A $M \times N$ binary secret image S.
Output: Two RGs R_1 and R_2.
$[R_1, R_2] = Encryption(S)$.

Algorithm 1.
Step 1: Construct a $M \times N$ matrix R_1 whose elements are randomly assigned the value 0 (white) or 1 (black).

Step 2: For each pixel at position (i,j) of S, compute

$$R_2(i,j) = \begin{cases} R_1(i,j), & \text{if } S(i,j) = 0 \\ \overline{R_1(i,j)}, & \text{otherwise} \end{cases}$$

where $\overline{R_1(i,j)}$ is the inverse of $R_1(i,j)$.
Step 3: Output the two shares R_1 and R_2.

Algorithm 2.
Step 1: Construct a $M \times N$ matrix R_1 whose elements are randomly assigned the value 0 (white) or 1 (black).
Step 2: For each pixel at position (i,j) of S, compute

$$R_2(i,j) = \begin{cases} R_1(i,j), & \text{if } S(i,j) = 0 \\ d, & \text{otherwise} \end{cases}$$

where d is randomly chosen from $\{0,1\}$.
Step 3: Output the two shares R_1 and R_2.

Algorithm 3.
Step 1: Construct a $M \times N$ matrix R_1 whose elements are randomly assigned the value 0 (white) or 1 (black).
Step 2: For each pixel at position (i,j) of S, compute

$$R_2(i,j) = \begin{cases} d, & \text{if } S(i,j) = 0 \\ \overline{R_1(i,j)}, & \text{otherwise} \end{cases}$$

where d is randomly chosen from $\{0,1\}$.
Step 3: Output the two shares R_1 and R_2.

Procedure $Encryption$ can be implemented by Algorithm 1, 2 or 3. To analyze RG-based VSS, light transmission, area representation and contrast are utilized, as defined as follows.

DEFINITION 1. *(Average light transmission). For a certain pixel r in a binary image R whose size is $M \times N$, the light transmission of a white pixel is defined as $T(r) = 1$. Whereas, $T(r) = 0$ for r is a black pixel. Totally, the average light transmission of R is defined as*

$$T(R) = \frac{\sum_{i=1}^{M} \sum_{j=1}^{N} T(R(i,j))}{M \times N}. \tag{1}$$

DEFINITION 2. *(Area representation). et $S(0)$ (resp. $S(1)$) be the area of all the white (resp. black) pixels in secret image S where $S = S(0) \cup S(1)$ and $S(0) \cap S(1) = \emptyset$. Therefore, $R[S(0)]$ (resp. $R[S(1)]$) is the corresponding area of all the white (resp. black) pixels in image R.*

DEFINITION 3. *(Contrast). The contrast of the reconstructed secret image $R_{1 \otimes \cdots \otimes n} = R_1 \otimes \cdots \otimes R_n$ with respect to the original secret image S is*

$$\alpha = \frac{T(R_{1 \otimes \cdots \otimes n}[S(0)]) - T(R_{1 \otimes \cdots \otimes n}[S(1)])}{1 + T(R_{1 \otimes \cdots \otimes n}[S(1)])}$$

where symbol $\otimes$ denotes the Boolean OR operation.

Contrast α is expected to be as large as possible. Secret information in the reconstructed secret image can be easily identified by naked eye with large α. Based on the $(2,2)$ algorithm, methods for constructing the $(2,n)$ [4], (n,n) [16] [4], (k,n) [5] and access structure [20] are developed. However, the light transmission of a share in the above-mentioned schemes is fixed at $\frac{1}{2}$.

3. THE PROPOSED ALGORITHMS

In this section, a generalized RG-based VSS for $(2,2)$ case is introduced, where the light transmission of a share can be manipulated. By recursively using the $(2,2)$ VSS for $n-1$ times, a (n,n) XOR-based VSS is constructed. Further, a XOR-based meaningful VSS is proposed.

3.1 The (2,2) generalized RG-based VSS

In reported RG-based VSS, the number of white pixels in a share is approximately half of the total number. Herein, we introduce the concept of generalized RG, where the percentage of white pixels in a share is adjustable. Primarily, a random bit generator is adopted, as given in Definition 4.

DEFINITION 4. *(Random bit generator). A random bit generator $b = g(x)$ is defined as a bit which is assigned the value 0 (resp. 1) with probability x (resp. $1-x$), as given by*

$$g(x): \; Prob(b=0) = x, \; Prob(b=1) = 1-x,$$

where procedure $Prob(A)$ represents the probability when event A is true.

Based on the random bit generator, a $(2,2)$ generalized RG-based VSS is constructed, as formulated in Algorithm 4.

Algorithm 4. Generalized RG-based VSS for $(2,2)$ case.
Input: a binary secret image S with $M \times N$ pixels, and three parameters u, v and d.
Output: two shares R_1 and R_2.
Step 1: For each position (i,j) in the secret image, Steps 2-3 are performed to generate two shared pixels $R_1(i,j)$ and $R_2(i,j)$.
Step 2: Construct a shared pixel $R_1(i,j)$ by

$$R_1(i,j) = g(\frac{u}{v}). \qquad (2)$$

Step 3: Construct the other shared pixel $R_2(i,j)$ by

$$R_2(i,j) = \begin{cases} R_1(i,j), & \text{if } S(i,j) = 0, \\ g(\frac{u}{v-d}), & \text{if } S(i,j) = 1 \text{ and } R_1(i,j) = 1, \\ g(\frac{u-d}{v-d}), & \text{if } S(i,j) = 1 \text{ and } R_1(i,j) = 0, \end{cases} \qquad (3)$$

Step 4: Output the two shares R_1 and R_2.

The three parameters u, v and d used in the $(2,2)$ scheme must satisfy the following conditions:

$$\begin{cases} d \geq 0, u > 0, v > 0, \\ v > u \geq d, \\ v \geq u+d. \end{cases}$$

In the following theoretical analysis, we prove that the $(2,2)$ scheme meets the security condition by Lemma 1 and satisfies the contrast condition by Lemma 2. Indeed, the security condition implies that insufficient shares give no clue about the secret and the contrast condition indicates that sufficient shares can disclose the secret. Theorem 1 formulates that the $(2,2)$ method is a valid construction of VSS when stacking operation is applied. The contrast of the $(2,2)$ method is analyzed in Theorem 2.

LEMMA 1. *Given two shares R_1 and R_2 generated from Algorithm 4, every share is a generalized RG, and gives no clue about the secret: $T(R_k[S(0)]) = T(R_k[S(1)]) = \frac{u}{v}$ where $k = 1, 2$.*

PROOF. Based on Equation (2), we get $Prob(R_1(i,j) = 0) = \frac{u}{v}$ no matter the secret pixel is white or black. By Definition 1, we have $T(R_1[S(0)]) = T(R_1[S(1)]) = \frac{u}{v}$. According to Equation (3), when $S(i,j) = 0$, $Prob(R_2(i,j) = 0) = Prob(R_1(i,j) = 0) = \frac{u}{v}$. When $S(i,j) = 1$, $Prob(R_2(i,j) = 0) = Prob(R_2(i,j) = 0 \wedge R_1(i,j) = 0) + Prob(R_2(i,j) = 0 \wedge R_1(i,j) = 1) = \frac{u-d}{v-d} \times \frac{u}{v} + \frac{u}{v-d} \times (1 - \frac{u}{v}) = \frac{u}{v}$. Hence, $Prob(R_2(i,j) = 0) = \frac{u}{v}$ is obtained no matter the secret pixel is white or black. By Definition 1, $T(R_2[S(0)]) = T(R_2[S(1)]) = \frac{u}{v}$ is achieved. Every share cannot disclose any information about the secret. □

LEMMA 2. *Given two shares R_1 and R_2 generated from Algorithm 4, the stacked result by the two shares $R_{1 \otimes 2} = R_1 \otimes R_2$ visually reveals the secret:*

$$T(R_{1 \otimes 2}[S(0)]) > T(R_{1 \otimes 2}[S(1)]).$$

PROOF. When $S(i,j) = 0$, $R_2(i,j) = R_1(i,j)$. If $R_1(i,j) = 0$, $R_2(i,j) = 0$. The stacked result is white if and only if the two shared pixels are white. Thus, we have $Prob(R_{1 \otimes 2}(i,j) = 0) = Prob(R_1(i,j) = 0 \wedge R_2(i,j) = 0) = \frac{u}{v}$. By Definition 1, we get $T(R_{1 \otimes 2}[S(0)]) = \frac{u}{v}$.

When $S(i,j) = 1$, $Prob(R_{1 \otimes 2}(i,j) = 0) = Prob(R_1(i,j) = 0 \wedge R_2(i,j) = 0) = \frac{u}{v} \times \frac{u-d}{v-d}$ according to Equation (3). By Definition 1, we obtain $T(R_{1 \otimes 2}[S(1)]) = \frac{u}{v} \times \frac{u-d}{v-d}$.

Therefore, $T(R_{1 \otimes 2}[S(0)]) - T(R_{1 \otimes 2}[S(1)]) = \frac{u}{v} - \frac{u}{v} \times \frac{u-d}{v-d} = \frac{u}{v} \times \frac{v-u}{v-d}$. Since $v > u \geq d$, we get $T(R_{1 \otimes 2}[S(0)]) - T(R_{1 \otimes 2}[S(1)]) > 0$. As a result, $T(R_{1 \otimes 2}[S(0)]) > T(R_{1 \otimes 2}[S(1)])$. The stacked result reveals the secret. □

THEOREM 1. *Algorithm 4 is a valid construction of the generalized RG-based VSS for $(2,2)$ case. It meets the following conditions:*

- *Every share is a generalized RG and gives no clue about the secret: $T(R_k[S(0)]) = T(R_k[S(1)]) = \frac{u}{v}$ where $k = 1, 2$.*

- *The stacked result by the two shares $R_{1 \otimes 2} = R_1 \otimes R_2$ reveals the secret: $T(R_{1 \otimes 2}[S(0)]) > T(R_{1 \otimes 2}[S(1)])$.*

PROOF. According to Lemmas 1 and 2, the two conditions are satisfied. Algorithm 1 is a valid construction of $(2,2)$ generalized RG-based VSS. □

THEOREM 2. *Contrast of the reconstructed secret image by stacking the two shares generated from Algorithm 4 is*

$$\alpha = \frac{u}{v+u-d}.$$

PROOF. Obtained from the proof of Lemma 2, we have $T(R_{1 \otimes 2}[S(0)]) = \frac{u}{v}$ and $T(R_{1 \otimes 2}[S(1)]) = \frac{u}{v} \times \frac{u-d}{v-d}$. According to Definition 3, the contrast of the reconstructed secret image is calculated by

$$\begin{aligned} \alpha &= \frac{T(R_{1 \otimes 2}[S(0)]) - T(R_{1 \otimes 2}[S(1)])}{1 + T(R_{1 \otimes 2}[S(1)])} \\ &= \left[\frac{u}{v} - \frac{u}{v} \times \frac{u-d}{v-d} \right] / \left[1 + \frac{u}{v} \times \frac{u-d}{v-d} \right] \\ &= \frac{u}{v+u-d}. \end{aligned}$$

□

When the average light transmission of a shadow is fixed (u, v are determined), parameter d is expected to be as large as possible so that larger contrast is achieved. The following two cases are considered: (1) $u \leq \frac{1}{2}v$ and (2) $u > \frac{1}{2}v$. When $u \leq \frac{1}{2}v$, the largest value of d is $d = u$. When $u > \frac{1}{2}v$, the largest value of d is $d = v - u$. Furthermore, we prove that the proposed $(2,2)$ scheme is a valid construction of VSS by Theorem 3 when XOR decryption is applied.

LEMMA 3. *Given two shares R_1 and R_2 generated from Algorithm 4, the XOR-ed result by the two shares $R_{1 \oplus 2} = R_1 \oplus R_2$ visually reveals the secret:*

$$T(R_{1 \oplus 2}[S(0)]) > T(R_{1 \oplus 2}[S(1)]).$$

PROOF. When $S(i,j) = 0$, $R_2(i,j) = R_1(i,j)$. When $R_1(i,j) = 0, R_2(i,j) = 0$ or $R_1(i,j) = 1, R_2(i,j) = 1$, the XOR-ed result is 0. The probability for $R_1(i,j) = 0$ and $R_2(i,j) = 0$ is $\frac{u}{v}$. And the probability for $R_1(i,j) = 1$ and $R_2(i,j) = 1$ is $(1 - \frac{u}{v})$. Thus, we have $Prob(R_{1 \oplus 2}(i,j) = 0) = \frac{u}{v} + 1 - \frac{u}{v} = 1$. By Definition 1, we obtain $T(R_{1 \oplus 2}[S(0)]) = 1$.

When $S(i,j) = 1$, the probability for $R_1(i,j) = 0$ and $R_2(i,j) = 0$ is $\frac{u}{v} \times \frac{u-d}{v-d}$. And the probability for $R_1(i,j) = 1$ and $R_2(i,j) = 1$ is $(1 - \frac{u}{v}) \times (1 - \frac{u}{v-d})$. Thus, we have $Prob(R_{1 \oplus 2}(i,j) = 0) = (\frac{u}{v})(\frac{u-d}{v-d}) + (1 - \frac{u}{v})(1 - \frac{u}{v-d})$. By Definition 1, we obtain $T(R_{1 \oplus 2}[S(0)]) = (\frac{u}{v})(\frac{u-d}{v-d}) + (1 - \frac{u}{v})(1 - \frac{u}{v-d})$.

Since $d \leq u < v$, $u - d < v - d$ is obtained. We have $0 \leq \frac{u-d}{v-d} < 1$. Further, since $v \geq u + d$, we get $v - d \geq u$. And $0 < \frac{u}{v-d} < 1$ is achieved. As a result, we obtain $(\frac{u}{v})(\frac{u-d}{v-d}) + (1 - \frac{u}{v})(1 - \frac{u}{v-d}) < (\frac{u}{v}) + (1 - \frac{u}{v}) = 1$. Finally, $T(R_{1 \oplus 2}[S(0)]) > T(R_{1 \oplus 2}[S(1)])$ is achieved. The XOR-ed result reveals the secret. □

THEOREM 3. *Algorithm 4 is a valid construction of XOR-based VSS for $(2,2)$ case. It satisfies the following conditions:*

- *Every share gives no clue about the secret: $T(R_k[S(0)]) = T(R_k[S(1)]) = \frac{u}{v}$ where $k = 1, 2$.*

- *The XOR-ed result by the two shares $R_{1 \oplus 2} = R_1 \oplus R_2$ reveals the secret: $T(R_{1 \oplus 2}[S(0)]) > T(R_{1 \oplus 2}[S(1)]).$*

PROOF. According to Lemmas 1 and 3, the two conditions are met. Algorithm 4 is a valid construction of XOR-based VSS for $(2,2)$ case. □

3.2 XOR-based meaningful VSS

Prior to formulating the XOR-based meaningful VSS, a (n,n) generalized RG-based VSS is given, where the n shares are constructed by recursively applying the $(2,2)$ scheme for $n-1$ times. Diagram of the share construction is illustrated in Fig.1. Description on the (n,n) scheme is given below.

Algorithm 5. Generalized RG-based VSS for (n,n) case.
Input: a binary secret image S with $M \times N$ pixels, and three parameters u, v, d.
Output: n shares $R_1, \cdots, R_n$.

Step 1: For each position (i,j) in the secret image, Steps 2 and 3 are performed to generate n shared pixels $R_1(i,j), \cdots, R_n(i,j)$
Step 2: By recursively applying the $(2,2)$ generalized RG-based VSS for $n-1$ times, n pixels $r_1, r_2, \cdots, r_n$ are constructed by

$$\begin{cases} [r_1, t_1] = GRG[(2,2), S(i,j), u, v, d], \\ [r_2, t_2] = GRG[(2,2), t_1, u, v, d], \\ \quad \vdots \\ [r_{n-2}, t_{n-2}] = GRG[(2,2), t_{n-3}, u, v, d], \\ [r_{n-1}, r_n] = GRG[(2,2), t_{n-2}, u, v, d], \end{cases} \quad (4)$$

where procedure GRG is implemented by generalized RG-based VSS, $(2,2)$ is the desired threshold, $S(i,j), t_1, \cdots, t_{n-2}$ are the input pixels, and u, v, d are the three parameters. Indeed, the $n-1$ pixels $r_1, r_2, \cdots, r_{n-1}$ are generated by the random bit generator $g(\frac{u}{v})$ in the $(2,2)$ scheme.
Step 4: The order of the n pixels $r_1, \cdots, r_n$ are rearranged and the rearranged n pixels are assigned to $R_1(i,j), \cdots, R_n(i,j)$.
Step 5: Output the n shares $R_1, \cdots, R_n$.

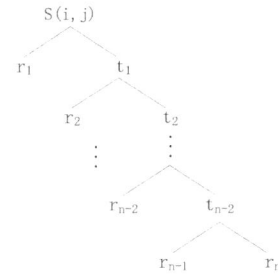

Figure 1: Diagram of share construction for Algorithm 5.

Based on the analysis of the $(2,2)$ scheme, we prove that Algorithm 5 satisfies the security condition by Lemmas 4 and 5, as well as the contrast condition by Lemma 6. Theorem 4 summaries the above-mentioned conclusions.

LEMMA 4. *Given n shares $R_1, \cdots, R_n$ generated from Algorithm 5, every share is a generalized RG and gives no clue about the secret: $T(R_k[S(0)]) = T(R_k[S(1)]) = \frac{u}{v}$ where $k = 1, \cdots, n$.*

PROOF. According to Algorithm 5, the n shared pixels $r_1, \cdots, r_n$ are constructed by recursively applying the $(2,2)$ scheme. Based on Lemma 1, every shared pixel is a generalized random pixel and cannot reveal any information about the secret pixel. Thus, we have $T(R_k[S(0)]) = T(R_k[S(1)]) = \frac{u}{v}$ for $k = 1, \cdots, n$. □

LEMMA 5. *Given n shares $R_1, \cdots, R_n$ constructed from Algorithm 5, the XOR-ed result by any $k < n$ shares $R_{x_1 \oplus \cdots \oplus x_k} = R_{x_1} \oplus \cdots \oplus R_{x_k}$ gives no clue about the secret:*

$$T(R_{x_1 \oplus \cdots \oplus x_k}[S(0)]) = T(R_{x_1 \oplus \cdots \oplus x_k}[S(1)]).$$

PROOF. Assume k shared pixels, denoted as $r_{x_1}, \cdots, r_{x_k}$, are collected from the n shared pixels $r_1, \cdots, r_n$, i.e.,

$$\{x_1, \cdots, x_k\} \in \{1, \cdots, n\}.$$

To prove that the XOR-ed result by any $k < n$ shared pixels do not reveal the secret pixel $S(i,j)$, two cases are considered: (1) $n \in \{x_1, \cdots, x_k\}$ and (2) $n \notin \{x_1, \cdots, x_n\}$.

(1) $n \in \{x_1, \cdots, x_k\}$. We consider $r_n \oplus r_g \oplus \cdots \oplus r_h$ with $g, \cdots, h$ being the indices in $\{x_1, \cdots, x_t\}$ besides n. Since the value t_{n-2} can be recovered by $r_{n-1} \oplus r_n$, assume that $n-1 \in \{x_1, \cdots, x_k\}$. We obtain

$$r_n \oplus r_g \oplus \cdots \oplus r_h = r_n \oplus r_{n-1} \oplus r_g \oplus \cdots \oplus r_{h-1}$$
$$= t_{n-2}^R \oplus r_g \oplus \cdots \oplus r_{h-1}$$

with $g, \cdots, h-1$ being the indices in $\{x_1, \cdots, x_k\}$ besides n and $n-1$, where t_{n-2}^R resembles t_{n-2} but meaningless.

Likewise, assume that $n-2, n-3, \cdots, n-k \in \{x_1, \cdots, x_k\}$, then

$$r_n \oplus r_g \oplus \cdots \oplus r_h = t_{n-2}^R \oplus r_g \oplus \cdots \oplus r_{h-1}$$
$$= t_{n-1}^R \oplus r_g \oplus \cdots \oplus r_{h-2}$$
$$= \cdots = t_{n-k}^R$$

is achieved where t_{n-k}^R resembles t_{n-k} visually but meaningless. Since $k < n$, the XOR-ed result by k shared pixels do not reveal the secret pixel. And it at most reveals a value t_{n-k}^R which is meaningless.

(2) $n \notin \{x_1, \cdots, x_n\}$. Since the k shared pixels are constructed by the random bit generator, the XOR-ed result by any k shared pixels give no clue about the associated secret pixel.

Based on the above analysis, the secret pixel cannot be recovered by conducting XOR operation on any $k < n$ shared pixels. As a result, the XOR-ed result of any $k < n$ shares $R_{x_1 \oplus \cdots \oplus x_k} = R_{x_1} \oplus \cdots \oplus R_{x_k}$ gives no clue about the secret: $T(R_{x_1 \oplus \cdots \oplus x_k}[S(0)]) = T(R_{x_1 \oplus \cdots \oplus x_k}[S(1)])$. $\square$

LEMMA 6. *Given n shares $R_1, \cdots, R_n$ constructed from Algorithm 5, the XOR-ed result of n shares visually reveals the secret: $T(R_{1 \oplus \cdots \oplus n}[S(0)]) > T(R_{1 \oplus \cdots \oplus n}[S(1)])$.*

PROOF. Let $S(i,j)$ be the secret pixel and let $r_1, \cdots, r_n$ be the n generated shared pixels. We first consider t_{n-2} which can be recovered from r_{n-1} and r_n. Let $t_{n-2}^R = r_{n-1} \oplus r_n$ be the reconstructed pixel. When $t_{n-2} = 0$, the probability for t_{n-2}^R to be 0 is 1. When $t_{n-2} = 1$, the probability for t_{n-2}^R to be 0 is $(\frac{u}{v})(\frac{u-d}{v-d}) + (1 - \frac{u}{v})(1 - \frac{u}{v-d}) < 1$.

Simply, we calculate the average light transmission of t_{n-2}^R by using another approach. Since r_{n-1} is generated by the random bit generator, we consider r_n. Let r_n^R be the reconstructed pixel which looks like r_n. Suppose that P_n^0 (resp. P_n^1) is the probability for r_n^R to be 0 when r_n is 0 (resp. 1). Therefore, we have $Prob(r_n^R = 0) = Prob(r_n = 0) \times P_n^0$ and $Prob(r_n^R = 1) = Prob(r_n = 1) \times (1 - P_n^1)$. Since r_n is a leaf node in the construction tree, we have $r_n^R = r_n$, which indicates that $P_n^0 = 1$ and $P_n^1 = 0$. Based on P_n^0 and P_n^1, we calculate the average light transmission of t_{n-2}^R. t_{n-2}^R can be represented by $t_{n-2}^R = r_{n-1} \oplus r_n^R$. When $t_{n-2} = 0$, the

average light transmission of t_{n-2}^R is computed by

$$T(t_{n-2}^R[t_{n-2} = 0])$$
$$= Prob(r_{n-1} = 0) \times Prob(r_n^R = 0) + Prob(r_{n-1} = 1)$$
$$\quad \times Prob(r_n^R = 1)$$
$$= Prob(r_{n-1} = 0) \times Prob(r_n = 0) \times P_n^0 + Prob(r_{n-1} = 1)$$
$$\quad \times Prob(r_n = 1) \times (1 - P_n^1)$$
$$= Prob(r_{n-1} = 0) \times Prob(r_n = 0) \times 1 + Prob(r_{n-1} = 1)$$
$$\quad \times Prob(r_n = 1) \times 1$$
$$= 1.$$

Similarly, when $t_{n-2} = 1$, the average light transmission of t_{n-2}^R is calculated by

$$T(t_{n-2}^R[t_{n-2} = 1])$$
$$= Prob(r_{n-1} = 0) \times Prob(r_n^R = 0) + Prob(r_{n-1} = 1)$$
$$\quad \times Prob(r_n^R = 1)$$
$$= Prob(r_{n-1} = 0) \times Prob(r_n = 0) \times P_n^0 + Prob(r_{n-1} = 1)$$
$$\quad \times Prob(r_n = 1) \times (1 - P_n^1)$$
$$= Prob(r_{n-1} = 0) \times Prob(r_n = 0) \times 1 + Prob(r_{n-1} = 1)$$
$$\quad \times Prob(r_n = 1) \times 1$$
$$= (\frac{u}{v})(\frac{u-d}{v-d}) + (1 - \frac{u}{v})(1 - \frac{u}{v-d}).$$

Further, let P_{n-2}^0 (resp. P_{n-2}^1) be the probability for t_{n-2}^R to be 0 when t_{n-2} is 0 (resp. 1). Actually, P_{n-2}^0 and P_{n-2}^1 are $T(t_{n-2}^R[t_{n-2} = 0])$ and $T(t_{n-2}^R[t_{n-2} = 1])$, respectively. Similarly, when $t_{n-3} = 0$, the average light transmission of t_{n-3}^R is calculated by

$$T(t_{n-3}^R[t_{n-3} = 0])$$
$$= Prob(r_{n-2} = 0) \times Prob(t_{n-2}^R = 0) + Prob(r_{n-2} = 1)$$
$$\quad \times Prob(t_{n-2}^R = 1)$$
$$= Prob(r_{n-2} = 0) \times Prob(t_{n-2} = 0) \times P_{n-2}^0 +$$
$$\quad Prob(r_{n-2} = 1) \times Prob(t_{n-2} = 1) \times (1 - P_{n-2}^1)$$
$$= (\frac{u}{v})P_{n-2}^0 + (1 - \frac{u}{v})(1 - P_{n-2}^1).$$

When $t_{n-3} = 1$, the average light transmission of t_{n-3}^R is calculated by

$$T(t_{n-3}^R[t_{n-3} = 1])$$
$$= Prob(r_{n-2} = 0) \times Prob(t_{n-2}^R = 0) + Prob(r_{n-2} = 1)$$
$$\quad \times Prob(t_{n-2}^R = 1)$$
$$= Prob(r_{n-2} = 0) \times Prob(t_{n-2} = 0) \times P_{n-2}^0 +$$
$$\quad Prob(r_{n-2} = 1) \times Prob(t_{n-2} = 1) \times (1 - P_{n-2}^1)$$
$$= (\frac{u}{v})(\frac{u-d}{v-d})P_{n-2}^0 + (1 - \frac{u}{v})(1 - \frac{u}{v-d})(1 - P_{n-2}^1).$$

Since $0 \le \frac{u-d}{v-d} < 1$ and $0 < 1 - \frac{u}{v-d} \le 1$, we have $(\frac{u}{v})(\frac{u-d}{v-d})P_{n-2}^0 < (\frac{u}{v})P_{n-2}^0$ and $(1 - \frac{u}{v})(1 - \frac{u}{v-d})(1 - P_{n-2}^1) \le (1 - \frac{u}{v})(1 - P_{n-2}^1)$. Therefore, $T(t_{n-3}^R[t_{n-3} = 0]) > T(t_{n-3}^R[t_{n-3} = 1])$ is obtained.

By the same method, we get $T(t_{n-4}^R[t_{n-4} = 0]) > T(t_{n-4}^R[t_{n-4} = 1]), \cdots, T(S^R(i,j)[S(i,j) = 0]) > T(S^R(i,j)[S(i,j) = 1])$ where $t_{n-4}^R, \cdots, S^R(i,j)$ are the reconstructed pixels. Based on Definition 1, $T(R_{1\oplus\cdots\oplus n}[S(0)]) > T(R_{1\oplus\cdots\oplus n}[S(1)])$ is obtained. The XOR-ed result by the n shares reveals the secret. $\square$

THEOREM 4. *Algorithm 5 is a valid construction of (n,n) XOR-based VSS. The following conditions are satisfied:*

- *Every share is a generalized RG and gives no clue about the secret:* $T(R_k[S(0)]) = T(R_k[S(1)]) = \frac{u}{v}$ *where* $k = 1,\cdots,n$.

- *The XOR-ed result by any k shares $R_{x_1\otimes\cdots\otimes x_k} = R_{x_1}\otimes \cdots \otimes R_{x_k}$ gives no clue about the secret:*
$$T(R_{x_1\otimes\cdots\otimes x_k}[S(0)]) = T(R_{x_1\otimes\cdots\otimes x_k}[S(1)]).$$

- *The XOR-ed result by n shares visually reveals the secret:* $T(R_{1\otimes\cdots\otimes n}[S(0)]) > T(R_{1\otimes\cdots\otimes n}[S(1)]).$

PROOF. Based on Lemmas 4, 5 and 6, the mentioned three conditions are satisfied. Algorithm 3 is a valid construction of (n,n) XOR-based VSS. $\square$

We adopt the concept of generalized RG to devise a XOR-based meaningful VSS, where the pixel expansion and random-looking problems are solved. In conventional VSS and XOR-based VSS, the shared pixels only carry the secret information. Hence the shares are noise-like. In the proposed XOR-based meaningful VSS, the shared pixels carry not only secret information but also cover image information. We utilize two different light transmissions to represent the white and black colors. The XOR-based meaningful VSS is described as follows.

Algorithm 6. XOR-based meaningful VSS for (n,n) case.
Input: a binary secret image S and a cover image, both with $M \times N$ pixels, and six parameters u_0, v_0, d_0 and u_1, v_1, d_1.
Output: n meaningful shares $R_1, \cdots, R_n$.
Step 1: For each position (i,j) in the secret image, Step 2 or 3 is performed to generate n shared pixels $R_1(i,j), \cdots, R_2(i,j)$.
Step 2: When the corresponding cover image pixel $C(i,j) = 0$, the n shared pixels are constructed by

$$[R_1(i,j),\cdots,R_n(i,j)] = GRG[(n,n),S(i,j),u_0,v_0,d_0], \tag{5}$$

where procedure GRG is implemented by generalized RG-based VSS, (n,n) is the desired threshold, $S(i,j)$ is the secret pixel, and u_0, v_0, d_0 are the three parameters.
Step 3: When the corresponding cover image pixel $C(i,j) = 1$, the n shared pixels are constructed by

$$[R_1(i,j),\cdots,R_n(i,j)] = GRG[(n,n),S(i,j),u_1,v_1,d_1]. \tag{6}$$

Step 4: Output the n meaningful shares $R_1, \cdots, R_n$.

To make sure that the generated shares resemble the cover image, the parameters must satisfy the following condition:

$$0 < \frac{u_1}{v_1} < \frac{u_0}{v_0} < 1.$$

Theorem 5 formulates that the Algorithm 6 is a a valid construction of XOR-based meaningful VSS for (n,n) case.

THEOREM 5. *et $R_1, \cdots, R_n$ be the n shares generated from Algorithm 6, Algorithm 6 is a valid construction of XOR-based meaningful VSS for (n,n) case. The following conditions are satisfied:*

- *Every share is a meaningful image which looks like the cover image :* $T(R_k[C(0)]) > T(R_k[C(1)])$, *and gives no clue about the secret:* $T(R_k[S(0)]) = T(R_k[S(1)])$, *where* $k = 1,\cdots,n$.

- *The XOR-ed result by any $k < n$ shares $R_{x_1\oplus\cdots\oplus x_k} = R_{x_1} \oplus \cdots \oplus R_{x_k}$ cannot disclose the secret:*
$$T(R_{x_1\oplus\cdots\oplus x_k}[S(0)]) = T(R_{x_1\oplus\cdots\oplus x_k}[S(1)]).$$

- *The XOR-ed result by n shares visually reveals the secret:* $T(R_{1\oplus\cdots\oplus n}[S(0)]) > T(R_{1\oplus\cdots\oplus n}[S(1)]).$

PROOF. When the cover image pixel $C(i,j) = 0$ (resp. $C(i,j) = 1$), the average light transmissions of the n shared pixels $R_1(i,j),\cdots,R_n(i,j)$ are $\frac{u_0}{v_0}$ (resp. $\frac{u_1}{v_1}$). Since $\frac{u_0}{v_0} > \frac{u_1}{v_1}$, we have $T(R_k(i,j)[C(i,j) = 0]) > T(R_k(i,j)[C(i,j) = 1])$ where $k = 1,\cdots,n$. By Definition 1, $T(R_k[C(0)]) > T(R_k[C(1)])$ is obtained. Every share is a meaningful image which resembles the cover image.

For the white area of the cover image, we calculate the corresponding average light transmissions of every share based on the first condition of Theorem 4, as denoted by $T(R_k[S(0)]) = T(R_k[S(1)]) = \frac{u_0}{v_0}, k = 1,\cdots,n$. For the black area of the cover image, we also get $T(R_k[S(0)]) = T(R_k[S(1)]) = \frac{u_1}{v_1}, k = 1,\cdots,n$. As a result, every single share gives no clue about the secret.

Based on the second condition of Theorem 4, the average light transmissions of the XOR-ed result by any $k < n$ shares are $T(R_{x_1\oplus\cdots\oplus x_k}[S(0)]) = T(R_{x_1\oplus\cdots\oplus x_k}[S(1)])$ when these XOR-ed pixels are corresponding to the white area of the cover image. Similarly, the same conclusion holds when these XOR-ed pixels are corresponding to the black area of the cover image. Hence, the XOR-ed result by any k shares do not reveal any information about the secret.

According to the third condition of Theorem 4, the average light transmissions of the XOR-ed result by n shares are $T(R_{1\oplus\cdots\oplus n}[S(0)]) > T(R_{1\oplus\cdots\oplus n}[S(1)])$ when these XOR-ed pixels belong to the white area of the cover image. And the same result holds as well when these XOR-ed pixels belong to the black area of the cover image. Thus, the XOR-ed result by n shares visually reveals the secret. $\square$

4. EXPERIMENTAL RESULTS

4.1 Feasibility

Simulation results by Algorithm 6 for constructing XOR-based meaningful VSS are provided in Figs.2 and 3. Figs.2 shows the $(2,2)$ scheme, where the six parameters are with the following configurations:

$$u_0 = 3, v_0 = 4, d_0 = 1 \text{ and } u_1 = 1, v_1 = 4, d_1 = 1.$$

The secret image and cover image are illustrated in Figs.2(a) and (b). Two generated meaningful shares which look like the cover image are demonstrated in Figs.2(c) and (d). The XOR-ed result by the two shares is shown in Fig.2(e), which reveals the secret.

Fig.3 illustrates the $(3,3)$ meaningful scheme. The six parameters used in experiment are configured as

$$u_0 = 2.5, v_0 = 4, d_0 = 1.5 \text{ and } u_1 = 1.5, v_1 = 4, d_1 = 1.5.$$

Figs.3(a) and (b) show the secret image and cover image, respectively. The meaningful shares are demonstrated in

Figs.3(c)-(e). The XOR-ed results by any two of the three shares are illustrated in Figs.3(f)-(h), which give no clue about the secret. The secret is reconstructed by conducting XOR operation on the three shares, as shown in Fig.3(i).

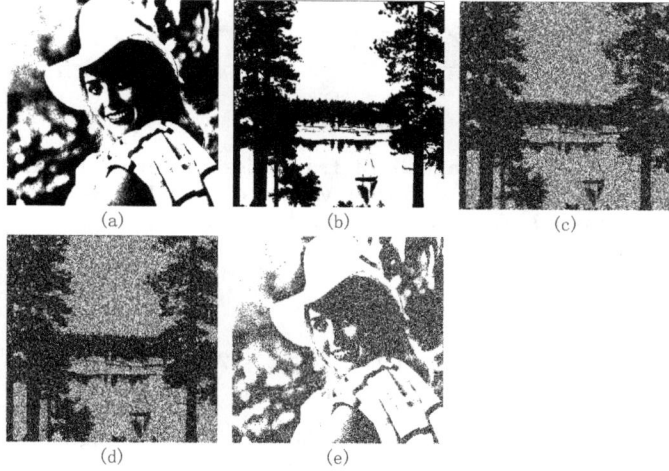

Figure 2: Simulation results of the $(2,2)$ XOR-based meaningful VSS by Algorithm 6. (a) The secret image, (b) the cover image, (c)-(d) two meaningful shares, (e) XOR-ed result by two shares.

4.2 Homogeneous conditions

Algorithm 6 is constructed by synthesizing two XOR-based VSS schemes with different values of $\frac{u}{v}$. But different values of $\frac{u}{v}$ would introduce different light transmissions. These light transmissions may vary from each other significantly, and lead to a consequence that the reconstructed secret image is not homogeneous. An example is shown in Fig.4 with the six parameters configured as

$$u_0 = 9, v_0 = 10, d_0 = 1 \text{ and } u_1 = 4, v_1 = 10, d_1 = 4.$$

Obviously, some reconstructed pixels which belong to the black area of the original secret image are darker than the others. The reason of resulting in inhomogeneous recovered secret image is that the light transmissions ($T^{\frac{u_0}{v_0}}(R_{1\oplus\cdots\oplus n}[S(0)])$ and $T^{\frac{u_0}{v_0}}(R_{1\oplus\cdots\oplus n}[S(1)])$) of the recovered secret image by value $\frac{u_0}{v_0}$ are significantly different from the light transmissions ($T^{\frac{u_1}{v_1}}(R_{1\oplus\cdots\oplus n}[S(0)])$ and $T^{\frac{u_1}{v_1}}(R_{1\oplus\cdots\oplus n}[S(1)])$) by value $\frac{u_1}{v_1}$. In this example,

$$T^{\frac{u_0}{v_0}}(R_{1\oplus\cdots\oplus n}[S(0)]) = T^{\frac{u_1}{v_1}}(R_{1\oplus\cdots\oplus n}[S(0)]) = 0,$$

but $T^{\frac{u_0}{v_0}}(R_{1\oplus\cdots\oplus n}[S(0)]) = 0.8$ and $T^{\frac{u_1}{v_1}}(R_{1\oplus\cdots\oplus n}[S(0)]) = 0.2$. $T^{\frac{u_0}{v_0}}(R_{1\oplus\cdots\oplus n}[S(0)])$ is different from $T^{\frac{u_1}{v_1}}(R_{1\oplus\cdots\oplus n}[S(0)])$ dramatically.

For obtaining homogeneous recovered secret image for the (n,n) XOR-based meaningful VSS, the four light transmissions should satisfy the following conditions:

$$T^{\frac{u_0}{v_0}}(R_{1\oplus\cdots\oplus n}[S(0)]) \approx T^{\frac{u_1}{v_1}}(R_{1\oplus\cdots\oplus n}[S(0)])$$

and

$$T^{\frac{u_0}{v_0}}(R_{1\oplus\cdots\oplus n}[S(1)]) \approx T^{\frac{u_1}{v_1}}(R_{1\oplus\cdots\oplus n}[S(1)]).$$

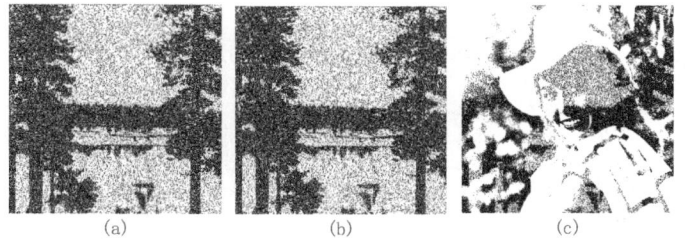

Figure 3: Simulation results of the $(3,3)$ XOR-based meaningful VSS by Algorithm 6. (a) The secret image, (b) the cover image, (c)-(e) three meaningful shares, (f)-(h) XOR-ed results by any two of the three shares, (i) XOR-ed result by three shares.

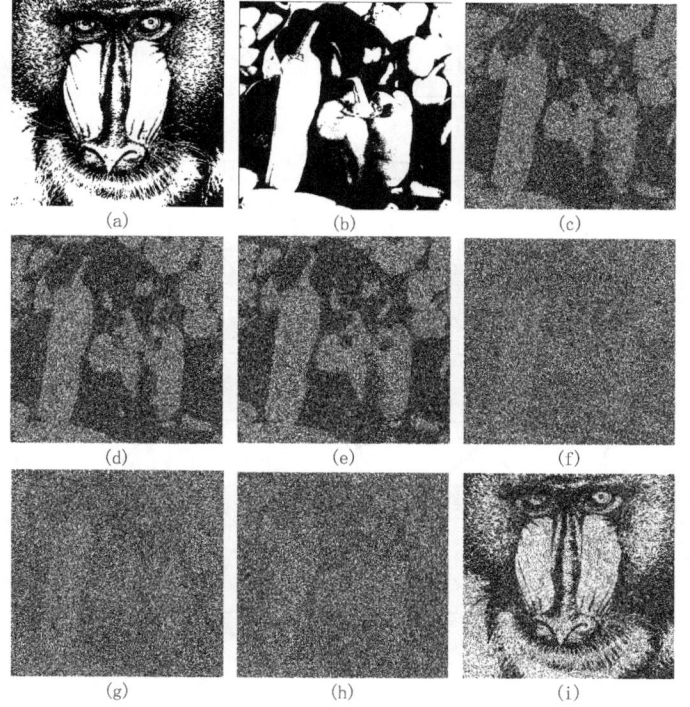

Figure 4: An example of $(2,2)$ XOR-based meaningful VSS, where the recovered secret image is not homogeneous. (a)-(b) Two meaningful shares, (c) the XOR-ed result by two shares.

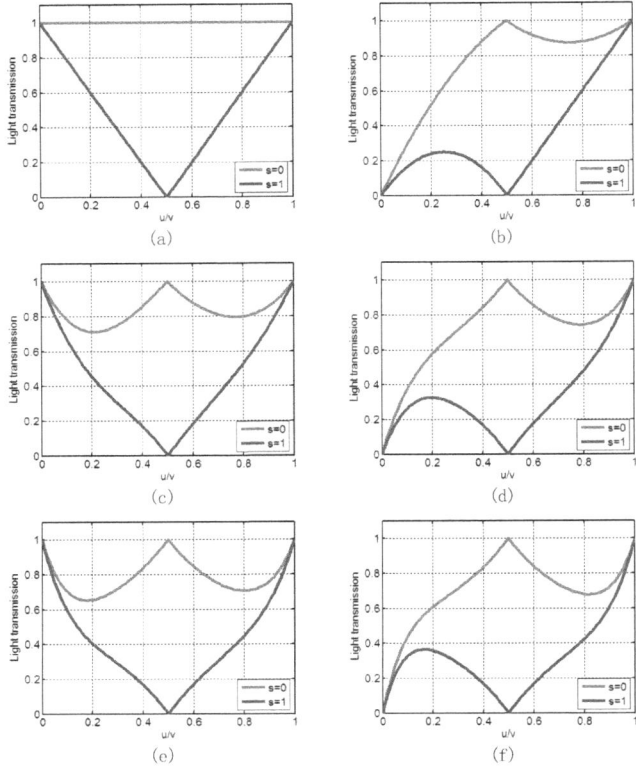

Figure 5: **Average light transmission curves of Algorithm 5 with different values of $\frac{u}{v}$. (a) The $(2,2)$ scheme, (b) the $(3,3)$ scheme, (c) the $(4,4)$ scheme, (d) the $(5,5)$ scheme, (e) the $(6,6)$ scheme, (f) the $(7,7)$ scheme.**

Based on the proof of Lemma 6, the average light transmissions of reconstructed results by n shares can be calculated iteratively. Herein, possible values of $\frac{u}{v}$ are adopted to compute the light transmissions of XOR-ed result by n shares in Algorithm 5, as demonstrated in Fig.5. Specifically, Fig.5(a) illustrates the average light transmission curves of the XOR-ed result by two shares in the $(2,2)$ scheme. To satisfy the homogeneous conditions, the values of $\frac{u_0}{v_0}$ and $\frac{u_1}{v_1}$ can be

$$\frac{u_0}{v_0} = 0.5 + t \text{ and } \frac{u_1}{v_1} = 0.5 - t$$

where $0 < t < 0.5$.

We further analyze the light transmission curves for schemes such as $(3,3), \cdots , (7,7)$, as shown in Figs.5(b)-(f). We notice that the curves in the $(3,3),(5,5)$ and $(7,7)$ scheme are similar. To meet the homogeneous conditions, the values of $\frac{u_0}{v_0}$ and $\frac{u_1}{v_1}$ can be 0.6 and 0.4, respectively. For the $(4,4)$ and $(6,6)$, values for $\frac{u_0}{v_0}$ and $\frac{u_1}{v_1}$ are suggested to be 0.6 and 0.4 as well. We further investigate the light transmission curves when n is much bigger, as demonstrated in Fig.6. According to the light transmission curves, suggested values for $\frac{u_0}{v_0}$ and $\frac{u_1}{v_1}$ which meets the homogeneous conditions are

$$\frac{u_0}{v_0} = \begin{cases} 0.5 + t, \text{ if } n = 2, \\ 0.6, \text{ otherwise,} \end{cases}$$

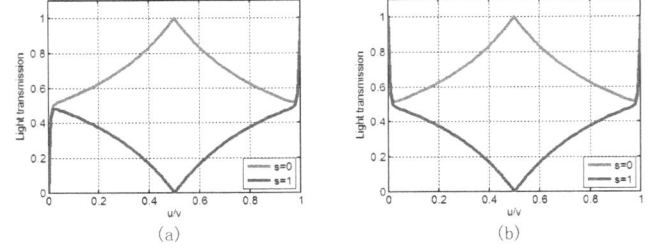

Figure 6: **Average light transmission curves of Algorithm 5 with different values of $\frac{u}{v}$, when large n is applied. (a) The $(99,99)$ scheme, (b) the $(100,100)$ scheme.**

and

$$\frac{u_1}{v_1} = \begin{cases} 0.5 - t, \text{ if } n = 2, \\ 0.4, \text{ otherwise.} \end{cases}$$

where $0 < t < 0.5$. Note that, the 0.6 and 0.4 are suggested values, some values near 0.6 and 0.4 are applicable as well.

4.3 Comparisons

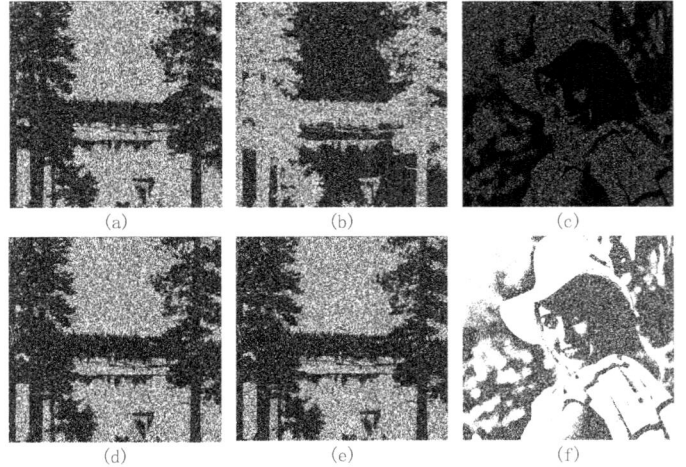

Figure 7: **Comparison of visual quality between Algorithm 6 and Chen and Tsao's method [6], where complementary shares are used in Chen and Tsao's method. (a)-(b) Two shares generated from [6], (c) the recovered secret image, (d)-(e) two shares generated from Algorithm 6, (f) the recovered secret image.**

Comparison of visual quality between Algorithm 6 and Chen and Tsao's meaningful RG-based VSS [6] is demonstrated in Fig.7, where complementary shares are used in Chen and Tsao's method. In their approach [6], the parameter which defines the portion of shared pixels in the meaningful share is set to be 0.5. In Algorithm 6, the six parameters are configured as

$$u_0 = 3, v_0 = 4, d_0 = 1 \text{ and } u_1 = 1, v_1 = 4, d_1 = 1.$$

Contrasts calculated from the shares and recovered secret image in this experiment are provided in Table 1. When

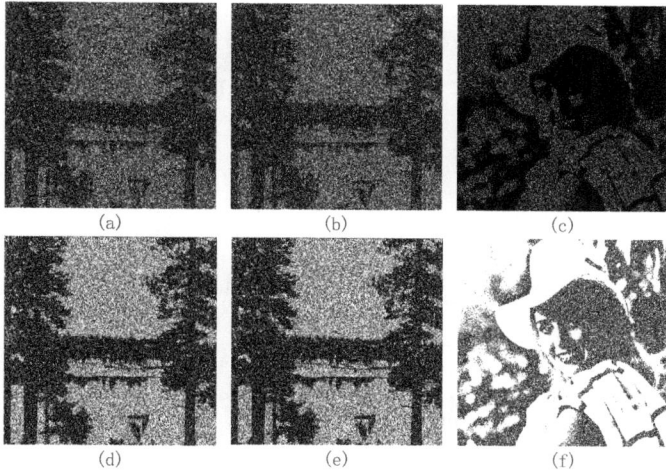

Figure 8: Comparison of visual quality between Algorithm 6 and Chen and Tsao's method [6], where complementary shares are not used in Chen and Tsao's method. (a)-(b) Two shares generated from [6], (c) the recovered secret image, (d)-(e) two shares generated from Algorithm 6, (f) the recovered secret image.

the shared image quality is approximately the same, optimal reconstructed image quality is provided by Algorithm 6. Further, adopting complementary shares is not suitable for practical applications, since the complementary share does not resemble natural image. More comparisons of visual quality between Algorithm 6 and Chen and Tsao's scheme [6] are exhibited in Fig.8 and Table 2. Obviously, superior visual quality is obtained by Algorithm 6.

Table 1: Comparison of contrast for the $(2, 2)$ case, where complementary shares are used in Chen and Tsao's approach [6].

Image	Contrast	
	Our	Ref.[6]
The first share	0.3963	0.3994
The second share	0.4008	-
Revealed secret image	0.3340	0.2506

Feature comparison among Algorithm 6 and related methods, including VC schemes and secret image sharing (SIS) schemes, is shown in Table 3. Major advantages of Algorithm 6 are that (1) shares are with meaningful contents and (2) superior visual quality is achieved. Meanwhile, merits such as no pixel expansion and no code book required are also maintained.

5. CONCLUSIONS

This paper first introduces a $(2, 2)$ generalized RG-based VSS, where the average light transmission of a share becomes adjustable. By recursively applying the $(2, 2)$ scheme for $n - 1$ times, a (n, n) generalized RG-based VSS is proposed. And the (n, n) scheme is proved to be a valid construction of XOR-based VSS but with meaningless shares.

Table 2: Comparison of contrast for the $(2, 2)$ case, where complementary shares are not used in Chen and Tsao's approach [6].

Image	Contrast	
	Our	Ref.[6]
The first share	0.3963	0.1986
The second share	0.4008	0.1997
Revealed secret image	0.3340	0.2510

Further, a XOR-based meaningful VSS is derived by synthesizing two (n, n) generalized RG-based VSS schemes with different values of $\frac{u}{v}$. Shares with meaningful contents are constructed, and superior visual quality of both the share and recovered secret image is obtained by the proposed method.

6. ACKNOWLEDGMENTS

This work was partially supported by Science and Technology Development Fund of Macao Special Administrative Region under Contract 006/2011/A1 and innovative talent training program of Sun Yat-sen University.

7. REFERENCES

[1] G. Ateniese, C. Blundo, A. De Santis, and D. Stinson. Visual Cryptography for General Access Structures. *Information and Computation*, 129(2):86–106, 1996.

[2] G. Ateniese, C. Blundo, A. Santis, and D. Stinson. Extended capabilities for visual cryptography. *Theoretical Computer Science*, 250(1-2):143–161, 2001.

[3] C. Blundo, A. De Santis, and D. Stinson. On the contrast in visual cryptography schemes. *ournal of Cryptology*, 12(4):241–289, 1999.

[4] T. Chen and K. Tsao. Visual secret sharing by random grids revisited. *Pattern Recognition*, 42(9):2203–2217, 2009.

[5] T. Chen and K. Tsao. Threshold visual secret sharing by random grids. *ournal of Systems and Software*, 84:1197–1208, 2011.

[6] T. Chen and K. Tsao. User-friendly random-grid-based visual secret sharing. *Circuits and Systems for Video Technology, IEEE Transactions on*, 21(11):1693–1703, 2011.

[7] S. Cimato, R. De Prisco, and A. De Santis. Probabilistic visual cryptography schemes. *The Computer ournal*, 49(1):97–107, 2006.

[8] R. Ito, H. Kuwakado, and H. Tanaka. Image size invariant visual cryptography. *IEICE Transactions on Fundamentals of Electronics, Communications and Computer Sciences*, 82(10):2172–2177, 1999.

[9] O. Kafri and E. Keren. Encryption of pictures and shapes by random grids. *Optics letters*, 12(6):377–379, 1987.

[10] I. Kang, G. Arce, and H. Lee. Color extended visual cryptography using error diffusion. *Image Processing, IEEE Transactions on*, 20(1):132–145, 2011.

[11] C. Lin and W. Tsai. Visual cryptography for gray-level images by dithering techniques. *Pattern Recognition etters*, 24(1-3):349–358, 2003.

Table 3: Comparison of feature among Algorithm 6 and related methods.

Schemes	Features Kernel Method	Meaningful Share	Pixel Expansion	Code book Needed	Decryption	Complexity Decryption	Visual Quality	Type of VSS
Ref.[17]	SIS	No	No	No	Computer	$O(n\log^2 n)$	High	(k,n)
Ref.[12]	SIS	Yes	Yes	No	Computer	$O(n\log^2 n)$	High	(k,n)
Ref.[18]	VSS	No	Yes	Yes	XOR	$O(n)$	Medium	(k,n)
Ref.[5]	VSS	No	No	No	Stack	$O(1)$	Low	(k,n)
Ref.[6]	VSS	Yes	No	No	Stack	$O(1)$	Low	(2,n),(n,n)
Algorithm 6	VSS	Yes	No	No	XOR	$O(n)$	Medium	(n,n)

[12] C. Lin and W. Tsai. Secret image sharing with steganography and authentication. *ournal of Systems and Software*, 73(3):405–414, 2004.

[13] F. Liu and C. Wu. Embedded extended visual cryptography schemes. *Information Forensics and Security, IEEE Transactions on*, 6(2):307–322, 2011.

[14] M. Naor and A. Shamir. Visual cryptography. *ecture Notes in Computer Science*, 950(1):1–12, 1995.

[15] S. Shyu. Image encryption by random grids. *Pattern Recognition*, 40(3):1014–1031, 2007.

[16] S. Shyu. Image encryption by multiple random grids. *Pattern Recognition*, 42(7):1582–1596, 2009.

[17] C. Thien and J. Lin. Secret image sharing. *Computers & Graphics*, 26(5):765–770, 2002.

[18] P. Tuyls, H. Hollmann, J. Lint, and L. Tolhuizen. Xor-based visual cryptography schemes. *Designs, Codes and Cryptography*, 37(1):169–186, 2005.

[19] Z. Wang, G. Arce, and G. Di Crescenzo. Halftone visual cryptography via error diffusion. *Information Forensics and Security, IEEE Transactions on*, 4(3):383–396, 2009.

[20] X. Wu and W. Sun. Visual secret sharing for general access structures by random grids. *IET information security*, 6(4):299–309, 2012.

[21] X. Wu and W. Sun. Improving the visual quality of random grid-based visual secret sharing. *Signal Processing*, 93(5):977–995, 2013.

[22] X. Wu and W. Sun. Random grid-based visual secret sharing with abilities of or and xor decryptions. *ournal of Visual Communication and Image Representation*, 24(1):48–62, 2013.

[23] C. Yang. New visual secret sharing schemes using probabilistic method. *Pattern Recognijion etters*, 25(4):486–494, 2004.

[24] Z. Zhou, G. Arce, and G. Di Crescenzo. Halftone visual cryptography. *Image Processing, IEEE Transactions on*, 15(8):2441–2453, 2006.

On the Intertwining of Information Hiding and Multimedia Security: A Personal Perspective

Anthony T.S. Ho
University of Surrey

Abstract

Over the past decade or so, the tremendous growth and proliferation of multimedia content has led to the important need to protect and verify the content integrity, particularly if the data are to be used for law enforcement, media, legal and financial applications. This has resulted in the research and applications of information hiding, and multimedia security and forensics becoming more and more integrated and intertwined and as clearly demonstrated, amongst other common activities, with the merging of the two prestigious and popular conferences of IH and ACM MMSec into ACM IHMMSEC 2013.

In this keynote presentation, I will present a personal perspective on some of the various changes, challenges, threats and opportunities in the areas of watermarking, steganography/steganalysis, and multimedia security and forensics that I have faced and experienced since I first stumbled upon digital watermarking and steganography some 16 years ago which I am still very much actively involved today. The talk with provide a chronological overview of some key milestones related to watermarking, information hiding and digital forensics, as well as including some personal events from setting up and managing a University spinout, to technology transfer and product commercialization.

Categories and Subject Descriptors [Computing Methodologies]: Image Processing and Computer Vision - *Applications*

Keywords: watermarking, steganography, authentication, forensics

Bio

Professor Anthony T.S. Ho holds a Personal Chair in Multimedia Security and is currently Head of Department of Computing, University of Surrey since 2010. He also leads the Multimedia Security and Forensics research group in the Department. He was the recipient of the Institution of Engineering and Technology (IET) Innovation in Engineering Award under the Security category for his research and commercialization work on digital watermarking in 2006. Professor Ho obtained his BSc(Hons) in Physical Electronics from Northumbria University in 1979, his MSc in Applied Optics from Imperial College London in 1980 and his PhD in Digital Image Processing from King's College London in 1983. After graduation, he worked in technical management positions in industry for 11 years in the UK and Canada.

From 1994 to 2005, Professor Ho was a Senior Lecturer and then Associate Professor at Nanyang Technological University (NTU), Singapore. While at NTU, he co-founded and became CEO of DataMark Technologies (DMT) in 1998, a company specialises in digital watermarking and steganography. DMT is now a subsidiary of Singapore Technologies Engineering. Professor Ho has published more than 130 articles in international journals and conference proceedings as well as 8 international patents granted related to watermarking and steganography. He recently received a best paper award for a co-authored conference paper on camera model identification from IEVC 2012. He is the Editor-in-Chief of the international journal Information Security Technical Report published by Elsevier.

Professor Ho was General Chair for the 8th International Workshop on Digital Watermarking (IWDW) held at the University of Surrey in 2009 and co-Editor for two Springer Proceedings on Digital Watermarking from IWDW08 and IWDW09. He is a Fellow of Institution of Engineering and Technology (FIET), Fellow of Institute of Physics (FInstP), Fellow of British Computer Society FBCS) and Senior Member of IEEE.

Natural Language Watermarking for German Texts

Oren Halvani[*], Martin Steinebach, Patrick Wolf, Ralf Zimmermann
Fraunhofer Institute for Secure Information Technology SIT
Rheinstrasse 75, 64295 Darmstadt, Germany
{FirstName.LastName}@SIT.Fraunhofer.de

ABSTRACT

In this paper we present four informed natural language watermark embedding methods, which operate on the lexical and syntactic layer of German texts. Our scheme provides several benefits in comparison to state-of-the-art approaches, as for instance that it is not relying on complex NLP operations like full sentence parsing, word sense disambiguation, named entity recognition or semantic role parsing. Even rich lexical resources (e.g. WordNet or the Collins thesaurus), which play an essential role in many previous approches, are unnecessary for our system. Instead, our methods require only a Part-Of-Speech Tagger, simple wordlists that act as black- and whitelists and a trained classifier, which automatically predicts the ability of potential lexical or syntactic patterns to carry portions of the watermark message. Besides this, a part of the proposed methods can be easily adapted into other Indo-European languages, since the grammar rules the methods rely on are not restricted only to the German language. Because the methods perform only lexical and minor syntactic transformations, the watermarked text is not affected by grammatical distortion and simultaneously the meaning of the text is preserved in 82.14% of the cases.

Categories and Subject Descriptors

H.3.1 [**Information Systems**]: INFORMATION STORAGE AND RETRIEVAL—*Content Analysis and Indexing, Linguistic processing*; D.2.11 [**Software Engineering**]: Software Architectures—*Information hiding*

Keywords

Natural Language Watermarking, Syntactic Analysis, Text Watermarking, Information Hiding, Performance

---

[*]Corresponding author.

1. INTRODUCTION

Natural language watermarking (NLW) is a subfield of digital watermarking. The goal of NLW is to embed watermark messages into text documents, using natural language components as the carrier such that the modifications are imperceptible to the readers and the embedded information is robust against possible attacks. NLW must not be confused with text or document watermarking. In the latter discipline the embedding process is performed by using modifications of the appearance of text elements (e.g. word/line spacing, fonts, etc.) rather than modifying the plaintext itself, [12].

One of the most important properties of NLW embedding methods is to avoid syntactic, semantic but also stylistic distortion. These can often occur when the text undergoes specific transformations as for instance lexical substitution or sentence paraphrasing. There are authors who state that their methods are resistent against semantic and stylistic distortions (e.g. [8]). This statement, however, is very complicated to prove, since semantics and especially style are subjective driven and hence, many independent test persons and texts among several domains (news texts, literature, etc.) are required in order to judge if embedding methods are truly able to preserve these two important properties. However, adequate watermark embedding methods can perform minor modifications to the text in that way, that the modified semantics and style are hardly perceived by a "normal reader". Such minor modifications could be for example reordering of conjuncts within enumerations or decomposing longer words into two or more smaller parts.

To date, a lot of effort in the field of NLW has been carried out for the English language. For the German language, however, to our best knowledge no previous research work has been done so far. In this paper we focus explicitly on the latter language since it offers many interesting possibilities to modify a natural language text and so, to embed watermark messages. We present four watermark embedding methods that make use of the flexible possibilities of the morphologically-rich German language, which partially can be also applied on non-German texts. Before introducing our methods, we set up the following notation that already has been used in [2] and extend it slightly.

Let $\mathcal{T}$ represent a natural language text consisting of n sentences $\sigma_1, \sigma_2, \ldots, \sigma_n$, $\mathcal{K}$ the secret key, $\mathcal{W}$ a watermark message consisting of m watermark bits $\mathcal{W}_{bit}$ and $\mathcal{T}'$ the resulting watermarked text. With this notation we can assess the following properties of a generic NLW system (portions taken from [2]):

- $\mathcal{W} \in \bigcup_{i \in \mathbb{N}}^{m} \{0,1\}^i$ describes a bitstring, which represents some kind of binary-encoded metadata (e.g. customer/license number, license-date, etc.).

- $\mathcal{T}'$ results from embedding $\mathcal{W} \circ \mathcal{K}$ through (at least one) embedding method, where $\circ$ stands for a mathematical compostion as for example the *xor* operation. The postcondition of the embedding process is that $\mathcal{T}'$ is semantically equivalent to $\mathcal{T}$.

- The probability that $\mathcal{W}$ is a "false positive" (when the watermark text occurs randomly) should be extremely small.

- $\mathcal{W}$ can only be obtained from $\mathcal{T}'$ if and only if someone knows $\mathcal{K}$.

- Unless someone knows $\mathcal{K}$, $\mathcal{W}$ is very hard to remove from $\mathcal{T}'$ without drastically changing its meaning.

The rest of this paper is organized as follows. Section 2 describes previous work on NLW. In section 3 we present our watermark embedding methods, where we explain the embedding process and give examples for all transformations performed by these methods. In section 4 we describe how we retrieve the embedded watermark message from the text. In section 5 we present the corpora we used for our experiments and also the results of our methods. Finally we outline our observations in section 6 and provide some ideas for future work.

2. PREVIOUS WORK

One of the first and probably the best-known approach in the past aimed to embed watermark bits through more or less "robust" synonym substitution as for instance in [5, 14, 15]. The major problem with this approach is that it relies on so-called partial-synonyms, which only have similar but no identical sense in the context where they appear. Partial synonyms occur very often in languages, such that synonym substitution sounds very tempting and straightforward. In contrast, absolute synonyms have identical sense (independent in which context they occur) but are extremely rare in a language [9] and thus are not sufficient to embed watermark messages. Chang et al. proposed in [5] their "Vertex Coloring Coding Method", which tries to take surrounding contexts of partial synonyms into account by using Google's *Web T1 n-gram corpus*. This approach, however, is unsatisfying since it operates on the sentence level (local) rather than on the document level (global). The following sample sentence σ demonstrates the problem of synonym substitution, when only local contexts are considered:

$\sigma = $ *Oren und Ralf* **reden** *über Watermarking.*

(*Oren and Ralf* **talk** *about watermarking.*)

According to the language database *Wortschatz Universität Leipzig* [3] the verb *reden* has the following ten partial synonyms: *äussern (express), bereden (discuss), besprechen (discuss), formulieren (formulate), sprechen (speak), plaudern (chat), artikulieren (articulate), unterhalten (talk), verbreiten (distribute)* and *vortragen (present).* In this case, only the synonyms **sprechen** and **plaudern** can be substituted one-to-one while simultaneously preserving the meaning of the sentence. The other eight synonyms however, are

inappropriate and thus not considered. Hence, the only two adequate substitution possibilities are:

$\sigma'_a = $ *Oren und Ralf* **sprechen** *über Watermarking.*

$\sigma'_b = $ *Oren und Ralf* **plaudern** *über Watermarking.*

Despite the fact that both transformations preserve the meaning of σ, it should be highlighted that **plaudern** is a colloquial expression and therefore is only suitable for a substitution if the writing style of $\mathcal{T}$ is also (entirely) colloquial, otherwise it would lead to a reading fluency disorder. Hence, the proposed method in [5] will fail in such cases, since no background knowledge regarding the global document writing style is taken into account, but only local contexts of synonyms. Another more general problem with the synonym substitution approach is that it depends on several lexical resources like lexicons/text meaning represenations (both described in [2]) or WordNet ([13]), in order to look up candidate words and their corresponding synonym sets. Such dependencies always result in a lack of coverage, since languages change constantly over the time. As a result of it some synonyms may become deprecated and thus are no longer appropriate for substitution.

Beyond synonym substitution other approaches developed over the years that tried to embed individual $\mathcal{W}_{bit}$ through constituent movement within the sentence structure (a constituent is a group of one or more words that forms a phrase within a sentence). Kim proposed in [8] for instance one approach that focussed on subject constituent movement within syntactic dependency trees. The idea behind this method is to reposition such constituents that include nouns or noun phrases to the position of their siblings. The central criticisms with this approach are two-folded. First the method relies on sentences that contain at least two subjects. This however, is unsatisfying since there are many sentences that include only one subject or not even one as for example imperative sentences. As a consequence the method is only applicable for a certain sort of sentences. The second point of criticism is that it relies on syntactic dependency tree construction, which in turn, requires full sentence parsing to obtain all available constituents in the text. According to Jurafsky et al. [4] the most accurate method to generate dependency trees is only able to reach 89% accuracy at the expense of time. When runtime plays an important role, the accuracy may become even lower. Hence, if performance issues matter (e.g. if transformations are made available through web services) Kim's method may be disadvantageous.

The methods we present in this paper follow another idea. Instead of performance-intensive operations like dependency tree construction or the error prone synonym substitution, our methods perform only minor lexical and syntactic transformations. The required components for the methods are wordlists, a trained classifier and a simple POS-Tagger to obtain word-categories (e.g. nouns, verbs or adjectives) within text documents. In contrast to full sentence parsing, current POS-taggers work both rapidly and reliably. Manning states in [11] an accuracy of 97.3% by using the Stanford POS-Tagger, which we also used for all our methods. In order to improve runtime, we implemented a multithreaded POS-Tagging technique, which is able to tag more than 1,000 sentences per second. Moreover, beyond POS-Tagging we do not depend on complex resources like WordNet or other lexical ontologies that were necessary in previous approaches. Hence, our system is even runnable on low-performing machines or in a web service environment.

3. EMBEDDING METHODS

In this section we present our watermark embedding methods, where we first explain which grammatical rule each method relies on and how exactly performed transformations look like. Moreover, we provide example sentences that show several problems the methods are confronted with and describe how to overcome these. At the end of each subsection we summarize the embedding process of each method. The result of all methods remains the same: A set of embedding patterns within $\mathcal{T}$ where each pattern represents a word or a constituent that is able to carry one $\mathcal{W}_{bit}$. Each method belongs to one of the following categories:

Lexical transformations: This category includes methods that manipulate $\mathcal{T}$ on the word level. The modifications can be for instance decomposition of morphemes or elimination of pre-, in- or suffixes.

Syntactic transformations: This category consists of methods that manipulate $\mathcal{T}$ on the sentence level. Typical modifications within this category are for instance reorderings of words or constituents.

At this point it should be mentioned that in general, embedding methods cannot guarantee semantic equivalence between $\mathcal{T}$ and $\mathcal{T}'$, since there are many factors that must be taken into account. However, it is possible to decrease the number of factors if embedding methods make use of several techniques from both worlds, linguistics and machine learning. Our methods follow this intuition, where the goal is to enable highly sophisticated transformations rather than many transformations of inferior quality.

Currently, all patterns identified by the embedding methods we describe in the following subsection are used for watermark embedding. As a consequence, the watermark key $\mathcal{K}$ is only used for message encryption, but not for watermark obfuscation. This leads to maximized capacity but limits security as an attacker can assume that all patterns suitable for embedding also have actually been used for embedding. This can easily be countered by adding an additional step in the embedding stage. The embedding methods search for potential embedding patterns and create a set of size n listing all patterns found and the corresponding methods. Then a key-driven pseudo-random selection of m patterns takes place. Thereby a number of embedding patterns are lost for actual embedding. On the other hand an attacker is now unable to identify the used patterns and needs to attack all potential patterns as long as he does not own $\mathcal{K}$. As it can be assumed that any embedding will feature a small but existing likelihood to cause quality loss, the attack will be likely to cause more quality loss than the embedding. Depending on the size of n and m, this can be sufficient to discourage attackers as the loss of quality in the attacked cover weights more than the chance to remove or modify the watermark.

As stated at the beginning of this paper our methods perform informed watermarking. This means that in order to retrieve $\mathcal{W}$ from $\mathcal{T}'$ we do not need $\mathcal{T}$, but instead the positions where $\mathcal{W}$ has been embedded. Thereby these positions become the side channel commonly required for informed watermarking. The original cover is not required for the detection process.

3.1 Enumeration Modulation

The first method we present is called Enumeration Modulation (EM), which is based on the grammatical rule "constituent movement" (described in [7]) and thus, belongs to the syntactic transformations category. This optional rule describes the ability to reorder constituents e.g. simple noun phrases within sentences. The following example demonstrates this for the sample sentence σ:

$$\sigma = Tina\ fuhr\ gestern\ das\ Auto\ in\ die\ Garage.$$

(*Tina drove the car into the garage yesterday.*)

Here, σ is divided into the following constituents v_1 - v_5 :

$$\sigma = \overbrace{Tina}^{v_1}\ \overbrace{fuhr}^{v_2}\ \overbrace{gestern}^{v_3}\ \overbrace{das\ Auto}^{v_4}\ \overbrace{in\ die\ Garage}^{v_5}.$$

In this case v_1, v_2 and v_3 are so-called irreducible constituents, which means that they cannot be separated further (in contrast to v_4 and v_5). Applying constituent movement on σ would make the following transformations possible: $\sigma_1' = (v_3\ v_2\ v_1\ v_4\ v_5)$, $\sigma_2' = (v_1\ v_2\ v_4\ v_3\ v_5)$ or $\sigma_3' = (v_5\ v_2\ v_1\ v_3\ v_4)$, while at the same time the meaning for each σ_i' is still preserved. The idea behind EM arose from such optional constituent reorderings, whereby EM only focuses on constituents appearing inside enumerations, e.g.:

$\sigma = In\ \textbf{Rumänien, Bulgarien, und Ungarn}\ leben\ viele\ arme\ Menschen.$

(*Many poor people live in **Romania, Bulgaria and Hungary**.*)

The bold enumeration in σ includes three country names (irreducible constituents), which are independent from eachother and therefore can be reordered. Simultaneously, this reordering preserves the correct grammatical structure and even the meaning and style of the sentence (at least on the sentence level). Hence, σ can be reordered as follows:

$\sigma_1' = In\ \textbf{Rumänien, Ungarn und Bulgarien}\ leben\ viele\ arme\ Menschen.$

$\sigma_2' = In\ \textbf{Bulgarien, Rumänien und Ungarn}\ leben\ viele\ arme\ Menschen.$

$\sigma_3' = In\ \textbf{Bulgarien, Ungarn und Rumänien}\ leben\ viele\ arme\ Menschen.$

$\sigma_4' = In\ \textbf{Ungarn, Rumänien und Bulgarien}\ leben\ viele\ arme\ Menschen.$

$\sigma_5' = In\ \textbf{Ungarn, Bulgarien und Rumänien}\ leben\ viele\ arme\ Menschen.$

In general, for n non-subordinating conjuncts there are always $n! - 1$ possible reorderings, which often preserve the meaning rather than only the grammatical structure. However, of course there are cases, where constituent movement might not be appropriate, since it would otherwise completely change the sentence semantics as for instance:

Table 1: Extract of $\mathcal{L}_{Pos}$

ρ_1	NE	NE	\$,	NE	KON	NE	VAFIN			
ρ_2	APPR	NN	KON	NN	\$,	APPR	CARD	NN		
ρ_3	KON	NN	\$,	NN	KON	NN	\$,	NN	KON	NN
$\vdots$	$\vdots$	$\vdots$	$\vdots$	$\vdots$	$\vdots$	$\vdots$	$\vdots$	$\vdots$	$\vdots$	$\vdots$

$\sigma = $ *Max Schautzer moderierte die Sendung* **Pleiten, Pech und Pannen**...

(*Max Schautzer moderated the show* **failures, flops and flippinhecks**.)

In this case the bold enumeration represents a wellknown idiomatic expression (originated from an old German TV show), which must not be reordered into e.g.:

$\sigma' = $ *Max Schautzer moderierte die Sendung* **Pech, Pannen und Pleiten**...

otherwise it would attract the attention of an experienced reader that something is strange with the sentence, even if semantic equivalence between σ and σ' is given. To counteract such cases we decided to use a list of idioms denoted by $\mathcal{L}_{Idioms}$, which includes $\approx 20,000$ lowercased n-grams of well-known idiomatic expressions and colloquialisms. It should be highlighted that all idioms are not written out in full, otherwise this would lead to a drastic decrease of potential matchings within $\mathcal{T}$ due to a lack of coverage. The following example clarifies this.

Let $\rho = $ *marmor, stein und eisen* (*marble, stone and iron*) be an idiomatic expression within $\mathcal{L}_{Idioms}$. Then ρ would match and thus EM would skip the below phrases:

"ρ bricht" ist der Titel eines(...)

(*"ρ breaks" is the title of*(...))

Die ρ-Tour in Tübingen ist(...)

(*The "ρ-tour in Tübingen is*(...))

To ensure a good performance during lookup of thousands of such patterns that might occur in $\mathcal{T}$, we adopted the Aho-Corasick string matching algorithm (proposed in [1]), which is able to look up a set of patterns in linear runtime. Beyond idiomatic expressions and colloquialisms there are other challenging cases where reorderings might distort the sentence meaning. One of these cases are for instance adjectives that initiate the enumeration and simultaneously are bound only to the first conjunct, e.g.:

$\sigma = $ *Er liebt* <u>*teure*</u> **Autos, Frauen und wilde Partys**....

(*He loves* <u>*expensive*</u> **cars, women and wild parties**.)

Here, the adjective *teure* (expensive) describes the noun *Autos* (cars) but not *Frauen* (women) and thus, reordering both words will "drastically" change the meaning of the sentence. To avoid such pitfalls, we used a blacklist $\mathcal{L}_{Pos}$ consisting of POS-tag patterns that include surrounding contexts. Table 1 shows an extract of this blacklist.

The Interpretation of a pattern like ρ_1 would be: [*Named Entity*] [*Named Entity*] [*,*] [*Named Entity*] [*Conjunction*] [*Named Entity*] [*Finite Verb*] and could prevent fatal transformations by EM as for example:

$\sigma = $ <u>**Andy**</u> <u>**Schleck,**</u> **Armstrong** **und** **Contador** *hat es erwischt.*

(<u>**Andy**</u> <u>**Schleck,**</u> **Armstrong** *and* **Contador** *were caught.*)

$\sigma' = $ <u>**Andy**</u> **Armstrong,** <u>**Schleck**</u> **und** **Contador** *hat es erwischt.*

In this case the names of the cycling stars **Andy Schleck** and **Armstrong** are mixed up and therefore the meaning of the sentence is completely distorted. Hence $\mathcal{L}_{Pos}$ should be always considered.

Once a potential pattern passes the multistage filtering process (lookup $\mathcal{L}_{idioms}$ followed by $\mathcal{L}_{Pos}$), it must finally be approved by a classifier to be considered as a highly potential enumeration pattern. To achieve this, we chose the Stanford Maximum Entropy classifier (MaxEnt), which we trained on adequate but also unsuitable enumeration patterns that have been selected manually by a team of three linguists. Using MaxEnt, we constructed a classification model which results in 82.67% accuracy by running a leave-one-out cross-validation. It should be highlighted that, due to its generalization ability, MaxEnt has been already used successfully in many previous NLP tasks like sentence segmentation, word tokenization or named-entity recognition. However, since the internals of this classifier are beyond the scope of this paper, we refer to [10] to gain a better understanding of the underlying algortihm. The entire process of EM is summarized as follows:

1. $\mathcal{T}_{Pos} \leftarrow$ Build POS-tag Annotation for $\mathcal{T}$.

2. $\mathcal{P} \leftarrow$ Extract "naive" enumerations from $\mathcal{T}_{Pos}$ based on simple regular expression patterns.

3. $\mathcal{P}' \leftarrow$ Filter $\mathcal{P}$ according to $\mathcal{L}_{Idioms}$.

4. $\mathcal{P}'' \leftarrow$ Filter $\mathcal{P}'$ according to $\mathcal{L}_{Pos}$.

5. $\mathcal{P}''' \leftarrow \forall \rho'' \in \mathcal{P}''$: Predict by using a classifier, if ρ'' tends to be a adequate enumeration. Reject ρ'' if the classifier predicts an inappropriate candidate, otherwise accept it.

6. Terminate and return $\mathcal{P}'''$.

3.2 Conjunction Modulation

Our second method we called the Conjunction Modulation (CM) method, which is also based on the "constituent movement" grammar rule (like EM) and therefore belongs to the syntactic transformations category. In contrast to EM, CM focuses only on two constituents, connected through an arbitrary conjunction, e.g. *und (and)* or *sowie (as well as)* that can occur anywhere in $\mathcal{T}$ except in enumerations (since these are blocked by EM). The constituents CM is looking for can be single words like nouns, verbs, adverbs or adjectives but also phrases consisting of two or more words. The following example demonstrates the idea behind CM:

$\sigma = $ **Viktor und Anna** *gingen abends romantisch essen.*

(**Viktor** *und* **Anna** *went to have a romantic dinner.*)

$\sigma' = $ **Anna und Viktor** *gingen abends romantisch essen.*

Table 2: Negated words and their expanded form

Negation form $\alpha\beta$:	Expanded form *nicht β*:
unwichtig (unimportant)	*nicht wichtig*
irrelevant	*nicht relevant*
intolerant	*nicht tolerant*
desinteressiert (disinterested)	*nicht interessiert*

Table 3: Features used by the PE method

Features and their description
f_1 : Left-sided context word of $\alpha\beta$
f_2 : $pos(f_1)$
f_3 : $pos(\alpha\beta)$
f_4 : β (the unnegated adjective)
f_5 : Boolean value if β occurs > 1 times in $\sigma(\alpha\beta)$
f_6 : Nearest verb within the left-sided context of $\alpha\beta$

Beyond identical syntax, σ' has also the same meaning as σ, such that this transformation is considered correct. However, in some cases the meaning or the style of a sentence might be distorted, if it contains well-known phrases that are affected by the transformation. The following example demonstrates such a case where sentence-style is distorted, while at the same time the meaning remains the same:

$\sigma = $ *In den legänderen Film "**Bonnie und Clyde**"...*

(At the legendary movie "**Bonnie and Clyde**")

$\sigma' = $ *In den legänderen Film "**Clyde und Bonnie**"...*

Here, the bold phrase in σ must remain immutable, since it forms a well-known title used in movies, books or the news. One straightforward possibility to handle this is to look up such fixed phrases within a blacklist $\mathcal{L}_{Fixed}$ (analogous to the previous method) and skip patterns that appear in $\mathcal{T}$. Like the EM method, CM has the same advantage to be adapted into many languages beyond German. The entire process of CM is summarized as follows:

1. $\mathcal{T}_{Pos} \leftarrow$ Build POS-tag Annotation for $\mathcal{T}$.

2. $\mathcal{P} \leftarrow$ Extract connected constituents from $\mathcal{T}_{Pos}$ based on simple regular expression patterns.

3. $\mathcal{P}' \leftarrow$ Filter $\mathcal{P}$ according to $\mathcal{L}_{Fixed}$.

4. Terminate and return $\mathcal{P}'$.

3.3 Prefix Expansion

The German language offers a wide range of possiblities to negate words, phrases or even complete sentences. Regarding words, negations can be expressed through pre- or suffixes as for instance (1) *unbeliebt* or (2) *leblos*. In (1) *un* is the negating prefix, while *los* in (2) represents the negating suffix. Our third method, which we call Prefix Expansion (PE) focuses on words, in particular adjectives, that contain negation prefixes. For this, PE (which belongs to the lexical transformations category) first looks up negated words of the form $\alpha\beta$, where $\alpha \in \{un, ir, in, des\}$ denotes a negation prefix and β an adjective, and then expands $\alpha\beta$ into the form *nicht β*, such that the meaning of the word and the sentence where it appears remains the same. Table 2 shows several examples for each α_i.

On a first view such transformations seem to be straightforward and easy to implement. On the second glance however, several problems became visible relating not only to the words themselves, but also to their left-sided context. The following sentence demonstrates for example one case where $\alpha\beta$ must not be expanded, due to its preceding word:

$\sigma = $ *Es war jedoch <u>nicht</u> **un**wahrscheinlich.*

(*However, it was **not un**likely.*)

The initial particle *nicht* negates $\alpha\beta = $ *unwahrscheinlich*, which itself is already negated. As a consequence PE will falsely transform σ into:

$\sigma' = $ *Es war jedoch <u>nicht</u> **nicht** wahrscheinlich.*

(*However, it was <u>not</u> **not** likely.*)

which is both grammatically and semantically incorrect. To overcome such cases we lookup the immediate left context of $\alpha\beta$ and make sure that there are no negation particles, otherwise PE skips this pattern. However, besides negation particles there are other pitfalls like preceding adverbs that can also cause grammatical and semantical distortion as for instance:

$\sigma = $ *Die statistische Information ist <u>äußerst</u> **un**befriedigend.*

(*The statistical information is <u>highly</u> **un**satisfactory.*)

In this specific case the adverb *äußerst* describes the adjective **un**befriedigend, such that a transformation of σ into:

$\sigma' = $ *Die statistische Information ist <u>äußerst</u> **nicht** befriedigend.*

(*The statistical information is <u>highly</u> **not** satisfactory.*)

would lead *äußerst* not longer to decribe *befriedigend*, but instead the negation particle *nicht*, which is incorrect in terms of grammar and meaning. Moreover, we have noticed cases where transformations are useless for specific verbs within the left context of $\alpha\beta$ as for instance *machen (make)*, *können (can)*, *zeigen (show)*, etc. To overcome these problems we trained, in analogy to EM, a MaxEnt classifier with sentences that contain the features given in Table 3. To increase readability we denote $\sigma(\alpha\beta)$ as the sentence, where the negated word $\alpha\beta$ occurs and $pos(\omega)$ as the POS-tag representation of the word ω.

The entire process of PE is summarized as follows:

1. $\mathcal{T}_{Pos} \leftarrow$ Build POS-tag Annotation for $\mathcal{T}$.

2. $\mathcal{P} \leftarrow$ Extract sentences from $\mathcal{T}_{Pos}$, where $\alpha\beta$ occur.

3. $\mathbb{F} \leftarrow \forall\rho \in \mathcal{P}$: Construct feature vectors $\mathcal{F}_1, \mathcal{F}_2, \ldots$ consisting of the features mentioned in Table 3.

4. $\mathcal{P}' \leftarrow \forall\rho \in \mathcal{P}$: Predict by using the classifier if ρ (respectively its corresponding feature vector $\mathcal{F}$) is suited to be transformed into the expanded form.

5. Terminate and return $\mathcal{P}'$.

Table 4: Compound segmentation examples

Rule:	Compound:	Segmentation:
(1)	*Kaffeeernte (coffee harvest)*	*Kaffe-Eernte*
(1)	*Bestellliste (order list)*	*Bestell-Liste*
(2)	*Midlifecrisis*	*Midlife-Crisis*
(2)	*Shoppingcenter*	*Shopping-Center*
(3)	*allgemeingültig (universally valid)*	*allgemein gültig*
(3)	*schwerkrank (seriously ill)*	*schwer krank*

3.4 Compound Segmentation

Our last method is called Compound Segmentation (CS) and belongs to the lexical transformations category. CS is based on three grammatical rules regarding *separate spelling* and *compound hyphenation* (both described in [6]). These rules are explained as follows:

- Rule (1) *"Schreibung mit Bindestrich"* - ([6], second rule from the top). This rule allows the hyphenation of two (or more) compound nouns. Among other things, this rule offers the possibility to separate words that include three consecutive repeated letters.

- Rule (2) *"Schreibung mit Bindestrich*" - ([6], third rule from the top). This rule allows the hyphenation of two (or more) connected anglicisms.

- Rule (3) *"Getrennt- und Zusammenschreibung 2"* - ([6], second rule from the top). This rule allows the separation of two connected (inflected) adjectives.

The idea behind these rules is that in the German language many words (especially nouns) can have a very complex structure, due to the ability that composing morphemes can be repeated (theoretically) infinite times. One extreme case for instance is the 63 characters long noun:

Rindfleischetikettierungsüberwachungsaufgabenübertragungsgesetz

(cattle marking and beef labeling supervision duties delegation law)

Besides such complex nouns, many anglicisms found a place in the German language, such that over time many words became almost unreadable by many readers. During 1996-2006 a spelling reform has been released which enables several optional rules to simplify (more or less) complex words through separation by hyphens or blank spaces. These optional rules inspired us to develop the CS method. Table 4 shows several examples among the mentioned three rules, to gain a better understanding behind CS.

In order to split such words we used the well-known Java library *JWordSplitter*, which splits German compounds into morphemes by using a recursive splitting function. The function takes a (compound) word, splits it into a left and a right part and then checks if the right part is a free morpheme (an independent word) by looking it up in a wordlist. If the right part has been found in the list, then the recursive method is called again with the left part as a parameter. If the method returns a list of words, then the splitting was performed successfully, otherwise the method concatenates the right part with the left-most character until it finds it in the list. If this fails, such that for all iterations the word parts cannot be found in the list, then the function returns the original word. *JWordSplitter* offers several parameters that have a strong influence on the resulting word splittings. The most relevant parameters are:

- par_1 = **Minimum word length** for each segmented part (morpheme).

- par_2 = **Hide interfix character(s)**, *true* = hide, *false* = show.

- par_3 = **Strict mode**, *true* = words will only be split if all parts are words, *false* = the splitting result might contain parts that are not words.

Despite the fact that *JWordSplitter* has many advantages, it also has several drawbacks. One of them is for example that a given compound word might have more than one possible decompositions as for example the word *Lottoannahmestelle (lottery agent's shop)*. In this case, if the above parameters are set to:

$$par_1 = 3, par_2 = true, par_3 = false$$

the splitting result would be *Lotto-Annahme-Stelle*, which is unsatisfying since this separation form is very uncommon in German texts. Therefore CS modifies the output of *JWordSplitter* in such a way that a compound always results in exactly two parts, where the first part is irreducible and the second part may be further separateable. Hence, CS would return *Lotto-Annahmestelle*, which is more common in German in comparison to *Lotto-Annahme-Stelle* (83,500 vs. 60,400 results, according to Google). Another problem with *JWordSplitter* is that it cannot handle anglicisms by default. Moreover, it was not intended to split adjectives and other word classes except nouns. Hence, we extended it with a list of anglicisms $\mathcal{L}_{Ang}$ ($\approx 6,000$ words) and a list of inflected adjectives $\mathcal{L}_{Adj}$ ($\approx 15,000$) which we crawled automatically from Wiktionary. At the same time we extended the existing blacklist of *JWordSplitter* with $\approx 8,000$ words that must not be splitted (although the grammatical rules allows this). The reason for this is to prevent stylistic distortion, even if only partial, due to the small number of words. Besides this, we further decided not to split words with the following interfixes:

$$(-e-, -s-, -es-, -n-, -en-, -er-, -ens-)$$

since the result might become unreadable in some cases. For example, the word *Gerichtsurteil (court decision)* can be splitted into *Gerichts-Urteil*. However, the latter form is very rarely used in German (859,000 vs. 8,430 results, according to Google) and thus might disturb the readability. The entire process of CS is summarized as follows:

1. $\mathcal{T}_{Pos} \leftarrow$ Build POS-tag Annotation for $\mathcal{T}$.

2. For rule (1): $\mathcal{P}_1 \leftarrow$ Extract nouns $(n_1, n_2, \ldots)$ from $\mathcal{T}_{Pos}$ while considering two types of nouns. The first type is a noun n_i that must include exactly three consecutive repeated letters inside the word and have at least a length of 8 characters. The second type is a noun n_i that must be at least ten characters long and include at least five vowels $v_i \in \{\ a, e, i, o, u, ä, ö, ü\ \}$.

3. For rule (2): $\mathcal{P}_2 \leftarrow$ Extract anglicisms according to $\mathcal{L}_{Ang}$ from $\mathcal{T}_{Pos}$.

4. For rule (3): $\mathcal{P}_3 \leftarrow$ Extract inflected adjectives according to $\mathcal{L}_{Adj}$ from $\mathcal{T}_{Pos}$.

5. $\mathcal{P} \leftarrow \mathcal{P}_1 \cup \mathcal{P}_2 \cup \mathcal{P}_3$

6. $\mathcal{P}' \leftarrow \forall \rho \in \mathcal{P}$: Apply *JWordSplitter* to segment ρ.

7. Terminate and return $\mathcal{P}'$.

4. WATERMARK RETRIEVING PROCESS

Our watermark retrieving scheme follows an non-blind manner, which means that the original text $\mathcal{T}$ is required to obtain the watermark message $\mathcal{W}$. However, instead of using $\mathcal{T}$ as an input for our algorithm, we use the tokenized form of the watermarked text denoted by $\mathcal{T}'_{tok}$ and a list of tuples $\langle (m_i, pos_i) \rangle$. For each embedded watermark-bit $\mathcal{W}[i]$ $m_i \in \mathcal{M}$ denotes the embedding method while pos_i describes the position of the token within $\mathcal{T}'_{tok}$, where the watermark-message begins. The entire retrieving process is decribed in Algorithm 1.

Input: $\mathcal{T}'_{tok}$ = the tokenized form of $\mathcal{T}'$ and
$\langle (m_i, pos_i) \rangle$ = the list of the
watermark-message index positions.

Output: $\mathcal{W}$

$offset \leftarrow 0$

$\mathcal{W}_{idx} \leftarrow sort(\langle (m_i, pos_i) \rangle)$ // Sort the list
// by ascending order according to pos_i

foreach (m_i, pos_i) *in* $\mathcal{W}_{idx}$ **do**
  $pos_{i'} \leftarrow pos_i + offset$;
  if $(m_i = EM)$ **then**
    if $(\mathcal{T}'_{tok}[pos_{i'} + 1], \mathcal{T}'_{tok}[pos_{i'} + 2]$ *and*
    $\mathcal{T}'_{tok}[pos_{i'} + 4]$ *are lexically ordered*)
    then $\mathcal{W}[i] = 0$;
    else $\mathcal{W}[i] = 1$;
  if $(m_i = CM)$ **then**
    if $(\mathcal{T}'_{tok}[pos_{i'} + 1]$ *and* $\mathcal{T}'_{tok}[pos_{i'} + 3]$ *are lexically*
    ordered)
    then $\mathcal{W}[i] = 0$;
    else $\mathcal{W}[i] = 1$;
  if $(m_i = PE)$ **then**
    if $(\mathcal{T}'_{tok}[pos_{i'}]$ *equals the negation word "nicht"*)
    then
      $\mathcal{W}[i] = 1$;
      $offset \leftarrow offset + 1$;
    else
      $\mathcal{W}[i] = 0$;
  if $(m_i = CS)$ **then**
    if $(\mathcal{T}'_{tok}[pos_{i'}]$ *includes a hyphen*)
    then $\mathcal{W}[i] = 1$;
    else $\mathcal{W}[i] = 0$;
end
return $\mathcal{W}$

Algorithm 1: Watermark retrieving algorithm

---

5. EXPERIMENTS

For our experiments we chose the "2010-news-1M" sentence corpus within the *Wortschatz Universität Leipzig* corpora collection [3], which consists of 1,000,000 sentences,

Table 5: Generall statistics

Total words:	3,209,791
Nouns:	785,205
Adjectives:	267,287
Average sentence (in words):	≈ 16
Min sentence length (in words):	3
Max sentence length (in words):	39

Table 6: Occurrences of words with length x

Length x:	10	11	12	13	14	15
Frequency:	133,935	110,701	78,422	56,522	42,039	31,073
Percentage:	4.12%	3.45%	2.44%	1.76%	1.31%	0.97%

crawled randomly from newspaper websites during 2010. Instead of using the entire corpus, we choosed only two segments where each segment includes 200,000 sentences. The first segment forms the training corpus denoted by $\mathcal{C}_1$ and includes the sentences with the ID's [1 - 200,000]. $\mathcal{C}_1$ was mainly used to train the MaxEnt classifier but also to generate blacklists and POS-tag patterns used by all embedding methods. The second segment forms the test corpus denoted by $\mathcal{C}_2$, which includes sentences with the ID's [200,001 - 400,000] and was used to evaluate our methods. In Table 5 and Table 6 we summarized the most relevant statistics regarding $\mathcal{C}_2$. After training the classifier and constructing the wordlists we applied the four embedding methods on $\mathcal{C}_2$. The results regarding the gained pattern frequencies are given in Table 7.

The total time needed for our system to perform POS-tagging, filtering, classification and finally to obtain relevant patterns from $\mathcal{C}_2$ took $\approx$ 30 minutes. For the most commonly used paper size in Germany (DIN A4 = 210 mm $\times$ 297 mm) which includes about 42 sentences, this would lead to a running time of $\approx$ 0.0063 minutes (or $\approx$ 0.378 seconds) per page. From here on we performed a manual evaluation, which has been carried out by 89 test persons across several target groups covered by students (from the fields of computer science, educational science, law and biology), linguists and co-workers. The test persons were not initiated by us regarding which sentence was original (σ) or watermarked (σ'). The scheme of our evaluation is described as follows: For any pair (σ, σ') we let a test person assess if both, the original and the watermarked sentence, are equal in terms of meaning and style. The conditions of the evaluation scheme are given in Table 5:

- If a test person decides that (σ, σ') are the same, then our evaluation scheme consideres this as a true positive.

- If (σ, σ') assessed twice by $\geq$ 1 test person(s) but the result differs, then the result is not a true positive.

Table 7: Pattern found by each method

Method:	Pattern frequency:
Enumeration Modulation:	1,198
Conjunction Modulation:	656
Prefix Expansion:	342
Compound Segmentation:	4,262
Σ	6,458

Table 8: Single and overall Accuracy

Method:	Accuracy:
Enumeration Modulation (EM):	82.55%
Conjunction Modulation (CM):	82.32%
Prefix Expansion (PE):	69.30%
Compound Segmentation (CS):	83.03%
Overall accuracy (method independent)	82.14%

- If (σ, σ') assessed $x > 2$ times, we apply a majority vote among the x assessments. If x is odd and the majority concludes that (σ, σ') are the same, then the result is also a true positive, otherwise not.

We calculate the accuracy of each embedding method as the number of true positives in relation to the number of the all patterns found by this method. The results are given in Table 8. Moreover, we have been interested to know how the assessments of all test persons perform by average and median. Hence, we calculated both measures among the 89 test persons and found out that in average each test person assessed (σ, σ') with an accuracy of 77.44% and 83.33% by median. The latter value implies that the majority of the test persons (substantially more than 50%) assessed that (σ, σ') are equal in terms of meaning and style.

However, we can conclude from the values in Table 8 that PE has the lowest accuracy among the other methods. After performing a deeper investigation it turned out, that the features were not sufficient enough, such that the patterns did not find wide acceptance by the test persons. Hence, the classification model needs more reliable features in order to improve the quality of the resulting patterns. One possibility could be to apply feature selection or extraction techniques, as for instance *Backward Elimination* or *PCA*.

6. CONCLUSIONS AND FUTURE WORK

We proposed in this paper four intuitive watermark embedding methods for the German language based on lexical and syntactic text analysis. Our methods have several benefits as for instance independence from complex NLP techniques and rich lexical resources (e.g WordNet/Collins thesaurus), which can only be constructed by experts. The only resources our system depends on are a POS-Tagger, a trained classifier and simple wordlists, which can even be edited by less technically-experienced users. Another benefit is that two of our methods (EM and CM) can be easily adapted one-by-one to other Indo-European languages (e.g. English, Spanish or French), since these languages have the same grammatical structure for enumerations or connected constituents like German. For non-Indo-European languages, however, more detailed background is required to adapt the other methods. One more benefit is that our system performs very fast in terms of runtime, as shown in the experiments. However, we could not compare our scheme against other NLW systems since, to our best knowledge, there are no standardized test corpora available for NLW embedding tasks (especially for the German language).

We can infer from the experimental results that our watermarking embedding methods are applicable for German texts, such that neither grammatical, nor semantic nor stylistic distortion have been observed by the clear majority of 89 test persons. However, one important question that could not be answered in this paper is how authors would react to the changes in their authored documents. Since this question is subjective driven, it would require a further empirical study, where authors should judge their acceptance at a given scale.

While currently our approach is informed watermarking, blind watermarking can also be realized for all embedding methods that allow setting a random watermarking bit. This includes EM and CM but excludes PE and CS as currently there is no inverse to this. This means that for the price of a reduced payload caused by fewer available embedding patterns, blindness can be achieved with the current embedding scheme.

In the near future we plan to improve the quality of all the methods (in particular PE) through extending the existing wordlists and POS-tag patters but also the classification model, which was used by EM and PE. Besides improving the embedding quality, we also plan to develop new embedding methods, which again operate only on the lexical and sytactic level of the text. One idea for instance is to swap two consecutive adjectives, which are independent from each other, e.g.:

$\sigma = $ *In der **oberen rechten** Ecke befinden sich...*

*(In the **upper right** corner are)...*

$\sigma' = $ *In der **rechten oberen** Ecke befinden sich...*

*(In the **right upper** corner are)...*

Another idea for a lexically oriented embedding method would be for instance to modify the spelling of certain words that contain similar sounding phonemes. One possible transformation could be for example:

$\sigma = $ *Junge Menschen interessieren sich immer mehr für die **Fotografie.***

*(Young people are increasingly interested in **photography**.)*

$\sigma' = $ *Junge Menschen interessieren sich immer mehr für die **Photographie.***

However, of course such reorderings have many pitfalls and thus, further investigation is needed.

7. ACKNOWLEDGMENT

This work was supported by the CASED Center for Advanced Security Research Darmstadt, Germany, funded by the German state government of Hessen under the LOEWE grant programme (www.CASED.de) and SiDiM, funded by the Federal Ministry of Education and Research.

8. REFERENCES

[1] A. V. Aho and M. J. Corasick. Efficient String Matching: An Aid to Bibliographic Search. *Commun. ACM*, 18(6):333–340, June 1975.

[2] M. J. Atallah, V. Raskin, M. Crogan, C. Hempelmann, F. Kerschbaum, D. Mohamed, and S. Naik. Natural Language Watermarking: Design, Analysis, and a Proof-of-Concept Implementation. In *Proceedings of the 4th International Workshop on Information Hiding*, IHW '01, pages 185–199, London, UK, 2001. Springer-Verlag.

[3] C. Biemann, S. Bordag, G. Heyer, U. Quasthoff, and C. Wolff. Language-Independent Methods for Compiling Monolingual Lexical Data. In *CICLing*, pages 217–228, 2004.

[4] D. Cer, M. catherine De Marneffe, D. Jurafsky, and C. D. Manning. Parsing to Stanford Dependencies: Trade-offs between Speed and Accuracy. In *In LREC 2010*, 2010.

[5] C.-Y. Chang and S. Clark. Practical Linguistic Steganography using Contextual Synonym Substitution and Vertex Colour Coding. In *Proceedings of the 2010 Conference on Empirical Methods in Natural Language Processing*, EMNLP '10, pages 1194–1203, Stroudsburg, PA, USA, 2010. Association for Computational Linguistics.

[6] Dudenverlag. Die neue deutsche Rechtschreibung kurz gefasst - Die wichtigsten neuen Regeln mit Beispielen). 2006.

[7] K. Hilbrig. Satzglieder. In *Grammatik der deutschen Gegenwartssprache*. Johannes Gutenberg-Universität Mainz - Deutsches Institut, 2009.

[8] M.-Y. Kim. Text Watermarking by Syntactic Analysis. In *Proceedings of the 12th WSEAS international conference on Computers*, ICCOMP'08, pages 904–909, Stevens Point, Wisconsin, USA, 2008. World Scientific and Engineering Academy and Society (WSEAS).

[9] G. A. Leonard Danglli. Absolute versus Relative Synonymy. volume 2/2, 2009. LCPJ Publishing, 2009.

[10] C. Manning and D. Klein. Optimization, Maxent Models, and Conditional Estimation without Magic. In *Proceedings of the 2003 Conference of the North American Chapter of the Association for Computational Linguistics on Human Language Technology: Tutorials - Volume 5*, NAACL-Tutorials '03, pages 8–8, Stroudsburg, PA, USA, 2003. Association for Computational Linguistics.

[11] C. D. Manning. Part-of-Speech Tagging from 97% to 100%: is it Time for some Linguistics? In *Proceedings of the 12th international conference on Computational linguistics and intelligent text processing - Volume Part I*, CICLing'11, pages 171–189, Berlin, Heidelberg, 2011. Springer-Verlag.

[12] M. Topkara, C. M. Taskiran, and E. J. D. III. Natural Language Watermarking. volume 5681, pages 441–452. SPIE, 2005.

[13] M. Topkara, U. Topkara, and M. J. Atallah. Words are Not Enough: Sentence Level Natural Language Watermarking. In *ACM Workshop on Contents Protection and Security*. ACM, 2006.

[14] U. Topkara, M. Topkara, and M. J. Atallah. The Hiding Virtues of Ambiguity: Quantifiably Resilient Watermarking of Natural Language Text through Synonym Substitutions. In S. Voloshynovskiy, J. Dittmann, and J. J. Fridrich, editors, *MM&Sec*, pages 164–174. ACM, 2006.

[15] J. Yang, J. Wang, C. Wang, and D. Li. Intelligent Information Hiding and Multimedia Signal Processing, 2007. IIHMSP 2007. Third International Conference on. volume 2, pages 481 –484, nov. 2007.

On Optimal Detection for Matrix Multiplicative Data Hiding [*]

Babak Moussakhani
Department of Electronics and
Telecommunications
NTNU, N-7491
Trondheim, Norway
babak@iet.ntnu.no

Mohammad Ali Sedaghat
Department of Electronics and
Telecommunications
NTNU, N-7491
Trondheim, Norway
mohammad.sedaghat@
iet.ntnu.no

John T. Flåm
Department of Electronics and
Telecommunications
NTNU, N-7491
Trondheim, Norway
flam@iet.ntnu.no

Tor Ramstad
Department of Electronics and
Telecommunications
NTNU, N-7491
Trondheim, Norway
tor.ramstad@iet.ntnu.no

ABSTRACT

This paper analyzes a multiplicative data hiding scheme, where the watermark bits are embedded within frames of a Gaussian host signal by two different, but arbitrary, embedding matrices. A closed form expression for the bit error rate (BER) of the optimal detector is derived when the frame sizes tend to infinity. Furthermore, a structure is proposed for the optimal detector which divides the detection process into two main blocks: host signal estimation and decision making. The proposed structure preserves optimality, and allows for a great deal of flexibility: The estimator can be selected according to the a priori knowledge about host signal. For example, if the host signal is an Auto-Regressive (AR) process, we argue that a Kalman filter may serve as the estimator. Compared to a direct implementation of the Neyman-Pearson detector, this approach results in significantly reduced complexity while keeping optimal performance.

Categories and Subject Descriptors

D.4.6 [**Security and Protection**]: [Authentication]; H.2.0 [**General**]: [Security, integrity, and protection]

Keywords

data hiding, watermarking, optimal detection, Kalman filter

[*]This work was funded by the MELODY Project, which is sponsored by the Research Council of Norway

1. INTRODUCTION

Watermarking refers to the process of embedding side information in a digital medium in a seemingly innocuous way. Its use is widespread in broadcast monitoring, covert communication applications and for preventing illegal use of the copyrighted data [2, 6, 10]. It is desired that the watermark is robust against attacks, and at the same time is inaudible, i.e. the change introduced by the watermark should be perceptually undetectable. Typically, this trade off needs to be satisfied for a certain data rate requirement [6].

The main stream methods for data embedding include additive and multiplicative schemes [4],[1]. Due to their robustness and compatibility with human visual/auditory systems, multiplicative approaches attract more interest [4], [3]. The methods introduced in [3],[1] utilize the optimal detector based on the likelihood ratio test to retrieve the embedded information. Solachidis et al. [11] have designed the optimal detector for multiplicative watermarks in the Discrete Fourier Transform domain for a signal with a first order separable autocorrelation function. In [9], the authors propose an optimal detector for a highly correlated first order Auto-Regressive (AR) host signal. In [12] an improved multiplicative spread spectrum data hiding method has been proposed. It tries to minimize the interference effect of the host signal. However, the investigation in [12] is limited to i.i.d host signals. To the best of our knowledge the optimal detector for an arbitrarily correlated (e.g. AR process of order r) host signal has not been investigated so far.

Most detectors in the literature assume that each sample within a frame of the host signal is identically and independently distributed (i.i.d.). This assumption imposes severe restrictions on the correlation structure, and for most real-world random signals it does not hold. Our work considers a host signal with an arbitrary correlation matrix. In addition, in contrast to e.g. [4], [1], we do not limit the attention to diagonal embedding matrices. Here, the embedding matrices can have arbitrary structure.

We derive the optimal Maximum Likelihood (ML) detector, and propose a block structure for its implementation which is flexible, and allows for reduced computational complexity. This structure divides the detection process into two main parts: signal estimation and decision making. This enables us to select an estimator according to the priori knowledge about the host signal, while preserving the optimality of the detector. The Bit Error Rate (BER) of the optimal detector is evaluated analytically, as the frame size tends to infinity. For the special case when the host signal is an AR process, we simplify the detector by invoking the Kalman filter as the estimator.

The rest of the paper is organized as follows: in section 2, the proposed watermarking method is introduced. The BER analysis of the optimal detector is given in section 3 and the implementation of the optimal detector is presented in section 4. Numerical and simulation results are given in section 5 and section 6 concludes the paper.

2. MATRIX MULTIPLICATIVE WATERMARKING

2.1 Watermark embedding

For data embedding, the host signal is segmented into non-overlapping frames of size N samples. The watermark is embedded by multiplying a matrix H_i to each frame of the host signal as follows:

$$\chi = \begin{cases} H_0 \mathbf{w} & \text{for embedding 0} \\ H_1 \mathbf{w} & \text{for embedding 1} \end{cases}, \qquad (1)$$

where H_i is a $N \times N$ matrix and i denotes the corresponding embedded bit. In (1), $\mathbf{w}$ and χ are $N \times 1$ vectors representing one segment of the host and the watermarked signals, respectively. We consider a general form of scaling based data hiding methods where only the statistical properties of the host signal are known. Moreover, we allow for arbitrary embedding matrices. Therefore, the method introduced in [4], [1] can be considered as a special case of (1) with diagonal H_i for both cases.

We will further assume that the watermarked signal is observed in Gaussian noise. This can either be seen as pure background noise, or as a deliberate attack. Thus, the received signal in each frame can be written as:

$$\mathbf{y} = \chi + \boldsymbol{\nu}, \qquad (2)$$

where $\boldsymbol{\nu}$ is the vector of Gaussian noise with $\mathcal{N}(\mathbf{0}, R)$ and it is assumed independent of the host signal.

2.2 Optimal Detector

The host signal has, in general, non-stationary statistics. Within a finite frame of N samples, however, we will assume that it can be regarded as a stationary with a known Gaussian distribution. We confine the analysis to one such frame of the host signal, $\mathbf{w}$, which is distributed as $\mathcal{N}(\boldsymbol{\mu}, G)$.

Assuming equally probable watermark bits, the test statistic for the ML detector is expressed as follows [8]:

$$T = \ln \frac{P(\mathbf{y}|H_1)}{P(\mathbf{y}|H_0)} \underset{H_0}{\overset{H_1}{\gtrless}} 0,$$

where $P(\mathbf{y}|H_1)$ and $P(\mathbf{y}|H_0)$ are the conditional probability density functions (pdf) of $\mathbf{y}$ given H_1 and H_0, respectively. From (2) it is clear that $\mathbf{y}$ has Gaussian distribution, thus

the test statistic has the following form:

$$T = \ln \frac{\frac{1}{(2\pi)^{\frac{N}{2}}|C_1|^{\frac{1}{2}}} \exp[-\frac{1}{2}(\mathbf{y} - H_1\boldsymbol{\mu})^T C_1^{-1}(\mathbf{y} - H_1\boldsymbol{\mu})]}{\frac{1}{(2\pi)^{\frac{N}{2}}|C_0|^{\frac{1}{2}}} \exp[-\frac{1}{2}(\mathbf{y} - H_0\boldsymbol{\mu})^T C_0^{-1}(\mathbf{y} - H_0\boldsymbol{\mu})]}, \qquad (3)$$

where C_0 and C_1 are the covariance matrices for $\mathbf{y}$ under the two hypotheses and they can be calculated as:

$$C_1 = H_1 G H_1^T + R,$$
$$C_0 = H_0 G H_0^T + R. \qquad (4)$$

Simplifying (3) results in:

$$T = \mathbf{y}^T(C_0^{-1} - C_1^{-1})\mathbf{y} + 2\boldsymbol{\mu}^T(H_1^T C_1^{-1} - H_0^T C_0^{-1})\mathbf{y}$$
$$+ \boldsymbol{\mu}^T(H_0^T C_0^{-1} H_0 - H_1^T C_1^{-1} H_1)\boldsymbol{\mu} + \ln\frac{|C_0|}{|C_1|} \underset{\mathcal{H}_0}{\overset{\mathcal{H}_1}{\gtrless}} 0. \qquad (5)$$

The ML detector decides 0 or 1 based on the sign of the test statistic given in (5).

3. ASYMPTOTIC PERFORMANCE ANALYSIS OF THE OPTIMAL DETECTOR

In order to evaluate the performance of the optimal detector, the pdf of T for both hypotheses are required. The quadratic form of the expression in (5) suggests that T follows a generalized Chi-Squared distribution (see e.g. [5]) which does not have a closed form pdf. Naturally, this complicates the analysis. However, when the frame size N becomes large, we may still characterize the performance rather accurately, as we shall see. To that end, it is convenient to rewrite (5) in a quadratic form as follows:

$$T = (\mathbf{y} + \boldsymbol{\beta})^T A(\mathbf{y} + \boldsymbol{\beta}) + \zeta, \qquad (6)$$

where A, $\boldsymbol{\beta}$ and ζ can be derived straightforward as:

$$A = C_0^{-1} - C_1^{-1},$$
$$\boldsymbol{\beta}^T = \boldsymbol{\mu}^T(H_1^T C_1^{-1} - H_0^T C_0^{-1})(C_0^{-1} - C_1^{-1})^{-1},$$
$$\zeta = \boldsymbol{\mu}^T(H_0^T C_0^{-1} H_0 - H_1^T C_1^{-1} H_1)\boldsymbol{\mu} - \boldsymbol{\beta}^T A\boldsymbol{\beta} + \ln\frac{|C_0|}{|C_1|}.$$

Now we derive the distribution of T for the hypothesis i, $P(T|H_i)$. Let $B_i = C_i^{\frac{1}{2}} A C_i^{\frac{1}{2}}$. It is easy to show that B_i is a symmetric matrix. Therefore, eigen-decomposition of B_i has the form:

$$B_i = P_i^T \Lambda_i P_i, \qquad (7)$$

where P_i contains the eigenvectors of B_i and Λ is a diagonal matrix of eigenvalues. In (7), i represents the hypothesis number. Using (7), the quadratic form of the test statistic can be written as:

$$\begin{aligned} T &= (\mathbf{y} + \boldsymbol{\beta})^T A(\mathbf{y} + \boldsymbol{\beta}) + \zeta \\ &= (P_i C_i^{-\frac{1}{2}}(\mathbf{y} + \boldsymbol{\beta}))^T \Lambda_i (P_i C_i^{-\frac{1}{2}}(\mathbf{y} + \boldsymbol{\beta})) + \zeta \\ &= \mathbf{z}_i^T \Lambda_i \mathbf{z}_i + \zeta. \end{aligned} \qquad (8)$$

It can be proven that

$$\mathbf{z}_i \sim \mathcal{N}\left(\boldsymbol{\mu}_{z_i}, I\right), \qquad (9)$$

where I is the identity matrix and

$$\boldsymbol{\mu}_{z_i} = P_i C_i^{-\frac{1}{2}}(H_i\boldsymbol{\mu} + \boldsymbol{\beta}).$$

From (8), (9), and because ζ does not depend on the observations, an equivalent test statistic is

$$T = \sum_{j=1}^{N} \lambda_{ij} \mathbf{z}_i(j)^2, \qquad (10)$$

where $\mathbf{z}_i(j)$ refers to the jth element of $\mathbf{z}_i$ with mean $\boldsymbol{\mu}_{z_i}(j)$ and λ_{ij} is the jth eigenvalue of B_i. From (10) it is clear that T is the sum of N Chi-square random variables with one degree of freedom. Based on the central limit theorem (CLT), when $N \to \infty$, we know that T becomes Gaussian distributed. In order to find the mean and covariance of that distribution, we derive the cumulants of T. The kth cumulant of T is obtained by the following equation which is in line with the result from [5]

$$\kappa_k^i = 2^{k-1}(k-1)! \left(\sum_{j=1}^{N} \lambda_{ij}^k + k \sum_{j=1}^{N} \lambda_{ij}^k \boldsymbol{\mu}_{z_i}(j)^2 \right). \quad (11)$$

Now, when $N \to \infty$, then T becomes Gaussian under both hypotheses:

$$P(T|H_i) \sim \mathcal{N}(\kappa_1^i, \kappa_2^i), \quad i \in \{0, 1\}.$$

Thus, the error probability for large N will approximately be

$$P_e = P(T \geq 0|H_0)P(H_0) + P(T < 0|H_1)P(H_1). \quad (12)$$

Assuming equiprobable watermark bits, (12) can then be written as

$$P_e = \frac{1}{2} \left[Q(-\frac{\kappa_1^0}{\sqrt{\kappa_2^0}}) + Q(\frac{\kappa_1^1}{\sqrt{\kappa_2^1}}) \right]. \quad (13)$$

These results were derived by assuming a frame size which tends to infinity. However, as we shall see in Section 5, they are very descriptive also for finite and quite moderate frame sizes.

4. OPTIMAL DETECTOR IMPLEMENTATION

Implementing (5) requires inverting $N \times N$ matrices, which is a tedious operation when the frame size is large. Also, in practice the host signal is typically a non-stationary process. This may imply a new matrix inversion for each frame. Thus, it is desired to express (5) in a format which results in a practical detector structure.

4.1 Wiener Filter Based Detector

Adding and subtracting $\mathbf{y}^T R^{-1} \mathbf{y}$ to the test statistic expression in (5), results in:

$$T = T_1 - T_0 + \ln \frac{|C_0|}{|C_1|}, \quad (14)$$

where T_i is defined as follows:

$$T_i = \mathbf{y}^T (R^{-1} - C_i^{-1})\mathbf{y} + 2\boldsymbol{\mu}^T H_i^T C_i^{-1} \mathbf{y} - \boldsymbol{\mu}^T H_i^T C_i^{-1} H_i \boldsymbol{\mu}. \quad (15)$$

From the matrix inversion lemma, (15) is simplified as:

$$T_i = \mathbf{y}^T R^{-1} H_i G H_i^T C_i^{-1} \mathbf{y} + 2\mathbf{y}^T C_i^{-1} H_i \boldsymbol{\mu} - \boldsymbol{\mu}^T H_i^T C_i^{-1} H_i \boldsymbol{\mu}. \quad (16)$$

On the other hand, it is known that the Minimum Mean Square Error (MMSE) estimation of $\mathbf{w}$, under H_i hypothesis, can be calculated by a Wiener Filter as [7]:

$$\hat{\mathbf{w}}_i = \boldsymbol{\mu} + G H_i^T C_i^{-1}(\mathbf{y} - H_i \boldsymbol{\mu}),$$

thus,

$$\begin{aligned} H_i \hat{\mathbf{w}}_i &= H_i \boldsymbol{\mu} + H_i G H_i^T C_i^{-1}(\mathbf{y} - H_i \boldsymbol{\mu}) \\ &= H_i G H_i^T C_i^{-1} \mathbf{y} + R C_i^{-1} H_i \boldsymbol{\mu}. \end{aligned} \quad (17)$$

Comparing (17) and (16), one can write T_i as:

$$T_i = \mathbf{y}^T R^{-1} H_i \hat{\mathbf{w}}_i + (\mathbf{y} - H_i \boldsymbol{\mu})^T C_i^{-1} H_i \boldsymbol{\mu}.$$

However, it is easier to implement T_i, using the following algebraically equivalent form:

$$T_i = \mathbf{y}^T R^{-1} H_i \hat{\mathbf{w}}_i + (H_i \boldsymbol{\mu})^T R^{-1}(\mathbf{y} - H_i \hat{\mathbf{w}}_i). \quad (18)$$

The block diagram of a detector which is based on (14) and (18) is shown in Fig. 1. In each branch of the detector, the MMSE estimation of the host signal is done using the Wiener filter with the corresponding H_i.

4.2 Sequential LMMSE Based Detector

For the detector structure in Fig .1, the matrix inversion problem is hidden in the Wiener filter blocks. However, if the noise is assumed to be AWGN ($R = \sigma_\nu^2 I$), the Wiener filter can be substituted by the sequential Linear Minimum Mean Square Error (SLMMSE) estimator with less complexity and the same performance [7]. Implementing SLMMSE for $\mathbf{w}_i$ consists of N iterations and each iteration includes two main steps as follows [7].

Estimator Update:

$$\hat{\mathbf{w}}_i(n) = \hat{\mathbf{w}}_i(n-1) + K_i(n)\left(y(n) - \mathbf{h}_i(n)\hat{\mathbf{w}}_i(n-1)\right), \quad (19)$$

where

$$K_i(n) = \frac{M_i(n-1)\mathbf{h}_i(n)^T}{\sigma_\nu^2 + \mathbf{h}_i(n)M_i(n-1)\mathbf{h}_i(n)^T}.$$

Here $\hat{\mathbf{w}}_i(n)$ is the estimate of $\mathbf{w}_i$ based on n observations, $(y(1), y(2), \cdots, y(n))$, and $\mathbf{h}_i(n)$ represents the nth row of the matrix H_i.

MMSE Matrix Update:

$$M_i(n) = (I - K_i(n)\mathbf{h}_i(n)) M_i(n-1). \quad (20)$$

The algorithm is initialized with $\hat{\mathbf{w}}_i(0) = \boldsymbol{\mu}$ and $M_i(0) = G$. Equations (19)-(20) do not involve any matrix inversion, but it does includes matrix multiplication of the size of $N \times N$ in each iteration. The next subsection considers a case where this can be avoided.

4.3 Kalman Filter Based Detector

In many applications, the host signal is mainly a low frequency component of natural image or an audio signal. This is commonly modeled by an AR process of order r. An AR(r) process has the following general forms:

$$w(n) = \sum_{k=1}^{r} a_k w(n-k) + u(n), \quad (21)$$

where a_k's are constant coefficients and $u(n) \sim \mathcal{N}(0, q)$.

A strong candidate for estimating an AR process disturbed by AWGN is the Kalman filter [7]. The causal nature

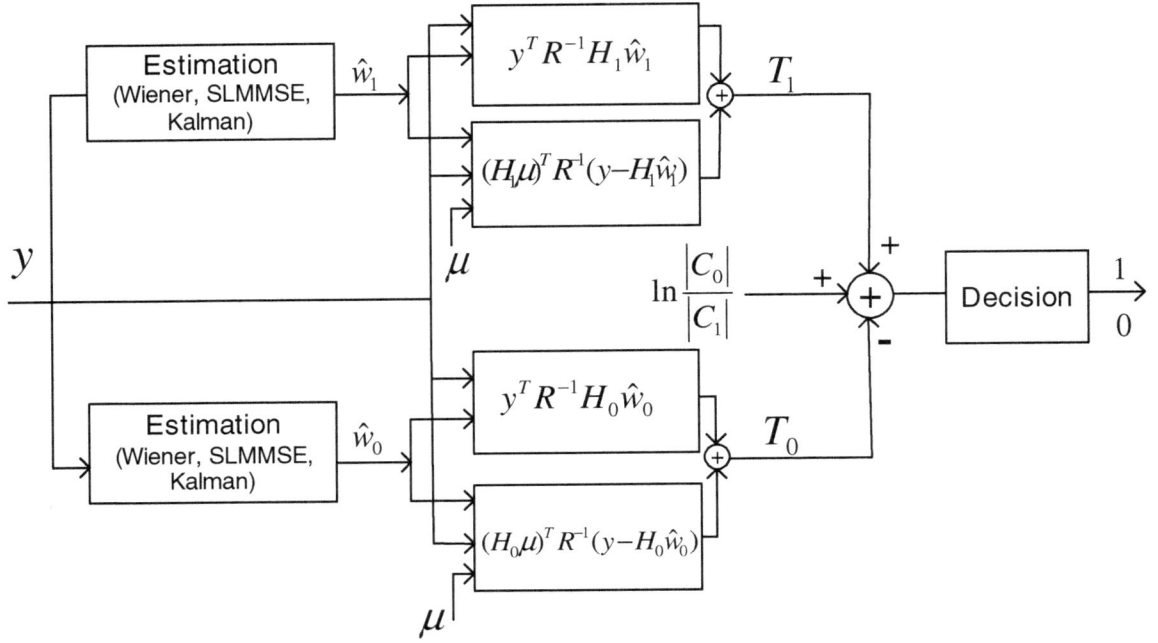

Figure 1: The detector block diagram.

of the Kalman filter results in a small performance degradation compared to the Wiener filter. However, as it will become clear, the Kalman filter provides substantial complexity reduction. To take advantage of the formulation in the Kalman filter, we define the following state vectors:

$$\mathbf{x}(n) = (w(n), w(n-1), \cdots, w(n-r+1))^T . \quad (22)$$

Thus, (21) can be written in the vector form as:

$$\mathbf{x}(n) = F\mathbf{x}(n-1) + \mathbf{u}(n),$$

where

$$F = \begin{pmatrix} a_1 & \cdots & a_{r-1} & a_r \\ 1 & \cdots & 0 & 0 \\ \vdots & \ddots & 0 & \vdots \\ 0 & \cdots & 1 & 0 \end{pmatrix}, \mathbf{u}(n) = \begin{pmatrix} u(n) \\ 0 \\ \vdots \\ 0 \end{pmatrix} .$$

Now each element of $\mathbf{y}$ in (2) for hypothesis i is calculated using

$$y(n) = \mathbf{d}_i(n)^T \mathbf{x}(n) + \boldsymbol{\nu}(n),$$

where

$$\mathbf{d}_i(n) = \begin{cases} \left(d_i(1), \cdots, d_i(n), \overbrace{0, \cdots, 0}^{r-n} \right)^T & n < r \\ (d_i(1), d_i(2), d_i(3), \cdots, d_i(r))^T & n \geq r \end{cases} .$$

Accordingly, by concatenating $\mathbf{d}_i(n)$, H_i is written as follows:

$$H_i = \begin{pmatrix} d_i(1) & 0 & 0 & \cdots & 0 & 0 \\ d_i(2) & d_i(1) & 0 & \cdots & 0 & 0 \\ d_i(3) & d_i(2) & d_i(1) & \cdots & 0 & 0 \\ \vdots & \vdots & \vdots & \vdots & \vdots & \vdots \\ 0 & \cdots & \cdots & d_i(r) & \cdots & d_i(1) \end{pmatrix} . \quad (23)$$

Using the Kalman filter one can estimate $\mathbf{x}$ as follows:

$$\hat{\mathbf{x}}(n) = F\hat{\mathbf{x}}(n-1) + K(n)\left(y(n) - \mathbf{d}_i(n)^T \hat{\mathbf{x}}(n-1) \right),$$

$$K(n) = P^+(n)\mathbf{d}_i(n)^T \left(\sigma_\nu^2 + \mathbf{d}_i(n)^T P^+(n)\mathbf{d}_i(n) \right)^{-1},$$

$$P^+(n) = FP(n)F^T + Q,$$

$$P(n) = \left(I - K(n)\mathbf{d}_i(n)^T \right) P^+(n), \quad (24)$$

where $Q_{r \times r}$, the covariance matrix of $\mathbf{u}_k$, is calculated as follows:

$$Q = \begin{pmatrix} q & 0 & 0 \\ 0 & 0 & \cdots \\ \vdots & \vdots & \vdots \end{pmatrix} .$$

Utilizing the Kalman filter to calculate $\hat{\mathbf{w}}_i$ in Fig. 1, reduces the computation load significantly. First, it does not involve any matrix inversion of size N and the estimation is done recursively. Second, defining H_i as (23) makes implementing (18) considerably simpler since instead of the matrix multiplication, $H_i\hat{\mathbf{w}}_i$ can be calculated using an FIR filter with r taps and zero initial condition for each frame.

5. NUMERICAL AND SIMULATION RESULTS

This section analyzes the performance of the proposed detector numerically. To that end we assume the following parameters. The frame size N is assumed to be 32. The host signal $\mathbf{w}$ is assumed to be an AR(2) process and it is generated using (21) with $a_1 = -0.4$, $a_2 = -0.1$ and $q = 0.005$. Later the mean value $\boldsymbol{\mu} = \mathbf{1}_{N \times 1}$ is added to the generated signal to fulfill the basic assumption of section 2.2. Based on the two chosen values for Document to Watermark Ratio (DWR), the corresponding values for the vectors $\mathbf{d}_i(n)$, to

Table 1: Selected parameters for two DWR realizations.

DWR	25dB	30dB
$(d_0(1), d_0(2))$	$(1, 0.05)$	$(1, 0.03)$
$(d_1(1), d_1(2))$	$(1, -0.05)$	$(1, -0.03)$

construct H_i, are selected from Table 1. Calculating DWR and Watermarks to Noise Ratio (WNR) is not trivial for the matrix multiplicative case and the detailed procedure for it, is explained in the appendix.

Fig. 2 portrays the BER performance of the optimal detector vs. WNR using the approximation introduced in (13) in comparison with the simulation results of the SLMMSE based and the Kalman based detector. The Monte-Carlo simulation results are obtained using the structure shown in Fig. 1 for the SLMMSE introduced by (19)-(20) and the Kalman filter introduced by (24). It is observed that the approximated BER of the optimal detector matches the simulation results using the SLMMSE based detector. This result indicates that the Gaussian assumption of the test statistics under the both hypotheses is rather accurate.

Moreover, it can be seen that the Kalman filter based detector performs essentially identical to the optimal detector. At the same time the Kalman filter in the structure given in Fig. 1 reduces the computational complexity significantly. In the case of having an AR(r) process, implementing the detector using Kalman filter has a complexity of order $\mathcal{O}(Nr^2)$. While the complexity of a Wiener based detector is of order $\mathcal{O}(N^3)$. In the our example, all operations in the Kalman filter are done on a vector of size two ,which is the size of the state vector, whereas in the SLMMSE based detector the same number of recursions are excused on a vector of size 32.

Our investigation indicates that the BER as function of WNR has a error floor. Such a behavior can be seen in Fig. 2 when DWR = 30dB. For DWR = 25dB the same behavior is expected for a lower BER which is out of the simulation range. The error floor exists because of the randomness of the host signal which is the basic assumption for blind watermarking technique. Therefore, even in the absence of noise the BER does not converge to zero.

The above parameters for the AR(2) process were chosen somewhat arbitrarily. We have also simulated with other values, but it does not really change the tendency of the outcome.

Finally we touch upon the problem of selcting H_i in order to obtain the best BER performance. This optimization problem is not trivial and to the best of our knowledge has not been solved. One approach to simplify the problem is to select H_i as follows:

$$H_0 = I - \alpha H,$$
$$H_1 = I + \alpha H, \qquad (25)$$

where α is a constant. It is desired to find H which minimizes the BER for a given WNR and DWR. By selecting H_i as in (25), the data hiding method can be considered as a generalized form of the multiplicative and scaling based data hiding introduced in [4] and [1]. Where, for random diagonal H and $H = I$, the methods in [4] and [1] are obtained,

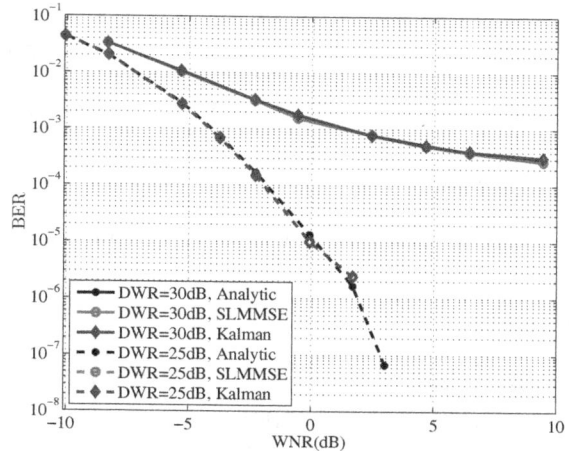

Figure 2: Simulated BER vs. WNR for the SLMMSE and Kalman based detectors and the analytical BER results of the optimal detector.

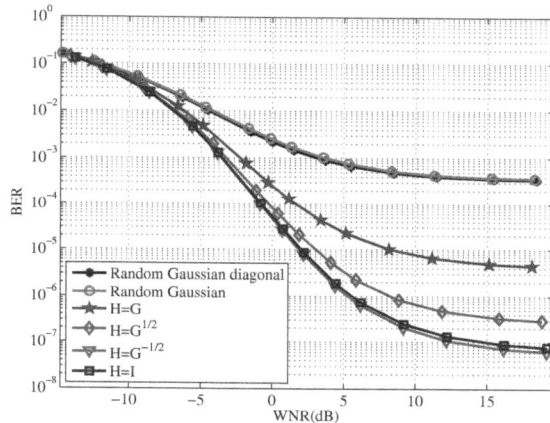

Figure 3: BER numerical results for the optimal detector with different matrix H.

respectively. Fig. 3 shows the BER performance of the optimal detector for different H. The DWR is set to 30dB and we use the same host signal as considered in Fig. 2. From Fig. 3, it is observed that the random Gaussian diagonal matrix results in the worst performance where choosing $H = G^{-1/2}$ and identity matrix give the best performance.

6. CONCLUSION AND FUTURE WORKS

In this paper, a matrix multiplicative data hiding scheme is presented and an optimal ML detector is proposed for retrieving the watermark data. The closed form expression for the BER of the optimal detector is derived and it is confirmed by the simulation results. A novel structure is proposed to implement the optimal detector with less computational complexity which divides the detection task into an estimation and a decision making subtasks. This unified structure holds for different assumptions on the signal correlation matrix while the estimation subtask can be simplified according to the assumptions on the host signal. As an example the Kalman filter is used in the detector structure to reduce the number of operations for AR(r) host signals and the simulation results show that the Kalman filter based detector performs essentially identically to the optimal detector. Finally, we investigate the design of certain type of the embedding matrices. The results indicate that a huge performance improvement is obtained by selecting the embedding matrices appropriately. As an extension to current work we aim to apply this method to a real data sets such as speech or image signals for a later journal version of this paper. Also it is desired to investigate the impact of the bit length on BER.

Appendix: Calculating DWR and WNR

The performance of a watermarking system is mainly expressed using WNR and DWR metrics. WNR is defined as follows:

$$
\begin{aligned}
\text{WNR} &= 10 \log \frac{E \left\| \mathbf{w} - H_i \mathbf{w} \right\|^2}{E \left\| \mathbf{y} - H_i \mathbf{x} \right\|^2} \\
&= 10 \log \frac{E \left\| \mathbf{w}^T \Psi_1 \mathbf{w} \right\| + E \left\| \mathbf{w}^T \Psi_0 \mathbf{w} \right\|}{2N \sigma_\nu^2}, \quad (26)
\end{aligned}
$$

where $\Psi_i = (I - H_i)^T (I - H_i)$. Calculating (26) is not trivial for non-diagonal H_i. However, they have the quadratic form of (6) which is computed using equations (7)-(11). Using the same parameters, DWR is defined as:

$$
\begin{aligned}
\text{DWR} &= 10 \log \frac{E \left\| \mathbf{w} \right\|^2}{E \left\| \mathbf{w} - H_i \mathbf{w} \right\|^2} \\
&= 10 \log \frac{2\text{Tr}(G) + 2\boldsymbol{\mu}^T \boldsymbol{\mu}}{E \left\| \mathbf{w}^T \Psi_1 \mathbf{w} \right\| + E \left\| \mathbf{w}^T \Psi_0 \mathbf{w} \right\|}, \quad (27)
\end{aligned}
$$

where the denumarator in (27) is calculated in the same manner as (26).

7. REFERENCES

[1] M. Akhaee, S. Sahraeian, B. Sankur, and F. Marvasti. Robust scaling-based image watermarking using maximum-likelihood decoder with optimum strength factor. *IEEE Transactions on Multimedia*, 11(5):822 –833, Aug. 2009.

[2] M. Barni and F. Bartolini, editors. *Watermarking Systems Engineering: Enabling Digital Assets Security and Other Applications*. CRC Press, 1 edition, Feb. 2004.

[3] Q. Cheng and T. Huang. Robust optimum detection of transform domain multiplicative watermarks. *IEEE Transactions on Signal Processing*, 51(4):906 – 924, Apr. 2003.

[4] I. Cox, J. Kilian, F. Leighton, and T. Shamoon. Secure spread spectrum watermarking for multimedia. *IEEE Transactions on Image Processing*, 6(12):1673 –1687, Dec. 1997.

[5] J. P. Imhof. Computing the distribution of quadratic forms in normal variables. *Biometrika*, 48(3/4):419–426, Dec. 1961.

[6] S. Katzenbeisser. *Information Hiding Techniques for Steganography and Digital Watermarking*. Artech Print on Demand, Dec. 1999.

[7] S. M. Kay. *Fundamentals of Statistical Signal Processing, Volume I: Estimation Theory*. Prentice Hall, 1 edition, Apr. 1993.

[8] S. M. Kay. *Fundamentals of Statistical Signal Processing, Volume 2: Detection Theory*. Prentice Hall, 1 edition, Feb. 1998.

[9] S. Sahraeian, M. Akhaee, and F. Marvasti. Information hiding with optimal detector for highly correlated signals. In *IEEE International Conference on Communications, 2009. ICC '09*, pages 1 –5, June 2009.

[10] J. Seitz, editor. *Digital Watermarking For Digital Media*. Information Science Publishing, May 2005.

[11] V. Solachidis and I. Pitas. Optimal detector for multiplicative watermarks embedded in the DFT domain of non-white signals. *EURASIP Journal on Advances in Signal Processing*, 2004(16):402942, Dec. 2004.

[12] A. Valizadeh and Z. Wang. An improved multiplicative spread spectrum embedding scheme for data hiding. *Information Forensics and Security, IEEE Transactions on*, 7(4):1127–1143, 2012.

Joint Watermarking and Progressive Geometric Compression of 3D Meshes

Ines Bouzidi
High Computer Scien Institute
2 Rue Abourayhae Elbayrouni
2080, Ariana, Tunisia
bouzidines@gmail.com

Azza Ouled Zaid
National Engineering School
of Tunis
SysCom Laboratory
1002 le Belvédère , Tunisia
azza.ouledzaid@isi.rnu.tn

Meha Hachani
National Engineering School
of Tunis
SysCom Laboratory
1002 le Belvédère , Tunisia
meha.hachani@gmail.com

William Puech
Montpellier University
LIRMM UMR CNRS 5506
161 rue Ada, 34392
Montpellier, France
william.puech@lirmm.fr

ABSTRACT

With the ever-increasing development of digital technologies and digital 3D models, the question of 3D mesh protection has becoming more and more important. One of the problems in digital watermarking, is to decide how to embed in a 3D mesh as many bits of information as possible while ensuring that the hidden information can be correctly retrieved after 3D mesh compression. This paper describes a hybrid watermarking/compression system, adapted to semi-regular 3D meshes. The central contribution is to integrate blind watermarking, to geometric progressive compression algorithm. The latter consists on semi-regular wavelet transform and zerotree coding approach. The proposed embedding method operates in the discrete wavelet transform domain using dither modulation principal. This work shows the ability of joint watermarking/compression scheme to guarantee watermark robustness against compression attacks while inducing a low quality degradation.

Categories and Subject Descriptors

H.4 [**Information Systems Applications**]: Miscellaneous; D.2.8 [**Software Engineering**]: Metrics—*complexity measures, performance measures*

Keywords

3D compression, blind watermarking, semi-regular 3D Meshes, wavelet transform, dither modulation

1. INTRODUCTION

The development of powerful computer systems and recent advances in 3D acquisition and reconstruction technologies facilitate the wide use of highly detailed geometric models in industrial, medical and entertainment applications. The extensive use of large and complex geometric models, triggers the need for efficient compression techniques in archiving transmission applications. On the other hand, security has become a major issue in 3D models delivery, particularly over public networks. Due to its potential applications in areas such as copyright protection, data authentication, and data hiding, 3D mesh watermarking has been widely studied during the past few years [1, 2, 3, 4].

It is therefore important to find an efficient system that allows the exchange of 3D objects between two parties while reducing the amount of data and protecting the integrity of content.

In most applications, watermarked 3D meshes are archived and/or transmitted in compressed format. Instead of treating watermarking and compression separately, it is interesting and beneficial to look at joint design of watermarking and compression schemes, which is the topic of this paper. In contrast with a vast amount of research in 3D mesh compression [5, 6, 7, 8, 9], there are only a few research works in the domain of joint watermarking and compression (JWC) [10, 11, 12]. This is principally due to the contrasting properties of both techniques.

Motivated by the need of hybrid watermarking/compression framework available in one consistent application, and taking into account the quality-compression-robustness requirements, we propose a JWC framework for 3D meshes. The proposed compression algorithm operates in the wavelet transform domain. The watermark embedding is performed on-the-fly during mesh compression. The computational cost to derive the transform domain a second time for embedding purpose can therefore be saved. Particularly, the watermark embedding phase is applied after wavelet transform and prior to zerotree coding [5]. As a result, recovery stage can be realized, either, after the zerotree decoding in the reconstruction cycle, or, whenever we apply the DWT to

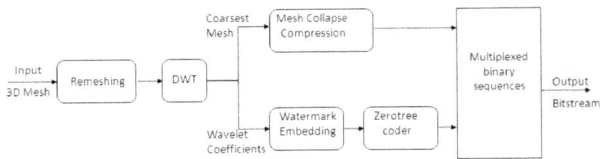

Figure 1: Schematic of the proposed JWC scheme for 3D meshes.

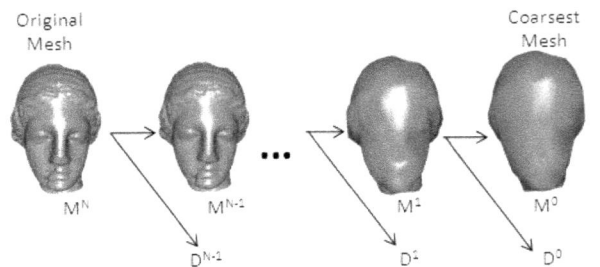

Figure 2: Illustration of the multiresolution representation of 3D mesh.

the reconstructed mesh. Furthermore, our watermarking approach can be coupled with several wavelet based progressive compression schemes.

Judging from our experimental results, the new hybrid watermarking/compression scheme is robust against compression attacks, while maintaining high performances, in terms of payload capacity, and imperceptibility requirements.

The paper is organized as follows. In Section 2, we present our 3D mesh JWC scheme, which is based on multiresolution analysis. In Section 3 we describe the watermarking strategy integrated to the proposed compression chain. In Section 4, we show some experimental results and comparisons with existing techniques. Finally, we conclude and point out future directions in Section 5.

2. PROPOSED JWC SCHEME

In this section we describe the proposed 3D mesh joint watermarking/compression algorithm which is depicted in a block diagram form as shown in Fig. 1. Our JWC mechanism is applied on 3D semi-regular meshes obtained by Guskov's remeshing method [13], which is based on global parameterization. As watermarking primitive, we chose the norms of the wavelet coefficient vectors (WCVs), at a certain appropriate resolution level.

Basically, after the 3D mesh is wavelet transformed, the watermark embedding is performed on the wavelet transform coefficients located at the 1th resolution level. Then, the totality of wavelet coefficients are progressive compressed using the zerotree coding algorithm. Finally, the generated code symbols are further encoded applying an arithmetic encoder. For high compression performance purpose, the coarsest level connectivity, which carries the most significant information about the mesh, is encoded using the Mesh Collapse Compression (MCC) scheme [14] which is widely considered to be state-of-the-art.

2.1 Wavelet Transform

As shown in Fig. 2, multiresolution analysis for triangles meshes provides a coarse mesh M^0 which represents the basic shape (low frequencies) and a set of wavelet coefficients which stands for details information at each resolution level (medium and high frequencies). The wavelet coefficients are calculated as the prediction errors for all the removed vertices and they are 3D vectors d^j, associated with each edge of the coarser mesh M^{j-1}. Several techniques for constructing wavelet transforms on semi-regular meshes have been developed. These are typically based on interpolating subdivision schemes such as Butterfly [15] and approximating methods like Loop subdivision [16]. In this work we retained the Loop based wavelet transform since it provides high order decorrelation and subdivision based reconstruction. Moreover, in compression applications, it has the same performances as

Butterfly, in terms of rate/distortion tradeoff, but has a visually more pleasing shape [5, 7]. In Loop based wavelet decomposition, a mesh is quaternary subdivided and deformed to make it fit the surface to be approximated. These steps can be repeated depending on the required number of resolution levels. In our implementation, we retain six wavelet decomposition levels.

2.2 Zerotree coder

To effectively exploit the fact that wavelet coefficients at finer scales tend to be smaller in magnitude than coefficients at coarser scales in the same region, three zerotree coders have been used to encode the components of wavelet coefficients separately. Arguing by analogy with the algorithm of Said and Pearlman [17] formerly implemented for images, these zerotree coders use quadtree definition for meshes. The main idea is to send the highest order bits of the largest magnitude coefficients first. These bits will make the major contribution towards reducing distortion. Specifically, zerotree algorithm groups all coefficients in hierarchical zerotree sets. Commonly, coefficients with high probability in a given set are concurrently below threshold.

The bits from all three coders are entropy coded, using an arithmetic coder, and interleaved to maintain progressivity. The adopted zerotree coding scheme has three basic concepts: (1) searching for groups of wavelet coefficients organized into spatial-orientation trees; (2) partitioning the wavelet coefficients in these trees into hierarchical zerotree sets; (3) coding and transmitting the highest order bits of the largest magnitude coefficients first. Differently from the image case, for semi-regular mesh hierarchies, wavelet coefficients have a one to one association with edges of the coarser mesh. Vertices do not have a tree structure, but edges do. Each edge is the parent of four edges of the same orientation in the finer mesh as depicted in Fig. 3. Thus, each edge of the base domain corresponds to the root of a zerotree; it comprises all the wavelet coefficients of a fixed wavelet subband from its two incident base domain triangles. A detailed description of zerotree coding mechanism adapted to semi-regular meshes can be found in [5].

2.3 Mesh Collapse Compression (MCC)

Appart from the wavelet coefficients, the compressed bitstream also includes the buffer corresponding to the encoding of the coarsest mesh connectivity. We have used the the MCC algorithm [14]. The latter performs a sequence of edge contractions until a single vertex remains in order to obtain bit rates of 1 to 4 bits per vertex (bpv). In what follows we will describe the watermark embedding approach.

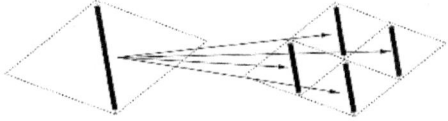

Figure 3: A coarse edge (left) is parent to four finer edges of the same orientation (right) [5].

3. WATERMARK EMBEDDING ENGINE

In our work, we developed a semi-regular 3D mesh watermarking method integrated to wavelet based progressive compression scheme. For embedding purpose, we retained the quantization strategy, because of its ease of implementation, high robustness to compression attacks, and large data payloads. Specifically, the embedding strategy is mainly inspired by our previous work [18]

the embedding stage was invoked after Discrete Wavelet Transform and prior to zerotree coding as illustrated in Fig. 1. The wavelet coefficients, to be watermarked, have been magnified by a predefined factor so as to resist quantization based embedding.

In their work, Chen and Wornell [19] presented the dithered quantization as a special case of quantization index modulation (QIM). Let $q(.)$ be a basic quantizer, and m the watermark message. In dither quantization, a dither vector $d(m)$ is added to the host signal s prior to quantization. The number of possible values of m determines the number of required quantizers. Therefore, m acts as an index which is assigned to a fixed quantizer value. The output of the quantization operation is denoted by:

$$x = q(s + d(m)) - d(m) = q^m(s)$$

For binary dither modulation with uniform scalar quantization ($m \in \{0, 1\}$), the output levels of the quantizers are given by:

$$x = \{ \begin{array}{llll} c_k^0 = & k \times \Delta + \frac{\Delta}{4} & \text{if} & m = 0 \\ c_k^1 = & k \times \Delta + \frac{3\Delta}{4} & \text{if} & m = 1 \end{array} \quad (1)$$

where $k \in \mathbb{N}$ and Δ is a quantizer step size.

The above dither modulation approach can be extended to a sequence of quantizers $q(s)$, where each q^m is a mapping from the real line $\mathbb{R}$ to a codebook $\mathcal{C} = \{c_1^m, c_2^m, \ldots, c_L^m\}$, where L is the size of codebook. The output values $\{c_k^m, 1 \leq k \leq L\}$ are referred to as reconstruction points. The robustness requirement suggests that all codebooks should be disjoint, otherwise it is not possible to determine the value of m.

Due to the distortion constraint and imperceptibility requirement in watermarking applications, the reconstruction points should be close to the host signal. In our work, we designed a watermarking system, based on dither modulation strategy, meeting these conflicting requirements.

For the embedding purpose, we only consider the set $D^j = [d_0^j, d_1^j, \ldots, d_{N-1}^j]^t$ of WCVs associated with the jth intermediate wavelet decomposition level. Thus, the payload of our watermarking approach is equal to the number of wavelet coefficients N in the considered resolution level. In our experiments, the embedding level (EL) corresponds to the first resolution level ($j = 1$), ensuring a balanced trade off between robustness and data payload. The cartesian coordinates of the coefficients d_i^j, $i \in \{0, \ldots, N-1\}$ are con-

verted to spherical coordinates $[r_i, \theta_i, \phi_i]^t$ where, $r_i = \|d_i^j\|$ denotes the norm of wavelet coefficient vector $d_i^j(x_j, y_j, z_j)$. It should be noted that the watermark embedding in the spherical coordinate system, especially in the radial component $r_i = \sqrt{x_i^2 + y_i^2 + z_i^2}$, has the advantage to be invariant to rotation and translation attacks.

Let us consider the watermark message as a binary sequence assigned by m $m = \{m_0, \ldots, m_i, \ldots, m_{N-1}\}$, with $m_i \in \{0, 1\}$. These bits are inserted by quantifying the WCV norms r_i according to equation 1. The binary decision results on two watermarked components c_0 and c_1 depending on the quantizer value Δ.

It is important to note that our watermarking scheme can support a quantization noise up to d_{min}. If ε is less than "d_{min}", the watermark can be entirely recovered without any confusion. Depending on the quantizer step size Δ, there is a trade-off between the embedding robustness and the compression error.

As our algorithm is applied on meshes after remeshing step, the reconstruction is not possible when a change of connectivity occurs. Hence it is sufficient for the watermarks in the semi-regular mesh to be robust to geometrical attacks. To increase the watermark robustness, the set $D^j = [d_0, d_1, \ldots, d_{N-1}]^t$ of WCVs can be divided into equally length sequences. Each sequence is independently quantized to encode one bit of the binary watermark message.

4. EXPERIMENTAL RESULTS

Our experiments were performed using a variety of 3D objects represented as semi-regular triangle meshes: Rabbit (107 502 vertices), Horse (112 642 vertices), Bunny (118 206 vertices), Venus (198 658 vertices) and Feline (258 048 vertices). Initially, we start by analyzing the watermarking impact on the reconstructed mesh quality. Secondly, we study the watermark robustness against zerotree compression and Laplacian smoothing attacks.

Concerning the choice of the quantized step size Δ, several values have been tested (ranging from 8 to 50). This choice is based on the best compromise between robustness against compression attacks and watermark invisibility. Based on the results obtained we retained $\Delta = 30$, which offers the best performances. The robustness is evaluated by the normalized correlation (corr) [20] between the extracted binary message and the original embedded one. The correlation value between recovered watermark bits $m_n^{''}$ and the original watermark m_n is calculated by means of

$$corr(m_n^{''}, m_n) = \frac{\sum_{n=0}^{N-1}(m_n^{''} - \bar{m}^{''})(m_n - \bar{m})}{\sqrt{\sum_{n=0}^{N-1}(m_n^{''} - \bar{m}^{''})^2 \times \sum_{n=0}^{N-1}(m_n - \bar{m})^2}} \quad (2)$$

where $\bar{m}$ and $\bar{m}^{''}$ indicate the average of m_n and $m_n^{''}$ respectively. The correlation value corr varies in the range of $[-1, 1]$. It measures the similarity between two strings and varies between -1 if both strings are orthogonal, and +1 if they are identical. Quality assessment was carried out using two distortion criteria: maximum root mean square error (MRMS), and mesh structural distortion measure (MSDM) [21]. The MRMS measure is an objective surface-to-surface distance between the original mesh M and its modified version M'. It is defined as follows:

$$d_{MRMS} = \max(d_{RMS}(M, M'), d_{RMS}(M', M)) \quad (3)$$

Table 1: Baseline evaluations of the proposed watermarking framework for Horse, Rabbit and Feline meshes (in the parentheses are the results of Wang *et al* robust watermarking method [23]).

	Horse	Rabbit	Feline
EL	1	1	1
Payload (bits)	64	64	64
MRMS (10^{-3})	0.071 (0.64)	0.12 (1.12)	0.168 (0.71)
MSDN	0.077 (0.07)	0.21 (0.098)	0.033 (0.11)

where $d_{RMS}(M, M')$ is the root mean square error (RMS) from M to M' given by:

$$d_{RMS}(M, M') = \sqrt{\frac{1}{|M|} \int \int_{p \in M} d(p, M')^2 dM}, \quad (4)$$

with p is a point on surface M, $|M|$ is the area of M, and $d(p, M')$ designates the point-to-surface distance between p and M'. The MSDM [21] is a perceptual metric that measures the perceptual distance between two 3D models. It is based on the concept of structural similarity that was proposed by Wang *et al.* [22] for 2D image quality assessment. The watermark message is a sequence of bits to be embedded in the norms of WCVs associated to the 1th resolution level (EL=1). The capacity payload adequacy depends on the content information in the 1th resolution level of the transformed mesh.

4.1 Baseline evaluation

In this section we evaluate the quality assessment of a 3D mesh after watermark embedding. The size of embedded watermark has been fixed to 64 bits so that we can compare our results to those obtained by the reference watermarking method [23]. Lossless compression mode has been enabled to measure only the amount of distortion due to watermarking. From the results reported in Table 1, we can notice that the embedded watermark is perceptually invisible. The induced MRMS is always less than 16.8×10^{-5}. Compared to Wang *et al* results, the distortion induced by our watermarking framework is globally lower, particularly for the Horse mesh. Fig. 4 corroborates the results presented in Table 1. In fact, the visual quality of watermarked and original meshes is undistinguishable.

4.2 Robustness evaluation

Tables 2 lists the robustness evaluation results against the Laplacian smoothing. Lossless compression mode has been enabled to measure only the amount of distortion due to watermarking and Laplacian smoothing. Comparisons with the robust watermarking algorithm proposed by Wang *et al* [23] have also been made. Based on the obtained *corr* values, we can assert that our watermarking framework is robust against smoothing attack. We can notice that all of the correlation values have positive contribution. Compared to Wang *et al.* watermarking algorithm [23], the watermarked models, obtained by our method have lower objective geometric distortion, For example, in the case of Horse mesh the MRMS value varies between 0.16×10^{-3} and 0.18×10^{-3} against a range of 0.21×10^{-3} and 0.80×10^{-3} with the reference algorithm [23]. However, the re-

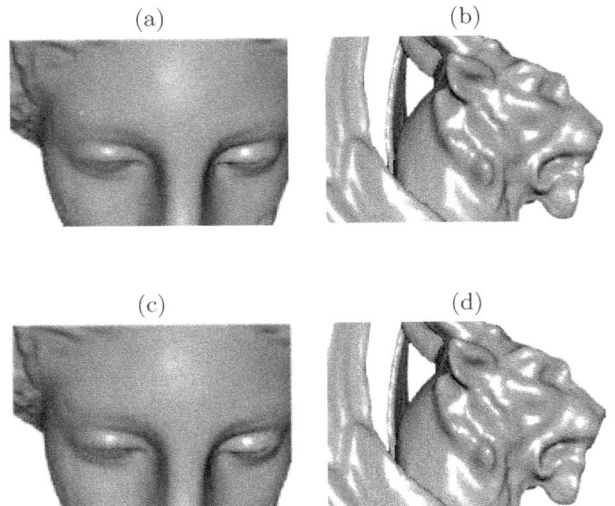

(a) (b)

(c) (d)

Figure 4: Close-ups of the watermarked semi-regular meshes (a) Rabbit and (b) Venus. The corresponding close-ups of non-watermarked meshes are also provided as (c) and (d) for comparison.

sults of the MSDM perceptual measure, obtained by Wang *et al* watermarking system [23] outperform those obtained by our method. Concretely, the objective MRMS distances introduced by our watermark embedding are smaller than those obtained by Wang *et al.*'s method. Though, these small-value objective distortions seem to be more perceptible since the induced mesh deformation in our embedding system is of low frequency while the reference algorithm [23] seems to introduce relatively high frequency distortions. Tables 3 and 4 show the performance of the proposed hybrid watermarking/compression scheme for a wide range of bitrates. The bitrate values are reported in bits-per-vertex (bpv) with respect to the number of vertices in the semi-regular mesh. Distortions between the original models and the reconstructed watermarked ones are evaluated by MSDM and the MRMS measures. The results presented in Table 3 and 4 demonstrate that the *corr* measure is influenced by the compression bitrate value. We can notice that for the tested meshes, watermark embedding is robust against zerotree based compression attacks with bitrates upper than 0.15 bpv. It is worth outlining that at bitrates of about 0.2 bpv, the compression process induces bad visual effects that are intolerable. Consequently, the watermark recovery will be no more necessary. Fig. 5 illustrates the quality deterioration of Bunny mesh according to three compression bitrates. We can clearly notice that at low bitrates the visual quality degradation is considerable.

Due to the nature of content information in 3D meshes, direct comparison with other related works is inaccurate. Nevertheless, based on Table 5, we can assume that compared to Lee *et al.* work, our compression method provides higher performance in terms of rate/distortion tradeoff. Table 5 also shows that for all the tested meshes, the capacity payload of our watermarking method is upper to that proposed in [12]. However, contrary to our watermarking scheme, the method introduced in [12] is reversible. Thus,

Table 2: Resistance of the robust watermark against Laplacian smoothing ($\lambda = 0.10$). In the parentheses are the results of Wang _et al._ robust watermarking method [23].

Mo el	e a ion	M M $_{(10^{-3})}$	M	corr
Rabbit	10	0.24 (0.24)	0.327 (0.15)	0 (0.90)
	30	0.23 (0.65)	0.388 (0.26)	0 (0.71)
	50	0.23 (1.03)	0.423 (0.31)	0 (0.45)
Horse	10	0.16 (0.21)	0.274 (0.15)	0 (0.97)
	30	0.17 (0.54)	0.381 (0.23)	1 (0.50)
	50	0.18 (0.80)	0.418 (0.28)	3 (0.35)
Feline	10	0.61 (0.33)	0.143 (0.12)	0 (0.74)
	30	0.73 (0.63)	0.223 (0.18)	2 (0.50)
	50	0.89 (1.59)	0.275 (0.31)	11 (-0.2)

Table 3: MRMS, MSDN, and _corr_ variations at different bitrate values using zerotree coder with watermarking for Bunny and Horse meshes.

	Bitrate $_{(bpv)}$	MRMS $_{(10^{-3})}$	MSDN	corr
Bunny	0.15	0.66	0.66	0.99
	0.2	0.45	0.62	1
	0.4	0.36	0.55	1
	0.6	0.35	0.51	1
	1	0.35	0.47	1
	2	0.34	0.38	1
Horse	0.15	0.33	0.64	0.88
	0.2	0.2	0.59	1
	0.4	0.14	0.51	1
	0.6	0.13	0.46	1
	1	0.12	0.4	1
	2	0.12	0.29	1

Table 4: MRMS, MSDN, and _Coor_ variations at different bitrate values using zerotree coder with watermarking for Rabbit and Venus meshes.

	Bitrate $_{(bpv)}$	MRMS $_{(10^{-3})}$	MSDN	Corr
Rabbit	0.15	0.23	0.66	1
	0.2	0.18	0.64	1
	0.4	0.17	0.59	1
	0.6	0.17	0.55	1
	1	0.18	0.51	1
	2	0.18	0.41	1
Venus	0.15	2.9	0.63	1
	0.2	2.7	0.61	1
	0.4	2.6	0.56	1
	0.6	2.6	0.53	1
	1	2.7	0.49	1
	2	2.7	0.41	1

Table 5: Compression bitrates and MRMS of our system with and without watermarking, data payload and correlation of watermark recovery are also provided (in the parentheses are the results of Lee _et al_ JWC method [12]).

	Horse	Bunny	Venus
With watermarking			
Bitrate $_{(bpv)}$	20 (21.18)	20 (19.47)	20 (17.95)
MRMS $_{(10^{-3})}$	0.16 (0.037)	0.14 (0.036)	0.95 (0.033)
EL	1 (2)	1 (2)	1 (2)
Payload $_{(bits)}$	330 (106)	359 (131)	582 (183)
Without watermarking			
Bitrate $_{(bpv)}$	20 (21.33)	20 (19.61)	18 (18.05)
MRMS $_{(10^{-3})}$	0.008 (0.037)	0.016 (0.036)	0.064 (0.033)

no comparison can or should be made regarding the distortion due to the watermark embedding. In order to perform a fair comparison with the reference method, the bitrate values presented in Table 5 are reported in bits-per-vertex (bpv) with respect to the original input mesh (irregular).

It is worth outlining that the performed experiments are quite preliminary. In particular, it is interesting to examine the watermark robustness against other attacks like random noise and geometric transformation. Since connectivity attacks destroy the semi-regular multiresolution connectivity of semi-regular meshes, the latter may not have to be resistant to such attacks.

5. CONCLUSION

In this paper, a quantization based watermarking method, based on dither modulation, is proposed. The watermark embedding is applied in the discrete wavelet transform domain, on conjunction with wavelet based compression algorithm. The latter accepts as input a semi-regular mesh. The simulation results demonstrated that the proposed wa-

termarking approach, integrated to wavelet based coding scheme, of 3D meshes, is promising. However, it is penalized by its sensitivity to transmission errors.

Future work is needed to extend the proposed JWC system to the following directions. Firstly, better compression performance could be achieved by formulating an optimization problem with both entropy and distortion constraints. Secondly, advanced error correcting codes can also be investigated to ensure the robustness of our watermarking scheme against transmission errors.

6. REFERENCES

[1] K. Wang, G. Lavoué, F. Denis, and A. Baskurt, "A Comprehensive Survey on Three-Dimensional Mesh Watermarking," _IEEE Transactions on Multimedia_, vol. 10, no. 8, pp. 1513–1527, 2008.

[2] F. Uccheddu, M. Corsini, and M. Barni, "Wavelet-based blind watermarking of 3D models," in _ACM Proc. of workshop on Multimedia and Security_, vol. 3719, pp. 143–154, 2005.

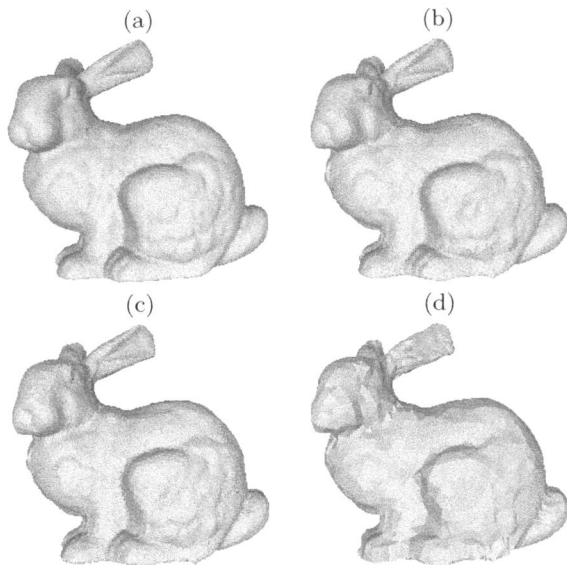

Figure 5: Watermarked/compressed Bunny model with different compression bitrates. (a) original Bunny model, (b) bitrate= 1 bpv, (c) bitrate= 0.6 bpv, (d) bitrate=0.2 bpv.

[3] M. Kim, S. Valette, H. Jung, and R. Prost, "Watermarking of 3d irregular meshes based on wavelet multiresolution analysis," in *Proceedings of the 4th Int. Conf on Digital Watermarking*, pp. 313–324, 2005.

[4] M. Luo and A. G. Bors, "Surface-preserving watermarking of 3-d shapes," *IEEE Transactions on Image Processing*, vol. 20, no. 10, pp. 2813–2826, 2011.

[5] A. Khodakovsky, P. Schroder, and W. Sweldens, "Progressive geometry compression," in *Annual Conference on Computer Graphics(SIGGRAPH)*, pp. 271–278, 2000.

[6] P. Alliez and C. Gotsman, "Recent advances in compression of 3d meshes," Research report 4966, INRIA, Sophia Antipolis, October 2005.

[7] C. Roudet, "A Study on Patch-Based Progressive Coding Schemes of Semi-Regular 3D Meshes for Local Wavelet Compression and View-Dependent Transmission," *ournal of Multimedia Processing and Technologies (MPT)*, vol. 1, no. 4, pp. 278–297, 2010.

[8] A. Maglo, C. Courbet, P. Alliez, and C. Hudelot, "Progressive compression of manifold polygon meshes," *ournal of Computers and Graphics*, vol. 36, no. 5, pp. 349–359, 2012.

[9] H. Lee, G. Lavoué, and F. Dupont, "Rate-distortion optimization for progressive compression of 3d mesh with color attributes," *International ournal of Computer Graphics*, vol. 28, no. 2, pp. 137–153, 2012.

[10] F. Denis, G. Lavoué, F. Dupont, and A. Baskurt, "Digital Watermarking of Compressed 3D Meshes," in *International Conference on Machine Intelligence (ACIDCA-ICMI)*, 2005.

[11] J. Cho, *Watermarking, Compression, and Their Combination for 3-D Triangular Meshes*. PhD thesis, INSA de Lyon, 2007.

[12] H. Lee, C. Dikici, G. Lavoué, and F. Dupont, "Joint reversible watermarking and progressive compression of 3D meshes," *Applied Mathematics and Computation*, vol. 27, no. 6-8, pp. 781–792, 2011.

[13] I. Guskov, "Manifold-based approach to semi-regular remeshing," *Graphical Models*, vol. 69, no. 1, pp. 1–18, 2007.

[14] M. Isenburg and J. Snoeyink, "Mesh collapse compression," in *Proceedings of SIBGRAPI*, pp. 27–28, 1999.

[15] D. Zorin and P. Schroder, "Interpolating subdivision for meshes with arbitrary topology," *Proceedings of SIGGRAPH*, vol. 96, pp. 189–192, 1996.

[16] D. Zorin, P. Schroder, and W. Sweldens, "Subdivision for modeling and animation," *Course Notes. ACM SIGGRAPH,*, 1999.

[17] A. Said and W. A. Pearlman, "A new fast and efficient image codec based on set partitioning in hierarchical trees," *IEEE Transactions on Circuits and Systems for Video Technology*, vol. 6, pp. 243–250, 1996.

[18] M. Hachani, A. O. Zaid, and W. Puech, "Robust mesh data hiding based on irregular wavelet transform," in *Proceedings of the 20th European Signal Processing Conference (EUSIPCO 2012)*, pp. 1742–1746, 2012.

[19] B. Chen and G. W. Wornell, "Quantization Index Modulation, A class of Provably Good Methods for Digital Watermarking and Information Embedding," *IEEE Trans. on Information Theory*, vol. 47, no. 4, pp. 1423–1443, 2001.

[20] I. Cox, M. Miller, J. Bloom, J. Fridrich, and T. Kalker, *Digital Watermarking and Steganography*. Morgan Kaufmann Publishers Inc., 2007.

[21] G. Lavoué, E. Gelasca, F. Dupont, A. Baskurt, and T. Ebrahimi, "Perceptually driven 3D distance metrics with application to watermarking," in *Proceedings of the SPIE Electronic Imaging*, vol. 6312, 2006.

[22] Z. Wang, A. Bovik, H. Sheikh, and E. Simoncelli, "Image quality assessment: From error visibility to structural similarity," *IEEE Transactions on Image Processing*, vol. 13, no. 4, pp. 1–14, 2004.

[23] K. Wang, G. Lavoué, F. Denis, and A. Baskurt, "Hierarchical Watermarking of Semiregular Meshes Based on Wavelet Transform," *IEEE Transactions on Information Forensics and Security*, vol. 3, no. 4, pp. 620–634, 2008.

Context Embedding for Raster-Scan Rhombus Based Reversible Watermarking

Dinu Coltuc
Electrical Engineering Dept.
Valahia University of Targoviste, Romania
coltuc@valahia.ro

Ioan-Catalin Dragoi
Electrical Engineering Dept.
Valahia University of Targoviste, Romania
dragoi@valahia.ro

ABSTRACT

The embedding not only into the current pixel, but also into the prediction context was recently proposed as an improvement of difference expansion reversible watermarking algorithms. So far it was shown that the effect of splitting the data between the current pixel and the prediction context decreases the embedding distortion, but increases the prediction error. This paper revisits the case of context embedding for the case of pixel prediction on the rhombus composed of the two vertical and the two horizontal neighbors. For this case it appears that the context embedding can be used not only to reduce the embedding distortion, but also to improve the prediction. The gain provided by the improvement of the prediction outperforms the one provided by the reduction of the embedding distortion. Experimental results are provided.

Categories and Subject Descriptors

D.2 [**Software Engineering**]: Software Arhitectures — *Information hiding*

Keywords

reversible watermarking, difference expansion, context embedding

1. INTRODUCTION

Reversible watermarking allows, at detection, the exact recovery of both the embedded data and the cover image. The most efficient reversible watermarking algorithms are the so-called difference expansion (DE) ones. The basic principle of DE reversible watermarking is to expand two times a difference and to embed a bit of data into the least significant bit of the expanded difference. While the original DE algorithms used the difference between adjacent pixels, [1]-[3], nowadays algorithms use the prediction error [4]-[11], etc. The better the prediction, the lower the distortion introduced by the watermarking. This is why most of the

research on DE reversible watermarking focuses on the improvement of the prediction.

A recent research direction aiming to reduce the embedding distortion of the prediction error expansion algorithms is the context embedding [8, 9]. Instead of embedding the entire amount of data into the current pixel, only a part is embedded into the current pixel and the remaining is spread over the prediction context. By splitting the data between the current pixel and the prediction context, the square embedding error decreases. The amount of data to be embedded into each pixel can be computed in order to minimize the overall mean square error.

On the other hand, some of the modified context pixels take part in the prediction of other pixels and, so on. By using both modified and original pixels for prediction, the prediction error can increase. The increase depends on the amount of data inserted into the prediction context. The larger the data, the greater the prediction error increase. The decrease of the embedding distortion and the increase of the prediction error have opposite effects. The trade-off between the part of the data embedded into the current pixel and the one embedded into the prediction context provides global optimization of the distortion introduced by the watermark.

In [8], the context embedding is investigated for median edge detector (MED), gradient-adjusted predictor (GAP) and simplified GAP (SGAP). In each case, the embedding into the context provides better results than the classical embedding. An interesting aspect is that the classical scheme using GAP is outperformed by the scheme with embedding into the context of SGAP. We remind you that GAP is a complex predictor. Its context is composed of 7 pixels. Based on local gradients and experimentally determined thresholds, the existence and the strength of a horizontal/vertical edge is detected, and the prediction is performed accordingly. When no edge is detected, GAP uses SGAP, a simple linear predictor with a context of 4 pixels. The results reported in [8] show that, instead of focusing on costly predictors, one can obtain very good performances by investigating some linear predictors and improving the embedding. This idea is also discussed in [9], where the embedding into the context is investigated for the case of JPEG4 predictor.

This paper considers a different predictor, the average of the 4-*neighbors* (i.e., the average on the rhombus composed of the two vertical and the two horizontal neighbors). The reversible watermarking difference expansion scheme based on the average of the 4-*neighbors* clearly outperforms the ones based on MED, SGAP or GAP. This is due to the fact that this approach estimates the pixel over the entire neighborhood and not only over a part of it. If one considers the usual raster scan ordering, a problem with the average on rhombus is the fact that, after the embedding by watermarking, a pixel takes part in the prediction of two other pixels. They are the right horizontal and the lower vertical pixels. More precisely, pixels are predicted by using two original pixel values and two modified ones. A solution to this problem is provided by the two stages embedding of Sachnev et al., [6]. The image is split in two equal halves in order to separate pixels and their prediction context. The pixels to be embedded into the first stage are estimated by using only original pixel values. The remaining pixels (embedded into the second stage) are estimated by using only modified pixels. On the entire image, the overall performance of the two stages scheme appears to slightly outperform the direct raster scan watermarking. The improvement is obtained at the cost of an increase in mathematical complexity.

The embedding into the rhombus context brings to light an interesting aspect. By using not the two stages scheme, but the simple raster scan, it appears that the context embedding can also be used for prediction error reduction. The gain provided by the improvement of the prediction outperforms the one provided by the reduction of the embedding distortion. Furthermore, the simple raster-scan schemes with context embedding can slightly outperform the two-stages scheme of [6]. The outline of the paper is as follows. The proposed rhombus context embedding reversible watermarking is presented in Section 2. Experimental results are presented in Section 3. Finally, the conclusions are drawn in Section 4.

2. RHOMBUS BASED PREDICTION ERROR EXPANSION

We shall briefly introduce the basic principles of the prediction error expansion reversible watermarking based on rhombus prediction. Furthermore, the proposed context embedding scheme is discussed.

2.1 Classical scheme

Let $x_{i,j}$ be the current pixel and let $\hat{x}_{i,j}$ be the estimated pixel by using the average of its four horizontal/vertical neighbors:

$$\hat{x}_{i,j} = \left\lfloor \frac{x_{i-1,j} + x_{i+1,j} + x_{i,j-1} + x_{i,j+1}}{4} + \frac{1}{2} \right\rfloor \quad (1)$$

Let $e_{i,j} = x_{i,j} - \hat{x}_{i,j}$ be the prediction error and let $e_{i,j}^*$ be the prediction error after the addition of the message bit, $b_{i,j}$. One has:

$$e_{i,j}^* = x_{i,j} - \hat{x}_{i,j} + b_{i,j} \quad (2)$$

The classical embedding proceeds by adding $e_{i,j}^*$ to the current pixel, provided that no overflow/underflow appears and the prediction error is less than a predefined threshold T. The threshold controls the embedding capacity and limits the distortions. The embedded pixel becomes:

$$X_{i,j} = x_{i,j} + e_{i,j}^* \quad (3)$$

The pixels where $e_{i,j} \geq T$ are shifted in order to provide, at detection, a prediction error greater than the one of the embedded pixels. The shifted pixels become:

$$X_{i,j} = \begin{cases} x_{i,j} + T, & \text{if } e_{i,j} \geq T \\ x_{i,j} - (T-1), & \text{if } e_{i,j} \leq -T. \end{cases} \quad (4)$$

The pixels that cannot be embedded or shifted because of overflow/underflow can be identified by using a map. The map is lossless compressed and embedded into the watermarked image in order to be available at detection.

At detection, the prediction error is computed:

$$E_{i,j} = X_{i,j} - \hat{X}_{i,j} \quad (5)$$

If the context is recovered without any change, one has $\hat{X}_{i,j} = \hat{x}_{i,j}$. Furthermore, one has two cases: embedded pixels and shifted pixels. For the embedded pixels, one has $-2T + 1 < E_{i,j} < 2T$. The prediction error appears as: $E_{i,j} = 2e_{i,j} + b_{i,j}$. The embedded bit is immediately extracted as the LSB of $E_{i,j}$ and the current pixel is recovered from equation (3). For the shifted pixels, the original values are recovered by inverting equation (4).

2.2 Context embedding scheme

The classical scheme introduces a square error of the order of e^2 for the embedded pixels and of T^2 for the shifted ones. The idea of [8] is to reduce the overall error by splitting the data for embedding and shifting between the pixels and their prediction context. Next we investigate the context embedding for the raster-scan rhombus based watermarking scheme.

The typical case discussed in [8] is the subtraction of a fraction of the prediction error from each pixel of the prediction context. This is the case of MED and GAP predictors. It should be noticed that MED and GAP are context adaptive predictors. Based on the context, one out of 3 (MED) or 7 (GAP) predictors is selected. The subtraction from all the context pixels of the same amount allows the selection of the same predictor both at embedding and at detection. The cases of SGAP (discussed in [8]) and JPEG 4 (see [9]) are much more flexible. The embedding can be done in any pixel or group of pixels from the prediction context. This is also the case of rhombus prediction.

In the case of raster-scan watermarking based on the rhombus predictor, it immediately appears that once embedded or shifted, a pixel takes part in the prediction context of two other pixels: the right horizontal and the lower vertical ones. Furthermore, if one investigates the prediction context, it appears that, after the embedding/shifting of the current pixel, only one out of the four context pixels will not take part in the prediction context of other pixels. This pixel is the upper vertical neighbor. This observation suggests us to use the upper vertical neighbor for context embedding.

Let a be the amount of data to be added to the current pixel. As discussed above, a can be the prediction error plus the message bit for the pixels that can be embedded and T (or $-T + 1$) for the pixels that should be shifted. Let us subtract a fraction δ of a from the upper vertical neighbor of the current pixel. One has:

$$X_{i-1,j}(\delta) = x_{i-1,j} - \delta a \quad (6)$$

Obviously, at detection one should recover the same prediction error as the one when the entire amount of data is added to the current pixel. Let $\hat{X}_{i,j}(\delta)$ be the estimated value of the current pixel after the upper vertical pixel is modified. In order to preserve the prediction error unchanged one should modify the current pixel, $X_{i,j}(\delta)$, so that: $X_{i,j}(\delta) - \hat{X}_{i,j}(\delta) = X_{i,j} - \hat{x}_{i,j}$. One has:

$$X_{i,j}(\delta) = X_{i,j} + \hat{X}_{i,j}(\delta) - \hat{x}_{i,j} \qquad (7)$$

$\hat{X}_{i,j}(\delta)$ is obtained from equation (1) where $x_{i-1,j}$ is replaced by the modified value, $X_{i-1,j}$, obtained by equation (6). $X_{i,j}$ is given either by equation (3) (embedded pixels) or by (4) (shifted pixels). Of course, there is the possibility that (6) will cause the overflow/underflow of $X_{i-1,j}$. In such cases the current pixel is left unchanged and its location is set into the overflow/underflow map.

In [8, 9], the optimization of the embedding error was investigated. We shall consider the same approach for the case of embedding into the upper vertical neighbor of the current pixel. One has $X_{i,j} = x_{i,j} + a$. If the rounding is neglected, one has $\hat{x}_{i,j}(\delta) - \hat{X}_{i,j} \approx \frac{\delta a}{4}$. Thus, one gets $X_{i,j}(\delta) = x_{i,j} + a - \frac{\delta a}{4}$. The local square error is determined by considering the error for $X_{i,j}(\delta)$ and $X_{i-1,j}(\delta)$, namely:

$$E^2(\delta) = \left(a - \frac{\delta a}{4}\right)^2 + (\delta a)^2 \qquad (8)$$

The minimum of $E^2(\delta)$ is obtained for $\delta = \frac{4}{17}$. One gets $E^2(\frac{4}{17}) = \frac{16a^2}{17}$. By subtracting from the vertical neighbor about a quarter of the amount to be added to the current pixel, the local embedding/shifting error is reduced by about $\frac{1}{17}$.

In [8], it was shown that by embedding into the context, the embedding error decreases and the prediction error increases. The increase of the prediction error yields an increase of the embedding error. It appears that the optimum embedding distortion is obtained as a compromise between the increase of the prediction error and the decrease of the embedding error. For the schemes investigated in [8], the current pixel will not take part in the prediction context of other pixels, while the modified context pixels do. They become, in their turn, current pixels and also take part in the prediction context of their neighbors. The predictors investigated in [8] are anticausal ones.

The rhombus predictor is neither causal, nor anticausal. As said above, with the raster-scan and the rhombus prediction, the current pixel takes part in the prediction context of two other pixels. On the other hand, its upper vertical neighbor, once out of the prediction context, does not take part in any other processing. By embedding into the upper vertical neighbor of the current pixel, the distortion of the current pixel decreases and thus, the further prediction errors computed with the current pixel can decrease as well. More precisely, for the case of raster-scan watermarking based on rhombus, the optimization problem should consider not only the minimization of (8), but also the one of the error introduced into the current pixel, $\left|a - \frac{\delta a}{4}\right|$.

Obviously, by increasing δ, the distortion of the current pixel decreases. Meanwhile, the increase of δ increases the distortion introduced into its upper vertical neighbor. The increase of δ can introduce more distortion than the one obtained by the normal embedding into the current pixel. By simple calculus, one gets $E^2(\delta) > a^2$ for $\delta > \frac{8}{17}$.

The direct minimization of the embedding distortion for the rhombus as investigated in [8] for the MED, GAP and SGAP predictors looks for δ in the range $\left(0, \frac{4}{17}\right)$. The search for a lower value than the ones that ensure the minimization of the embedding for the current pixel is motivated by

Figure 1: Test images: *Lena, Barbara, Jetplane, Mandrill, Couple* and *House*

the reduction of context distortion. The fact that the embedded context pixel does not take part in other processing would yield to the selection of $\frac{4}{17}$. The analysis shown above suggests that the effect of prediction error reduction should be investigated as well. Therefore, one should search for $\delta \geq \frac{4}{17}$.

The case $\delta = \frac{8}{17}$ corresponds to the case when the embedding error for context embedding is equal to the one for classical embedding into the current pixel, but the current pixel is less distorted than for the classical embedding. Since the current pixel takes part in the prediction context of two other pixels, the advantage could be a reduction of the further prediction errors and thus, an overall lower distortion. If the decrease of the prediction error counts more than the increase of the local embedding error, one can also admit $\delta \geq \frac{8}{17}$.

3. EXPERIMENTAL RESULTS

Next, experimental results of the context embedding prediction error expansion scheme based on rhombus prediction are presented. Six classical graylevel test images of size 512×512 are considered, namely *Lena, Barbara, Jetplane, Mandrill, Couple* and *House*. The test images are presented in Fig. 1.

As said in Section 1, the raster scan reversible watermarking based on rhombus prediction outperforms the algorithms based on other classical predictors as MED or GAP. Meanwhile, the two-stages scheme based on the same rhombus predictor, [6], can slightly outperform the simple raster-scan scheme. An example with results for MED, GAP and average on rhombus for the test image *Lena* are provided in Fig. 3. It can be seen that the results for the raster-scan and the two-stages schemes are almost identical.

We investigated the results of the context embedding scheme with respect to δ. We first considered the case $\delta = \frac{4}{17}$ and then, we increased δ up to the value that provides the best performance, δ_o. The results have been further compared with the classical raster-scan embedding ($\delta = 0$). The results are presented in Fig. 2.

On three out of the six test images (*Barbara, Jetplane* and *House*) we have a visible increase in PSNR compared with the classical embedding scheme for the entire bit-rate do-

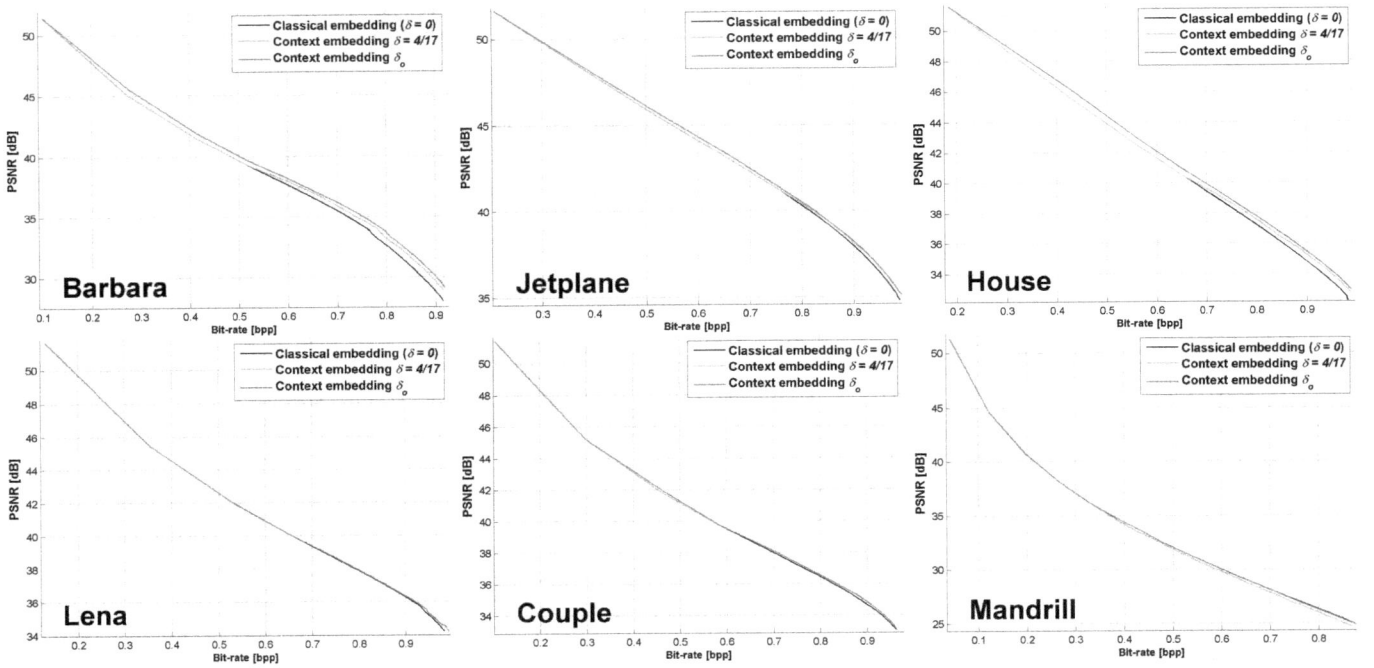

Figure 2: Experimental results of the proposed context embedding scheme.

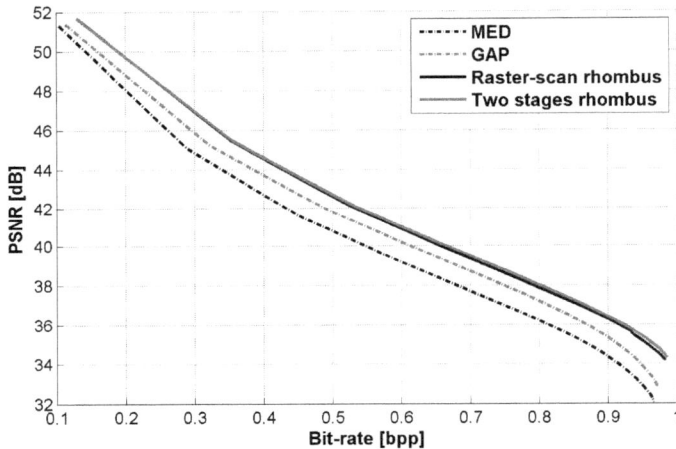

Figure 3: Results for MED, GAP and the rhombus prediction on *Lena*

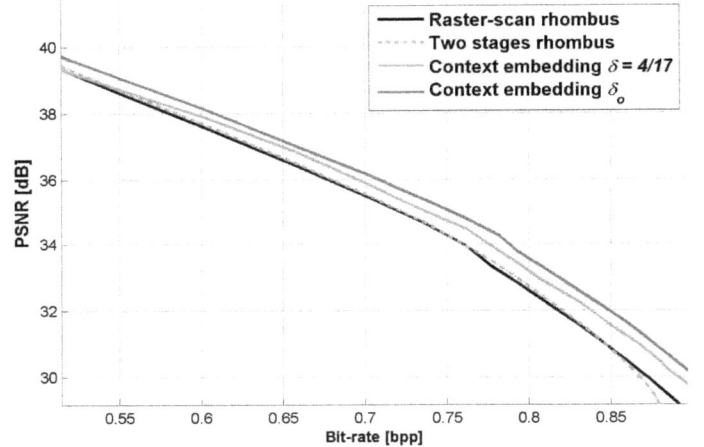

Figure 4: Context embedding compared with raster-scan and two stage rhombus on *Barbara*, zoomed

main. Thus, one has an average of 0.6 dB with a maximum increase of 1.25 dB on *Barbara*, 0.5 dB with a maximum of 1.12 dB on *House* and 0.27 dB with a maximum of 0.4 dB on *Jetplane*. On these three test images, the optimal results were obtained using $\delta_o = \frac{11}{17}$ for bit-rates less than 0.55 bpp and $\delta_o = \frac{8}{17}$, otherwise . The high values of δ_o indicate that, at low embedding capacity, for these test images a better prediction context is more important than the additional distortion introduced into the upper vertical pixel. We remind you that a lower distortion of the central pixel produces a less distorted prediction context for the next pixels considered for embedding (the current central pixel directly affects the prediction for its right and bottom neighbors, which in turn affect their neighbors).

$\delta_o = \frac{11}{17}$ is partially caused by a side effect of context embedding. Before context embedding, the upper vertical neighbor was already distorted by embedding or shifting. There is a certain probability that the context embedding actually corrects the distortion of the upper vertical neighbor.

On two test images (*Couple* and *Lena*), we have slightly better results than the classical embedding scheme. For *Couple* we still have a visible gain in PSNR of 0.12 dB in the range [0.35 − 0.55] bpp and 0.15 dB in [0.65 − 0.96] bpp. The maximum increase on *Couple* is of 0.2 dB. On *Lena*, we have a negligible increase up to the 0.85 bpp interval and, for [0.85 − 0.99] bpp, there is an average gain of 0.17 dB with a maximum gain of 0.34 dB. On both images we have

$\delta_o = \frac{8}{17}$ for low bit-rates (under 0.55 bpp) and $\delta_o = \frac{4}{17}$ for the rest of the interval.

Finally, on *Mandrill* there is almost no improvement in PSNR. The best results are obtained for low values of the context embedding fraction, $\delta_o = \frac{2}{17}$ for low bit-rates (under 0.45 bpp) and $\delta_o = \frac{1}{17}$ otherwise. An interesting aspect is that we have an increase in bit-rate of 0.0076 bpp (approximately 2000 extra pixels are embedded). The increase in bit-rate means an improvement of the prediction. On the other hand, the slight improvement of the prediction should also correspond to a gain in PSNR. For *Mandrill*, the expected gain in quality appears to be canceled by the additional distortion introduced by the context embedding. It should also be noticed that slight increases of the embedding bit-rates appear for all the test images.

The proposed scheme can provide better results than the two stages scheme of [6]. Thus, one has better results on *Barbara, Jetplane* and *House*. On these images the results of the two stages scheme are similar to the ones of the raster-scan one. Thus, for bit-rates lower than 0.85 dB, the two-stages scheme outperforms the raster-scan one with 0.05 dB on *Barbara*, 0.02 dB on *Jetplane* and 0.005 dB on *House*. For bit-rates greater than 0.85 bpp, the raster-scan appears to slightly outperform the two stages scheme. Context embedding managed to obtain better results on these images: an increase of 0.55 dB over the two stages embedding on *Barbara*, 0.25 on *Jetplane* and 0.5 dB on *House*. The results on *Barbara* are presented in Fig. 4. On the other test images (*Lena, Couple* and *Mandrill*) context embedding does not bring improvement over the two stages scheme.

On all the test images, δ_o takes higher values at lower embedding bit-rates. Since δ is a fraction of the prediction error (equivalently, of the threshold), at low thresholds δ should be higher in order to have effect. Otherwise, the integer value of δa is zero.

The results presented above were obtained by varying δ between $\frac{1}{17}$ and 1 with a step of $\frac{1}{17}$. A finer variation of δ does not produce any changes in bit-rate or PSNR.

4. CONCLUSIONS

The newly proposed reversible watermarking method with embedding into the prediction context has been investigated for the case of rhombus context and raster-scan watermarking. It is shown that the embedding into the upper vertical pixel of the context can not only reduce the embedding distortion, but also improve the prediction. The paper discusses the trade-off between the improvement of the prediction and the reduction of the embedding distortion. The experimental results show that the gain provided by the proposed technique is mainly due to the improvement of the prediction. The proposed scheme not only outperforms the classical raster-scan scheme, but also can outperform the classical two-stages scheme of [6].

5. ACKNOWLEDGMENTS

This work was supported by UEFISCDI Romania, project PN-II-PT-PCCA-2011-3.2-1162.

6. REFERENCES

[1] J. Tian. Reversible data embedding using a difference expansion. *IEEE Trans. Circuits Syst. Video Technol.*, 13(8):890–896, 2003.

[2] A. Alattar. Reversible watermark using the difference expansion of a generalized integer transform. *IEEE Trans. Image Processing*, 13(8):1147–1156, 2004.

[3] D. Coltuc and J.-M. Chassery. Very fast watermarking by reversible contrast mapping. *IEEE Signal Processing Lett.*, 14(4):255–258, 2007.

[4] D. Thodi and J. Rodriguez. Expansion embedding techniques for reversible watermarking. *IEEE Trans. Image Processing*, 16(3):721–730, 2007.

[5] Y. Hu, H.-K. Lee, and J. Li. De-based reversible data hiding with improved overflow location map. *IEEE Trans. Circuits Syst. Video Technol.*, 19(2):250–260, 2009.

[6] V. Sachnev, H.-J. Kim, J. Nam, S. Suresh, and Y.-Q. Shi. Reversible watermarking algorithm using sorting and prediction. *IEEE Trans. Circuits Syst. Video Technol.*, 19(7):989–999, 2009.

[7] X. Li, B. Yang, and T. Zeng. Efficient reversible watermarking based on adaptive prediction-error expansion and pixel selection. *IEEE Trans. Image Processing*, 20(12):3524–3533, 2011.

[8] D. Coltuc. Improved embedding for prediction-based reversible watermarking. *IEEE Trans.Inf. Forensics Security*, 6(3):873–882, 2011.

[9] D. Coltuc. Low distortion transform for reversible watermarking. *IEEE Trans. Image Processing*, 21(1):412–417, 2012.

[10] C. Dragoi and D. Coltuc. Improved rhombus interpolation for reversible watermarking by difference expansion. In *EUSIPCO'2012 Signal Processing Conference*, pages 1688–1692, August 2012.

[11] G. Coatrieux, W. Pan, N. Cuppens-Boulahia, F. Cuppens, and C. Roux. Reversible watermarking based on invariant image classification and dynamic histogram shifting. *IEEE Trans.Inf. Forensics Security*, 8(1):111–120, 2013.

Watermarking Road Maps against Crop and Merge Attacks

Kai Jiang   Kenny Q. Zhu
Shanghai Jiao Tong University
Shanghai, China
jkai@sjtu.edu.cn,
kzhu@cs.sjtu.edu.cn

Yan Huang
University of North Texas
Denton, TX, USA
huangyan@unt.edu

Xiaobin Ma
1 Sybase Dr
Dublin, CA 94568
xiaobin@cs.umn.edu

ABSTRACT

Past research on watermarking digital road maps has been focused on deterring common attacks such as adding noise to the whole map so as to destroy the embedded watermarks. This paper focuses on two less common but increasingly used types of attack: crop attacks and merge attacks. Crop attack crops a fragment of the original map and uses the fragment as a new map. When the new map is much smaller than the original map, it is called massive cropping. Merge attack merges maps from various sources together to form a new map. Conventional watermarking techniques fail against these attacks either because they require global information from the whole map or they must add too many local watermarks and affect the usability of the maps. This paper proposes a novel quad-tree based blind watermarking scheme that partitions the original map according to the quad-tree and plants just one single bit in each sub-region of the map. The approach achieves almost 100% detection accuracy for moderate crop and merge attacks, and over 80% accuracy with more than 95% of the original map cropped and removed. Furthermore, the method introduces very little distortion to the original map: to effectively protect a 23.5MB Minneapolis-St.Paul map against crop and merge as well as other common attacks, only 423 bits or 53 bytes of watermark is required. [1]

Categories and Subject Descriptors

D.2.11 [**Software Architectures**]: Information hiding

Keywords

Watermark, digital road map, quad-tree, crop attack, merge attack

1. INTRODUCTION

Digital watermarking is an important technique to protect the copyrights of digital products such as images, audios and videos. A watermark is small amount of digital noise embedded into the digital representation of the products. Watermarking is different from

---

[1]Kenny Q. Zhu (the corresponding author) is partially supported by NSFC grants 61033002 and 61100050.

encryption, another method used to protect digital content from unauthorized access. Watermarks embedded in a product should not be *perceived* by the user or the application and hence don't affect the normal use of the product, whereas encrypted product cannot be used unless the user has the means to decrypt the product, usually with the help of a secret key. Once the content is decrypted, unlimited illegal copies of the product can be made and used as if they were legal copies. Digital watermarking complements encryption. By embedding some watermarks that are hard to remove, one can always claim the ownership of the product after detecting the watermarks.

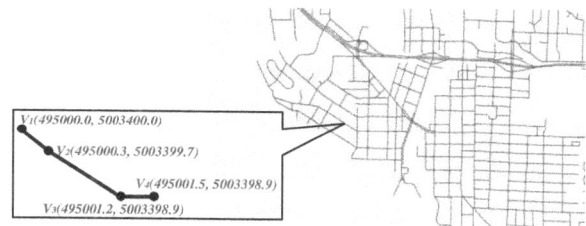

Figure 1: A Digital Road Map for Part of Anoka County, MN

In this paper, we are concerned with the protection of copyrights of digital road maps by watermarking. A digital road map is a vector graph representation of roads in a geographical region. Such maps are widely used in Geographic Positioning Systems (GPS) and other GIS or location-based applications. Figure 1 shows an example of a snippet of a road map of Anoka County, MN in the United States. In this map, a road is represented by a *polyline*, shown in the blow-up image, where a polyline is a sequence of connected straight line segments. Each line segment is presented digitally by its two end vertexes in terms of (x, y) coordinates, where x and y are latitude and longitude of the point on earth, respectively. Very wide two-way roads (e.g., freeways) with central dividers are represented by two (often) parallel polylines, which are also shown in Figure 1.

The standard watermarking framework for digital road maps (shown in Figure 2) also adopts a two-step approach. The two key modules in the framework are the watermark insertion and detection algorithms. These two modules typically share some common secret keys which are only known to the algorithms. Some detection algorithms require the original map while others don't. When digital road maps are unlawfully copied for commercial use, they often undergo various modifications or transformations in hope that the original watermarks are either removed or become undetectable. Such modifications to the map is called *attacks* on the watermarks. Existing attacks include attempts to remove or alter the watermarks,

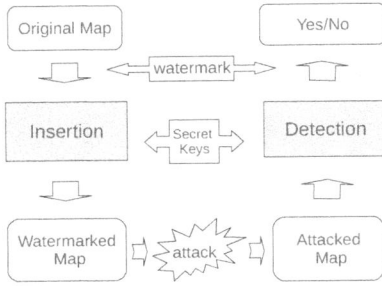

Figure 2: General Watermarking Framework For Road Maps

adding more noises to the map, cutting a map into smaller pieces or merging multiple maps from different sources. The last two attacks, which we call *"crop attack"* and *"merge attack"* are less common, and they are the focus of our research in this paper.

A scenario of a crop attack goes like this: an attacker obtains a big map, e.g., the map of the state of Minnesota, and crops out the Minneapolis - St.Paul area to create a "new" twin-city map. In the case of a merge attack, the attacker extracts maps for various counties in Minnesota from several different digital maps and composes a new Minnesota map by aligning these sub-maps properly together. The first attack is easier to implement, while the second attack is more difficult to carry out in practice and harder to defeat.

Existing watermarking techniques come in two categories, *global watermarking* and *local watermarking*. In global watermarking, the insertion module computes an overall watermark based on the global information of the data, and inserts this watermark over the whole data. Detection requires the reconstruction of the original watermark which requires global information as well. As such, these techniques cannot handle crop or merge attacks.

In local watermarking, the insertion module generates many watermarks for different regions of the data, and each watermark is computed from the local information of the corresponding regions. For example, one can partition a map into many smaller regions, and insert a watermark according to the properties of the data in each region. Local road map watermarking schemes [15, 16, 23] have the potential of surviving crop attacks. However, to handle "massive cropping", i.e., cropping out a very small piece of the original map, existing local schemes have to resort to fine-grained partitioning and the insertion of many more watermarks which may affect the perception of the map. Moreover, many of these techniques require coordination between the detection of watermarks in adjacent sub-regions (e.g., some repetitive patterns) to conclude the authenticity of the overall map. Such coordination may fail if it happens at the boundary of the cropping. Such massive cropping attacks are real, since in our previous example, the Twin-Cities area is much smaller than the whole state of Minnesota.

None of the existing local methods can defeat the merge attack because all of them compute a global confidence score based on the watermarks extracted from individual sub-regions. If a significant part of the map comes from a foreign source without the inserted watermarks, these methods typically give a low confidence score and fail to identify part of the map as being authentic. Without a proper data structure, these methods also suffer from high computation complexity if they attempt to "guess" where the watermarked region is in the map.

In this paper, we propose a novel local watermarking approach which partitions the original map by a modified quad-tree structure. The depth of the tree is determined by the road density in the region. We compute the local watermark for each partition by

the total length of the roads in that partition and each watermark is represented by *one bit* change in the original data. During detection phase, our approach can reconstruct the quad-tree and identify the potential locations of the embedded watermarks, and can report with high confidence if a given attacked map (be it traditional attacks or crop/merge attacks) contains a sub-region which carries the original watermarks as well as reporting that sub-region itself. In addition, the detection method in our approach doesn't require the original map, but only needs a "secret grid boundary" which serves as the key. The size of this key is negligible compared to the original data. Watermark detection scheme without the need for original data is also known as "blind watermarking."

This paper makes the following key contributions:

- *The framework defeats massive cropping and merging attacks with high accuracy.* Our experiments show that our approach achieves 100% detection accuracy for moderate cropping and more than 80% accuracy with more than 95% of the original map cropped, whereas the accuracy of two other state-of-the-art approaches degrades to around 20% with similar massive cropping. Our method outperforms the peers by similar margins under merge attacks.

- *The framework incurs little distortion.* The map is partitioned into sub-regions of various sizes *on demand*. Watermarking position is calculated by information inside these sub-regions. We use a one-bit watermark to represent that the sub-region is watermarked. Consequently, to effectively watermark the whole Twin-Cities 7-counties map (23.5MB), our approach merely modified 423 *bits*.

- *The framework is lightweight.* It is a blind watermarking method which requires no original map for watermark detection, and the time complexity of both the insertion and detection algorithm is $O(|V|log\mathcal{L})$ where $|V|$ is the number of vertices in the map and $\mathcal{L}$ is the total length of roads in the map.

The remainder of this paper is organized as follows. Section 2 introduces some preliminaries about the watermarking GIS digital data and formalizes the problems of interest. Section 3 discusses the proposed digital watermarking approach in detail. Section 4 describes the experiment setup and presents evaluation results on a real digital map data set. Section 5 discusses the related work, and we conclude the paper with some further work in section 6.

2. PROBLEM DEFINITION

In this section, we first define digital road maps and distortions to the map. We then give the problem definition of watermarking digital road maps in terms of the interfaces of two functions, *insertion* and *detection*. Finally we describe some common attacks on digital maps with special emphasis on the two difficult attacks: crop and merge attacks.

2.1 Digital Road Map and Its Distortions

A digital road map, M, is a *view* of a graph G with a set of vertices V and a set of edges E. M consists of a set of k roads R_i, where each road is a *polyline* represented by a sequence of vertices in the form of (x, y) coordinates in a geographical coordinate system (e.g., latitudes and longitudes). Formally,

$$G = \{V, E\}$$

$$M = \bigcup_{i=1}^{k} R_i, \text{where } k \geq 1; \text{ and}$$

$$R_i = [V_1, V_2, \ldots, V_m]$$

$$\text{where } m \leq |V|; \forall i \neq j : V_i \neq V_j;$$

$$\forall i \in [1, m] : (V_i, V_{i+1}) \in E; \text{ and}$$

$$\forall i \in [1, m] : V_i = (x_i, y_i).$$

Whether we are watermarking or attacking a given map, we are essentially changing the original map, or adding distortion. In order to maintain usability of the map, the amount of distortion must not be larger than a threshold η known as *perception tolerance*. We consider three types of distortion one can make to a map: *perturb* some vertices, *insert* some new vertices into a road, or *delete* some vertices from a road.

Given a road R, and a changed road R', let P be the set of nodes in R which are perturbed, and I be the set of nodes in R' which are newly inserted, and D be the set in R of nodes which are deleted, the distortion between R and R' is defined as

$$\delta(R, R') = \delta(P) + \delta(I) + \delta(D)$$

where

$$\delta(P) = \sum_{V_i \in P} ||V_i' - V_i||$$

$$\delta(I) = \sum_{V_i \in I} d(V_i, R)$$

$$\delta(D) = \sum_{V_i \in D} d(V_i, R')$$

and

$$d(V_i, R) = \begin{cases} ||V_i - V_{i+1}|| & \text{if } i = 1, \{V_i, V_{i+1}\} \subseteq R \\ ||V_i - V_{i-1}|| & \text{if } i = |R|, \{V_i, V_{i-1}\} \subseteq R \\ |||\boldsymbol{\alpha}|| \sin \langle \boldsymbol{\alpha}, \boldsymbol{\beta} \rangle| & \text{if } \{V_{i-1}, V_i, V_{i+1}\} \subseteq R \end{cases}$$

where $\boldsymbol{\alpha} = V_i - V_{i-1}$ and $\boldsymbol{\beta} = V_{i+1} - V_{i-1}$, and $\langle \boldsymbol{\alpha}, \boldsymbol{\beta} \rangle$ means the angle of intersection between vectors $\boldsymbol{\alpha}$ and $\boldsymbol{\beta}$. Here $d(V_i, R)$(see Figure 3) means the distance between a node V_i and the line segment (V_{i-1}, V_{i+1}), or if V_i happens to be the end of a road, the distance to its adjacent node in the road.

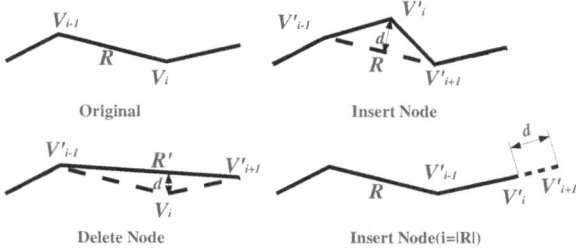

Figure 3: Distance Measurement function d(V, R)

The distortion to the whole map is hence the total distortion to all its roads, normalized by the total lengths of all roads:

$$\delta(M, M') = \frac{\sum_{R \in M, R' \in M'} \delta(R, R')}{\sum_{R \in M} length(R)}.$$

In the remainder of this paper, we use δ_w to represent the $\delta(M, M')$ caused by watermarking, and use δ_n for $\delta(M, M')$ due to noise.

2.2 Insertion and Detection of Watermarks

For a digital road map M, watermark W, and some secret key K (to enhance robustness against attacks), the interface of watermarking process can be represented by two functions $\mathcal{I}$ and $\mathcal{D}$.

$$\mathcal{I} : (M, W, K) \rightarrow M'$$
$$\mathcal{D} : (M, W, K) \rightarrow \{T \mid F\}$$

where M' is the watermarked map, $\delta(M, M') \leq \eta$, and detection process returns a boolean value of either *true* or *false*.

2.3 Attacks

There are many different attacks on digital road map. In this section We focus on into three types: the first type is a common attack which introduces random noises into an illegal copy of the map. The other two types are more complex attacks which involves cropping a given map into smaller pieces and merging pieces together from various sources.

Noise Attack

An attacker disturbs the watermarks in a map by selecting a subset of the nodes in the map and perturb the position of these nodes slightly. The subset could be small compared to the whole map:

$$noise(M) = \{noise(R) \mid R \in M_1\} \cup M_2$$

where $M_1 \cap M_2 = \emptyset$, $M_1 \cup M_2 = M$, $noise(R) = [perturb(V) \mid V \in R]$, where $[f(V) \mid V \in R]$ a list comprehension constructed from another list R.

Crop Attack

An attacker crop a geographical region from the watermarked map and use it as if it's a new map. The crop attack can defeat almost all global watermarking techniques because the global information can be destroyed by the cropping. Even for many local watermarking techniques, the resistance against cropping is limited if just a small piece of the map is cropped. We define cropping attack as:

$$Crop(M) = \{subseg(R) \mid R \in M'\}$$

where $M' \subseteq M$ and $subseq(R)$ returns a subsequence of road R.

If M' is a very small subset of M, we call the attack "massive crop" attack. None of the existing watermarking approaches can handle massive crop attack.

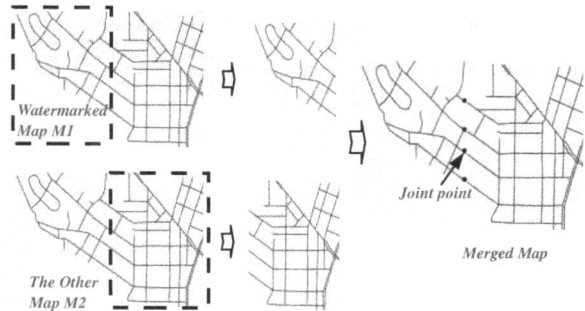

Figure 4: Merge Attack

Merge Attack

This attack involves the merging of multiple maps from different sources (see Figure 4). Maps from various sources differ by either precision of measurement, the granularity of road segmentation, or minor details of roads due to changes to the road over time. However, maps of the same region will be largely identical. This enables the attacker to crop parts from different maps and piece them together to make a new map. There might some slight distortion or inaccuracy at the boundaries but the resulting map is usable. We define the "merge" of two maps as:

$$Merge(M_1, M_2) = M_{sep} \cup M_{con}$$

where

$$
\begin{aligned}
M_{sep} &= \{R_1 \mid R_1 \in M_1 \text{ and} \\
&\qquad \forall R_2 \in M_2 : connect(R_1, R_2) = false\} \\
&\cup \quad \{R_2 \mid R_2 \in M_2 \text{ and} \\
&\qquad \forall R_1 \in M_1 : connect(R_1, R_2) = false\} \\
M_{con} &= \{join(R_1, R_2) \mid \forall R_1 \in M_1, R_2 \in M_2, \\
&\qquad connect(R_1, R_2) = true\}
\end{aligned}
$$

and $connect(R_1, R_2)$ is a boolean function that evaluates to true if two roads R_1 and R_2 share a name and an endpoint. $join(R_1, R_2)$ returns a road that joins two connected roads with identical name. M_{sep} and M_{con} are two sets of roads that make up the merged map, where M_{sep} denotes those roads from the original maps which are disjoint and M_{con} denotes a set of roads from the boundaries of the two input maps which are joined together.

3. OUR APPROACH

In this section, we propose a novel watermarking approach, which can effectively survive "massive crop" and "merge" attacks. Our watermarking method inserts negligible watermarks (one-bit only) to locations which are determined by a spatial partitioning algorithm. Then during detection time, the same spatial partitioning algorithm is used with the help of a secret key, which ensures that the resulting segmentation of the space and the input map is almost identical to that of the watermarked map, even though no original map is available. In the following, we first introduce the secret keys used in this framework, then present the space partitioning algorithm, watermark insertion and detection algorithms, before giving analysis of the algorithms. All symbols used in the algorithms are summarized in Table 1.

Table 1: All Symbols Used in Algorithms

Symbol	Definition	Symbol	Definition
G	master grid	PO	sub-region list
M	original data-set	T	MQtree
$\mathcal{R}$	partitioned region	l	secret square size
θ	road length threshold	k	secret hash key

3.1 Secret Keys

The secret keys, often randomly generated, are used to decide where to insert the watermarks. In the proposed algorithm, we use three secret keys: a master grid, a secret minimum bounding rectangle (MBR) and a secret square size.

The *master grid* G is a secret coordinate system which is only known to the map producer. The grid has an origin which is certain position on earth with precise latitude and longitude, and it has a step size which defines the granularity of the grid (see Figure 5):

$$G = \{Origin(x_0, y_0), Step\}$$

Given an original map to watermark, it can be laid out on the master grid, according to the coordinates of the vertices in the map. The *secret MBR* is then the smallest rectangle which coincides with the grid lines and completely encloses the whole map. The red rectangle in Figure 5 is one such secret MBR of the blue road map. In our algorithm, we partition the space according to a modified Quadtree. The MBR of the map serves as an initial of the partition process, which will improve the robustness of our algorithm.

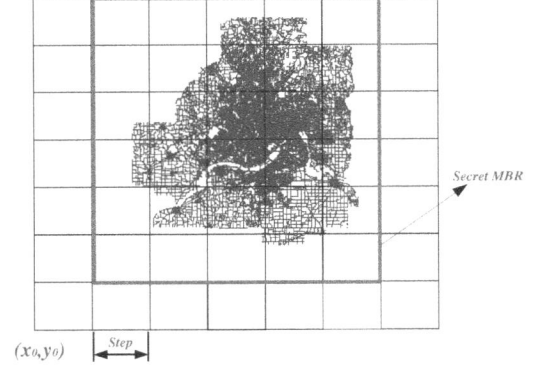

Figure 5: Master Grid and MBR

The *secret square size* is an integer number l that determines the size of a square box that we used to select a small neighborhood of road segments from which to compute the watermarks. More details of the use of l will be presented in Section 3.3.

3.2 Space Partitioning Algorithm

Algorithm 1 is used in both insertion and detection of the watermarks. It recursively partitions the space bounded by the secret MBR for a map into small regions using a modified quad-tree structure (known as MQtree) according to the density of the roads. Each node in MQtree represents a sub-region of the map. A leaf node represents a region in which the total length of road segments within is between θ and 4θ meters. Figure 6(b) illustrate a MQtree created from partitioning an MBR shown in Figure 6(a).

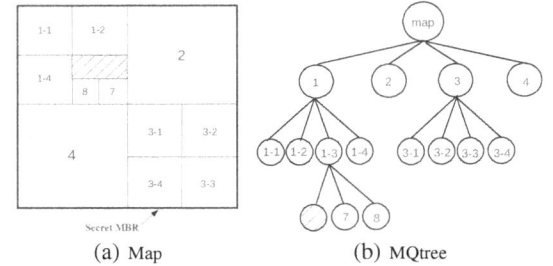

(a) Map   (b) MQtree

Figure 6: MQtree

In Algorithm 1, the secret MBR is generated from the master grid(see Figure 5). Then the map area is partitioned iteratively according to the density of roads such that finally the total road length included in every subregion has more than m meters and less than $4 * \theta$ meters. Finally, we output all of these subregions. Here we modify Quadtree by merging one subregion with less roads with its smallest neighbor when the road length of it is less than θ. Road length of an area cannot be changed arbitrarily due to the constraints of perception tolerance which must be observed by both the watermark producer and the attacker. No matter a watermarked map is cropped or merged with other parts from different maps, this method still produces almost the identical partition results for the watermarked part.

Algorithm 1 Partition

Input: G, M, T, θ
Output: PO, T
1: **function** PARTITION(G, M, T, θ)
2:      $L|PO|T \leftarrow$ new queue|new list|$MBR(G, M)$
3:      $L.Push(T)$
4:      **while** L is not empty **do**
5:          partition region $\mathcal{R} \leftarrow L.pop$ into $\mathcal{R}_i, i \in \{1, 2, 3, 4\}$
6:          **for** each $\mathcal{R}_i$ **do**
7:              **if** road length in $\mathcal{R}_i < \theta$ **then**
8:                  merge $\mathcal{R}_i$ with its smaller neighbor
9:              **else if** road length in $\mathcal{R}_i > 4\theta$ **then**
10:                  $\mathcal{R}.children_i \leftarrow \mathcal{R}_i$
11:                  $L.push(\mathcal{R}.children_i)$
12:              **else**
13:                  $\mathcal{R}.children_i \leftarrow \mathcal{R}_i$
14:                  insert $\mathcal{R}_i$ to PO
15: **return** PO

3.3 Watermark Insertion Algorithm

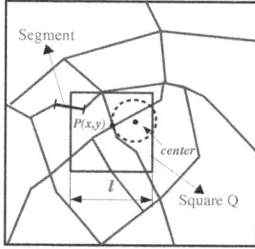

Figure 7: Insertion Strategy

Algorithm 2 first generates a set of sub-regions by partitioning. Then it inserts one watermark into each sub-region at the leaf nodes of the MQtree. The watermark is inserted into a road vertex $P(x, y)$ which is closest to the center of the sub-region (marked by the black box in Figure 7). To compute the exact watermark to be inserted, the algorithm then draw a square box of size l (the other secret key) centered at $P(x, y)$ (the red box in Figure 7). Let sl be the length of road segments that intersects the square box, and let j be a value hashed from sl. We then set the jth least significant bit in x coordinate of P to "1". The hash function in this algorithm must guarantee to hash to the same value before and after watermarking. Even if the watermarked map is attacked (i.e., some end points of those segments intersecting Q are altered), the hash function must still hash to the same j. To this end, we design this function with a tolerance to possible distortions. Assuming that the biggest possible distortion of a single end point is the change of J_{max} least significant bits of the coordinates, then

$$j \quad = \quad Hash(Trans(sl), k)$$

$$\text{where} \quad Trans(x) = x \wedge \underbrace{11\ldots1}\overbrace{00\ldots0}^{J_{max}}$$
$$\underbrace{}_{bit\_length(x)}$$

Algorithm 2 Insert Watermark into Map

Input: G, M, l, k, θ
Output: M
1: **procedure** INSERTION(M, G, l, k, θ)
2:      $PO \leftarrow$ PARTITION($G, M, NULL, \theta$)
3:      **for** each region $\mathcal{R}_i \in PO$ **do**
4:          **if** road length in $\mathcal{R}_i > \theta$ **then**
5:              $P \leftarrow$ point closest to $\mathcal{R}_i.center$
6:              draw a square Q of side length l centered at P
7:              $sl \leftarrow$ length of line segments intersecting Q
8:              j $\leftarrow$ Hash(k, sl)
9:              j^{th} LSB of $P.x \leftarrow 1$

3.4 Watermark Detection Algorithm

In Algorithm 3, we partition the map using the same strategy as insertion. Then we select the data points closest to the center of the regions to detect whether the watermark exists there. Each sub-region which is detected to contain a watermark casts a vote which collectively contributes to the final decision of whether a larger area is watermarked as a whole. For leaf nodes of the MQtree, if the bit value at the right position is "1", we mark this sub-region as a "match". Function STATS(T) (Algorithm 4) computes two statistics for each node of the MQtree: the total number leaf nodes underneath the node (T.total) and the total number of nodes which has been marked as "match" (T.match). If the detection confidence $conf(T_i)$ is larger than a threshold ξ for for any non-leaf node T_i, the watermark in the map is successfully identified. We define the detection confidence of T as

$$conf(T) = 1 - \sum_{i=n}^{N} \binom{N}{i} \left(\frac{1}{2}\right)^{N-i} \left(\frac{1}{2}\right)^i \quad (1)$$

where N is T.total and n is T.match. In our approach, the data points where we select to insert watermark may already contain "1" at the specified bit position. Here we assume uniform distribution and hence the probability of "1" being already present is 1/2.

Algorithm 3 Detect Watermark from a Suspicious Map

Input: G, M, l, k, θ
Output: Yes/No
1: **function** DETECTION(M, G, l, k, θ)
2:      $T \leftarrow$ new MQtree
3:      $PO \leftarrow$ PARTITION($G, M, \&T, \theta$)
4:      **for** each region $\mathcal{R}_i \in PO$ **do**
5:          **if** road length in $\mathcal{R}_i > \theta$ **then**
6:              $P \leftarrow$ point closest to $\mathcal{R}_i.center$
7:              draw a square Q of side length l center at P
8:              $sl \leftarrow$ length of line segments intersecting Q
9:              j $\leftarrow$ Hash(k, sl)
10:              **if** j^{th} LSB of $P.x$ is 1 **then**
11:                  Mark $\mathcal{R}_i$ as "match"
12:      STATS(T)
13:      **for** each non-leaf node T_i of T in depth-first order **do**
14:          **if** $conf(T_i) > \xi$ **then return** Yes
15: **return** No

If the watermarked map is attacked by "massive crop" attack, the MQtree structure partitioned by detection algorithm is just a part of the insertion MQtree. However, it will be almost the same as the corresponding part of the MQtree for the whole map. An example of the detection process is illustrated in Figure 8. Assuming that

---

Algorithm 4 Compute Stats For a Given MQtree

1: **procedure** STATS(T)
2:    **if** T is not a leaf node **then**
3:       **for** each $T_i \in T.children$ **do**
4:          STATS(T_i)
5:          T.match←T.match+T_i.match
6:          T.total←T.total+T_i.total
7:    **else**
8:       **if** The region of T is "match" **then**
9:          T.match←1
10:      **else**
11:         T.match←0
12:      T.total←1

---

the shaded parts of Figure 8(a) is cropped from the watermarked map, the corresponding MQtree is shown in Figure 8(b).

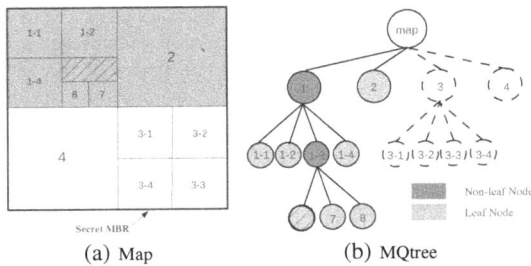

(a) Map   (b) MQtree

Figure 8: Detection Strategy

If the watermarked map is attacked by "Merge Attack", the detection MQtree will be almost the same as the insertion one. However, we can find the watermark only in part of the MQtree. In this case, the algorithm reports the sub-regions that are watermarked. We can make a depth-first traversal of the detection MQtree to find the largest watermarked region.

3.5 Analysis

The time complexity of Algorithm 1 is

$$\mathcal{T} = O(|E| \log \mathcal{L}),$$

where $\mathcal{L}$ is the total length of all roads in map M. Since the number of edges connected to a vertex is bounded a small number q, that is, $|E| \leq (q \times |V|)/2$, $\mathcal{T} = O(|V| \log \mathcal{L})$.

The time complexity of Algorithm 2 and Algorithm 3 is $\mathcal{T} + O(|V|)$, or $O(|V| \log \mathcal{L})$.

The detection confidence in (1) essentially represents the probability of correctly identifying watermarks in a given map (attacked or not). We now attempt to give a lower bound to the detection confidence. Intuitively, as θ decreases, the map is divided into more subregions and therefore more watermarks will be inserted while the accuracy of watermark detection should be enhanced. We thus have the following lemma.

LEMMA 3.1. *Given a map M with total length $\mathcal{L}$ and an algorithm threshold θ, the minimum detection confidence for M:*

$$conf_{min}(M) = 1 - \sum_{i=\lceil \rho\mathcal{L}/4\theta \rceil}^{\lceil \mathcal{L}/4\theta \rceil} \binom{\lceil \mathcal{L}/4\theta \rceil}{i} \left(\frac{1}{2}\right)^{\lceil \mathcal{L}/4\theta \rceil}$$

where ρ is the ratio between the number of leaf nodes that match and the total number of leaf nodes in M.

PROOF. Straightforward as the total number of leaf nodes is no less than $\mathcal{L}/4\theta$. □

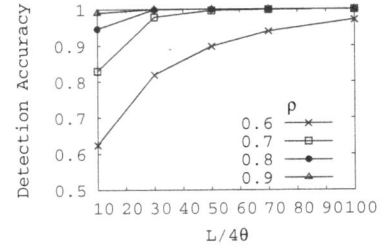

Figure 9: Accuracy of Detection

Figure 9 plots the relationship between minimum detection confidence against $\mathcal{L}/4\theta$ for different values of ρ, which coincides with our previous intuition. However, smaller θ translates into more watermarks and hence larger distortion to the map. It also causes the watermarking to be more time-consuming. This trade-off should be carefully considered when applying our approach.

4. EVALUATION

In this section, we present some experimental results from the proposed framework.

4.1 The Experimental Setup

We implement and test the performance of the algorithms under different potential attacks. All algorithms are implemented with C and all experiments are conducted on Core PC with 2.0 GHz CPU and 2 GBytes of memory running the Ubuntu 12.04 operating system.

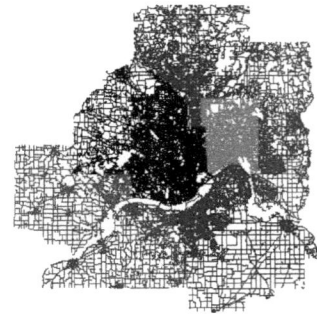

Figure 10: Twin-Cities Seven-County Road Map

We use MN state base map of seven counties, namely, Anoka, Carver, Dakota, Hennepin, Ramsey, Scott, Washington, as our real data set for this experiment. In this data-set, there are in total 415,651 line segments and 372,466 different points. Figure 10 shows the visual map of digital data for these seven counties. This data set can be downloaded from the MN/DOT web site[1].

In order to evaluate the robustness of our watermarking algorithms (which is called Jiang in the rest of this section), we illustrate the performance of our proposed watermark approach under different attacks with different settings. In this part, we compare the proposed approach with two other watermarking algorithms proposed by Pu[17] and Voigt[23]. Both methods are blind watermarking algorithms and provide some resistance to crop attack. We control the accuracy lost of the experiment data caused by different methods and compare the performance of them under noise attack, crop attack and merge attack. In this section, "crop ratio" and "merge ratio" mean the area ratio we crop from the total watermarked map. We set ξ as 0.95.

4.2 Performance under Noise Attack

Noises are added to randomly selected subsets of watermarked maps. Meanwhile, to keep the usability of a map, those subsets could not take too much proportion of the total map. In this experiment, we watermark the map of St. Paul area and attack the watermarked map with some random Gaussian noise, perturbing the map with different accuracy lost.

In this noise attack experiment, we watermark the map with algorithms of Pu[17], Voigt[23] and Jiang in certain distortion. After that we attack the watermarked maps with different noise distortion. For each noise distortion, the noise will be added in different methods for 20 times. For all three methods, the noise added is "exactly" the same each time. At last, we detect the watermark and calculate detection accuracy for three algorithms. We set distortion δ_w added by the watermarking as 10.5×10^{-6} (Jiang), 10.8×10^{-6} (Voigt) and 9.8×10^{-6} (Pu). Take the size of map into consideration, these distortion can be deemed at the same level. On the other hand, the noise distortion δ_n is changed from 5.12×10^{-3} to 2.56×10^{-2}. Actually, δ_n here is large enough that almost changes all vertexes of the map. Figure 11 shows the results.

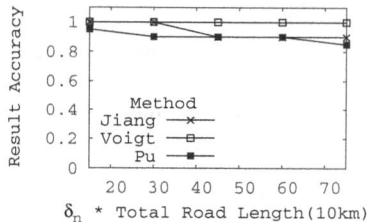

Figure 11: Performance under Noise Attack

In this experiment, we set the standard of positive detection as correctly decide the whole map is watermarked. However, in fact, according to the detection method of our algorithm, some more assistance can be obtained. Even the whole map is failed to be detected, the result could be a series of sub-regions that is suspicious. The results show that our algorithm successfully survived noise attack. On one hand, we watermark certain bits which will not be directly affected by the noise if perturbing for individual vertex is under certain strength. Meanwhile, even the perturbing for individual vertex is powerful enough, θ and the hash function of sl in partition and insertion algorithms provide a good tolerance for it.

4.3 Performance under Crop Attack

In our experiment, on one hand, each county out of seven is selected to be detected. On the other hand, some certain proportion of the map is selected to evaluate the performance of our algorithm.

In this experiment, the parameter θ is set as 30,000.0 ($\delta_w = 10.5 \times 10^{-6}$) and the square side length is 100.0 for both insertion and detection. We partition the whole map of Minneapolis-St. Paul Metropolitan area. Then the watermarked map is split according to the boundary of different counties. After that, we impose our watermarking algorithm on these "partial" maps, trying to decide whether the maps are parts of our original map. Table 2 shows the results of this experiment.

Table 2: Crop Attack Detection

County	Total	Match	Confidence	Result
Anoka	55	51	1.000	positive
Carver	28	23	0.999	positive
Dakota	68	61	1.000	positive
Hennipin	141	137	1.000	positive
Ramsey	58	56	1.000	positive
Scott	29	25	0.999	positive
Washington	46	43	1.000	positive

By analyzing the insertion algorithm, we can easily get the notion that the partition criterion θ has a large influence on the result of our watermark algorithm. We also design a series of experiments to figure out the influence of the θ. In this experiment, we watermark the map with different distortion (2.1) by adjusting θ (see Figure 13(a)) and then select the crop ratio of $1/2$, $1/4$ and $1/8$ of the map to detect. Each ratio is detected for 20 times. Figure 13(b) show the result of experiments. Insertion (Figure 13(c)) and detection (Figure 13(d)) time for different distortion is also measured.

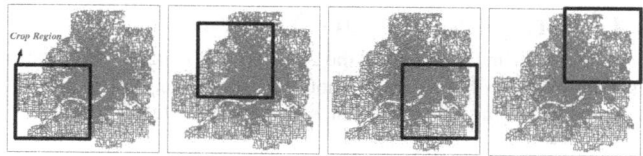

Figure 12: A Showcase of Crop Ratio 1/4

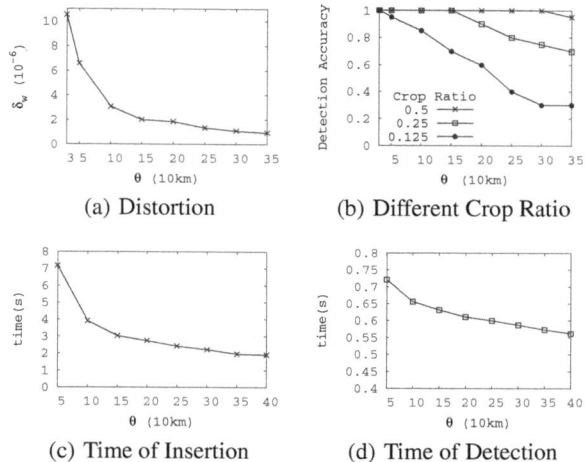

(a) Distortion   (b) Different Crop Ratio

(c) Time of Insertion   (d) Time of Detection

Figure 13: Experiment Results under Different Distortion

In the following experiment, we watermark a map with certain distortion, here we set $\theta = 30,000$. After that we crop different ratio from the map to evaluate the performance of our algorithm. For each crop ratio, we select different parts of the map to detect up to 20 times. We randomly select different parts of the watermarked map to detect (see Figure 12) and calculate the detection accuracy. Here we also implement Voigt's and Pu's methods to make a comparison. Distortion δ_w added by the watermarking is 10.5×10^{-6} (Jiang), 10.8×10^{-6} (Voigt) and 9.8×10^{-6} (Pu). The distortion of all three methods are almost at the same level. Figure 14(a) gives the results.

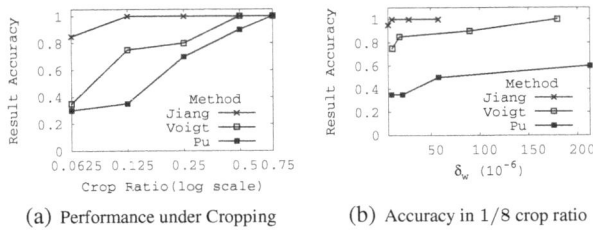
(a) Performance under Cropping   (b) Accuracy in $1/8$ crop ratio

Figure 14: Performance under Crop Attack

According to the experiment result, we can find that our algorithm keeps a perfect result when the crop ratio is up to $1/8$, while the comparison methods show a significant accuracy degradation. And when crop ratio is $1/16$, we still contain a high accuracy. We also test the detection accuracy under different distortion in $1/8$ crop ratio (see Figure 14(b)). In this experiment, our algorithm can attain a 100% detection accuracy with just little distortion. Since the detection accuracy of our algorithm quickly attain to 1, it is not necessary to plot too many points in Figure 14(b).

4.4 Performance under Merge Attack

In this experiment, we select the 2012 TIGER map of Minneapolis-St. Paul Metropolitan area as another data source, which can be downloaded from the United States Census Website[2]. The coordinate system of TIGER map is different from MN dot base Map. We transform the coordinate system of TIGER map to make it same as the former data source. Figure 15 is the overlap of these two maps of Anoka county after the synchronization.

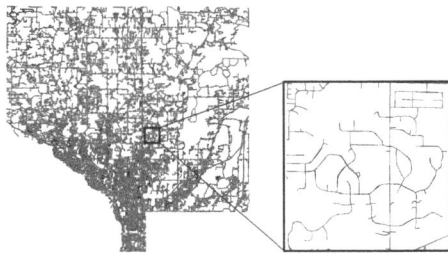

Figure 15: Overlap of Two Maps

We crop a watermarked map ($\delta_w = 6.60 \times 10^{-6}$) and merge part of it with TIGER map to make a "new" map (see Figure 16(a)). The result of the merge detection: suspicious regions and detection confidence is shown in Table 3. Here we select those regions which have at least 10 points tested. From the corresponding visual figure (see Figure 16(b)), we can see that our algorithm almost "exactly" decides the suspicious regions.

Table 3: Merge Attack Detection

Region	Total	Match	Confidence	Result
1	147	122	1.000	positive
2	12	11	0.997	positive
3	23	18	0.994	positive
4	15	12	0.983	positive

We also watermark the Minneapolis-St. Paul Metropolitan area and then split this watermarked map into the same small portions as cropping experiment above. After that we merge these maps with

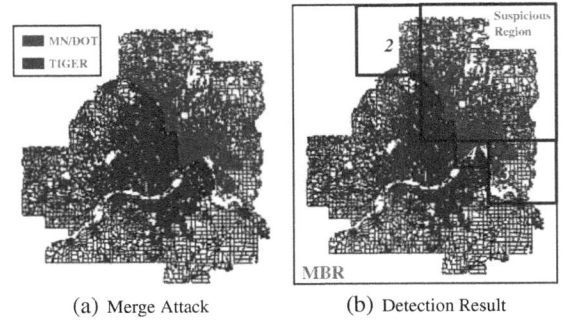
(a) Merge Attack   (b) Detection Result

Figure 16: Merged Map

the complementary parts of map from TIGER to create some new digital road maps. In this experiment, we also implement the two other method to make a comparison. Distortion δ_w added by the watermarking still is 10.5×10^{-6} (Jiang), 10.8×10^{-6} (Voigt) and 9.8×10^{-6} (Pu). Figure 17(a) shows the result of our experiments.

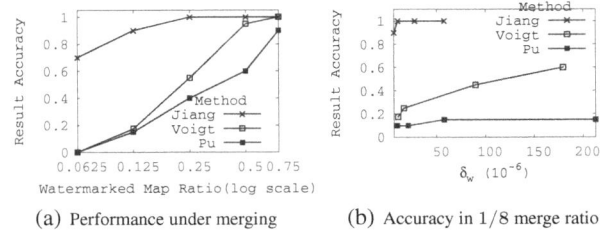
(a) Performance under merging   (b) Accuracy in $1/8$ merge ratio

Figure 17: Performance under Crop Attack

Comparing with the cropping experiment, we can obviously find the performance of our proposed algorithm is almost not affected by the complementary part of the map. However, the detection accuracy of the other two methods decrease significantly. The reason is the complementary map provides sufficient disturb to watermarked data. Similarly, we also implement another experiment to evaluate the relationship between detection accuracy and watermark distortion δ_w. From this figure, we can see that our algorithm still can quickly attain a quite high detection accuracy. However, when δ_w increases for Pu's and Voigt's method, the detection accuracy doesn't changed significantly. The reason for Pu should be that it's global liner correlation is destroyed by "merge" attack. For Voigt's method, though more watermark information is used for detection, more "merge" noise will will also be added to the detection process. Thus increase of detection accuracy for them is not significant.

5. RELATED WORK

Many efforts have been made to protect the copyrights of multimedia products such as images, movies and music. Digital road maps is a special vector graphics data which contains important geographical and spatial information. In the rest of this section, we will focus on GIS spatial data watermarking but will also briefly touch on related techniques in some other domains. The technique proposed in this paper benefits from or is inspired by some of these methods.

5.1 GIS Spatial Data Watermarking

Several studies have touched on the watermarking of GIS spatial data such as digital vector maps. Even though digital vector maps are represented by node coordinates which can also be treated as relational tables, techniques developed for relational data ignore the spatial properties of road maps such as spatial distances and geo-localities. These distinct features of GIS spatial data call for special treatments in watermarking techniques. According to Niu [14], the existing methods of digital vector map watermarking is classified into two categories: algorithms in spatial domain and algorithms in frequency domain. Depending on whether to require the original map for detection, these methods are also classified as the not blind and the blind. In addition, algorithms can also be categorized into *global* or *local* depending on whether global information of the map is needed when computing each watermark.

The spatial domain algorithms embed watermarks based on the geometric properties of polyline and polygon objects. It is often easier to control the amount of distortion added by the watermarks. They are also more robust against rotation, scaling and noises, while preserving the utility of a map. Existing methods in spatial domain usually lack of robustness against massive cropping and merging. The method proposed in this paper falls into the category of spatial domain algorithms.

The frequency domain algorithms essentially transform the original data into frequency domain, usually by Discrete Fourier Transform (DFT) [11, 21, 22] or Discrete Wavelet Transform (DWT) [13], add noises in the frequency domain and then transform it back into the spatial domain. The critical drawbacks of frequency domain techniques are the difficulty of controlling the amount of distortion in the spatial domain and the lack of robustness against data cropping and data reordering, due to the fact that it is actually a global watermarking scheme.

5.1.1 Non-Blind Methods in Spatial Domain

Some watermarking methods [7, 15, 16] require the original map or watermarked map as a reference to detect watermarks from a suspicious map. This kind of methods are called "non-blind" algorithms. The main weakness of these methods is that road maps can be updated over time and a map producer may have many versions of the same map in its database. Moreover in the same database, there could be many maps which have overlapping regions, say map of the Twin Cities, map of Minnesota, map of the United States, etc. When the map database is big, and when the suspicious map could have been subjected to cropping and merging, it is not easy to identify the original map.

Ohbuchi et al.[15] partitions the space of the digital map into rectangles such that every rectangle contains almost equal node numbers. Then the vth vertex inside the rectangle is modified to include a watermark. In another method [16], all vertices are connected into a single mesh by Delaunay triangulation. Then a mesh Laplacian is formed and the mesh is partitioned into patches using the same method as in the former one[15]. Mesh-spectral coefficients are calculated for every patch and the watermark is embedded into these coefficients.

Both of the above algorithms disperse watermarks locally and have some robustness against crop attack. However, them are highly dependent on the validity of the original data. When extracting the watermark, the suspicious map is aligned onto the original map. All inserted nodes have to be deleted, and all removed nodes have to be correctly recovered.

5.1.2 Blind Methods in Spatial Domain

Some other watermark framework are proposed which required no original or watermarked map as a reference. Some of these methods [9, 8, 24, 12] insert watermark globally. Yan et al. proposed a key point based algorithm [24]. Key points are those nodes in the map which have more important geometric aspects than the other ones, for example cross joints and those in sharp curve. They are not likely to be removed or edited by the attackers because removing them will render the map useless. This method uses a dynamic programming algorithm [6] both in insertion and detection steps. Key points in the map are used for inserting and detecting watermarks. This kind of algorithms are robust against some attacks like noise and vertex simplification, but are still vulnerable to crop and merge attacks.

Other blind watermarking algorithms [23, 18, 17, 5, 10] provide some limited resistance against crop attacks to some extent. Voigt et al.[23] proposed a feature based watermarking algorithm which is relies on statistical detection. This method partitions a map into small rectangular regions called "patches". It then randomly selects two subsets of the patches called set A and set B, respectively. Next, it calculates a reference point for each patch in the two set. During watermark insertion, all nodes in set A are shifted *toward* the reference point in their respective patches, while all nodes in set B are shifted *away* from the reference point. The amount of shift is governed by an F-distribution [3] which is also used to detect the watermark. Pu et al. proposed a blind algorithm [17] which divides the map into mesh segments, and then embeds the watermark in each segment with a fixed order. In the detection step, each segment is evaluated by a correlation parameter, which is a linear correlation of the watermark and the watermarked data. To survive crop attack, a global correlation based detection method is applied as an optimization. This algorithm watermarks maps according to their topological relations.

While these algorithms present some resistance against cropping attack, they cannot survive cropping at larger scale. Take Voigt[23] as an example, when the watermarked map is massively cropped, many patches that are marked may be removed. Thus F distribution of watermarked points may be destroyed. Therefore, the method is not robust enough against "massive crop". Furthermore, if the map is cropped and then merged with others, the information added by the merge will defeat the watermarking more easily.

5.1.3 Methods in Frequency Domain

Solachidis et al.[21] proposed a blind watermarking scheme embedding a single bit into a polyline by modifying the discrete Fourier coefficients of polyline's coordinate sequence. This method embeds the watermark in the magnitude of the curve's Fourier descriptors to exploit its location, scale, and rotation invariant properties. Due to the amplitude frequency features of discrete Fourier transform, the algorithm is inherently robust to many attacks such as map translation, rotation, scaling and changing start vertex. Similar to the DFT method[21], Li et al. proposed a blind scheme [13] embedding multi-bits into a vector map in DWT domain. These frequency domain methods rely on the integrity of map and order of data points. When part of map data is removed or the order of data points is changed, the coefficients will also be changed, which makes them extremely vulnerable to crop and merge attacks.

5.2 Watermarking in Other Domains

Some research attention has been given to relational data[4, 20]. Rakesh Agrawal proposes a framework of watermarking relational databases[4]. According to this approach, a primary key is stored in some significant tuples of relational data. The altered attribute index and bit index for the selected attribute are randomly selected according to secret keys. Their approach is highly dependent on the primary key of the data tuple and randomly selects a subset of tuples to watermark. This approach in fact disperses one bit watermark into different position of relational data. It provide some resistance against crop and merge attack to some extent. Some ideas in this framework actually inspired the work in this paper, e.g., modifying least significant bits and computing the confidence of detection. However, this framework is for relational data and hence does not consider the special properties of spatial attributes in GIS spatial data. In our method, information which is adjacent to each other in geographical space collaborate to decide the watermarking positions. However, in relational data, different tuples are completely independent to each other, even though they are stored together, because they form a set. Other work[20] extends the framework[19] to relational databases. In that paper, numeric dataset are first hashed to another dataset with a secret order. Then the new dataset is grouped into different chunks according to their order. Finally, the average value and standard deviation is calculated for every chunk. According to these statistics and watermarking data, a small number of data points are altered. This approach still disperses the watermark globally. One of the serious drawbacks for this global watermarking approach is that it completely fails a "massive crop" attack.

6. CONCLUSION

In this paper, we proposed a new blind watermarking scheme for digital vector road maps. The scheme produces and detects watermarks according to local information with the help of three secret keys of negligible sizes but without referring to the original map. The algorithm dynamically partitions a given map according to road density and inserts one-bit watermarks to one of the least significant bits of points determined by the secret keys. The amount of distortion brought by watermarks is arguably much smaller than existing methods. Our preliminary evaluation shows that this algorithm is resilient to massive crop and merge attacks and significantly outperforms two other state-of-the-art vector map watermarking approaches in terms of detection accuracy.

7. REFERENCES

[1] MN/DOT. http://www.dot.state.mn.us/.

[2] TIGER. http://www.census.gov/.

[3] M. Abramowitz and I. Stegun. *Handbook of mathematical functions: with formulas, graphs, and mathematical tables*, volume 55. Dover publications, 1965.

[4] R. Agrawal and J. Kiernan. Watermarking relational databases. In *VLDB*, pages 155–166, 2002.

[5] S. Bird, C. Bellman, and R. v. Schyndel. A shape-based vector watermark for digital mapping. In *Proceedings of the 2009 Digital Image Computing: Techniques and Applications*, pages 454–461. IEEE Computer Society, 2009.

[6] D. H. Douglas. Algorithms for the reduction of the number of points required to represent a line or its a caricature. *The Canadian Cartographer*, 10(2):112–122, 1973.

[7] P. Han, J. Gong, and L. Cheng. An improved adaptive watermarking algorithm for vector digital maps. In *Geoscience and Remote Sensing Symposium,IGARSS*, pages 2844 –2847, 2006.

[8] X.-J. Huo, T.-Y. Seung, B.-J. Jang, S.-H. Lee, and K.-R. Kwon. A watermarking scheme using polyline and polygon characteristic of shapefile. In *ICINIS, 2010*, pages 649 –652, 2010.

[9] H. Kang, K. Kim, and J. Choi. A vector watermarking using the generalized square mask. In *ITCC*, pages 234–236. IEEE Computer Society, 2001.

[10] J. Kim, S. Won, W. Zeng, and S. Park. Copyright protection of vector map using digital watermarking in the spatial domain. In *Digital Content, Multimedia Technology and its Applications (IDCTA), 2011 7th International Conference on*, pages 154 –159, aug. 2011.

[11] I. Kitamura, S. Kanai, and T. Kishinami. Copyright protection of vector map using digital watermarking method based on discrete fourier transform. In *Geoscience and Remote Sensing Symposium, 2001. IGARSS '01. IEEE 2001 International*, volume 3, pages 1191 –1193 vol.3, 2001.

[12] S.-H. Lee and K.-R. Kwon. Vector watermarking scheme for GIS vector map management. *DOI10.1007/s11042-011-0894-y SpringerLink*, 2011.

[13] Y. Li and L. Xu. A blind watermarking of vector graphics images. In *ICCIMA '03: Proceedings of the 5th International Conference on Computational Intelligence and Multimedia Applications*, page 424, Washington, DC, USA, 2003. IEEE Computer Society.

[14] X. Niu, C. Shao, and X. Wang. A survey of digital vector map watermarking. In *2006 International Journal of Innovative Computing,Information and Control Volume 2*, 2006.

[15] R. Ohbuchi, H. Ueda, and S. Endoh. Robust watermarking of vector digital maps. In *ICME (1)*, pages 577–580, 2002.

[16] R. Ohbuchi, H. Ueda, and S. Endoh. Watermarking 2d vector maps in the mesh-spectral domain. In *Shape Modeling International*, pages 216–228, 2003.

[17] Y.-C. Pu, W.-C. Du, and I.-C. Jou. Toward blind robust watermarking of vector maps. In *ICPR (3)*, pages 930–933, 2006.

[18] G. Schulz and M. Voigt. A high capacity watermarking system for digital maps. In *MM&Sec*, pages 180–186, 2004.

[19] R. Sion, M. J. Atallah, and S. Prabhakar. On watermarking numeric sets. In *IWDW*, pages 130–146, 2002.

[20] R. Sion, M. J. Atallah, and S. Prabhakar. Rights protection for relational data. In *SIGMOD Conference*, pages 98–109, 2003.

[21] V. Solachidis and I. Pitas. Watermarking polygonal lines using fourier descriptors. *Computer Graphics and Applications, IEEE*, 24(3):44 – 51, may-jun 2004.

[22] H. Sonnet, T. Isenberg, J. Dittmann, and T. Strothotte. Illustration watermarks for vector graphics. *Computer Graphics and Applications, Pacific Conference on*, 0:73, 2003.

[23] M. Voigt and C. Busch. Feature-based watermarking of 2d-vector data. In *SPIE,Security and Watermarking of Multimedia Content.Santa Clara,*, pages 359–366, 2003.

[24] H. Yan, J. Li, and H. Wen. A key points-based blind watermarking approach for vector geo-spatial data. *Computers, Environment and Urban Systems*, 35(6):485–492, 2011.

Author Index

www.ingramcontent.com/pod-product-compliance
Lightning Source LLC
Chambersburg PA
CBHW061409210326
41598CB00035B/6146